THE NEW

MONTINIAN CHURCH

THE NEW

MONTINIAN CHURCH

THE REVEREND
JOAQUIN SÁENZ Y ARRIAGA, PH.D.

Translated by
Edgar A. Lucidi, M.D.

EDGAR A. LUCIDI, M.D.
La Habra, California 90631

Copyright © 1985 by Edgar A. Lucidi, M.D.

All rights reserved. No part of this book may be reproduced or transmitted in any form or by any means, electronic or mechanical, including photocopying, recording or any information storage or retrieval system, without permission in writing from the translator.

Printed at the Lakeside Press by R.R. Donnelley & Sons Company
    1st English Edition
    1st Printing—August 15, 1985

This is copy No. _____ of a limited edition of 2,000 copies, translated from the second revised Spanish edition that was published in Mexico, by Editores Asociados on March 13, 1972.

Order From—
    Edgar A. Lucidi, M.D.
    410 W. Central Ave.—Suite 101
    Brea, California 92621

ACKNOWLEDGMENTS

The translator wishes to acknowledge his indebtedness to Fernando Bosch, Thomas Serpico and Faye Anderson for their invaluable aid in translating and editing this book.

DEDICATION

I wish to dedicate this book to Fr. Nicholas Ruffo, Fr. Charles Kropp and all my former Franciscan and Augustinian mentors; to my beloved cousin, Yolanda; to my grandfather, Alfredo; to Czar Nicholas II and his descendants; to my worldwide brothers of the Sovereign Order of Saint John of Jerusalem; to the traditional dedicated minority of the Catholic clergy and hierarchy, including Cardinals Lucidi, Ottaviani and Vagnozzi; to all divinely oriented traditionalists; and, lastly, to my beloved wife, Rose Marie, my children Celeste, Michael, Mark and John, and all my living and departed friends and relatives.

TO THE MEMORY

OF THE RENOWNED

MONSIGNOR RAFAEL RUA ALVAREZ,

FORMER PRIEST OF ORIZABA,

UNTIRING APOSTLE AND

INTREPID DEFENDER

OF THE CATHOLIC FAITH,

BELOVED BROTHER AND ADMIRED FRIEND.

Lay this flower
Upon his glorious grave;
Its perfume is that of a rose,
For it is a symbol of love.

The Reverend Joaquin Sáenz y Arriaga, Ph.D.
Mexico, August 15, 1971

TABLE OF CONTENTS

Chapter	Page
PROLOGUE	xv
I. THE EUCHARISTIC CONGRESS OF BOGOTÁ AND THE NEW POST-CONCILIAR CHURCH	1
II. THE 39TH INTERNATIONAL EUCHARISTIC CONGRESS, THE PAPAL VISIT, AND REVOLUTIONARY ACTIVISM	9
Marvelous Harmony of Church and Government	12
According to Public Opinion, What Was the Meaning of the Papal Visit?	13
Propaganda During the Eucharistic Congress	20
Christ	21
Camilo	21
Ché	21
The Apostolic Nuncio to Cuba Speaks	27
Fidel's New Attitude	28
With the Oppressed or With the Oppressors?	37
Revolutionary Activists Disclose Their Projects	39
Camilo Analyzed	43
The Apostolic Administrator of Bogota, His Excellency Monsignor Anibal Munoz, Welcomes the Foreign Pilgrims	47
III. THE INAUGURATION OF THE CONGRESS	49
IV. THE SOCIAL PROBLEM IN LATIN AMERICA	53
V. WELCOMING SPEECH BY THE APOSTOLIC ADMINISTRATOR TO THE LEGATE AND CONGRESS	59
VI. THE AWAITED SPEECH OF HIS EMINENCE GIACOMO LERCARO	65
VII. REMARKS ABOUT CARDINAL LERCARO'S SPEECH	71
Our Humble Remarks About His Eminence's Rhetorical Speech	71
VIII. THE CHURCH SUFFERS PROFOUND CHANGES	81
IX. REVOLUTION: THE ONLY SOLUTION FOR LATIN AMERICA?	83
X. THE CHANGE OF STRUCTURES AND THE DEMOGRAPHIC EXPLOSION	87
Neo-Nativism	93

Chapter	Page
XI. LAMEC IS A MATTER OF LIFE OR DEATH FOR THE CHURCH	95
Renovating Wind at the International Eucharistic Congress	96
Renovating Wind	97
Discrimination of Churches	97
Explosive Meaning	97
Social Opinions	98
Voices of Protest	98
Revolution	98
LAMEC: The Beginning	99
Monday, August 19	
Ecumenical Day	100
The Experts Anticipate What the Pope is Going to Say at the International Eucharistic Congress	113
XII. A DANGEROUS TURNABOUT	127
Confidential Letter to the Most Eminent Cardinals, Most Excellent Archbishops, and Bishops of Spain, Portugal, and Latin America	127
Dangerous Turnabout of Vatican Policy	128
Let Us Clear Up Some Points	133
Not Always Loyal and Accepted Advisors	135
What Pius IX, Leo XII, Pius XI, and Pius XII Have Taught	135
Decree of Excommunication of Communism by the Supreme Sacred Congregation of the Holy Office	139
A Bit of Reasoning	140
An Explanation by the Vatican Broadcasting Station	142
The Harmonious Set of Enemies	145
Some of the Most Important Documents Which Form the Basis for our Reasoning	147
The Light of the Great Architect of the Universe Enlightens The Vatican	147
Ghostly Dialogue Between John XXIII and Maximilian Robespierre	151
Prologue from The Plot Against the Church	157
Introduction to the American Edition	157
Important Information for the Reader, Plot Against The Church, *Introduction to the Italian Edition*	159
Foreword to the Austrian Edition	163
Preface to the German Edition	166
Introduction to the Spanish Edition, A Sensational Book	167
European Documents	170
Background that Should be Known	173
Final Words	174

Table of Contents x

Chapter *Page*

XIII. OUR RETURN TO THE EUCHARISTIC CONGRESS......... 177
    What Father Arias Published in Spain About the Pope's Journey........ 177
        Do Not Come! 178
        Day of the Sacraments of Christian Initiation 182
        Material from Cuernavaca and Religious Progressivism in Mexico 186
        My Christ is Not the Vatican's Christ 187
        The Form of Consecration Said in the Tridentine Mass............... 200
XIV. FATHER ARRUPE AND THE JESUITS AT THE
      EUCHARISTIC CONGRESS IN BOGOTÁ, AND THEIR
      ROLE IN THE SUBVERSION OF LATIN AMERICA....... 205
        To the Senior Superiors of Latin America 215
    Catholic-Marxist Dialogue and the So-Called Third Way
        Between Communism and Capitalism 219
XV. LETTERS SENT TO THE POPE
      BEFORE HIS ARRIVAL IN BOGOTÁ 233
        Open Letter to Paul VI from Colombian Progressivists 233
        Another Open Letter to Paul VI, from Argentina 236
        Why Must the Pope not Come to Colombia or
            any Other Latin American Country?......................... 238
        Message from the National Liberation Army of Colombia to Paul VI 241
XVI. THE POPE COMES TO AMERICA 245
        The Journey of Paul VI 249
XVII. THE NEW THEOLOGY OF THE
      BOGOTÁ INTERNATIONAL CONGRESS 253
        Other Words by the Papal Legate, Cardinal Lercaro................... 257
        The New Communal Ceremonies of Penance....................... 259
        The Cardinal-Legate Pays a Visit to Bogotá's Model Prison............ 263
XVIII. THE ARRIVAL OF THE POPE IN COLOMBIA............. 265
        Some Historical Background on Eucharistic Congresses 268
        Returning to the Pope's Flight..................................... 270
        President Lleras' Speech 275
        The Pope's Greeting to the People of Latin America.................. 278
XIX. MONSIGNOR HELDER CAMARA ARRIVES IN
      COLOMBIA AND ISSUES STATEMENTS 283
XX. PAUL VI IN BOGOTÁ, and
        His Relationship with the Hebrews................................ 293
XXI. THE AMULET OF POPE MONTINI 299
XXII. PAUL VI AND HIS RESPONSIBILITY FOR THE
      CURRENT CHAOS IN THE CHURCH 315
        A Letter from Father Calmel...................................... 319
        A Letter from Father Barbara 319

Chapter	Page
XXIII. PAUL VI—A LEGITIMATE POPE?	325
An Article by Dr. Carlos A. Disandro	325
An Article by Abbe Georges de Nantes—Some Opinions	330
From M. Feuillet	331
From *Civis Romanus*	331
From the Abbe Dulac	332
Concerning the Pope's Intention to Abdicate	333
From Herald Zimmermann	334
From Brazil	337
From Monsignor Spadafora	337
From the Abbe Georges de Nantes Himself	338
Should the Pope Be a Heretic, There Is No Need to Quit the Church, Which Is Not His Church, or Any Man's Work; It is Necessary to Remove Him	339
My Opinion About These Opinions	342
Statements by Alfred Cardinal Ottaviani	344
Statements by Cardinal Tisserant	346
Some Comments by Father Raymond Dulac	347
The Archbishop of Genoa, Cardinal Siri, Speaks	348
Opinions Replace Truth	348
Is Gnosis Reappearing?	349
What is Most Urgent?	350
XXIV. IS JOHN BAPTIST MONTINI A TRUE POPE?	351
Prospects of Larger Communion between Lutherans and Catholics	380
XXV. IS JOHN MONTINI A TRUE POPE? THE AUTHOR'S AND OTHER OPINIONS	385
My Personal Opinion of Pope Paul VI	385
A Plot Against the Church	393
XXVI. PAUL VI SEEKS ALLIANCES WITH COMMUNIST COUNTRIES	401
Loyal to His Program, Paul VI Seeks Alliances with Communist Countries	401
A Message from the World Conference on Religion and Peace	403
The Common Heritage of All Religions	404
The Scandal of the Arms Race	404
All Religions Must Unite for the Sake of Peace	405
XXVII. POPE PAUL VI AND THE PEASANTS	409
Development Day at Bogota—Paul VI's Speech to the Peasants of America	409

Table of Contents

Chapter	Page

**XXVIII. POPE PAUL VI, HERESY, AND
PAPAL SUCCESSION AND INFALLIBILITY** 423
   Abbe Dulac Exposes Pope Montini 423
   The Vatican Suppresses the Concept of Heresy 424
   Cardinal Willebrands and Pontifical Infallibility 425

**XXIX. PAUL VI, LAMEC, AND THE
NEW THEOLOGIANS** 427
   Discourse of the Pope at the Shrine of the Congress 427
      Latin America's Problems 427
   The Pontiff Also Inaugurated the New Seat of LAMEC 433
   The Christian Family Movement 436
   The Cursillo Movement 436
   *The Inauguration of the Second Assembly of LAMEC,
    and the Speech of Paul VI* 437
   The Institutional Church and the Charismatic Church 452
   Hans Kung, Bold Theologian 453
   What I Think of Hans Kung's Theology 454
   About Jacob Maritain 459
   A Further Critique of Pope Paul VI's Speech 460
      Groups Deserving Particular Attention 461
         The Priests 461
         The Youth and the Students 462
         The Workers 463
      Social Guidelines 464
         Encyclicals and Teachings of the Episcopate 464
         Pastoral Technique 464
         Witness of Poverty 466
         Christianity and Violence 469
         Peace 470
         Love and Transformations 471
         On the *Humanae Vitae* 472
   *A Speech by John Cardinal Ricketts,
    Archibishop of Lima* 473
      The Pilgrim of Peace 474
      Latin American Collegiality 474
      Deep Transformations 474
      Rapprochement with Man 475
      Latin American Liberation 475
      Task of the Meeting 475
      The Signs of the Times 475
      Need for a New Order 476

Chapter	Page
XXX. LAMEC DOCUMENTS, RESULTS, AND THE TRUTH ABOUT PAUL VI	481
Some Documents of the Second Latin American Episcopal Conference	481
A Document by Monsignor Mark McGrath, Bishop of Santiago de Varaguas, Panama	482
A Document by Monsignor Samuel Ruiz, Bishop of San Cristobal de las Casas, Chiapas	492
Violence	503
The Results of the Assembly in Medellin	507
The Truth about the Pontiff	510
XXXI. TITO'S VISIT	513
XXXII. PRIESTS' MOVEMENT FOR THE THIRD WORLD	521
XXXIII. THE DEATH OF GOD	529
What is "The Death of God?"	530
The Secular Life	530
Priests Before the Vatican	531
Mission of the Churches	532
Argentinian Catholicism	533
The Post-Conciliar Church	533
The Originality of Christ's Message	535
XXXIV. SOCIALIZATION IN MEXICO	539
XXXV. THE NEW THEOLOGY OF THE POST-CONCILIAR CHURCH	543
I—Crisis of Values: Authority and Obedience	543
II—Further Critique of the Crisis of Values	548
XXXVI. THE PRIESTHOOD, THE NEXT SYNOD, AND THE PREPARATORY INQUESTS	553
Thirty-Nine Spanish Bishops Deny Their Supposed Unanimity	556
XXXVII. FATHER ARRUPE VISITS THE UNION OF SOVIET SOCIALIST REPUBLICS	559
XXXVIII. THE TRAGEDY OF CHILE, TREASON WITHIN THE CHURCH, AND EXAMPLES TO BE IMITATED	567
My Comments on the Alarming Treason Against Our Catholic Faith	571
An Example to be Imitated and Intercessors Who Will Help Us from Heaven	572
XXXIX. THE GREAT TREASON	575
XL. DIVINISM, POPELATRY, AND THE DOCTRINE OF THE LESSER EVIL	591
FOOTNOTES	595

PROLOGUE

I didn't write this prologue; public opinion did. The number of copies of *The New Montinian Church* that are circulating in Mexico and abroad, and the rapidity with which they were sold, are imposing phenomena in the religious book field. *The New Montinian Church* seems to answer an imperious, urgent, and compelling biological and psychological need. It seems to answer a void in a desert of authentic ideas in our present world. Actually, with respect to the drama of the Universal Church, there exists a terrifying void in the minds and souls of men and an immense yearning to nourish themselves with the desperately necessary food of spiritual ideas which, as expressed by Christ, constitute an immortal bond between the Church and the Catholic Faith.

These ideas always constituted something uniform, fixed, compact, solid, and unique. To be a Catholic was to be the same at whatever point in time and space. Independent of this, Catholicism, without divisions of artificial and malevolent concessions, was always and continues to be the unalterable representation of transcendent truth. This is that truth that conducts and assures us of immortality to enjoy the presence of God and to be reunited with our loved ones who, in passing, left us in a sorrowful but temporary absence; that gave us that certain and consoling feeling of being a part of one united Christendom which emanates from one common Creator, who is Father, Redemptor, and Judge; that makes us children of the same sublime celestial Mother, in whose womb the Word incarnated as true God and true man to spill His redeeming blood in a sacrifice perpetuated in the Holy Mass where the same drama is neither related, commemorated, nor analyzed, but re-enacted in a real but unbloody manner; that attaches us, from pole to pole, to the Holy Eucharist, i.e., to that certain and effective, material and substantial presence of Christ Himself in the holy form by means of the ineffable mystery of the Transubstantiation, effected by God Himself in the words, "*This is my body, this is my blood,*" whereby He gave the apostles the power to do likewise.

Life on earth is a passage to eternal life, and from this earth we pray for our departed brethren who, in turn, are praying for us. All these eternal truths give us a common origin, destiny, and law within which to live. We Catholics have always had the immutable conviction that to enter any church on earth was to enter a common home, and that to pray together was to form one flock under the same pastor, the Pope, who in speaking to us as Pope, i.e., as pastor, teacher, and universal guide about exclusive matters of faith, was speaking to us through the Holy Spirit, thereby maintaining the monolithic unity of the doctrine deposited in the custody of Peter and his successors. All this is grandiose, solemn, august, and congruent with this short life and the other eternal life; all this was, is, and has always been something expressible in a simple angelic form, fully and beautifully, in the *Apostles' Creed*.

All this has now been interdicted, placed in doubt, and become an object of discussion and contradiction. All the sacred teachings have become objects of ignoble treatment, of approximations, of "broad-minded" interpretations, of aberrations, in short, of heresies that at the base signify an immense, gigantic and inconceivable betrayal of Christ Himself. In brief, we are beginning to live a life of *universal apostasy*, which is the universal negation of revealed truth.

The contemporary world has turned its back on Christ. It begins at the same altar where at first it is the people of God and later becomes its own god. We live in an iconoclastic world for whom its sacred images are idols, and for whom saints and sanctity are myths and regressions.

We live in a world much more tremendous than candid, in which one does not conceive faith and science to be in harmony but of faith to be like a loose rock in the mountain of science; a world of vanity, pride, arrogance, and corruption of customs and ideals; a world in which the law of pleasure and the law of the jungle are joined together; in brief, a world which demands the accommodation and servitude of Christ and His Church, rather than that the depraved and amoral world regenerate itself by a definitive readjustment to the law of God. In effect, God is relegated to the service of the world, in a world created and ruled by Him! By slow degrees, the modernist church with its weak or infiltrated Pope and hierarchy have entered upon a terrifying and desolate road, taking Catholics along with it, not the true Church which God Himself guides, but the false one which makes of revealed truth a motif of constant limping revision and accommodation.

Today the Church no longer feels called to conduct man to eternal life but to worthless pursuits. It feels itself called only to make man happy on earth. It is no longer the Ten Commandments that are of importance but rather class struggle, better salaries, unions, irresponsible liberty, unbridled youth and sex, wanton eroticism, heresy, and aiding and abetting Communism in its goal of world domination. In the face of barbarity, the Church does not Christianize but chooses to barbarize itself.

Against all these aberrations there arises Fr. Saénz Arriaga's book, *The New Montinian Church*, which, like a potent flying flag, challenges the retreat of the fraudulent Church.

Until this book was written, the world could have thought of itself as being deluded into following the path of error, but now God has provided to him who wishes to avail himself, all the information necessary to lift himself out of the dark abyss. We neither know nor can know the solution, as we are but creatures in the hands of God. Nevertheless, we have a history that originates in Christ and over which Christ Himself presides, a Gospel that speaks to us through Him and in which He speaks to us, a handful of apostles that represented the yeast of the earth, a centuries-old faith that inflamed our hearts, and a pleiad of saints who showed us the way that vain men now wish to change. Let us enter and get to the heart of the matter! Let us be Christians of one faith and dogma, and of one solid doctrine of salvation. Let us conduct ourselves as men, in body and soul, just as Christ told us through the prophets of the Old Testament and confirmed with His blood in the New Testament.

The world has one history: toward the cross and away from the cross. Those who choose the flesh over the spirit for a few miserable days of arrogance and pleasure, forget that each of us has but a few remaining years of life. We should not come before God with empty hands but, at the very least, present Him with the rich humility of an attempt, an intention, and a solicitude of being with Him till the end of time.

For this I have put my heart and soul into writing this long prologue, binding myself to the thesis of this book so that it may surge forth like a lantern of light and orientation from the hands of its author.

I am but a humble journalist. In God's name, let us unite my small effort to this gigantic effort in defense of the One, Holy, Catholic, and Apostolic Roman Church!

In closing, we wish to remind our readers that we are not against the Papacy but against one Pontiff (Pope Paul VI) who, for reasons only God knows, worked against the Papacy itself.

René Capistrán Garza

Addendum: On February 22, 1972, a precise and appropriate document appeared and was published in various newspapers with the title, "Violence is not the Way, Condemn Guerillas and Kidnappers," which the Archbishop of Monterrey, Alfonso Espino Silva, addressed to his parishioners as a Lenten message.

Reading and analyzing said important document, one clearly understands the pure doctrine of the Catholic Church with its immutable divine principles unchanged by political interests and untainted by the universal Communist subversion. In this document, violence is condemned, kidnappers rebuked, bank robberies censured and terrorism rejected, along with its underlying doctrine of the "new redemption," whose aim is not only to terrorize society but also to change the existing public order.

This is the Church which we traditionalists love and support, being ever faithful to the authentic spirit of the Gospel. On the other hand, the "same" Church has produced many inconceivable declarations of bishops and priests whose authority is maintained by the same Pontiff who has nominated, aided, and abetted them or who, at least, does not condemn them either openly or secretly.

Concrete and irrefutable examples:

1. "To oppose change is to be guilty of violence—Jesuit confirms to the clergy of Chihuahua." (*Excelsior*, Feb. 11, 1972, p. 1). In that declaration, signed by fourteen Jesuit priests headed by the provincial, Enrique Gutierrez, S.J., this distinguished clerical group makes a concrete eulogy for violence as well as for peremptory and revolutionary structural change, adhering without the least modesty and scruples to the same thesis which has just been sustained by Bishops Almeida of Chihuahua, and Talamás of Juárez, as well as the Reverend Fr. Arrupe, supreme leader of the Society of Jesus.

2. Adherence to the same conduct, principles and orientations on the part of the Bishop of Juárez, Manuel Talamás Camandari. (Article by Antonio Rius Facius, *El Universal*, Feb. 11, 1972, p. 6).

3. Previous declaration by the Archbishop of Chihuahua, Alberto Almeida, affirming that "institutional violence" is the cause of political subversive violence. (*Excelsior*, Jan. 29, 1972, p. 4).

4. Bishop Mendez Arceo, of Cuernavaca, joins with Archbishop Almeida of Chihuahua, in statements entitled: "He Who Wishes to Leave Cuba is not Necessarily Bad." (*Excelsior*, Jan. 31, 1972, p. 4).

The following brief, but substantial annotation is important: There exists in Mexico an apostolic delegation whose function is, or is supposed to be, to keep the Vatican informed of the activities of the bishops on a daily basis. Another small observation, which many will consider to be treacherous, appears to be of relative importance: Comparing the faithful and orthodox declaration of Bishop Espino Silva, of Monterrey, with the turbulent and seditious statements of Bishops Almeida of Chihuahua, Talamás of Juárez, and Méndez Arceo of Cuernavaca, can one not legitimately deduce that there presently exists in Mexico, as in the rest of the world, both a false and another true Church? In the meantime, how do we reckon with the centralized authority of His Holiness Paul VI? Well, they tell us something about these disturbing manifestations which will soon explode throughout the world. In this ecclesiastical melange which we are tragically experiencing, the world is being crucified under the hammer and sickle ... and the cross. In the history of Christian mankind, this is like a frontal assault by the synagogue, not only to conquer, but also to erase Calvary and the redeeming punishment of mankind itself from the map.

René Capistrán Garza

TRANSLATOR'S PREFACE

Fr. Joaquín Sáenz y Arriaga, S.J., Ph.D. was born October 12, 1899, ordained a Jesuit priest in April, 1930, and died in April, 1976. An acclaimed sentinel and guardian of the Rock of St. Peter, he held doctorates in philosophy, theology and Canon Law. An active and prodigious traditionalist writer, he authored or co-authored more than fifty books exposing the neo-gnosticism of the Post-Conciliar Church, including such well-known texts as *Sede Vacante (The Vacant Chair), For Christ and Against Christ, The New Mass Is Not the One Catholic Mass, The Plot Against the Church,* etc. A dedicated servant of Christ, his love of God and mankind propelled him to write the present comprehensive exposé against the occult conspiracy. A shining star of the Jesuit Order and the Order of Saint John of Jerusalem, he first published *La Nueva Iglesia Montiniana* on the Feast of the Assumption, August 15, 1971. This was subsequently translated and published in Italian, creating such a furor within liberalized Church circles that it even brought about an invalid excommunication, handed down by a bishop who did not have jurisdiction over Fr. Sáenz and who did not call a tribunal to hear the case.

It is hoped that the timely and long-awaited publication of this book on August 15, 1985 will provide the reader with enough historical insight to appreciate the nature of the pagan anti-Christian conspiracy which is at work against the Church. For further elaboration, I refer the reader to the following indispensable books:

1) *The Plot Against the Church,* Maurice Pinay. (Nom de plume of Fr. Sáenz and several co-authors).
2) *Freemasonry and the Vatican,* Léon de Poncins.
3) *The World Order,* Eustace Mullins.
4) *The Unholy Alliance,* Frank Perida.
5) *Secret Societies and Subversive Movements,* Nesta Webster.
6) *Liturgical Revolution,* Michael Davies.
7) *Dope, Inc.,* Goldman, Steinberg & Kalimtgis.
8) *The New Dark Ages Conspiracy,* Carol White.
9) *Spiritual Communism,* Helen Peters.

In conclusion, it is to be made clear that neither the author nor the translator are indiscriminately attacking or vilifying any religious, racial, national, political or social group, per se, but only those elitist individuals and opportunists who, in order to keep their position of world power and control, are using their power of office, influence and money to transform mankind from an active, healthy and divinely oriented progressive society, to a sick, drugged state of moral regression, secular humanism, political impotence, social anarchy and economic slavery. This so-called *"New World Order"* is, in reality, a continuation of the old pagan Babylonian world order system, as exemplified by the League of Nations and the United Nations. This *"New Dark Age Conspiracy,"* which is centered in London, the capital of the "neo-pagan Roman Empire," must be stopped in order to prevent a return to a one world barbaric slave state under a rigid elitist control. The destruction of religion, the decimation of half of the world's population, and the abject enslavement of the remainder are but three unholy facets of their satanic pentagram, the other two being the evils of both *material* and *spiritual* Communism, which they have been promoting under the guise of their Hegelian dialectic. Now is the time for all men of good faith and good will, Christian and non-Christian, to learn, to know, to teach and to act, not only for ourselves and the present, but for our children and the future of all mankind, for whatsoever we sow on Earth, we shall reap in Heaven.

THE NEW
POST-CONCILIAR
OR
MONTINIAN CHURCH

CHAPTER I

THE EUCHARISTIC CONGRESS OF BOGOTÁ AND THE NEW POST-CONCILIAR CHURCH

Most chronicles and reports about the International Eucharistic Congress held in Bogotá at the end of August, 1968, and enhanced by the presence of His Holiness Pope Paul VI, the first Pope to have stepped on Latin-American soil, were, without a doubt, extremely flattering, insofar as certain liberal Catholic media are concerned. The Congress, according to these media, was extremely successful, "a triumph without triumphalism," as the *Osservatore Romano* remarked.

Setting aside partisan exaltation, however, and analyzing just the reality of facts, I conclude that this most important religious event showed confusing, disquieting, and dangerous features. If it were not for the possibility that my words could be construed and censored as being contemptuous or critical, I would almost dare to summarize my opinion of the Colombian Congress by defining it as a second and spiritual "Bogotazo" that shattered and is still shattering not only Colombia but all of Latin America. This Congress was the call to arms of the planned subversion of the Latin American countries. Its consequences are still not predictable, as they depend upon the energy with which the legitimate governments of our countries will defend our jeopardized sovereignties.

In my opinion, the Congress was a solemn and official introduction of the program and goals of the reformed post-Conciliar Church to the Catholic and non-Catholic world. The air was saturated with liberal progressivism, and the Eucharistic issues were either eliminated or relegated to a secondary position. Human and social problems were given priority over the divine problems of the glory of God and the salvation of souls.

Of course, the Holy Eucharist was mentioned, but not in order to probe its ineffable mysteries, to praise its excellence, to help us appreciate the inexhaustible treasury of the love of Christ, to invite us to live more Eucharistic lives, or to adhere more closely to the cross and the Master's life. Such issues were used as convenient bait, so as to focus the issues and deeds of the Congress toward human and secular subjects, such as underdevelopment, the misery of the poor classes, and the socialization of Latin America, which had been decreed during secret talks at the Vatican. At the Congress and at the subsequent Latin American Episcopal Conference (LAMEC) meeting, it was easy to notice the decisive influence of the "Conciliar experts," luminaries of modern theology who, for the sake of peace, development, and material progress, are ready to silence the voice of faith, to conceal and deny some of our cherished dogmas, and to even become allies of the sons of iniquity.

In order to understand the extreme positions already taken by Colombia's priests, we may refer to an extremely disconcerting fact that has no precedent in the history of Catholicism. The second general conference of the Latin American bishops, held in Medellín, Colombia, and solemnly inaugurated by the Pope at the Cathedral of Bogotá on the eve of the Congress, was the culmination of the program and the evident and concrete goal of these religious events, i.e., to bring about an actual revolution in Latin America, without violence or bloodshed, if possible.

In the religious field, one of the revolutionary aspects of this program, and certainly not the least important, was our prelates' overflowing, inconceivable, surrendering ecumenism at the Eucharistic Congress and the subsequent Medellín LAMEC conference.

By means of a moving message, five non-Catholic "observers" (today's name for wolves in sheep's clothing) asked permission from the august assembly to receive Holy Communion along with the bishops. The names of these soliciting observers were: David B. Reed, Anglican Bishop of Bogotá; Prof. Manfred K. Bahmann, a Lutheran from Buenos Aires; Br. Roberto Giscard, of the Taizé community; the Reverend Dana Green; and Dr. Kurtis F. Naylor. Their apparently humble and moving supplication reads as follows: "The conference being almost at an end, may we request the exceptional privilege of communing, at least once, along with all our Christian brothers gathering here."

As grounds on which the "separated people" based their request, they cited the Ecumenic Directory, No. 55, which states that the Church may allow a separated brother to receive the Sacraments if there are sufficient reasons. It also defines some cases of urgent need, and goes on to say that "we are being pressed by the most urgent conceivable reason, that of charity. Hence, moved by loyalty, we are discretely and confidentially addressing this Conference to the presidency itself, asking it to take into account that the unity of faith about the sacraments on which the Directory bases its doctrinal denial, is not lacking on our part. We confess that the Eucharist is that certain and efficacious sign of the personal presence of Christ, the sacrament of the body and blood of Christ, the sacrament of His real presence."

In answer to this petition, Rafael Moya García, right-hand man of Fr. Enrique Maza, S.J., a prominent Mexican progressivist, commented that "the presidency of the second Latin American Episcopal Conference could not and did not want to reject this petition which undoubtedly opens new and promising avenues toward the unity of all Christians."

To me, this incomprehensible fact is an appropriate consummation of the second "Bogotazo" trying to revolutionize all Latin American structures. Although they invoke fraternal charity to justify this fact, I cannot restrain my just indignation, as a Catholic and as a priest, when faced with this outrageous and sacrilegious political gesture by the Latin American prelates who, like new Judases, betrayed their Master. This fact is not at all justified by the presence of His Eminence Antonio Cardinal Samoré.

It is no longer time to be cautious. We may no longer be quiet in the face of this dreadful abomination. We must clarify the above-mentioned fact urgently, and then analyze it in order to draw logical and evident conclusions therefrom.

Who made the petition to the LAMEC prelates? What was asked, and why? What are the theological and apostolic implications of the unbearable concessions that the Latin American bishops granted these "separated brothers" through their official proxies?

Sincere answers to these questions will provide a correct interpretation of that fact and will simultaneously underline the shepherds' terrible responsibility before God, conscience, parishioners, and history. Because of incompetence, cowardice, servility, lack of faith, or temporal interests, they not only betrayed our Master and scandalized the flock, but also gave up the most precious heritage we had received from our ancestors, our Catholic unity.

The petitioners were self-confessed heretics, that is, people who not only do not accept, but also reject and repudiate much of the truth as revealed by God, as stated by the Church's Magisterium and belonging to our Catholic Faith. The churches or ecclesiastical communities to which they belong are but branches that have been severed from the trunk of the only Church that Christ built. Such branches differ considerably not only from us but also among each other, because of their various origins, doctrines, and spiritual lives.

With respect to the relations of the separated brothers with the Catholic Church, Chapter 1 on the Ecumenism of Vatican II says:

> Ever since the beginning there appeared schisms within this one and only Church of God (cf. I Cor. 2:18-19, Gal. 1:6-9, I John 2:18-19), but the apostle repudiated them as seriously damnable. In the centuries that followed, new and wider schisms arose; large communities seceded from the full communion of the Catholic Church, sometimes because of the faults of men on both sides. However, those who are now born within these communities and are nourished by Christ's faith may not be blamed for the sin of secession, and the Catholic Church embraces them with fraternal respect and love, for those who believe in Christ and have been duly baptized enjoy a sort of communion, albeit imperfect,

The Montinian Church

with the Catholic Church. Certainly, various discrepancies standing between them and the Catholic Church in structural, doctrinal, and disciplinary matters are in the way of their full ecclesiastical communion, but the ecumenical movement is trying to remove such obstacles. Since faith justified them by virtue of their Baptism, they belong to Christ and fully deserve to be honored with the name of Christians; hence, the sons of the Catholic Church correctly recognize them to be brethren in the Lord.

In addition to the elements or goods that jointly compose and give life to the Church itself, some and even many very valuable ones can be found outside of the visible circle of the Catholic Church: the written Word of God, the life of grace, faith, hope, charity, and other inner gifts of the Holy Spirit. All of these things, which come from Christ and lead to Him, belong *de jure* to the only Church of Christ.

In my opinion, these enigmatic words, which can be subject to disastrous interpretations, are plainly incomprehensible. Evidently, those who are now born within these heretical or schismatic communities can or cannot be personally guilty of their sad condition, in the same way that we are not *individually liable* for Adam's sin, in which we are all born. In like manner, those who suffer from hereditary diseases are not guilty of the vices from which their parents became so terribly ill. Such reasoning, however, cannot efface the fact that they were born in sad circumstances. Similarly, the absence of personal sin does not mean that those who are born into these sects should not be separated from the trunk of the Church, through which we receive fruitful sap from Christ's redemption. For how can they be nourished in Christ if they are separated from the Christ-built trunk of the Church? Can Christ be divided into pieces? It is all or nothing at all. Christianity requires a sincere acceptance of the *entire* doctrine that God revealed. One cannot be friend and foe at the same time. The "separated" do not sincerely and faithfully believe in part of the revealed and defined truth; they even attack, deny, and sneer at it. These structural, doctrinal, and disciplinary discrepancies obstruct the way toward a full ecclesiastical communion and, while they last, prevent the participation of these individuals in the life of the Church. In exceptional cases, where they adopt wrong attitudes in good faith and obey the moral law faithfully, we may reasonably believe that they participate invisibly, but without our being able to feel sure of this. The words of Christ are peremptory: *"He who believes shall be saved; he who does not believe shall be condemned."*

I cannot understand what this "sort of communion . . . with the Catholic Church" that the Council mentions, consists of. There is no communion insofar as doctrine, hierarchy, and sacraments are concerned. The Council says that the "separated brethren" belong to Christ by virtue of their Baptism, to which I object because the Church has always been distrustful of the validity of the sects' baptismal rites. That is why the members of those sects who converted to Catholicism were *sub conditione* administered Catholic Baptism, a sacrament which our Lord Jesus Christ instituted. The Church, therefore, was not sure of their truly belonging to Christ. In fact, some of them do not even believe in Christ's divinity. Their Christianity is mutilated, incoherent, and based on a liberal examination and interpretation of the holy Scripture. The Catholic Church recognizes them as "brethren in the Lord" because they have been created by God and called by God to participate in the divine life that the Incarnate Word brought to us, and not because she recognizes in them an adoptive supernatural *filiation*, for in such a case they would not be separated brethren, but sons of the Church.

I am not denying the possibility that an exceptional few of these "separated brethren" may become justified through Jesus Christ, i.e., that they receive sanctifying grace, infused theological virtues, and other inner gifts from the Holy Spirit. *De internis non judicat Ecclesia*; only God penetrates the intimacy of souls. However possible these rare and isolated cases may be, they cannot serve as an argument to discard the Catholic affirmation that *outside of the Catholic Church there is no salvation.*

In facie ecclesiae, before the visible church, those who requested that unheard-of privilege in Medellín were heretics.

What, then, did those gentlemen ask of our venerable prelates? Nothing less than taking the Most Holy Sacrament without being and without wanting to become Catholics. Had their petition been sincere, they would have applied for a full conversion to our Catholic Faith, since their supplication itself shows us that they knew perfectly well the Holy Church's requisites to receive the Sacraments. In their demand they implicitly avow that they are not members of the Church and that they do not even intend to become such, but, nevertheless, they asked permission to commune or to concelebrate with our bishops, in spite of not deserving it, as the above circumstances show.

The apostle Paul requires that man prepare himself properly in order to be worthy of this august Sacrament, for he who eats and drinks of the body and blood of our Lord without deserving it, *judicium sibi manducat et bibit*, eats and drinks his own judgment. Were those petitioners personally pure, and exempt from deadly sins? A well-known, non-Catholic Mexican newspaper commentator rightly affirms that the LAMEC prelates' concession implies their acceptance of the thesis of the Bishop of Cuernavaca, according to which one may receive Holy Communion in the state of mortal sin, and without grace, confession, or even being a Catholic.

Ecumenism was the reason that the "separated brethren" gave for their absurd request: "May we suggest [they do not affirm it to be so, they just suggest] that we are being pressed by the most urgent conceivable reason, that of charity." Evidently this suggestion does not refer to charity with respect to

God, but to charity with respect to human beings. Is charity for human beings conceivable, however, when it is not based on charity for God? Moreover, can there be charity for God on the part of those who, being so close to the truth, do not even move to approach it? They do not get closer to the truth nor do they accept it, but they actually deny it and secretly intend to fight it. These Protestant ministers, by not publicly and sincerely renouncing their errors in order to accept the integrity of revealed truth, are really telling us that they intend to fight the dogmas of our religion that they do not accept, with the goal of converting Latin American Catholics to their beliefs.

On the other hand, even if we were to avow, and it would be a big avowal, that these "observers" have the same beliefs that we Catholics have with respect to the Sacraments, this would not be enough ground to declare them ready to receive Christ's body and blood, not symbolically, but really and truly. For, in order to duly receive the Holy Sacrament of the Eucharist, one not only needs to be in a state of grace but also to confess his sins, if he is conscious of them. Did the "separated brethren" qualify?

Having studied the request of the so-called "Protestant pastors" in depth, I do not believe it imprudent to affirm that they were not sincere. They did not ask for Communion because they believed in it or because they wanted to give public testimony to the truth of our Catholic Faith, but because they wanted a license, a passport, and an endorsement from our prelates in order to continue proselytizing our simple and ill-prepared Latin American people. They were in a position of everything to gain and nothing to lose or sacrifice; in fact, they made great strides toward eliminating our people's legitimate and healthy resistance to their preaching.

In the theological field, the gracious concession of our venerable LAMEC bishops seems to be a profanation and a politically-inspired sacrilege, designed to fit in with the ecumenical movement whereby we gave up everything without receiving anything in exchange. As the Protestant writer of the Mexican newspaper *Excelsior* remarks, it also signifies an implicit acceptance of the strange thesis of bishops from Cuernavaca and Torreón, according to which one does not need sacramental confession to duly receive Communion, even if one's soul is not in the state of grace. Theologically speaking, then, we are in error, but this has been disregarded for political reasons by our venerable prelates.

In the pastoral field it simplifies the task of our "separated brethren" to proselytize among our Catholic people. Our simple and unknowing people, on seeing the Protestant ministers concelebrating or receiving Communion with our Catholic bishops, logically concluded that we are all one and the same, that Catholics and Protestants are already united, and that any way may be chosen to go to Heaven. They are also led to such conclusions by the teachings of the "separated ones," by the multiple changes they see in the Catholic Church, and by the "new post-Conciliar teaching" of the priests, which the people do not understand. Apostolically speaking, then, the concession of the LAMEC bishops of Medellín efficaciously contributed to the Protestantization of Latin America or to the establishment of "religious pluralism," *according to the signs of the times.*

Chapter II

THE 39TH INTERNATIONAL EUCHARISTIC CONGRESS, THE PAPAL VISIT, AND REVOLUTIONARY ACTIVISM

Pope Paul VI, in the announcement of his coming to Colombia to attend the 39th International Eucharistic Congress, to be held in Bogotá from August 18-28, 1968, said the following:

Most beloved sons and daughters:
We wish to announce to this audience that, God willing, we will go to Colombia next August to attend the closing of the International Eucharistic Congress and to start the general conference of the Latin American Episcopate, sincerely lamenting that we are unable to accept the kind invitations that other countries of that continent have sent us.
What is the meaning of the Pope's trips? They mean that the ways of the world are open to his ministry; they indicate a wider circulation of charity; and they evidence the unity and catholicity of the Church.
By means of our trip to Bogotá we wish to unequivocally give testimony of the Faith to all of the Church in the triple sanctifying virtue of the Eucharist: a reminder of His Redeeming Passion, the real wonder of Christ's sacramental presence, and the promise of His final coming.
We are also pleased that this religious affirmation is taking place in our most beloved Latin America, where faith is reviving great social charity and where we anticipate growing civil justice and greater Christian prosperity.
Henceforth, we extend our apostolic blessing *to all you wholehearted people* of the immense Latin American world.

In this address of Paul VI, in which he announced, *Urbi et Orbi*, his intention to fly to Latin America to participate in the 39th International Eucharistic Congress, the Pope is declaring his intentions which, in addition to the customary goals of his Pontifical trips (to show the world that all paths are open to his pastoral ministry, to spread charity, and to give witness to the unity and catholicity of the Church), the Pope came to Bogotá to attest to the aforementioned triple sanctifying virtue of the Eucharist. In keeping with the objectives and guidelines of previous international Eucharistic congresses, His

Holiness wanted his presence and his words to intensify Eucharistic life in Latin America, for it is mainly through the Eucharist, unfailing source of all sanctity, that the most precious fruits of Christ's redemption come to us. According to these words, the Pope seemed to have definite Eucharistic, and not political or social, goals in mind for the forthcoming Congress. Nevertheless, this brings to our attention something which we must henceforth keep in mind that the Pope did not mention *sacrifice*, without which the Eucharist would not exist in the Church.

The circumstances His Holiness mentioned, that "this religious affirmation" should take place in Latin America, wherein the Pontiff saw a *growing civil justice and a greater Christian prosperity*, do not seem to have changed the specific finality of all these international meetings, which have always been solemn and public ratifications of our Eucharistic beliefs and of the fundamental dogmas of our Catholic faith: the Sacrificial Eucharist, the Eucharistic Sacrament, and the real Eucharistic Presence of Christ in the consecrated species.

Nevertheless, the appointment of Cardinal Lercaro, former Archbishop of Bologna, as papal legate to the Congress, made many observers, Italian and otherwise, afraid that the great event was going to have an end quite different from the one being proclaimed by the media and the invitations. Just as the document which John F. Kennedy signed in Bogotá to establish an "Alliance for Progress," was a crafty plan to establish socialism in Latin America, said document almost literally coinciding with the *Populorum Progressio* of Paul VI, the International Eucharistic Congress could be the start, the beginning of that continental revolution that would bring rapid and audacious "structural" changes to all the Latin American countries, thereby putting an end to their underdevelopment.

The Pope's letter to Cardinal Lercaro reads as follows:

Most eminent Giacomo Cardinal Lercaro, *Legato a Látere:*

We have decided to commit to you the task of representing us as a legate at the 39th International Eucharistic Congress which will take place next month in Bogotá, Colombia, with the certainty that this Congress, *the first one since the Council*, will benefit from your magisterial authority and your apostolic zeal.

May the Church still enjoy your valuable experience for many long years in this new phase of your life, rich in doctrinal accomplishments and in experiences acquired through the faithful exercise of your sacerdotal and pastoral duties. Your appointment as legate to Bogotá publicly confirms our feelings and special deference toward you.

The Papal Visit and Revolutionary Activism

The "red" Cardinal, as the former Archbishop of Bologna is called worldwide, was given this important appointment as legate a latere. His open sympathy or "Christian understanding" toward Communism, his democratic rapprochement to the needy classes, his not always discrete cooperation with Marxist activities in his diocese, and his efforts to eliminate or to soften the Church's ancient sternness and intolerable condemnations against atheistic Marxism, had turned this cardinal whom Paul VI appointed as his legate in Bogotá into one of the leading representatives of "religious progressivism." Neither must one forget his radical liturgical reform, which practically effaced all ancient rites and ceremonies of the pre-Conciliar Church, in order to eliminate all prejudices and to ensure that the people would fervently accept the new ideas and the new religion.

The letter from Pope Paul VI to the Cardinal is more than a simple appointment, as its text goes beyond the ordinary forms used in these occasions. The Pope appoints Lercaro as his legate, feeling sure that *this Congress will benefit from his magisterial authority and his apostolic zeal*. Apart from the cardinal's background of open accommodation to Marxism and his liberality in destroying the multi-centennial venerable rites in which the Catholic Church's wisdom and holiness, under the light of the Holy Spirit, had crystallized Catholic worship, we do not know of any other merits by which he deserved to be so solemnly proclaimed *master and apostle* of Latin America and of the whole world. What contribution did the Pope expect from the wisdom and apostolic zeal of the former Archbishop of Bologna?

As if the above praises were not enough, the Pope ends his letter by hoping that the Church may "still enjoy your valuable experience for many long years in this new phase of your life, which is rich in doctrinal accomplishments and in experiences acquired through the faithful exercise of your sacerdotal and pastoral duties."

In this magnificent eulogy, His Holiness avows that advanced age is no obstacle for cardinals, bishops, and priests to render service to God, the Church, and the salvation of souls, thereby contradicting his post-Conciliar politics and his famous *Motu Proprio* on the age of cardinals. In fact, what he had affirmed of Cardinal Lercaro could be applied, on identical grounds, to all the venerable prelates who, because of the unpardonable sin of age, had been removed from their sees, in spite of the valuable experience they had acquired through the exercise of their sacerdotal and pastoral duties. No sign of special deference came from Christ's Vicar, however, for those dismissed pastors who have been deprived of both office and benefits, committed to their parishioners' charity in their old age and poverty, and who look like a living picture of the Church of the past.

The Montinian Church

MARVELOUS HARMONY OF CHURCH AND STATE

One of the circumstances that was especially brought to the attention of many foreigners attending the thirty-ninth International Eucharistic Congress, was the complete collaboration and perfect harmony between civil and ecclesiastical authorities, the former giving full support to the latter for the celebration of this internationally significant event. It is no exaggeration to say that everybody, from the president of the republic down to the lowest Colombian soldier, was at the disposal of the promoters and organizers of the Congress.

This was paradoxical, inasmuch as the "Maritainian" opinions which have invaded the Church reject all concordats or privileges, as well as all sorts of cooperation with governments, so that the Church might be able to develop its apostolic work in a more independent way.

It was also paradoxical that the purple robes of the cardinals, the flaring cassocks of bishops and monsignors, the religious habits, the *aggiornated* dresses of nuns, and the uniforms of Catholic pupils clashed and mixed with the uniforms of generals, soldiers, policemen, and traffic officials. Beside the Pope stood the president of the republic, beside the cardinals, the secretaries of government and high-ranking officers of the Colombian army. I wondered: could this Congress of so many cardinals, bishops and religious, including the Pope himself, have been possible without the union, harmony, and endorsement of the government? Could the visit and declarations of the Rev. Father Pedro Arrupe, S.J., have been possible? Without those old established structures that they had audaciously decided to demolish, could the ecclesiastics, the venerable members of LAMEC, and the worldwide progressivists have had this brilliant occasion to start the fire of revolution that they had boldly decreed for Latin America?

It was the prevailing oligarchy, which many think must be eliminated in order to establish real Christianity, that made the Congress possible by ensuring its splendor and safety in spite of a restless milieu, where it seemed that the ghost of Camilo Torres was sinisterly reflected on the Colombian Andes. It was the same rich exploiters who, by means of generous gifts, paid for the large expenditures involved in the preparation, organization, and realization of all the acts of that Congress.

The following quotation from a medical report by Dr. Juan Mendoza Vega describes a single item of the large disbursements the Colombian government had to make in order to appropriately prepare the country to host so many thousands of people coming from various regions and countries:

> The International Eucharistic Congress is a public health *emergency* for Bogotá and for the whole country. Last January, the Department of Public

The Papal Visit and Revolutionary Activism

Health appointed a special committee with the aim of forecasting the sanitary problems the Congress would entail, to the extent that such forecast is scientifically possible, in order to take effective preventive steps in advance.

The secretary himself presides over it and its six divisions, each of which has subdivisions that are responsible for a total of nineteen aspects of the potential health problem. Starting in January, the whole team began to elaborate a general services plan; afterwards, several weeks were devoted to the financing of *ten million pesos* for the purchase of ambulances, medical appliances, and other supplies which are to be distributed to hospitals once the Congress is over.

Now, taking into account the government's constant untiring support of the hierarchy, clergy, and lay organizations of the Congress, again I ask: Could the planning and celebration of this event have een possible without this aid? If the government and the wealthy classes had not contributed generously, could the Pope and the hierarchy have even *thought* about undertaking such a vast project?

ACCORDING TO PUBLIC OPINION, WHAT WAS THE MEANING OF THE PAPAL VISIT?

Various comments were issued about the Pope's projected visit to America. The Eucharistic idea did not appear very convincing, especially after the legate was appointed. The *Osservatore Romano*, official organ of the Vatican, tried to deny a prevailing opinion that the Congress and the Pope's visit were a long-range political gesture. This is the UPI text issued at the Vatican on August 20, as it appeared in the *El Tiempo* of Bogotá on August 21, 1968:

> THE VISIT OF PAUL VI IS RELIGIOUS, NOT POLITICAL. *Severe Reply of the Vatican to Leftist Groups' Criticism.* Vatican City, August 20 (UPI)—Today the Vatican replied to leftist criticism about the forthcoming Pope's trip, stressing that the tour is religious and not political.
>
> It appears as if political and social definitions, instead of a religious message, are to be expected from the Pope, says the *Osservatore Romano*, official organ of the Vatican today.
>
> It deplores the wide publicity given by the left-wing press to the criticism made of a Pontiff's first trip to Latin America.
>
> The Vatican newspaper points out that, instead of concentrating on giving journalistic information about extreme situations, eccentricities, and polemic dissidences within the Latin American Catholic Church, it is essential to link the Pope's tour to the local bishops' constant efforts toward renovation and pastoral coordination.

The Montinian Church

As a reply to the charge that the Pope is indifferent to the penury of millions of Latin Americans, it points out that the Pope, in his last Sunday sermon, called for an end to social injustice, idle privilege, and dreadful poverty.

It also mentions previous socially concerned papal documents, such as the recent and controversial encyclical on birth control.

"In his constant and firm pastoral teachings, Paul VI has never evaded these problems," according to the Vatican newspaper in answer to left-wing attacks, including that of *L'Unita*, official organ of the Italian Communist Party, which says that the Pope's trip could not be of any help to relieve Latin American poverty.

The Pontiff keeps on preparing his three-day trip *to the world's most Catholic continent* . . .

Vatican sources stated today that the texts of the speeches Paul VI will deliver at the 39th International Eucharistic Congress and at the Latin American Episcopal Conference (LAMEC) on Thursday, Friday, and Saturday are already complete, together with their translations into the leading languages.

The above text of the UPI dispatch from Vatican City clearly shows that in both Europe and America the Pope's trip was considered to be a socio-economic and political tour, instead of a pious and exclusively religious peregrination. There were other circumstances that seemed to justify such predictions, such as: the intense propaganda coming from Fr. Ricardo Lombardi, S.J., whose ideas of redemption are well-known; the meeting of the General of the Jesuit Order with the Latin American provincials and the ratified documents emerging therefrom; and the Pope's social ideas, as contained in his many speeches and, above all, in his encyclical *Populorum Progressio*.

By means of these predictions, the leftists pressed the Pope to openly condemn *prevailing injustice* in all of Latin America, in favor of progress and a more equitable distribution of wealth, to quickly and effectively eliminate the dreadful poverty, famine, and underdevelopment. In this manner, the Church became ideologically bound to and engaged with leftist forces that, for a long time, had been planning *Castroite* subversion, chaos, and propaganda throughout Latin America. In turn, the leftists sought the Pope's benevolent approval for the redeeming activity of the guerillas.

We real Catholics also feared the Pope's visit. What was the Pope going to say in his numerous speeches? What was his legate going to tell us? What would Helder Cámara, Sergio Méndez Arceo and other similar prelates tell us? What would the prelates of the Latin American Episcopal Conference decide? The prelude was not too reassuring. In the powder keg of Latin America, the voice of the Catholic hierarchy could be the fuse that would explode the bomb.

"It is essential," the Vatican newspaper said, "to link the Pope's tour to the local bishops' constant efforts toward renovation and pastoral coordination." Given the vague and wide meaning of these two words, *renovation* and *pastoral*, it was not easy to ascertain the meaning of the Pope's tour and to link it to the local bishops' *constant efforts*. If, from the onset of the Council, we study the episcopal activity, the documents issued, and the ratifications rendered by the conferences, we must conclude that our prelates disregarded some of Christ's spiritual gospel and His high interest in the salvation of souls, in order to dedicate themselves to the material welfare of our people.

In his address of August 17, Paul VI had said: "It pleases us that this religious affirmation should take place in our beloved Latin America, where the faith is reviving a great social charity and where we anticipate a growing civil justice and a larger Christian prosperity." These words clearly explain the link between the *Pope's tour* and the local bishops' *efforts toward renovation and pastoral coordination*.

The Pope came to Latin America to endorse, orient, and promote the pastoral efforts of the bishops who, having realized that the evangelizing and pastoral work of previous centuries was a failure, wanted to effectively remedy the huge and most urgent needs of our indigent and underdeveloped poor classes, so as to begin a new evangelization of Latin America by means of a *complete rectification of the past*.

Nobody believes the Pope to be indifferent to the indigence of millions of Latin Americans. In fact, His Holiness has called for an end to social injustice in more than one of his speeches. What really surprises me is the Vatican newspaper's definition of "social injustice:" "*idle privilege*" on the one hand and "*dreadful misery*" on the other. This is the impressive way by which demagogues or the ignorant are accustomed to describe Latin American underdevelopment: a Latin America comprised of two social classes, the unjust, oppressive, and merciless, rich oligarchy, and the starved, oppressed, underdeveloped masses who are seen as too feeble to put an end to their "dreadful misery."

This regrettable situation results from several centuries of slavery, during which the underdeveloped people have been victimized by some merciless exploiters. The Church of colonial times, as well as the Church after independence, was, unfortunately, associated with this caste of soulless tyrants. The wrongs of this ignominious past must be confessed by means of a *mea culpa* of deep repentance, and effaced by means of redeeming actions.

L'Unita, official organ of the Italian Communist Party, knowingly lied when it affirmed that the Pope's tour could not be of any help to relieve misery and poverty in Latin American countries. It knew that the Latin American bishops and clergymen were already *engaged in an immense venture designed to change the political and social structures* that exist today in those countries. The "idle privilege" had to be eliminated and the "dreadful misery" had to be replaced by audaciously implanting new structures, liquidating the ignominious and shameful past. The Pope's tour was supposed to have reinforced the bishops' efforts toward "renovation" and "pastoral coordination."

Despite the changes that legislation has imposed on government attitudes, however, and despite the new mentality that has been introduced by prelates and clergymen, the Catholic Church, its bishops and its priests, continue to exercise a decisive influence over the underdeveloped sector of Latin America.

The Pope's trip, the previous gatherings of the LAMEC leaders and of the Jesuits, the apostolic tours of Fr. Lombardi and his Society for a Better World, and the entire program of the Congress definitely had a *more social and political* character than a religious or Eucharistic one.

At the Argentinian Embassy in Rome on October 18, 1968, at a meeting attended by His Eminence Antonio Cardinal Samoré, president of the Pontifical Commission for Latin America, Msgr. Eduardo Pironio, Argentine bishop and secretary of LAMEC, and Msgr. Giovanni Benelli, it was disclaimed that there had been *any tendency favoring violence* at the recent general meeting of the Latin American bishops in Medellín. According to His Eminence, prelates, priests, and laymen voluntarily joined with the Pope, who, when visiting Colombia last August, *condemned violence as a means of changing the political and socio-economic structures of Latin America.*

This information from the Associated Press confirms that the international comments were continuing to follow the idea that the Pope's trip to South America was a political tour whose main purpose was to boldly change the political and socio-economic structure of Latin America. It is evident, however, that some of the bishops, priests, and laymen boldly surpassed the Pope's program, in the belief that violence is not only unavoidable, but helpful. The presence of certain bishops such as Helder Cámara and Sergio Méndez Arceo, Mexican priests such as Pedro Velázquez, Enrique Maza, Felipe Pardinas, the Spanish refugee Ramón de Ertze Garamendi (present canon of the Cathedral of Mexico), as well as the former French priest-worker, Fr. Agustín Desobry, O.P., should suffice to demonstrate that the LAMEC Conference *was definitely infiltrated by advocates of violence.*

A letter from the Brazilian Bishop Helder Cámara to the mother of the guerilla-priest Camilo Torres supports my accusation which is aimed solely at unmasking subversion in disguise under cover of the apostolate. It reads as follows:

Recife, 7/27/68
Mrs. Isabel Restrepo de Torres
Bogotá, Colombia

    Only yesterday did I receive your letter of July 9. Please try to understand

The Papal Visit and Revolutionary Activism

why I cannot accept your fraternal invitation.

I wish to stay in Bogotá as modestly as possible. I will be there on my way to Medellín, just in time to attend the opening of the second meeting of the Latin American hierarchy, as well as the closing procession of the International Eucharistic Congress.

Even in Medellín, I will do my utmost to avoid much attention. *What is important is teamwork and united effort. I am certain that Camilo understands, approves, and blesses me from Heaven.*

At Holy Mass I will always pray for you.

Your friend and admirer in Christ,

Helder Cámara

This letter from the well-known, restless, and communizing Archbishop of Recife, friend and fellow-traveler of the Bishop of Cuernavaca, shows the former's intimate support, sympathy, and commitment to the cause of the late guerilla-priest, the poor Camilo Torres. His tactics are based on concealment; he wants "to stay in Bogotá as modestly as possible;" he wants to do his utmost "to avoid much attention." These precautionary tactics, however, are designed *to undertake a teamwork* in Medellín; in other words, he wants to impose his fighting methods on those very good prelates who are presiding and attending the LAMEC gathering. These are artful and cunning Marxist tactics which secretly undermine and destroy under the cover of programs of progress and redemption. That is why Don Helder affirms in his letter that Camilo "understands, approves, and blesses" him, if he is actually able to bless anyone in his present state.

How, then, are we to correlate Cardinal Samoré's denial of pro-violent tendencies at the recent conference in Medellín, with the regrettable violent events that occurred a few weeks after the LAMEC meeting? The confidential letter from the Archbishop of Recife to Camilo Torres' mother is the key to understanding the game, in which His Eminence surely took no part.

What occurred in this subcontinent after the Eucharistic Congress and the Medellín conference is extremely serious and revealing, for it represented one of the worst periods of social and political turmoil in all of Latin America. Looking from the outside, it cannot be doubted that the Vatican, the Jesuits, many bishops, priests, and Catholic laymen who lead national and international organizations, were convinced of the urgent need for *a bold change of socio-economic and political structures* in all of Latin America. The clergymen, however, did not wish to suggest or to ask for these bold changes but rather to lead the revolutionary movements either with, without, or against the respective governments. This decision of those ecclesiastics, even if we deem it to be holy, just, and apostolic, was, nevertheless, *an order to use violence.*

Violence came in the most serious and bloody conflicts of college students in Uruguay, Brazil, and Mexico. The Bolivian President, General René Barrientos, announced to the nation and the world that the guerillas had reappeared on the Bolivian scene. In Costa Rica, banana laborers set fire to the fields and premises, and in Argentina, the number of violent and bloody clashes between workers and soldiers increased dramatically. In Panamá and Peru, the presidents were overthrown by a *coup d'etat*; it is interesting to note that General Velasco of Peru attempted to justify his coup on the basis of *an urgent need to change structures*. Later on we will comment on the speech given by the Cardinal-Archbishop of Lima before the Pope at the Cathedral of Bogotá, on the day that the Latin American Episcopal Conference was inaugurated.

The immediate and particular causes of these revolutionary events and their external manifestations have varied, depending on the social, political, and economic problems of each individual country. Nevertheless, the coincidence of time and objectives among all of them indicates a common factor and demonstrates the direct or indirect influence of the participants at Bogotá and Medellín.

In the face of these facts and pronouncements, we may not doubt that Catholics and progressive clergymen feel themselves pre-destined to bring about the change of structures that the poor and underdeveloped Latin American countries require.

In an article published in Hermosillo, Sonora, on January 1, 1971, by Fr. Jose Esteban Sarmiento, one of the unconditional followers of Msgr. Quintero, already famous for his cunning progressivism, the following concepts of the "new theology" are voiced:

> In yesterday's commentary we were not quite in agreement with interclassicism, namely, the philosophical position of those who, accepting the world as something already made, without possibility of change, believe that the only thing to do is to do nothing. The acceptance of one's role in this human drama, even if it be that of a wretch, would be for them the ideal goal as it signifies the submission of the human will to that of the divine, which, they say, comprises perfect sanctity.
>
> We do not deny or doubt the above nor do we affirm it to be the precise bourgeois position. We do believe, however, that the world in which we live is not a world already made and that it is within the sense of history and Providence that we make it and continuously improve it.
>
> Within this world that is in the process of being built in the material, scientific, technical, social, and human spheres, there are antagonistic classes which are not only different but opposed to each other. This fact has penetrated all of human history to the extent that some people are always on the bottom and become alienated as a result of abuse by those on top.
>
> Acceptance of the fact, however, that there are struggling classes or classes

The Papal Visit and Revolutionary Activism

that can start their struggle at any moment, does not imply acceptance of class struggle as a method. The Church rejects such struggle, and it must do so if this struggle is inspired by hate and revenge and if its sole goal is to unshackle violence. Once hate is removed, however, class struggle inspired by love for one's neighbor, rich or poor, must be accepted, because one fights for love too.

If one loves the poor, words do not suffice and must be replaced by a true effort to liberate them. If one does not love, one will not do anything to transform the "system" which generates evil for so many people. Love and battle can go together. Because of love, one fights against those who want to maintain the system, against those who, because of self-interest, reject change, and against rich and privileged people who drop their privilege only when they lose the fight.

That is why, from a Christian standpoint, one must not fight against persons but against evil actions. We must all love one another, but we are also obliged to reject and even to hate evil. Moreover, it is *deeds* which are evil, for, in this world, differences do not arise so much from differences in talent as from sin. Rich people and oppressed people exist because of injustice, avarice, and arrogance; poor people exist because of oppression, vice, and irresponsibility.

The fight for love is the fight against sin in which one must not recognize allegiances. Should we tolerate oppressive exploiters just because they are Catholics? No; our duty is to denounce injustice, even at the risk of losing the protection they are willing to pay for the complacent silence of the Church. If the price be that of forgetting the poor, the Church's prosperity serves no useful purpose.

The struggle, however, must not be a violent one. The Church condemns the desperate violence of the poor as much as the institutional violence of the rich. In this struggle it is love that matters. The revolution of hate attempts to settle everything by means of an intense social cataclysm. The revolution of love, however, whose manifesto is the Gospel, is perhaps slower, but it has been pushing forward for almost two thousand years, and is now the only sign of freedom and hope.

Here we have a typical "progressivist" sermon which includes unheard-of statements that are apparently contradictory and openly subversive. They do not agree with "interclassicism," but later they implicitly say that it is necessary to eliminate all social classes. The world has not been completely made but must continue to be made in a constant "becoming" in which its builders are men, not God.

The goal of this constant evolution is a classless society. This is the meaning of "history and Providence." I would rather say that this is the meaning of Marxist dialectics and of that giddy illusion of all Communists and their progressivist confréres. They do this by means of sophistic reasoning, for the world has already been made, not by us, but by God. In this world, we men must work to improve our spiritual condition and to save our souls, which is a great personal task; then, and only then, must we attempt to improve our material condition, always keeping in mind the law of life by which *"thou shalt earn thy bread by the sweat of thy brow."*

We must not forget, however, the words of St. Pius X: "It is in conformity with the order established by God that in human society there be rulers and the ruled, masters and workers, rich and poor, wise and unwise, noblemen and plebeians." (*Pontifical Doctrines, Social Documents*, Madrid, 1959, p. 464).

The classes are not inherently antagonistic; they have been made so by the Communist revolution which the ecclesiastical progressivists have joined as fellow travelers. Moreover, to make "love" an inspiration for this fight is plain celestial music. The Communist struggle is never made for the sake of love, nor with sprinkling holy water, with episcopal smiles, or with "compromising" phrases uttered from pulpits or written in newspapers, but rather with hate, rifles, machine guns, bombs, blood, fire, and destruction.

According to the new redemptors, it is the "system" and the "structures" which impede them from helping the poor; in actuality, however, it is they themselves who are unwilling to spare a meal, a walk, a cigarette, or the least bit of help for them. For them, the "system" includes the government, the constitution, the laws, the courts, the police, the army, our institutions, nationalism, and love of country; these, then, are the obstacles that must be destroyed to establish a classless society of the proletariat dictatorship. The rest of Fr. Sarmiento's article is verbiage taken from the sermons of a novice seminarian.

Taking these arguments into consideration, we do not believe it contemptuous to affirm that His Holiness' trip to Latin America was designed to concretely apply his opinions and doctrine, as stated in the *Populorum Progressio*.

PROPAGANDA DURING THE EUCHARISTIC CONGRESS

Besides the official propaganda distributed to the pilgrims by the central office, there was subversive propaganda which circulated publicly and profusely. Copies of the Communist newspaper *United Front (Frente Unido)*, were sold at every corner. The founder of this newspaper was the infamous guerilla-priest, Fr. Camilo Torres Restrepo, and its editor was Mr. Germán Guzmán Campos. Three pictures stood out on the front page, that of Paul VI in the middle, with Camilo Torres on one side and "Ché" Guevara, the notorious guerilla leader killed in Bolivia, on the other.

Three thoughts by Christ, Camilo, and "Ché" Guevara, summarize the message of the newspaper:

The Papal Visit and Revolutionary Activism

CHRIST

1. Christ, my leader, taught . . . *"I have not come to the world to bring peace, but war. Only the violent will enter the kingdom of heaven."*

According to these statements, which falsify Christ's Gospel, the goals of Christianity are violent revolution and war.

CAMILO

2. The worst ballast for the Colombian Church is to have wealth and political power, which compel it to base its decisions on human, rather than divine, wisdom. . . .

It is very difficult to serve two masters: God and mammon. . . .

The Colombian clergy is the most reactionary in the world, even more so than that of Spain. It becomes evident that *the only progressivist churches of the world are the poor ones.*

3. Let me tell you, even if it sounds ridiculous, that a true revolutionary is led by true feelings of love. It is impossible to conceive of a real revolutionary without this quality. Perhaps this is one of the leader's great dramas, in which he must add a cool mind to his passionate spirit in order to make painful decisions without tightening a muscle.

Our vanguard revolutionaries must idealize their love for the people and its most sacred causes, so as to make it unique and indivisible. . . .

The leaders of the revolution have children who, when they begin to babble, are unable to name their fathers, women who must take part in this great sacrifice of their lives so as to bring about the revolution to its destiny and no friends outside of their fellow revolutionaries. There can be no life outside of the revolution.

"CHÉ"

At the end of the page, we read this astonishing synthesis of progressivist thinking:

The duty of every Christian is to be a revolutionary . . . the duty of every revolutionary is to make the revolution! The duty, then, of every Latin American Christian is to work for immediate revolution. Some say it should be violent, others, peaceful. But everyone agrees that today one cannot be a good Catholic if one does not fight for the revolution in his own way.

On the following page we read:

The Montinian Church

The message of Inti Peredo: THE BOLIVIAN GUERILLAS ARE NOT DEAD. *They have just started.*

Inti Peredo, political commissary of the Bolivian National Liberation Army which its founder, "Ché" Guevara, defined in his diary as a growing political and revolutionary force, has just released a piece of information designed to let the people of Bolivia and the world know that the guerilla movement in Bolivia is not dead, thereby refuting all allegations coming from revisionists, traitors, pseudo-revolutionaries, and pro-imperialists, about the supposed failure of the revolutionary road chosen by "Ché" and the fighters who died with him. For the benefit of the readers of *United Front*, we are publishing fragments of this transcendental message:

The Bolivian guerillas are not dead; they have just started!

The Bolivian guerillas are marching steadily, and we do not hesitate to forecast their brilliant final success *which will establish SOCIALISM in Latin America.*

From the beginning, our country has lived through a *revolutionary experience whose continental consequences are unimaginable.* The beginning of our fight, however, was accompanied by a tragic setback in the irreparable loss of our friend, comrade, and commander, Ernesto "Ché" Guevara, together with many other fighters. They who constituted the purest and noblest part of generations of our continent, did not hesitate for a moment to offer their lives on the altar of human redemption.

But all these painful episodes, far from intimidating us, fortify our revolutionary consciousness, strengthen and increase our decision to fight, and enable us to produce, in the crucible of war, new fighters and leaders who will render glorious honor and homage to the fallen.

We know why we are fighting. We are not making war for the sake of war, nor are we deluded visionaries. We trust human beings as such, and we are not fighting to satisfy personal or party ambitions. *Our sole and final goal is the liberation of Latin America, which is not only our continent, but also our fatherland, temporarily divided into twenty republics.*

We are convinced that the dream of Bolivia and "Ché" to politically and geographically unify Latin America can only be fulfilled by means of an armed struggle, which is the only worthy, honest, glorious, and irreversible way of motivating people. There is no other purer way than armed combat, of which guerilla warfare is the most efficient.

That is why, as long as there be an honest man in Latin America, the guerillas will not die, and armed struggle will develop vigorously until such time that all the people will awaken and rise up in arms against their common enemy—U.S. imperialism.

The Bolivian guerillas are not dead but have just begun. . . . For us, guerilla warfare is a form of prolonged combat that people use to take power, and whose essential feature is to control the duration.

The first stage of any guerilla struggle consists in surviving until it can root itself in the people, particularly among the peasants. Starting from this nucleus, its power will renew itself until it reaches such a degree of development that it becomes an invincible force. . . .

In our case, the budding guerilla was not able to surpass this first stage, but other buds will sprout and reach complete development, until the enemy is completely crushed.

From this circumstantial fact, our critics drew the conclusion that it is the way which is wrong. They refuse to pay attention to or to analyze the causes that provoked our partial and temporary defeat, for to do so would mean that they would have to judge themselves. . . .

They watched our fight from afar, and, above all, they isolated it, refused to aid it, and spread anti-guerilla propaganda in the hearts of their militant followers. Then, to feign "anti-imperialism," they issued two communiqués of "solidarity" with the guerillas. In actuality, however, they limited their solidarity to empty talk about their polite moral support of a small group of "romantic dreamers."

The Bolivian Communist Party leaders talk about getting the party ready to take power by *using all known methods*. All people must participate in the takeover of power, and, since they must be prepared for that, one must not talk to them about "using all known methods" when one is preparing a takeover. When the party or a group plans a takeover of power, it chooses a particular way; to do otherwise is not to take itself seriously.

They graciously pretend to give up the guerilla way because of its first defeat, but they promote the "democratic" or "reformist" way, in spite of the *continuous* failures of the latter. Let us discard the electoral problem! *No true revolutionary can believe that this is the way to take control of Bolivia or any other Latin American country.*

. . . We are not against people fighting for their economic recovery, but we are sure that this could be much more fruitfully and effectively achieved if they were to face a government that has been intimidated and weakened by the actions of a guerilla nucleus. . .

It is this guerilla nucleus that shows the people, by means of facts, that it is possible to face the might of imperialism and its puppets, and not only to face it but to defeat it.

People, especially peasants, do not support anything that they do not believe to exist. To expect their support for a non-existing armed struggle is to play a game, the way some theoreticians of armed struggle do when they demand massive support beforehand. The peasants will effectively support a guerilla nucleus when it shows strength, and only then.

That is why, at the first stage, the goal of the guerillas is to become strong and to survive in the field of operations, none of which is possible without an uninterrupted flow of aid from the cities. In our case, this aid was refused to us by the political forces which knew of the existence of our movement.

. . . Some people think we are disbanding. They are fooling themselves. We are reorganizing our regiments to fight in the mountains, because we firmly believe that this is the only way to liberate our country and Latin America from the clutches of Yankee imperialism.

We do not seek to create a political party, but an armed force capable of facing and defeating the army, which is the main supporting tool of the existing regime.

Neither will we become the armed instrument of any political party. . . .

We are fully convinced that guerilla warfare is not an auxiliary tool of any other "superior form of struggle." On the contrary, as international experience has borne out, we believe that it will govern and direct the emancipation of all our people.

. . . No single group or political party can fulfill the task of liberating our people. In this we agree with the left wing. We need a broad, anti-imperialistic front. The question is how to set it up. . . .

Our brief experience has shown us that much more has been accomplished in a few months of armed struggle than in many years of sitting at round tables.

. . . The sectarianism of the vanguards is also shown by their desire to subordinate the guerilla leadership to the political. One might ask: to whose political leadership? . . .

Are they, by chance, trying to divide the conflict into a military and peaceful struggle and to subordinate the former to the latter? . . . Or are they intending to use the armed conflict merely as a pressure device for the benefit of the *"political struggle" in the cities*? . . . We prefer a unique, military-political leadership, taking into account that the conduct of guerilla warfare must be the responsibility of the most capable revolutionary squadrons.

The conflict in the cities must assist the guerilla action. Therefore, the guerillas cannot be led from the cities. It is the guerillas themselves who must lead; to do otherwise is to condemn them to ignorance, inaction, and failure. It is the struggle itself that will progressively create its leaders. The real leaders of the people will arise in the midst of the struggle, and no one who is a true revolutionary may request the leadership or be afraid of being deprived thereof. . . .

The Papal Visit and Revolutionary Activism

Throughout the world, the forces of national liberation are dealing heavy blows to their common enemy: imperialism. The cruel Vietnamese war, despite its militarization and stabilization of the United States' economy so as to prevent a crisis, is creating a serious problem for that country. All the Yankee military might is already impotent to stop that glorious people under arms.

The struggle of our Vietnamese brethren is the struggle of all the revolutionaries of the world. They are fighting for and with us, who must create a second Vietnam, thus fulfilling the legacy of our heroic Ernesto "Ché" Guevara.

Contrary to the way our enemies and the pseudo-revolutionaries depict it, the thesis of creating several Vietnams is neither whimsical nor the fruit of a warlike mentality, but one which corresponds to the reality that imperialism will never give up its positions voluntarily. And in our continent, through its department, the Organization of American States, it will push its lackeys in the various countries to join forces to crush any rebellions of the people.

This [is] the epoch of continental revolution . . .

We have lost one battle, and in it fell the top leader of the oppressed, Commander Ernesto "Ché" Guevara.

But the guerillas are one, and we will never stop, for we who fought beside "Ché" do not know the meaning of the word "surrender." His blood and that of the fighters who shed their blood on the Bolivian countryside will germinate the seed of liberation and convert our continent into a volcano of fire and destruction against imperialism.

This will be the victorious Vietnam which the romantic, visionary, and heroic "Ché" dreamed and loved.

To achieve these ideals we are ready to win or die.
To achieve these ideals our Cuban comrades died.
To achieve these ideals our Peruvian comrades died.
To achieve these ideals our Argentinian comrades died.
To achieve these ideals our Bolivian comrades died.

All honor and glory to Tania, Joaquín, Pablo Chang, Moisés Guevara, Jorge Vásquez, Aniceto Reynaga, Antonio Jiménez, Coco Peredo, and to all those who fell bearing arms. . . .

Let not imperialism and its lackeys sing of victory, because the war has not ended; it has just begun. Let us return to the mountains! Once again, our cry of VICTORY OR DEATH will shake Bolivia!

Undoubtedly, this document has capital importance for the purpose of understanding and evaluating the internationally planned program of intense Communistic subversion in Latin America. Those who still believe the

Communist menace to be a myth, something no longer in existence, or a product of feverish and sickly minds, will perhaps open their eyes to the real, imminent and most active danger faced by all Latin American countries, especially Mexico. To quote Inti Peredo: "The ... guerillas are not dead, they have just started! ... [w]e do not hesitate to forecast their brilliant final success [and that of the revolutionary forces] *which will establish SOCIALISM IN LATIN AMERICA.*"

According to the document which we have just analyzed, the guerilla warfare of "Che" Guevara was a revolutionary experience whose continental consequences are still unpredictable. The forces of subversion do not deem it to have been a failure or a decisive triumph of the free world but, on the contrary, a fruitful experience for the militants of international Communism. "Che" will become a martyr and a world hero of revolutionary socialism.

I believe that one of the most powerful and frightful weapons of the Latin American guerillas is their mysticism which unfortunately, the free world no longer has, for those in charge of fomenting and preserving it for future generations have been most active in fighting and destroying it. What would we give for that same firmness, unity, and fearlessness in our own Catholic youth? Unfortunately, the combat spirit of that glorious Mexican Catholic Youth for Action (ACJM) of the time of Fr. Berguend is already over! It pains me to say that it was the bishops who killed the old spirit in order to create a new, flexible, accommodating, and compromising ACJM.

Inti Peredo said: "... [All] these painful episodes, far from intimidating us, fortify our revolutionary consciousness, strengthen and increase our decision to fight, and enable us to produce, in the tough crucible of war, new fighters and leaders who will render glorious honor and homage to the fallen." *If only those of us who believe in God and fight for freedom were to speak like this!*

When Inti Peredo compares the attitude of the active, militant guerillas who face death, with that of the urban Communists who sympathize with the former and aid them to some extent while avoiding danger, he makes an observation that we can apply to our own people. Many there are who say they are enemies of Communism and cautiously aid those who fight ideological, moral, social, and political subversion, but how few are those who dare to participate in the battle and to jeopardize, if not their lives, at least their social position, economic interests, and comforts!

Inti Peredo's document must be deeply studied and understood, so as to assure us of a legitimate defense.

On the other hand, the most upsetting and embarrassing document for the Church in its struggle between liberty and slavery is the one published in that same issue of *United Front (Frente Unido)*, which was widely circulated in Bogotá at the time of the International Eucharistic Congress. We have read it

The Papal Visit and Revolutionary Activism

before because *Excelsior* had previously published it in Mexico. It deserves to be reproduced:

THE APOSTOLIC NUNCIO TO CUBA SPEAKS

Monsignor Cesare Zacchi, Apostolic Nuncio to Cuba, is a post-Conciliar bishop: young, tall, congenial, and with an unobtrusive intellectual manner.

Between 1959 and 1960, entire communities of priests and nuns abandoned Havana and other cities, either as a protest to alleged restrictions to freedom of worship (their migration performing the function of stimulating a political crisis, anyway) or because of governmental requests, in the face of indisputable evidence of their involvement in counter-revolutionary activities. Since 1959, and even after the Bay of Pigs invasion, deposits of weapons were discovered behind main altars. In the years which followed, priests were involved in almost every disclosed conspiracy, including one in which several Franciscans took part in a plot to murder the prime minister (some of them are still in prison). The government, in turn, modified numerous ecclesiastical privileges in the past nine years: priests were forbidden to wear their garb in public following the manner of the Mexican Revolution; vast church properties were confiscated (the wound has still not healed); and religious school teaching has been constrained.

Since his arrival in Havana in 1960, Monsignor Zacchi has had to face this complicated dispute. The Church maintained a humble and stubborn stance, considering itself persecuted, while the government refused to deem it innocent and dissociated from its former protectors, the members of the large oligarchy which had been thrown out of the country, and considered it to be an accomplice of the designing United States interventionists. The Nuncio himself avows that this situation had (and has) little to do with the problem of religious expression itself. Catholic worship has never been prohibited in Cuba. Even in 1961 after the invasion, Father Pardiñas, Chaplain of the Rebel Army, celebrated a field Mass for thousands of believers at the civic plaza in Havana.

The last issue of *Charity Almanac*, a Catholic magazine that has been published in Havana for 84 years without interruption, indicates that 200 churches, 15 male religious communities, and 16 feminine orders are functioning normally in this country. In the province of Havana alone, there are three medical care centers (two of which are foundling homes) and four hospitals under the control of religious orders, as well as three Catholic book stores.

Fr. Hilario Chaurrondo, C.M., editor of the *Almanac*, writes in the same issue:

The priests are working harder, taking care of six or seven churches. Catechetical schools are flourishing and finishing schools are being organized.

The Montinian Church

The liturgical movement is comforting; now, almost everyone prays aloud and knows what he is praying.

Fidel's New Attitude

Until last year, the hierarchy consisted of the two Archbishops of Havana and Santiago de Cuba, and four bishops. At the end of 1967, the Vatican appointed bishops for three more auxiliary dioceses without consulting the government, which accepted the appointees. Moreover, during this time, Monsignor Zacchi was anointed Bishop of Zella. Dignitaries of the Canadian Church came to Havana for the formalities, which took place at the 400-year-old cathedral. The government provided cars and various other facilities for the visitors and the Nuncio to travel over the country. Thus, almost forgotten pictures were seen again in Cuba: Fidel Castro at a party, surrounded by bishops and archbishops of the Cuban dioceses, and church prelates riding in Soviet-made military jeeps through the countryside.

Since freedom of worship is not involved, the clash between the Cuban clergy and the revolutionary government is political, rather than religious. It is the Church's millenary wisdom which speaks when Zacchi says that the Church must accommodate to all kinds of systems in order to save souls and lead the flock. This is the thesis which the Nuncio is applying in Cuba, with positive results for the Vatican, insofar as its goals, to remain and to preach, are concerned.

I asked Monsignor Zacchi if this orientation comes from specific guidelines provided by the Vatican Council. "Not at all," he answered. "It came before the Council, although it coincides, to some extent, with what the Council decided."

I then asked him if he considers himself as a neutral third party, as an arbiter in the quarrel between Church and government. He does not deny it. "I am not impartial, of course, but, because of my diplomatic position, I am in touch with governmental spheres, whereas such contacts are still forbidden to Church officials. Therefore, I have unwillingly become a sort of voice of the Church before the government. At the same time, I advise the hierarchy as to what I believe to be the regime's opinion on these problems."

Question: "Have the grounds for the government's distrust of the Church and clergy disappeared?"

Answer: "The emigration of dissidents to the United States relieved some of the pressure being exerted on the clergy. Since the *worms* [counter-revolutionaries] were the main link between clergy and society, their political ideas were unavoidably adopte'by them. The clergy, therefore, usually got a distorted picture of the revolutionary movement. As these persons began to leave, the priests began to get in touch with other Catholics, and, as a result,

The Papal Visit and Revolutionary Activism

they are now able to judge things from a different viewpoint." (The italics in this section, concerning Monsignor Zacchi have been added by the author.)

Question: "Does this mean that the clergy is in the process of becoming integrated?"

Answer: "No, we are still far from that possibility, but, on the other hand, some priests have changed their minds, partially as a result of certain governmental acts of tolerance. For example, some priests who had emigrated for political reasons have been allowed to return and work at their parishes."

Question: "What improvements, then, do you see in the situation?"

Answer: "In the past few years, both parties have realized some basic changes in their convictions. *The Church has realized that the revolution is irreversible.* A few years ago, the priests considered it to be temporary, that any moment conditions would change and the atheistic, socialistic regime would turn out to be but a nightmare of the past. But now, socialism has been institutionalized, and the revolution has proven to be perpetual. In this stabilized situation, the Church has had to plan how to enter the new society. The government, in turn, has detected this new mentality. Through the Nuncio it speaks with the Church or at least gets first-hand information about how it is currently thinking. This is the beginning of mutual confidence. Many things can improve if the Cuban Church realizes that this is its country, and if the government becomes aware of the Church's willingness to work together with it."

Question: "Can you easily see Fidel Castro when you deem it necessary?" It has been said that the Nuncio and Castro are personal friends but nevertheless, Monsignor Zacchi is cautious.

Answer: "I last talked to him two years ago when he came to a reception at my residence. Last year he accepted another invitation but cancelled his visit because of the outbreak of the Middle East war. As you may know, he seldom visits Western embassies, and the Vatican may be no exception; there are, however, other channels to reach the governmental level."

On one hand, the answers of this subtle, new-style, diplomatic Bishop are quite sincere with respect *to the revolutionary fact itself.*

Question: "You have lived in Cuba long enough to see all the stages of a revolution now entering its adult age. In the beginning, you saw the condition of this country under the previous regimes. Do you think things have improved, and that the people have benefited by the revolution?"

Answer: "The people have experienced radical changes in their material condition, so much so that they now have a standard of living which they did not have previously. *Redistribution of wealth and social justice* now prevail, in contrast to the past."

Question: "Do you think a Catholic must be an integral part of the revolution?"

The Montinian Church

Answer: "I affirm this all the time. Catholics must join the mass organizations of the society in which they live. They must cooperate in voluntary works, join the miitias, join sport and cultural organizations, and also be active in *student movements and professional entities.* This will naturally promote mutual influences, with the result that certain Catholic ideals and concepts of life will penetrate the concepts of the revolution. Thus, the revolution will become truly representative of all the forms of feeling in this nation."

Question: "Would you accept a young Catholic joining the Communist party?"

Answer: "Well, here there is only one party, the Communist party, and its cadres perform *important concrete functions designed to carry out social change.* I see no inconvenience in a Catholic accepting the Marxist economic theories for the practical purpose of this activity within a revolutionary cadre."

Question: "What about the contradiction, in such a case, between dialectic materialism and Christian concepts concerning certain processes and their origins, between free will and determinism, and between certain collectivistic approaches and religion-endorsed individualism?"

Answer: "I think that for practical purposes those contradictions would not be at stake but would only be subject to theoretical discussion. A Catholic thus integrated would of course always maintain certain reserves with respect to specific demands." This answer notably defines the Nuncio's new viewpoint with respect to the giddy process of the revolution.

Question: "As you know, Fidel Castro was educated at a Jesuit school and was a Catholic while an adolescent. Taking into account his present behavior, would you consider him to be a Christian?"

Answer: "Of course he is not an ideological Christian, for he has declared himself a Marxist-Leninist, but I do consider him to be ethically Christian."

The above statements of the Nuncio to Havana, which have been published in *Excelsior* from Mexico and *United Front* from Bogotá, are indisputable evidence of the Vatican's regretful turnabout toward the socialist and communizing left wing. They also explain the real meaning of the *change of structures* which was mentioned so often in Bogotá and Medellín and appears so frequently in episcopal documents and in spontaneous statements of progressivistic lay leaders, such as Alvarez Icaza and Alejandro Avilés. Communism and its preceding stage, socialism, which the previous Popes had deemed to be intrinsically evil, incompatible with Catholic doctrine, and dreadful monsters from Hell, have been revised and subtly revalued according to new Conciliary views. The progressivist ecclesiastics have willingly agreed to dialogue about salvation with the representatives of the sinister might of Hell. Peaceful coexistence between love and hate, truth and error, liberty and slavery, plunder, spoils, firing squads, legalized crime, misfortune, ruin, inexpressible suffering, desperation, and the death of uncountable past and present victims of Communism in Cuba and throughout the world, has, according to this diplomat of the Vatican, been put into practice in the Cuba of Fidel Castro.

What did Monsignor Zacchi really say? The following are the principal points covered by the questions and answers above:

1. The 1959 and 1960 exodus of priests and religious from Cuba was due to their disagreement with the new regime and to their counter-revolutionary activities, not to religious persecution. Besides, their migration was intended to provoke a political crisis.

2. Caches of weapons were found behind main altars.

It is curious to notice the lack of perspicacity of the alleged conspirators who unanimously chose temples and main altars as hiding places for their weapons. Of course, we think the Castro government ought to have widely disclosed what the material evidence was.

What an eloquent argument to annihilate the reactionary forces! We also believe that the Cuban patriots, provided they found a more convenient hiding place, were exercising their legitimate right in hiding weapons they intended to use to resist international Communism's bloody tyranny.

3. The Nuncio admitted that Fidel's government has imposed severe restrictions on Church activities, among which the prohibition of religious school teaching was not the least. But these are just *peccata minuscula*!

4. The position of the Nuncio, since his arrival in 1960, was extremely delicate, as he found himself caught between two equally intransigent rivals, the Church and the government. The Church felt it was being persecuted, while the government considered the Church to be guilty and allied with its former sponsors, the rich, the oligarchs, and the imperialists.

This has always been the pretext of those who persecute the Church. When Calles[1] expelled bishops, shot priests, profaned temples, sent Catholics to jail, etc., he was supported by statutes he himself had enacted, and whose practical goal was to destroy the Catholic religion of Mexico. He said, "I do not persecute religion; I persecute rebel clergymen who do not abide by the law." He failed to say that the law denied religion, the Church, and the clergy.

As a matter of fact, it was Cuban ecclesiastics like Archbishop Peréz Cerantes of Santiago de Cuba, who not only saved the lives of Fidel Castro and the handful of plotters accompanying him, but also rendered possible the Communist revolution. These ecclesiastics thought they were aiding liberators while, in fact, they were aiding Communism. When Castro triumphed, the *Osservatore Romano* congratulated the Cuban people on behalf of the Vatican.

5. The Nuncio, although a diplomat, cannot be an impartial observer or an arbiter of this kind of dispute. Even though he is a diplomat, he is, above all, a Catholic, a priest, a bishop. His diplomatic status is that of a representative of

the Pope, of the Vicar of Jesus Christ, and head of the Catholic Church. When he affirms that he is impartial, he ceases to be a diplomat, because he ceases to be a Catholic and a representative of the Pope. *"He who is not with Me, is against Me,"* said Christ.

6. Worship has never been prohibited in Cuba. Avowing this to be true for argument's sake, it does not mean that the Catholic Church may take liberties in the performance of its highest, divinely prescribed duties. We have already seen that governmental restrictions have enslaved the *silent Church* in Cuba, as in all Communist countries. If the Nuncio contends that the present condition of the Church in Cuba had and has little to do with religious expression, namely with the freedom of the Church on that island, it means that, despite his diplomatic status, His Excellency has not realized what the real condition of the Catholic Church in this country is. Perhaps he believes Cuba to be a peaceful paradise where progressivist religion enjoys complete freedom because he is judging in accordance with the diplomatic privileges the Castroite tyranny graciously awards him. The same applies to Hungary, Poland, and other Communist-ruled countries.

That famous field Mass celebrated by the ill-famed chaplain of the rebel army, Father Pardiñas, was the last hoax Fidel and his men used to try to conceal their Communist ideology and their links with the Soviets from the Cuban people and the world.

7. To help deceive us and to justify the Papal Nuncio's scandalous statements beforehand, the journalist quotes precise figures he takes from the newest issue of *Charity Almanac*, a Catholic magazine that has been published on the island for 84 years:

> Presently, there are 210 churches, 15 male religious communities, and 16 feminine ones. In Havana alone, there are three medical care centers. Catechetical schools are flourishing and finishing schools are being organized. The liturgical movement is comforting; three new bishops have been appointed by the Vatican with the consent of the government. To facilitate the celebration of the consecration of the Nuncio, the government provided army jars and jeeps for the nunciature, so that the consecrating Canadian bishops could be at ease during their stay in Cuba.

We cannot help admiring the candor of this journalist who, without any further examination, accepts figures provided by Castro's police and research sources. Is it possible he knows nothing about the subtle, deceitful tactics Communists use to paralyze their enemies' defense and to turn such defense into unconditional support of their own goals? In spite of his efforts to use smooth expressions, the Papal Nuncio is not able to convince us that the Cuban Church has not been or is not being persecuted. His is a surrendering attitude.

8. "I have unwillingly become a sort of *voice of the Church* before the government," says the Nuncio. "At the same time, I advise the hierarchy as to what I believe to be the regime's opinion on these problems." Thus, the role of the Nuncio is that of a receiving and transmitting radio station. He conveys the Church's wishes to Fidel, and the regime's replies to the bishops. In this way, the Communist government, through minimal concessions, gets a most important information office, that of the Nuncio. It is thus understandable how Fidel and the Nuncio can sit at the same banquet tables. What would we have thought of Patriarch Pérez, if he had accepted the role of an intermediary between Calles and the Mexican Catholic bishops and people, during the fateful days of religious persecution?

9. The Nuncio says that the emigration of the dissidents to the United States relieved some of the pressure being exerted on the clergy, and that the *worms* living in Cuba constituted the clergy's main link with Cuban society. He further states that, as a result, the clergy almost always got deformed pictures of the revolutionary process, and that, as these people began to leave, the priests began to get in touch with a different kind of Catholic, with the end result that they were now able to judge from a different viewpoint.

History will record the Nuncio's shameful words as degrading evidence of *a most abject servility*. Is it possible for the Pope's representative to label as "worms" the faithful Catholics and former benefactors of the Church, whose only crime was not to accept Communism? We may conclude with this example that the same priests who today dine at the tables of the wealthy and receive their generous aid for their apostolic works and their personal benefit, may tomorrow be associated with their benefactors' enemies, who will insult them and call them *worms*.

According to the Pope's official representative, before those miserable "worms" emigrated, the clergy had wrong ideas and could not evaluate the revolutionary process correctly because of the pressure exerted by their stupid parishioners. Now, on the other hand, having been brainwashed and freed from the obscurantist pressure of the "worms," they judge things from a different standpoint and not only resign themselves to bow to the beneficial yoke of Communism, but also efficaciously cooperate in the fulfillment of the Communist program. They are not yet integrated, but it is certain that some priests have changed their way of thinking, partly as a result of Castro's scattered and opportune generous acts.

10. "... [b]oth [opposing] parties have realized some basic changes in their convictions." This affirmation is unintelligible. Does it mean that Communism, ceasing to be Communism, is beginning to accept the eternal Catholic truth? Or, on the contrary, that the Church is beginning to lose its fear of Communism, is studying it, and is finding it to be today's concrete fulfillment

(as Bishop Sergio Méndez Arceo[2] would say) of Christ's redemption? "The church," says the Nuncio, "has realized that the revolution is *irreversible*." Really, Monsignor? May the Church believe that *the gates of Hell have prevailed upon Jesus Christ's work*, against His Holy Church? May it accept that truth has been irreversibly defeated by error, justice by monstrous injustice, and love by hate? No, it cannot, for up until a few years ago, did we not firmly believe, in spite of the apparent successes of Communism in Cuba, Hungary, Czechoslovakia, Russia, and China, that this situation would not last indefinitely, that things would have to change in Cuba, that what you call *institutionalization* of bloody, atheistic Marxism will end, and that the way of thinking and talking like His Excellency will be over, as has happened with so many storms that have menaced Peter's bark?

This dialogue that the Nuncio carries on with the atheistic, irreligious, and criminal government of Cuba may not and does not mean the beginning of a state of confidence in this government on the part of any Cuban who really loves his country or of any individual who loves freedom. Confidence in destruction? Confidence in slavery? Confidence in the imponderable tragedy of his fatherland? To think like this, Mister Nuncio, you have to be an Italian Christian Democrat leader, not a Latin American Catholic!

The Church may not get criminally involved in Communist work, as this would be equivalent to complicity with the satanic work of the Antichrist. The Church can endure the relentless torment that its cruel enemies inflict on the aching flesh of Christ's mystical body, but the Church, Mister Nuncio, will never work with this tyranny or endorse it!

In Cuba, it is said that this bishop whose style is all but new, this diplomat in charge of a subtle task, is a personal friend of Fidel Castro. Like all diplomats, he neither affirms it nor denies it. What I believe can be affirmed, without exaggeration or lie, is that this most extraordinary Nuncio has become one of the most valuable and efficacious props of the Communist regime that is oppressing Cuba. I think that *His Excellency's overture to Communism is without parallel or precedent, and that this subtle Vatican diplomat has baptized atheistic Marxism*.

11. Logical and consistent in these thoughts and actions, the Nuncio affirms that, having lived in Cuba long enough to see all the stages of the Communist revolution, he now sees it entering "its adult age." Since his personal status and *modus vivendi* are safe, it is natural that he estimates the Communist revolution to be mature, even though people are starving and the number who voluntarily leave their fatherland in search of peace and freedom is growing. "The people," he says, "have experienced radical changes in their material condition . . ." That is true, Mr. Nuncio, very true, but it was a change from abundance to famine and most dreadful need, from the island's typical joy to inexpressible and sad desolation. Hasn't anyone told His Excellency about

The Papal Visit and Revolutionary Activism

the patient, silent lines of people waiting for bits of rationed, stale bread? Or about the secret, continuous and heart-breaking tears being shed in so many homes that have been destroyed by the mature, successful revolution? Mr. Nuncio, I know you have everything, and that the army jeeps are at your disposal any time you need them, but not all Cubans, including bishops and priests, are papal nuncios or friends of Fidel Castro.

12. "[The people] now have a standard of living which they did not have previously," says the Pope's representative. Moreover, according to Monsignor Zacchi, *"Redistribution of wealth and social justice now prevail,* in contrast to the past."

It is pitiful that he speaks like this for, taking into account his training and his episcopal position, he ought to be an authentic witness for objective truth. Everyone knows of the precarious situation of Cuba, including individuals, families, and the country itself. Wealth has not been distributed, for nobody owns anything in Cuba. Everyone lives at the expense of the government, which is the sole proprietor, and at the expense of those who rule the country and contemptibly violate everybody's rights. Maybe the Nuncio himself, who now proclaims the success of the Communist revolution, will be eliminated as soon as his "services" are no longer needed by the Communist rulers. He will then be treated as harshly as those who refused to bow to the yoke of the powerful ones. If the present condition of the Cubans is the so-called social justice that progressivists proclaim, then *we abhor it and we will fight it as long as we live.*

13. Another unheard-of affirmation by the Nuncio is that Catholics must integrate the revolution and that they must join unions, cooperate in voluntary works, join the militias, join sport and cultural clubs, and be active in student movements and professional entities. In other words, the Nuncio affirms that all Cuban Catholics must set aside religious prejudice, personal resentment, independent criteria, and their wishes of freedom, if such feelings are incompatible with the full success of the revolution, in order to actively belong to the revolution. Since there is only one party in Cuba and since its cadres perform *important concrete functions* designed to carry out social change, it follows that all Catholics must become members and *activists* of the Communist party. What about the excommunication decree of Pius XII, Mr. Nuncio? I'm sorry, I almost forgot that such doctrines have been overruled by the prevailing progressivism. The Pope's representative sees no obstacle to a Catholic becoming a Marxist, for the practical purpose of his own safe conduct and privileges as a pillar of the revolution.

14. Unfortunately, the Nuncio surprises us again with his post-Conciliar view that the contradiction between dialectic materialism and Christian beliefs cannot hinder peaceful coexistence, dialogue, or even cooperation of Catholics with Communism, since these differences are merely theoretical, not practical.

Naturally, a Catholic will have internal reservations. In other words, this Vatican diplomat does not deem it necessary that there be a perfect concurrence between thinking and behavior, faith and works, theory and practice. Dissimulation, feigning, and hypocrisy would be admissible and praiseworthy in these circumstances.

A Catholic thinker once said: "We have to live the way we believe, or we will end up believing the way we live." That is true, for when our works are not consistent with our beliefs and convictions, the latter end up vanishing. There can be no better way to peacefully establish atheistic Communism, irreligiosity, and moral depravity, than by authorizing and spreading a separation between religion and life. The Nuncio to Cuba is a most valuable collaborator of Castro's militant Communism, and an apologist as well. For him, Fidel's atheism and Communism are no obstacles because ethically, he is still a Christian. His crimes, sacrilegious profanations, sexual immorality, and vandalism in Latin America are no obstacles either, for this Cuban dictator continues to be an ethical Christian. Mr. Nuncio, *what do you consider to be Christian ethics?*

The way the Papal Nuncio thinks shows us how flexible today's ecclesiastics are in changing their minds and doctrine in order to accommodate and adapt to changing circumstances. The dynamics of Vatican II have apparently penetrated even the deepest layers of the clergymen's consciousness, for today our prelates defend what the Popes energetically and conclusively condemned yesterday, as though such condemnations had lost value and strength.

What did the previous Popes say about Communism? That "Marx's evolutionary materialism is intrinsically perverse" (*Divini Redemptoris* 9, 58); that "this doctrine is contrary to natural law" (*Qui plur.* 8); that "it is socialism's heir" (*Quadragesimo Anno* 43); that "its nature is impious and unjust" (*Quad. Anno* 43; *Rerum Novarum* 3); that "it is a monster of civil society" (*Diuturnum* 25); that "it fights everything that is divine" (*Div. Redemp.* 22); that "it intends to establish a godless society" (*Div. Redemp.* 12); that "it rejects all hierarchies and authority" (*Div. Redemp.* 10); and that "it deprives man of his freedom" (*Div. Redemp.* 10).

I know quite well that progressivists have, as they are used to saying, "surpassed" these prejudices or opinions of previous Popes, whose value, if any, was merely *circumstantial* and belonging to past times. But, right from the beginning, I expose progressivism as being Communism's most efficacious past and present ally, and I also affirm that these pretexts are just a disguise our enemies designed to fool naive Catholics in search of orientation in the middle of today's confusion.

Communist tactics have changed, but Communism's nature remains the same. Today, like yesterday, it remains the chief enemy of individuals, families, countries, and God's Church.

Shameful, humiliating, and most sad is the spectacle of the Papal Nuncio to Cuba. He transgresses his episcopal, sacerdotal, diplomatic, and even his human duties in order to justify Castro's Communist regime; he looks down on the tragedy of a humanly hopeless country; and his absurd opinions infect all of Latin America. But of what importance is our people's misfortune, when compared with this young Nuncio's "diplomatic career?"

WITH THE OPPRESSED OR WITH THE OPPRESSORS?

The following editorial in *United Front* demonstrates the tremendous pressure exerted by Communists and progressivists in order to take advantage of the Eucharistic Congress and get things done their own way:

> The International Eucharistic Congress is a crowd-gathering religious event, promoted by the Catholic Church, whose central figure is the Pope.
>
> To begin with, a predominantly religious people have the right to manifest their faith. But such faith may not be exploited in such a way that it narcoticizes the masses, for it would be a circus trick to keep the masses oppressed, neutral, and resigned to a *false social order*, where an oligarchic minority exploits an immense majority.
>
> With the exception of very small sectors, people do not have social consciousness yet. They are *fatalists, conformists,* and *fetishists.*
>
> *Fatalists,* because they think that the false social order is unmodifiable, since those who enjoy it have everything—money, power, command, and weapons.
>
> *Conformists,* because misery, which has been basically determined by the cleverness of a few, prevents their rebelling against the same misery.
>
> *Fetishists,* because they see the rulers, oligarchs, and members of the exploiting class as fetishes or demigods who are deserving of their homage and submission.
>
> If the Congress continues to keep the people thinking along these lines, it can be considered as treasonous to their cause and best interests. Moreover, if the Congress does not promote the spirit of change and *if it does not act as a spur to stimulate their rebellion against injustice,* it may be concluded that the exploiters turned this Congress into an opiate for the people.
>
> *Christian love does not consist of exploiters continuing their exploitation, but of the exploited rebelling against those who exploit mankind.*
>
> It is absurd to talk about a "love bond" (such was the theme of the Congress) while the system and powerful groups produce misery, beggars,

forsaken children, prostitutes, violence, illiteracy, and starvation. The Catholic Church faces a dilemma: either it *joins with the oppressed majority*, or it *remains bonded to an oligarchic structure* by a tie of love. It is either the real Church of Christ or the false institutional church.

The big press, which is the servant of the exploiters, talks about bishops who do not lodge among the poor living in the slums, but at the homes of the oligarchs and the rich, in residential areas where luxury and sumptuousness prevail. Judging by this aspect alone, this is certainly not *the Church of the poor*.

This same Church, which is the most powerful spiritual force in Latin America, will accomplish nothing with empty definitions and theoretical calls for justice. Either it *condemns present structures* by means of facts, or it *remains allied to these structures*. As a matter of fact, the hungry and the poor can no longer be deceived by Eucharistic congresses where farce and lies prevail and where Christ is used as a pretext of control and as a device to conceal the Church's nefarious intimate connection with oppressors and plutocrats. What matters most is not to please the ruling class, but to remove oppression from the poor; this, of course, is very displeasing to the dominant class.

The Pope is the central figure of the Congress. He comes to the Latin American continent, which belongs to the Third World. He comes to attend the Congress, yet he will not attend the LAMEC reunion (Latin American Episcopal Conference). He will spend forty-eight hours in Bogotá.

Two comments arise immediately: one, our America deserves better treatment, and two, many people wish to see the Pope working together with the hierarchy at Medellín, and analyzing this continent's problems in depth for the first time.

The briefness of his visit gives the impression of a travel tour, of something which he is doing for the sake of duty and protocol.

Paul VI knows America's revolutionary situation quite well. He knows that some nations already have guerilla movements in existence or in the process of formation. These movements have been created by circumstances and not by mere personal whim. If he were to condemn the revolution explicitly, he would ignore things like the following:

    A. The dominant classes have imposed violence upon the oppressed.

    B. When such is the case, violence becomes the right of the oppressed.

    C. We are being dominated by imperialism, which is essentially brutal and warlike, as was shown in Vietnam and Santo Domingo. The issue before the people is that they either resign themselves to be crushed or that they plunge themselves into rebellion with the sole aim of assuming power. Neither blessings nor damnations will be able to stop them.

Germán Guzmán Campos

In Colombia, as in Europe, Communism pressured the Pope to endorse violence, guerilla warfare, and bloody changes of structures. They did not want words; they wanted deeds and they wanted total war against the rich and the imperialists. A Eucharistic congress which did not constitute a trumpet call to start the war would be a nefarious opiate to narcoticize the people.

Mr. Germán Guzmán Campos did know that the planned International Eucharistic Congress was not designed to keep people *fatalist, conformist, and fetishist,* as he had said. He also knew that this religious event was not treasonous to the interests of the poor and that the progressivist currents violently invading a segment of the Latin American ecclesiastics, especially young individuals and the Jesuits, had already oriented the program and spirit of the coming Congress toward endorsing immediate and audacious change of social, economic, and political structures.

He was also well aware that such change did not exclude the religious field, but, nevertheless, he and his party wanted to press the Pope to have the Congress *justify guerilla warfare* and to act as a spur to stimulate rebellion of the Latin Americans against injustice. In other words, *United Front,* the Communist Party, and its progressivist allies wanted the Congress to start a continental Communist revolution and to implicitly accept guerilla warfare and the Castroite projects for Latin America.

For these false Christs, social inequality is an intolerable oppression which gives basis to the almost divine right of the "have-nots" to use violence against the "haves," and oppressed against their oppressors. This is the essence of Marxism: *violence, brutality, deprivation, destruction,* and *death,* its final goal being to establish a most brutal tyranny upon the human race and to strip it of all its rights.

REVOLUTIONARY ACTIVISTS DISCLOSE THEIR PROJECTS

On the 158th anniversary of the proclamation of independence, delegates of various regional revolutionary organizations which represent the workers' movement, as well as peasants, students, professionals, writers, *revolutionary priests,* and *religious,* participated in a historical meeting which was devoted to making an objective examination of the cause of the Colombian revolution and to selecting a way of tactically and strategically uniting the historical forces of national liberation. They all identify themselves with the thinking, work, and exemplary life of Camilo Torres Restrepo, and they feel obliged to jointly fulfill the mandate arising from his sacrifice and from the heroic parable described by "Che" Guevara, who is the heart and spirit of all the people who fight imperialism.

Aware as they are of the scope of the concrete tasks the Colombians confront in the present situation, they have decided to set up working teams as a first step toward constituting a National Liberation Front. These teams will take care of the fundamental struggle, while an auxiliary rearguard, acting in the mass sector, will ensure the participation of our people in the *violent battle* against colonial and neo-colonial imperialism.

Conscious of the long-standing struggle for liberation in our country, they have decided to cooperate in the planning of the giant effort of mobilizing and organizing the popular classes for the takeover of power. This will include persistent efforts to develop national consciousness, education, scientific research, and participation in the life and struggle of the people, as well as ideological struggle against deviations and trends that harbor reformist illusions.

As a result of today's need to turn from words to deeds, from thinking to work, from ideas into material force, and from the weapon of criticism into "armed criticism," they have pledged to join all efforts, be they small, humble, or anonymous, so that the nascent struggle of liberation may become the struggle of all Colombians.

The statement of motives and immediate concrete tasks to be undertaken is recorded in the following Deed of Pledge:

> *We*, the revolutionaries of Colombia, conscious of our responsibility before the people and the revolution, and whereas:
>
> 1. Our country, having achieved independence from Spanish colonialism one and a half centuries ago through the efforts of the masses and the armies of liberation, remains, nevertheless, backward and dependent because it has been subdued by American imperialism whose rapacious exploitation plunders our wealth, deforms our culture, and dominates our public power.
>
> 2. The dominant classes consist of an oligarchic, inept, and voracious minority which is an ally and agent of imperialism. This minority is being nourished by a false social order which breeds misery, violence, unemployment, malnutrition, alcoholism, prostitution, vice, and lack of opportunities to acquire health, culture, and shelter.
>
> 3. This false oligarchic social order is a barrier for the flourishing of our nation's material and spiritual wealth and for the realization of our historical destiny.
>
> 4. It is only through deep and radical change of social, economic, and political structures and the revolutionary takeover of power by the popular classes that Colombia will be able to overcome its present 20-year-old crisis.
>
> 5. This repressive, apparently powerful apparatus that protects and supports the oligarchic-imperialistic system, has declared a preventive war, led and financed by the Yankee military machine, in order to stop the inexorable course of history toward liberation of the masses; this force is not invincible, however, and will become impotent when it faces the unified and conscious

resistance of our country in arms.

6. The Colombian revolution is not the concern of a single group, political party, or social class but of all the people, that is to say, all social classes and groups who are being victimized by an oppressive system based on semi-feudal theories of agricultural production and false neo-colonial capitalistic development.

7. The revolution will result from the joint efforts of all those sectors that believe in the power of the people, really want national liberation, and effectively work to bring about a human, socialist, and authentically Christian society by means of Marxist-Leninist principles.

8. Taking into account imperialism's global and continental strategy, our revolutionary struggle must not become isolated from the rest of Latin America, or from those people in Asia, Africa, and Europe who are striving to liberate mankind from alienating and adulterated structures, the most degenerate and corrupt of which is American imperialism.

9. Although we recognize the necessity to use all available open and legal means of fighting while it is possible, it does become evident that imperialism and the prevailing oligarchy are blocking our peaceful struggle more and more each day, thereby granting the people the right to fight reactionary violence with an armed revolutionary force.

10. The most important problem that must be resolved by the Colombian revolution does not lie in the might of the prevailing classes, but in the disunity and dispersion of the forces called to overthrow them. Consequently, the basic task is to promote unity between the revolutionary sectors and the vanguards on the basis of fighting reformism, revisionism, and opportunism, thereby paving the way for unification of strategic goals and tactical actions.

On the basis of these declarations, we believe it to be our duty to build revolutionary working teams to realize the following concrete tactical actions:

1. To promote the thinking and actions of genuine revolutionaries toward unity of aims.

2. To strengthen and develop the solidarity of the masses with the vanguards which strive for national liberation in Colombia, Latin America, North America, Asia, and Africa.

3. To support and defend the politically persecuted, to render assistance to their families, and to grant safety to those who perform revolutionary tasks.

4. To mobilize the people and to transform their consciousness through education and enlightenment so that they *accept the necessity of change*, and to convince them of the possibility of such change through the application of higher forms of political struggle.

5. To promote scientific research of the social and economic structures by going to the people and participating in their lives to take care of short- and long-term solutions, and to prevent deceptive actions on the part of the so-called civic-

military action, peace corps, etc.

6. To coordinate the work of the existing revolutionary groups and to organize the marginal sectors.

7. To make efforts to ensure efficacious revolutionary actions and to help develop a true revolutionary vanguard.

8. To spread the thoughts, words and deeds of Camilo and Ché, so that they may become examples of revolutionary behavior.

9. To develop working teams to put the above postulates into practice at the local, regional and national levels.

Bogotá, 20 July 1968

Some leading points of this revolutionary program, which coincided with the LAMEC program, were circulated profusely not only in Bogotá but all over Colombia. It is continental in scope and is designed to promote *bold changes of socio-economic and political structures* in all Latin American countries. What the LAMEC document conceals or disguises is disclosed here. The LAMEC document talks about the imperious necessity of a bold change of structures without specifying which ones need to be changed or which ones are to take their place. The document of the National Liberation Front, however, does explain which structures have to change and which ones will replace what they call *colonial and neo-colonial forms of imperialistic domination*. It is only through deep and radical changes of social, economic, and political structures that Latin America will be able to cope with its present total crisis and problem of underdevelopment.

These new structures are *socialism* and its offspring, *Communism*, which represent the revolutionary takeover of power by the masses. It is necessary to eliminate the ruling oligarchy; it is urgent to effect a fair distribution of wealth in order to establish social equality, after having suppressed all privileges. That is why this revolution is not the concern of a single group, political party, or social class, but of the people as a whole, that is to say, the combination of all social groups and classes who are victims of oppression. This is the new gospel of love and Christian fraternity. That is why the struggle is worldwide; it is not Colombian or Mexican, but of all Latin America, Asia, Africa, and Europe; and the common enemy is American imperialism. The problem is international. All the sectors that have faith in the power of the people, without distinction as to race, country, or religion, and all those people who really want national liberation and effectively work to bring it about, must participate in this joint effort to improve this world by means of Marxist-Leninist principles which, stripped of their atheism, basically express the Christian message.

In order to convert this redeeming program into reality, the Camilo Torres Restrepo Latin American Foundation has just been established in Bogotá, in the house where Father Torres and his mother used to live.

The Papal Visit and Revolutionary Activism

This foundation will be the Camilist scientific and cultural (?) center, and will function at national and international levels. Its principal function will be to organize and intellectually develop all activities based on the work of the *"immortal priest-guerilla leader,"* whose life as a social scientist and whose activity as a real revolutionary are examples for millions of Christians who now follow his teaching throughout the world.

Union and student leaders, peasants, writers, and priests are among the founders of this entity designed to fill a vacuum in the present revolution of the Latin American people, oppressed by famine, illiteracy, disease, and all other evils provoked by the international exploiting class, which will be progressively unmasked as the revolutionary science advances.

Camilo Analyzed

Camilo's words: "What is the essential task for the masses in order to assume power? First, one of the main conditions is to work toward the development of a common consciousness among the masses." (Lecture at the Bavarian Union, July, 1965).

Camilo's guidelines are very clear: the masses must assume power. The first required condition is that they have a common consciousness, that is to say that they be of one class and they have a strong consciousness of class.

1. What is power? What does "taking power" mean? Why is it that it must be the masses who are to take power? Why must they take power?

2. Camilo says that the masses must have a common consciousness. What is the meaning of "common consciousness?" In regard to which objectives must the masses have a common consciousness? Are the masses convinced that they must take power? Since there is no clear consciousness, why is that so? What prevents the masses from having a common consciousness? What means could be employed to develop it among them? What is the meaning of the words *consciousness* and *consciencizing*?

3. What is the way by which the masses are to take power? The following data must be taken into account: (a) The oligarchy shields itself with force to maintain its power. (b) The oligarchy and the working class are antagonistic to each other. (c) The oligarchy has set up a class dictatorship which it disguises with "legality" and defends with weapons. (d) The bourgeois oligarchic farce must be replaced with a socialist democracy. (e) American imperialism supports the bourgeois oligarchic democracies with money and military aid. Whenever it finds it convenient, it places a "gorilla" into power. (f) The subject can be stated in this way: either national liberation or a dictatorship of the privileged, either a military control by the people or by the Yankee Pentagon. Any other statement would be reactionary and reformist. (g) The bourgeoisie will resort to violence to prevent the coming to power of the people. The

following option will then arise: either a pro-imperialistic, dictatorial, bourgeois regime or a violently-achieved revolutionary government of the masses.

Each Time More... More... and More Political Prisoners!

Camilo also had these things to say:

The foundation of the National Liberation Front starts a new wave of persecution and violence against the more honest citizens of our country. This new stage includes sophisticated techniques taught by Americans in short courses held in Colombia and abroad, as well as permanent advice given by United States Secret Service technicians in espionage and infiltration.

Large expenditures are incurred by the public treasury to support the judicial and repressive apparatus which personifies persecution, prison, torture, and death. Thanks to these, the government police keep the jails of Bogotá, Bucaramanga, Armenia, Ibagué, Popayán, and Chaparral, as well as the penal colonies of Acacías, Araracuara, and Gorgona full of political prisoners, many of whom have been sentenced to more than 30 years of confinement, while others have not yet been interrogated.

The government's continuous arbitrary acts openly show its anti-democratic nature, which defies the principles of the human rights declaration and of the National Constitution.

The depravity of the Colombian penal system is a secret to no one; political prisoners, and many times their relatives, are known to be submitted to moral and physical torture.

The political prisoners are not an exception to the revolutionary patriotic struggle. All acts of freedom give rise to arrogance and cruelty on the part of the individuals in power, who are striving to stop the progress and liberation of the people.

The political prisoners, by reason of their participation in the revolutionary process, become symbols of resistance and human courage, as well as living exponents of a struggle that neither humiliation nor jail and death are able to stop.

That is why we, who are still free, who are candidates for arrest or court-martial, are obliged to make public the great significance of the political prisoners. To defend and aid them and their families constitute tasks that belong to all the people, as well as being moral and material obligations of all real revolutionaries.

Moreover, the defense of the political prisoners is another way of unmasking a dictatorship that brags about being democratic, of accentuating its dissolution, and of encouraging more fighters among the people to take over power for the masses.

In order that our arrested comrades find positive reward for their sacrifice, it is essential that they enjoy as much esteem and encouragement as they deserve; continuing our fight against the oligarchy and American imperialism is the best way of giving thanks to those who, in the regime's dungeons, are paying for their love of country and the popular cause.

These documents which, as I have already mentioned, were widely circulated in Bogotá during the days of the Eucharistic Congress, give us an idea of the ideology, determination, and the radical program of Communist subversion, which is now being spread all over Latin America. The same vocabulary, ideology, and tactics have been used in Mexico and other Latin American countries. To bring about a bold and urgent change of structures it is necessary that the masses take power. To take power they must launch the revolution, and this revolution must be violent, for the oligarchy (as they call the present ruling class and legitimate authorities who represent and defend law and order) resorts to force to remain in power. This "class dictatorship," therefore, must be fought with arms. Only by means of weapons will the assault of power be possible. And what next? A new authority, law, and dictatorship which will uphold the new structures. Without force, Communism would not be able to remain in power, as the sad cases of Hungary, Czechoslovakia, and Cuba demonstrate.

There is a false premise in all these arguments. Not all legitimate governments are dictatorships. It is not true that the repression legitimate authorities use to fight subversion is abusive. Legitimate authority and subversive movements are necessarily antagonistic. As long as legitimate authorities are in command, under law and conscience, the subversive forces have to use violence to overthrow and destroy them; but once brutality and violence have succeeded, once they have climbed to power, they establish their own law, which is no law at all, for it is neither rational nor is it designed to favor public interests, but to uphold their inconsistent power by means of force and abuse, such power being exerted for the exclusive benefit of those who incarnate the new structures.

Communism is violent in its conquests and in the preservation of its conquests. The option, therefore, is the following: either an orderly government that energetically curbs violent subversion, or a Communist dictatorship that enslaves all of us through a most terrifying violence. Either we use antibiotics to fight disease, or the disease dominates and kills us.

This struggle is unavoidable and necessary, and the governments, acting under the law, must repress license and anarchy which, pretending to be emancipating, provoke Communist subversion. The authorities must also suppress the personal freedom of those who, by means of violent and criminal

The Montinian Church

acts, endeavor to take power and proclaim the Communist dictatorship of the proletariat. These are the so-called "political prisoners," individuals who have committed real crimes which could in no way be promoted by the principles of human rights. As the President of the Mexican Republic, Dr. Gustavo Díaz Ordaz, judiciously said in his report, "Political prisoners and imprisoned politicians are different animals." It is no crime to endorse such and such political ideas, or to be a militant of such and such political party, provided that the party's program or activities are not subversive or criminal; no one goes to jail because of this. But to commit criminal offenses and to violate the rights and legitimate interests of individuals or society, even under the banner of the redemption of the poor, are not political but criminal activities which the authorities must curb and punish in order to protect the society that they rule.

In fact, the democratic spirit has made the governments of many countries tolerate the legal functioning of Communist parties and maintain diplomatic relations with openly Communist governments. They disregard the fact that such generosity sooner or later results in serious riots, gory fighting, and bloody conflicts that jeopardize social peace. Communism intrinsically means violence, subversion, and anarchy. It is unable to succeed or to remain in power through legal means.

I admit, of course, that such prisoners become symbols of resistance and living exponents of subversion for the Communist cause. Their mystique is fiery and contagious, and party members consider the most violent, destructive, and criminal acts as heroic actions and brave sacrifices. That is why the political prisoners or, better yet, the imprisoned politicians who have been found guilty under the law, are considered heroes, victims, and martyrs by the accomplices of subversion.

The end does not justify the means. Even if the goals of Communist subversion were good, we could not accept or applaud the torturous and criminal means they use to achieve such goals. Were they reasonable men, subversives would have to understand that the legitimate authorities need drastic means in order to curb subversion. For Communists, the triumph of their cause is not only good, but eminently so; for legitimate authority, the defense of law and society is not only good, but an inescapable duty.

In all civilized countries, the defense of prisoners in court is not only legitimate but necessary, provided that the evidence is not altered and the legal norms granting peace and social welfare are not violated. To Communists, all legitimate governments are tyrannies and unbearable dictatorships which is why they justify all means aimed at destroying the safety of the government and propagating violence and other crimes that they resort to in order to succeed.

The Papal Visit and Revolutionary Activism

THE APOSTOLIC ADMINISTRATOR OF BOGOTÁ, HIS EXCELLENCY MONSIGNOR ANIBAL MUÑOZ DUQUE, WELCOMES THE FOREIGN PILGRIMS.

I could not help noticing that His Eminence Cardinal Luis Concha, Archbishop of Bogotá, was assigned to an inferior rank. This is a curious but unfortunately commonplace phenomenon in the post-Conciliar Church, namely, that archbishops, bishops, and even cardinals who resist the *aggiornamento* or who do not adapt themselves to the new ideology and practices are eliminated or at least, as was the case in Bogotá, are paralyzed through the appointment of coadjutors or apostolic administrators who assume command and relegate to second rank the person and position of the prelates who frown upon the new Church's giddy evolution. The case in Bogotá is widely known.

The newspapers amply informed us about the rebellion of some priests who longed for most radical changes and who had to confront His Eminence Luis Cardinal Concha, whose ideas and attitudes were considered too old-fashioned and conservative. The appointment of Msgr. Muñoz Duque as Apostolic Administrator of the Archdiocese of Bogotá solved the problem. The Cardinal kept his title but the administration of the archdiocese was put into the hands of the Apostolic Administrator. The welcome speech was not delivered by Cardinal Concha, but by the Apostolic Administrator. Its text reads as follows:

> You are arriving in Bogotá on the days that the world Christian community is being summoned to celebrate the 39th International Eucharistic Congress. This event draws an immense crowd of Catholics who are intimately united with Pope Paul VI to celebrate the Eucharist, which is a bond of love, and to strongly consolidate the faith of all the Church in the triple sanctifying virtue of the Eucharist, the Memorial of the Redeeming Passion, the sacramental presence of Christ, and the promise of His final coming. May you receive our cordial welcome in the Christian embrace of peace, that expression of love which the Spirit circulates among the brethren, and in the friendly hospitality of this city of Bogotá, a sign of how sincerely we Colombians love you.

This welcome speech undoubtedly has a distinct post-Conciliar taste. "Crowd," "bond of love," "Christian embrace of peace," "love which the Spirit circulates among the brethren," are all commonplace post-Conciliar and progressivist terms. It also calls to our attention that the Apostolic Administrator does not mention the Eucharistic *Sacrifice*. This is integral humanism, which seems to place man before God.

Dr. Virgilio Barco Vargas, Mayor of Bogotá, also delivered a salutation

The Montinian Church

to the visitors:

> It is Bogotá's privilege to receive you illustrious visitors, who have wanted to extol the celebration of the International Eucharistic Congress and to share your faith and religious fervor with that of our people.
>
> This unique occasion will make us witnesses to an extraordinary occurrence which will turn our city into a center of convergence for transcendental events, which will be definitively recorded in the history of the Catholic Church. It is the wish of the citizens of Bogotá, and mine as well, that the fondest and kindest memories of this event will remain everlastingly impressed in your hearts and souls.
>
> Bogotá is proud to receive you, and cordially and affectionately invites you to enjoy the same degree of confidence and safety that you have in your own home.

Without a doubt, all of us who spent those days in Bogotá can attest to the hospitality and friendly reception that we received from our brethren in Colombia. The Colombian families generously opened their doors to welcome and entertain all visitors. This welcome was not merely polite; it was a sincere, warm, and generous fraternal embrace.

Nevertheless, we cannot understand the words of the Mayor when he tells us, "This unique occasion will make us witnesses to an extraordinary occurrence which will turn our city into a convergence for transcendental events, which will be definitively recorded in the history of the Catholic Church." What type of extraordinary event is that? What are these transcendental happenings which will be definitively recorded in the history of the Catholic Church? I do not believe that the International Eucharistic Congress we attended in Bogotá deserves such adjectives. Apart from the Pope's visit, nothing in the Congress was religiously extraordinary. Nowhere did we behold the transcendental happenings the mayor mentioned. To be frank, in the religious field and Eucharistic order, the Congress was dull and devoid of faith and enthusiasm. That which was floating in the air was not about the Eucharist or problems of faith, but of *bold solutions to the so-called social problem and radical change of structures*, which was what the progressivists urgently demanded. Maybe in this sense the Congress was extraordinary and the LAMEC resolutions transcendental and quite similar to the practical principles of the National Liberation Front, which is fighting to incorporate itself into the history and structure of the Catholic Church. Time seems to have already proved it.

But let us comment on the program of the Congress itself, which officially started on Sunday, August 18, 1968.

Chapter III

THE INAUGURATION OF THE CONGRESS

The inauguration ceremony scheduled to take place at the "Eucharistic Field," was designed to welcome the brethren coming from all over the world, according to the official program. The newspapers of Bogotá forecast that two hundred thousand people would attend this event. The President of the Republic, Dr. Carlos Lleras Restrepo, his wife, Sra. Cecilia de la Fuente de Lleras, and the Secretary of Foreign Affairs, Alfonso López Michelsen, accompanied the Cardinal Legate to the Pontifical shrine. To the left of Cardinal Lercaro was Msgr. Muñoz Duque, Apostolic Administrator of Bogotá. The other twenty cardinals, as well as almost six hundred archbishops, bishops, priests, monks, and nuns were already waiting for the Pope's legate.

After the Pontifical and Colombian national anthems and a religious concert by professional choirs were heard, the formal opening of the Congress took place through the reading of the Pontifical brief. It read as follows:

> To Cardinal Giacomo Lercaro, our beloved son, greetings and apostolic blessing.
> Bogotá, capital and bulwark of conspicuous Colombia, a city made illustrious by its beautiful location and by the feats surrounding its noble origin, as well as by the bright, ingenious, and noble feelings of its inhabitants, and even more by its adhesion and observance of the Christian religion, has been chosen as a worthy see for the celebration of the International Eucharistic Congress this coming August.
> It will be pleasant to be able to see for ourselves what we now know by hearsay.
> We had long ago decided to pay a visit to Latin America, and this singularly important religious event affords us an appropriate occasion of putting our wish into practice. Then we will travel to Bogotá. This brief and fast flight will be, God willing, joyful and safe, and we have grounds to forecast that our peregrination will be beneficial for the Catholic faith.
> We prepare our spirit in advance to reach you, beloved sons of Colombia, through the abundance of the blessing of Christ's Gospel, which is a source of great joy and hope for us.
> It being impossible for us to preside during the entire Eucharistic

The Montinian Church

Congress, for our thinking and concern must go toward other fields, and especially toward the opening of the General Conference of Latin American Bishops, we have decided to choose one of the members of the Sacred College of Cardinals to represent our person at the most solemn celebrations of the august Sacrament.

Therefore, this letter will appoint and vest you, beloved son, as our legate a *látere*, so that, vested of our authority and on our behalf, you will preside at the ceremonies and carry the paternal prayers of our benevolent spirit.

We bestow upon you the commission of proclaiming that we know and are pleased to know that in Colombia, and particularly in Bogotá, the devotion to the Holy Eucharist increases every month, and that its sincere adorers compete in worshipping this mystery and look forward to approaching the Bread of Heaven, in order to find life and to taste the Lord. The height of the Eucharistic Mystery is so sublime that the mind nearly faints when studying and contemplating it, so much so that words are absolutely inappropriate to praise its greatness. The Sacrament of the Altar is the Sacrament of Charity, the bond of perfection and the source of life.

In reality, what the heart is in the human body, and what the most Sacred Heart is in Christ's body, the Eucharist is in the Church. Since the Eucharist is Christ's body, it performs the vital function of the heart of the Church. Thus, the august Sacrament of the Altar is like the sun and the life-nourishing principle of the Church. Its warmth fills and covers everything, visible and invisible, and unites time and eternity.

In the Last Supper, the night He was given up, our Saviour instituted the Eucharistic Sacrifice of body and blood to perpetuate the Sacrifice of the Cross throughout the centuries, until the date of His coming, thus handing over to His spouse, the Church, the Memorial of His death and resurrection, the Sacrament of Piety, the sign of unity, the bond of love, the Paschal banquet, where one receives Christ, where one's soul is filled with grace and where one is given a pledge of future glory.

In light of these considerations, my dear son, we invite you to encourage the participants to the Congress to follow the tradition of their ancestors, making efforts to turn the worship of the Eucharist into a sign of faith, a defense against errors, and *a stimulus for virtuous activity in the social realm as well*.

In this respect, you will talk not only to Colombians, but to all those people who are coming to Bogotá from various parts of the world, so that, lifting up their prayers to God, they take breath and strength from the holy Eucharistic Congress *to adequately and agreeably solve the present social problems*.

May prayer and action attain Christian peace in the kingdom of Christ of Latin America. May feelings of fraternity flourish; may righteousness and honesty spread; and *may justice abound*, not through violent means, which often engender worse evils, but through healthy statutes *primarily aimed at favoring the*

The Inauguration of the Congress

less privileged classes, and also by spreading Christian truth and the fulfillment of the commandments.

May the heavenly gifts of peace and charity be bestowed by the Blessed Virgin of the Rosary, who is venerated at the sanctuary of Chiquinquirá as patroness and glorious Queen of Colombia and Mother of grace, hope, and holy joy, in whom reliance never faints, and from whom one always receives more than what one expects, for, maternally magnificent as she is, she desires more for her indigent sons than what they pray to receive.

In the confidence that you will discharge your functions as a legate a *látere* with maximum dignity and splendor, we wholeheartedly bestow the apostolic blessing upon you, beloved son, and upon the Cardinal Archbishop of Bogotá, his episcopal brothers, the authorities, and all of our sons who are coming from various nations to participate in the Congress.

Given in Rome, at the Church of Saint Peter, on July 16, 1968, in the sixth year of our Pontificate. Paulus PP VI.

On hearing the first part of the Papal brief, we really believed that our fears were unfounded and that the Congress we were attending was going to be, by the grace of God, a real international Eucharistic congress in which the traditional Catholic faith of our parents would fill our souls with an intense and practical love for the divine Eucharist. A Eucharistic congress is, above all, a reaffirmation of our Catholic faith concerning the sublime truth of this Mystery of Faith. Now, more than ever, when in various countries progressivism is trying to obscure and impugn the Eucharistic dogmas, when the human community at the "assembly" seems to have done away with the sacrificial essence of the Holy Mass; when the dignified reception of such a divine sacrament is so profaned by modern opinions and practices which, like an infection, have come from Europe to these poor and underdeveloped Latin American countries; and now, when the Real Presence in the consecrated Host is denied by many of the new theologians, we expected the Congress to declare our traditional beliefs to the world and to issue a public and solemn statement of the immutable Faith of the one and true Church of Christ. The dogmatic definitions of Trent gave birth and splendor to the ancient Eucharistic congresses, such as those of Madrid, Budapest, Chicago, and Argentina, which, in turn, ought to have given life and orientation to the Congress of Bogotá.

Moreover, the Supreme Pontiff not only wanted to increase Eucharistic worship but also to primarily stimulate *a virtuous activity in the social field*. He also wished that everyone should take "breath and strength from the Holy Eucharistic Congress *to adequately and agreeably solve the present social problems*." This he expected to be achieved not through violent means, but through wholesome laws.

The problem was stated: a revolution was now necessary to change the structures of Latin America. There were two paths: *violent revolution*, which, according to the Pope, often engenders worse evils, or *peaceful revolution* through law. Paul VI chose the latter. I believe that, in addition to the reason given by the Holy Father for rejecting violence because it often engenders worse evils, one can say that these destructive means are *intrinsically* evil. The end cannot justify the means, even if it be lofty.

Chapter IV

THE SOCIAL PROBLEM IN LATIN AMERICA

Before continuing our analysis of the 39th Eucharistic Congress in Bogotá, perhaps the last one of the post-Conciliar Church, we must stop for awhile to study the "social problem" which so much concerns the Catholic hierarchy. Because of it, they have decided to reconstruct the entire Church founded by Our Lord Jesus Christ in order to accommodate it to the moods and demands of the modern world. I will try to be clear and concise, so as not to prolong my digression.

1. *The social problem*, like sociology, the new science of human knowledge founded by Comte, is an imprecise problem that may have and, in fact, does have as many meanings as the number of schools, ideological trends, and various parties that refer to it. Communism and its mitigated forms of socialism, for example, consider the social problem to be private property which must be fought and extirpated in order to establish a paradise on earth. There will be a social problem as long as there is private property or capitalists. For many others, who secretly favor Communist doctrine, the social problem consists of the unfair distribution of wealth and temporal goods. As long as there are rich and poor there will be a social problem, and the greater the economic, cultural, and social inequality, the more serious the social problem. May we say that this is the prevailing modern tendency, which manifests itself as *religious progressivism* within the Church. The progressivists do not seem to want to eliminate all private property; they just want earthly goods to be distributed fairly. They want to eliminate all poverty so there will be no more poor people, in accordance with the Communist thesis: "From each, according to his ability; to each, according to his needs." Their goal seems to be the earthly paradise and the lost Eden which progressivism will reconstruct by means of "social justice," a "bold and total change of structures," revolution, and even violence, if the latter is inevitable.

2. Let us pose the following question, not with the thought of delving deeply into the subject, but of clarifying my statement: Is economic, cultural and social inequality a phenomenon provoked by the abuse of human freedom and, therefore, capable of being eliminated? Or, on the contrary, does it constitute a fact of human nature itself, forecast by God and decided by His

ineffable providence, which we may alleviate but never eliminate?

History teaches us that there has always been a consistent social inequality among all peoples. Even the most superficial observations show that such inequality frequently appears among members of the same family. The undeniable fact that there exist among men the intelligent and the stupid, the healthy and the sick, the workers and the idlers, as well as the honest and the corrupt, makes social equality an unstable condition, even though human laws try to maintain equilibrium. The famous *"equality"* preached by the French Revolution is one of the myths of history.

I am not trying to deny that sometimes the ablest men abuse their positions and power to iniquitously exploit the weak and the inferior who are dependent upon them in one way or another. Such abuses, already condemned by divine law and the Church, as well as by reason and conscience, must obviously be fought by means of just statutes that render social life possible. The Catholic social doctrine does not and may not have any other objective than to remind and urge people to fulfill the duties imposed by divine law, thereby preventing the damnable abuses to which we are driven by human concupiscence. The idea that the Church's social doctrine seeks to eliminate human inequality is utopic, has no solid basis in the Gospel, and can only be advocated and spread by compromised and compromising demagogues.

Let us recall the words of St. Pius X: "It belongs to the order established by God that human society include governors and governed, bosses and laborers, rich and poor, wise and ignorant, nobles and plebians." (*Pontifical Doctrine. Social Documents*, Madrid, 1959).

3. In Latin America, the so-called "social problem," like the human inequality which it seeks to remedy, has specific features which have nothing to do with what the "experts" have detected in European countries. Fundamentally it is an *ethnological* problem, as old as the days of the Spanish conquest, which has been recognized as such and earnestly fought by the rulers ever since. Only because of ignorance, demagoguery, or bad faith, can it be affirmed that for four centuries, our humble social classes, especially the natives, have been intentionally and maliciously subjected to plunder, exploitation, and abandonment so as to keep them underdeveloped and as slaves in disguise. The underdevelopment of our natives was not ignored, but actively combatted by the Church and the Crown.

The "social problem" in Italy, France, or any other European country has nothing to do with *our* "social problem." In Europe, perhaps, the fundamental social problem may be an economic one, which could be solved by means of progressive wage increases, social security, and uniform codes that regulate the social function of capital. In Latin America, however, *the social problem is not basically economic* and, therefore, cannot be solved by means of continuous wage increases that seriously jeopardize the existence of private

The Social Problem in Latin America

enterprise, nor through the progressive and continuous distribution of land. These demogogic measures can only provoke economic crises that increase poverty and unemployment.

It was not colonialism that provoked social and economic inequality among us. On the contrary, it was the interruption of Spain's fruitful and positive work that brought about this condition of unfair privilege which Paul VI exposes and regrets in his speeches and in his encyclical *Populorum Progressio*. Such situations normally exist in all countries in different degrees. Now we attack Yankee imperialism and blame it for all our misfortunes, but let us remember that, for more than a century, we thought all of our endemic evils were a disastrous consequence of the colonial period. We were the victims of a monstrous hoax, instigated, promoted and skillfully spread by the secret seats of Masonry and international Jewry.

We parted from Spain; we broke the chains that bound us to her and stupidly fell into an even more inhuman, insatiable, and absorbing sort of "colonialism" (I say *more* to adopt the same viewpoint of people who talk about "colonialism," not because I am convinced it was bad). *We are victims of an evil that we call "Yankee colonialism" but which is really an international conspiracy that enslaves both the United States and Latin America.*

I respectfully differ with some of the Pope's statements about colonialism in his encyclical *Populorum Progressio*. I believe that, in justice, an impartial investigation of those remote colonial times will show that *the benefits we received from Spain immensely surpassed the loss of our exaggerated pre-Hispanic civilization*. Many centuries of progress stand between the colonial monuments and the indigenous ruins we admire.

The Latin American people are integrated by three evidently distinct, if not antagonistic, racial and cultural groups. Racial integration takes time, and the lower the culture and civilization of the dominated races, the longer the process of incorporating them into the top levels of a superior culture and civilization. First, we have Europeans and people of European or similar descent; second, we are fortunate to still have indigenous tribes; and third, we have many *mestizos* of mixed combinations.

The so-called social problem of economic inequality is found in all three groups, although in different degrees. There are poor natives, just as there are poor *mestizos* and poor people of European origin, even though they don't all endure poverty equally nor have the same causes for their indigence. When talking about the needy, many refer only to our lower classes, the Indians, and forget that there are cases of concealed and overlooked poverty that can be even worse. But let us limit the problem to the working class of workers and peasants, consisting mainly of Indians and *mestizos*.

This circumscribed "social problem" can be efficaciously and constructively solved only if three exigencies are fulfilled, namely, the conditional needs of prevention, education, and of creating new sources of production to grant productive work to these members of our community, and adequate circulation of material goods.

    a. Above all, these people must be *educated* in an integral manner. It is not enough to alphabetize them, to teach them reading, writing, and arithmetic so as to have them learn a trade, a profession, and a way of earning their living, but to create morality and good working habits. It is necessary to develop their sense of responsibility and their voluntary compliance with the legitimate demands of law, authority, and conscience. It is also necessary to have them understand their obligations towards their wives and children, so as to not only provide for their peremptory needs but also to continually improve their standard of living. It is imperative to build such education upon a solid and stable basis, which exists only when religion is known, cherished, and faithfully practiced. Morality can apparently survive without a religious foundation, but the daily struggle of existence finally kills it.

    b. Before education or at least simultaneously with it, comes what we call the *prophylactic* condition. To render such education enduring and possible, it is necessary to urgently introduce hygiene and prophylaxis among our humble classes. It is also necessary to eradicate the hereditary diseases that they contracted through the life habits, vices, and malnutrition of themselves and their predecessors. They must be taught to eat what foods they need to make a balanced diet, so as to invigorate this deteriorated race. Many times it is not that they do not have enough to eat, but that they eat harmful things or refuse to eat what they need. It is also urgent and imperative to develop their habit of temperance, especially with respect to lower quality alcoholic beverages that are almost always poisonous and toxic to the point of insensibility and destruction. Above all, it is most urgent to teach them personal, practical, and household hygiene. How many diseases, especially parasitic ones, could these poor people avoid by means of adequate hygiene and cleanliness!

    But mental hygiene is as indispensable as body hygiene. It is necessary to root out of these people their many fraudulent beliefs, absurd prejudices, witchcraft, irrational hatreds, and wrong views of life and the universe. Such mental hygiene is, in a way, more necessary than the other, for without it, the resistance to physical hygiene would be impossible to overcome. This has been evidenced by the poor results of all works done without this previous mental conditioning.

    I remember that, when the epidemic of aphthous fever obliged the Mexican and U.S. governments to take radical measures to stop the spread of this disease among cattle, in some regions peasants revolted against the members of the sanitary brigades and even killed some of the individuals who performed these sanitary tasks.

    c. Finally, the third conditional need of the so-called "social problem" of

The Social Problem in Latin America

Latin America is to *create new sources of production* that guarantee everyone fruitful work. It is criminal to try to deceive people by means of destructive promises of progress and development for the needy while simultaneously eliminating the sources of abundance and social welfare. Without capital, private initiative, and free enterprise, there can be neither sources of work and production nor real social progress. Experience shows that ferocious and greedy statism, whose chief exponent is the socialist state, dries up the sources of production, uses up the benefits it promises, and submits people to a most unmerciful slavery.

New sources of constructive and fruitful work will be created in our fatherland only when there is the stimulus of a fair profit, of free enterprise not excessively restrained, harmony between labor and management, and when the government does not seek to asphyxiate work and its sources through unjust and burdensome taxes.

It was necessary for me to determine the meaning and scope of the social problem because, as we have already seen, the approach of the Eucharistic Congress was aimed at solving this problem. The Pope himself, in his brief read at the opening of the said Congress, clearly said that this event should be *"a stimulus for virtuous activity in the social realm as well . . ., primarily aimed at favoring the less privileged classes. . . ."*

Although it would be dangerous and reprehensible to overlook the social problem and to paralyze this "virtuous activity" that the Pope mentions, it would be even more dangerous to falsify the true meaning of this problem in each country and to seek a solution to the problem, however virtuous the intent, by wrong means.

Potentially, Latin America is a continent of vast resources. The crisis it is suffering today is being demagogically exaggerated and provoked by invisible hands which, acting from abroad and through the complicated machinery of international finance, as well as for their own profit, unscrupulously exploit the wealth of these countries, whose leaders, perhaps, have not had sufficient courage or vision to defend their own countries' legitimate interests.

Chapter V

WELCOMING SPEECH BY THE APOSTOLIC ADMINISTRATOR TO THE LEGATE AND CONGRESS

Once again, it was the Apostolic Administrator of Bogotá, Msgr. Muñoz Duque, instead of the primate Cardinal-Archbishop, who delivered the welcoming address. His discourse deserves to be reproduced before commenting on its principal points:

> Most Eminent Cardinal Giacomo Lercaro, His Excellency the President of the Republic of Colombia, Most Eminent Cardinals, Ministers of State, Most Excellent Archbishops, Bishops, and other Prelates, Ambassadors and Special Envoys, His Honor the Mayor of Bogotá, Brethren in Christ:
> On so solemn a day I am deeply moved, as a prelate, Colombian and American, in welcoming you to this fruitful and promising land, starred by bells and towers, and sown with schools and colleges, factories and farms, where prayers and work harmoniously unite to worship God and serve mankind.
> The Christian traditions that have enriched the current of our history and dignified and exalted the American people for four centuries, must join this International Eucharistic Congress that strives for these two supreme goals.
> Since that dawn, when the cross and the host were lifted up to Heaven as signs of redemption and progress, up until our distressed but hopeful days, Christ has been governing our history. The faith and religious spirit of the American evangelizers pushed them beyond the mirage of El Dorado to the inestimable treasure of the souls redeemed for Christ.
> Faith that ennobled the conquest, saved us from failure, and enabled so many sacrifices to bear fruit, now lifts us to this international altar. Without the moral strength and the noble stimulus that religious consciousness creates, the huge epics of the conquest and settlement of our lands would never have been written.
> The missionaries, heroes of the cross, divine Quixotes, served as mediators in the bloody clash between the original race and the conquerors, standing as severe judges of the victors and protectors of the vanquished.
> The evangelization of our America was, in fact, a mystic crusade with the blood of the martyrs set off against the blood shed by the warriors' swords, and a

The Montinian Church

sparkling crusade with gentle and peaceful light sufficient to cause the red brilliance of fires and battles to grow faint. Right then began the cultural and educational work of the Church, which has attached itself to every glorious and dangerous feat ever since. It helped enforce humanitarian legislation to protect the rights of the Indians, and, in the face of cruel and despotic human egoism, it raised the torch of charity, the standard of idealism, and the supreme reality of the spirit.

For two and a half centuries popular education was the integral and exclusive work of the Church. And what about the colonial artistic vitality, totally impregnated with religious idealism, full of mystical meaning, promoted and favored by the Church?

When these nations lifted up their own spirits and their lush, juvenile profiles, they heroically conquered freedom, that holy fruit of the tree of Calvary. Moreover, inspired by doctrines taught in cloisters and universities, in the books of the great masters of the theological school, such as Suárez, Victoria, and Belarmino, to mention only the most famous ones, our people reassumed the sovereignty and fully recovered their rights.

From the densely populated cities to the silent corners of distant villages and the dawn of discovery to present times, all vigorous enterprises as well as all progressive ideas and works of welfare, even when deficient or notoriously imperfect, have been inspired or endorsed by the Church.

Your Eminence and brothers in Christ, I have found it to be right and just, in this world apotheosis, to render thanks and homage to the craftsmen of this unity of faith and culture, to prelates and religious, priests and catechists, rulers and lawyers, and to extol the past glory by means of a hymn of praise, not as a mere illusory dream or a vain sterile reminder, but as a new obligation and a stimulus for the present. For the grandeur of the past is always the basis of the sublime achievements and brave enterprises of the present and the future.

Strengthened by this rich social and religious heritage, we have come here to celebrate the Eucharist, the love bond; to sincerely scrutinize the signs of the times through fraternal dialogue; to adapt our thinking and actions to the needs and demands of the times; and to proclaim our love of God, our Father, and of our brethren, getting involved in activities of service to the latter, and helping them to get rid of the slavery of sin, ignorance, and misery, so they may fully enjoy dignity and freedom as God's children.

As the Apostolic Administrator of Bogotá, I, the most lowly attendant to this inaugural, want to cordially thank you and convey to you the greetings of Bogotá and Colombia and, above all, to the Pontifical mission headed by you, Most Eminent Cardinal Lercaro, legate a *látere*, who have come in place of and on behalf of the supreme Pontiff, to preside over this 39th International Eucharistic Congress with singular authority and worthy prestige.

You provide it with your masterly voice and your apostolic position. Your

Welcoming Speech to the Congress

distinguished life, which is nearing the accomplishment of its goals and which has been enriched by the greatest spiritual attributes, has been integrally spent in the service of God's people. The richness of your devotion and Eucharistic doctrine and the most clear example of your sacerdotal and pastoral ministry that you have fulfilled with loyalty to the venerable tradition of the Church and the urgent need of the new age, will give us light and warmth for the great journeys we have to undertake in regard to the adorable reality of the Eucharistic Mystery.

Your presence among us is another precious gift for which we must thank you and the Holy Father's supreme kindness. Your assumption of the chairmanship of the Congress becomes nicer and more pleasing because of the resemblance of the features of your personality to those of Pope Paul VI. The firmness of your doctrine, your bravery in facing the new situations of this contemporary world, your enlightened love for Christ and His Church, your efforts to renew the liturgy, and your respect for human dignity make you similar to the most noble and attractive figure of Paul VI, who now leads the Christian flock with universal praise.

I fraternally embrace the cardinals, archbishops, and bishops who came to solemnize this grand Congress and brought messages of faith and hope from all over the world: from Europe, whose missionaries, doctors, and saints brought us the holy seed of Christianity and of Western culture, and who made efforts to have it take root in our soil to produce an abundant harvest; from Asia, Africa, and Oceania, where the Catholic faith is developing and spreading in spite of difficulties and sacrifices, a sign of future success; from North America, where Catholicism is growing rich and powerful in content and community spirit; and from Latin America, so close to us by virtue of historical links of blood, culture, origin, and common fate, and so united to us in the struggle of the present.

America is gathering here to review its structures and analyze its problems, in search of appropriate solutions within the directions given by the Magisterium of the Church.

I cordially greet the priests, religious, and laymen from distant and neighboring countries who responded to our call and endeavor to re-evaluate our faith and tighten the links of charity emanating from the Eucharist.

In greeting all Colombians with patriotic fervor, I wish to give testimony of my particular gratefulness to them: to the government officials of our fatherland, especially to the president of the republic and the Mayor of Bogotá, whose admirable Christian spirit and sense of civic duty helped give prestige and splendor to the Congress; to the members of the commissions and executive committees of the Congress who, acting tenaciously and in harmonious intelligence, brought about this so difficult but hopeful result; and to all the persons who, in some way or other, cooperated to turn this hour into reality and to hold this event that will certainly mark a new age in the development of our history.

This first meeting of God's people is the prelude of luminous days for which we have constantly prayed. To our distressed and chaotic world these days will mean a bright revival of Christian consciousness which will be submerged in works of love, solidarity, development, and progress. Egoism leaves only a trail of foam or a wake of blood, hatred, violence, and injustice, but where Christian charity passes, the track of its creative fruitfulness remains forever.

May the divine Eucharist, bond of love, sign of unity, and Sacrament of Piety radiate the light of hope, confraternity, justice, peace, and liberty on all of us and on those who are not present but who are accompanying us spiritually through the media of radio and television.

Were we to judge the rhetorical speech of the Apostolic Administrator of Bogotá by its external appearance, we would find it old-fashioned, triumphalistic, and pre-Conciliar. It is not as emaciated and crude as our present sacred oratory and evidently includes all the finesse of 19th and early 20th century academic oratory. Studying its contents and manifest objectives, however, we realize that His Eminence Muñoz Duque did indeed attend Vatican II and knew how to assimilate the new and renovating doctrines that were expounded and advocated by the so-called Council "experts."

From the beginning, without leaving any doubt, the Apostolic Administrator defined the two goals of the Congress: *worship of God and service to mankind.* These two goals, God and man, cannot be separated without upsetting the harmonic balance of the universe, but when one speaks of man, one must refer to the integral human being of matter and spirit, to the existential human being, not projected throughout eternity, but in time.

I must avow and enthusiastically praise, however, his meritorious award of tribute, even if dissimulated, to Spain's grandiose work, which was the only tribute I had seen or heard. To have omitted the name of the mother of all the Latin American countries would have been an unforgivable sin in such an important event! It is true that Msgr. Muñoz Duque did not mention Spain directly and seems to attribute all the marvelous work of colonizing and civilizing America to the unselfish missionaries who, identifying themselves with Spain, its government, and its people, carried out these marvelous feats of evangelization and incorporation of Latin America into Western Christian civilization. Great are the merits of our missionaries, but no less great are those of the crown, in spite of some of the faults, weaknesses, and much publicized cruelty of some of the conquistadores.

We cannot and must not continue to accept this unjust condemnation of the prodigious work of Spain which, in less than three centuries, implanted us with the faith, culture, and civilization of immortal Spain. This campaign to denigrate the Spanish feat in America seeks to ultimately disintegrate our

Welcoming Speech to the Congress

Spanish heritage, which is the firmest link of unity among the Latin American countries. Msgr. Muñoz Duque is right in saying, "The Christian traditions ... have enriched the current of our history and dignified and exalted the American people for four centuries...." Such Christian traditions, however, did not sprout spontaneously in the virgin lands of Latin America, but germinated and grew out of the work of Spain, its missionaries, warriors, legislators, theologians, rulers, and all its sons who, in one way or another, contributed to this marvelous crusade of the colonization of America. It was Spanish arms that lifted up the cross and the host for the first time in the new world, as *"signs of redemption and progress,"* as the Apostolic Administrator eloquently says.

In his discourse, His Excellency does not fail to acknowledge that it was spiritual, rather than material values, that accomplished this grandiose epic of the conquest and colonization of our land. The evangelization of America was not only a religious, spiritual, and mystic task but also a civilizing, human, and constructive work which, in less than four centuries, gave birth to the twenty nations of Latin America. The Church inspired and aided the evangelization, but Spain enacted human codes designed to protect the rights of the Indians. We cannot dissociate Spain from the Church, as far as those golden centuries are concerned.

We also thought it fair and just, in the world apotheosis that the Congress aspired to be, to give thanks and homage to the craftsmen of this community of Christian faith and culture, which constitutes the essence of the Latin American countries. The underdevelopment of our countries, which so much preoccupies the progressivist leaders, is to a large extent offset by this rich heritage and spiritual patrimony which we received from Spain and which is lacking in today's developed countries.

A phrase by Msgr. Duque is quite frequent in present-day progressivistic talk and very enigmatic to me: "... [W]e have come here to celebrate the Eucharist, the love bond; [and] to sincerely scrutinize the signs of the times through fraternal dialogue...." We are already disgusted with so much of the love, dialogue, and fraternity of today's progressivists. May I remind you of the words of the apostle Saint John: "Little children, let us love not so much with words, but with works and truth." I am still unable to decode the semi-cabalistic meaning of Msgr. Duque's phrase, as I find it neither in holy Scripture nor in the secular Tradition of the Church. Naturally, I find it unacceptable to make the revealed truth, the immutable doctrine of the eternal Gospel, or Catholic morality a function of the indefinite "signs of the times." "Heaven and earth will pass away," said Jesus Christ, "but my words will not pass away." The "signs of the times," as far as I know, are the fashions, customs, regimens, human criteria, and all those changeable human things, but not those which God has taught or commanded us.

The ecclesiastics gathered in Bogotá and Medellín could well study, through fraternal dialogue, the various, changing circumstances of Latin America in order to straighten the twisted, heal the sick, and revive the Christian spirit that, unfortunately, is dead to a large extent; on the other hand, however, they should not adapt the divine work to human whims and demands according to the signs of the times, using particular criteria as personally construed.

At the end of his speech the Apostolic Administrator of Bogotá seems to have exceeded his gracious diplomacy in bestowing so much praise upon Cardinal Lercaro, the Pope's legate a *látere*.

Physically, of course, there does not seem to be any resemblance between His Eminence, the former Archbishop of Bologna, and Pope Paul VI. Ideologically, it is possible that there is some similarity but at the very least, it is indisputable that Cardinal Lercaro enjoys the Pope's substantial support.

Chapter VI

THE AWAITED SPEECH OF HIS EMINENCE GIACOMO LERCARO

The text of the speech which Giacomo Cardinal Lercaro, who represented Pope Paul VI at the Latin American Episcopal Conference, gave, is as follows:

Holy people of God's Church, pilgrims of Colombia, Latin America, and the world, may the grace of our Lord Jesus Christ, the love of God the Father, and the fellowship of the Holy Spirit be with you all. Amen.

To His Excellency, the President of the Republic, my respectful homage; to you, my beloved and venerable brothers in the episcopate, my kiss of peace; to all the respectable authorities whose presence from the very beginning of this Congress does honor to me, my deferential greetings in the name of the only Lord Jesus Christ, sole name in which salvation can be expected and in which we are gathering here; to all of you members of God's people whom the regenerating grace of Baptism turned into brethren in God's family, effacing all race, color, and social differences, my wishes for prosperity, justice, peace, truth, and grace; to the poor, miserable, sick, old, and suffering, and to the children, my embrace, the maternally solicitous embrace of the Church and the embrace of Christ, our brother and Saviour.

As you well know, however, I am only a guest who is representing the Vicar of Christ who sent me here, and to whose solicitude is entrusted all of the Lord's flock. He is present here in this universal concert, and his august words, to which we have piously listened, set a standard for the activities and solemn celebrations of our meeting. But he will personally join us in a few days as the first successor of Peter to step on this Latin American earth and on this nation, the only one to bear the name of the great Genoese who planted the cross of Christ on American soil.

But we are gathered here, and the Holy Father will be with us, to celebrate the Eucharist which is, above all, the living and present Memorial of the Redeeming Sacrifice where Christ, Son of God, became our brother and offered Himself as a victim to God's justice to expiate our innumerable sins and reconcile us with God. Centuries ago the prophet Isaias wrote: "Surely he hath borne our infirmities and carried our sorrows; and we have thought him as it were a leper, and as one struck by God and afflicted. But he was wounded for our iniquities, he was bruised for our sins; the chastisement of our peace was upon him, and by his bruises we are healed." (Is. 53: 4-5).

In the Mass, as in the cross, His body is immolated by us and His blood *is shed for the remission of all sins* and as a ratification of the new and eternal covenant of reconciliation and alliance between God and man.

On the altar of the Mass, according to John the Baptist, Jesus is the "Lamb of God, who taketh away the sins of the world." Just as in the Apocalypse the apostle Saint John saw Him on the altar of heaven, dead but erect and victorious in such a way that only He, the Lamb, can break the seals of the book where the fate of nations has been recorded, likewise, on the altar, as a victim immolated to God's majesty but resurrected and victorious over death, He becomes our source of life, mercy, and peace. "Lamb of God, who takes away the sins of the world, have mercy on us, grant us peace. . . ."

Have mercy on us sinners who are burdened with the anxiety of being far from God and, in our anguish, despite our pride, realize that instead of using the means at hand to build a humanly suited home in the world, we often use them to excavate abysses and to sow ruins.

But when John the Baptist announced the revelation of the Lamb of God who takes away the sins of the world, to make way for His imminent appearance he preached penance, to which he gave credence by his body exhausted by fasting, his disarranged hair, and his rough clothing. He even demanded penance by means of threats: "The axe is laid to the root of the tree . . . and in his hand he has a trident." He condemned those arrogant and vain men who boasted that they were just because they belonged to the chosen people and were of the seed of Abraham. He demanded a strict sense of justice from the publicans who were attracted by the charm of money to the extent of becoming unjust. From the imperial soldiers, easily inclined to abuse their invincible power, he required a clear and conscious respect for freedom. He admonished the restless multitudes, crowded at the borders of the Jordan River, to generously make common cause with the needy: "He that hath two coats, let him impart to him that hath none, and he that hath food, let him do likewise. . . ." (Luke 3:10 ff).

This exhortation of the Gospel is also addressed to the Christian world of our century and to us who have come to adore the Lamb who takes away the sins of the world. As a forerunner of Christ's Vicar in this land of America, I endorse this exhortation at the start of this grandiose Congress which is taking place within a historic context full of misgivings, promises, hope, and fear. We are being asked what John the Baptist asked in that moment of anxiety and expectation, a *metanoya*: "Repent ye; for the kingdom of Heaven is at hand." (Matt. 3:2).

The Awaited Speech of Cardinal Lercaro

Metanoya - penance; a revision of our conscience, way of life, criteria, individual spiritual attitudes, and social behavior; a revision made face-to-face with the light of the Gospel.

The Gospel is the word of life and of eternal life, but better yet, as the apostle Saint Peter asserted to Jesus, the *sole* word of eternal life (John 6:69). It is the word that shall remain even if Heaven and earth pass away (Matt. 24:35). Eternal as it is, this word does not cease to illuminate and fertilize the transitory moments of time.

That is why the Church, as depository and interpreter of Christ's word, and in exerting its Magisterium throughout the centuries, never ceases to refer contingent historical situations to the Gospel.

Everyone of us must compare our life and internal state with the Gospel, and, insofar as our own functions are concerned, we must also compare our historical condition and our community and social structures with it.

We must compare them in the humble way of the human being who knows his weaknesses and the strength of his perennial proneness to elude the requirements of "the kingdom of God and his righteousness" (Matt. 6:33) in order to abandon himself to his own individual and collective egoism which tempts him to legalize and legitimatize, under cover of established law and order, *the most infamous phenomena of injustice, exploitation, and hatred..*

We have to compare ourselves with the everlasting Gospel especially when, as today, the signs of the times reveal that the dawn of a *new world* is at hand. No one, in fact, can fail to notice that scientific and technical progress, along with the use of new and powerful means of communication, has drastically modified mutual relations among countries, rendering unification of the large human family more possible and prompt, but simultaneously, because of mysterious reasons that only the burden of sin can explain, such progress gives rise to a most deep and deadly egoism to such an extent that dreadful and threatening inequality, bloody differences and quarrels, and even genocide are authorized or commanded. Our present time is one of oppositions in which we experience the acute pains and joyful hopes of pregnancy. (John, 16:21).

So then, we who are gathered around the Lamb who takes away the sins of the world, are being asked, as the crowds were asked by the forerunner, to profoundly and imperiously feel and live up to the responsibility of belonging to God's people, that is to say, of being the true seed of Abraham and responsible Christians because of which "we are called and are children of God" (1 John 3:1), linked by a fraternal tie that reinforces and sublimates the unity of our common nature.

It is also particularly demanded of us that we show the utmost respect for justice and freedom in relations with our neighbors, in ordinary behavior, in the practice of our professions, as John the Baptist required of the publicans who were responsible for collecting taxes, and in the relations between the various social categories, classes, and races, as the forerunner required of the imperial soldiers who were admonished not to harass the subdued people.

We are demanding social justice with respect to the essential needs of life: adequate food, clothing, lodging; suitable work, social security, health care; access to freedom, culture, and education; and participation in social life. We also ask that these goods be fairly distributed lest one owns two robes while another has nothing to wear; lest one eats plentifully while another is hungry; lest one widely enjoys the fruits of culture, nature, and the work of others while another is absolutely deprived of everything and submitted to a condition that is offensive to human dignity, poisons life, and blocks all proper perspective and hope.

Surpassing His forerunner's pressing call, Jesus later said that "blessed are they who hunger and thirst for the sake of justice." (Matt. 5:6). The Savior's vocabulary is not so emphatic, as He does not talk about hunger and thirst when He proclaims the other blessings, but He does talk about them when He announces this one, which encounters serious obstacles in personal and collective egoism.

All those who are proud of being Christians or, better yet, those who are conscious of human dignity, must try their best to cultivate their hunger and thirst for righteousness, to perseveringly implore them to God and to watchfully and consciously feel them, despite the temptation of disregarding the condition of others. It was Cain who insolently asked: "Am I my brother's keeper?" Moreover, the Apostle Saint John teaches that "the charity of God is not in him that, having property in this world and looking upon his brother's misery, closes his entrails to him." (I John 3:17).

Let us be of a clear conscience and feel hunger and thirst for justice against all types of discrimination as to race, class, category, or group and against thirst for power and aspirations for revenge or retaliation. But above all, he who is in charge of others must aspire to interpret the hunger and thirst for righteousness, and the more elevated his position, the stronger his desire must be. As I am a bishop, this thought makes me tremble, and in one way or another, I now call it to the attention of those who are vested with authority, first of all to us whom the Holy Spirit appointed to rule God's church, so that our preaching, teaching, and evangelical life become fertile yeast so that the longing for justice and the internal rebellion against egoism and dominance ferment and ripen in the soul and conscience of the community. May the divine germ of charity ferment and ripen in them, for without charity, justice will not be achieved and, if it were, it would be inappropriate and almost inhuman, with features of revenge and hatred which, therefore, would render it an injustice.

With due respect and charity, but exercising all my apostolic rights, I remind the leaders of the civil community to examine the situations that have

The Awaited Speech of Cardinal Lercaro

been created by separated processes in the light of the Gospel that the Church has always preached and is preaching now more than ever in this dawn of a new age. I also remind them of their obligation of responsibly renovating the structures wherever necessary, with spirits free from injustice or irrational pressure.

The forerunner's threats to the leaders of God's people, who felt confident because of their being Abraham's children and custodians of the tradition, sound, even more so today than in the past, comprehensible and up-to-date: "See that the axe is laid onto the root of the tree . . . [and] that the one that cometh hath the pitchfork in his hand to separate the wheat from the chaff." (Luke 3:9, 17).

With the outbreak of a rapid succession of social upheavals, a widespread protest movement, and the universal rise of the new generations ready to reshape the world, *a consciousness is swiftly . . . awakening to fight the injustice and inequality that have been tolerated for centuries.*

A common desire for freedom and dignity announces that the yeast of the kingdom is entering the world through mysterious, and sometimes unimaginable ways, and is fermenting and ripening the world, despite the fact that exaggeration, disadjustment, imprudence, and instrumentalization may change the genuine features of this process here and there.

But what we are really glimpsing is the image, even if distorted, of the kingdom of God, expected and prophesied by Isaias, who attributed the following program to the Messiah: "The spirit of the Lord is upon me because the Lord hath anointed me; he hath sent me to preach to the meek, to heal the contrite of heart, and to preach a release of the captives and deliverance to them that are shut up." (Is. 61:1).

Jesus adopted this program in his speech at Nazareth (Luke 4:17 ff) and in his answer to John the Baptist's messengers. Christ says that the good news he announced to the poor is the unmistakable sign that the kingdom of God has been established. (Matt. 11:5).

Vatican II, primarily in the constitution *Gaudium et Spes*, as well as the great encyclicals of the last two popes, has applied that prophetic and evangelical message to the present situation.

The Lamb of God, worthy of receiving all honor, majesty, and the kingdom by nenewing the immolation of the cross on the altar for our salvation and redemption, affirms and exalts charity, which is the most perfect stage of justice, for it is the essence of the law. (Matt. 22:40). But the immolation of the cross also reminds us that Christ did not come to be served, but to serve, even to the extent of giving up His own life; giving up one's life is the supreme pledge of charity. (John 15:13). That is why Christ affirms that service is the unmistakable sign of love, of that love He Himself has had for us and about which He has given us a new commandment that characterizes and identifies the New Covenant, His commandment, whose fulfillment by us will show the world our fidelity to the Gospel. (John 13:35, 15:12).

In the last night of His mortal life, in the intimacy of the cenacle, at the foot of the table where the Eucharist had been celebrated for the first time and left as a perpetual memorial until the day of the great return, the Lord laid aside His garments, took a towel, girded Himself, and washed His disciples' feet. This was the regular service rendered by the slave to the honored guest. "You," Jesus remarked to His astonished disciples, "call me Master and Lord, and you say well, for so I am. But I have given you an example, that you should do as I have done to you. Love one another as I have loved you."

Let us serve one another. Be the first to serve so that we can know who, in a way, is the Lord and Master. (John 13:13-17). Authority is service, and service is love. It is a concrete pledge of love, and therefore involves renunciation, sacrifice, the cross, and the altar; but it accepts and embraces them, for because of Christ's cross, the cross of service is just as fruitful.

Our solemn celebration of the Eucharist introduces and leads us to this eminently evangelical climate, so profoundly and positively human. It is, then, with this generous overture to the teaching of the Gospel that we of ardent faith, open the celebration of this week's activities which will offer to our eyes and, even more, to our spirits, that admirable Sacrament of the whole Church through which Christ, the only Savior, continues His redeeming work.

As a vortex of all the activities of the Church and source of all its energy (*S.C.* 10, *Deh.* 17), root and axis of the community life (*P.O.* 5, *Deh.* 1254), we can contemplate the Eucharist, perpetual memorial of the loving Sacrifice of the Cross, treasure of the Church, "to which all the sacraments, ecclesiastical ministry, and apostolic work are tightly united and directed." (*P.O.* 5, *Deh.* 1253).

May the Holy Spirit, who fired the cenacle with His resplendent and strengthening flame, also inflame our blessed city wherein God's Church is manifesting itself today by the presence of its authorized and devout representatives. May He fill the hearts of the parishioners and light the flame of love in them, and may the intercession of the ever Virgin Mother of God and the Lord Jesus Christ, whose presence and prayer supported the apostles while they were waiting for the effusion of the Spirit, make efficacious our prayer.

Chapter VII

REMARKS ABOUT CARDINAL LERCARO'S SPEECH

I cannot refrain from commenting on this speech by the Cardinal Legate *a látere,* since in it I find not only unmistakable traces of triumphalistic progressivism but also the theme and the preconceived, prefabricated format for all of the activities of the 39th International Eucharistic Congress. Cardinal Lercaro was sincere, and, in the midst of his oblique, opportune references to the Eucharist and the Gospel, which were somewhat strained, he almost plainly introduced his reformist and *socializing* aspirations.

OUR HUMBLE REMARKS ABOUT HIS EMINENCE'S RHETORICAL SPEECH

1. After the usual greetings to his distinguished listeners, a remembrance of pre-Conciliar times whereby His Eminence showed his diplomatic skill, his classical education, as well as his deep consciousness, at those moments, of the enormous mission with which he had been entrusted, he announced and reminded all of his listeners of the coming visit of His Holiness Paul VI, the first successor of Peter to step on Latin American soil.

2. Having flattered his listeners with his opening announcement, the Cardinal presents a brief synthesis of the Eucharistic Mysteries, relating the bloody sacrifice of Calvary to the bloodless Sacrifice of the Altar. This was a recollection of the most solid, immutable, and infallible doctrine of the Council of Trent, where the unfailing light of the Holy Spirit taught us the definitive concrete dogmas of revealed truth concerning those supreme effusions of Christ's love toward men.

3. After these meritorious comments comes the skillful transition whereby the Legate insinuates the basic theme of his discourse: "[We humbly] . . . realize that instead of using the means at hand to build a humanly suited home in the world, we often use them to excavate abysses and to sow ruins."

That is why we are begging mercy, not so much because of our sins against almighty God—our dishonesty, prevailing irreligiosity, and the terrible sacrileges which, under cover of *aggiornamento,* profane our temples and the most sacred ceremonies of our liturgy—but also because of our insolent and haughty attitude in condemning the Church of the past with its very dogmas, venerable traditions, discipline, most wise regulations, ancient definitions of previous councils, and the supreme teaching of the Magisterium as stated by the Popes preceding Pope John XXIII.

We are not begging mercy because of the ideological confusion surrounding us, because of the apostasy of so many priests and bishops who have retired from the holy ministry to abandon themselves to the pleasures of the bride-chamber without any hindrance, nor because of the deep, profound, irreconcilable division among Catholics with respect to vital points of doctrine and morality that have torn the seamless robe of Christ. Neither is it because of the wreckage of the religious life in exemplary communities in whose bosom the most heroic and perfect virtues of Christian life used to flourish, nor today's rebellious attitude of some people and episcopal conferences toward the teaching of the Pope, even in regard to the encyclical *Humanae Vitae*, wherein the Pope does not teach or enact anything new but just states that the natural law and God's eternal law condemn all contraceptive devices, be it among Catholics, Jews, Protestants, or pagans.

Though all of these enormous sins estrange us from God, they do not cause us as much anguish as our discovery that, despite our enormous possibilities, we have not been able to construct a better world, *a more humanly suited home*, instead of *excavating abysses and sowing ruins*.

Holy Scripture teaches us that we do not have a permanent city here on earth, that we are pilgrims of eternity, and that our suffering in this life "cannot be compared with the future glory that has been revealed to us." But this is a wrong picture of life, because man cannot live on hope alone. That is why His Eminence wants to change those decrepit ideas of ours, in order to offer us a better world, a more human world, a world without abysses and ruins, a world of integral humanism wherein the threat of war will disappear forever and where the harmonious development of the economy and culture of all countries will, with the aid of a friendly and continuous dialogue, turn this valley of tears into the lost paradise.

4. Using a bold rhetorical figure of speech, the Legate compares himself to John the Baptist, to interpret his sermon of penance and to render his own version, for those moments were so exceptional that, in a way, they presaged a new coming of the kingdom of God. The Baptist announced the coming of the Messiah and His imminent revelation to the world. His Eminence, coming as a precursor of the Vicar of Christ to this American land, renders his own interpretation of John's sermon as an invitation to the people to radically transform their lives by penance, in order to duly pave the way for the coming of the Lord, in this case, the forthcoming and imminent visit of His Holiness, Pope Paul VI.

Remarks About Cardinal Lercaro's Speech

Penance, for Cardinal Lercaro, is a *metanoya*: a revision of our consciousness, way of life, criteria, individual spiritual attitudes, and *social behavior*, a revision made in the light of and face-to-face with the Gospel.

5. This revision, according to the Legate, is more necessary than ever, particularly at the start of this grandiose Congress, which is taking place within a historic context full of misgivings, promises, hopes, and fears.

This is the expectation of progressivism which is convinced that a new world and a new humanity are being born. We are seeing the dawn of a new and splendorous day, of a pleasant, radiant spring of the world and the Church where injustice, social inequality, and the old structures will disappear in order to establish the beneficial reign of socialism which, according to the Bishop of Metz, "is a grace, an inevitable fact of history." (*Bulletin officiel de l'évêché de Metz*, No. 134, Sept. 1, 1967).

6. To carry out this revision we must go back to the "sources" so that it can be made in the light of and face-to-face with the Gospel. The Church, as depository and interpreter of the word of Christ, never ceases to refer contingent historical situations to the Gospel. We must compare ourselves with the everlasting Gospel, especially when, as today, the signs of the times reveal that the dawn of a new world is at hand.

All this cabalistic jargon is obviously similar to the auguries of the Bishop of Metz, whose words presage the rhetorical statements of the former Archbishop of Bologna. The French Bishop of Metz says:

> The change of civilization we are experiencing involves modifications not only in our external behavior but also in the conception of the creation and salvation which Jesus Christ brought to us. These most fundamental premises not only require new pastoral efforts but something deeper, a more evangelical, personal, and communitarian conception of God's design for the world.

These propositions, which adequately express the heresy of the 20th century, are not positive at all, but purely methodological and negative. They do not tell us what the new religion consists of; they only say that the contemporary world and its drastic changes require that we discard what we used to deem immutable.

7. What do the sign of the times mean to His Eminence? What do they proclaim and foretell? Let us repeat his words:

> No one, in fact, can fail to notice that scientific and technical progress, along with the use of new and powerful means of communication, has drastically modified mutual relations among countries, rendering unification of the large human family more possible and prompt but simultaneously, because of mysterious reasons that only the burden of sin can explain, such progress gives

rise to a most deep and deadly egoism to such an extent that dreadful and threatening inequality, bloody differences and quarrels, and even genocide are authorized or commanded.

These are the signs of the times in which progressivism has read the future of the world. The world is at the center of this complete, rapid, and destructive evolution. The task of the Magisterium is to faithfully interpret these signs, that is, the demands of the world which include, of course, all that the world is and means, even if this implies a disregard of the other world of grace and immortality and even if we have to pay no attention at all to God and His eternal law. Moreover, Cardinal Lercaro and his zealous disciples have interpreted these signs of the times as forecasting a time of opposition when we will experience the intense pain and joyful hope of pregnancy, which will bring about the perfect unification of the great human family.

Whatever separates or divides human beings must be suppressed, be it social or racial inequality, religion, property, family, or fatherland. We must go back to evangelical purity and make a new religion, a religious syncretism which will accommodate and fuse together all the beliefs of mankind. Then, and only then, will we have the "perfect unity of the great human family" upon which, according to the Cardinal, the success of Christ's redemption depends.

The Argentinian, Víctor Eduardo Ordóñez, is correct in affirming that:

> Christian Modernism, a prisoner of nature, cannot escape from the scheme of existentialism which continues to build its freedom step-by-step, minute-by-minute. Its Christianity, to the extent it survives, is imminent instead of transcendent. The new Christianity approaches mankind and the divine from the aspect of life as a triumphal cosmic explosion and from the constant risk of non-being. Moreover, it would be said that Christ is scarcely but a mere historical support, a technical reference, a working hypothesis; the cross, but a metaphor; and redemption, but a dialectic enterprise. Nothing is or exists but my effort to lift myself up and elevate my nature which is to be considered as the framework of my freedom, as my trench against grace from which I must redeem myself.

According to His Eminence, the bond of fraternity which underlies and sublimates the unity of our common nature is the lively, profound, and imperious longing to belong to the city of God, which is of the true seed of Abraham. However, neither being of the city of God nor of the true seed of Abraham can be the basis for such prerogatives, but only our justification through Jesus Christ, our incorporation into Him, and the faithfulness with which we follow His doctrine and commandments. "No one who says Lord, Lord, will enter into the kingdom of Heaven but he who obeys the will of my eternal Father."

More than the utmost respect for justice and freedom in relations with our neighbors, in ordinary work, and in the practice of our professions, must be required to fulfill our duties toward God because, without love for God, the so-called love of neighbor is but egoism in disguise. It is not the natural but the supernatural virtues which make us children of God and brothers in Christ.

The very recommendations of John the Baptist imply a natural inequality among men that exists by virtue of disposition or divine command. If it were not for someone having two robes, no one would be able to dispose of one as a gift for the needy. If it were not for the existence of the chosen people and the seed of Abraham, the Jews would not have any basis for their arrogance and vanity. If it were not for the publicans, the demand for strict justice would have been groundless. If it were not for the Roman soldiers in Palestine, John could not have requested a clear consciousness of respect for freedom.

Human inequality, which has always existed and always will exist among men, is the condition foreseen and ordained by divine Providence to give us an opportunity to cultivate those supernatural virtues that constitute the essence of Christian life. In the process of universalizing the requirements of Christianity, Cardinal Lercaro does not duly distinguish between *natural* and *supernatural* virtues, and promises the unity of the great human family as an already tangible fruit, which is the mistake of *naturalism* and a distortion of evangelical doctrine. When the Sermon on the Mount speaks of the "hunger and thirst for justice," it certainly does not refer to that *social justice* among men that has driven so many priests crazy, but to that justice which Christ brought us in the divine life, in our justification, and in our complete submission to God's Will.

8. The example of Cain is also farfetched. It cannot be applied to each one of us to ask or, better yet, to demand that we fulfill the material needs of our fellow men. If it were so, we would not have enough means at our disposal to resolve all of our neighbors' economic needs. Depending upon my circumstances, I can help some people, but not all. Since we are not divine Providence, we are unable to resolve all the needs of others. If we gave away everything we had to spare, who would then be able to giveanything to the indigent who will always be with us? Social equality would render impossible the observance of the most sublime and generous virtues of Christian life.

9. "We are demanding social justice," says His Eminence, "with respect to the essential needs of life, [and] that these goods be fairly distributed lest one owns two robes while another has nothing to wear, lest one eats plentifully while another is hungry, lest one widely enjoys the fruits of culture, nature, and the work of others while another is absolutely deprived of everything and submitted to a condition that is offensive to human dignity, poisons life, and blocks all proper perspective and hope."

The Montinian Church

This social program of the Cardinal is absolutely utopic. Even if we distributed all of our robes, there will always be those who lack robes or who do not want to wear any. Even though we were to give away all of our food, there would always be people who would be hungry. There are persons who are never satisifed, no matter how much they eat, and others who are never hungry, in spite of what little they have. Indigence, on the other hand, is often due to laziness and a refusal to work. Is Cardinal Lercaro forgetting that work is the rule of life? One has to accept any available job, in case one is unable to find a better one. Let him who cannot work as a factory manager be a worker, a sweeper, and he will eat. Not all of us are good at everything and, therefore, must resign ourselves to what God has given us; we must remember, however, that nearly everyone is good at something.

Let us remember the parable of the talents. One was given five, another three, and another only one; the last one, for not having bargained, was later demanded the fruit of his work and, bound hand and foot, was thrown into the outer darkness. It is preposterous to pretend that we are all equally cultured. Such a phenomenon is not to be found even among the members of a single class or family because it is completely opposed to the reality of human nature in its fallen state. There are, always have been, and always will be, the cultured and the uncultured, the educated and the ignorant, the talented and the untalented. The possibilities for study, when there is a true aptitude and inclination, depend upon one's firmness and skill in seeking them, as experience shows. A large majority of youngsters who succeed in their studies are not rich, but middle or lower class students who resolutely strive to overcome their indigence.

10. It was not so much the manifest intention of the Cardinal's speech, however, to awaken a hunger and thirst for social justice and the righteousness of the kingdom of Heaven among God's people, but among the authorities in charge of the community. His Eminence wanted a legal and peaceful change of structures which could be brought about only by the authorities. Was this not the program of LAMEC which was worked out before the Congress? "... [A]bove all," says the legate, "he who is in charge of others must aspire to interpret the hunger and thirst for righteousness, and the more elevated his position, the stronger his desire must be." In the socialist countries, the authorities have interpreted that hunger and thirst for justice in their own way and in accordance with the doctrine of Marxism, thereby depriving everyone of everything, in order to establish the social equality of which the Cardinal of Bologna dreams. To a lesser extent, in the other countries where socialism has not been definitively established, a voracious statism has been confiscating private property and taking possession of the sources of production through unbearable taxes and statutes. Insensibly or peacefully, socialism has been establishing or preparing its implantation. In the United States, despite its immense resources, growing taxes have introduced a sort of socialism for the

majority of Americans, so much so that the abundance of loans and credit has enslaved those unconscious multitudes with invisible handcuffs.

Ever since the beginning of the Congress, and in a diplomatic way, His Eminence became the advocate for the *socialization* of Latin America and for a *change in its social structures*. His message was evident. According to the Europeans, the increasing number of conflicts in Latin America indicate a lack of proper structure, which is a lamentable remnant of colonial times, and for which, therefore, the only remedy is to destroy and wipe out the past, completely change the social structures, and peacefully or violently establish beneficial socialism. The authorities, says the Papal Legate, must interpret this hunger and thirst for justice and must help bring about this essential and urgent transformation.

His Eminence, from the time he became a bishop, and despite his smiling face, trembles because of his enormous responsibility. That is why his preaching, his teaching, his melodious, frank words, have unhesitatingly defended Italian Communism, so much so that his weekly magazine is one of the most active focuses of Communistic propaganda.

11. In just one paragraph, Cardinal Lercaro summarizes his thought, message, and command to act not only in Colombia, but in all of Latin America: "With due respect and charity" (pure rhetoric), "but exercising all my apostolic rights" (post-Conciliar pastoral), "I remind the leaders of the civil community to examine . . . in the light of the Gospel" (going back to the sources and Gospel as interpreted by progressivism), "that the Church has always preached" (not in the progressivist way or language), ". . . now more than ever in this dawn of a new age. . . ." (the dawn of socialization and Communism), ". . . to examine the situations that have been created by separated processes . . ." (confusing words, subject to different and opposite interpretations), ". . . with spirits free from injustice or irrational pressure. . . ." (To whom is His Eminence referring? Is it the hateful oligarchy that has been exploiting the needy for so many years?), ". . . [and] of responsibly renovating the structures wherever necessary" (energetically, coldly, firmly, and demolishingly).

His Eminence neither mentions the structures that need to be renovated or changed, nor the ones that are to replace the old. But he does consider John the Baptist's threats to be comprehensible and up-to-date, more so today than in the past. He perceives himself as a forerunner, if not of Christ, as least of Paul VI, whose thoughts he wishes to convey.

12. According to Cardinal Lercaro, we are witnessing a quick "succession of social upheavals . . . and the universal rise of the new generation ready to reshape the world," and a "consciousness [which] is swiftly . . . awakening to fight the injustice and inequality that have been tolerated for centuries." These gloomy words of His Eminence very much resemble the

forecasts of Communism which, condemning and rejecting all of the past as unbearably unjust, wants to liberate the human being from inequality, be it social, racial, cultural, religious, or above all, economic. According to the Cardinal and those who have joined his ranks, there will be no Christianity as long as there is social inequality.

Parting itself from the Gospel, the Church tolerated and concealed these inequalities for centuries. It was progressivism which bravely exposed this intolerable situation. That is why the threats of the forerunner or, rather of the two forerunners, are now more comprehensible and up-to-date.

13. But the Legate's rhetoric reaches its zenith when he affirms that "[a] common desire for freedom and dignity announces that the yeast of the Kingdom [of God] is entering . . . and is fermenting and ripening the world . . . through mysterious, and sometimes unimaginable ways. . . ." This is how the naturalistic, new religion of progressivism interprets the Gospel. The yeast of which Christ speaks is not meant to ferment the material world but the spiritual. The evangelical metaphor is clear in that the world ferments and ripens when it approaches Christ, accepts all of His teachings, and lives as He did, not when it recites revolutionary mottoes such as "liberty, equality, and fraternity."

The present world, despite scientific progress, technology, and rapid means of communication, is not ripe. The material world has suffocated the spiritual, and our exaggerated conquests seem to imitate the tower of Babel, from which the new man wants to defy God Himself. What one sees is not the semblance, even blurred, of the Lord, but the dreadful profile of the Antichrist.

The evangelical poverty that announced the coming of the Messiah and was praised by the divine Master in His beatitudes is not material, but spiritual. It means that one must place the eternal before the secular benefits of this world. Moreover, Jesus did not come to liberate those who are imprisoned because of their crimes, but those of us who suffer the slavery of sin, death, and Hell.

That is why some documents of Vatican II, especially the Constitution, *Gaudium et Spes*, and the great encyclicals of the two most recent Pontiffs, on which His Eminence bases his new sociology, are so ambiguous and engender so many mistakes. I cannot believe the present condition to be the fulfillment of the prophetic and evangelical message, as Cardinal Lercaro thinks.

14. It is indisputable that the service God rendered to mankind is an unmistakable sign of love. In this respect, I agree with His Eminence, but on the other hand, we must not confuse servile service with the kind of service the Gospel mentions. There is no merit before God when one serves because of salary or because of merely material motives. In the hierarchy of evangelical values everything must lead to God, for only in this way can the cross of service, which so concerns the Cardinal, ever be fruitful.

Remarks About Cardinal Lercaro's Speech

15. There is still another central idea of progressivism which the Cardinal unequivocally expressed in his opening speech. The Eucharist, he says, is the "root and axis of the community life." The words of institution that Christ said on the night of the great mysteries preceding His death, do not support this. Since He told His apostles, "Do this in memory of Me," the sacrificial Eucharistic Sacrament is, before all and above all, a Memorial of the Passion and death of our Lord. More than an assembly of God's people or a love feast, it is, according to the Council of Trent, which was not pastoral but positively and definitively doctrinal, a true and real sacrificial prolongation of the sacrifice at Calvary. This sacrificial character is the essence of the Holy Sacrifice of the Mass.

This idea of making the Eucharist into the root and axis of the communal life has given birth to all of those sacrilegious abuses by means of which it is intended to attract crowds and to turn the Holy Sacrifice into a diversionary spectacle.

After having read and meditated upon Cardinal Lercaro's speech, we realize how impetuously he dared to destroy the venerable liturgy that had stimulated the solid faith of Catholics for centuries. It took an unscrupulous mentality and will like that of His Eminence, to even endeavor to bring about the spectacular and scandalous changes which have caused so much harm to priests and laymen. Now the liturgical unity and the dogmatic, universal, and immutable meaning of the Eucharistic Mysteries are gone. The apparent unity with the Church of the past has been demolished forever and we now have a new religion of the *aggiornamento*.

Chapter VIII

THE CHURCH SUFFERS PROFOUND CHANGES

The following questions were asked of the Paraguayan Bishop, Msgr. Aníbal Mena Borta, one of the most dangerous of the South American prelates, during an interview he granted to national and foreign press representatives upon his arrival in Bogotá to attend the International Eucharistic Congress. They reveal the misgivings, reservations, and internal divisions among Catholic and non-Catholic observers, as a result of the spectacular changes in Christ's Church. These quotes are taken from the August 20, 1968, edition of the Bogotá publication, *El Espacio:*

Question: "Do you believe the progress of the new Church to be opportune in regard to traditional and conservative thinking?"

Answer: "This is a stage we are witnessing. After Vatican II, the Catholic Church, including the Latin American Church, has been going through an age of transformation and change."

Question: "Is it true that the Paraguayan bishops have serious reservations about the LAMEC proposals?"

Answer: "Just some misgivings. We have prepared a brief document in which we explain our position."

Question: "Are fundamental changes being solicited?"

Answer: "No, but we are asking some important ones."

Question: "Must the Church get involved in a vast social enterprise?"

Answer: "The Church is already involved. What we are seeking is to increase such involvement."

The New Church is the name given by reporters to the reformed church which grew out of the Council of John XXIII and Paul VI, and which is irreversibly destroying the traditional and conservative viewpoint. This doctrinal assault is compelled to efface and destroy the past, inasmuch as these two mentalities are irreconcilably opposite. Is this the *self-demolition* of the Church that Paul VI regretted in one of his pathetic allocutions, by means of which he is seemingly trying to stop the avalanche of heresy and schism?

The progressivists are not out to fight traditional and conservative theses but the immutable dogmas of our Catholic Faith upon which the structure of the Church, its preservation, and its very essence are based. His Excellency the Archbishop of Paraguay avows and accepts that the stage through which we are going after Vatican II is one of transformation and continuous change. What remains standing after that storm? When will the changes be over?

What is the present guideline between the contingent and the immutable, between the circumstantial, transient truth and the infallible? What yesterday we denied, today we accept and impose. At the Council of Trent it was declared that, "If anyone affirm that the Mass be celebrated in the vernacular, let him be anathema." Today, on the contrary, the episcopal conferences want to impose the vernacular language not only on the Mass, but also on all the liturgy.

The blueprint which LAMEC prepared in advance for the Medellín meeting provoked serious misgivings not only among the bishops but also among the laymen who got to know it. The Church, or better yet the hierarchy, became involved in a vast social enterprise. The transformation that the ecclesiastics wanted for the Church and for God's work seemed to embrace the very goals of the Gospel. Now, one no longer looked so much for *the kingdom of God and its justice but for the kingdom of man and its social justice.*

Chapter IX

REVOLUTION: THE ONLY SOLUTION FOR LATIN AMERICA?

Taking into account these earthly aspirations, the observer can easily understand the fighting and revolutionary mood of so many ecclesiastics and lay leaders of the Church. The following quotation on this subject was taken from the August 21, 1968 edition of *El Tiempo* of Bogotá:

> A group of 30 priests, religious, and laymen from Bogotá have just submitted a transcendent and interesting analysis to Msgr. Abelard Brandao Vileda, president of LAMEC, which hurls a series of criticisms at the proposals of the second episcopal conference at Medellín. This investigating team affirms that being "deeply interested in the proposed change of structures for Latin America and in the responsibility and commitment of the Church thereto," they had carried out a study about the Latin American structures.
>
> Among other considerations, this investigating team, coordinated by Fr. René García Lizarralde, pastor of the district of Florencia in Bogotá, affirms that the great tragedy of the best Latin American rulers arises from their ignorance of structures. Coincidentally, the plans for the transformation of Latin America almost textually coincide with the *programs of action of the postwar Communist parties*. All of these attempts have failed, despite their scientific basis, because of their having adopted foreign patterns that are valid under different circumstances.
>
> In analyzing the chapter on "Latin American Reality," particularly in regard to the demographic situation, the study says that to blame the *demographic explosion* for the socio-economic disturbances is to avoid the real solution, which lies in the transformation of the means of production. In facing the demographic problem, some people do not hesitate in confronting others with the option of choosing between faith and life. At the scientific level there is another solution, namely *The Revolution*, which will create new means of production that will permit men to preserve their life and religion. Population control in the countries whose development is being prevented must be analyzed in light of the fact that the developed countries want to maintain their privileged social status, for which they will not hesitate to destroy all institutions through their program of *family planning*.

The Montinian Church

Since the LAMEC document affirms that the marginal population of Latin America represents 80% of the total, the Bogotá research group points out that if 80% of the population be marginal, this means that the so-called marginal people are not marginal and that the privileged 20% constitute the elites living off foreign-made schemes.

It is not true that this large population lacks social cohesion and organization. Their pre-Columbian tradition permitted them to survive despite the conquest, the violent Creole war of independence, and the civil wars.

Today they are bearing the oppression of international capitalism and its local agents who are preparing their liberation. It is unfair to suppose that people prevented from developing will remain underdeveloped, for their centuries-old accumulated capabilities will turn them into the hope of the human race.

The predominant culture in Latin America is not occidental, although it is presented as such in order to conceal the truth and overshadow the invisible logic of indigenous thought, which is the cultural reserve that will flourish in the future.

The youth of today are the most numerous and belligerent social group, due to the influence of the technological revolution and the vast development of international communications, which make them oppose the statism of our culture and society.

I was astonished to read the above opinions in the Bogotá newspapers, precisely on the days of the Eucharistic Congress, for they basically imply not only a break with, but a condemnation of, the Christian and Spanish Latin American past. Those secret meetings of clergy, nuns, and laity, so numerous and frequent after the closing of Vatican II, and which claim to be the genuine manifestation and definite fulfillment of the Conciliar mentality and the pastoral program arising therefrom, have provoked a tragic and regretful revolution within the Church. This revolution has made clergymen and laymen lose their faith and even episcopal conferences rebel against the immutable teachings of the Magisterium.

The secret meeting at Bogotá, apparently headed by Fr. René García Lizarralde, publicly endorses the bold, deep, and radical changes of Latin American structures, thus agreeing with the evolutionary program of Cardinal Lercaro. Perhaps the signers of the research report handed to Msgr. Abelard Brandao Vileda were more explicit, for they did say what the structures are that need urgent change. In the preamble they state the problem clearly and without circumlocution:

> Being deeply interested in the change of structures in Latin America, in the responsibility of the Church and its engagement therein, we have carried out a study about Latin American structures.

Revolution—The Only Solution?

From the beginning they assume and take for granted that it is imperious, urgent, and undeferrable to change the structures not only in Colombia, but in all Latin American countries. They do not say why, but we know that it was because it was so decreed by LAMEC and taken for granted by the progressivists who are presently allied with Marxist dialectic materialism. Moreover, they believe that the Church must be committed to and responsible for accomplishing this change. Why should the Church be responsible? Is it perhaps its mission to draft, change, or perfect the social, political, or economic structures of the countries? Cs not this task contradictory to Christ's words: "Render unto Caesar what is Caesar's, and to God what is God's?" It is not the Church that is committed; it is the ecclesiastics who are determined to baptize Communism and to become allies of the deadly enemies of God and the Church.

Resting on this false and unstable basis, they draw up a research report on behalf of the committed Church. One has to be really stubborn or committed to higher powers to launch such a far-reaching research, particularly when one's views are certainly narrow and lacking in knowledge and training. I do not think that even the venerable LAMEC prelates, in spite of their high position, age, and Conciliar studies, had the minimum social, economic, and political knowledge to assume such a tremendous responsibility and convey it to the Church. They became unconscious puppets of the wise "experts" who, since the time of the Council, have been paving the way for the enemy.

Ignorance is almost always bold and presumptuous. The participants who set up the research report have boldly and collectively judged all past and present Latin American governments to make a universally adverse verdict. "... [T]he great tragedy," they say, "of the best Latin American rulers arises from their ignorance of structures." This judgment refers to the *best rulers* and, *a postiori*, must also cover the *average* as well as the *worst* ones. Ergo, they all ignored the structures and they all governed in the dark!

But today the light of development and progress that these young brains project will dissipate the darkness and make us see with transparent clarity the only way for us to go. "Coincidentally," as these inspired reformers affirm, "the plans for the transformation of Latin America almost textually coincide with the *programs of action of the postwar Communist parties*."

To which plans do these paladins of liberty and progress refer? To the Alliance for Progress of Kennedy, Betancourt, and Figueres? To the LAMEC document? To the program that Fr. Arrupe and the Latin American Jesuit provincials worked out in Rio de Janeiro? To the *Populorum Progressio*? According to the compilers of the research report, it is a *coincidence, just a coincidence*, that the plans for the transformation of Latin America are similar to, inspired by, and virtually identical with the plans drawn up by the leaders of the postwar Communist parties. I would say, following the theological thought of the Bishop of Cuernavaca, Don Sergio Méndez Arceo, that such convergence is not fortuitous, but logical and wonderfully revealing.

These plans for the rapid, bold, and total transformation of all Latin American structures demand that we know the *true names and lineage* of all those *paid Communist agents* who cautiously militate within the Church and *have infiltrated the clergy, the Catholic organizations, and the very hierarchy itself*. That is why their programs do not seem to be inspired by Christ or His Gospel, but by Marx, Lenin, and the orders issued by the top leaders and masters of all these postwar Communist parties who may change their tactics but never relinquish their goals.

To play the game of *"peaceful coexistence,"* the Communists changed their tactics, whereupon their generous allies could now tell all the naive that Communism has lost its belligerency and now has positive aspects, that socialism is unavoidable, and that it is impossible to stop the triumphal advance of the proletariat. Moreover, the battling Bishop of Cuernavaca, in a moment of contagious lyricism, tells us that Communism is now so identical to Christianity that it is the only practical way of putting Christ's redemption into practice. As to the "fellow travelers" or "useful idiots," as Marxists call them, they will end up believing this fabulous story and will enthusiastically work out plans on their own to change the structures of Latin America; such plans, of course, will incidentally coincide with the programs of action of the postwar Communist parties.

Chapter X

THE CHANGE OF STRUCTURES AND THE DEMOGRAPHIC EXPLOSION

Reports on the Latin American social condition have exposed the so-called "demographic explosion" as one of the most lethal causes of our chronic underdevelopment. The proponents of economic liberalism acclaim that it is necessary to stop the constant increase in births and to widely spread scientific birth control by means of various contraceptive methods which the government must teach and spread among the masses.

From a different point of view, the progressivist theologians joyfully endorsed this contraceptive propaganda that flattered the increasingly impudent and daring passions of the crowds, who no longer tolerate the restrictions of chastity. Faced with the evidence that the new birth control pills prevented ovulation and did not escape, therefore, from the solemn and definite condemnation of the Magisterium of the Church, they sought a new, progressive, theological approach to Christian morality whereby they affirmed that the primary and essential goal of marriage was not, as it had been said, *the procreation and education of children*, but mutual love between the spouses, with such love being understood in a completely human, and above all, carnal and sexual way. Some of the progressives said more than that; they even denied the validity of the natural law as if it were old-fashioned and medieval.

The encyclical *Humanae Vitae*, long awaited by the orthodox, provoked a veritable revolution in many sectors, including several episcopal conferences. This was to be feared. At the Council itself, respectable voices were heard of cardinals and bishops who claimed to speak on behalf of the national or regional groups to which they belonged, and who called for a reform of conjugal morality, particularly in regard to this point. Right from the beginning when the Conciliar Fathers were about to re-examine the Church's rules on mixed marriages, Cardinal Döphner of Munich, endorsed by Cardinals Léger of Montreal and Suenens of Belgium, demanded major changes in all of the regulations concerning conjugal life.

The doctrinal aspect of marriage was handled within the scheme on "The Church in the Modern World," held during the third meeting of the Council. On October 28, 1964, the moderator, Cardinal Agaganiani, made public that some points had been reserved for the Pope-appointed Special Commission on

Birth Control. Nevertheless, the Conciliar Fathers were free to hand in their written observations and could feel sure that the papal commission would pay them due attention.

On October 29, 1964, during the debate on article 21 of the scheme entitled, "Sanctity of the Marriage and Family," Cardinal Léger of Montreal affirmed that "today many theologians believe that the difficulties related to the doctrine of matrimony *have their origin in an inadequate explanation of the goals of marriage*." To him, fertility should be considered as a permanent duty of the conjugal "state," and this state should be considered abstractly and collectively, not concretely, in the particular acts that the individual couple might perform.

"It is absolutely necessary," Cardinal Léger said, "that human love between spouses, and I am talking about human love that embraces both body and soul, be considered as one of the essential goals of matrimony as something good in itself, as something that has its own needs and rules." His Eminence was pleased that the *proposed scheme* avoided calling procreation the "primary and essential goal" of matrimony, and conjugal love the "secondary goal." This omission, however, would be immaterial if the scheme did not mention conjugal love except in connection with fertility. The scheme ought to state, said this Canadian Cardinal, that one of the "primary and essential goals" of *conjugal love* is the intimate union of the couple and, therefore, the act of the couple is "legitimate, even though it not be oriented to procreation."

Joining his colleagues, Cardinal Suenens of Belgium said that the words of the holy Scripture, "Grow and multiply yourselves," had been overemphasized to the extent that another phrase, also God's word, had been forgotten: "And they shall become two in one flesh." Both are true and essential, both are contained in the holy Scripture, and therefore, said the Cardinal, they each must serve to clarify the concrete meaning of the other. As a concrete and practical resolution, the Belgian primate asked that the names of all the persons the Pope had appointed as members of the Commission be published, so that "all God's people" could get in touch with them and give them their personal views concerning marriage and birth control.

On the following day it was His Eminence Cardinal Ottaviani who spoke. "I do not agree," he said, "with the affirmation included in the text of the scheme that conjugal couples may determine the number of children they will have. *This was never heard before in the Church*." His Eminence is the eleventh child in a family of twelve. "My father was a worker, but nevertheless, the fear of having too many children never entered my parents' minds, because they trusted in God's Providence."

Cardinal Ottaviani concluded his brief defense of the traditional doctrine of the Church by expressing his amazement at what his colleagues had said:

> Yesterday, at the Council, it should have been said that it is now being

The Change of Structures

questioned whether the pre-Conciliar Church has had the correct guidelines to establish the principles regulating marriage. Does this mean that we are doubting the infallibility of the Church? Was not the Holy Spirit with the Church, in past centuries, to enlighten the minds concerning this basic doctrinal point?

On September 29, 1965, at the fourth session of the Council, the Auxiliary Bishop Kazimierz Majdanski of Poland spoke energetically about these aberrations of contemporary man. He said:

> The modern world, . . . abhors the shedding of blood in war but views with indifference the destruction of the unborn child. The number of abortions performed in one single year surpasses the number of persons killed during World War II.

The final scheme on the doctrine of marriage covered 152 pages and was distributed to the Conciliar Fathers on Friday end Saturday, November 12 and 13, 1965. The bishops were supposed to have used the weekend before the voting to revise the schematic text, but instead, 500 of them took advantage of a free trip offered to them to attend the celebration of the seventh centennial of Dante's birth in Florence. So went things at the Council!

Addressing the Sacred College on June 23, 1964, the Pope said:

> For the present we do not have sufficient grounds to judge and declare past edicts invalid [the norms of previous Pontiffs], at least until we earnestly feel obliged to modify them. Since this is so flerious an issue, it is fitting and proper that Catholics follow the authoritative law of the Church and, therefore, that no one assume the right of contradicting the present norm.

Pius XI and Pius XII unequivocally declared that no one can change what God Himself has established; this is the natural law, a reflection of the eternal. The Pope's words are stunning at first sight. May the natural and the eternal divine law be overruled and rendered invalid? Catholics, evidently, must follow the authoritative and infallible voice of the Magisterium. Once it has spoken, however, they cannot expect a change that nullifies or, as is being said today, "surpasses" the immutable teaching of the conscience that imposed the rulings of the natural law which, as I have already said, is a reflection of the eternal law of God Himself. As Cardinal Ottaviani clearly pointed out, what Cardinals Döphner, Léger, and Suenens said at the Council implied that it is now being questioned whether the pre-Conciliar Church and the faithful had the right norms to establish the principles regulating marriage. Using the Cardinal's own words, again we ask: Does it mean that we distrust the *infallibility* of the Church and that the Holy Spirit has abandoned His Church temporarily? This is the great aberration of progressivism, that it tries to overlook, deny, or "surpass" the immutable doctrines of the past. In principle, Paul VI seems to accept this new doctrine, at least in possibility.

On October 6, 1965, in his famous speech at the United Nations in New York, although His Holiness did not utter the last, promised, and expected word on birth control and birth control pills, he was very explicit:

> Human life is sacred; no one may dare to violate it ... your task is to provide mankind's table with sufficient bread, instead of favoring artificial and irrational birth control which would reduce the number of guests at the banquet of life.

In October of 1966, at the 52nd National Congress of the Italian Society of Obstetrics and Gynecology, Paul VI expressed his thoughts once again:

> We shall only remind you of what we stated in our speech of June 23, 1964, ... namely that the thinking and norms of the Church have not changed and that the traditional teaching of the Church still prevails. The recent ecumenical council has provided the Church with some very *useful* views that can enrich Church doctrine in such an important field, but which are *insufficient* to change its basic concepts. Such views are convenient, however, to exhibit and to show, through authoritative arguments, that the Church is extremely interested in the problems of love, marriage, birth rate, and the family.... Meanwhile, as we said in that speech, the rules given by the Church and enriched by the wise guidelines of the Council require faithful and generous compliance. They may not be deemed non-obligatory, as though the Church's Magisterium mistrusted them now, while the study and reflection on what has been deemed worthy of careful consideration are underway.

Finally, the Pope returned to solemnly touch upon a document of great renown, his encyclical *Populorum Progressio*, in which he discussed the ever-burning question of birth control. In this encyclical, without uttering his final word on this vital matter that kept the Catholic and non-Catholic world greatly agitated, the Pope spoke about *"responsible paternity,"* which seemingly left up to the conscience of each couple the decision as to the number of children desired and the means of avoiding the undesired ones. We assume that this was not what the Pope meant; it was certainly not the explicit answer that everyone hoped and expected to hear from the definitive and conclusive voice of the Magisterium that would have put an end to the unhealthy speculations of the "experts."

In this same encyclical, His Holiness seems to authorize governments to intervene, for the sake of educational information, in this most serious matter of conjugal morality. Taking into account the irreligion and sectarianism of most governments, such information given by governmental agencies could not be expected to comply with God's law, but to elude it. All over Latin America, the United States State Department had by that time organized an intense "educational" campaign designed to extensively spread the techniques of birth control with the goal of banishing the menace of the Latin American demographic explosion to the peace and welfare of America. Clinics were opened in all our countries in which well trained and financed personnel divulged and distributed contraceptive information and devices.

When *Humanae Vitae* was finally released, it was all but natural that it should arouse noisy protests on the part of the ultra-radical progressivists, for the Pope had spoken definitively and had closed the door in favor of the natural law, God's eternal law, and the permanent teaching of the past. Some individuals were convinced that the Pope would not mention this subject again, or that his opinion would be entirely consistent with the unanimous views of the "experts" endorsed by the "new wave" of the Society of Jesus, some Dominicans, and other renowned religious groups.

In fact, *Humanae Vitae* does not enact a new law or decision of the present Pontiff. Since it is the natural, immutable, universal law that condemns the use of contraceptive measures during marital intercourse, *neither the Pope nor the Council may change what God Himself has established*. Progesterone may be used for therapeutic purposes, to afford rest to the ovaries for example, but never to prevent conception, even if its use be designed to spare the patient serious disturbance.

The revolutionary uprising provoked by the encyclical of Paul VI not only strives to defend birth control, but to attack the very authority and infallibility of the Church itself, thereby destroying the very basis of conjugal morality and most seriously jeopardizing the faith of its followers.

It was not expected that certain opposition to the encyclical *Humanae Vitae* was going to manifest itself at the Eucharistic Congress the Pope was going to attend. Neither was anyone able to forecast that in a milieu so full of "changes of structures" could the violent and widespread reaction to Paul's document be ignored. However, the priests, religious and laymen who conducted the Bogotá research program did not follow this current, but rather that of those who favored their revolutionary plans.

Let us go back to the document on which we have previously commented: "To blame the demographic explosion for the socio-economic disturbance is to avoid the real solution, the transformation of the means of production. In facing the demographic problem, some persons do not hesitate to confront people with the option of choosing between faith and life." What the promoters of these destructive campaigns seek is to divorce religion and life. They want to *plan life* according to the criteria of the "new teachers" Saint Paul referred to, those who flatter our wits, stimulate our passions, divert us from truth, and lead us to a fairy-tale world.

But the authors of the famous research of Bogotá do not accept the solution of the mafia which wants to reduce the population of the Latin American countries in order to relieve the developed countries from the unbearable load they are carrying, thus helping them maintain their *privileged position*. At the scientific level, the Colombian priests, religious, and laymen say there is another solution: *The Revolution*. They do not explain what this revolution consists or must consist of, nor do they explain whether it will be peaceful or violent. Be that as it may, it will be an audacious and violent change of the political structures of Latin America, a complete alteration with new forms, new structures, and something radically different from what we have experienced, what our parents forecast, and what have been the rules of our existence until now. This revolution, affirm the authors of this document, "will create new relations of production, namely, new social, economic, and political structures that will permit human beings to preserve their life and their religion."

The authors of the document presented to LAMEC are right in believing that our world still has immense resources to feed the eventual generations that neo-Malthusianism is sacrificing. The governmental attitude of the developed countries, which, in order to maintain their privileged position, want to destroy all institutions through family planning, is certainly criminal. I have never been nor am I now an ally of economic liberalism nor can I support those who seek to solve the demographic problem (if indeed this menacing and troublesome problem actually exists as it is depicted), by means of birth control as an easy and safe solution to the personal, domestic, and social difficulties of this much-publicized problem.

It would be interesting to investigate what the source of this campaign is and whose invisible hands have spread this net throughout the world, disseminating intense propaganda, and wanting to destroy life in its very sources, in order to dominate, enslave, and exploit us. Modern technologists are only tools of a *secret mafia to which we unconsciously give aid* in carrying out this perverse plan.

The way of stably and peacefully solving the social problem in Latin America is not to kill and hinder life, but to feed, educate, and integrally develop the underdeveloped people. No other kind of revolution can ever be peaceful, but can be carried out only through violence, guerilla warfare, destruction, and death.

Whatever their percentage may be, the marginal people referred to in this document have existed, exist now, and will always exist on the surface of the earth. That is why the work of the Church to improve their condition has been, is, and will always be intense, sincere, and efficacious, although it may never succeed in eliminating misery.

The Change of Structures

There are, in fact, marginal people everywhere. Some people exceed the ideal unit that we can pretend is the average; others represent only a fraction. The Church and the ecclesiastics take advantage of those "elites living out of foreign-made schemes," as the document calls them, to improve the condition of those who need help and protection. Neither the Church nor the ecclesiastics would be able to do anything to aid the marginal people if it were not for the generous souls that exist within those elites who give up everything for the sake of faith, because they love the kingdom of Heaven.

NEO-NATIVISM

As quoted before, the sociologists who conducted the previously-mentioned research wrote:

> It is not true that this large population lacks social cohesion and organization. Their pre-Columbian tradition permitted them to survive despite the conquest, the violent Creole war of independence, and the civil wars.
>
> Today they are bearing the oppression of international capitalism and its local agents who are preparing their liberation. It is unfair to suppose that people prevented from developing will remain underdeveloped, for their centuries-old accumulated capabilities will turn them into the hope of the human race.
>
> The predominant culture in Latin America is not occidental, although it is presented as such in order to conceal the truth and overshadow invisible logic of indigenous thought, which is the cutural reserve that will flourish in the future.

The Colombian progressivist sociologists who wrote this document have drawn up revolutionary plans that include a breach with the past and the present, going back to the times, the culture, and the true and constructive logic of the native thinking, because it is the hope of the human race and the cultural reserve for the future. According to these writers, the work of Spain and the Church, as well as Christianity, has done nothing for Latin America. Using oppression, they buried the indigenous resources in order to set up the decadent and destructive Christian civilization upon those ruins. But from those ashes the vivifying and redeeming flame of native culture and its centuries-long accumulated capabilities will rise again. The Inca, Maya, and Aztec empires will come back, as will human sacrifices, cannibalism, and ferocious wars of extermination. It is necessary to go back to the purity of the "sources," and it is urgent to begin history again, wiping off Christ, His Church, Spain, and the adventurous friars who fraudulently perverted our aboriginal culture that now appears as the hope of the human race.

One of the biggest aberrations of the change- and reform-greedy progressivists is to deny all past positive work, in order to go back, as they say, to the purity of the "sources." They forget the evangelical parable in which the kingdom of Heaven is compared to a mustard seed that grows and develops until it becomes a bush on whose branches the birds of the sky perch their nests. Life is growth, and it would be absurd to begin the same journey all over again.

But the authors of the research report do not intend to go back to the crystalline sources, but to eliminate all the Christian period in order to throw us back again into the indigenous period. According to them, ours is not the occidental or the Christian culture, but the indigenous culture that has survived "despite the conquest, the violent Creole war of independence, and the civil wars."

The consequences of this revolutionary doctrine are clear: Latin Americans are not one family or a new race. Conquered and conquerors remain totally separated, mutually opposite. The conquerors must either leave America, for it does not belong to them, or give up their European heritage and their Christian principles in order to completely assimilate themselves into the indigenous culture which is to reign throughout Latin America. *Christianity is superfluous in America,* and it is the cause of our countries' underdevelopment.

Fortunately, progressivists are illogical and contradict themselves. The last paragraph of the document on which we have commented recants the previous paragraphs:

> The youth of today are the most numerous and belligerent social group, due to the influence of the technological revolution *and the vast development of international communications* that make them oppose the stability of our culture and our civilization.

Why should we look abroad for what we have at home? Did they not say that our own and independent native culture, having been able to survive the conquest, the violence of the Creole wars of independence and the civil wars, was the hope of the human race?

Yes, today's youth *is* the most numerous group! This is precisely one of the tragic features of the time in which we live, that we are in the hands of inexperienced, passionate, dissatisfied, dull youngsters, who not only are able to do without the past but who, in order to build a new, better, and a more human world, must smash the structures our ancestors bequeathed us. When inexperienced youth becomes disoriented, the equilibrium of a nation is endangered.

Chapter XI

LAMEC IS A MATTER OF LIFE OR DEATH FOR THE CHURCH

In the August 20, 1968, edition of *Der Spiegel*, a weekly news magazine published in Hamburg, Germany, an article is devoted to the Pope's trip to Bogotá, and emphasizes the following words by Abbe René Laurentin concerning the episcopal meeting of the LAMEC in Medellín: *"For Latin America and for the Church, the hour of life or death has come."*

According to this German weekly, "Pope Paul VI can become the *obstetrician* in this birth of a social-revolutionary Church." The article refers to famine and underdevelopment in Latin America, but also to the progressivist Church, which has been encouraged by the encyclical *Populorum Progressio*.

It mentions the prodigious work of Don Helder Cámara and Bishop Waldir Caldheiro. It makes reference to the birth control pill and affirms that, according to the *Guardian*, the Pope's visit to Latin America can be stormy. The following quotation from a report appearing in *El Espacio* from Bogotá on August 20, 1968, give us an idea about the heat that the Pope's visit, the LAMEC document, and the restless activity of the progressivists, especially the Bishop of Recife and Olinda, Brazil, Don Helder Cámara, had produced in Europe and America:

> The well-known name of the Bishop of Recife and Olinda, Brazil, has been the most outstanding feature ever since various rumors spread about his arrival in this country to attend the second international conference of bishops at Medellín ... The belligerent attitude of the Brazilian Archbishop has been the subject of numerous comments on the part of clergymen.

Below I copy the letter from Mrs. Isabel Restrepo de Torres to Don Helder, taking into account that I have previously quoted the letter from the Archbishop to Doña Isabel:

Bogotá, 7/7/68.
Helder Cámara, Archbishop of Recife and Olinda, Brazil.
Dear Father Helder Cámara,
    I am sure you will come to Colombia to attend the Eucharistic Congress. It

would be my great honor if you would accept my cordial invitation and be my guest at home, where my son Camilo Torres used to live. He died because he externalized his ideas—that I know to be yours too—following Christ's steps to defend the poor. I should appreciate your prompt answer, that I hope will be affirmative.

I remain, your sister in Christ,
Isabel Restrepo de Torres.

This letter, in which we find all the sincerity of a mother who has lost her son, tells us that Don Helder and Camilo, the priest-guerilla leader, were quite intimately related as far as ideology and activity are concerned. Don Helder, like the Bishop of Cuernavaca, conceals his feelings, thoughts, and actions when he sees fit. Camilo Torres, says his mother, "died because he externalized his ideas," which Doña Isabel knows are also Don Helder's.

Camilo's ideas were guerila warfare, violent revolution, and audacious and radical change of the structures. These are also supposed to be Don Helder's ideas, but His Excellency lacks the necessary boldness, bravery, and courage to put his redeeming program into practice.

But, beware! This ideology of the bullets, this activism by fire and sword, are not Christ's program to aid the indigent! "*If you want to be perfect go and sell what you have and give it to the poor.*" It is not obligatory, but voluntary; it is advice which Christ gives. Nowhere in the Gospel does our Lord advise us to take up arms, to engage in guerila warfare and provoke subversion of the social order to relieve the needs of the indigent. Christ-revolution, or Christ as a revolutionary, is ficticious, a hoax through which Communism seeks to make converts.

Is this the birth of a social-revolutionary Church which the famous Abbe Laurentin, well-known French progressivist, announces? Will Pope Montini volunteer to be the obstetrician in this child-birth as the German weekly magazine asked in commenting on the coming trip of Paul VI to Colombia?

RENOVATING WIND AT THE INTERNATIONAL EUCHARISTIC CONGRESS

Some of the more conservative prelates of Latin America feared that the Pope's visit would have explosive consequences for the future of the Church in America, and wanted to raise dissident voices at the Eucharistic shrine. An important question was on their minds—would LAMEC be the real beginning of many revolutions in Latin America?

From the newspaper *El Vespertino* from Bogotá we quote as follows:

Bogotá, August 20 (UPI)—A vast outcry of disagreement, anxiety,

LAMEC—A Matter of Life or Death?

nonconformity, and wish for transformation is paving a rocky road for the historical trip of Paul VI, the first Roman Pontiff to step on Latin American soil in the history of mankind.

Dissident voices, but not shy or discordant, have invaded the sacred field of liturgy, spreading opinions that just a few years ago *would be voiced only in leftist or markedly heterodox newspapers or platforms.*

This fact has turned the International Eucharistic Congress and the Pope's forthcoming visit into a dramatic landmark that *can point to a vast renovation in the history of the Latin American Church.*

Renovating Wind

Although many observers and responsible ecclesiastic sources believe that Paul VI will stay within the framework of moderate renovation as indicated by this encyclical *Populorum Progressio (People's Progress)* and the conservatism of his most recent papal document, *Humanae Vitae (Human Life),* some people believe that he will not be able to escape the renovating hurricane that has let itself be felt during the two first sessions of the International Eucharistic Congress.

Discrimination Of Churches

When Paul VI arrives at Bogotá at about ten o'clock a.m. next Thursday, he will find that the Eucharistic field (the shrine built for the chief acts of the Congress and consecrated for one of the most impressive Mass ceremonies of Catholicism) has already been used to expose Latin American and especially Colombian discrimination against other Christian religions, by virtue of a concordat with the Holy See.

On the other hand, the Pope's words will have been preceded by social statements of numerous cardinals and bishops who consider the Latin American economic and social systems as oppressive, unjust, and, in certain cases, *even justifying violence.*

Explosive Meaning

The ecclesiastic observers consider that it is impossible that the Holy Father can withdraw himself from this environment, and think, therefore, that he will frankly and boldly attack these incandescent subjects. This has given birth to the belief that his visit to Bogotá will be something more than an act of love towards Latin America and that *it will be charged with explosive consequences for the future attitude of the Church in this part of the world.*

Authoritative ecclesiastic sources point out that at least one of the Pope's speeches will help refute the intense criticism poured forth ever since he conveyed to the world his judgment opposing all sorts of artificial birth control methods several weeks ago. In Latin America the issue of demographic explosion has provoked serious division within governmental, political, and even religious sectors, which are carefully studying the eventual consequences of an unruly population increase before the social and economic condition in this region of the world is improved.

Social Opinions

For the Latin American people however, the demographic problem is secondary. What the Pope has to say concerning the people's progress will probably be more important to them. The ecclesiastical circles that reported the event say that this will be the second greatest speech Paul VI has delivered, and possibly the one that will have the most intense repercussions on expectant Latin American Catholics.

Voices of Protest

The third great issue the Pope will attack is the Church's *ecumenism*, that is, the Catholic rapprochement to other Christian religions, some of whose spokesmen have enjoyed a seat and voice at the Eucharistic shrine and at the religious ceremonies having been performed so far.

Going through the wide gate which Vatican Council II opened, the Eucharistic Congress celebrated an ecumenical journey during which an Anglican pastor *exposed* the Latin American discrimination against creeds other than Catholicism, and a Lutheran bishop pointed out that the revolutionary *aggiornamento* in today's Church *is just a second edition of the Reformation which Protestants effected four centuries ago.*

Such views are not new, but on being voiced within the consecrated precinct of the Eucharistic shrine, they certainly made the ultraconservative sectors of the Latin American Church shiver.

Revolution

These sectors have been regarding the Eucharistic Congress as distrustfully as if it were a revolution designed to alter the traditional strata of the Latin American Church. They have been scared mostly by the frequence and impudence with which the word *revolution* has been used by cardinals, bishops, priests, and theologians who are discussing metaphysical subjects in the ancient Columbus Theatre, the oldest in Bogotá, usually devoted to opera and ballet, and today turned into the stage of a politically and socially transcendent religious

LAMEC—A Matter of Life or Death?

discussion.

Even so, the ecclesiastical observers forecast that the visit of Pope Paul VI to Bogotá will not bring about a total change in the direction of the Latin American Church.

LAMEC: The Beginning

On the other hand, they expect that such changes will begin to take place at the meeting of the Latin American bishops in Medellín at the beginning of next week. This meeting will be personally opened by the Pope at Bogotá, but the work sessions will be transferred to Medellín and begin next Tuesday.

As a basis for their activities, the bishops will have a document that has been exposed as *revolutionary* even by moderately liberal segments of the Church. This document, charged with using left-wing vocabulary, denounces the exploitation of workers, attacks the conditions imposed by foreign capital, and in a veiled manner exposes the oppressive, capitalistic system in the underdeveloped world.

These many reasons make one expect that the visit of Pope Paul VI will push toward goals other than endorsing a series of liturgical rulings that have transformed the external functions of the Church, and which have also been attacked by the most conservative groups.

The above article reproduced from the Bogotá newspaper *El Vespertino* gives us a precise idea about the tension, muffled strife, fear, and hope prevailing in Bogotá two days prior to the beginning of the innovative Eucharistic Congress where, as we have already pointed out, little was said about the Eucharist and much about *change of structures, revolution*, and *violence*. The imminent visit of the Pope was expected by some people to bring dreams of redemption, and feared by others as the spark that could have exploded a bomb on all Latin American structures. Progressivists believed the Pope would energetically, clearly, apostolically and boldly speak their own language. Conservatives were afraid that the Pope's visit was going to be the trumpet-call that announced the start of a continental revolution that would knock down all the religious, social, and political Latin American structures. The *Populorum Progressio* and the *Humanae Vitae* indicated two opposing directions in the mind and activity of the reforming Pontiff.

The Pope could not ignore the socio-economic and political background of the International Eucharistic Congress and, in such circumstances, it was impossible that the Holy Father *not* frankly and boldly treat these burning subjects. *Social justice, demographic explosion,* and *ecumenism* were the most fervent issues being discussed, under Eucharistic guise, at the numerous international congresses being simultaneously celebrated at Bogotá during those days.

Paul VI had already spoken about the first two issues in his controversial encyclicals, *Populorum Progressio* and *Humanae Vitae*, whose directions were opposite, with the former pointing to the left and the latter to the right. Evidently in preparing both documents His Holiness took Latin America and his deeply beloved Third World into account. In due course we shall see what he said in Bogotá about these subjects.

Let us say something now, however, about the third issue of ecumenism, since, in the schedule of the Congress, the second day was especially devoted to it. Let us quote the new and unusually interesting schedule:

MONDAY, AUGUST 19

Ecumenical Day

Concelebration at the parishes.
Theme: *Christian Unity*
Conscious that the holy goal of reconciling all the Christians of the one and only Church of Jesus Christ exceeds the human forces and capabilities, in this celebration we base our hope on Christ's prayer for the Church, the love of the Father for us, and the virtue of the Holy Ghost. Just as we now have the same Lord, the same beliefs, the same Baptism, and the same Heavenly Father, one day we shall become a single body partaking of the same bread.

Let the reader excuse my interrupting the quotation in order to make some comments on such a strange beginning. The progressivist vocabulary is so confusing and ambiguous that its thought also becomes uniformly equivocal.

Do we *really* have the same Lord, the same beliefs, the same Baptism, and the same divine Father? Evidently not, for if such unity existed, the progressivist-promoted ecumenical movement itself would be unnecessary, and the ecumenical celebration on the second day of the Congress would have been meaningless. The statement is, then, at least grammatically incorrect. Maybe they intended to say: "If we now had the same Lord, etc., then we would be a single body. . . ." This is a conditional sentence whose nature must be explained for such an affirmation to be made. The "separated" people must first convert and sincerely accept all the truth of our religion; they must then participate in our Sacraments; and they must abide by the authority of our legitimate shepherds and submit thereto, in order to constitute with us one body, and one flock under one Shepherd.

How dangerous ecumenism is when trying to flatter the "separated brothers!" It insinuates that their secession is accidental instead of substantial, that basically we are the same stuff, or almost the same stuff, and that it was past

LAMEC—A Matter of Life or Death?

stubbornness and inquisitorial intransigence which created dissent and deepened our division.

Now, let us go back to the program:

ENTRANCE SONG
Psalm 99

Antiphon: Come before the Lord
singing hymns of joy.

Verse I: Let all the earth cry out to God,
Serve the Lord with joy,
Rejoice in Him.
(Other songs: see hymnal, page 117.)

GREETING

President: The Lord be with you.
People: And also with you.

PENITENTIAL ACT

President: Forgive, O Lord, all our faults against your love, that give birth to our discord.
Choir: Christ, have mercy.
People: Christ, have mercy.
President: Give us your grace so that we can better reward your design of love and unity.
Choir: Lord, have mercy.
People: Lord, have mercy.

PEOPLE'S PRAYER

President: Almighty and eternal God, you gather what is scattered; look at the sheep of your flock, so that all who were consecrated in the same Baptism remain united by the integrity of the Faith and the bond of love. Through Jesus Christ Our Lord.
People: Amen.

FIRST READING

A reading from the letter of the apostle Saint Paul to the Ephesians. "Brothers: I therefore, the prisoner of the Lord, beseech you that ye walk worthy of the vocation wherewith ye are called.

"Be always humble and meek, with longsuffering and forbearing one another in love, and endeavoring to keep the unity of the Spirit in the bond of peace. There is one body,

The Montinian Church

and one Spirit, even as ye are called in one hope of your calling; one Lord, one faith, one baptism; and one God and Father of all, who is above all, and through all, and in you all."

MEDITATION SONG

Antiphon: One Lord, one Faith, one Baptism, one God and Father.

Verse: 1. Called to preserve the unity of the spirit through the bond of peace, we sing and proclaim.

2. Called to constitute a single body in the same spirit, we sing and proclaim:

3. Called to share the same hope in Christ, we sing and proclaim.

SECOND READING (John 17:20-26).

A reading from the Holy Gospel according to Saint John. "At that time Jesus lifted up His eyes to heaven and said, Father, neither pray I for these alone, but for them also which shall believe on me through their word; That they all may be one, as thou, Father, art in me, and I in thee, that they also may be one in us, that the world may believe that thou hast sent me. And the glory which Thou gavest me I have given them, that they may be one, even as we are one: I in them, and thou in me, that they may be made perfect in one; and that the world may know that thou hast sent me, and hast loved them as thou hast loved me. Father, I will that they also, whom thou hast given me, be with me where I am; that they may behold my glory, which thou hast given me, for Thou lovedst me before the foundation of the world. O righteous Father, the world hath not known thee, but I have known thee, and these have known that thou hast sent me. And I have declared unto them Thy name, and will declare it, that the love wherewith Thou hast loved me may be in them, and I in them."

HOMILY

President: ... O God, source of unity and love, look upon us who are gathering in Christ and through Him hear our prayer.

Deacon-Commentator: For all the shepherds of your Church, so that they loyally fulfill their mission of serving the unity and concord of men.

People: ... We beg you, Lord:

LAMEC—A Matter of Life or Death?

For the peace of the world, so that all wars and divisions among the members of the human family be at an end.
For the brothers of all the churches, so that our common faith in Christ unite us in sincere charity and service.
So that the glittering unity of faith of Latin America ripen into the effective integration of its nations.
So that love, which we show by eating the same bread, be exempt from nationalistic, racial, and social class boundaries.
So that all the pilgrims be as brothers and united in the same Faith and the same love among us.

OFFERTORY
Antiphon: Glory to you for all the centuries. (Other songs: see hymnal, page 120.)

PRAYER OVER THE GIFTS
President: Almighty God, we are aware of our weakness and trust your might; Send us the joy of being always united under your love. Through Jesus Christ Our Lord.
People: Amen.

EUCHARISTIC PRAYER
President: The Lord be with you.
People: And also with you.
President: Lift up your hearts.
People: We lift them up to the Lord.
President: Let us give thanks to the Lord, our God.
People: It is right to give him thanks and praise.
Holy, Holy, Holy ...
President: Through Christ, with Him, in Him, in the unity of the Holy Spirit, all glory and honor is yours, Almighty Father, forever and ever.
People: Amen.
Our Father; Lamb of God.

COMMUNION SONG
Canticle of Charity. (See hymnal, page 124.)
You are my Shepherd. (See hymnal, page 126.)

POST-COMMUNION PRAYERS
President: O Lord, pour out your spirit of charity upon us, so that, fed with the Paschal sacraments, we remain united by the grace

The Montinian Church

                of your love.
People: Amen.

CONCLUDING SONG

              ECUMENICAL CELEBRATION OF THE WORD
                (At the Eucharistic Field—The Shrine.)

In the dialogue with Christians of all confessions, the love and veneration of the Holy Scriptures are precious instruments in God's mighty hand, in order to achieve the unity that the Savior offers all men. The common celebration of God's Word will be the expression of the fundamental unity of all Christians, and a search for a more complete unity.

                Choir of the Presbyterian Church.
                Choir of the Baptist Church.
                Choir of the Anglican Church.
                Mixed choir of other churches.
                Antiochian Singing Society.

We decided to present in total both the program and the peculiar liturgy of the *Ecumenical Day* before making any comments on one of the most discussed, controversial and, to be sincere, scandalous issues of the Colombian Eucharistic Congress. The Catholic Church, our Church, the only one Jesus Christ founded according to our beliefs, was, on that ecumenical day, not only assimilated, but was subordinated to, the sects that claim to be Christian but do not profess the doctrines the Divine Master taught. It is evident that the Church wants and seeks the salvation of all men, since this is the great aspiration of Christ's heart, but this wish may not lead to the condemnation of our own Church or to the abandonment of its apostolic doctrine. Either the "separated brothers" convert to our religion and integrally accept the Catholic doctrine, or the ecumenical union Vatican II preached and sought will be only a sweet dream whose fulfillment will be impossible.

"One Lord, one Faith, one Baptism, one God and Father." This is the program, and the great aspiration of Christ's heart. This is *potentially, in actu primo* so to speak, the redeeming work, but this is not the reality expressed by the churches that claim to be Christian but do not have the same faith, nor perhaps the same Christ and God we Catholics have.

Had we Catholics and Protestants of various denominations and doctrines "one Faith," the consequence would be that those of our dogmas they do not accept would not belong to the *deposit of revealed truth,* or that such truth could be partially or totally impugned, omitted, or denied by anyone bearing the name of "Christian," that is to say, accepting Christ's person, even if distrusting or denying His divinity.

Following this trend of most liberal ecumenism, we might say that all religions that include a God and a belief, have a faith that is the *same* faith we Catholics have. This might include monotheism or polytheism, acceptance or rejection of the Trinity, an imminent or transcendent god, cosmic and evolutionary Christ, or a Christ who is extraordinary as man, but who is not God. All of these are the same in ecumenical syncretism, the sole grantor of peace and fraternity for the large human family.

When speaking about the sacrilegious communion of the Protestant ministers in Medellín, thanks to the concession of His Excellency Antonio Samoré and the pious LAMEC leaders, I remarked that the Catholic Church, our Church, does not even accept the baptism of the "separated people" as safe; hence, it requests that the members of those sects who convert to our Catholic Faith be baptized again, *sub conditione.* Thus, we *cannot* affirm that ours is *the same Baptism* as theirs.

The "Penitential Act" opening the very peculiar liturgy prepared for this unheard-of ceremony of the Congress of Bogotá was but a *mea culpa* of the Catholic Church, since it is the Popes, bishops and Catholic believers who are charged with the awesome responsibility of having provoked the secession of the "separated brothers." The president of the Mass says:

> Forgive, O Lord, all our faults . . . that give birth to our discord. . . . look at . . . all who were consecrated in the same Baptism [so that they may] remain united by . . . the Faith and . . . love.

Was it the Catholics' fault that division had risen among men, thus frustrating Christ's design for love and unity? In the face of heresy, sacrilege, offenses against God, impugnation and denial of the revealed truth, must we have dialogue, be silent, not even mention our dogmas, conceal our beliefs, and accommodate our sacred rites to the Protestant services and customs, to avoid hurting our "separated brothers," even though our weakness and cowardice hurt Christ Himself?

The mission of the shepherds of the real Church of Christ is not serving the "unity" and harmony of men, as is said in the ecumenical liturgical prayer invented by Cardinal Lercaro, but to be servants of God, keeping intact the deposit of the divine revelation. Moreover, if it is necessary to condemn heresy and punish the heretics in order to keep the sacred deposit untouched, they must do so, even if the heretics have to leave Christ's flock. Merciful tolerance towards people who have plunged into error or sin, but later repent, is very different from tolerance with respect to ideas that are opposite to truth or to persons who stubbornly endorse and spread error. We may be tolerant to people provided we do not jeopardize our faithfulness to God by seeming to accept what God Himself condemns, or by exposing our brothers in the Catholic Faith to the risk of thinking that it is permissible to compromise with heresy, because tolerance of false ideas is apostasy and infidelity to God and His Church.

Peace is desirable, and we must persistently pray for it to the Lord, but sometimes war is not only just, but necessary. As long as we remain in the state of "fallen nature" in which original sin left us, wars are to be taken for granted. The progressivists themselves, who so insistently seek this Octavian peace, forget it when endorsing or justifying "violence" as the sole efficacious means of rapidly and radically changing the structures which they believe, in turn, to be the basis on which progress and the only acceptable human way of living together are based.

I believe I have shown that our Faith is not the same faith as that of our brothers of the other, so-called Christian Churches. Otherwise there would be no "separated brothers" to concern Vatican II so gravely. I may render services to and be a friend of these separated brothers, provided I do not jeopardize my own faith or that of my brothers. My charity and services to men should always be subordinate to my charity and service to God.

I cannot understand what His Eminence Cardinal Lercaro meant, in this innovative ecumenical gathering, with the following prayer he had the assembly intone: "So that the glittering unity of faith of Latin America ripen into the effective integration of its nations." What kind of integration did he refer to? Religious integration? Racial integration? Social and economical integration? Political integration, designed to efface all borders and identify us all into a single nation under a single government? All sound alike; all lead to the destruction of our identity and essence, and melt us together into a continental mass. It seems to be defined by the following prayer of the assembly: "So that love, that we manifest in eating the same bread, be exempt from nationalistic, racial, and social class boundaries." What bread is this prayer referring to? To the earthly bread, fruit of human hands, or to the Heavenly Bread, the divine Eucharist?

"Effective integration of its nations." This phrase is confusing, but, given the Communistic leaning of the former Archbishop of Bologna, I do feel I can catch his idea. This is no *ecumenical* prayer; this is a *Communist* prayer!

But the most regretful, humiliating and scandalous feature of that ecumenical day was, no doubt, the "Ecumenical Celebration of the Word," as the program named the liturgical (?) ceremonies which took place on that day at the Eucharistic shrine. We quote again the words with which the program was justified to the perturbed and sincere Catholics who witnessed this most sorrowful spectacle:

> In ... dialogue with Christians of all confessions, the love and veneration of the holy Scriptures are precious instruments in God's mighty hand, in order to achieve the unity that the Savior offers all men. The common celebration of

LAMEC—A Matter of Life or Death?

God's Word will be the expression of the fundamental unity of all Christians, and a search for a more complete unity.

Do Catholics and Protestant "free thinkers" love and venerate the holy Scriptures in like manner? How could such heterogeneous and contradictory preaching bring about the unity the Savior offers all men? In avowing there is *"fundamental unity"* or a common denominator between the Catholic religion and the Protestant sects, we are giving up our principles, mixing up truth and falsehood, and incurring religious syncretism, are we not? What does such *"fundamental unity"* consist of, taking into account that many "separated brothers" do not even recognize the divinity of Jesus Christ?

This joint celebration of God's Word, which Catholics and Protestants interpret in such different and diametrically opposite ways, does not seem to be a precious instrument in God's mighty hand to convert mistaken people or to achieve the unity the Savior longed for, for all his people. The words may be the same, but their meanings will change according to the various interpretations the numerous Protestant denominations give to the sacred texts.

Next to the Pope's Legate, in liturgical robes and in scandalous equality, sat the Orthodox priest, Gabriel Stephen, the Lutheran so-called Bishop of Bavaria, Dieszelbinger, and the Anglican priest or minister, Samuel Pinzón. Truth matched falsehood; the One, Holy, Catholic and Apostolic Church founded by Jesus Christ at the same level as its enemies, the sects! In the presence of such an unusual show, I thought about Christ's crucifixion, when Our Lord at Calvary hung from the cross between two thieves.

The Anglican minister, taking the opportunity of using such an uncommon occasion to put things his own way, denounced "Latin American discrimination against creeds other than Catholicism." According to him, the provisions of the concordats between the Latin American countries and the Holy See should be abolished. All Protestants and non-Protestant propagandists should be given wide opportunity to spread their errors and unmercifully attack the most sacred dogmas of our religion. This imperious and crude demand was to be seen in large type in the profuse advertisements stuck to the walls of Bogotá during the celebration of the Eucharistic Congress, while the Catholic shepherds in charge of the sheep ignored, implicitly accepted, and, in some cases may have looked upon them with satisfaction. So their sophisticated ecumenism made them deserving of promotions in their ecclesiastical careers! Rather than a Catholic Pope, Paul VI is an ecumenical Pope.

The Lutheran "bishop" recalled that the revolutionary *aggiornamento* of today's Church is but a "second edition of Luther's Reformation." In other words, according to this "separated brother," the Church is becoming *Protestant;* it is now accepting what it has been condemning for four centuries. Where is the indefectibility of the Church? Where is its infallible Magisterium? The

Council of Trent, with its definitions and condemnations, lacks all meaning and value.

The Lutheran "bishop" of Bavaria, who delivered the first homily (?), brought prolonged applauses from that naive or drowsy audience, the first applauses heard at the Eucharistic shrine during the Ecumenical Celebration of the Word. Below are the words of that "separated brother," who raised so much enthusiasm among that heterogeneous crowd:

> I belong to the church that thanks God for the Lutheran Reformation, and today I am able to greet the International Eucharistic Congress in this great Catholic country of Colombia, in this beautiful city of Bogotá.
>
> How has this been possible? Above all let us thank God and the Holy Spirit, who, in these days, have mobilized all Christendom on earth. Everywhere He has made the long-forgotten truth shine again, that Christendom is the One, the only, Holy, Catholic, and Apostolic Church. He has disclosed the unfairness of self-sufficiency, in which we Christians of *all* creeds and doctrines have lived for such a long time....
>
> His precious life is astonishing for it discloses separated segments in Christendom. Under the pressure of Hitler's regime, He brought about a mutual rapprochement of Catholics and evangelicals in Germany. Both groups have found from experience that it is precisely pain which unites separated people and that pain is a great ecumenical force.

This "bishop" contended that by means of Vatican II, John XXIII gave a new strength to ecumenism, and that the resulting movement has continued until now, like circles created by a stone cast into water.

He recalled *the participation of our Catholic Church in the World Council of Churches* and called for a second meeting to bring about even more concrete achievements.

He argued that it is very pleasant to know that, from Vatican II on, the Roman Catholic Church has been opening itself to the ecumenical movement, thus creating a more definite hope.

This German "bishop" said that in many religious sectors, not only the Lutheran Reformation, but the word *Reformation,* has been adopted, and that the word *Reformation* is being introduced even into the Roman Catholic Church.

This speech, that cannot and must not be called a homily, a sermon, or evangelical preaching, was delivered by a gentleman who, though he claims to be one, is *not* a bishop, for he was not consecrated by an apostolic successor. The speech basically meant the total wreckage of the counter-Reformation carried out in God's Church, the only one Christ founded under Peter's direction and leadership, with its wonderful saints with whom God endowed

His Church to reinforce it in the face of its enemies.

This so-called "bishop," who thanks God for the Lutheran Reformation, was officially invited by the Catholic hierarchy and presented to Catholics coming from all over the world before the Pope's Legate and proxy at the International Eucharistic Congress, not in order that he avow and confess the mistakes of the Reformation and accept truth as defined at Trent as the immutable dogma of our Catholic and Apostolic Faith belonging to the deposit of the divine revelation, but to proclaim that the union of all the churches that claim to be Christian, although differing as to doctrine, is Christendom, the only, Holy, Catholic and Apostolic Church. This means that the Roman Church improperly assumed those titles, features, or signs that characterize the One, True Church instituted by Jesus Christ. It was unfair, according to the Lutheran "bishop," that we Catholics had secluded ourselves in this exclusiveness. No matter what their creed, all Christian denominations belong to Christendom, that is, to the One, Holy, Catholic and Apostolic Church founded by Jesus Christ.

The Lutheran "bishop" says that the oppression of Hitler's regime united Catholics and evangelicals. This pain that he mentions, this sentimentalism, is the key to understanding this most peculiar compromise between Truth and error, between the Catholic Church and the Protestant churches. Herculean lie! The hoax of the six million Jews slain by the Nazis! *Look* magazine was right in its famous article, "How the Jews Changed Catholic Thinking." They did so to such an extent that at Bogotá it appeared as if the Reformation and Trent had publicly made up. *Jesus autem tacebat!* (And Jesus kept quiet!).

Our participation in the World Council of Churches, painful enigma for those of us who are still faithful to the monolithic belief of yesterday's Church, is not and must not be just more than a polite gesture, an expression of goodwill designed to help the "separated brothers" avow their errors and accept the healthy and genuine doctrine which the Magisterium of the Church has consistently taught. A world council in which all Christian denominations and the One True Church of Christ took part with equal rights would be impossible, because valid councils must be convened by the Pope, they must be dogmatic, and all their definitions and resolutions must be ratified and enforced by the Pope. In other words, all the members of these councils must be Catholic and must abide by the supreme and definitive authority of the Roman Pontiff.

It cannot be denied that, after Vatican II, there remained a kind of *Conciliar psychosis,* a thirst for continuous change, a desire to mold the doctrine, morality, liturgy, discipline, asceticism, and mysticism of the Church. This was to bring about "even more concrete achievements," according to the Lutheran "bishop," who implied a world council wherein we all have a voice and a vote, where the democratic and collegiate vote, according to the principle of co-responsibility enunciated by the Belgian primate, enforces the new creed and the new religious structure of the Church, the beatific fraternity of love and peace, namely, the religion of Universal Brotherhood.

In his speech, the Lutheran "bishop" hints that Luther's Reformation has already been accepted by the Roman Catholic Church. This is what the reformer Bishop of Cuernavaca, Don Sergio VII, endorsed by his brothers in the episcopate, said: "Luther was right; his mistake consisted of having tried to make his Reformation outside of the Church."

After the speech by the Lutheran "bishop" and going on with the program, the Latin American Lutheran minister, Antonio Lara, (I do not think it an exaggeration to suspect he is a Catholic renegade) intoned an ecumenical prayer that was meekly echoed by all the attending Catholics, headed by their Excellencies and Most Reverend Eminences.

Then came the second "homily" and ecumenical speech, by the Anglican minister, Samuel Pinzón. Neither his first nor his last name appears to be quite Anglican, but his faith was. He defined the points around which his Anglican Church could accept unity and said that undoubtedly unity could be accomplished only around the word of the Gospel (as construed by them, naturally). He demanded a "change of structures," not only in governments, but also in the churches. He endorsed Cardinal Lercaro's ideas about people's development as stated by that Catholic hierarch at the opening of the 39th International Eucharistic Congress. He explained that in Colombia the unity of the churches is unthinkable as long as the concordat on the mission of territories and other exclusive rights is in force. These are his words:

> It is necessary that the Catholic Church face the other churches in sincere dialogue, which must be carried out not only at the episcopal and clerical level, but also at the popular, lay level. The Colombian Christians who do not belong to the Roman Church notice a big difference between the ecumenical relations of the Roman Church with the other churches in Europe and North America, in contrast to those in Spain and Latin America, especially in Colombia. We find the Vatican Council's statement on religious freedom and human rights as proclaimed by John XXIII, to contradict the limitations in force in those countries. It is necessary to suppress anything that lies in the way of free dialogue. We hope that when the second conference of bishops (LAMEC) discusses the Latin American socio-economic and religious problems, the agenda will also include the Concordat of 1887 and the agreement on missions, as being obstacles to a true ecumenical dialogue.

Analyzing the above words spoken by an Anglican minister at a Catholic ceremony to which he had been invited by the Catholic hierarchy, we discover what the words of John XXIII on human rights, contained in *Pacem in Terris,* the statement on religious freedom of Vatican II, and "Ecumenical Dialogue" of Paul VIth's *Ecclesiam Suam* mean to the "separated brothers." All these pastoral statements mean not only *de facto* but *de jure* religious pluralism to the "separated brothers." To avoid annoying divisions and fraternal feuds, we ought to accept the apostolic proselytism of Protestant sects, Jews, and propagandists of other religions among our Catholic people.

This basically means making all religions equal. All the legitimate defenses which the preservation of our Faith requires and which so wisely and zealously the pre-Conciliar Church established have to be eliminated to please the "separated brothers." Let the poison be within reach of everybody, even though many intoxicate themselves and die!

"Dialogue" is always dangerous. So it was ever since that first time, when the woman began to have dialogue with the snake. In order that it be fruitful, both parties to a dialogue should be equal and always have the same sincerity and good faith. As far as this case is concerned, the Catholic Church, being infallibly sure of its doctrine, cannot adopt the position of the "separated brothers," even if they could be deemed quite sincere. The Church, being and having to be, confident about the doctrine which it professes and teaches as true, must notice the error in which, unfortunately, those who claim to be Christian but fail to follow the real religion of Christ find themselves. In turn, the "separated brothers" feel that it is they who are right and we who are wrong. For their dialogue with the Church to be sincere and fruitful, they should begin by at least questioning their own positions. If they do not doubt, the Church must at least sow the seed of doubt within them to try to convince them otherwise. Rather than a dialogue, the apostolic work of the Church must use the apologetical monologue which it has always used to convert those who find themselves outside the truth. Christ did not say to His apostles: "Go and dialogue," but "go and teach."

Today, even our dialogue with atheists is being promoted, a plain contradiction. Is dialogue possible between a sincere, clear, and resolute affirmation and an equally determined denial? Tactically, Communists can simulate and pretend to accept dialogue in order to deceive naive people. Communism would cease to be Communism from the very moment it sincerely accepted dialogue with believers.

Dialogue has been and is being grossly abused. Those who ask the Church and its Tradition to enter into dialogue do not tell the truth; on the contrary, they intend to defend their error and spread confusion. Moreover in such cases, the talking parties do not speak the same language, for, as we have already pointed out, the same words have different meanings, and modern terminology, unable to resist the force of constructive reasoning, is good only for digressions.

Cardinal Lercaro ratified his excessively wide position when, in his speech, he said:

The Montinian Church

So far, in a world poisoned by naturalism, we Christians of today have deemed the attitude of the primitive community of Jerusalem to be too simple. Today however, when mankind wants to at least approach the possibility of establishing *a single community,* the question is not only optional and human, but calls for the only possible solution to the dramatic dilemma, namely, everybody's sharing in the attainment of earthly goods, or destruction. The world that the mass media have made smaller, cannot afford the gap between the well-fed third and the starving two-thirds of mankind.

These grave and threatening words by the Pope's Legate show us what ecumenism means to him: choosing between a force of salvation that can prevent the impending slaughter, or Communism; following the example of that primitive Christian community of Jerusalem, or destruction and death. Either we become one in belief, liturgy, customs, and possession of earthly goods, or we will face the serious danger of nuclear war. It is no longer possible that some people have much and others, little or nothing. All must be yielded for salvation's sake. Communism—economical Communism, ideological Communism, political Communism, religious Communism—is the only salvation for our poor world. Recalling the small and primitive Christian community at Jerusalem, the ecumenical Cardinal Lercaro conceives mankind as reduced to a "single community" in which we will all be equal, own the same things, have the same universal religion, the same rites or the same freedom to invent them, and a single government, *the Messianic world-government of international Jewry.*

After the speeches, readings, and songs included in the schedule of the celebration of this ecumenical day, the representatives of the Christian Churches blended in a communitarian prayer for perfect ecumenism. Did the "separated brothers" at the moment think over even the possibility of embracing our faith and relinquishing their errors? Surely not. Such celebrations could only foster their belief, help them gain confidence in their faith, and consider that the Catholic Church wanted to humbly confess its past intransigence. That was why Don Sergio from Cuernavaca affirmed that the Church was not the sole depository of truth! *That ecumenical day will be recorded in the history of Latin American Catholicism as gray and disquieting.*

The following churches and communities had been fraternally invited: United Bible Societies, Provisional Committee for Latin American Evangelical Unity, Greek Orthodox Church, Council of Latin American Methodist Bishops, National Council of Churches of Christ - Latin American Division, South American Archbishopric of the Moscow Patriarchate, Episcopal Church, Latin American Public Seminar, Taizé Community, and the Lutheran World Federation.

In *L'Osservatore Romano,* the French priest Charles Boyer, head of the

LAMEC—A Matter of Life or Death?

International Ecumenical Organization, "Unitas," severely criticized Catholics who commune with non-Catholics in violation of the teaching of the Church. This article of *L'Osservatore* (August 19, 1968) mentions two recent events in which Catholics joined non-Catholics in taking Communion. The first of such events took place in Paris, on Whitsunday, and the second in Upsala, during the recent conference of the World Council of Churches. Father Boyer says that the Catholic Church maintains that the Eucharist is "the sign of unity" and, therefore, mixed Communions are not permitted as long as the Churches remain separated. "The Churches being separated," he writes, "the show of unity at mixed Communions is merely external, and the division stands; in fact, it is even more noticeable." Could we not apply such words to these ecumenical ceremonies of the Eucharistic Congress at Bogotá, where the representatives of the "separated brothers" remained apart and distant from us, their presence among us in so solemn an event being good only for confusing and disorienting our Catholic people?

THE EXPERTS ANTICIPATE WHAT THE POPE IS GOING TO SAY AT THE INTERNATIONAL EUCHARISTIC CONGRESS

From the Bogotá newspaper *El Tiempo* of August 19, 1968, we quote as follows:

Pope Paul VI will deliver his most important speech at the cathedral to open the discussions of the second general assembly of LAMEC. Since this fact has repeatedly been affirmed by experts in Vatican affairs who have had indirect access to the documents, questions have arisen about what of such importance the Pope will say at Bogotá.

Talking with *El Tiempo*, Fr. Cipriano Calderón discloses his forecasts about the issues His Holiness Paul VI will treat during his public speeches at Bogotá. This Spanish priest is particularly qualified to talk about this, for he is a Vatican correspondent for Spanish newspapers. He has just been appointed editor of the Spanish edition of *L'Osservatore Romano*, is the author of the first biography of Paul VI published after his coronation as Pope, and, as a correspondent of the Madrid newspaper, *Ya*, he forecast that Cardinal Montini would become Pope when he was appointed Archbishop of Milan.

According to Father Calderón, whom another veteran journalist, Fr. Martin Descalzo, seconded during the talk, the statements of Pope Paul before LAMEC will be even more advanced than those of his encyclical *Populorum Progressio*. Father Martin Descalzo says:

People who got to know these speeches during their preparation affirmed that they would belittle even Msgr. Helder Cámara, *The revolutionary attitude* which the Pope will adopt in his speeches is characterized by his defense of active non-violence as a Christian answer to the problems of the Latin American continent.

"The Pope will preach *the Gospel revolution* whose ways are love and active non-violence," adds Fr. Calderón.

Referring to the two addresses by the Pope the following Friday, to the peasants in the morning, and to the youth, workers, and businessmen in the afternoon of the so-called development day, the priest-journalists explained that, since the subject of full development had already been stated by *Populorum Progressio* and the Pope himself had already blocked some possible ways through *Humanae Vitae,* in which he called inhuman development the "limitation of the number of guests to the banquet of life," the Pope's Bogotá discourses will show *other ways that remain open* and lead to the complete development of man and mankind.

Both priests said that the Pope, faced with the temptation of violence, will emphasize the *way of active pressure,* whose spokesman in our continent is the Archbishop of Olinda and Recife, Msgr. Helder Cámara.

Finally, they disclosed the active intervention in the composition of the speeches of certain Latin American prelates and LAMEC leaders such as Msgr. Avelar Brandao, Msgr. Marcos MacGrath, and Msgr. Eduardo Pironio, as well as the chairman of the Vatican Commission on Latin American Affairs, former Nuncio to Colombia, Cardinal Antonio Samoré.

This interview, and the opinions and revelations delivered by the two well-known ultra-progressivist Spanish priest-journalists, give us an idea about the climate of exultation prevailing in Bogotá on the first days of the Congress. It was not the Eucharist, its elevated mysteries, or the renewal of Christian life which these two well-informed priests announced would be the subject of the Pope's speeches. *"The Pope will preach the Gospel revolution. . . . "* If the Pope is faced with the temptations of violence, both journalists affirmed that he will emphasize the way of *active pressure,* whose spokesman in our continent is the Archbishop of Olinda and Recife, Msgr. Helder Cámara. In other words, His Holiness will endorse Don Helder and his revolutionary thesis, which has so scandalized the world. This is the same thesis that the ultra-progressivist Bishop of Cuernavaca, friend and faithful disciple of the Brazilian Archbishop, preaches in Mexico, with some variations in regard to violence and totalitarianism.

In a lecture entitled "Human Solidarity" Don Helder delivered in São Paulo in May 1970, the Archbishop of Recife said:

> When, after three centuries of persecution, the Greco-Latin world became

LAMEC—A Matter of Life or Death?

Christian to a large extent, and when the Christians came out of the catacombs to the dangerous glitter of the basilicas and the imperial court, the rumor began to spread that the barbarians were coming.

Curious word, *barbarians!* It showed the Greco-Roman self-sufficiency and, at the same time, the dread of facing the destruction of a civilization that seemed indestructible.

Nothing was more expressive than the sight of the great Saint Augustine at the end of his life, wrapped in dread. Notwithstanding his almost univeral vision, he was not able to catch the final meaning of this event. He thought it was a catastrophe, but on the contrary, it was the beginning of a new world.

The recollection of this historical episode dominates my mind in the face of the attitude of the Western World with respect to the socialist world. That world boasts to be Christian when it suits its interests.

The socialist world was the easy target of similar attacks from the Western World. Philosophically socialism embraced Marxism, which seemed to be the synonym of a supreme, alienated, alienating, materialistic, and combative anti-religious force.

In the Union of Soviet Socialist Republics (USSR), atheism became militant, aggressive, and official. After the Iron Curtain was erected, it was easy to talk about the abuse of human personality in a climate of permanent accusations and terrorism. Insurrections were crushed by fire and sword, and the Berlin Wall separating East and West is still standing. When Red China appeared, the USSR adopted an appearance of prudence and balance.

The Western World created and disseminated some myths that are difficult to eradicate today: anti-Communism, preached as the crusade of our time, and fear of the USSR as the number one enemy of liberty, democracy, Christian civilization, God, fatherland, and family. The Russians took the place of contempt and dread that used to belong to the Jews, the deicide people. Today the USSR has become, to some people, the number two enemy, with Red China having surpassed Russia in its thirst for domination and destruction.

The United States, champion of Christian civilization, democracy, and liberty, appeared as the opposite of the USSR and China. Many people believe the U.S. to be the chosen people, since they have twice saved the world. Many people acknowledge their right and duty to intervene in any country in danger of becoming Communist, and consider any economic or military measures of theirs to prevent Communist expansion to be just and healthy. Many people accept any kind of war in which Americans engage, and find a way to consciously accept and endorse any escalation, including new Hiroshimas and Nagasakis.

This type of mentality will always help deepen the abyss existing between the socialist world and the Western, so-called Christian, World. With these myths we will make World War III inevitable, with unforeseeable consequences for mankind, and with this view it will be practically impossible for us to understand the need and urgency of *world solidarity* . . .

Do not let passion blind us. Let us not confuse the clash of economic interests with religious wars or ideological struggle. How long will Latin America stand the imposition of keeping its sister Cuba excommunicated? The Cuban rebels wanted only to see Cuba free from underdevelopment and misery. At the beginning, they knocked at the doors of Canada and the United States; those who ignore an isolated and locked people are liable for their raving attitudes.

It is said that dialogue with Cuba means exposing Latin America to the terrible danger of Cubanization. How long will democracy be unable to face dialogue? How long will we be naive enough to believe that isolating Cuba, punishing it for the crime of wanting to put into practice the self-determination which in theory we boast to respect, means to abandon it forever within the orbit of Soviet imperialism and to create in our youth the myth of Cuba as a pattern of revolution and departure from underdevelopment?

In this speech by the Bishop of Recife and personal friend of Paul VI, we can find all the vocabulary and poison of marching progressivism. Don Helder's premise is that the Constantinian Church of past times, the Church of "the dangerous glitter of the basilicas and the imperial court" that the lecturer insinuates, became corrupt in a short time, was scared of and defended itself from the implacable advance of the barbarians, and marked for itself "the beginning of a new world."

The seemingly indestructible Greco-Roman civilization fell, but another purer, more consistent and humanistic civilization was born out of that apparent wreckage. So it is now, Don Helder insinuates, that the civilization which the Constantinian Church has been raising for sixteen centuries is falling, but we are on the eve of the *birth of a new world. The new barbarians are the Communists.* The Church has anathematized them, but will end by concluding a perfect alliance with them. "The recollection of this . . . episode [of the barbarians]," says the Archbishop, "dominates my mind in the face of the attitude of the Western World [and of the pre-Conciliar Church] with respect to the socialist world." According to him, this recollection shows that the fears which the Church and the Free World have of advancing Communism are groundless and unreasonable.

Don Helder also intimates that Marxism *seems* to be a synonym of materialism and of war against religion, yet nothing could be falser than this! In a recent book, our illustrious writer José Porfirio Miranda y de la Parra, friend and comrade in arms of Don Helder and Don Sergio of Cuernavaca, has proven that Marx's thinking is the same as that of the Bible. As to the fight against religion, the Polish organization "PAX," the Pope's Nuncio to Cuba, the recent establishment of diplomatic relations by the Vatican with some Communist countries, and the luxurious and courteous party Paul VI provided Tito, the murderer of so many Croation and Yugoslavian Catholics, all show that the wild beast can be tamed. As a matter of fact it *has* been tamed, and these new barbarians will erect a new civilization, the *socialist* civilization, where there will be no classes, no religions, no barriers dividing the members of the large human family, and where we shall live under the paternal, not paternalistic, regime of international Jewry.

It follows that "anti-Communism" is a myth. Pius XI, the hot-headed Pius XI, almost proclaimed "anti-Communism" a new crusade to save Christ's religion and Christian civilization, but since all hostile movements are more absurd and harmful than what they try to fight, the antibiotic is more lethal than the infection. Besides, as the Archbishop of Mexico said: "anti-Communism" prevents pastoral work among Communists, who are sheep of his flock, too.

The USSR was militantly, aggressively, and officially atheistic, but now, after the visits of Russian officials to the Vatican, things have changed. Russia's aggressiveness is over. It has been substituted by meetings of heads of government, diplomatic activity, new peace treaties, and peaceful coexistence. Now it is only the number two enemy. Don Helder also hints that, in fact, the USSR is no longer, nor has ever been, our enemy, and neither is China, which some people consider more dangerous than Russia as far as thirst for domination and destruction are concerned.

So by means of a false and sophisticated exposition, this Catholic Bishop, a hireling of our enemies who preaches poverty and has the money to travel all over the world preaching Marxism and displaying his restless destructive activity, depicts Communism and socialism as the builders of a new world, a better world, a more human and, therefore, a more Christian world. According to this mitered Brazilian, Communism is performing a historical role, which is similar, as Don Rodrigo García Treviño says, to that of early Christianity two thousand years ago, or to that of the barbarians who founded a new empire, the Holy Roman Empire, when the Greco-Roman empire fell.

In face of this sweeping, triumphant, and implacable movement, Don Helder introduces a decrepit, cruel, and inhuman imperialism, that of the United States of America. Many people consider Americans as the chosen people, since the two last wars were won because of their intervention. Many people acknowledge their right to intervene in any country being jeopardized by Communism. They are the world's police force. But the danger of American imperialism to which this Archbishop alludes, is greater than that of the USSR and China, as Hiroshima and Nagasaki demonstrate.

"This . . . mentality," [of inevitable war and misunderstanding], as Helder Cámara warns, "will always help deepen the abyss existing between the socialist world and the Western, so-called Christian, World." The third war is becoming inevitable, and the only solution is *world solidarity*. In other words, in

The Montinian Church

these crucial times, there is no solution for the world and for the Church, but *solidarity with Communism*. Although the thesis of peaceful coexistence was useful in the past as a working instrument for ending antagonisms and starting the motion towards understanding, today it is extinct. Communism is irreversible and is winning everywhere. We have no choice but to associate with Communism, make common cause with Communism, and become Communists. This attitude is defeatist, cowardly, anti-Christian, and unworthy of a man, especially of a Christian. In a bishop this attitude means treason and apostasy. In spite of the fact they are mitered men, Don Helder Cámara and Don Sergio Méndez Arceo are no longer worthy to be shepherds of Christ's Church.

What goals did Helder Cámara move toward with this totally political speech, that was subsequently delivered at the Kremlin? It was intended to justify the Cuban revolution and Communism, which "wanted only to see Cuba free from underdevelopment . . .," in which all Latin American countries have been criminally submerged, as Paul VI had diagnosed. ". . . *[T]hose who ignore an isolated and locked people,"* he says as a skilled statesman and expert in mankind, and as Paul VI would say at the United Nations, *"are liable for their raving attitudes."* (Italics added by the author).

Cuba, however, is not isolated. It is quite well protected by the military might of the USSR. It is not the free world then, that defends itself, but the Communistic, imperialist allies of Fidel's Cuba who are liable for the Cubans' frequent and condemnable raving attitudes, which are an authentic demonstration of what Communism means. To have dialogue with Cuba, to open the doors to Communist Cuba, is to lift the sanitary quarantine, to let the "Trojan horse" enter our countries, to allow the spread of guerilla movements, and to permit Communism to dominate us. To quote Garcí Treviño:

> If, in theory, Fidel intended to rid Cuba of underdevelopment and misery, in fact he has tremendously augmented the latter, for such is not and cannot be development. Although he claimed he wanted self-determination for the island, to remain in power he made it much more dependent on Russia than it was on the United States.

Cuba is a real, not a fictitious, danger for all Latin America, because it is in Cuba that guerillas, kidnappers, and terrorists are trained and receive financial support, and Cuba exports the leaders of subversion, as the legendary case of "Ché" Guevara demonstrates.

Both the above speech by Don Helder and my comments on it should be borne in mind, so that I am able to prove the thesis of my book. My thesis is that the progressivist elements, especially the *ecclesiastical* progressivists, are responsible for Latin America's great tragedy.

LAMEC—A Matter of Life or Death?

In this connection, may I copy a letter to the Bishop of Cuernavaca from Dr. Agustin Reyes Ponce, dated August 31, 1971:

His Excellency the Bishop of Cuernavaca
Don Sergio Méndez Arceo
Cuernavaca, Morelos
Dear Sir,

I want you to feel sure I am no conservative, but I am no self-called progressivist either. In such a mood, I was pleased and proud of one of our prelates, the Bishop of Cuernavaca, who spoke firmly and originally five or six times at the Council. Certainly I regretted not to be able to endorse some elements of his ideas, but I felt that, in addressing the other bishops of the world convened by the supreme Shepherd, some contradictory ideas had to be formulated as a necessary and fruitful means of having good things finally arise, even though each isolated opinion lacked definitive value, must as is the case with the contentions of the prosecutor and the counsel for the defense. The Council was only the means of arriving at the real conclusions, for only its constitutions, decrees, and statements are the voice of the Council.

Unfortunately, I had to change my mind at a gradually accelerated pace. I think your success at the Council (?) and the appeal, especially to non-Catholics, of your systematic thirst for innovation, have pushed you to a kind of exhibitionist attitude. There is no subject, no problem, no place about which a phrase, a statement, etc., by the Bishop of Cuernavaca fails to be published almost every week. This is serious, not only because of your episcopal title, but above all, because the tone of your words leave the impression that it is not a private person, a theologian, a bishop, or a politician who speaks, but the *Universal Church* or, at least, the *Catholic Church in Mexico*.

I believe that we Mexican Catholics *have the right to be represented* before the other creeds, the nation, and the world *only by our legitimate shepherds*, instead of by a person who because of smartness, extroversion or audacity, his good intentions notwithstanding, conveys a judgmental and really improper image of himself. Naturally, I am not referring to what he does at his diocese and for his diocesans. [Poor diocesans and poor priests, who are persecuted by His Excellency's dogs whenever they fail to submit to him! *This is a note from the author as are the italics in this section.*]

The last and fully unfortunate expression of this exhibitionist spectacle and of his growing involvement in flocks that have not been entrusted to him, consists of what we might call "the Puebla affair." The Bishop of Cuernavaca fulfilled his wish to give pastoral orientation to other shepherds' sheep (I cannot believe he had done it by request), at a public meeting you mention under the headline, *"Don Sergio at the Street."* I have seriously meditated about the grave harm and deep disturbance your attitude and your statements were going to cause, for you said it is socialism that will prevail. Moreover, your statement against ecclesiastic celibacy, which I considered to be theologically low and improper of a bishop, was the joke (?) with which the newspapers credited you: "What I wish for married priests is that they show good taste when choosing."

... I am writing to you because of my somewhat innate rejection of the attitude of a bishop who speaks on behalf of the Church in Mexico and its believers, despite his not having been charged with such a commission. I am not aware that the Pope, the episcopal conference, the Archbishop of Puebla, or even the majority of the Catholics from Puebla, had conferred it upon you. If a group of them was anxious to be oriented by you, you could easily have convened them to your diocese to enlighten them, but you might not go to another's flock to indoctrinate them.

To justify your behavior, maybe you will invoke the episcopal collegiality, since *Lumen Gentium* points out that "As members of the episcopal college and legitimate successors of the apostles, all of them must have the solicitude that Christ's institutions and regulations require with respect to the Universal Church." Let me remind you, however, that the same document states that each one of the bishops who is in charge of a particular church *discharges his pastoral activity within that portion of God's people that has been entrusted to him, not within the other churches or the Universal Church.*

Furthermore, the constitution *Christus Dominus* (No. 11) states:

> The diocese is a segment of God's people entrusted to a bishop for him to graze... Each one of the bishops upon whom the care of a particular church has been conferred, grazes his sheep in the name of the Lord, and in them he performs his tasks of teaching, ruling, and sanctifying.

I do not think it necessary to add Conciliar-type arguments... to prove that his regretful intrusion in Puebla, which was the culmination of his continuous intervention in other people's affairs and jurisdictions, flows from his mission as Bishop of Cuernavaca. I think that most elementary education, which arises out of the dignity of the human personality you defend so much, will indicate to you that no person should intrude into another's home, nor exercise functions with which he has not been charged...

Nobody should object if the Bishop of Cuernavaca, inside his diocese in addressing his parishioners or talking about their business, divulges conservative or progressivist, wise or incoherent, ideas, as long as he remains the bishop of that diocese, confirmed as such by the same Church and its hierarchical authorities. We may object to what he says, insofar as ideas that permeate other sectors and give good or bad examples to other dioceses are concerned, but not because he oversteps his episcopal functions. His growing intrusions, however,

LAMEC—A Matter of Life or Death?

and his appearing as the only person in Mexico skilled to amend or complete the other bishops, contradicts not only ecclesiastical and Conciliar provisions, but elementary good manners, and attempts to create a state of division, consternation, and confusion among the believers.

Your objections, according to the information published by *Excelsior,* follow the regular pattern of superficial arguers in these lowly times, namely, to use showy words and phrases. What you attack in Msgr. Márquez and his pastoral work is his "triumphalism," his "resting on Pontifical documents not having been previously and thoroughly analyzed" and his "lack of confidence in the spirit."

But there is a somewhat more explicit chapter on Marxism. The phrase opening this section reads as follows:

> *Nowadays, Marxism is the world's mightiest ideology. Let us discover its symbolic force....*

The above letter depicts in fine outline the picturesque character of the already famous Bishop of Cuernavaca. After my book *Cuernavaca and Religious Progressivism In Mexico* had provoked astonishment, dread, and almost Pharisaical scandal from the many chicken-hearted people among us, many persons brushed aside their fears and volunteered to tell Don Sergio Méndez Arceo some of the many things that could be said about his person, deeds, and statements. The above letter alludes to some leading subjects deserving comment in my present book, whose approach is wider and more inclusive. In former times, Don Sergio Méndez Arceo might have been cast into oblivion, as was the case with his brother, Don Eduardo Sánchez Camacho, the unfortunate Bishop of Tamaulipas, in the episcopate and in the Masonic lodge. Nowadays, however, in our times of *aggiornamento,* "ecumenism," "dialogue," "freedom of conscience," "acquittal of the Jews for the crime of deicide," and in these times when "Luther has been revaluated" to such an extent that it has been possible to affirm the "convergence of this heresiarch with Vatican II" (these are not my words, but those of Cardinal Willebrands), Don Sergio peacefully remains in charge of his diocese, surrounded by scandal, to the astonishment of Catholics and non-Catholics alike. This is not all, for as Dr. Agustin Reyes Ponce remarks in his letter, what is particularly striking, inexplicable, and grave is that Don Sergio, using the many passenger buses he anonymously owns, travels all over Mexico and abroad performing his modern apostolate of pastoral subversion throughout all the states and all the dioceses of the republic. And why all this? Because, as he himself proclaims, he is a personal friend of Paul VI and is endorsed by almost all of his brothers in the episcopate. According to some people, especially to the Jesuits of Río Hondo and all those of the "new wave," Don Sergio is a *superman*; he is the most outstanding member of our venerable episcopate, including the two cardinals. That is why he is so free to travel, and to indoctrinate and graze (the metaphor sounds evangelical) sheep from other flocks. After the Council Don Sergio feels almost like a Pope; he suffers from Council psychosis and feels he is always on the popular or Conciliar tribune, with his indefectible voice defending his brothers, "the children of our father Abraham," and all the activities of these children of the covenant.

The chief thesis contained in Don Sergio's harangue at Puebla was the one conveying the core of his dynamics, attracting the episcopal endorsement and the Pope's friendship: *"Nowadays, Marxism is the world's mightiest ideology."* This is equivalent to saying: The Christian message, though we thought it was everlasting, has been "overridden" (this word is theirs) by the message of Karl Marx, the new Messiah, the new Christ, who will save the world from the threat of nuclear war. Don Sergio is now the new Lazarus, not the one of the resurrection, but of Jiquilpan—his relative, party comrade and friend—who, mitered or not, disseminates intense propaganda within his diocese, to the tourists who attend his show of "Panamerican Mass," and to public college students and members of the Rotary and Lions' clubs. Even at the Masonic lodges this new Lazarus gets a tribune of his own. Such is the world's condition!

After having said something about these two most important characters who of course, attended the Bogotá Eucharistic Congress and were present and active in Medellín, let us go on commenting on the forecast by those two Spanish priest-journalists, Fr. Cipriano Calderón and Fr. Martin Descalzo. Certainly their estimate of what Paul VI would say in his speeches at Bogotá was quite accurate.

These Spanish priest-journalists assumed that the Pontiff would delve into the leading subject of "development," that is the emancipation of Latin America, the underdeveloped countries, and the Third World. But, "faced with the temptation of violence" (this terrible and persistent temptation that besieges the conscience of today's ecclesiastics!), the Pope will emphasize the *solution of active pressure*, whose spokesmen in our continent are the Archbishop of Olinda and Recife and his venerable brother, the Bishop of Cuernavaca.

"Active pressure." What does this consist of? Upon whom will it be exerted? Those Spanish priests did not say this, but the answer may be inferred from subsequent events. It was a question of actively pressing governments, presidents, and also laymen—businessmen, workers, landowners, and peasants—though each in a different way. It was necessary to strike the liberty bell, to destroy the old and decrepit structures, thus hastening the birth of the coming world announced by the unmistakable signs of the times. Genesis says that God made man in His image and likeness. Now, we say that we have to make God in man's image and likeness.

LAMEC—A Matter of Life or Death?

The following observation will close my comment on the prophecies of those "experts" in the affairs of the Vatican and mankind. Both are priests and Spaniards; this makes their words more incomprehensible and shameful. "The statements of Pope Paul before LAMEC will be even more advanced than those of his encyclical *Populorum Progressio*. ...[His] speeches... would belittle even Msgr. Helder Cámara."

Spain knows what Communism means. A war in which one million people die, cannot and must not be easily forgotten. The Spanish priests suffered militant atheism's sternness and cruelty, but now some of them, including a lot of Jesuits (who could have foretold it?), flirt with their deadly enemies, use their language, accept their doctrines, celebrate their successes, and promote their mandates. They have secretly or publicly joined them in order to establish the dreamed-of paradise of an egalitarian, classless society.

False and treacherous obedience, contradictory to the attitude and the doctrine of its great theologians, has led Spain to accept reforms that have demolished its national unity; opened its gates to the enemy, by now inside Spain; facilitated the Protestantization of countless Spaniards; emptied its seminaries and novitiates; secularized the clergy and even some bishops; made many, especially the young, lose their faith; suppressed the solid, learned, and fruitful godliness of Spanish Catholics; and paved the way for immorality and license, thus destroying the very essence of Hispanicism. I do not want to criticize Spain, which I have always loved filially, but I cannot help regretting the passive tolerance, cowardice, and treason that the Spanish clergy, including the sacerdotal brotherhood from which so much could be expected, showed in accepting the Eucharistic profanations that can be seen in the peninsula today as profusely as in other countries, or even more.

When progressivism began to show its real face during the first session of Vatican II, I flew to Spain and talked with cardinals, bishops, theologians and even members of the Spanish government. *I trusted Spain.* I felt sure the Spanish theologians and prelates would engage in battle, as at Trent, to expose the enemy who, having infiltrated the Church, wanted us to make an alliance with Communism, Masonry, and International Jewry. This time, however, Spain was not equal to its historical background, tradition, and wisdom. The Spanish bishops were afraid of getting involved, of making themselves ridiculous, or displeasing the Pope. Because they knew the enemy had climbed to the top, they accepted what their wisdom and conscience rejected. The compromise started in Spain, and was also carried on in the American countries of Spanish descent.

It is not the exclusive fault of the ecclesiastics, for the Spanish government had forgotten the exploits of the past and had made an alliance with those it had previously fought against.

Unbelievably, virulent progressivism has spread all over Spain. I am not

The Montinian Church

referring to the exceptions, the remaining wonderful resistance, but to the *turba magna,* the majority. Many priests, feigning pastoral motives, have rebelled against the civil and ecclesiastical authorities and have merged with the numerous secret Communist groups and even with Communist international organizations. There is more Communism in Spain than is generally believed. The regime represses, arrests and tries, but last year the trial of some members of a terrorist organization in which two bishops and the Pope intervened before the judgment of the military court had been passed, shows that, with the aid of subversive priests, Montserrat monks, and leftist bishops, a sudden spark could turn Catholic Spain into a battleground. Now the mystique of the past war seems no longer to exist, for the field has been very much tilled and undermined by the enemy.

Even more dangerous, however, is the *moderation, cautiousness* and *equilibrium* of some Spanish rightists who are aware of the danger and claim to be fighting it but refuse to acknowledge the dreadful reality of today's world. I have said "world," but this applies especially to Spain, which in the 16th century set up the counter-Reformation, and in the 20th century is scarcely able to maintain its theological equilibrium or defend itself against the present "Reformation," which is indisputably more harmful and destructive than Luther's "overridden" Reformation.

College students in Madrid smash a crucifix that used to hang in their classroom. Madrid is not shattered by this event; it does not alter the pace of its business, fun, and feast life. Friars and priests take off their robes to avoid being recognized and to conceal their clerical investiture, mix with the people, go to the movies, attend parties, and take part in street rallies and riots when circumstances require. Religious freedom has permitted the opening of numerous Protestant churches, particularly those of the Jehovah's Witnesses, and not a few synagogues, for the decree of expulsion enacted by the Catholic monarchs has been revoked. What would Isabel and Don Fernando, Cardinal Cisneros, Saint John of Avila, and all the theologians and saints with whom Spain endowed the world, think about it? Poor Spain! Its very prelates deprived it of its religious unity, the bond of social and political solidarity that united and strengthened its people.

Those Spanish "experts" or journalists who announced the subjects Pope Montini intended to treat in his well-meditated speeches, seemed to be dominated by a peculiar kind of euphoria when they wrote that the Pontiff's statements before LAMEC would be even more advanced than those of the encyclical *Populorum Progressio,* and that the Pope's speeches would "belittle" even Msgr. Helder Cámara. These affirmations published by the Bogotá newspapers did not surprise me. The freedom and scandalous impunity enjoyed by Don Helder Cámara, Don Sergio Méndez Arceo, the Belgian and Dutch prelates, not to mention the episcopal conferences, including the Spanish one, show that these meddlesome spokesmen are being substantially backed. The question the new, post-Conciliar Church poses to our Catholic consciences is, plainly speaking, terrible and anguishing. I believe in and profess the luminous dogma of Peter's primate as defined by Vatican I. I most sincerely stick to the Catholic doctrine of the primacy of Peter's successor as to jurisdiction and Magisterium. I believe in the ecumenical and dogmatic Vatican Council I. These inveterate beliefs of mine, however, do not prevent me from noticing the human factor, the thick shades that are presently darkening Peter's chair.

Chapter XII

A DANGEROUS TURNABOUT

At the risk of diverting the reader's attention, I shall reproduce a confidential letter and some reports published in Madrid in 1963, shortly before the beginning of the second session of Vatican II. These were handed out in Rome to all of the cardinals, archbishops, and bishops of Spain, Portugal, and Latin America. This information will be helpful for those who want to accurately interpret both the Bogotá Eucharistic Congress and the present tragedy afflicting the world, especially Latin America. They call the reader's attention to a dangerous turnabout in our beloved Catholic Church.

CONFIDENTIAL LETTER TO THE MOST EMINENT CARDINALS, MOST EXCELLENT ARCHBISHOPS, AND BISHOPS OF SPAIN, PORTUGAL, AND LATIN AMERICA.

Following is the text of a confidential unsigned letter written to the most eminent cardinals, most excellent archbishops, and bishops of Spain, Portugal, and Latin America:

Most Excellent and Most Reverend Sir:

With due respect and submission to the Church and its hierarchy, solely moved by the aim of serving God and the salvation of souls, I wish to present to His Most Reverend Excellency a piece of information and reasoning on vital issues for the future of the people of the Church itself.

I must inform His Most Reverend Excellency that this attempt of mine to render a service to God's Church enjoys the approval of several Mexican bishops and the blessing of some European prelates.

The circumstances have obliged me to print this information and reasoning. Otherwise, it would have been almost impossible for me to make all the necessary copies. The printing was discrete and carefully checked.

Kissing your pastoral ring and humbly requesting your blessing, I remain,

Sincerely yours in Christ,

The Montinian Church

DANGEROUS TURNABOUT OF VATICAN POLICY

I was astonished in reading the following Associated Press dispatch out of Vatican City, dated June 28, two days prior to the coronation of the new Pontiff:

> It is estimated that Paul VI is studying a way of making arrangements with Communist governments in order to improve the condition of the 60 million Roman Catholics living beyond the Iron Curtain. Since he was appointed to occupy Saint Peter's throne a week ago, the Pontiff has been preparing the re-establishment of Vatican relations with Communist governments. It has been reported that Pope Paul is interested in re-establishing the links that were cut off after the Second World War, rather than keeping alive the old feud with the Communists.
>
> This follows the trend initiated by John XXIII, who stimulated Cardinal Joseph Midzenty's exit from the United States Legation in Budapest to come to the Vatican in exchange for an easing of the restrictions imposed on the Church by the Hungarian government.
>
> In diplomatic circles it was emphasized that the Vatican opposes the Communistic ideology as it has always done, but the Pope is faced with the political conditions of the time, and in order that the Church be able to attain its goal of taking care of its flock, he will have to promote better relations between the Holy See and the countries belonging to the Communist side. (*Ultimas Noticias*, June 28, 1963, Year 27, Vol. 3, No. 8,688).

As a ratification of the above words by Associated Press, in the same copy of the newspaper, I read a report about the effusive and enthusiastic message His Holiness had sent to Nikita Khrushchev as an answer to the congratulations the Soviet head had expressed to the Pontiff:

> We give loyal and sincere thanks to your Excellency for your congratulations and good wishes. Your message brings the image of the Russian people and their human and Christian history to my soul. We pray to God that this people, *in their prosperity and organized life* [italics added by the author], may be able to make an important contribution to the real progress of mankind and to the world's just peace.

Again, on the same page of the same copy, as a piece of biting criticism to such policy, I came across a brief comment by Pomares Montleón: "Marxists and democratic Christians merge in Italy. The cross and the Devil [go] arm-in-arm along the Via Apia."

Few times, if ever before, have I felt so deeply and intensely moved. It was as if suddenly the light that used to lead me had been extinguished, my very faith had been intensely shaken, and existence itself had lost any interest or reason for me. How terrible it is to feel that one has no support, that one's life has no stable and immovable basis, and that we are now extending friendly hands to those whom up until yesterday we had firmly and loyally fought as God's enemies and militant denyers of everything we believe in, and that now we offer them a seat at our side!

The subtle distinctions of modern casuistry are unable to stop the avalanche of objections and the vehement and angry protestations rushing out of my mind and heart, as priest and believer that I am. It is evident that there is a wide gap between the definite, precise, forceful approach of Pius XI and Pius XII on the one hand, and the distressing and soft approach of John XXIII and Paul VI on the other.

Aldo Baroni wrote the following impressive words, characteristic of how lay people and non-Catholic thinkers have commented on the new Vatican policy, in the July 18, 1963 edition of *Excelsior*:

> A comment by Prezzolini, Papini's great comrade, on the encyclical *Pacem in Terris*, has come to me with great delay, the delay of the cheapest mail service, maritime mail. It reads as follows:
>
>> The encyclical *Pacem in Terris* has provoked much noise. It is only too natural that it be so, particularly in Italy. The Papacy is the only political organization that has survived in Italy since the Roman Empire. In the formation of this aristocratic democracy and this absolute, electoral monarchy, the Italians have contributed their utmost political wisdom and organizational skill. In addition, this encyclical's contents are basically economic and social. The comments which I have read refer mostly to this point: The Church's Great Turnabout.
>>
>> To survive, the Church has always compromised with political winners, and *now since the socialist forms of government seem to be bound to prevail, it is convenient to enter into dialogue with them, to try to find a compromising formula* [italics added by the author]. Many people are concerned, because this time the question does not relate to the Gallic clergy, the French monarchy, the whim of independence of the Venetian republic, or Napoleon's transient empire, but to Russia, *a state that is also a religion that absolutely excludes any other religion* [italics added] save that of the state itself.
>>
>> From the religious point of view this encyclical is very important. In it His Holiness contends that every human being has reason inside himself, and this reason grants him the capability of achieving a national and international order and through it the greatest earthly good of peace. What

The Montinian Church

the encyclical fails to mention is that, due to original sin, man has lost the capability of persevering in good works to the extent of being able to achieve the greatest earthly good of peace, *without the aid of God's grace.* [italics added].

This encyclical approximately endorses the position of Pelagius who, in the fourth century after Christ, maintained that man is able to save himself by means of reason and morality alone. It also says something similar to what the 18th century rationalistic movement contended, that an honest man, even if a disbeliever, might take a seat beside the saints, just as Socrates may be sitting beside Jesus. I cannot find any reference to original sin or God's grace in this encyclical. These concepts very much dismay some "new wave" Catholics, who appear to intend to free religion from what they call "Medieval ballast." This reminds me of a recent romance by Mr. Saviene, who tells the story of a bishop who, when dying, dreams of his being a Pope and infallibly announcing that there is no Hell.

What I have read about the young, sacerdotal Italian "new wave," headed by a crazy spendthrift by the name of La Pira and by Msgr. Capovilla, makes me think that the new Pontiff will have to resort to most severe means to put the derailed people back on the right track. His gaze is severe, his appearance is healthy, and this affords hope. As for the rest, the apostle Matthew already said it: "*Et portae enferi non praevalebunt*." ("and the gates of Hell shall not prevail against it").

So be it.

The above was not the only comment on the great and evident turnabout of the ecclesiastic authorities I had read. In the section entitled "Broadcasting" of *Latest News (Ultimas Noticias),* Mexico, August 9, 1963, I read the following words, that bring uneasiness and dread to the Catholic Faith:

Nowadays, when even the European clergy of cities exceptionally consecrated by Western religion, art, and civilization such as Florence, show buds of Catholic Marxism waiting for the occasion of exporting their poison to the Americas, it would be convenient that unifying factors intervene in order to prevent the basically disintegrating factors of red fascism from destroying our life. This broadcaster shivers with fear of the red infection menacing the world in such delicate and dangerous areas as Rome itself, where the supreme head of the Christian religion resides. Taking into account the unbelievable slides of high Catholic personalities and the dangerous embrace of the chairman of the Council of Ministers of the Italian Republic with leftist radicals, a clever writer has just closed an interesting article with the following ominous words:

A Dangerous Turnabout

>One must get to know whether the Church still supports the Free World and fights Communist atheists, or is marching toward Communism in the belief it will succeed in coexisting with the winner. *We should like to know who is sitting on Peter's chair, the Vicar of Christ or a timorous heir of Pontius Pilate.* [italics added].

Our beloved readers will certainly understand if we confess the above words have suddenly wrapped us in dread and fear.

This broadcaster has good cause to be shaken by the above, published in so widespread a newspaper of the Mexican Republic. I myself have experienced indescribable feelings when quoting it to give the Spanish-speaking prelates complete information about the confusion prevailing in today's world.

The Canon Dr. Don Rafael Rúa Alvarez wrote another most interesting article, "The Catholic Church Cannot Be Communist," which conveys the impression that its author piously defends the policy being overwhelmingly imposed upon us from above. After having concisely and masterly described the unforeseeable and burdensome scientific, social, economic, and political surprises the 20th century has brought us, he turns to the ecclesiastical changes:

>The Church could not fail to join this historical current. The tough traditionalism which was the solid basis for the teaching of uncompromising truth, non-demagogic justice, integral righteousness, freedom without abuse, and peace without destructive coexistence is broken.

It is most evident, then, that the Pontifical attitude toward international Communism suffered a dizzy and almost radical change. It is said that at the speculative, Platonic level the antagonism remains unchanged, but at the *practical* level, at the level of human relations, the Pope contended that:

>... [T]o improve the condition of the 60 million Catholics living beyond the Iron Curtain it is preferable to prepare for the re-establishment of the Vatican's relations with the Communist governments ...

Prezzolini was right in affirming that *this is the Church's great turnabout!* [italics added]. I should rather say: "*the great turnabout of Vatican politics.*"

The goal of helping our 60 million brothers endure slavery and vexation beyond the Iron Curtain is certainly apostolic and praiseworthy, but one has to take very much into account the concern of many people, "because this time the question does not relate to the Gallic clergy, the French monarchy, the whim of independence of the Venetian republic, or Napoleon's transient empire, but to

Russia, *a state that is also a religion that absolutely excludes any other religion*, save that of the state itself." I might add that one of the basic and central principles of the intensely proselytizing program of this nihilistic and pulverizing doctrine is to fight God, because God is a nefarious and antiscientific myth, and to destroy every dogmatic and positive religion, because religion is the opiate of the people.

This is the vital problem we are facing and the logical solution of which we are unable to find. In his above-quoted article, "The Catholic Church Cannot Be Communist," my admired friend, the Canon Rúa, whose death has caused so much sorrow, wrote:

> The ... reconstructive [I would rather say: reformist] papal dynamics have provoked regretful errors, which created two trends: *a rightist and a leftist.*
>
> The *rightist* current is alarmed, and considers that the Vatican's moral softness will bring about the breakdown of the world's moral structure through the peaceful coexistence of truth and error, justice and injustice, good and evil, freedom and slavery. Unarmed, handcuffed peace will apparently be armed and destruction-greedy peace.
>
> A superficial reading of the press leads some modern, analytical thinkers who know logic and history in depth, as well as some philosophers and sociologists, to the conclusion that such a process implies the conceptual destruction of the philosophical order, the consequences of which are still unpredictable. Essentially opposite terms merge in that the universal identifies itself with the particular, and *being* puts itself on the same plane as *non-being.*

One might add: affirmation and denial seem reconciled in the flexible, gelatinous, and compromising casuistry of human convenience, as though one's most noble and urgent needs could justify one's nebulous means, namely, the disquieting policy of the "extended hand."

Contrary to what my friend piously says, this fearful disorientation and darkening of conscience have not been provoked by false information, ignorance of the history and canonical structure of the Church, by the irrevocable basis of its martyred, tested faith, or by theology and other ecclesiastical subjects.

It is because we know theology, because we are aware of the history of the Church, because we have read, meditated on, and experienced the Pontifical documents, that we have been stricken with dizziness. That is why we lift up our impotent voice. That is why we struggle for light.

A Dangerous Turnabout

LET US CLEAR UP SOME POINTS

My words must not lead to the conclusion that I lack adequate respect for Christ's Vicar, Peter's successor, God's representative on earth, be his name Pius, John, or Peter. Thanks be to God, my endorsement of the Pontificate has always been deep and sincere, for it is based upon and backed by my Catholic Faith. However, to understand my present confusion and that of many others, the following points must be borne in mind:

1. The Pope is infallible only "when speaking *ex cathedra*, that is when performing his job as shepherd of all Christians in defining, with his supreme apostolic authority, the doctrine of faith or morality that the whole Church has to believe... Henceforth his definitions are unamendable by themselves, not because of the Church's consent" (Vatican Council I, 4th session, c. 4.). From this definition of Vatican I it follows that the Pope does not always enjoy the privilege of infallibility, that such privilege does not mean personal, but *didactic* infallibility, and that, in order that we accept what the Pope infallibly defines as true, four conditions have to be present:

    a. That the Pope speak *ex cathedra*, as Shepherd and supreme Master of the Church, and expressly and unequivocally state so.

    b. That the issues pertain to doctrines of faith or morality.

    c. That he define, that is that he tell us that a *definite and concrete piece of truth* is contained in the deposit of the divine revelation.

    d. That he impose upon all of us Catholics the duty of believing in what he has defined, as a matter of faith and on pain of everlasting condemnation.

    It follows from the definition of Vatican I, contrary to Cardinal Suenens' and other progressivists' contentions, that to become unreformable and dogmatic pieces of truth, such Papal definitions do not require any ratification from the Church's ecclesiastics or believers. If the four conditions stated by Vatican Council I are fulfilled, such Papal definitions are unreformable by themselves and become articles of faith and immutable dogmas of our Catholic religion.

2. Independent of his *ex cathedra* definitions on the doctrines of faith and morality in which the Universal Church must believe, the Pope indisputably enjoys the assistance of the Holy Spirit as far as the fulfillment of his most high duties is concerned. This regular assistance, however, does not make the Pope personally infallible or impeccable. This ordinary divine assistance requires previous personal and free correspondence from human liberty, and the Pope, as a man, can fail to correspond in such a way.

3. As to the ordinary Magisterium of the Popes, they are infallible when stating pieces of truth previously defined either by former Pontiffs, or by ecumenical councils, or when teaching and repeating the doctrine *quam semper*

et ubique tenuit Ecclesia, that has always and everywhere been accepted and believed in by the Universal Church. For Christ has infallibly promised that the Church cannot universally fall into error.

4. As a private person, the Pope is not necessarily infallible. He can err, not only in purely human matters, but also in matters related to faith. Consistent with the logical consequences arising from the nature and restrictions of the Pope's prerogative of didactic infallibility, prominent theologians have felt that the Pope can also, as a person, incur heresy. However, the Church's "inerrancy" reassures us that, even in such exceptional circumstances, the Pope could not define as revealed truth and as a matter of faith, an error he privately professed.

5. Acting as supreme Pontiff, but not defining when he speaks, by virtue of his full apostolic authority about doctrines that do not have to be believed as dogmas by the Universal Church, his opinions are neither dogmatic nor definitive, infallible or obligatory as a matter of faith. However, provided they do not contradict the doctrine of Catholic Faith, or above all, the submission we owe God, we Catholics must bestow upon them our external submission, our *obsequium religiosum*.

6. The Pope, besides his being the supreme and infallible Master of the Church, is the Head of a human and visible, though spiritual, society, which is intimately related to the other purely human societies and especially to the nations and governments thereof. For this reason, the Popes have regained their political independence, striven for the conservation and defense of their Pontifical states, and signed the Lateran Treaty, whereby Italy recognized the full sovereignty and autonomy of Vatican City. For this reason, in conducting their foreign affairs the Popes have followed a policy of their own that sometimes led to alliances of war or the acceptance of peace agreements, according to not only the most high interests of God's kingdom, but also the requirements of the Papacy's own interests or those of the people and governments allied thereto.

7. Just as the Popes, before formulating their definitive and unappealable opinions in the exercise of their ordinary or extraordinary Magisterium, resort to the services of specialized theologians, and sound the feelings and moods of the Church's bishops and major theological schools in order to pave God's ways, they also, as Heads of this visible society in order to rule the Church and conduct their administrative and practical policies, must necessarily consult the advice and direction of outstanding and skilled persons. In some cases they may attach these people to their administration because of pressure being exerted from without by non-Catholic, and even heretical, schismatic, and sometimes secret or public enemies of God's Church. This is a great danger and the obvious explanation for the undeniable errors incurred by the Vatican while conducting its international policies.

A Dangerous Turnabout

NOT ALWAYS LOYAL AND ACCEPTED ADVISORS

At the Catholic international level it became evident that outstanding but bombastic "expert" theologians, as well as monsignors of the Roman Pontifical court and of the Vatican diplomatic body, acted in suspicious connivance with left-wing and Communistic political groups to exert their nefarious influence upon Vatican II. Their ideology and activities provoked unjustifiable transactions with God's enemies and prevented authentic Catholic forces from intervening and defending the doctrine and very existence of the Church, despite the fact that their struggle was most noble and necessary. It appears as if the advice of the Masonic regime at the White House weighed more upon them than the millenary teaching of the Christian Tradition.

A personal dispatch President Franklin Roosevelt sent to His Holiness Pope Pius XII through his representative to the Vatican, Myron Taylor, reads as follows:

> However, I feel that the Russian dictatorship is less dangerous to the other countries' sovereignty than the German-type dictatorship. The sole weapon the Russian dictatorship employs outside of its borders is Communistic propaganda which, I naturally avow, has been oriented in the past to overthrow other nations' forms of government, religious beliefs, etc. Germany, however, not only has employed, but is employing this kind of propaganda also and in addition, has resorted to all kinds of military aggressions abroad, with the aim of conquering the world by force of weapons and propaganda....
>
> I believe that Russia's survival is less dangerous for religion, for the Church as such, and generally speaking, for mankind, than the survival of the German-type dictatorship. Moreover, I feel the heads of all American churches should agree with my view and refuse to aid Germany in achieving the goals it is proposing through its attitude....

Pius XII and his advisors could not take seriously this ill-intentioned and evil statement by the President of the United States. The Church's experience with both the doctrinal and miliary aspects of Communism had been bitter enough not to let itself be deceived by flattering promises for the future and ignore contemporary reality. Therefore, the attitude of that great Pontiff who saved Rome was consistent with those of his predecessors, Pius IX, Leo XIII and Pius XI.

WHAT PIUS IX, LEO XIII, PIUS XI, AND PIUS XII HAVE TAUGHT

Even Gregory XVI, in his encyclical *Mirari Vos* dated August 15, 1832,

The Montinian Church

gave us a dreadful description of the prelude to today's hecatomb:

> Indeed we feel sad and sorry to have to address you, whom we know to be overwhelmed with anguish in considering our time's threat to the religion you love so much. In fact we might say that this is the hour of the power of darkness, when the children of the elect will be sifted as wheat (Luke 22:53). Yes, *the earth is overcome by grief, and seems to be vitiated by the corruption of its inhabitants, for they have violated the rules, modified the law, and broken the eternal covenant* (Is. 23:5) [italics added]. We are referring, venerable brothers, to the things your very eyes can see, and because of which we all cry with the same tears. This is the victory of unrestricted malice, impudent science and unlimited license. The sanctity of the sacred and the majesty of divine worship are looked upon with contempt. Henceforth, holy doctrine is being corrupted, and errors of every type boldly disseminated. Neither the sacred laws, nor the rights, institutions, and holy teachings are safe from the attack of malicious tongues.
>
> Peter's See, whereupon Christ laid the foundation of the Church, is being tenaciously fought. The bond of unity is being dissolved and broken every minute. The divine authority of the Church is being challenged, deprived of its rights, and submitted to earthly reasons. Utmost injustice is making it the target of people's hatred and reducing it to infamous servitude. Its bishops are being denied due obedience and their rights challenged. In universities and colleges, roars the noisy din of new opinions which no longer secretly and deceptively, but crudely and openly, defy and declare nefarious war upon the Catholic Faith. Once the hearts of youth are corrupted by the doctrine and example of their teachers, destruction of religion and perversion of morals grow out of bounds. That is why, when holy religion, the sole force whereby kingdoms survive and the strength of every might is ratified, has been broken, that the ruin of public order, the fall of governments, and the destruction of all legitimate power increase progressively. The origin of so many calamities is to be found in the conspiratorial activities of those societies into which converged, as if to an immense sewer, all the sacrilege, subversion, and blasphemy that heresy and the most perverse sects of all ages had accumulated.

Addressing the bishops, this illustrious Pontiff wrote:

> Since we acknowledge that at the stage where we find ourselves it is not enough to regret so many evils, but we must strive to remedy them with all of our capabilities, we resort to the aid of your faith, venerable brothers, and invoke your solicitude for the salvation of the Catholic flock.... It is our duty to raise our voice and engage all means, so that neither the wild boar nor the rapacious wolves are able to sacrifice the flock. It belongs to us to lead the sheep only to healthy grass, where there is not even the slightest danger. In the name of God,

A Dangerous Turnabout

do not permit, dearest brothers, that among such serious evils and danger, the shepherds fail to fulfill their duty and wrapped in fear, abandon their sheep or, disregarding the caretaking of their flock, lazily rest. Therefore, in the full unity of the same spirit, let us defend our common cause, or better said, God's cause, and combine care and efforts to fight our common enemy, for the benefit of Christian people.... You will quite fulfill your duty if, as your job requires, you scrutinize yourselves as much as your doctrine, always bearing in mind that the whole Church is harmed by any innovation (St. Caelest., Pope, ep. 21 *ad Episcopos Galliarum*) and that, according to Saint Agaton, nothing must be taken out of what has been defined, nothing must be changed, nothing must be added, but must be kept pure, in both words and meaning. (Ep. ad Imp., ap. Labb. v. 2, p. 235, Mansi ed.).

You must, therefore, diligently work and watch, in order to preserve the deposit of faith, particularly in the midst of this conspiracy of impious people, upon whose efforts to loot and ruin everything we look with sorrow....

Now we want to stimulate your religious zeal against the shameful league that is harming clerical celibacy and grows continually, because our century's fake philosophers find the support of some ecclesiastics who forget their own dignity and state, and, drawn by thirst of pleasure, have fallen into such a licentious condition that in some places they publicly dare and repeatedly ask the Sovereigns to suppress that disciplinary regulation. It provokes embarrassment to speak so much about such filthy issues. Trusting your zeal, and according to the canons, however, we recommend that you make all efforts to integrally and obstinately protect, replenish, and defend this so important law, against which licentious people cast their darts from everywhere.

Out of this muddy source of indifference pours the absurd and erroneous, or better said, crazy defense of *freedom of conscience* at any price and for everybody. This pestilential error is making its way, shielded by *immoderate freedom of opinion*, which is spreading more and more everywhere, thus ruining both religious and civil societies. Some people are impudent enough to contend that the cause of religion derives great benefit therefrom. "For the soul there is no worse kind of death than the freedom of error!" (Saint Augustine ps. *contra art. Donat*)... Such is the origin of present spiritual instability, corruption of youth, people's contempt for holy things and for most respectable laws and institutions, in brief of the virulent and deadliest social plague, because even the oldest experience teaches how nations that flourished because of their wealth, might, and glory, succumbed to the sole evil of *immoderate* freedom of opinion, freedom of speech, and thirst for novelties.

I want to dispense with details of Pius IX's most clear condemnations of *socialism, Communism, secret societies, Bible societies, and societies or gatherings of the then-called liberal clergymen* (modern progressivists). For the

benefit of scholars, let us cite just the following references:
> Encyclical *Qui Pluribus*, of November 9, 1846.
> Allocution *Quibus Quantisque*, of April 20, 1849.
> Encyclical *Nostis et Nobiscum*, of December 8, 1849.
> Allocution *Singulari Quadam*, of December 9, 1854.
> Encyclical *Quanto Conficiamur Moerore*, August 1, 1863.

In his encyclical *Divini Redemptoris*, Pius XI tells us that Communism is "intrinsically perverse." He also condemns it in the *Syllabus* and calls it a "nefarious doctrine, contrary to natural law itself." In his encyclical *Quod Apostolici Muneris*, Leo XIII defines it as "a mortal plague infiltrating the most intimate articulations of human society and exposing it to the danger of death." Pius XI points out that "the atheistic trends amid the popular masses in the age of technology have been originated by that philosophical tendency that has striven for centuries to separate science and life from faith and the Church." The great Pontiff of Catholic Action is also the author of the encyclicals *Miserentissimus Redemptor, Quadragesimo Anno, Caritate Christi, Acerva Animi* and *Dilectissima Nobis*, which are resounding alarms, vigorous condemnations, and precise definitions of the unchangeable position of the Church with respect to the imminent threat of international Communism.

In *Quadragesimo Anno*, Pius XI says:

> Therefore we deem it superfluous to warn the good and faithful children of the Church about the impious and unjust nature of Communism, but we cannot help feeling profoundly sorry for the indolence of those who seem to ignore this imminent danger, and dominated by a kind of passive laziness, permit the wide dissemination of doctrines that will smash society by violence and death.

In *Divini Redemptoris*, this great Pontiff categorically affirms:

> *Communism is intrinsically perverse* [italics added], and it cannot be accepted that those who want to save Christian civilization cooperate with it in any respect. If some people, by mistake, cooperate in the victory of Communism in their countries, they would be the first victims of their error. Moreover, the older and bigger the Christian civilization of the regions Communism succeeds in penetrating, the more devastating the hatred of the godless people will be.

One might say that Pius XI was contemplating the dreadful tragedy of modern times.

We shall dispense with mentioning Pius XII, because the progressivist elements of our upsetting age cannot stand his matchless and grandiose personality and deeds. Let us just mention the decree of excommunication of Communism by the supreme Sacred Congregation of the Holy Office that is so

A Dangerous Turnabout

persecuted, slandered, and discredited today.

DECREE OF EXCOMMUNICATION OF COMMUNISM

by the Supreme Sacred Congregation of the Holy Office

The supreme Sacred Congregation of the Holy Office has been asked:

1. Is it permissible to join Communist parties or favor them?
2. Is it permissible to publish, propagate, or read books, periodicals, journals, or booklets favoring Communist doctrine or activities, or write them?
3. May those believers who consciously and deliberately carried on acts of those kinds mentioned under numbers 1 and 2 be admitted to receive the holy sacraments?
4. Do those believers who profess the Communist, materialist, and anti-Christian doctrine, and especially those who defend and spread it, automatically incur the excommunication especially reserved to the Apostolic See, as apostates of the Catholic Faith?

The most eminent and most reverend Fathers who take care of the defense of faith and morality, having listened to the vote of the most reverend advisors at the plenary session on Tuesday, June 28th, 1949, decreed that they had to answer as follows:

To the first point: No. Since [Communism] is *materialistic* and *anti-Christian*, and, although its leaders sometimes contend that they do not fight religion, their very doctrine and deeds demonstrate that they are enemies of God, true religion, and Jesus Christ's Church.

To the second point: No, as a matter prohibited by the law itself (see canon 1399).

To the third point: No, according to the ordinary principles of denial of the holy sacraments to those who do not qualify to receive them.

To the fourth point: Yes.

On the 30th of the same month and year, our most Holy Pontiff by divine Providence, Pope XII, in an ordinary audience granted to the most excellent and most reverend advisor of the Holy Office, approved this opinion that the most eminent Fathers had presented to him, confirmed it, and ordered it to be published in the Official Commentary of the Acts of the Holy Apostolic See, dated in Rome, July 1, 1949.

The Prezzolini-mentioned turnabout between the positions of Gregory

XVI, Pius IX, Leo XIII, Pius XI, and Pius XII on the one hand, and the conciliatory policies of John XXIII and Paul VI, on the other, is, then, clear and indisputable.

A BIT OF REASONING

The above-mentioned Canon Rafael Rúa Alvarez, writes:

> Leftists say [that] the Catholic Church has professed socialism, John XXIII was a pro-Communist, and the Vatican is a friend of the world's Communist governments. Then, changing their tactics with the swift intelligence that characterizes them and following the advice of their ideological ancestors, they hypocritically smile to the Vatican, write to it, applaud it, sympathize with it, and as a pledge of sorrow for John XXIII's death, they even celebrate a mournful Pontifical Mass in Moscow, and lower the flags to half-mast in Cuba.

> All these evidently opposite and contradictory proceedings and opinions urgently demand a concrete, coherent and convincing answer to the following questions which the sincerity of our faith and the logic of our reason pose upon us:
> 1. Has Communism ceased to promote a denial of God, an attack on religion, destruction of the family, permanent conspiracy against authority, law, and institutions, and an unbearable slavery and death of the dignity of the human personality, natural law, and inalienable rights which the Creator granted mankind?
> 2. Or is it the Church, which, *in order to survive before the inevitable world triumph of socialism and Communism,* yields and pretends to accept what it so emphatically and frequently used to condemn?
> I quite understand the subtle distinction between the *speculative order* and the *practical order* which has been used to explain the new Vatican position: as to principles, no change; practically, however, one has to face the reality of the modern world, in which Communizing socialism will dominate us. Notwithstanding the above, a comparison now strikes me, and I state it as a question: Let us suppose moral evil and dissolution of customs increase and propagate alarmingly and evidently. Should we, in such a case, accommodate ourselves to disorder in the practical realm, although we remain inflexible in the intellectual realm? Pius XI affirmed that in no respect is it permissible that those who want to save Christian civilization cooperate with Communism!!
> 3. May relations be maintained or established with those who have sowed desolation in the Lord's house? Is not this confusion, this soft and courteous policy of apparent acceptance of the most dreadful and brutal tyranny on earth which has usurped by brute force the functions and position of a true and

legitimate authority, sufficient grounds for *just scandal?*

4. They seek to save 60 million Catholics living in the silent Church, but I shall pose these questions: First, are we not in danger of losing the rest of the flock by letting the blood-thirsty wolves in sheep's clothing enter Christ's flock with confidence? The Free World's biggest error was to accept the Bolsheviks in the League of Nations many years ago, when they had become a tyrannical and usurping government. Moreover this policy increases confusion, and confusion is the best field for quick and safe Communist conquest. Second, I ask: Would it not be self-defeating and discouraging for our enslaved brothers to have them see the Holy See maintain relations with their very tormentors? Could the Cuban Catholics have been aided by the inexplicable presence in the island of the papal nuncio precisely at the time priests and bishops were being outsted, harassed, arrested, and persecuted, all Catholic schools closed and confiscated so that their children and youth could be given up to Moscow's implacable corrupters, and at the time when the most execrable profanations of God's house were being committed by the leaders of evil turned into government? This is a typical democratic-Christian policy, a very subtle one or, better said to us of Spanish origin, a more sincere, realistic, and Machiavellian one.

5. Is *peaceful coexistence* possible between the Catholic Church and atheistic Communism? May there be coexistence between the Gospel's integral affirmation and Communism's totalitarian denial, between charity and hate, between light and darkness? "He who is not with Me is against Me," said the divine Master, and His eternal words have the same authority and meaning now as they did two thousand years ago.

What does this "coexistence" mean? In the publicized feud said to have arisen between Russian and Chinese Communists, Russian Communists are right in contending that Communism's final victory does not require war with its horror, danger, and large expenditures. There are more efficacious and less risky means of dominating us. Russia will achieve better results by means of diplomatic relations, and compromising and deceiving activities, than through violent aggression.

The thesis and policy of the United States, that proclaim peaceful coexistence as a reasonable and beneficial solution to the East-West conflict, have apparently been accepted and implemented by Moscow and the Vatican, this giving birth to the "coexistence axis" of Washington-Rome-Moscow and Kennedy-John XXIII-Khrushchev.

What does coexistence mean to each side? To the West it means tolerance, fulfillment of its international treaties, the abandonment of war, and the paralyzing confidence of an apparent truce. But to the Communists, this coexistence means numerous and unexpected ways to carry on their conquest and destructive work within society, especially with respect to the conscience of youth and children. Let old people pray *while the militant denial of God lets the young generations grow up without Christ!* Let private enterprise go on building factories and edifices, confidently expanding their business projects, while greedy statism, labor conflicts, and ideological disorientation prepare their future ruin and desolation! Let temples remain open, while freedom is restricted and the altar's servants imperceptibly become bureaucrats! The new liturgy will pave the way, first for democratization, later socialization, and finally for the disappearance of the Church! Let diplomatic bargaining and willingness go on, while the "Trojan horse" is skillfully infiltrating the governmental and even ecclesiastical centers!

In the long run, however, if Communism does not change and abandon its will to proselytize and universally expand, violence will come, and sporadically, progressively, and unavoidably, terrorist, destructive surprises will repeat themselves, for there is no nation or people who have called for or are calling for a Communist dictatorship. Communist dictatorships can be imposed only by deceit, force, treason, bloody revolutions, or military coups, as were the cases in the European satellite countries and our sister republic of Cuba. The more careless and confident the governments and people, the more successful such attacks are. Peaceful coexistence is the best kind of preparation for destructive and paralyzing surprise attacks by the Communists.

Meanwhile as we coexist or maintain diplomatic relations with the bloody, criminal Communist dictators who rule the satellite countries, will we ignore our brothers who are being enslaved and starved, their rights and human dignity brutally trampled, and who *hopelessly await their future redemption*? If not treacherous, this policy at least implies cowardly surrender.

AN EXPLANATION BY THE
VATICAN BROADCASTING STATION

Some days ago, the press announced that, taking these protests into account, the Vatican had determined its position towards Communism. From the August 2, 1963 edition of *Ultimas Noticias*, a newspaper from Mexico D.F., we take the following report:

> Rome says *there may be no compromise with [Communism], for its doctrine completely contradicts Catholicism* (Vatican City, Aug. 2, 1963, AFP). The Vatican broadcasting station declared that "Marxism and its political expression Communism" are inadmissible "both to Christianity as well as to the free conscious world."
>
> "To promote, endorse, and stimulate motions that favor peace among nations," added the broadcaster, "is our duty, but it is also our duty to keep constant and tireless watch over Marxist ideology. No international solution or

A Dangerous Turnabout

relaxation of tension or historical pretext may justify our indulgent or compromising attitude toward Marxist Communism."

After referring to the "motions" Marxist Communism makes use of in order to "reduce sympathy and breed doubt," the Vatican broadcasting station affirmed that "Marxist Communism is the antithesis of Christianity" and "the denial of freedom, truth, justice, and peace. Its compromising attitudes inspired by continually changing reality do not mean any change in Communism's doctrine or practical activity, but a tactical and dialectical adaptation to the particular circumstances."

This comment by the Vatican broadcasting station concluded by making reference to Pope John XXIII's encyclical *Pacem in Terris*, which underlines the necessity that Catholics always remain watchful and consistent with themselves so that there can never be any compromise on religion or morality at the level of natural law, "[w]here Catholics have a broad field for contacts and agreements."

After having studied, analyzed, and meditated on the above press version of the meddlesome statements by the Vatican broadcasting station, we are able to draw the following conclusions:

1. This unexpected statement is certainly designed to attain a goal as it follows a design. The Vatican has realized that the Pontifical *statements and policies* had provoked disquieting disorientation in the really believing and faithful Catholic world.

The applause, approval, smiles, and repulsive flirtation of the children of falsehood and iniquity toward the persons and attitudes of the two latest Popes, John XXIII and Paul VI; the Havana "diplomatic" banquet with which the papal nuncio celebrated the coronation of the new Pontiff and which was attended by Fidel Castro, in a friendly, polite, and diplomatic mood, and the Soviet Ambassador, who watches over, advises, and leads Castro's administration; the "diplomatic" words exchanged by John XXIII and the recently appointed Cuban ambassador to the Holy See, a Spanish refugee, a priest murderer, and member of the Masonic sect, burdened all the world's believers with vague uneasiness. All of these also gave rise to a torrent of questions, comments, doubts, and even respectful protests which, no doubt, reached the top levels of the Vatican and demanded those meddlesome statements by its broadcasting station.

2. The Vatican broadcasting station repeats, quite consistently with Pius XI and Pius XII, that "Marxismand its political expression Communism" are inadmissible "both to Christianity as well as to the free conscious world." But I ask: What do Marxism and its political expression, Communism, mean to the broadcasters of the Vatican broadcasting station? Its ideas, its doctrine, or the activity of the party leaders? Once again, conceptual and verbal accuracy is necessary to avoid confusion and the most serious danger it entails.

The Montinian Church

Since Communism is inadmissible "both to Christianity as well as to the free conscious world," how can alliances or diplomatic rapprochements be admitted, taking into account the fact that simple, unprepared, and sincere people might interpret them as an implicit acceptance, if not of the doctrine, at least of the criminal and bloody activities that the party conducts everywhere?

3. The Vatican broadcasting station affirms that "to promote, endorse, and stimulate motions that favor peace among nations *is our duty*..." [italics added]. Again we notice a kind of verbal and conceptual vagueness. Of course, the purpose of the Vatican broadcasting station is clear in explaining to us the aim of the aforesaid moves designed to promote diplomatic relations between the Holy See and the Communist countries, namely, "[t]o promote... peace among nations...." But what kind of peace is this we are seeking? Is such peace possible? Is such peace desirable? Is such peace decorous, permissible, Christian? Is this the peace Christ came to bring the world, or the peace the world claims to be able to give us? Is this peace at any cost? In this fight, two opposite, irreconcilable terms can be found. Each of them openly endeavors to exterminate and absolutely eliminate its rival. Catholicism, using the weapon of truth, wants, tries, and apostolically endeavors to eliminate Communism, which is Satan's earthly kingdom. In turn, Communism efficiently, practically, and criminally wishes the total annihilation, not only of Christianity, but of all religion, belief, and divine worship. In this conflict there may be no compromise, equivocal positions, or disquieting and dangerous truces which are good only for favoring the tactics and perverse intentions of the "godless" army.

The motions and agreements the high secular Eastern and Western powers could make, the pacts Moscow and Washington could have concluded or may conclude, have some ground and meaning, although they arouse misgivings and just suspicion on the part of sincere people, for many of us fear that these political games cover *a harmony that is understood and directed by secret hidden hands who run both sides*. This cannot be the case of the relations, agreements, and secret understanding that could exist between us who believe in God and Christ, and those who vehemently deny God and fight Christ and His Church in an impudent, cruel, and unbearably wicked way.

4. The Vatican broadcasting station categorically avows that Communism is "the antithesis of Christianity" and "the denial of freedom, truth, justice, and peace." It also avows that "no international solution or relaxation of tension or historical pretext, may justify our indulgent or compromising attitude towards Marxist Communism." The Vatican broadcasters also avow that "[i]ts compromising attitudes inspired by continually changing reality do not mean any change in Communism's doctrine or practical activity, but a tactical and dialectical adaptation to the particular circumstances."

A Dangerous Turnabout

Communism, then, is incompatible with our religion, as it is with man's fundamental rights, our basic freedom, and the dignity of the human personality. Communism is essentially unjust and opposite to world peace. Hence, Communism is on a war footing, and we cannot talk about peace or peaceful coexistence without betraying ourselves and most dangerously favoring the success of our enemies which would mean slavery, destruction, and death.

To postpone the solution and maintain hesitant and dangerous attitudes cannot help remove danger or paralyze the enemy's belligerency. On the contrary this imperils our defense and gives our foes the opportunity of achieving a complete and decisive victory. Ours is a clear and inevitable option: *Catholicism or Communism, freedom as God's children, or Satan's slavery and Hell.*

Some people believe that Soviet Communism, after fifty years of bitter experiences, has lost virulence while the Stalinist drastic methods and radical solutions belong to the past. Those who affirm this certainly forget Hungary's dreadful tragedy and the crimes of Castro Ruz and his gang. They forget Khrushchev's frequent threats and screams, as they forget the recent tragedy of Czechoslovakia. By dialectically avowing it to be so, Russia's maturity does not and cannot mean it has relinquished its doctrine, methods, goals, and intensely revolutionary and destructive program. It must be borne in mind that, above the men, even the leaders, is the Communist Party, and above the Party is the *secret invisible government.*

Neither the Church nor Communism can relinquish their respective programs that they embrace and accept. That is why the final, decisive battle will be fought by Catholicism, or truth, and Communism; by Christ and the Antichrist. In this final battle, there is no doubt that the eternal victory will be Jesus Christ's.

THE HARMONIOUS SET OF ENEMIES

There is a most grave and meaningful point on which there have been some comments, but such remarks have lacked the sincerity, equanimity, and clearness the subject requires and deserves. I am referring to the noisy and exceptional repercussion the writings and deeds of Popes John XXIII and Paul VI, and the two events separating and linking their Pontificates (the former's death and the latter's election and coronation) provoked among the fellow travelers of Masonry and Communism. This phenomenon has no parallel or precedent in the Church's recent history. Its dimensions are universal and scandalous. In Italy, as well as in France, America, Germany, Spain, Portugal, Mexico, Russia, and Cuba, all the underground destructive and hateful currents publicly and impudently merged, in order to praise what they called the progressivist leaning of both Popes and intone a mournful elegy before the grave of the Pontiff of Tolerance. It was *The New York Times* which started this campaign.

To explain this confluence of the voices of the enemies of the Church, many Catholics smile and say, "It is only natural that they try to put things their own way. The words and attitudes of the two latest Popes, and especially those of Pope John XXIII, have been malevolently and wrongfully construed, as if they meant acceptance of rationalism, materialism, Masonry, and Communism."

1. Such an explanation is a childish and inadmissible oversimplification. Never before had Masonry or Communism accepted or praised the Popes' personalities, encyclicals, or activities. Leo XIII, Pius XI, and Pius XII clearly and masterfully stated the Church's social doctrine, immutably based on natural law and the everlasting Gospel's divine teachings, but their wonderful documents have been ignored, if not distorted and intentionally challenged, by the agents of error and iniquity.

2. The scandalous phenomenon on which we are commenting, involves the existence of a common source or impelling force spreading its tentacles all over the world. This is no isolated process. If it were so, maybe it could be explained in a different way, but it is a universal fact, wherein we find perfect harmony of concepts, activities, and even words. Our foes themselves have pointed it out in their comments.

3. In addition, logic teaches that, if our enemies joyfully applaud and recommend reading the Pope's documents, it is because in them they have found a terminology, a style, and ideas that they, by mistake if you wish, contend and try to prove are their own.

4. Amidst this ideological confusion in which it is difficult to determine our position, many people's faith is in trouble, wavers, and is in danger of being lost. Coexistence of error and truth is as absurd as the ontological identity of being and non-being.

5. We cannot deny that envy, prestige, pride, or ambition could perpetuate feuds that perhaps were reasonable in the past, but today are *anachronistic*, but we may not confuse this kind of dissension with that covering *dogmatic points, immutable principles* and *pieces of truth* already defined by the Church's authentic and infallible Magisterium. Should we relinquish our doctrinal intolerance and our definite and invariable position, our faith would crumble, and we would betray Christ Himself as well as His Church.

6. All the above discussion and the large number of national and foreign, Catholic and non-Catholic documents on the subject that we have read, seem to convincingly prove the thesis Maurice Pinay sustains in his famous book, *The Plot Against the Church (Complotto Contro la Chiesa)*, which we got to know in Europe and which, at the proper time, was distributed to all the Conciliar

A Dangerous Turnabout

Fathers at the beginning of Vatican II. This writer exposes a conspiracy plotted by the political forces of world Zionism against the Catholic Church, taking advantage of the twenty-second ecumenical council. The preface of this book is the anticipation of what had been planned and was going to happen at that synod. Since we deem it to be the most important among other documents, we shall include our translation into English of this preface, which is a summary of the whole book. It was curious to see how evident was the coincidence of the ideas the preface contained and the contents of the numerous documents I had examined by that time.

7. Finally, I have included a substantial synthesis of European documents which, as the reader will notice, show the reason for the disturbances that have shaken the faith of countless members in the teaching, and especially in the speaking Church at this crucial time.

SOME OF THE MOST IMPORTANT DOCUMENTS WHICH FORM THE BASIS FOR OUR REASONING

1. I quote from the June 4, 1963, edition of *The Reporter (El Informador)*:

> The Great Western Mexican Lodge of Free and Accepted Masons, on the occasion of the death of Pope John XXIII, makes known its sorrow for the disappearance of this great man who revolutionized the ideas, thoughts, and forms of the Roman Catholic liturgy.
>
> His encyclicals *Mater et Magistra* and *Pacem in Terris* have revolutionized the concepts favoring human rights and liberty.
>
> Mankind has lost a great man, and we Masons acknowledge his high principles, his humanitarianism, and his being a great liberal.
>
> Guadalajara, Jal., Mexico, June 3, 1963
> Dr. José Guadalupe Zuno Hernández

2. Below we quote two articles taken from the *Masonic Bulletin*, official organ of the Supreme Council of the 33rd Degree of the Ancient and Accepted Scottish Rite, for the Masonic District of the United States of Mexico, located at 56 Lucerna Street, Mexico, D.F. (Year 18, No. 220, May 1963).

THE LIGHT OF THE GREAT ARCHITECT OF THE UNIVERSE ENLIGHTENS THE VATICAN

Generally speaking, the encyclical *Pacem in Terris*, addressed to all men of goodwill, has inspired comfort and hope. Both in democratic and Communist countries it has been universally praised. Only the Catholic dictatorships have frowned upon it and distorted its spirit.

To us many concepts and doctrines it contains are familiar. We have heard them from illustrious rationalist, liberal, and *socialist* brothers. After having carefully weighed the meaning of each word, we might say that, the proverbial and typical Vatican literary rubbish notwithstanding, the encyclical *Pacem in Terris* is a vigorous statement of Masonic doctrine. As partial addressees of this encyclical, since we are *men of goodwill*, we do not hesitate to recommend its thoughtful reading.

The "peace" slogan has been adopted by most Pontiffs, despite the fact that their deeds are not always consistent with their words. Historian Lafuente, definitely a Catholic, wrote that the Church hierarchs have been warriors rather than religious. As skilled in the use of the sword as they were in that of the sprinkler, they often forgot they should have been at church, rather than at the battleground encouraging their warlike hosts. For many centuries there were battles, at times between the cross and the half-moon, and at others between the Reformation and counter-Reformation. These were implacable battles, lasting centuries and rendered pleasant by regular and well-known witch hunts and burnings of heretics at the stake. Some Pontiffs were, by temperament, brave warriors; Julius II for example, used to wear his cuirass and sword more often than his cloak and crosier.

During the Spanish Carlist wars the priests were ferocious guerillas, just as they were during the battle between the republican government and fascism, in which they took such a prominent part. Moreover, the Mexican revolutionaries should remember their bloody fight against the "Cristeros" (Christists). The encyclical of John XXIII does not confine itself to a routine prescribed invocation of peace and a Platonic condemnation of war that did not prevent his predecessors, personally or through their bishops, from blessing armies on their way to battle. Rather John XXIII asks for *peace based on truth, justice, charity, and freedom, an end to the armament race, a ban on nuclear weapons, and a general agreement on progressive disarmament with an efficacious control system.*

The Jewish heritage of the implacable God of Sinai who, just as the Homeric gods personally enjoyed engaging in battle, yields to the Christ of peace and forgiveness. This Holy Week a God has been buried, who, we hope, will never rise again: the implacable God of war. According to the encyclical, *Santiago Matamoros* must sheathe his sword.[3]

John XXIII adds that *the universal common good poses problems of universal scope that cannot be properly attacked or solved except through the efforts of public authorities who are in a position to effectively work on a worldwide basis.* This is the old idea of a world government, formulated at the end of the last century by the Grand Master Léon Boreois, president of the French Government and Nobel Prize winner, and, in our century, by our brother Briand, who conceived the idea of creating the United States of Europe.

John XXIII praises virtue and human dignity and declares that "every man has rights and obligations derived from his nature that are, therefore, inviolable and inalienable. Their human dignity makes all men equal, and he who has such rights is obliged to vindicate them as a pledge of his dignity." The consequences of this statement are that he proclaims democratic regimes and political constitutions as *the best form of government in our times.* He declares that *no* State may develop by aggrieving other States, and reminds us of Saint Augustine's words: "What are kingdoms without justice, but bands of thieves?"

Consistent with such theories, he clearly condemns dictactorship and says:

> Although authority comes from God, men have the right to choose who will rule the state, decide the form of government, and determine both the way of exercising authority and the limits thereof. If any man does not acknowledge or violates human rights, he is not fulfilling his obligations, and his orders lack juridical force. Any human society established under a government of force must be considered inhuman, because the personality of its members is restricted or repressed.

For their having said much less than this, thousands of persons are in jail in Spain, Portugal, and several Latin American countries. We guess that the beloved children in Christ of Pope John XXIII—Francisco Franco, Oliveira Salazar, Stroessner, Somoza, etc. have blushed in shame in reading the above words, provided that tyrants can turn red for reasons other than the stains of their victims' blood!

"The natural law," says John XXIII, *"provides that every human being has rights that are consubstantial with his personality."* Then, we may point out, human rights have not been granted by God or by heads of government anointed with God's grace. They arise from natural law, which is a doctrine of Rousseau, rather than Catholic doctrine. Among the rights that the Pontiff mentions are *"freedom to search the truth and to express and convey one's opinions, the right to life and the development thereof, the right to clothing, shelter, rest, and social security for illness, incapacity, widowhood, old age, and unemployment."* We say that these rights have been conquered, thanks to labor unions and bloody revolutions during the last third of the past century and the present century. But what did the Catholic Church do to make its believers respect such rights during the first nineteen centuries of its existence? What did the *revealed truth* say about them?

"Throughout the world, the workers," says the Pope, *"refuse to be treated as irrational objects deprived of freedom and to be at others' arbitrary disposal."* Who treated them like this? The Catholic feudal lords, the monarchs of God's grace, the bosses and big capitalists, faithful dischargers of tithes and first fruits, and stubborn rebels against social laws.

As an innovation to the Catholic tradition, John XXIII speaks about woman's human dignity and her equality with man as to rights, *both in domestic and public life.* It is worth remembering the Church's tradition in order to celebrate even more, this change of mind. Eve, taken out of Adam's extra bone to be his mate, ruined the human race, and it was her fault that divine damnation had fallen upon her children from generation to generation. Numerous saints, whose complexes the humblest disciple of Freud could explain, dedicated a thousand compliments to women: "No wild beast is more harmful than woman," proclaimed Saint John Chrysostom. "She is a frustrated man, an occasional being," affirmed Saint Thomas. "She is a beast, neither firm nor stable," added Saint Augustine. No doubt the ideas of these saints that so many women venerate on the altars, influenced the Fathers of the Church to such an extent that, at a council, it was discussed whether women had souls or not. This misogynous tradition has been overridden; to this the Marian worship has no doubt contributed. Now, John XXIII has given the accolade to our eternal muse and mate. In this respect, maybe some Masons have something to learn.

Although placed at the beginning of his encyclical, the following statement deserves our final comment, for it is the very essence of the Masonic doctrine: *"Every human being has the right to worship God according to the promptings of his honest conscience."* For espousing this very principle, thousands of rationalists and believers were burnt during the Inquisition; for saying the same, we Masons were excommunicated by Clement XII and seven more Pontiffs. Since John XXIII's affirmations of tolerance and freedom of conscience have been delivered at the moment that the great hierarchs of the Church are preparing their conclusions for the Vatican Council, let us assume that maybe the Catholic Church is abandoning its policy of fanatic intolerance. Mankind would profit from such a change.

John XXIII ends his encyclical by affirming that *these doctrinal principles provide Catholics with a basis for understanding both their separated brothers and those who have not been enlightened by Christ's faith but have been endowed by the light of reason and a natural and practical integrity.*

We praise the goodwill of the Pontiff of Tolerance. His humanistic doctrine deserves our respect. We assume that, for the sake of mankind's welfare, the cause of peace, disarmament, ban of atomic weapons, and enforcement of the rights to life, freedom, and human dignity, not even one man of goodwill will fail to enter into dialogue. We dare say that those who will reject dialogue are his beloved children in Christ, those who condemn their people to hunger, desperation, and misery, those who suspend indefinitely the constitutional guarantees, the mongers of holy things, and the priests and bishops who are still guarding their arms at the trenches of counter-Reformation.

A Dangerous Turnabout

Out of the same *Masonic Bulletin* previously mentioned, we take the following:

GHOSTLY DIALOGUE BETWEEN JOHN XXIII AND MAXIMILIAN ROBESPIERRE

It was a stormy March night. Stubborn rain and hurricane winds whipped the panes of the papal chamber. In the dim light of a lamp and the intermittent glitter of lightning, Pope John XXIII lay on his bed after a hard working day. Father Francis leaned back against an armchair and looked upon the majestic sight of the sky, where the dense clouds were being torn by frequent bolts of lightning.

Fr. Francis: What a storm, Holy Father! It is said that it was under a storm like this that the First Vatican Council sanctioned the dogma of the Pope's infallibility.

John XXIII: Also amid thunder and lightning was formulated the Mosaic law on Sinai.

Fr. Francis: I have also learned that it was a stormy evening when our Lord Jesus Christ appeared to your holy predecessor. Do you, Holy Father, believe in apparitions?

John XXIII: Our Holy Church is based on one of those. Do you remember when Jesus appeared to Peter, when he was fleeing from the city, and made him return to Rome, where he was sacrificed at the cross?

Fr. Francis: Yes, I do. *Quo vadis, Domine?* Sister Pascualina says she could hear the dialogue between Pius XII and Our Lord. She says she was entering the chamber, carrying a cup of coffee, when she heard Pius XII saying: "Do not abandon me yet, my Jesus," and asked Sister Pascualina for another coffee. Do you believe in this, Holy Father?

John XXIII: To the Lord, there is nothing impossible. Jesus, after His resurrection, attended a dinner at Emmaus.... May I deserve the privilege of His inspiration for the encyclical I will address to the faithful this Holy Thursday.

Fr. Francis: You may rest, Holy Father; your encyclical will not be inferior to *Mater et Magistra*.

The Pontiff's tired face progressively acquires the serenity of sleep. A pleasant, lethargic sleep comes over Fr. Francis, too, while rain keeps on rattling the panes.

Near the Pontiff's bed, the ghost of a well-known figure of the convention becomes increasingly recognizable. His head is covered by a delicate and powdered wig, his forehead is ample and cloudless, his eyes are stretched, his cheek bones are prominent, and his chin is roundish. He is wearing a blue dress coat, a white shirt, and high boots. On his white vest large bloodstains can be seen and around his neck, a marked and deep red line is perceivable.

John XXIII: It is not you, Robespierre, who was supposed to give me inspiration.

Robespierre: If you wish, I shall quit. And excuse me, Holy Father, for thouing you. The terrorist and atheist Hebert, whom I had guillotined, obliged us at the convention to do so. And a dead person finds it so difficult to change his habits!

John XXIII: Address me as you like. To talk with you does not disturb me. While in France, I, Nuncio Roncalli, paid several visits to the Carnavalette Museum, where there are many souvenirs of yours. I saw your proclamation for insurrection, bearing just the first two letters of your last name . . . It was then that you were shot. I have always been curious about your personality and ideas; Nuncio Roncalli was a friend of great masters such as Marsoudon, Ramadier, Mendes-France, and Guy Mollet. A few days ago I received Adzjubei, and perhaps soon I will receive Khrushchev. These are atheists, but you believed in the Supreme Being and the immortality of the soul. You were a religious man.

Robespierre: Great was the feast I organized to honor the Supreme Being! I wore this very costume, the one I wore afterwards in Thermidor. I went ahead, then came the deputies to the convention, and behind us, several hundred thousand citizens. I set the firing torch to the hideous statue of atheism and waited until the gifts of reason and virtue had come out of the flames. Previously, in my speech to the convention, I had praised the worship of the Supreme Being as a deadly strike against fanaticism and religious intolerance. I spoke about a religion without tormentors or victims, where all souls merged in love to the Creator of nature, the great Architect of the Universe. I proclaimed *every man's right to worship God according to the promptings of his own conscience,* in other words, *to search for truth in the ways his reason prompts him.* I was, just as my master Rousseau, a great humanist. We both trusted the innate goodness of man for it was society which had made us evil. The best way to worship the Supreme Being is for man to fulfill his duties. Such is the sole guarantee of social happiness.

John XXIII: I am surprised that the champion of the rights of man speaks like that.

Robespierre: Both concepts are reciprocal and arise from our very nature. That is why they are universal, inviolable, and inalienable. You know that the Philadelphia Declaration of the Rights of Man was masterminded by our august order. Later on the convention proclaimed the Declaration of Rights of Man and of Citizens, of which I was one of the authors. "The equality of the rights of man," we said, "is based on nature. The people are sovereign, and the government is their proxy. The law is equal for everybody. Nothing must be

A Dangerous Turnabout

above the general will." I no longer remember which words were Rousseau's and which ours, but they are the essence of the liberal and rationalist doctrine which the Catholic Church has deemed to be sinful. Nevertheless, our revolution has been for mankind what the compass is for the vessel; it cannot see the harbor, but it leads it there.

John XXIII: Today the rights of man have been acknowledged by all political constitutions. Yours was the success, but many centuries before Jesus had proclaimed the equality of all men.

Robespierre: Christ proclaimed all men equal under God, but we have made them equal under the law.

John XXIII: The Church has always defended human rights and received inspiration from Christ's love for His neighbors.

Robespierre: Doctrinally, yes. But you have permitted the so-called Catholic heads of government to disregard and ridicule them. The articles of the constitutions stating such rights have been suspended for decades and in cases, for periods lasting more than twenty-five years. The Church has supported and promoted dictatorial regimes in Spain, Portugal, and most American republics. All dictators, who continually violate human rights, are most beloved children of yours. No Pope has ever excommunicated a dictator. Some of them have been awarded the Golden Rose by the Pope.

John XXIII: Not by me. It is true that Pius XII awarded it to General Franco, represented by his wife, and that in Spain no constitution stands. But my illustrious predecessor, whom the world has named Pope of Peace . . .

Robespierre: Excuse me; do not praise Pius XII. No Pope has ever delivered so many speeches or issued so many encyclicals as he did, but in them you will not find a word of protest against the concentration camps, mass deportations, gas chambers, or the extermination of the Jewish people and the Masons.

John XXIII: This sentimentalism on the part of him who set up The Terror surprises me.

Robespierre: Tu quoque, Pater mi! Throughout the whole period of The Terror there were fewer victims than in just one of Napoleon's glorious battles, fewer than those burned by Dominic of Gusmán, who is standing on your altars. I defended peace at the Jacobins, contrary to the opinion of the overwhelming majority of the French people. I defended human virtue and dignity, and fought immorality and corruption. I was attacked because people demanded power for me, the most righteous one, the only one who could have saved France. My ideas saved my people from being enslaved in the name of liberty. I preferred to die rather than assuming the dictatorship.

John XXIII: I hate dictatorship, too. As you know, I am infallible; however, I have convened the Council, my Convention. I do not know what the Church is going to say in the way of doctrine. Ah! May all my collaborators be

The Montinian Church

like Lienart, Bea, and Méndez Arceo! There are still many of them who would like to feed the blazes of the Inquisition. I wish you had met Ottaviani and the Spanish bishops, imitators of Torquemada!

Robespierre: But I met Fouché, Fouquier Tinville, Barras, Talien. Watch over your enemies as I did over mine.

John XXIII: Nothing worries me, yet. I leave a social doctrine and the spirit of tolerance, and I hope these will not fade away. I am already very old. You, in turn, died so young!

Robespierre: Those who have to fulfill their historical destiny die when such destiny has been fulfilled.

Little by little, the figure of "The Incorruptible" fades out....

John XXIII: Father Francis, turn on the light. During my dream, some ideas have come up to my mind that I want you to take down for my encyclical. In due course, you will give them proper shape. Write: *"Every man has the right to worship God according to the promptings of his own conscience. In other words, to search his own truth in order to express and convey his opinions."*

Fr. Francis: I beg your pardon, Holy Father! The Council of Trent said ...

John XXIII: I am not here to keep religious battles alive, but to bury the counter-Reformation. I want to speak about tolerance, human rights and duties, human virtue and dignity. I want to expose dictatorial systems and proclaim that human equality arises from nature, and that all peoples must aid each other.

Fr. Francis: How kind you are, Holy Father! You, like Saint Francis, would kiss a leper!

John XXIII: I want to do even more than that. Your holy patron called the wolf a brother but, so far, nobody from Saint Peter's chair has called man a brother. I mean human beings regardless of race, national belief, or religious differences. I want to address my encyclical to all men of goodwill.

Father Francis has lifted up his head in astonishment. His eyes appear frightened. From his aquiline nose, his spectacles have fallen, and his hand has dropped his pen.

It dawns. At the dim light of dawn, the scene we have just portrayed becomes ghostly and mysterious.

[*Author's Note:* These two documents taken, as mentioned previously, from the *Masonic Bulletin*, official organ of the Supreme council of the 33rd degree of the Ancient and Accepted Scottish Rite, are sensational and revealing, and amply explain the dreadful crisis Christ's Church is suffering. These documents demonstrate that it is Jews and Masons who inspire the anti-Church in the genuine religious revolution we are facing. It is not the Holy

A Dangerous Turnabout

Spirit, but Robespierre who masterminded *Mater et Magistra, Pacem in Terris* and other, more recent documents promoting nonconformity with the past, change of all structures, and guerilla warfare. It is not the doctrine of Christ but the doctrine prefabricated by international Judaism and its Messianic materialism, meekly adopted by the Masonic lodges, that now appears in these innovative documents! For the sake of brevity we shall dispense with a minute analysis of the contents of the documents of John XFIII, Paul VI, and Vatican II, in which the 20th century's new Catholic doctrine is stated. In many fragments, the parallels are perfect.]

Below we reproduce, from Supplement Number 33 of *Always (Siempre)*, a Mexican pro-Communist magazine, of October 3, 1962, some paragraphs of an article entitled "Catholics and Marxists Enter Into Dialogue."

> On September 11, at the School of Political and Social Science of the National Autonomous University of Mexico, a round-table discussion was devoted to the subject of "Cultural Cold War." It was attended by two Catholic philosophers, Jorge Portilla and the Dominican Friar, Alberto de Escurdia, and by two st philosophers, Adolfo Sánchez and Víctor Flores Olea.

From what that ill-famed ex-Dominican Father, Alberto de Escurdia, said, we quote the following:

> Neither Marxism nor Christianity are locked ideological systems. Marxism has to be perfected by action, but so does Christianity. According to the Marxist doctrine, human freedom and happiness will be achieved within the community; such is the case with Christianity, too, with the difference that Christianity's history is transcendental, but Marxism's is not. But both are imminent in that Marxism affirms that man's cooperation will transform the universe and increasingly the physical world whereas Christianity knows that God put nature at men's disposal in order that they dominate and make use of it, thus serving each other, and that they must render an account of such efforts at God's judgment seat.

From the July 17, 1963 edition of *New Mexico (Mexico Nuevo)*, a college magazine issued by pro-Communist groups of the University of Mexico, we quote as follows:

> Lately, this has been the case with religious thought: our Catholic and Guadalupan people have found ferocious opposition to their struggle for independence, reform, and revolution, especially as to agrarian reform, on the part of the social form of religious thought, namely, the Church. But in the long

run, economic changes prevailed, and the colonial economy, the semi-feudal economy, and the imperialist-dependent economy perished, as did the divorce between religious thought and colonial, Malinchist thought.

The Catholic Church had to adapt itself to all the changes that economic relations suffered throughout the world. Pope John XXIII, through his encyclicals *Mater et Magistra* and *Pacem in Terris*, started the most extraordinary *turnabout* the Church has recently accomplished, in order to survive in a world of accelerated change threatened by total destructive war.

Facing the imminent danger of violent change, the religious suprastructure could not help modifying all its forms of social existence, and calling for unity, it started the inevitable reforms of ritual and liturgy at the unfinished ecumenical council. It called for world peace based on dogma and an unusually humble viewpoint.

Being a man of rural origin and of humanistic, realistic, and popular thought, the late Pope used a universal language everyone understood and praised, and started *the great turn to the left,* in accordance with the laws of historical development.

But inside the Christian world, at the decisive moment, voices of dissent about the thought and orders coming from the Vatican have been heard. The dwarfs of thought showed up on the street, in working places, in political trends shattering the country, and even in newspaper articles that *Opinion (Dictamen)*—the top corrupter in the national press—has not hesitated to publish.

But this is no use. The new forms of thought and religious politics will follow the new tendency and accompany the world's economic development from behind.

No doubt the new Pope will have to pursue the way devised by John XXIII.

On Tuesday, January 29, 1963, *Excelsior* published an article entitled "The Jews and the Council," written by the Spanish Republican Father Ramón de Ertze Garamendi. Previously this priest, sponsored by the fraternal order of the B'nai B'rith, had delivered a lecture on the same subject. From the *Excelsior* article we quote as follows:

> With Catholic thinkers having paved the way, Vatican Council II attacked the issue of relations between Jews and Christians during the last meetings of the Council's first session. Previously, at the general congregation held last December 6, the Bishop of Cuernavaca, Monsignor Sergio Méndez Arceo, spoke about Jewish and Masonic problems. As to the Jewish problems and *pressed by his conscience,* this Mexican Conciliar Father made the following remarks:

A Dangerous Turnabout

I frequently wonder how the children of our father Abraham who still do not believe in Jesus Christ, picture our Church . . . . I do know that the Roman Pontiffs, especially nowadays, have won the confidence of the Jewish people, but I do not know whether all shepherds and believers, despite possible negative attitudes, treat Jews with love or, unconsciously, engage in anti-Semitic practices.

Words to be meditated.

Finally, we present a significant remark showing the confusion that all these compromising tendencies have provoked, delivered by a Spanish Jesuit at the shrine of the Sacred Heart the Society owns at Serrano Street, Madrid: *"We, children of Ignatius Loyola, who in the 16th century set up the counter-Reformation, will be the first to dismantle it."* We can dispense with this by saying that this is one of the characters of the "new wave" of the Society of Jesus, shameful antithesis of the Ignatian work!

PROLOGUE FROM
THE PLOT AGAINST THE CHURCH

Below I reproduce the wonderful prologue of Maurice Pinay's book, *The Plot Against the Church,* the Italian version of which I read in Rome at the beginning of Vatican II. I believe the occurrences that followed its publication fully supported the evidence and the lucid views of this work. The Conciliar Fathers ought to have read it before voting democratically at the various sessions of the Council.

This prologue consists of five parts as given on pages 13 through 30 of the American edition of *The Plot Against the Church,* published by St. Anthony Press, Los Angeles, in 1967. The titles are: (a) "Introduction to the American Edition," (b) "Important Information for the Reader, *Plot Against the Church,* Introduction to the Italian Edition," (c) "Foreword to the Austrian Edition," (d) "Preface to the German Edition," and (e) "Introduction to the Spanish Edition - A Sensational Book." The reader's attention is called to the fact that English spellings are used throughout this prologue, and that it is, in large part, unedited for its use in this book.

Introduction to the American Edition

This historically important book will, in all probability, be attacked as being anti-Semitic. Let nobody be led astray or distracted, however, from a serious and scientific consideration of the incontrovertible facts here set out. We are concerned with a major factor of history, and more especially of the history of the Christian Church. No crude, negative and destructive anti-Semitism comes into question. That the Jews have played a tremendous and not always beneficial role in the whole story of mankind is obvious; that their activities were not always friendly to Christianity and to the non-Jewish peoples is equally obvious, and there is an enormous fund of evidence from Jewish as well as other sources of unshakable authority to prove this.

This work of great erudition displays not alone a knowledge of events past, but shows also that its compilers had had knowledge of events to come in some immensely important respects. As readers will see from the foreword to a German-language edition, the first edition of this work, in Italian, began by stating that its authors knew that the purpose of calling the Second Vatican Council was to persuade it to declare that the Jews were not responsible for the Crucifixion of Our Saviour, i.e., they were not guilty of deicide, and this book appeared *before* the first session of the Council. Subsequently, as forecast, this proposal was put forward, great pressures were applied to get it accepted, and something, even if diluted, was agreed upon at the end.

Now it cannot be denied, even apart from the essence of the proposal itself, that the fact that any Jews, however representative or otherwise of most of their co-religionists and co-racialists, could do what they had done at the very highest levels of the Catholic Church, is a matter of tremendous significance to Catholics and all others, even to non-Christians.

And not only was it possible to find men at the summit of the Hierarchy to further this project, but the Council appeared to contain a large number of Bishops who, at the very least, did not seem to understand the importance of the problem.

None can sit in judgment on those concerned; it is understandable that the Jews want to "improve their image," especially as they have the power to do so. The lessons to be drawn are, surely, not that the Jews as such or any who have been misled should be the objects of severe criticism, but that the facts, the truth concerning all matters of great importance, and especially when they affect the purity and influence of the Church, should be made widely known. In this all Churches should help with a sense of urgency.

However, it should be pointed out to the Jews concerned that instead of trying to improve their reputation and increase their influence by fostering deceptions and attacking basic Christian traditions, they would serve their own true interests best by first setting their own hearts and attitude toward others aright. Again and again they have overreached themselves over the centuries, and then complained at the results for which they alone were responsible.

In particular, this recent initiative in Rome has merely served to draw the attention of intelligent and decent men to a matter of immediate concern to all. It is the obvious duty of all who may read this book to make its contents known and to encourage all their friends to acquire, read and spread it.

A Dangerous Turnabout

Important Information for the Reader,
Plot Against the Church,
Introduction to the Italian Edition

The most infamous conspiracy is in progress against the Church. Her enemies are working to destroy the most holy traditions and thus to introduce dangerous and evil-intended reforms, such as those ... Calvin, Zwingli and other false teachers once attempted. They manifest a hypocritical zeal to modernise the Church and to adapt it to the present day situation; but in reality they conceal the secret intention of opening the gates to Communism, to hasten the collapse of the free world and to prepare the further destruction of Christianity. All this is intended to [be] put into effect at the coming Vatican Council. We have proofs of how everything is being planned in secret agreement with the leading forces of Communism, of world Freemasonry and of the secret power directing these.

It is intended to first carry out a probe and to begin with the reforms which encounter less resistance from the defenders of Holy Church, in order to then gradually extend the range, as weakening resistance allows this.

In addition, we have confirmation of what will still be unbelievable for those who are not initiated, namely that the anti-Christian forces have at their disposal in the ranks of the Church dignitaries, a veritable "Fifth Column" of agents who are the unconditional tools of Communism and of the secret power directing it. For it has been revealed that those cardinals, archbishops and bishops, who form a kind of "progressive" wing within the Council, will attempt to bring about a breakthrough of shameful reforms, whereby the good faith and the eagerness for progress of many devout Council Fathers will be deceived.

The assurance has been given that the Progressive block forming at the beginning of the Synod will be able to count upon the support of the Vatican, in which, so it is said, those anti-Christian forces possess influence. This appears unbelievable to us and sounds more like boastful arrogance by the enemies of the Church than sober reality. However, we mention this, so that one sees how far the enemies of Catholicism and of the Free World risk revealing themselves. Apart from the dangerous reforms in the doctrine of the Church and her traditional policy which stand in open contradiction to what was approved by the preceding Popes and Ecumenical Councils, it is desired that the Excommunication Bulls uttered by his Holiness Pope Pius XII against the Communists and their lackeys be declared nullified.

In this manner the effort is made to establish a peaceful coexistence with the Communists, which on the one side would be harmful to the regard for Holy Church in the eyes of Christians who fight against materialistic and atheistic Communism and on the other side weaken the morale of these [sic] fighters, hasten their defeat and as a consequence cause dissolution in their own ranks, in such a way so as to ensure the world-wide triumph of Red totalitarianism.

The Montinian Church

Concern is taken that Protestants and Orthodox who fight heroically against Communism, are in no way invited, but rather only those Churches and Church counsellors who stand under the influence of Freemasonry, Communism and the secret power directing them. In this manner, the Freemasons and Communists disguised in priestly robes, who have usurped the leading posts in such churches, work together concealed and in a subtle way, but also very effectively, with their accomplices who have infiltrated into the Catholic clergy.

On its side the Kremlin has already decided to refuse known anti-Communist prelates an exit visa, and only to allow their unconditional agents or those who have bowed out of fear of Red reprisals, to travel from the satellite states. Thus, at the Second Vatican Council, the Church will experience the silence of those who could defend her best of all and could enlighten the Holy Synod concerning what takes place in the Communist world.

This will undoubtedly seem incredible to those who read it; but the events at the Holy Ecumenical Council will open their eyes and convince them that we are speaking the truth. For it is there that the enemy intends to play a trump card, whereby it, so we are assured, will have on its side unconditional accomplices among the highest Church dignitaries. A further disastrous plan, which is being prepared, is that the Church shall contradict itself, so as a result to sacrifice its regard with the faithful; for later it will be broadcast, that an institution which contradicts itself cannot be divine. With this proof they wish to desolate the Churches and achieve that the faithful lose their confidence in the clergy and abandon them.

It is intended to cause the Church to declare that what it has represented for centuries as bad, is now good. Among such manoeuvres spun for this purpose one particularly stands out on account of its importance, and refers in fact to the conduct of Holy Church towards the damned Jews, as Saint Augustine calls them; and this in reference both to those who nailed Christ to the cross, as well as to their descendants who are both archenemies of Christianity. The unanimous doctrine of the great Church Fathers, that *"unanimus consensus Patrum"* which the Church regards as a source of faith, condemned the unbelieving Jews and declared the struggle against them to be good and necessary.

For example, in this struggle, there participated, as we will prove by means of irrefutable evidence, the following Saints: Saint Ambrose, Bishop of Milan; Saint Hieronymus, Saint Augustine, Bishop of Hippo; Saint John Chrysostom, Saint Athanasius, Saint Gregory of Naziancus, Saint Basil, Saint Cyril of Alexandria, Saint Isidor of Sevilla, Saint Bernhard and even Tertullian as well as Origenes, the latter two during the period of their indisputable orthodoxy. In addition the Church fought energetically for nineteen centuries against the Jews, as we will likewise prove by means of reliable documents, and among which are found the following: Papal Bulls, Protocols of the Ecumenical and Provincial Councils as well as the highly renowned Fourth Lateran Council and many

A Dangerous Turnabout

others, the teachings of Saint Thomas of Aquinas, Duns Scotus and of the most important doctors of the Church. In addition we will quote Jewish sources of indisputable authenticity, like the official Encyclopedias of Jewry, the works of famous rabbis as well as of the most well known Jewish historians.

The Jewish, Freemasonic and Communist plotters now have the intention at the coming Council of utilising, as they assert, the lack of knowledge of most clergy concerning the true history of the Church, in order to execute a surprise coup, by their adopting the standpoint at the assembled Council that anti-Semitism must be condemned, as well as every struggle against the Jews who, as we will elaborate, are the wirepullers of Freemasonry and of international Communism. They would like that the infamous Jews, whom the Church has regarded as evil for the course of nineteen centuries, to be declared as good and beloved of God. As a result the *unanimus consensus Patrum* which laid down exactly the opposite, would be contradicted, as well as that which was expressed through various Papal Bulls and Canons of Ecumenical and Provincial Councils.

Since the Jews and their accomplices pillory every struggle within the Catholic Church against their wickedness and their plots directed against Christ, our Lord, — as anti-Semitism, we will likewise reveal in this book, that Christ himself, the Gospels and the Catholic Church can be included among the sources of anti-Semitism, since they campaigned for nearly two thousand years against those who denied their Messiah.

With the condemnation of anti-Semitism, which at times is called anti-Semitic racialism, it is wished to attain that His Holiness the Pope and the assembled Council in condemnation of anti-Semitism experience the catastrophic event that the Church contradicts itself, and therefore without giving account to this, silently also condemn Christ, our Lord, himself, as well as the Holy Gospels, the Church Fathers and most Popes, among them Gregory VII (Hildebrand), Innocence II, Innocence III, Pius V, and Leo XIII, who as we will show in this book, have fought bitterly against the Jews and the "Synagogue of Satan."

With such condemnation it would be successful to simultaneously place countless Church Councils in the dock, among them the Ecumenical Councils of Nicaea and the Second, Third and Fourth Lateran Council, whose Canons we will subject in this book to a thorough investigation, and which carried on an energetic struggle against the Hebrews. To put it in few words, the infamous plotters have the scheme in mind that Holy Church, by its condemning anti-Semitism, condemns itself, whereby one can easily amplify the disastrous consequences.

It was already attempted at the last Vatican Council, even if in disguised form, to alter the course of the traditional doctrine of the Church, when it was successful by means of a surprise manoeuvre and lasting pressure, to influence countless Church Fathers to sign "a Postulate in favour of the Jews." Misusing

The Montinian Church

the Apostolic zeal of the devout prelates, it was first spoken of as a summons for the conversion of the Israelites, which, regarded from the theological viewpoint, is an intention without fault; but later they inoculated the secret poison in the form of assertions, which as we will reveal in the course of this work, stand in open contradiction to the doctrine which Holy Church has laid down in this respect.

But upon this occasion, when the "Synagogue of Satan" believed to have secured the approval of the postulate on the part of the Council, God, who always stands by his Church, prevented that the mystical body of Christ contradict itself and fructify the plots of its thousand year old enemy. The Franco-Prussian war broke out unexpectedly. Napoleon had to hastily withdraw the troops protecting the Pontificate, and the army of Victor Emanuel prepared to take Rome. Therefore, the 1st Holy Vatican Council had to be hastily dissolved, and the prelates returned to their dioceses, before a general discussion concerning the postulate in question was able to begin.

This was, however, not the first time that divine providence held up such a misfortune by means of something extraordinary. History shows us that this has occurred numerous times, usually involving the Popes and devout prelates as divine agents. Among the latter we include Saint Athanasius, Saint Cyril of Alexandria, Saint Leanero, Cardinal Aimerico, and even such humble monks as Saint Bernhard or Saint John of Capistranus. In other cases than those previously mentioned, it even made use of ambitious monarchs, as the example of Victor Emanuel, the King of Italy reveals.

When in the middle of the past year we experienced how the enemy was preparing renewed attempts to unleash a plot which would open the gates to Communism, prepare the collapse of the free world and deliver Holy Church into the claws of the "Synagogue of Satan," we began, without losing any time, to collect documents and to write the following work which is intended to be less a book with a certain disputed tendency, than far more an ordered summary of Council records, Papal Bulls and all kinds of documents and sources, with which we leave out those whose reliability or truthfulness is doubtful, and select only those which possess indisputable truth.

In this book not only is the plot which Communism and the "Synagogue of Satan" have established against Vatican Council II uncovered and subject to a thorough illumination, but also the preceding conspiracies which were recorded in the course of nineteen centuries as cases of precedence. For what is intended to occur at the newly assembled Holy Synod, has already occurred repeatedly in the past centuries. In order to grasp what will occur to the full extent, it is therefore unavoidable to know the cases of precedence as well as the nature of that hostile "Fifth Column" infiltrated into the bosom of the clergy. This purpose is served by the extensive investigation of the Fourth Part, which rests upon a faultless proof of sources.

A Dangerous Turnabout

Since, in addition, attention is drawn to [the prediction] that the Holy Chair and the Second Vatican Council might abandon certain traditions of the Church, in order to grant aid to the triumph of Communism and of Freemasonry, we lay as a basis of the first two parts of this work, a minute study where we cite the two most serious sources concerning what one can call the quintessence of Freemasonry and of atheistic Communism, and investigate the nature of the secret power directing it. Even if the fourth part of this book is the most important, nevertheless the first three and, above all, the third will elucidate the plot threatening Holy Church [sic] in its entire circumference. This plot is not restricted to its activity during the coming universal Synod but extends far more to the entire feature of the Church. For the enemy has already calculated that if for some reasons at the Holy Synod, strong defensive forces awaken against its planned reforms and these should bring about the failure of its intentions at the Second Vatican Council, it will use at a later point any kind of opportunity to return to its plan, in which respect it would know how to utilise the strong influence which it pretends to have with the Holy See.

We are naturally convinced of the fact that in spite of the intrigues of the enemy, the support which God always grants His Church, will also cause its criminal machinations to fail this time. It is also written: "The Powers of Hell shall not triumph over them!"

Unfortunately for writing this very documentary book we have used more than fourteen months, and there remain only two until the opening of the Second Vatican Council. God will help us to overcome all resistance, in order to have ready the printing of this work either by the beginning of the Synod or at least before the enemy can cause the first harm. If we are also aware that the Lord God will not permit a catastrophe, then we must nevertheless keep before our eyes, what an outstanding Saint expressed: that although we know that all depends upon God, we should nevertheless act as if everything depended upon us. And as Saint Bernhard said in a similar grave crisis to that of the present: "Pray to God and hit out with the stick."

The second volume of this work will comprise Part V and VI of the same. Its publication will naturally be awaited so that the reactions of the enemy and their customary slanders, can be answered in an impressive and decisive way.

Rome, August 31, 1962. The Author.

Foreword to the Austrian Edition

On grounds of numerous requests, which have reached us from the ranks of the Austrian and German clergy, we have decided to print the Austrian edition of the book *Plot Against the Church*.

The Fathers of the Second Vatican Council, to whom this work was dedicated, had occasion to establish in the course of the Holy Synod, that our

The Montinian Church

warning voice with regard to the existence of a veritable plot against the most holy traditions of the Church and its defensive powers in the face of atheistic Communism found their full justification through the course of the first part of the Holy Council. This shows that our assertions correspond to a tragic truth.

The events of the coming months will provide our readers with the confirmation that our revelations rest upon an incredible but regrettable reality. The enemies of the Church renewed the attempt at the first sitting of the world-embracing Synod, by means of their accomplices in the high clergy, to abnegate or to narrow the tradition of the Church and its character as source of revelation. This had already been striven for before them by the Waldenses, the Hussites and other Mediaeval heretics, as well as later by Calvin, Zwingli and additional false teachers; only that this time all this is fought for under the cloak of the high ideal, inspiring us all, of Christian unity, while the heretics of those times cited for substantiation of the same thesis further diverse and sophistic arguments.

To attempt [sic] that the Church deny the tradition of its character as source of doctrine and to admit such an attribute only to the Holy Bible, comes more or less equal to the intention of causing it to contradict itself. This would accordingly mean that that was declared to be black which had been maintained for almost twenty centuries to be white; and in fact with the devastating result that the mystical body of Christ on grounds of contradiction would sacrifice its respect with the faithful, since indeed an institution which contradicts itself in its essence, can only with difficulty be called divine.

A step of this kind would bring Holy Church into such an impossible situation, that it could not be justified through the wishful image of the longed for Christian unity, whose realisation at the moment would be very problematical. But should this dream become fact upon such an absurd basis, then this would signify that Holy Church recognises [itself] to have been caught up in error, and its faithful would as a result turn in masses to Protestantism, whose essential postulate has always been from of old, to recognise solely and alone the Bible as source of true revelation and to refuse such a character to the tradition of the Catholic Church.

It is incomprehensible that the enemies of Catholicism and their accomplices in the high clergy have possessed the audacity to go so far. This also proves that what was prophesied in our book written before the Holy Council, has found its confirmation through the launching of the same and that the enemy possessed infiltrated accomplices in the high clergy, who occupied the highest positions. As we in fact learned from well-informed sources, upon the appearance of this book and after its distribution among the Council Fathers, the enemies first made a halt from bringing before the Council more daring proposals, which apart from the programme of the day they had kept in readiness for the last few days of the Council. Among such proposals was found that which had the aim of demanding the lifting of the Excommunication Bulls directed by

A Dangerous Turnabout

Pope Pius XII against the Communists and their lackeys, as likewise the establishing of a peaceful coexistence between Church and Communism and finally, the condemnation of anti-Semitism

This step in retreat, which was forced by reason of the accusation in this book, may only be of partial duration. It is hoped that a careful propaganda worked out in agreement with the Kremlin, will soften the resistance of those defending Holy Church in favour of the setting up of a peaceful coexistence with atheistic Communism. It is intended to attempt to weaken the defensive powers of the Church and of the free world, in which the support of the Red dictator can be relied upon, who in return would release the prelates imprisoned for many years, direct letters of good wishes to His Holiness the Pope and display further signs of visible friendship towards the Church. All this in order to bring weighty arguments in favour of the accomplices of the Kremlin, who have infiltrated into the high clergy, to give power to a lifting of the Bulls of Excommunication and to bring about a pact of the Holy See with Communism.

In alliance with certain accomplices, who have nested themselves in the highest spheres of the Vatican, it is even planned in Moscow to take up diplomatic relations between Holy Church and the atheistic, materialistic Soviet State under the pretence that as a result an easing of religious persecution in Russia could be introduced.

In reality, it is the aim of the Kremlin and its agents from the ranks of the Church hierarchy, to demoralise Catholics as well as the heroic clergy, who in Europe and the rest of the world are fighting heroically against Communism, so as to provide the impression that the latter is in fact not so bad. This, of course, will occur only after the Holy See has decided to take up diplomatic relations with the Soviet Union and other Communist states.

It is, therefore, also intended to cripple the fighting spirit of the North American anti-Communists, for through this step they would see themselves weakened in their struggle against the dark forces which seek to draw even the United States into the Communist chaos. In a word, it is intended, as we have already made clear in the introduction to the Italian edition, to cripple the defensive powers of the free world and to level the way for the final triumph of atheistic Marxism.

But the arrogance of Communism, Freemasonry and Jews goes so far, that they already speak of bringing the next Papal election under their control with the intention of placing one of their accomplices in the dignified College of Cardinals on the throne of Saint Peter. Therefore, they intend, with the aid of the influence which they claim to have in the Vatican, to exercise a pressure upon His Holiness the Pope, whose health is under uch strain, in order to occasion him to appoint a large number of new Cardinals, even if the latter should exceed the maximum limit. In this manner they will attain the necessary number of supporters, which is intended to secure the election of a Pontifex to transform the

The Montinian Church

Holy Church into a satellite in the service of Communism, Freemasonry and the "Synagogue of Satan."

But the forces of the Antichrist do not reckon with the support which our Lord God will grant to His Church, in order to prevent that such a manoeuvre gain the upper hand.

It suffices to recall that this is not the first time in history that such an attempt has been experienced. As we prove in this book by means of undoubtedly authentic documents, the powers of the "devilish dragon" were successful enthroning a Cardinal as Pope, who was not only directed by the forces of Satan but at times also gave the appearance as if the latter might be the Lord of the Church. Christ, our Lord, who has never abandoned His Church however, provided and armed devout men like Saint Bernard, Saint Norbert, Cardinal Aimerico, the Fathers of the Councils of Etampes, Rheims, Pisa and the Second Ecumenical Lateran Council, with the courage to act. They all divested Cardinal Pierleoni, this wolf in sheep's clothing who for many years usurped the throne of Saint Peter, of his Papal dignity, excommunicated him and attributed to him the role of Anti-Pope, a fitting appellation.

The plans of the Kremlin, of Freemasonry and of the "Synagogue of Satan," are, however advanced they may seem, nevertheless nullified by the visible hand of God. For, as in all times, men will arise like Saint Athanasius, Saint John Chrysostom, Saint Bernhard and Saint John Capistranus, who hold firm to the inspiration and strength which Christ, our Lord, chooses to provide them, so as to cause their disastrous plots to fail, which once again the dark forces of the Antichrist are instigating to bring about the world-wide triumph of totalitarian Imperialism from Moscow.

We saw ourselves compelled in the first Italian edition, to leave out eleven chapters of the fourth part of this book because of our compelled hast in distributing this work among the Fathers of the Second Vatican Council, before the beast could cast forth the first blows of its paws. But since we have more time at our disposal in the printing of this edition, we have added the eleven chapters in question, which are of fundamenental importance for the better understanding of the devilish plot which threatens Holy Church in our days.

Preface to the German Edition

The following book was compiled by a group of Idealists, who are Catholics of strict belief and who as Catholics firmly believe that the Catholic Church is now passing through one of the most dangerous periods in its history.

In order to reveal what dangers threaten the Catholic Church, in particular from International Communism and also from other International organisations, this Idealist group undertook the enormous task of compilating and editing this book with numerous documents from the Middle Ages and recent times.

A Dangerous Turnabout

The Italian edition has already appeared and [is] already in the hands of the high clergy and other interested . . . [parties]. Editions in other languages are in preparation.

The authors believe that it is vital that the German Catholic Church have this work in its hands, in order from the documents summarised in this work, to be able to gain authentic information concerning historical facts from the struggle and life of the Catholic Church.

The authors must beg forgiveness that it was not possible to once again edit the German work stylistically. They know that the style in many chapters leaves much to be desired, and that repetitions also occur, which could have been prevented. The authors can only promise their highly esteemed readers that all these faults will be avoided in an eventual new edition. But they hope, nevertheless, that this work will find recognition and interest, and that their idealistic and selfless work for the well-being of our Catholic Church have at least the success that the German leaders of the Catholic Church become informed about historical facts which are certainly completely unknown to the public.

Madrid, 1963. The Authors.

Introduction to the Spanish Edition, A Sensational Book

The facts confirm that the term "sensational," applied to the book, *Plot Against the Church (Complot Contra La Iglesia)*, is not exaggerated. Following the first Italian edition, distributed in the Fall of 1962 among the Fathers of the Second Vatican Council, the press of different countries of the world began to make commentaries on this book, the reading of which is of capital importance not only for Catholics, but also for all free men.

It can be stated without fear of exaggeration, that no book in the present century has been the object of so many commentaries in the world press; virulently unfavorable were those of communist newspapers and those controlled by Masons or Jews; and extremely favorable were those commentaries of some Catholic newspapers, which are independent of those obscure forces, and which have had, in addition, the courage and the possibility to express their points of view freely. Even one year after the distribution of the first Italian edition in the Vatican Council, the press of different countries of the world is still occupied with this extraordinary book—a thing truly unusual in matters of publicity.

In order that the reader may be informed of the importance of this work, we quote here some interesting paragraphs that the Rome correspondent of the Catholic newspaper *Agora* of Lisbon, edition of March 1, 1963, page 7, tells his readers:

The Montinian Church

We are going to refer to a publication which came out some time ago in Rome. In addition to other information, we were able to obtain a copy of this book, which in two months became a bibliographic rarity .... The book was printed in a Roman publishing house, but when the present authorities in Italy, the Christian Democrats, favorable to Marxism, took note of its publication, the copies of the thick volume of 617 pages had already been distributed among the Fathers of the Ecumenical Council. This produced alarm both in the Vatican government and the diplomatic world as well as in the parties of the left. For several days the printing house was visited by the highest police authorities, who obtained only the statement that the printing of the book had been ordered, and that the cost of the edition had been paid in full. The leftist press attacked it furiously ....

The exceptional importance of the book resides principally in one fundamental element, and that is, whether the book has one or several authors. Any person of elemental culture can divine that the compilation has been made by clerics. Naturally, the most diverse versions have appeared in respect to this matter. There are those that affirm that they (the authors) were Italian prelates in collaboration with elements of English catholicism; others speak of a group of priests including some bishops from an unidentified country of South America .... This work, because of the enormous importance of its scrupulous, erudite, and minutely detailed documentation, is not just one more of those products of anti-Semitism based on the "Protocolos [sic] of the Learned Elders of Zion" (which are in no way used in the book). In conclusion, in the pages, arguments, and style of the book, is revealed the presence of Catholic clerics in battle against the eternal heresy which has always tended to subvert the religious, ethical, and historical bases of Catholicism, successively employing Simon the Magician, Arius, Nestor, the Albigenses and, in the present day, the leftists of the Ecumenical Council.

So much for the quotations of the interesting commentary made about *The Plot Against the Church*, by the Catholic Portugese [sic] newspaper *Agora*.

Nevertheless, the version predominant in Rome as in the world press, is that the sensational book was prepared by no more nor less than distinguished elements of *the Roman Curia*, which is, as is known, *the supreme government of the Church*, the auxiliary of His Holiness the Pope in the highest functions. It is repeatedly affirmed that the work *The Plot Against the Church* is one of the greatest efforts *of the Roman Curia* to cause the destruction of those reforms which *the left wing of the Catholic clergy* is attempting to bring out, reforms which, if realized, would completely subvert *the bases* on which the Holy Church rests. There are newspapers which have been even more explicit, which affirm that it was the so-called *"Syndicate of Cardinals"who prepared the book*. It is necessary to explain that *the Masons, the communists, and their accomplices* have given the name "Syndicate of Cardinals" to the heroic group of Cardinals of the Roman Curia who are struggling in *the Second Vatican Council* to prevent *a group of the clergy*—which in a strange manner is found *at the service of Masonry and communism*—from imposing on the Holy Synod a whole series of subversive or heretical theses, designed to ruin the Church. Such ruin will never be consummated, because it is written: "the gates of Hell shall not prevail against her," although the Apocalypse of Saint John also prophesises [sic] that such infernal forces will achieve great temporal triumphs, after which they will be conquered and destroyed.

So as not to prolong this Prologue, we will only transcribe in continuation that which an important Latin American newspaper has to say regarding Masonic and communist tendencies. We refer to the weekly *Tiempo* published in Mexico City by Mr. Martin Luiz *Guzman*, a distinguished *Hierarch of Masonry*, who says in referring to the Bishops called progressive:

> The rebellion of the Bishops was considered as the beginning of heresy by Ottaviani and other Cardinals of the "Syndicate." Even the possibility that the Council would depose the Pope if it considered him a heretic, was mentioned in *L'Osservatore Romano*. The "Syndicate" (of Cardinals) then edited, October 1962, a libel entitled *Plot Against the Church*, having the pseudonym, *"Maurice Pinay."* (Number 1119, Volume XIII, page 60, October 14, 1963).

Thus for the comment of the above mentioned newspaper.

What gives this book definite, provable worth is that it deals with a magnificent and imposing compilation of documents and sources of undeniable importance and authenticity, which demonstrates *with no room for doubt the existence of a great conspiracy*, which the traditional enemies of the Church have prepared against the Holy Catholic Church, and against the Free World. These (enemies) are attempting to convert Catholicism into *a blind instrument in the service of communism, Masonry, and Judaism,* in order to weaken free humanity with it and to facilitate its ruin, and with this ruin, the definite victory of atheistic communism. The most useful instruments in this conspiracy . . . [are] those Catholic clergymen who, betraying Holy Church, attempt to destroy her most loyal defenders, while at the same time they assist *Communists, Masons and Jews* in their subversive activities in every way they can.

In this edition, we attempt to alert not only Catholics, but also *all* the anti-communists of Venezuela and of Latin America, so that they may realize the grave dangers which at present threaten not only the Catholic Church, *but Christianity and the free world in general*, and so that they may offer all their support to that deserving group of Cardinals, Archbishops and Bishops who are now fighting in the Vatican Council and in their respective countries against the external and internal enemies of the Holy Church and of the free world; those enemies which, with satanic perseverance, are trying to destroy the most sacred traditions of Catholicism, and to submerge us and our children in frightful communist slavery.

The Editor, *Caracas, Venezuela, December 15, 1963.*

EUROPEAN DOCUMENTS

Plenty of documents evidence the universal sorrow for the death of John XXIII. Top Communists, Masons, Jews and other representatives of anti-Christianity in today's world, sent messages to the Vatican. Numerous Catholics exclaimed: "What hypocrisy! Excommunicated people, murderers of Catholic populations cannot be sorry!"

Unfortunately, those messages of condolence were sincere. The death of John XXIII was neither the first nor the last occurrence which anti-Christian voices made use of to praise him; the campaign continues to support political actions not related to religion, but based on his words or deeds. Let us read the following quotation, taken out of the last June issue of the renowned *Ecumenical Christian Action* bulletin, about some opinions of Communist leaders concerning the encyclical *Pacem in Terris:*

> The Polish *Zycie Warszawy* newspaper of April 11, affirms that "it can be safely considered as the encyclical of peaceful coexistence (to use the still standing Leninist-Stalinist terminology), and it is the most effective weapon of the socialist revolution at the present stage of imperialism and proletarian movement."
>
> The General Secretary of the British Communist Party, John Gollan, before television cameras, on April 21, said that the "Paschal encyclical had surprised and gladdened" him and, therefore, he had externalized his "most sincere satisfaction at the recent 28th Party Congress."
>
> Prior to this, on April 11, the official organ of the French Communist Party, *L'Humanité*, after a long summary of the encyclical, published an article by Gilber Mury, to which the following paragraphs belong:
>
>> To the extent that the Pope's cry of alarm interprets the deep feelings of huge Christian masses, it will unite and strengthen the side of the men who are striving to avert catastrophe. The way to achieve this necessary unit is open. Certainly this does not turn religious idealism into a progressive force, but it is immensely comforting to see the *top Catholic authority joining the wider movement of the masses.*

A Dangerous Turnabout

From Moscow on April 14, *Pravda* pointed out:

> The democratic people and the peace-loving Italians have welcomed Pope John's encyclical. Of course, the encyclical contains ideas we cannot possibly endorse. However, what matters is that this encyclical is aimed, basically, at preventing the danger of war.

Finally, to end this inventory of Communist congratulations, let us look at Palmiro Togliatti, general secretary of the Italian Communist Party, who, at a press conference with foreign journalists and correspondents, gave his opinion about the encyclical:

> This is a document whose importance goes beyond the electoral campaign in Italy. ... [I feel that the most important feature of this document is referred] to the new political concept of history, of the history that has been made by man and human intelligence, and of which we are an integral part. The leading facts of contemporary history are the liberation of the colonized countries and the creation of the socialist states. The Pope's encyclical and his call for the preservation of peace mean an important step forward in line with human efforts to save our civilization.

I have still another document at hand, and reproduce it below, for I strongly believe that all the truth has to be said to help clear up present confusion. On June 13, 1963, under the title, "Msgr. Roncalli's Work During the Persecutions," the *Hebrew Weekly Magazine (Settimanale Ebraico)*, edited by the Israeli community in Rome, contained an article whose last four paragraphs I quote below:

> In 1944, Hirschmann was in the Balkans as a personal envoy of the American President Roosevelt, to help the Jews of those countries. That very year, Nuncio Angelo Roncalli was the apostolic delegate to Turkey. Hirschmann requested an audience with the future Pope, to ask the then-still-powerful Catholic Church in Nazi-invaded Hungary to help save the Jews from mass destruction. "I have never met a man with such a radiant cordiality and human warmth," declared Hirschmann, recollecting that conversation.
>
> After they had drunk two glasses of wine together, the Nuncio listened to Roosevelt's envoy. Then he asked Hirschmann: "Do you think the Jews over there would agree to go through the rite of Baptism?"
>
> The American felt he could assert they would, in order to avoid persecution. Then the Nuncio decreed that the Hungarian clergy take action to baptize the Jews, and give them corresponding certificates. As Catholics, the

The Montinian Church

Jews had the opportunity to be safe within the Church or pursue their own way (that is to say, remain Jews).

Hirschmann added that afterward, some groups of Jews who were operating in the underground in Hungary, *printed thousands of certificates of Baptism without performance of the Catholic rite. According to Hirschmann, Msgr. Roncalli knew this, but never objected.* "That was a loving service by a great man," Hirschmann commented.

The above document must force a cry of alarm from us, bearing in mind that now a group of most eminent cardinals and bishops are working, under pressure from Jewish-controlled, political, economic, advertising, international organizations, to make the Catholic Church review its attitude toward the people who rejected Jesus as Messiah and who, throughout all their generations, have furiously fought His work. The design was to make the Vatican Council consider the anti-Semitism issue, disregarding the fact that the Church itself, from the first day of its existence, has had to take defensive steps against Jewish cobwebs, heresies, and crimes. The aim is to exculpate Jews from the crime of deicide, casting it upon the Romans, which is opposite to the Church's eternal teaching and most strict historical accuracy. The goal is to conclude alliances with the Masonic sects, which, as the books by famous ecclesiastics evidence, have been created and are run by Jewry. The aim is, finally, to enter into an agreement with Communism, the overwhelming majority of whose ideologists, promoters, and leaders are Jews, as numerous books having the necessary documents teach us.

The authorization conceded by Nuncio Roncalli, according to Hirschmann's undisputed witness and published in Rome itself, is an incredibly shameful deed, for it is the justification of a sacrilegious simulation of Baptism, a sacrament of the Church, in order to rid the Jews of supposed Nazi persecution. The goal, even if it were a noble one, may not justify intrinsically perverse means.

It is no exaggeration to affirm there were Jewish-Masonic infiltrators in the Church before Vatican II. The international press itself has referred to it. On October 13, 1962, *Paese Sera,* a Roman Communism newspaper, on page 12, under a headline that read: "Towards a Revision of the Charge of Deicide Fired at the Jews," gave details about an agreement between the Catholic hierarchy and members of the Universal Israelite Alliance. On February 1, 1963, *Il Giornale d'Italia,* another Roman newspaper but of Catholic leanings, published a long article by Filipo Pucci, wherein, under the headline, "Vatican II Examines the Problem of Anti-Semitism," it reported the previous day's meeting of Cardinal Bea and the world president of the B'nai B'rith, Mr. Label Katz. The Cardinal was unbelievably eulogistic about the Jewish people, and promised that the Secretariat for the Unity of the Christians he presides over would endorse the Jewish petitions, a research report having been prepared to that effect. In other words, under the guise of the unity of Christians, the head of the top Jewish-fraternal organization is received, and the harshest anti-Christians are praised and offered support.

The Conciliar Fathers are already aware of the aforesaid, for it will be remembered that, on December 6, 1962, during one of the last sessions of God's Parliament, the Mexican Bishop Méndez Arceo proposed that the Church's attitude towards Masonry and Abraham's children be reviewed, as reported by *Civiltà Cattolica* magazine of January 19, 1963.

BACKGROUND THAT SHOULD BE KNOWN

This is not the first attempt to attain a rapprochement, truce, implicit alliance, or *entente* between the Church and its deadly enemies, Masonry and Communism. In a well-known work by Albert L'Antoine, "Letter to the Sovereign Pontiff" *("Lettre au Souverain Pontife"),* an accomplice of sacrilegious acts and murder accuses the Pope as follows:

> Countless times, moved by noble indignation, the Papacy has condemned the abominable proceedings of which the Jews were victims throughout the years. Why is it that it has failed to censor, in an equally generous mood, the atrocities and jeers our [Masonic] order has suffered in various countries? It appears that, at the time Mussolini's hordes assaulted the Masonic temples in Italy . . . , the Vatican condemned such behavior. . . . It is possible, and I would rather believe it, for it is an honorable person who affirms it. I only regret that your voice had not resounded beyond the City of the Seven Hills.
>
> Please silence those priests from Brittany, Anjou, and other superstitious regions, who still depict us as murderers and devils. Dare to tell those priests, as I tell Freemasons, that it is time to put an end to mutual slander. We shall be equal when, taking advantage of our disagreement on ideology and faith, the merchants of the temple asphyxiate our feuds under the gag of slavery (pp. 50-52).
>
> You, Sovereign Pontiff, serve a God in whom I do not believe. What is this? Heresy? Let us put away this outdated word. We are charged with killing your faith. Reflect that it is heresy itself which we Masons have mortally injured. From the day when, *thanks to the spread of our tolerance, heresy obtains the right of citizenship,* it ceases to exist. Do not reproach us for this; maybe your Church owes it to us to be still glittering (p. 53).

It is very surprising that it was precisely a most recent event that led to a rapprochement of Jesuits and Freemasons. After a certain degree of willingness to come to an agreement had been evident for a long time, full-scale bargaining began in June, 1928. In a dialogue at Aachen there participated, on one side, Fr. Herman Gruber, the Jesuit who knows most about Freemasonry, and, on the other, Ossian Lang, the general secretary of the Great Lodge of New York, Dr. Kurt Reichl, the Masonic philosopher from Vienna, and the writer Eugene Lennhoff, author of a work on Freemasonry containing many documents (René Füllop Müller: *Power and Secrets of the Jesuits*).

On September 15, 1933, the "Letter to the Sovereign Pontiff" was answered by the Jesuit, Joseph Bertelott, as quoted on page 394 of the *Revue de Paris*:

> History, that great master of education, teaches us how, under a huge common blow or a grave and imminent danger, the children of a country faithful to the same faith, generally forget all feuds in order to face danger as a single block and undergo the test fraternally.
>
> Are we on the eve of such a situation, if not of a similar unity at least of a better understanding and intelligence, between the two rivals of Catholicism and Freemasonry that opinion deems irreconcilable? That is what, from a purely historical standpoint, we want to examine here.

The policy of an "extended hand" to Catholics was encouraged by George Dimitrov, Stalin's spokesman and General Secretary of the Komintern (Communist International), at its VIIth World Congress held at Moscow beginning July 25, 1935. "Truce" or a "Regimen of Peace" between Masonry and the Church is just the Masonic version of Moscow's "extended hand" policy or the introduction of the Masonic-Marxist Trojan horse into world Catholicism.

We are no longer surprised by the audacious phrase by H.J.B. Clavel, as quoted by L'Antoine, that "Christianity and Masonry are complementary, and can be reciprocally helpful for the future of mankind." According to Disraeli, "Christianity is either the complement of Judaism, or is nothing. . . ." And now, Christianity complements and is complemented by Jewish Masonry.

FINAL WORDS

In the present critical moments, we Latin American Catholics who have not entered into any agreement with United States Masonry and keep the very faith of Ignatius Loyola, Francis Xavier, Theresa de Jesús, and all saints and heroes of immortal Spain, turn our heads and terrified hearts to Spain, our motherland and to heroic Portugal, in search of inspiration and guidance for the battle.

Spain saved Christendom against the might of the Half-Moon at Lepanto and against the Protestant Reformation at Trent. Spain gave a world to Christ and His Church. Spain was victorious in her crusade against the Communist

A Dangerous Turnabout

hosts. Spain may not betray its providential mission in history.

Finally: *To God: My being, my life. To the Church, Pope, and hierarchy: My filial bond. To the enemies of Christ and the Church: A war without respite.*

Thus we have finished commenting on my "Confidential Letter to the Most Eminent Cardinals, Most Excellent Archbishops, and Bishops of Spain, Portugal, and Latin America." This letter fell on deaf ears, but events have shown the tangible reality of the Jewish-Masonic conspiracy.

Chapter XIII

OUR RETURN TO THE EUCHARISTIC CONGRESS

Let us go back to Bogotá and its socio-economic and socio-political Eucharistic Congress.

WHAT FATHER ARIAS PUBLISHED IN SPAIN ABOUT THE POPE'S JOURNEY

Using large type, the Madrid newspaper *People (Pueblo)*, published an article by its correspondent to Rome, Fr. Arias, entitled: "The Pope is Going to Hell." A quotation from that article follows:

> The nearer the date of the transcendental trip of His Holiness Paul VI to Colombia, the bigger the expectation this event excites. The social condition of this Latin American country gives the Pontiff's travel very special meaning. Undoubtedly this trip, before its having taken place, has given birth to speculations, argument, and various politically meaningful controversies.

The report by the *People* correspondent to the Vatican informs us of an article which appeared on the pages of *L'Espresso*, under the showy headline: "The Pope is Going to Hell." To the Latin American oligarchies, who sponsor conditions of infrahuman capitalistic exploitation, this trip provokes fear, for they are afraid of a public and energetic exposure of such conditions. Left-wing advocates, on the other hand, interpret the Pope's visit to Bogotá as an endorsement and legitimization of the unbearable conditions they are fighting. But despite misunderstanding and pressure, the Pope said: "I am going as a prophet who would never betray the gospel of the poor." This implies an arbitration between the apostles of nonviolence and the mystics of revolution, between exploiters and the exploited. This is a difficult and worthy task, for, as an apostle of peace, Christ's Vicar on earth sees himself compelled, twenty centuries after Christ, to reincarnate the Gospel paradox: *"I have not come to bring peace, but war."*

The text of the article by Father Arias as it appeared in the Madrid newspaper, *People*, is given below:

The Montinian Church

Rome, August 16, 1968. (A chronicle, via telex, by our correspondent to the Vatican, Father Arias): "The Pope is Going to Hell." Equally journalistic is the headline of a great color report which this week's *L'Espresso* publishes about Paul VI's trip to Colombia, and which contains a fourteen-page text, written in Bogotá by its special envoy, Giovanni Gozzer.

If what this famous journalist says is true, if the pictures he publishes are genuine, Colombia is undoubtedly a small hell of injustice and pain waiting for the Pope as hungrily and anxiously as everyone who suffers intense pain waits for his Messiah.

If it is true that in today's Colombia, each year, thirty-six thousand children die from starvation, that the average lifetime is 35 years, that 50 families keep millions of human beings in misery and illiteracy, that a document has been handed in to the government in Bogotá exposing the crimes committed by the plantation owners against the Indians, that reads: "Some of them are proud of having killed up to five hundred natives," and that Luis Enrique Morín, an Arauca latifundist, is mad at the police who arrested him to question him, and affirms: "It is only now that we are aware that killing an Indian is a crime, for we used to consider them as deer or rabbits"—if all this is true, and I am speaking just about Colombia (one would disbelieve it had it not been published by the information media), one can easily understand the pressure coming from both sides, to have the Pope remain quietly at his Vatican. Those whose hands are red with blood and injustice are greatly agitated at the thought that he might read them his *Populorum Progressio* again, perhaps with a second, amended, and expanded edition thereof... Those who fight and even give up their lives in order to provide less inhuman conditions for millions of unjustly exploited people, priests and laymen who even fall into the temptation of bearing arms when they feel defenseless in the presence of the giant of misery, those who are calm but honest and suffer the pain of their oppressed brothers in their own flesh, all these are afraid that Paul VI will arrive in America as a luxury guest, and that he will be monopolized, blessed, and kissed by those who are engendering the monster of revolution.

Do Not Come!

While some people tell him not to go to Colombia, because Colombia is the land of Camilo Torres, the priest-guerilla whose life terminated in an ambush and whose picture as a rebel priest stands behind the great stage of the Eucharistic field altar; because the mother of this guerilla priest, of the "Ché" Guevara of priests, is waiting for the Pope with a letter demanding her son's body and, if possible, that he be canonized; and because Marxist propaganda could turn this religious trip into a political event, others have merely written Paul VI: "His Holiness must not come to Colombia. May you accept this supplication

Our Return to the Eucharistic Congress

coming from our sincere Catholic consciences."

The Pope must not come to Colombia or anywhere in America, because:

1. Colombia is a *pilot laboratory* of neo-colonialism in the Third World. Less than one percent of Colombians own 75% of the land. It would be hard to find any other country in America that deserves the most grave condemnation by *Populorum Progressio* as much as the 50-family-exploited Colombia does.

2. Its Department of Colonies has already ordered its presidents to gather in Bogotá, Colombia, to pay [the Pope] homage. Believe they in God or the Devil, in the Eucharist or the dollar, they will participate in another farce devised against the American people. Most of them do not believe in God but do believe in the Pope's influence upon the people. They will communicate with what they may not believe, in order to profit from that which they *do* believe.

Do not lend yourself to this ignominy. Do not come. Otherwise, the oppressors' hoax would complete the criminal history of white, black, and national slavery. May God enlighten you!

But the Pope has said: *"I am going."* And he will go, as a prophet who would never betray the gospel of the poor. At his arrival, he will see the great manifesto of the Congress where, on a red background, white and black strokes loom and converge in the Congress' motto: *"Seed of Concord and Unity."* The Pope will stand among those white and black strokes, among the apostles of nonviolence and the preachers of the new theology of revolution. A hard mediation will belong to this frail and brave Pope, a disconcerting Pope, said to be shy and brave enough to enter the very core of the Hell of violence. In front of white and black people, as an apostle of peace and an intercessor for the poor, his hands will lift up the Eucharistic bread, the very substance of Christ who, disconcerting like none other, let Himself be led to death "like a sheep being led to slaughter," and whose words remain mysterious to us after twenty centuries of preaching.

The above document which Father Arias, Vatican correspondent of the newspaper *People* from Madrid, sent from Rome to Spain, is full of slander, hatred, and explosive hints. It is pitiful that a correspondent to the Vatican, a priest and also a Spaniard, had so lightly and villainously reproduced what *L'Espresso* from Italy dared to publish. Could this *People* correspondent give supporting evidence of his terrible charges against a whole nation? Like Pilate he washes his hands by stating he is just translating what *L'Espresso* has published. This is the way the slanderous legend to which Communists resort to try to justify their attacks and sow hatred takes shape. Those who read and accept such lies fail to notice the contradictions incurred by this mercenary slanderer and his faithful Madrid echo. For, if 50, not 51 or 49, families own 75% of the tillable land, how is it possible that 96% of the oil and 70% of the coffee belong to American imperialists?

Provided that thirty-six thousand children die yearly *from starvation* in Colombia, we may assume that the adult yearly mortality figure must be awful. How could undernourished bodies, incapable of resisting endemic or epidemic diseases, victims of inhuman exploitation, exist for months, not to mention years? According to this report, the average lifetime in Colombia is only 35 years. During my last trip to Colombia, however, and two previous ones I made to this republic, I could see countless old people, men and women, over seventy and eighty.

But the most serious point is: why did the Colombian Church permit these unheard-of crimes? I am not referring to the existence of 50 rich families, but to reducing these millions of human beings to a condition of misery and illiteracy. Was it necessary that Vatican II and both of the latest Popes' revolutionary encyclicals should come to dissipate the darkness of infamy and deceitful silence which the Colombian hierarchy and ecclesiastics maintained for so many years in the presence of so much anti-Christian injustice? Particularly in question would be the Jesuits, who through their San Bartolomé School and their Xavieran University controlled the prevailing oligarchy.

Why do *L'Espresso* and the Vatican reporter fail to reproduce the document handed in to the government in Bogotá, whereby the crimes of the latifundists (some of them boasting of having killed five hundred natives) are exposed? The reproduction of this document and, above all, the verification of its authenticity, would have been the best kind of denunciation for those accusers who wanted to terrorize the Pope and oblige him to be more energetic than in *Populorum Progressio* in condemning these injustices in the "pilot laboratory" of the Third World.

Believe they in God or the Devil, in the Eucharist or the dollar," say these international slanderers, "they will participate in another farce [we assume they are referring to the Eucharistic Congress], devised against the American people. Most of them do not believe in God but do believe in the Pope's influence upon the people. They will communicate with what they may not believe, in order to profit from that which they *do* believe."

Unintentionally, these progressivists have disclosed their diabolical Marxist tactics. Their pragmatism uses most sacred things, in which they certainly do not believe, to attain the concrete goals they cherish. The end justifies the means! What matters is solely to achieve one's goals, even if one has to trample most holy things or simulate a liturgical reform. And they assume we believers act in the same way. That is why to them, the International Eucharistic Congress and the Pope's visit to America did not have, nor could have had, any other purpose than fostering, blessing, and supporting the hideous oligarchy and Yankee imperialists who, so they say, are engendering revolution and violence.

To the progressivists, Paul VI is "a disconcerting Pope," for they think that he, after having stated the premises, hesitates to draw the conclusions arising therefrom. He is a Pope *said to be shy* but brave enough to enter the very core of the Hell of violence. And to justify this apparently ambiguous and contradictory attitude, they make reference to Christ Himself, who, if on the one hand let Himself be put to death "like a sheep being led to slaughter," on the other hand said, "I have not come to bring peace, but war." Paul VI, shy Paul VI, came, according to the progressivist most reverend Father General and the reverend Latin American Provincial Fathers of the Society of Jesus, to bless the liberating guerilla movements of Colombia and the other Latin American countries. His were words of peace, but his deeds were warlike.

From the most conservative newspaper of Bogotá, *The Century (El Siglo)*, we quote as follows:

> His Holiness, Paul VI, head of the Catholic Church, pleaded that the poor be dispensed strict justice, but repeated his rejection of violent means which he considers to provoke even worse evils.

In other words, the Pope accepts and avows the existence in Latin America of a most grave evil, social injustice, which unavoidably leads to revolution and civil wars. But His Holiness recommends ways other than violence, for this brings evils worse than the one being cured.

The progressivists also contend that:

> If social injustice exists, if peaceful means cannot alleviate it, for the oligarchy will not consent to being deprived of what it has owned for centuries, there is no way left to attain equality, except by violence, guerilla warfare and the smashing philosophy of terror.

They think that this transistory, though most grave evil of civil turmoil, is preferable to social injustice.

Change! Change! This still appears to be the countersign of all those who want to improve the condition of the disinherited classes. We must humbly admit our errors. All the past was wrong, unjust, cruel, and inhuman. One has to demolish the old structures, which were not inspired by the Gospel nor gave the poor equal justice. But, again I say: What a tremendous responsibility of the Church and the people of the Church who, in the presence of such an unbearable abuse, kept quiet because of cowardice, acceptance of, compromise, or full identification with that criminal oligarchy! Were not the children of such aristocrats educated in their schools? Such a grave and persistent lameness on the part of Popes, bishops, and priests, if true, would certainly mean a claudication in the very essential doctrine of the Church.

Progressivism is, to use the Pope's own words, the auto-demolition of

Catholicism!

DAY OF THE SACRAMENTS OF CHRISTIAN INITIATION

"Using new Catholic rites," says one of the newspapers from Bogotá, "the Pope's legate, Cardinal Giacomo Lercaro, baptized, confirmed, and administered the first Holy Communion to fourteen natives and six youngsters from various regions of the country...." The newspaper continues:

> The application of the new rite for Baptism and Confirmation was rather exotic for the attendants of the Eucharistic celebration, for the catechumens of Sierra de Perijá (at the Venezuelan border), and the Motilona.
> These persons, who had been trained to enter Catholicism and afterwards were confirmed in the Faith by Cardinal Lercaro, wore drilling clothes, for they were very poor people. The natives, along with the six youngsters from different provinces, went ahead in a disordered row, for they were bashful, and watched the cadets of the military academy in luxurious uniforms, and the central 15-meter cross with the crowds as a background. Once they entered the shrine, they became inscrutably serious. After the catechumens came their godparents. For the 14 natives there were two godparents: Don Juan José Ramírez and his wife, Teresa de Ramírez. The applicants for Baptism entered through an honor guard formed by the academy of cadets and local police. Once on the steps of the shrine, under the television and movie lights, they waited for some minutes until His Holiness' legate introduced them to the acts of Christian initiation, Catholic according to the rite.

The official program of the Congress tells us about the novel meaning, according to progressivist and post-Conciliar terminology, of Baptism and the new rites which His Eminence Cardinal Lercaro invented, performed, and authorized. To quote:

> Through Baptism and Confirmation, the catechumen gets to participate in Christ's spirit of love, thus entering the Church, where he expresses his faith and obliges himself to bear witness of it in the world. But Christian initiation, that is, the incorporation of a person into the Christian community, is not complete as long as he has not entered, through the Eucharist, into the full participation in ecclesiastical fellowship. Christian initiation is a task for the whole Church community, hierarchically constituted, which receives new children. The holy people, the deacons, the presbyters, and the bishop, each of them according to his own function, accepts the new Christians, and then the whole community celebrates the Eucharist.

Our Return to the Eucharistic Congress

The old theology taught us that Baptism is one of the sacraments of the new alliance, a tangible sign instituted by Christ that represents and awards grace, through which we acquire the *justification* which Christ brought us. That is to say, the old man, the man of sin, dies within us, and we rise with Christ to the divine life, which begins with time and lasts throughout eternity, if we do not lose it through grave personal sin. Baptism, then, gives us a new life, different from the human and natural life we received through our parents. Just as our human nature is the source of all of our activities as men, so also is *the sanctifying grace* given to us at Holy Baptism a new nature, the new source of supernatural activities, exceeding and surpassing the capabilities of our human nature. Just as our human nature has different faculties to display the various human activities belonging to the human being, so it is that along with sanctifying grace, *three infused virtues*, called *theological virtues*, are given to us at Baptism. These faculties or powers of sanctifying grace, the virtues of faith, hope, and charity are the means by which we display the various supernatural activities that transcend time and gaze at eternity. When born to this divine life, we become God's children, His adopted children, and, "if children, heirs, heirs of God, and co-heirs of Christ."

I cannot understand how Christian initiation could be "a task for the whole Church community." The spiritual reception awarded to the neophytes by the holy people, the deacons, presbyters, and bishops in accordance with Cardinal Lercaro's liturgy, did not initiate them into Christianity at all. To be received by the holy people would be no use for them, had they not been previously regenerated and justified by Christ in the Church.

Progressivists however, are excited about their new ecclesiastical theology of the "holy people," the charismatic and prophetic "ecclesiastical community." That is why they empower the communal assembly with the very power of initiating the catechumens into Christianity. Following the great theologians, I would say that it is Christ who justifies, regenerates, and initiates, and that these catechumens became members of God's people as a result of Holy Baptism.

I cannot agree with another progessivist affirmation either, namely that "the incorporation of a person into the Christian community is not complete as long as he has not entered, through the Eucharist, into the full participation in ecclesiastical fellowship," according to Cardinal Lercaro. Through Baptism, we are incorporated fully and perfectly into Christ and, as a result, into the ecclesiastical community. The essential goal is become incorporated into Christ; the resulting and secondary goal is to become integrated into the ecclesiastical community. The Eucharist is the sacrament Christ instituted for the conservation and growth of the divine life that we receive at Baptism, not to perfect our incorporation into the Christian community. The ecclesiastical community hierarchically receives and shelters the new children of God, but it

The Montinian Church

does not make them.

The progressivist program of Bogotá ends by saying that *"the whole community celebrates the Eucharist"* [italics added]. What could these words mean? Does the whole community celebrate the Holy Mass? Who is the celebrant, the priest or the believing people? Things become clear if we accept the famous definition of the *Instructio Generalis* of the *Novus Ordo Missae:* "The Lord's Supper, the Mass, is the holy assembly of God's people gathered under the *presidency* of the priest to celebrate the Lord's Memorial." Strictly speaking, there is neither sacrifice, victim, nor a real priest. There is a sacred assembly (despite the Church's de-sacralization); there is a "president;" there is a celebration, a supper, or a love feast. Furthermore, in this analogical and commemorative sacrifice, nothing hinders the possibility that all the members of the holy people concelebrate. According to the socializing times in which we are living, the charismatic theology of God's people and the communal assembly have thus abolished the Sacrament of Ordination.

In that day's "penitential act" of the "Eucharistic action", as experts would say, or in the liturgy set up by Cardinal Lercaro for the concelebration at the parishes, as we pre-Conciliar people would say, again we find this *integral humanism* that characterizes the new, post-Conciliar religion. The president of the assembly said:

> Grant us, O Lord, your mercy, for we have failed to be a new ferment of love and unity *in an always growing and progressive world.*

The Church is a function of the growing and progressive world, "Christ-genesis" compared to "cosmogenesis." Materially, the world grows and progresses, but it keeps moving away from Christ and His eternal Gospel, because "the world is founded on iniquity," says Saint John, and, because "in the world, everything is concupiscence of the flesh, concupiscence of the eyes, and haughtiness of life."

The president of the assembly then adds:

> Forgive also the outrages to human dignity committed by the Christian community which prevent other men from recognizing Christ's face in the Church.

We do not beg pardon for the offenses committed by the Christian community and the president of the assembly to God Himself through so many and such grave sins as all men have committed, nor do we beg mercy for the outrages which we have individually inflicted on the Lord, but for "the outrages to human dignity committed by the Christian community."

His Eminence's chief theme also shows up unequivocally in a penitential cry: "Forgive us, O Lord, for we have allowed many of your children to suffer hunger, misery, and injustice." It is we who, individually or collectively, have caused misery, hunger, and injustice in the world. It is we who have broken God-created social equality. It is we who are guilty of the existence of lazy, deranged, sick, vicious, foolish, abnormal people and the whole range of human inequalities which in turn necessarily provoke the hunger and misery that the progressivists want to impute to us at any price in order to justify guerilla warfare, revolution, violence, and organized, legal plunder of private property. *"Anything superfluous is theft.... All private property is a fruit of plunder or oppression"* and in consequence, injustice against mankind. All? Well, there are exceptions! All except that of the new apostles of the social gospel.

Moreover, in order that there could be no doubt about the Cardinal's leading thought, at the communal prayer of the faithful all repeated:

> So that the Congress we are celebrating may encourage a more integral human development all over Latin America and the world, so that, amidst today's world's science and technique, we may discover the meaning of God and His providence, so that our active presence may grant AUDACITY and PRUDENCE to the accelerated changes in our world.

This means an audacious change of structures, brought about by our *active*, I would rather say, *revolutionary*, presence in the world, and especially in Latin America which is the "pilot laboratory" of *Populorum Progressio*. The documents we have already read and commented on in this book clear up the meaning, not only of this unusual prayer, but of the whole International Eucharistic Congress of Bogotá.

The liturgical changes, cautiously started by the Vatican Council and pompously and spectacularly brought about afterwards by the Council presided over for a time by His Eminence Cardinal Lercaro, have torn Christ's robe, as Tito Casini[4] would say. Many people have welcomed such changes enthusiastically, for they believe the Catholic religion has become more human and the Holy Mass more comprehensible. As if the human mind might ever be able to fully understand the Divine Mysteries! Others attach secondary importance to these changes, disregarding the essential relationship of our religion with *revealed truth*, as stated and taught by the Church's living, authentic, and infallible Magisterium. Progressivists contend that, without these radical liturgical transformations, the Conciliar *aggiornamento* of Pope John would have been unattainable. José Alvarez Isaza, the Judaizing Christian who, along with his friend and party comrade Alejandro Avilés, seeks to monopolize the faith of the Mexican and even Latin American people, dared say that if the Church had failed to carry out these changes it would have ceased to exist in ten years. According to these "experts," the liturgical changes were the *sine qua non* condition for the Church's conservation and life.

It was necessary to eliminate Catholic triumphalism expressed by that most beautiful liturgy, with which faithful believers imitated the angelic canticles. It was imperative to turn the Eucharist into a communal love feast instead of a sacrifice, in order to suppress all inequalities among men. Out with Gregorian music! Out with Pope Pius Xth's regulations on sacred music! Out with those boring ceremonies! Now altar and priest face the people complete with mariachis, jazz, and ballet, the show! In Bogotá, that most special liturgy prepared by Cardinal Lercaro definitively broke the outdated obscurantism contained in the Church's liturgy.

MATERIAL FROM CUERNAVACA AND RELIGIOUS PROGRESSIVISM IN MEXICO

Permit me to transcribe the following from my book, *Cuernavaca and Religious Progressivism in Mexico* published two years ago:

> It is a secret to no one that one of the most ancient and cherished goals of the Jewish mafia and the international organizations it founded and controls (Masonry, Communism, and the international, financial, and political organizations) is the establishment of a world government, which would gather all the economic, socio-political, and religious institutions of the various nations into socialistic syncretism.
>
> The current offensive against the Catholic Church is but a stage of a boldly executed maneuver designed to infiltrate and destroy Christ's Church from within and to associate it, at its upper levels, with its very enemies.
>
> Abbé Roca (1830-1893), a graduate of the Carmelite School and ordained as a priest in 1858, was appointed honorary canon of Perpignan in 1869 . . . He was the worst kind of apostate, and was a member of the most important secret societies and an element consciously disposed to destroy the Church. We deem it pertinent to quote some of his writings in which he anticipates today's dreadful crisis. In a letter to a Jew, Oswald With, dated August 23, 1891, he says:
>
>> [There will come] a new, sublime, wide, deep, really universalist, absolutely encyclopedic Christianity, which will end by having all heavens come down upon earth, as Victor Hugo said, by suppressing borders, sectarianism, local, ethnical, and zealous churches, divisional temples, the alveoles that retain the aching molecules of Christ's largers social body as prisoners of the Pope. . . . (*Glorious Centennial*, p. 123).
>
> What Christendom wants to build is not a pagoda, but a universal worship embracing all worships. (*Ibid.*, p. 77).

Our Return to the Eucharistic Congress

Is not this the "ecumenism" on which we commented, in the previous liturgy of Cardinal Lercaro? But let us return to Abbé Roca:

> My view is that mankind coincides with Christ in a much more real way than what the mystics had believed so far. If Christ-Man, as Incarnate Word, is God's only Son, He is also, therefore, the whole universe and especially all mankind or, better said, the countless series of travelling humanity. (*Ibid.*, p. 188).

Here we have the origin of the Teilhardian *cosmic Christ*. Disavowal by the initiates notwithstanding, this concept, whereby progressivism associates and merges with all religions in the immanent god of pantheism, was worked out within the Jewish-Masonic dens.

> An incarnation of the uncreated reason in the created reason, a manifestation of the absolute in the relative, the personal Christ is a central symbol, a sort of a physical *hieroglyph* who always speaks and acts in a peculiar way. He is the Man-Book mentioned by both the Kabbala and the Apocalypse.
> What the sages call evolution, the enlightened priests call redemption, disincarnation, death, and ascension. (*Glorious Centennial*, p. 237).

At the International Spiritualist Congress held September 9-16, 1889, at the Grand Orient of France under the honorary presidency of the Duchess of Pomar, Canon Roca said:

MY CHRIST IS NOT THE VATICAN'S CHRIST

> With the world and because He is the world, Christ evolves and becomes transformed. Nobody will be able to stop Christ's whirlwind. Nobody will be able to brake the course of evolution that Christ leads all over the world and will overwhelm everything. The dogmas evolve with it, since they are living things, like the world, like man, like all organic beings. Since they are echoes of the collective conscience, they follow, as it does, *the course of history.*

Here we have Teilhard's integral evolution, and also the progressivist dogma of evolution. It is the basis of the *aggiornamento*, whereby the Church is considered as a world's function evolving with the world and accommodated to the stages of the world wherein we live. Dogmas must evolve with the world. They are not immutable pieces of truth, but *"echoes of the collective conscience."*

In his book, *The End of the Ancient World*, on page 327, Roca announced the Church's present crisis:

The Montinian Church

What is being prepared in the Universal Church? Not a reformation. I dare not call it a revolution, for this word would sound inexact, but an evolution.

I recall having heard the following fearful exclamation from Cardinal Ottaviani: *"What we are contemplating is a dreadful revolution."* Was not Paul VI expressing the same idea when he said the Church's current crisis appeared as the *"auto-demolition"* of Catholicism? And an AP dispatch out of Vatican City, dated October 28, 1970, read as follows:

> Today Pope Paul VI voiced a warning against the "catastrophic consequences" that would arise from acceptance of any radical change as a means of attaining progress.
>
> "People wonder whether religious truth and dogmas are changing," said the Pope during his weekly audience at Saint Peter's Basilica. Is it possible that now, nothing is permanent?
>
> An answer must be found, at least to avoid the catastrophic consequences arising from the avowal that no rule, no doctrine may remain forever, and that all changes, even if radical, can be adapted as a progressive, controversial, or revolutionary device.
>
> Provided we do not want our civilization to end in chaos and the Christian religion to lose all justification in the modern world, we must all clearly state that "something" remains and must remain while time passes.

The basis and immovable fundamental of our Catholic Faith is not the personal or collective convenience of avoiding the catastrophic consequences of the continuous change of our ideas, but the authority of God, who revealed to us the truth in which we believe. What remains and must remain is not "something," but *all* that God taught us, all of our dogmas, for, if a single dogma falls, all the others must logically accompany it in its collapse. What the Pope regrets is but the inevitable consequence of having let the ax fall upon what the Church's Magisterium taught as Catholic dogmatic truth.

Let us explain further the diabolical plans of the Jewish-Masonic conspiracy, as explained by Canon Roca in the last century:

> The Papacy's present shape will disappear. The Pontiff of the divine Synarchy will look like today's Pope as much as the latter resembles the pope of Salt Lake City ... The new social order will be established without Rome, despite Rome, and against Rome.
>
> The old Papacy, the old priesthood will willingly yield to the future Pontificate and to priests, who will be the old ones converted and transfigured for the purposes of the scientific organization of our planet according to the Gospel.
>
> Moreover, although this new Church may, perhaps, not keep anything

> belonging to the ancient scholastic discipline and rudimentary shape of the ancient Church, *it will receive its consecration and canonic jurisdiction from Rome.* (*Glorious Centennial*, pp. 452, 456).
>
> *The Roman curia will not be forgiven.* This political institution, known as the Roman curia or the Vatican, has juxtaposed and, at times, superimposed itself on the divine institution. The Vatican is not the Church, nor is Canon Law the Gospel. (*Ibid.*, p. 452).

Does not this description of the Church given by Roca resemble the post-Conciliar Church which progressivism has bequeathed us? Does it not appear as if "collegiality" and "co-responsibility" have caused the ancient Papacy to disappear? Have we not seen the old Papacy, the old bishops and priests, willingly give us their hierarchical and sacred nature to become "assembly presidents?" What is left of the Roman curia? Moreover, the new hierarchs, the *aggiornated* priests, and the progressivist bishops receive their consecration and canonic jurisdiction from Rome!

Roca tells us that it is *the clergy,* the infiltrators, who will bring the revolution into the bosom of the Church. Two parties will develop inside the Church, that of the followers of the old Papacy, whom he calls reactionaries or ultramontanists, and that of the new priests who adhere to the revolution. Modern language calls them "traditionalists" and "progressivists."

> By now they form a ring, which will break in its middle, and each of its halves will form a new ring. The schism is about to occur whereby there will be a "progressivism" ring and a "reactionary" ring. (*Glorious Centennial*, pp. 446-447).

With absolute certainty, the apostate Roca foretold the internal schism that the Church is now experiencing. The unity of the Church is not only jeopardized but is already lost. The progressivist Church no longer is the traditional and Apostolic Church. The infiltrators, the fifth column, the Trojan horse, opened the gates to the enemy.

> And we priests, let us pray for, bless, and glorify the wonderful task of bringing about the scientific, economic, and social transfiguration of our religious mysteries, symbols, dogmas, and sacraments. Maybe you do not realize our forms are outdated and we are worn out, abandoned by the Spirit and alone; our hands are full of empty shells and dead letters. (*Glorious Centennial*, p. 102).

Roca's words have the flavor of the present time. It appears that progressivist ecclesiastics want science, economy, and sociology to "override" the Church's Mysteries and, so they say, take the place of doctrinal,

The Montinian Church

sacramental, and liturgical immovability, through sociological and socializing pastoral activity. This is the way they interpret *aggiornamento*. As a confirmation, let us quote the leader of the "new wave" Jesuits, the diabolical Teilhard de Chardin, father of the post-Conciliar Church. In his famous and explicit letter of October 4, 1950, to his friend, the ex-Dominican Max Corce, who professed the same doctrine he did, and who published Teilhard's letter in his book, *The Council and Teilhard, The Eternal and the Human* (Messellier, ed., Neuchatel, Switzerland, pp. 196-198), Teilhard said:

> Basically I consider, as you do, that the Church (as every living reality after a period of time) has reached a stage of "molting" or necessary reformation. After two thousand years, this is unavoidable. Mankind is in the process of molting. How could Christianity fail to do likewise? More precisely I consider that such reformation (a much more profound one than that of the 16th century) is not merely a matter of institutions, but of *faith*. In a way, our image of God has unfolded. Transversally, so to speak, besides the traditional and transcendental God from *above*, a God appeared to us a century ago who is moving forward towards something "ultra-human." To me, this is all. To man, the question is to re-conceive God, no longer in terms of cosmos, but of cosmogenesis, God who can be adored and reached only through the end of the universe, which is illuminated and given irreversible love by Him from within. Yes, yes, *the upward and the forward movements are synthesized from within* . . .

Consistent with what Roca said and maybe because he followed his secret school—for both belonged to the secret conventicles that then as now, infected Paris and were fostered and sponsored by the lodges—Teilhard announces a total reformation of Christianity, a more profound one than that of the 16th century. Mankind and the world are in the process of molting. How could Christianity fail to do likewise? As if Christianity were the work of men and a function of human changes!

This *reformation* has to begin with the liturgy. Let us quote S. de Guaita (*Essai de Sciences Maudites*, pp. 588-589), who forecast esoteric Christianity:

> O rites! O dead symbols! Your soul will return to you when Christianity, strengthened again by the sap from its source, will be transfigured; when the eternal religion that manifests itself uttering the restoring wind of its intimate esotericism (occult doctrine, known only to the initiates) will revive the dead letter through the kiss of the immortal spirit.

To the occult sects of the past and present centuries, among them gnosticism, to which not a few high-ranking ecclesiastics belong, the Sacraments, the Church's liturgy, the very Eucharistic Sacrifice have grown old, for the supernatural no longer explains anything. Human intelligence is self-sufficient, and by itself, through its intrinsic nature, it receives the divine directly. What do those vehicles of Christ's grace mean, then? Roca tells it to us:

> As long as Christian ideas remained in a state of sacramental incubation, in our hands and under the veil of liturgy, they were unable to exert any efficacious and scientifically decisive social effect upon the organic constitution and public government of human societies. (*Glorious Centennial*, p. 162).

The religious goal of the modern world is not God's glory and the salvation of souls, but "to exert ... [an] efficacious and scientifically decisive social effect upon the organic constitution and public government of human societies." That is why it was necessary to make a complete liturgical change that had the *sacramental incubation* ripen into *social action*, organic constitution, and public government of human societies. That is why the mariachis were necessary, why the altar and priest have to face the people, why the Lord's Mass or Supper has to be de-sacralized and de-mythified. A de-sacralized, humanized liturgy is the only one that suits the "progress" of God's people. *Socialization is conceived as the final and supreme stage of Mankind.*

In the last century, Jewish-Masonic anticlericalism also forecast the suppression of the religious cassock and robes. Roca, in his book, *Christ, the Pope, and Democracy* (pp. 105-107), announced:

> When society beholds our archaic and queer clothing in the public square, the effect is that of a masquerade or carnival ... we are ridiculed. In satiric magazines and on the theatrical stage, the cassock and the bonnet are food for the crowd's scorn.

Jesus Christ was also the target of nasty mockery on the part of His enemies. It is not surprising at all that priests and religious are ridiculed and scoffed by the enemies of God and His Church. It was a long time ago that noxious and sectarian literature began a campaign to de-sacralize the Lord's ministers, not only depicting their human side with grotesque strokes, but effacing and denying the supernatural features of their sacerdotal ministry in order to make them equal with other men. The most outstanding of these books are the ones that humanize the sacerdotal life to such an extent that they turn it into hateful and perverse hypocrisy. Remember the works by Morris West (*The Devil's Advocate, The Shoes of the Fisherman*, etc.), which de-sacralized the Church and slandered its hierarchy.

In the new Church, foretold by Roca, it is evident that priestly celibacy was to become a target for unmerciful attacks. Let us quote this renowned apostate again:

The Montinian Church

> I am an outlaw, a Roman priest, a pariah, a eunuch. There is no place for me in the familial household. I have no place under the sun of civilization. I am a plaything of fatality.

In a letter addressed to the Pope, Roca writes:

> Due to the vile reputation celibacy has cast upon us and which has tied us to the gibbet, due to the humiliating heritage it has bequeathed us and the regretful situation in which it puts us in present times, we find ourselves, Holy Father, miserably exiled from all living and fruitful circles in this world... lonely, despised, banished from everywhere, isolated on earth, and secluded in our rectories like lepers, we are accompanied all day long by the hateful "me," which deforms us and makes us selfish. *(Christ, the Pope and Democracy*, p. 1103).

Today, sacerdotal celibacy is also being fought by all the followers of progressivism. Msgr. Méndez Arceo, Don Sergio VII, the outstanding Bishop of Cuernavaca, after having campaigned and gathered signatures and adepts for the abolition of celibacy, in his harangue to young university students at Puebla, said that tomorrow's celibacy will be optional, and the only thing he asked of newly married priests was to have good taste when choosing spouses. Another good-spirited and wise priest, in the presence of so many priests who, in the endless procession, abandon the sacred ministry everywhere to enjoy the pleasures of the bride-chamber, told me that he felt the Church could end by yielding and allowing incontinent priests to get married. But this proves too much; therefore, it does not prove anything. Facetiously, one might say that so many offenses are committed against chastity, that it would be good to suppress the sixth commandment of the Decalogue. So many are the sins against the moral law, that it would be good to proclaim the moral law outdated. Thus would human dignity and freedom be more adequately respected!

During the first half of 1964, an article by an ecclesiastic, quoted by *Nouvelles de Chrétienté*, moved to allow the marriage of isolated priests in charge of rural parishes, while clergymen living in communities would remain celibate. This idea does not belong to Méndez Arceo or the said French ecclesiastic; it is very old. It was advanced by the apostate, Roca, who, in his book, *Glorious Centennial*, on page 434, proposed the creation of "a mixed apostleship, *composed of celibate and married priests.*"

But Roca's prophetic vision went beyond this. He announced a change in the priests' pastoral ministry. Their useless works would be substituted by intense social activity for the masses' benefit, as was demanded by "international progressivism" in Colombia.

Our Return to the Eucharistic Congress

Priests will become the leaders of unions, mutualities, cooperative production, consumer agencies, work retirement funds, and social security programs. *(Glorious Centennial,* p. 20).

"Following this trend," says Pierre Virion, "the new priest," as this famous Mason announces it, "will put out stars in the sky that will never light up again." Their example, doctrine, and pastoral activity will show that Heaven does not exist beyond this world, but down here.

The kingdom of Heaven, that is the impersonal and Divine kingdom of truth in liberty, of justice in equality, of social economy in fraternity, is that which constitutes the Holy Trinity of evangelical synarchy. *(Glorious Centennial,* p. 20).

But the ideological parallelism of the ex-Canon, Roca, with the "ultra-progressivist" triad from Cuernavaca and all those who are endeavoring to build a new Church upon the ruins of the old one, is even more perfect than this. All of them describe the coveted, anticipated priest of the future according to the blueprint masterminded at the bottom of the secret laboratories of the counter-Church at the end of the last century. To quote Roca:

No, no, Monsieur Veuillot! Mankind is not becoming *de-Christianized* but *de-clericalized,* so that the priest will become more human, and both will become Christian in the Gospel's real sense. *(Christ, the Pope and Democracy,* p. 81).

It is curious to hear today's reformers, such as Illich, Lemercier, Pardinas, Enrique Maza S.J., and the famous and applauded Bishop of Cuernavaca, repeat Roca's very words of "de-Christianization," "de-sacralization," "de-mythification." All of these sound alike and mean the same thing, denial of traditional, apostolic Catholicism and the auto-demolition of Christianity designed to aid "integral humanism" according to the primitive sources and to the Gospel's real meaning which the Church lost and the sects have found again.

Let us quote the following from Pierre Virion's revealing book, *The Church and Masonry:*

Through the disclosure of Cretineau-Joly, the project of the Alta Vendita of the Carbonari became known: to seize Rome with the aid of priests who were conspiring against the Church. This disclosure, as well as the openly Masonic recruiting methods used by the Carbonari, did not fail to help wreck those plans. . . . *The Abbess of Jouarre* wrote that the religious reforms (a euphemism used to name the religious and moral revolution) *would be brought about by*

The Montinian Church

leading characters of the Church, and will be entirely consistent with regulations. In other words, in a future council, the regular and non-separate clergy, under the influence of a new Christianity and open to the modern currents of thought, will end by favoring their own integration into the ecumenism of the lodges.

In turn, in his work *Abbé Gabriel*, Roca wrote the following prophetic words:

> I feel that divine worship, as regulated by the liturgy, ceremonies, rites, and rulings of the Roman Church, will suffer a transformation soon, at an ecumenical council. It will return the Church to the venerable simplicity of the apostolic golden age, and harmonize it with *the new stage of modern conscience and civilization*.

"It was also," says Pierre Virion, "the illusion and almost an hallucination, of the conversion of an eventual Pope to a movement opposite to the Syllabus, *that would approve the new spirit of the world* (sic)."

Further, Roca says:

> Something will happen that will astonish the world and make it kneel before its Redeemer. This "something" will be the demonstration of the perfect consistence between the ideals of modern civilization and the ideals of Christ and His Gospel. This will mean the consecration of the new social order and the solemn baptism of modern civilization. (*The End of The Ancient World*, p. 282).

Perfect consistence between the ideals of modern civilization and the ideals of Christ and His Gospel" and the "baptism of modern civilization." What do these cabalistic expressions mean? Let us go on. Roca still has more dreadful expressions, by means of which he seems to try to describe future Catholicism, as designed by the lodges. In his book, *Glorious Centennial*, on page 13, he writes:

> *I affirm that we are arriving at the final complete collapse of the ancient religious, political, and economic order, and foresee new viewpoints on the state, family and all other circles of human activity.*
>
> An immolation is being prepared, that will solemnly expiate... *The Papacy will succumb; it will be killed by the holy knife forged by the Popes of the last Council. The Papal Caesar is a host crowned for the sacrifice.*

What will come after this immolation? A new Christianity without temples, altars, or liturgy. An esoteric Christianity. A religion whose Gospel will be "social justice." To quote Roca:

Our Return to the Eucharistic Congress

The convert at the Vatican will not have to reveal to his brethren in Christ a new teaching. He will not have to propel Christendom or the world as a whole along ways other than those followed by people under the inspiration of modern civilization, whose essentially Christian evangelical principles, ideas, and works have, despite us, become the principles, ideas, and works of the regenerated nations before Rome even dreamed of advocating them. The Pontiff will be limited in confirming and glorifying the work of the Spirit of Christ or the Christ-Spirit on the public spirit and, thanks to his privilege of personal infallibility, will canonically declare *urbi et orbi* that the present civilization is a legitimate child of the holy gospel of social redemption. (*Glorious Centennial*, p. 111).

I wanted to quote the apostate Roca and his followers at length, because a complete panorama was necessary in order to understand the spectacular changes in our Catholic liturgy which, no doubt, culminated at the International Eucharistic Congress of Bogotá. If we analyze Roca's contentions as expressed in the above quotations, we find a whole program of internal demolition of Catholicism which undoubtedly coincides with the terminology and program of progressivism.

To undertake the complete reformation of the institutional Church, it was necessary to begin with those audacious liturgical changes that the apostate Roca forecast and announced, because to the people the liturgy is the tangible manifestation of the truth of our religion. The liturgy is not the dogma, but is or must be the authentic expression of the dogma, according to the principle of Catholic theology that reads: *"Lex orandi, lex credendi,"* i.e., the law of the believers' prayer is the law of faith.

It is evident that the sacred rites and ceremonies of our liturgy, as well as our very dogmas, have experienced slow evolution throughout the centuries under the guidance of the Holy Spirit and the solicitous leadership and surveillance of the Church's Magisterium. The deposit of the divine revelation was definitively closed by the death of the last apostle, but this did not paralyze the vital activity of Christ's Church. "The kingdom of heaven is like a grain of mustard seed, which is the least of all seeds, but when it is grown, it is the greatest among herbs, and becometh a tree, so that the birds in the air come and lodge in the branches thereof."

This slow and secular evolution of the dogmas, liturgy, discipline, and the whole life of the Church had, then, been anticipated by the divine Master. The case is not that the Church invents new dogmas, but that its living, authentic, and infallible Magisterium progressively teaches us new pieces of truth that were contained in the deposit of the divine revelation and that, according to the necessity of the times, must be explained to us, either to condemn new heresies or to increase our knowledge of the divine things.

It would be preposterous and contradictory to lay aside the evolution or growth the Church has attained so far, as if it were the result of the exclusive activity of men, and begin the whole process again, neglecting the richness accumulated throughout the centuries. This would be *primitivism* or *archaism* which, contrary to God's design, endeavors to reconstruct the whole life of the Church and its organic evolution according to the criteria of modern "experts" and the demands of the contemporary world. This is not to return to the sources, but to ignore them and establish an inadmissible parenthesis of twenty centuries in the very life of the Church, during which Christ failed to fulfill His promises and the Holy Spirit failed to furnish assistance.

The contradiction incurred by the reformers is clear: they impute to the Holy Spirit all the spectacular changes which they have implemented at the Council and after the Council, in liturgy, morality, formulation or suppression of certain dogmas, discipline, and the traditional teaching of the Magisterium. Simultaneously, they deny that the Church had had any divine assistance during the past twenty centuries of its life. Charismatic and prophetic progressivism feels itself to be exclusively assisted by the Holy Spirit and the sole depository of revealed truth. Have these innovators forgotten what was defined at Trent and Vatican I, to mention just the two last councils prior to Vatican II? Have they forgotten the condemnations by the Syllabus, and the condemnation of Modernism by St. Pius XI? Have they forgotten the liturgical rulings issued by recent Popes, especially Saint Pius X and his most excellent successor, Pius XII? How is it that in just a few years they could have lost sight of the wise teachings and precise precepts of *Mediator Dei* which, only twenty years ago, condemned the absurd contentions of these demolishers with complete accuracy and wisdom? Either the Holy Spirit was wrong some years ago, is wrong now, or has changed His mind in view of the data of the electronic computers of Vatican II. I find all three hypotheses to be absurd. Is that not so, all you progressivist gentlemen?

But there is much more. Radical liturgical changes introduced by the reformers grant such a degree of freedom that unbelievable extravagances which seem to emulate theatre plays or pagan rites have been implemented. Indeed, Roca's words in his work, *Abbé Gabriel*, would seem prophetic, were they not revealing the nefarious plans prepared by the lodges and occult sects in order that the infiltrators in the Church could realize them in due time. Let us quote such words again:

> I feel that divine worship, as regulated by the liturgy, ceremonies, rites, and rulings of the Roman Church, will suffer a transformation soon, at an ecumenical council. It will return the Church to the venerable simplicity of the apostolic golden age, and harmonize it with *the new stage of modern conscience and civilization*.

Our Return to the Eucharistic Congress

No doubt to Roca the progressivists, the Patriarch of Cuernavaca, and the venerable simplicity of the apostolic golden age requires turning our temples into cold sheds without any spiritual Christian message and without images, tabernacles, flowers, candles or incense which, *mutatis mutandis*, in due time become centers for dancing, boxing, or political meetings.

I cannot imagine mariachis or jazz at Christian meetings during the era of the catacombs. Nor can I associate the psychedelic clothing Don Sergio VII wears to celebrate his Panamerican liturgy at his "model" cathedral at Cuernavaca, with the impressive figures of the first Popes who presided over the primitive Christian community. The same music heard the night before for joy and amusement at nightclubs and sinful places, is heard the next day at the temples to celebrate the greatness of the Lord.

It is convenient to quote some fragments of His Holiness Pius XII's *Mediator Dei*, since this encyclical, enacted November 20, 1947, does not have circumstantial, but *doctrinal* significance:

> In every liturgical act, its divine Founder is present along with the Church. Christ is present at the august Sacrifice of the Altar both in the priest, who represents Him, and, most singularly, in Himself, under the Eucharistic Species. With His divine virtue, He is present in the Sacraments to which He has conveyed supernatural efficiency so that they become instruments of holiness. Finally, He is present in the praise and supplication we address God, according to these words of His: "Where two or three people gather in My name, I will be amidst them."
>
> The holy liturgy constitutes then, the public cult which our Redeemer, the head of the Church, renders the celestial Father, and which the society of the Christian faithful offers its divine Founder and, through Him, the Eternal Father. To put it briefly, it integrally constitutes the public worship of Jesus Christ's Mystical Body, of his head and limbs.
>
> The universal worship the Church owes God must be both external and internal. *External*, indeed, for it arises from man's nature, comprising both body and soul . . . ; since divine worship must involve not only individuals, but also the human community, it must also be *social* . . . . Hence this public and social worship manifests the unity of the Mystical Body in a particular way . . . . The chief element of divine worship, however, must be the *internal* one, because it is always necessary to live in Christ and always devote oneself to Him so that, in Him, with Him, and through Him, the Heavenly Father be given due glory.
>
> Those who affirm therefore, that the holy liturgy, as a part of divine worship, consists just of the external and sensible manifestation, the decorative pomp of the ceremonies, are absolutely wrong and turn away from the authentic doctrine. . . . [N]o less wrong are those who affirm that the holy liturgy is the sum of laws and rulings which the hierarchical Church has enacted in order that

The Montinian Church

the sacred rites be performed and ordered.

The efficacy of both the Eucharistic Sacrifice and the Sacraments arises first from the Sacrifice itself and the Sacraments themselves, *ex opere operato*, but, if we consider the very activity of Jesus Christ's undefiled spouse, who adorns with prayers and holy ceremonies the Eucharistic Sacrifice and the Sacraments and if we consider the "sacramentals" and the other rites having been instituted by the ecclesiastic hierarchy, then their efficaciousness derives, rather, *ex opere operantis Ecclesiae*, from the activity of the very Church itself, for, it being holy and most tightly united with its Head, it acts united to Christ.

It is impossible to reproduce the text of *Mediator Dei* in its entirety here, but since this encyclical not only contains precious and clear teachings for the Catholic, but also contradicts the whole modern progressivist liturgical doctrine, we cannot help saying something about the Holy Sacrifice of the Mass. Pius XII says:

> The head and kind of a center of the Christian religion is the mystery of the Most Holy Eucharist, instituted by the High Priest, Christ, who commands that it be perpetually renewed in the Church by its ministers. The Sacrifice of the Altar is not merely a simple memorial of Jesus Christ's crucifixion and death, but a true, genuine sacrifice in which, through a bloodless immolation, the High Priest now does what He did on the Cross, giving Himself up to His eternal Father as a most acceptable host....

Using the above words, perfectly consistent with what was defined at Trent, Pius XII teaches us three pieces of truth of our Catholic Faith which the progressivists would now like to conceal or weaken, namely:

1. The Mass is a real and true sacrifice, not merely a simple memorial.
2. The same Priest who offered the sacrifice at Calvary offers the Sacrifice of the Altar; the hierarchical minister acts on behalf of Christ, with the power of Christ.
3. The Victim who was immolated at Calvary is the same Victim who is immolated on the altar, Christ Jesus.

That is why Pius XII says:

> The priest is the one and the same Jesus Christ, whose holy person is represented by His minister. The latter, by virtue of the sacerdotal consecration he has received, symbolizes the High Priest and has the power to act by virtue and by the person of Christ Himself. That is why, in a way, his sacerdotal activity *lends Christ his tongue and extends his hand*. (Saint John Cris., *Hom.* 86, 4).

It is not then, all the believers, the "assembly," who celebrate, who consecrate, and who summon Christ as a victim upon the altar, but only the hierarchical priest who received, along with Christ's power, the representation of Christ at his Holy Ordination.

The Pope goes on to say:

> The victim is also the one and same divine Redeemer in His human nature and in the reality of His body and blood.

Here we have the *Mysterium Fidei* which today is omitted in the consecration. Here we have the Transubstantiation, Christ's real presence *sub speciebus panis et vini*, under the appearance of bread and wine. There would be no real sacrifice but for this complete Transubstantiation.

> Christ gives Himself up in different ways. On the cross, He gave Himself up to God completely with all His suffering, and this immolation of the Victim was carried out through a bloody death ... in exchange, on the altar, due to the glorious state of His human nature, *death hath no more dominion over him* (Rom. 6:9) ... but the divine wisdom has found a wonderful way of expressing the sacrifice of our Redemption by means of external signs that are symbols of death, for, thanks to the Transubstantiation of the bread into Christ's body and the wine into Christ's blood, both His body and His blood are really present. In this way the Eucharistic Species under which He is present, symbolize the bloody separation of body and blood. In this way, the memorial of His death, which really took place at Calvary, repeats itself in each of the Sacrifices of the Altar, for, through various signs, Jesus Christ shows up and appears in the state of a Victim.

There is a difference, then, in the way in which the Sacrifice of the Cross and the Sacrifice of the Altar are performed. At the cross there is blood and death, but not at the altar, because the resurrected Christ cannot die, suffer, or shed His blood; but the Transubstantiation and Real Presence, after the consecration, turn Him into an acceptable victim on the altar.

Then the Pope explains that this Eucharistic Sacrifice, just as the sacrifice at Calvary, affects the goals of a real and proper sacrifice, namely: God's glory—sacrifice of divine worship; thanksgiving—Eucharistic Sacrifice; expiation and propitiation—propitiatory sacrifice; and impetration—supplicatory sacrifice. But there is an essential and most important difference regarding the intention Christ had in offering both of these sacrifices, for on the cross, He redeemed us, and at the altar, he makes the inexhaustible fruits of His redemption applicable to us.

The Pope says:

The Montinian Church

It can be said that at Calvary Christ set up a pond of purification and salvation filled with the blood that He shed, but if men do not bathe and wash up the stains of their iniquity in it, they will certainly not get purified and saved. To this effect, that all sinners be purified in the blood of the Lamb, *their own cooperation is necessary*. Even though Christ, generally speaking, has reconciled the whole human genre with the Father through His bloody death (this is the redemption for *everybody*), nevertheless, He wanted everybody to approach and be carried to the cross through the Sacraments and the Sacrifice of the Eucharist, *in order to be able to obtain the fruits of salvation He had gathered at the Cross*....

According to this doctrine, which is the very doctrine of the Council of Trent, Christ, when setting up the Eucharistic Sacrifice, endeavored to bequeath us the most efficient and concrete way of partaking of the inexhaustible fruits of the Redemption. He, so to speak, put them at our disposal, at the disposal of all men who wanted to make use of them, through the sacraments and the Holy Sacrifice of the Altar. But the fact that not all men would lend their necessary personal cooperation explains Jesus Christ's words, according to the Gospel, when he set up the Holy Sacrifice: "... [I]t will be shed for you and for *many* [not for *everybody*], so that sins may be forgiven." Luther was logical in denying the necessity of the Holy Sacrifice, since he believed Christ's redemption alone saved us. This is the doctrine of *faith without works*. But against this Lutheran doctrine we have the infallible doctrine of Trent. I shall not quote its canons but rather the Catechism of Saint Pius V, also called that of the Council of Trent, because its publication started at this ecumenical council. All or most of the Conciliar Fathers of Trent helped write it, three of them summarized it, and a decree of this Council ordered it published, though leaving it in the hands of the high Pontiff. It is also called the Roman Catechism, for it was named so by Pope Clement XIII. This Catechism was solemnly acknowledged by another ecumenical council, Vatican I.

THE FORM OF CONSECRATION SAID IN THE TRIDENTINE MASS

Hic est enim Calix Sanguinis Mei, novi et aeterni Testamenti,

Mysterium Fidei,

qui pro vobis et pro Multis effundetur in remissionem pecatorum.

For this is the cup of my blood, the blood of the new and everlasting testament, the Mystery of Faith, which will be shed for you and for *many*, so that sins may be forgiven.

In this form of consecration of the chalice, that will not be found in the vernacular translation of the *Novus Ordo Missae*, the distinction between the Sacrifice of the Cross and the Sacrifice of the Altar according to Christ's design, that is between the dogma of the Redemption and the dogma of Salvation appears clearly. Christ alone makes the Redemption; that is why He died for *all* men, giving us all the possibility of making use of this redemption, while we attain salvation by joining our freedom to the divine grace. That is why not *everybody*, but *many* are the ones who are saved.

Following is additional material taken from the Tridentine Mass:

> In consequence, it must be believed that this (the form) is included in the following words: *"This, then, is the cup of My blood, the blood of the new and everlasting covenant, Mystery of Faith, which will be shed for you and for many, so that sins may be forgiven."* Many of these words have been taken out of the Holy Writ, and many of them kept in the Church by apostolic tradition. The words, *"This is my cup,"* are to be found in Saint Luke and the apostle Paul; as for the words, *"of my blood,"* or, *"my blood of the new testament, which will be shed for you and for many, so that sins may be forgiven,"* some were written by Saint John and others by Saint Matthew, but the words *"everlasting"* and *"Mystery of Faith"* have been taught to us by Holy Tradition, which is the interpreter and defender of Catholic truth.
>
> And nobody may doubt regarding this form, taking into account what was said about the consecratory form used as to the bread. For it is evident that the form used for this element is included in the words that express that the substance of the wine is contained in the Lord's blood. Since those words are clear, it is evident, then, that no other form may be determined. For in addition, they refer to certain admirable fruits of the blood shed in the Lord's Passion that most especially concern this sacrament. The first one is the entrance into the eternal heritage, which comes to us through the right of the new and everlasting covenant. The second one is the possibility of justification through the Mystery of Faith, for God proposed Jesus Christ as *a propitiatory victim, by virtue of His Blood, by means of the faith . . . so that He be the just and He who justifies those who live by the faith of Jesus Christ.* The third one is the forgiveness of sins.
>
> But since these very words of consecration are full of mysteries and very much concern our subject, it is convenient to study them attentively. The words *"This, then, is the cup of my blood"* must be understood as follows: *This is My blood* contained in this chalice. It is right and opportune to mention the cup with reference to the believers' beverage. For it could not be understood that this blood were exactly a beverage if it were not contained in a cup, Then, *"of the new and everlasting testament,"* this phrase was certainly added so that we may

understand that the blood of our Lord Jesus Christ is not figuratively given to all men, as in the Old Testament (for in the apostle's letter to the Hebrews we can read that that testament could not have been consecrated without blood), but really and truly, as pertains to the New Testament. Thus, the apostle said: *"For this Christ is the mediator of a new testament, so that, through His death, those whom God has called, receive the everlasting heritage."* The word "everlasting" refers to the everlasting heritage that belongs to us *dejure*, because of the death of the eternal testator, Christ Our Lord.

The words that follow *"Mystery of Faith"* are not opposite to the reality of this sacrament; on the contrary, they mean that what is so covered and far from the sense of sight must be firmly believed. But the meaning of these words here is different from the one they have when applied to Baptism. One says "Mystery of Faith" because through faith we get to see Christ's blood under cover of the species of wine. We, the Latin Church, are right in calling Baptism the Sacrament of Faith, and Greeks the Mystery of Faith, for it comprises the whole profession of Christian faith. On different grounds, we also call the Lord's blood "Mystery of Faith," because human reason finds it extremely difficult and troublesome to believe that Christ Our Lord, God's real Son and, at the same time God and man, suffered for us, His death manifesting itself through the Blood Sacrament.

That is why, more properly here than in the consecration of the body, the Lord's Passion is recalled through the following words: *". . . that will be shed so that sins may be forgiven."* For blood, separately consecrated, has much more strength and efficacy to represent in our minds Our Lord's Passion and death and the way He suffered.

As to the accompanying words: *"For you"* and *"for many,"* the first were taken out of Saint Luke, and the others out of Saint Matthew, but the Holy Church, under the guidance of God's Spirit, united them. And they are quite appropriate to manifest the Passion's *fruit and advantages,* for, as to the value of the Passion, one has to avow that the Savior shed His blood for *everybody's* salvation (this is the dogma of Redemption). If, however, we take into account the fruit all men would receive therefrom (this is the dogma of Salvation), we will easily understand that its usefulness does not reach "everybody," but only "many." Then, when he said *"for you,"* he meant either those present or the chosen ones among the Jewish people, such as his disciples, save Judas, with whom he was talking. When he said, *"for many people,"* he wanted us to understand the rest of the chosen ones of the Jews and Gentiles. Quite wisely, then, the Savior did not say *"for everybody,"* for he was talking just about the *fruits* of his Passion, which produces *fruits of salvation only for the chosen ones.* The apostle's words refer to this: *"Christ was once offered to bear the sins of many"* (Heb. 9:28); so did the Lord's, according to Saint John: *"I pray for them [now]: I pray not for the world, but for them which thou hast given me, for they are*

Our Return to the Eucharistic Congress

thine" (John 17:9).

The above words from the Tridentine Catechism, the faithful and clear expression of the dogmatic doctrine of the Council of Trent, give us the translation into the vernacular languages of the consecration of the chalice that we find as follows:

> *Take this, all of you, and drink from it: For this is the cup of My blood, the blood of the new and everlasting covenant, which will be shed for you and for all men so that sins may be forgiven.*

This contains a fraudulent adulteration, not merely grammatical but doctrinal and dogmatic, which confuses the dogma of Redemption *(Christ died for everyone)* and the dogma of Salvation *(not everyone receives the fruits of the Redemption)*, just as Protestants do. Since the Mass, the Eucharistic Sacrifice, was specifically set up by Christ in order that we might participate in the fruits of His Passion, and since not *all* but only *many* will avail themselves of the fruits of the Redemption, for the others fail to use the means of Salvation instituted by Jesus Christ, we cannot accept any form inspired by fake "ecumenism" or the Protestant doctrine of salvation through faith without works which, contrary to Christ's doctrine, hints that the redeeming fruits of the Eucharistic Sacrifice belong to *all men*. If we contend that such words mean Christ's redemption on the cross, then we would have to deny that the Mass is an actual and true sacrifice but at best, an anological sacrifice of praise and thanksgiving, since the Redemption has already been *consummated* at Calvary. Consummated, but not applied; to apply it, Christ set up the Sacraments of the Holy Sacrifice and the Altar to be consummated for *everybody*, but applied only to *many*.

We have spent much time commenting on Cardinal Lercaro's specially-made theatrical liturgy of the innovative Congress of Bogotá. This is a most important feature of the New Montinian Church we could not lay aside. Now let us focus our attention to the activity displayed during the preparation of the Congress of Bogotá and the subsequent LAMEC meeting at Medellín by Fr. Pedro Arrupe, Provost General of the Society of Jesus. From this we will be able to better understand the socio-economic, socio-political, and socio-religious aspects of the program of the 39th Eucharistic Congress where deliberately, as we have said before, very little was said about the Eucharist, *but much about revolution, violence, and change of structures.* We love the Society and have always loved it, but we mean Saint Ignatius' Society, not this hideous deformity that has been engendered for a long time and now circulates all over the world with the *Imprimi potest* protection and most active solicitude of Father General Fr. Pedro Arrupe.

Chapter XIV

FATHER ARRUPE AND THE JESUITS AT THE EUCHARISTIC CONGRESS IN BOGOTÁ, AND THEIR ROLE IN THE SUBVERSION OF LATIN AMERICA

No doubt one of the phenomena that has especially surprised and impressed all Catholic and non-Catholic observers who have eyes and do not close them to reality even though it be sad and painful, consists of the spectacular, demolishing, and to me, incomprehensible changes that have occurred over the past few years in one of the most renowned and meritorious religious orders, the Society of Jesus. It appears as though, having forgotten the counter-Reformation fight, their most noble mottoes, "to the greater glory of God," and "the inner law of charity that the Holy Ghost writes and prints in every heart," as well as the very Ignatian rules and spirit, the new Jesuits, have become not one of the instruments, but *the* most efficacious and efficient instrument of the socio-economic, socio-political, socio-moral, and socio-religious "revolution" that has overturned our world. Please be reminded that I am not speaking about the old, marginated Jesuits who impotently cry out their tragedy, and who are "exclusively dedicated" to the *"apostolate of social justice,"* as their General himself said.

This is no local or circumstantial phenomenon which affects isolated Jesuits. It is a world process, programmed, led, and fostered by the Father General and all the heads of the Order. It seems that Fr. Arrupe, the Provost General of the Society of Jesus, and his assistant advisors follow directions coming from above, which they use to justify the unheard-of changes that are adulterating the work of Ignatius of Loyola before their own consciences and before all the members of their Society. My suspicion was supported by a conversation I had at Rome with Fr. Arrupe in his very room, not long ago. Using my characteristic clearness and frankness, and my rights as a trainee of the Jesuits for more than thirty years, during which time I gave up the best part of my life to God's service within the Society, and taking into account Fr. Arrupe's position as successor of Saint Ignatius, I stated the sad condition of the present Society—divided, secularized, and absolutely turned aside from the literal meaning and spirit of its constitution. Father Arrupe listened to me with evident quietness and, let me say, benevolence. Then he asked me: "What can I do?" The Father General did not know what to do! At the end, he very graciously gave me a medal and a picture of himself. On the medal and in the picture, Fr. Arrupe is kneeling before Paul VI, who is blessing him. This photograph and medal appeared to me as a complete answer and the very justification that the Jesuit superiors use to defend their administration: *"The Pope wants it; the Pope orders and blesses it; and we, by virtue of our special oath of obedience to the Pope, must obey."*

There is still more evidence supporting this interpretation of mine. Not long ago, I talked with a relative of Fr. Enrique Maza, the Jesuit who conducts subversion in Mexico. We spoke about the sad case of Fr. Felipe Parinas, still a Father, despite his dispensation, and who by now has a son whom he named John Ernest, *John* after the Pope of Tolerance and *Ernest* after "Ché" Guevara. Enrique's relative agreed with me in regretting and censoring Felipe's cynicism, with which he wanted to conceal his infidelity. I took the opportunity of our chat to let Enrique's relative know what many people think about Enrique's ultra-radical progressivist mood. He is following, I said, the same path that Fr. Pardinas did. My interlocutor agreed with my sad augury and prognostication that Enrique was following the path that had led Felipe not only to marriage but to his new and strange "experiences" of Christ. However, the common blood finally reacted and the person with whom I was speaking tried to defend Enrique, contending he was just obeying orders he had received from the Father Provincial.

"What are you saying, Madam?" asked I, disturbed. "Do you mean the Father Provincial not only conceals, but authorized and orders Enrique to follow this path?"

"That is correct!" answered that respectable lady. "The Father Provincial told Enrique to follow such a path and that he would support him."

I suspected so! Given the vigilance and censorship that has always existed in the Society, continuous defiance is just impossible, especially concerning such public things as Felipe's and Enrique's speeches over television and their writings in journals and magazines. It would be childish to think that the superiors, engaged in their most high duty of fulfilling orders from above, lack the time to get to know this rubbish that scandalized and continues to scandalize all of Mexico. The consequence, then, is simply terrible: it is the superiors of this modern "official" Society who support and disseminate world subversion, in which Pardinas and Maza are but mere suitable instruments.

"But," our readers might ask, "who is Fr. Arrupe?" We will give a summary of his background. Pedro Arrupe was born in Bilbao, Spain, on November 14, 1907. His father was a most famous propagandist of Saint Ignatius Loyola's Exercises. Every year he recruited a team of men from his acquaintances in Bilbao who gathered at Loyola during Holy Week. One may suppose the idea of giving that region a Catholic newspaper, today known as *Northern Gazette (La Gaceta del Norte)* came from one of these teams, specifically, that of 1901. Mr. Arrupe was one of the co-founders of said newspaper.

Pedro Arrupe studied at the Colegio de los Escolapios for six years (1916-1922). From 1918 on he was a member of the Marian congregation of said city. He soon became a member of the governing body, first as head of the dramatic section, and then as a vice-prefect. The magazine *Flowers and Fruits* recorded his first contributions.

In 1922 he moved to Madrid to study medicine at the university, but on January 14, 1927, he interrupted his study of medicine to join the Society of Jesus, entering the Loyola novitiate. He was studying philosophy at Oña, when the decree of dissolution of the Society in Spain in February of 1931 caused the educational centers of the order to move abroad, in this case to Marneffe, Belgium. Without getting his master's degree, he began his theological study at Valkenburg, Holland, where, under similar circumstances, the Theological School of the Province of Lower Germany was located. He was ordained a priest at Marneffe in 1936, but he still lacked one year of theology which he took at St. Mary's in Missouri, U.S.A. He spent one summer of initiation into the sacerdotal ministry in Mexico, and went back to the United States for his third probation in Cleveland, Ohio. He then devoted three more months to the ministry, this time in New York among the Spanish-speaking population. On October 15, 1938, he arrived in Japan.

After an indispensable period of learning the language at Tokyo, he spent several months working in a social project at Sophia University. In 1940 he became a missionary and pastor at Yamagushi, where he baptized the man who would later become the first professed member of the Jesuit province of Japan. During wartime he had to spend some months in jail "on security grounds." From 1942 to 1954, he was vice-rector and master of novices, then vice-provincial and, from October 18, 1958 on, the first provincial of the newly created province of Japan. He was master of novices when the atomic bomb exploded over Hiroshima. Finally, on May 22, 1965, he was appointed General Provost of the Society of Jesus, during the already agitated times of the last ecumenical council. Now, he is also the President of the Confederation of Religious Communities.

What about Fr. Arrupe's thought? Let us begin with his statements about the attitude of Jesuits regarding *Humanae Vitae* as depicted by the newspaper *El Tiempo* of Bogotá, on August 23, 1968:

> There is no problem in accepting the Pontifical document, for *faithfulness to the Pope is precisely one of the essential duties of the Society of Jesus*. I consider that this encyclical contains the authentic papal Magisterium, although the Pope avoided speaking *ex cathedra* about this subject. This encyclical has to be studied carefully and responsibly. It contains very important and profound

anthropological concepts. The Pope's guidelines cannot be discovered through an oblique, cursory reading. One single reading is not enough, and nobody must hasten to comment on it without previous reflection. It is the point of departure to delve deeply into integral anthropology. The Holy Father has provided energetic and clear guidelines.

Father Arrupe's obscure terminology is the complicated, sophisticated, and confused language of today's progressivism. What has anthropology, the science of man, to do with the natural law, the divine law, the science of God? Was, perhaps, the papal encyclical addressed to the scientists and the experts in anthropology? Or is it, rather, a document of the Church's Magisterium in which the Pope expounds to all believers the certain, safe, most clear doctrine arising from the divine law? In such a delicate subject there is no place for ambiguity or philosophical disquietude requiring metaphysical, physical, or moral analysis on the part of the poor people to whom the encyclical was supposed to have been addressed.

But, according to the Society's General, "The Pope's guidelines cannot be discovered through an oblique, cursory reading" [of the encyclical]. What does one *need* to catch Paul VI's thought? Perhaps anthropological training that allows us to find the *licet* within the *non licet*, affirmation within denial? In Fr. Arrupe's integral anthropology it seems possible to adjust the prohibition of contraceptives to tolerance thereof, in cases of human conflicts of opposing duties. Now we understand the rebellion of so many episcopal conferences and the Pontiff's benevolent tolerance.

The journalists, the magnates of the fourth estate, posed Fr. Arrupe another question upon his arrival at Bogotá in the Pope's airplane: "What do you think about the socializing tendencies to be noticed in a goodly part of the clergy?" Fr. Arrupe, whom *The Times* from London considers a compromiser rather than a pacifier, began with the distinction between thesis and persons. This is a very non-committal political attitude and, therefore, very suitable for a General of the Society of Jesus:

> I dare not judge persons, for there are always subjective factors in their behavior that we do not know and which prevent us from issuing opinions; nevertheless, the Church may not accept violence. No doubt some socio-economic conditions cannot be accepted; they have to change. But this may not lead to succumbing to the temptation of violent revolution which not only destroys, but also fails to provide a building program.

Father Arrupe defends himself before anybody accuses him; he does not want to judge persons, because in Colombia by then, the sinister ghost of Camilo Torres seemed to project itself over the capital, decked out for the

Congress. But neither could he join the side of the exploiting oligarchy, which he had previously abandoned at the famous meeting of Rio de Janeiro and in the official documents he had written as Provost General of the Society of Jesus. That is why he says: "No doubt some socio-economic conditions cannot be accepted; they have to change." This thesis is brilliant, provided the hypothesis is right. We were in America, in the afflicted Third World, in the underdeveloped countries. Though too late, this situation was publicly and officially acknowledged by the Father General and the Latin American Provincial Fathers. It took the Jesuits too long to diagnose the evil and apply the urgently-needed remedy. Most necessary were the frequent and spectacular trips of the indefatigable Father Lombardi in order that Rome, insensible Rome, the Vatican, and the General's curia of the renowned Saint Ignatius' militia could wake up to the reality of the dreadful tragedy of millions of human beings dying from famine each year due to the slavery imposed by the selfish oligarchies, among which stood the members of the high clergy.

After the diagnosis that coincided perfectly with the radical thesis of *Populorum Progressio*, it was necessary to apply the remedy: a revolution and audacious change of structures, but without violence, "which not only destroys, but also fails to provide a building program." This was a wise answer which, without committing itself, insinuates the indispensable remedy! Father Arrupe continues:

> ... [C]ontact between oppressors and oppressed, to amend all that has to be amended. This reform is a duty of conscience. At any rate, the real solution must carry a building program. For actually, violent revolution poses a dilemma: either it destroys everything without building anything, or it simply provokes another violent reaction that prevents building."

But I wonder: What kind of contact does the Father General propose? Perhaps there is no contact between "oppressors" and "oppressed" as he calls them. We guess Fr. Arrupe wants a confrontation of conscience, for he discards violence. This confrontation would presuppose a certain intellectual, moral, and cultural equality between ruling and ruled classes, which he prejudges as "oppressors" and "oppressed" which, unfortunately, is not the case. Then in the presence of the oppressors' institutional violence, there is no way except guerilla violence on the part of the oppressed. And Fr. Arrupe seemed to prudently hint this when he said:

> I believe that the Latin American condition has to change. I insist I cannot judge Camilo Torres, because I do not know the subjective reasons that caused him to act as he did. What I do know is that violence cannot be admitted under any circumstances.

The Montinian Church

The above seems to be a categorical answer which, however, is very ambiguous. The Latin American situation has to change; that is certain. He cannot judge Camilo Torres, because he does not know the subjective reasons that caused him to act as he did. Then, according to Fr. Arrupe, there can be subjective reasons that exculpate Camilo Torres Restrepo's violence. Furthermore, can there be any nobler goal than pursuing a social design such as the Father General proclaimed? If the Latin American condition has to change and there is no remedy except violent revolution, it follows that violence is not only necessary, but legitimate. His last phrase is superfluous: "... violence cannot be admitted under any circumstances." It is dangerous to walk along on a loose rope!

Then the journalists posed another spiny problem to Fr. Arrupe, perhaps more spiny than the social problem they had mentioned before:

> What will the Jesuits' attitude be with respect to the conflict between traditionalists and progressivists?

This question shows that there are two increasingly opposing parties within the Church. There are two mentalities, two antagonistic positions around vital points, that astonish the world with good cause. These are the pre-Conciliar Church and the post-Conciliar Church. Those who strive to identify both positions fail to understand them in depth.

Father Arrupe answered this question:

> The Society of Jesus is trying to make a synthesis, for the Church needs both currents, that of the elders' somewhat traditionalist experience, and the dynamism and ardor of the young, who are usually progressivists. The solution of this conflict is, once again, dialogue. Both sectors have to acknowledge their own limitations, for out of dialogue always arises mutual understanding, at the very least. Dialogue brings about mutual respect which is the best course for the Church. You know that, if a locomotive has no tracks, it loses control and crashes, but if a rail is set up, it can use all its might and run at full speed without danger of crashing. The locomotive consists of zealous youngsters, and it belongs to the others to set up the rail. They need each other, for they are complementary.

This is plain dialectics, the dialectics of age: the elders are the thesis, the young the antithesis. The Society searches for the synthesis. The way is dialogue. The Father General's answer skillfully avoids the stated problem, which is not a problem of age but of ideology. Some young members of the Society think as traditionalists do, in accordance with the Church's old and Holy Tradition as well as the ancient rules that have bettered Saint Ignatius' institute. There are also old Jesuits who, inexplicably, think as progressivists do. They have betrayed what they had learned for so many years, perhaps in order to keep their privileged status and administrative position even if it be in the kitchen. Better to be the head of a mouse than the tail of a lion!

Old people have limitations, but I believe that generally speaking, they are less important than those of young people, notwithstanding the latter's ardor. Wisdom acquired through experience can be provided only by age, and, as to juvenile ardor, swift and non-subdued passions often darken the very light of reason.

There is a profound division in the Society of Jesus. It has caused the most respectable Fathers of Spain and other places to ask Fr. Arrupe and even the Pope for separation between those who keep on thinking as Saint Ignatius taught them, and those who have accommodated to the new mentality and freedom of Fr. Arrupe's "aggiornated" Society. How could dialogue be possible between those who fulfill yesterday's regulations and the "new wave" of licentious Jesuits? Both groups live together, but are mutually alien. In the past, the enemies of the Society used to say the Jesuits entered the Society without meeting each other, lived without loving each other, and died without weeping over each other's death. Such a saying was slanderous with respect to the true and holy Society, but I believe that presently, the avant-garde progressivists at the bottom of their hearts look down upon old people, who, they feel, hinder their aspiration of maintaining a life adapted to the modern world's demands. Even the Spiritual Exercises written by St. Ignatius have been amended by the innovators!

Poor, marginal old people, illustrious saintly men, whose edifying regular observance, wisdom, and apostolic work enhanced the Society of yore and supported St. Ignatius' work! Now, their labor is over, and "... it belongs to [them] to set up the rail" for those sweeping and uncontrollable locomotives to keep on destroying what their predecessors in the Order had built up.

"Why is it," the journalists asked Fr. Arrupe afterwards, "that young priests are so impatient?" Father Arrupe replied:

> Because young people feel the world is changing, and they are right, for *structures and mentalities have to be changed.* But such change is, to a young priest, deeper, precisely because his vocation causes him to live everything more intensely.

So speaks progressivism whose main contention is the change and metamorphosis of the world. The change of mentality Fr. Arrupe mentions is a change of faith. Never did the Gospel or the Catholic Tradition teach that the Church, the religious life, the sanctity and the salvation of souls were functions of the world. Saint Ignatius taught just the opposite. He used the following words to summarize what his institute was: "The Society asks the world for crucified men for whom the world itself is crucified." Like all progressivists, Fr. Arrupe affirms that the *change of structures* is necessary, urgent, undeferrable, but he does not say what structures need change, nor which ones will be substituted for the old structures that will be removed by those young people whose vocation causes them to live so intensely. Young Jesuits live so intensely that an increasing number of them quit the Order either because in their disappointment, they fail to find the way of saving and sanctifying themselves, or because an intense and quick *aggiornamento* makes them fall into unforeseeable abysses from which the old regular obedience would have saved them! In Spain, the Order's birthplace, the novitiates have been closed due to lack of vocations. Vocation to religious life is no call to demagoguery, license, or organization of student conflicts, but a call to give up oneself to God's service and to work for the salvation of souls.

Father Arrupe still treated another most important point in his press conference. Guilefully, for they knew his thought in advance, the journalists asked him what he thought about Fr. Teilhard de Chardin. He replied as follows:

> No doubt Chardin is a great son of the Society of Jesus and one of the most influential men within and without Catholicism. But it must be borne in mind that Chardin was no theologian, and therefore, some expressions of his, while valid as scientific terminology, may be somewhat inaccurate from the theological viewpoint. Chardin's theses form a modern and attractive projection of very deep ideas, but said ideas can be argued when operating in a field that is not theirs.

To the most reverend Father General of today's Jesuits, Fr. Pierre Teilhard de Chardin is *a great son of the Society,* notwithstanding his most grave and undeniable errors against revealed doctrine, its very theodicy, and his experiences with women, to which he himself bore witness and verified his well-known relations with his female confidants and co-workers. Former superiors of the Society became obliged to prohibit the publication of his writings, which had been condemned by the Holy Office, not only once, but several times. Teilhard pretended to obey, but, cunning as he was, he found a way to avoid prohibition and censorship and published his works, which merited all praise and recommendation from Fr. Pedro Arrupe, more valuable than the *imprimi potest.* Now the net result is that the top ideologist of progressivism is none other than "a great son of the Society." He was, added Fr. Arrupe, "one of the most influential men within and without Catholicism." The Provost General fails to disclose what kind of influence this was, although out of the context of his statements it can be clearly inferred that such influence was helpful and enlightening for mankind. Finally we have found the lost link, not by means of

Diogenes' lantern, but by the illuminated mind of this portentous Jesuit who, against faith and reason, has been able to prove integral evolutionism, imminent pantheism, the mysterious identification of life and non-life, and of spirit and matter. Using his supreme authority, Fr. Arrupe authorizes and blesses Teilhard's work, aimed at making a most profound amendment to old Christianity "from within," since Christianity, during its two-thousand-year existence, had lost its strength and message for the modern world.

". . . [I]t must be borne in mind that Chardin was no theologian. . . ." Maybe be didn't study his theology before being ordained as a priest? How could his superiors let him be ordained if they were certain he was deeply ignorant about divine science? Moreover they ought to have been aware of his gross errors, despite their concealment under scientific or poetic terminology. Father Arrupe explains this apparent paradox: *". . . therefore, some expressions of his, while valid as scientific terminology, may be somewhat inaccurate from the theological viewpoint."* Not "somewhat inaccurate," Fr. Arrupe, but very inaccurate and absolutely opposite to natural and dogmatic theology! They are incompatible with the idea of a transcendent and personal God, with creation (which Teilhard believed did not exist), with the soul's spirituality, and many other fundamental truths of natural and supernatural religion. *Teilhard's cosmic Christ is not the Vatican's Christ.*

I regret very much that a Provost General of the illustrious Society of Jesus appears as justifying opposition between real theology and real science, between faith and reason, e.g., "some expressions of his, while valid as scientific terminology, may be somewhat inaccurate from the theological viewpoint." The above premises now help me understand the ideological confusion prevailing among the Society's many sages as well as the dreadful instability of its new theologians, who teach divine science and other ecclesiastical subjects at the educational centers of the Order.

"Chardin's theses," insists Fr. Arrupe, "form a modern and attractive projection of very deep ideas, but said ideas can be argued when operating in a field that is not theirs." This means that such deep ideas, modern and attractively projected, are true, categorical, and irrefutable from the scientific standpoint, although in the theological field, they turn out to be not only disputable, but false. Said opposition turns theology into a myth and an absurdity that cannot resist scientific analysis.

The Jesuit's Father General was posed yet another question by the foreign journalists who were visiting Colombia at the time of the Congress. To quote:

> What might the link be between the Pope's visit and the working up of a concrete doctrine of the Church designed to solve the problem of underdevelopment?

The Montinian Church

Perhaps no one is better qualified than Fr. Arrupe to answer this disquieting question that was circulating in Bogotá prior to the Pontiff's arrival. He enjoys Paul VI's full confidence and in addition, had traveled to Colombia with the Pope in the latter's own aircraft. But the Father General was able to answer without exposing his own position, or the Pope's. His answer could be interpreted both ways, thus calming some and satisfying others:

> About the second point, I just don't know. I feel the Pope's visit will be a great inspiration for Latin America. The Holy Father's presence can give a charismatic and spiritual impulse to the tasks Latin America wants to perform. But I warn you, the solution will not be a technical and concrete one, for this is not the Holy Father's mission. It is possible that, besides what the Pope will say during these days in his speeches, homilies, and even encyclicals, the Holy Father may provide some orientation later on.

To subversives, who hoped the Pontiff's speeches would endorse guerilla warfare, the Father General's words would be encouraging: "... the Pope's visit will be a great inspiration for Latin America ... [and] can give a charismatic and spiritual impulse to the tasks Latin America wants to perform." In order to comprehend the hidden meaning of these words, we ought to define some terms this Father uses, namely, "inspiration," "charismatic and spiritual impulse," "tasks Latin America wants to perform." All this terminology sounds very much like that of the IDOC, the charismatic and prophetic Church, which wants to take the place of the institutional Church in order to pave the way for socializing Communism or Communizing socialism.

Father Arrupe seems to support said hope with the words with which he ended his answer:

> It is possible that, besides what the Pope will say during these days in his speeches, homilies, and even encyclicals, the Holy Father may provide some orientation *later on*." [italics added].

It is *as though* he were saying:

> Take it easy; things will run as you wish. The Pope has some surprises in store for us, but this Congress cannot be as explicit as he would like. The orientation for the tasks Latin America wants to perform will come *later on*.

To those who feared that Paul VI's words could be interpreted by the guerillas and their allies as approval and apostolic blessing of subversion, Fr. Arrupe says: "... [T]he solution will not be a technical and concrete one, for this is not the Holy Father's mission." Again, this is plain dialectics; the thesis is that the Pope approves the tasks, but the antithesis is that his solution will not be technical, or concrete; as to the synthesis, it will come *later on*.

But to catch the Father General's thought about these thorny issues, one has to know some documents unknown to many people and, therefore, worth quoting. Public opinion has applied the term, "The Black Pope's Social Encyclical" to three documents of his, namely, a letter addressed to the superiors of Latin America, the statutes of the Society's Centers for Research and Social Action (CRSA) and a letter to all Jesuits working in these Centers. To said documents, I shall add the letter he addressed to the North American Jesuits regarding the black people's racial problem in the United States. The following is the first of such documents:

To the Senior Superiors of Latin America

As everybody knows, from July 25-29, 1966, the first meeting of the Latin American Centers for Research and Social Action (CRSA) was held in Lima and attended by the priest-directors and some priests who were members of the CRSA. I attached so much importance to this congress, that I wanted it to be celebrated despite the many obstacles and difficulties we had to face. I did not hesitate to have myself accompanied by the two assistant priests for Latin America and also decided that the assistant Father for Germany and a Father from the Institute of Social Sciences of Gregorian University should attend the gathering, to give the discussion a wider basis and more extensive outlook. The aim of said meeting was to have the priests meet each other, jointly analyze what had been done so far, create a common consciousness of the social problems and their feasible solutions, and, as a result of their work, hand in their findings and answers to me.

Here we have, then, the most reverend Father General of the Society of Jesus acting as top commander, gathering the senior officers of an intercontinental organization in order to have them meet each other, analyse what had been done so far, and create *a common consciousness* of the *social* problems and their feasible solutions. He keeps the final approval of the findings of the congress for himself.

Two documents were compiled by the participants and sent to the Father General. The first one contained the conclusions of the congress. The second one, entitled: "The Society's Official Position with Respect to the Latin American Social Conflict," asked the Father General for "a statement that went beyond the documents designed for our [Society members'] exclusive use." Both documents "were sent to the Provincial Fathers and to some experts, so that they could give the Father General their opinions." Once the answers were received and studied, the assistants consulted, and finally the Lord's light asked,

The Montinian Church

Fr. Arrupe decided to enact the statutes of the CRSA of Latin America, which would stand from then on.

> The foreword of the statutes contains an extensive selection of texts almost literally taken out of the Vatican Council *(Gaudium et Spes)*, which stress the *need for a mental and structural reform,* [italics added], designed to curb the scandal of excessive economic and social inequality. Since said inequality is not limited to mere monetary compensation for one's work, it cannot be eliminated by bare monetary increments of such retribution, for instance wage increases. Father Janssens, the Belgian who preceded Fr. Arrupe as General, did not hesitate to expose them on the whole as *"repugnans evangelio"* (contrary to the Gospel) and *"intolerabilis"* (unbearable). The Council, in turn, calls them: "contrary to justice, fairness, human dignity, and social peace."[5]

Mental and structural change! This is the synthesis and imperious prerequisite for all the reforms introduced by the Council and the post-Council, which have provoked a complete revolution in the Church. This change is indispensable to eliminate human inequality. "Ultimately," says Vatican II, "the new society we are longing for is merely a society wherein each individual could increasingly become a human person. In other words, not that he *have* more, but *be* more" (*Gaudium et Spes,* 35).

Father Arrupe is more explicit:

> Social justice is not accomplished merely by occasional alms or soothing wage increases. A social order that prevents the exercise of self-initiative and responsibility is unjust to human dignity, even though such social order grant people a just and equitable monetary compensation.

We feel the above words by the Council and Fr. Arrupe are absolutely demagogic, absurd, and utopic. The equality they seek sounds like the echo of the *equality* proclaimed by the French Revolution, which could be attained only by the leaders, those who controlled power, but never by the enslaved crowds. No doubt the system of fair wages the Church pointed out to businessmen as a duty of conscience used to give the best qualified workers, employees, and peasants who took advantage of it, legitimate opportunities to gradually improve their personal and domestic condition. We have mentioned it before, that human inequality does not always arise from injustice, oppression, or abuse on the part of the ruling classes but from wounded human nature itself. What does Fr. Janssens want? What does Fr. Arrupe and the post-Conciliar mentality suggest to shatter economic and social conformity and to remedy the dangerous, unbalanced conditions that consume society and the human personality?

To repeat from the above, "A social order that prevents the exercise of self-initiative and responsibility," the Jesuits' Provost General categorically affirms, "is unjust to human dignity, even though such social order grant people a just and equitable monetary compensation." This solution, for the last two Generals of the Society, "is unbearable and opposite to the Gospel." The Council, in turn, calls it "contrary to justice, fairness, human dignity, and social peace."

Any just social order must render possible the exercise of self-initiative and responsibility. But, let me ask: do all men have self-initiative and a deep sense of responsibility? I am not referring just to people in the process of becoming integrated into a culture, but even to people more homogeneously civilized. Now then, if not all men have self-initiative and real responsibility, how is it possible for them to give what they do not have? Could we even imagine such an imaginary equality?

When asked who the active agents are who would build up the new society, according to Alfonso Carmín (a familiar name to most exponents of the Church's social doctrine), Fr. Arrupe rejects all *paternalistic* options in favor of entrusting the reconstructive work of the "revolution from above" to the so-called marginal classes. It is time to put our civilization's most complicated machinery into the proletariat's calloused hands, so that workers and peasants may successfully lead the boat of society to its right destination. In Fr. Arrupe's words:

> Remodeling the society according to a fairer, more equitable and human pattern affects mostly the poor, the workers, the peasants, and the social classes forcibly kept outside of society without any possibility of adequately enjoying its goods and services and participating in its decisions, which ought not to be taken without their active presence, precisely because such decisions affect most directly these same poor and neglected people. Nobody must substitute for them in dictating the basic decisions concerning their own interests, not even with the excuse of doing it better than they.

I cannot understand what Fr. Arrupe and his illustrious Society of Jesus have to do with the human and secular work of *"remodeling"* the social, economic and political features of society. Neither do I understand what the relation might be between secular and human remodeling of the society, and the duties with which the religious life charges Jesuits according to the constitution Saint Ignatius gave them, of bringing about the primary and essential goal of their vocation. This goal is, in the words of the Order's saintly founder: "Not only to strive towards the salvation and sanctification of one's own soul, with the aid of divine grace, but, by means of said grace, also to tend to the salvation and sanctification of one's neighbor." I guess that Fr. Arrupe, his advisors, and assistants have run off the track and, concerned for what does not belong to

The Montinian Church

them, have abandoned the rule of their Order, to the grave detriment of its members. The Father General has realized this and, to avoid jeopardizing himself too much, commits "the poor, the workers, the peasants, the social classes forcibly kept outside of society" to actively search for a drastic solution to this irregular and unbearable situation.

But just to mention such a solution in a letter containing guidelines for the Society's superiors means to assume the entire responsibility for its contents. The Father General's letter is no sociological, economic, or political treatise that can or cannot be followed according to the reader's personal criteria, but a letter with a program of action issued by the Provost General and addressed to all Jesuits, who, by virtue of the oath of obedience, has to awaken, impel, and lead the aforesaid reformist activity of the Society he rules. No doubt Fr. Arrupe relies upon the prestige and enormous influence of the Order within some social segments, accustomed to believe every Jesuit to be a sage and a saint and that, above the Society, there is only the Pope and his *yes-men*.

Is it the poor and indigent who, generally speaking, lack not only intellectual and moral capability, but far-seeing vision for selecting able and adequate means of remodeling society, who must carry on this dangerous and most delicate enterprise "with ... their active presence?" So affirms Fr. Arrupe, who, in a definitively demagogic phrase states that "Nobody must substitute for [the poor and indigent people] in dictating the basic decisions concerning their own interests, not even with the excuse of doing it better than they." This phrase is "consistent with the most pure and up-to-date prophetic denunciation, a denunciation prepared and elaborated according to the style and problems of our historic times," as A.C. Comín tells us, and, moreover, comprises a total program of social subversion of incalculable consequences, of which Fr. Arrupe cannot be unaware. What kind of initiative can those unprepared, indigent, and neglected people provide to remedy their own country's abnormal and unjust social condition, except through violence, guerilla warfare, destruction of others' property, and murder of the hateful oligarchies which, for centuries and without any right, have been violating their rights? There is only one way for the General's rules and suggestions to become a reality, and that is revolution, violent, destructive revolution, even though the victorious will later fall into the hands of even more inhuman and cruel dictatorships.

Indeed Mr. Comín is right in that Fr. Arrupe's letter is "consistent with the most pure and up-to-date prophetic denunciation," in other words, with the prediction of *"materialistic messianism"* and its apocalyptic horsemen who will carry desolation and death everywhere, thus preparing for the Jewish world government, to whom the Father General has subordinated the select militia of Christ's Church. Father Arrupe "unhesitatingly and totally enters the place of danger, that is of the social revolution of the disinherited classes and peoples, denounces conformism, and announces the great hope that this revolution kindles."

In other words, the General's program for all of his sons, especially his Latin American sons, is to arouse the classes that have fallen into a lethargy and to preach the new gospel of social justice, which can and must be brought about only through the poor, neglected, and marginal people's revolution designed to rid our society of improper inequality. In a Church in a state of "diaspora," according to Fr. Karl Rahner (one of the worst Vatican II "experts," if not the worst one, and a very dedicated member of the Society of Jesus), Fr. Arrupe talks about a world in the process of reconstruction into which the Church has to plunge, but, above all, he talks fearlessly, for, to Fr. Arrupe, the ghost of *défaitisme* (defeatism) does not exist.

That is why we question what Fr. Arrupe writes:

> In today's world, the envoy of the Spirit, the apostle, is completely naked. At the level of human values, civilization, culture, technique, education, art, aid, etc., he brings nothing that the world to which he has been sent does not already have in advance and to a degree better than his, while the sole thing that is really his, the announcing of the coming of God's kingdom in Christ the Lord, has no value at all to this world.

This is indeed defeatism, denial of the everlasting life of God's word, which places human achievements before God's work! This is equivalent to ignoring the fact that man has a transcendental mission to fulfill. Even as eternal values surpass temporal values, so this mission of man greatly surpasses the human value that has impressed Fr. Arrupe to the extent of making him lose the vision of life which is given by the first meditation of the Spiritual Exercises, namely, the meditation on the *Principle and Fundamental!*

I take the following from the November, 1970 issue of *Word (Verbo)*, a magazine from Spain:

CATHOLIC-MARXIST DIALOGUE AND THE SO-CALLED THIRD WAY BETWEEN COMMUNISM AND CAPITALISM

Hard upon the heels of a discussion about "Christians and Marxists in the Modern World" between Cardinal Daniélou and the "heterodox" Marxist Roger Garandy, broadcast last May by one of the French television networks, Louis Salleron published an article entitled "The Third Way" *("La troisième voie")*, in *Itineraries (Itineraires)*, No. 145, July-August), in which he commented on both subjects. Below we reproduce the core of said article:

I had expected the Cardinal to stand on the religious field the way

The Montinian Church

Garandy did on the Marxist field. On the contrary, both the movie he presented and his participation in the subsequent discussion concentrated on the social question, and he seemed to clarify the social issue according to Christian guidelines. Practically speaking, the conclusion the average listener could draw was the following: If Communism accepted Christianity, it would be perfect . . . .

He compared Capitalism and Marxism without making any proposal, which means he leaned toward the "Marxist analysis," and could not reply anything when Garandy called his attention to the fact that the Church condemns Communism as "intrinsically evil" while, on the other hand, it condemns only the capitalistic *abuses*. "I would prefer," said Garandy, "that you had condemned the principles of Capitalism and the perversion of Communism."

It was painful or, at least I suffered at the sight of a greatly intelligent and deeply Christian (?) man as Cardinal Daniélou corralled by such questions. I also suffered because, having accepted the presentation of Christianity in its economic and social aspect, which certainly is not the Cardinal's specialty, he was unable to remember that the Christian solution is what the journalist of *The Cross (La Croix)* called the "Third Way."

Ah! I well know why. Above all he does not know the subject well. Secondly, he is evidently convinced Communism has won the game in advance, and the sole issue is to "recover" it, topping it with a Christian sauce that transforms it into *democratic socialism*, the kind of socialism of which everybody dreams, although nobody is able to design even an approximate pattern.

May I point out to the Cardinal, my old friend Daniélou, that the arch of triumph that opens the third way is to be found in the first paragraph of the second chapter of th encyclical *Mater et Magistra*. In vernacular language, it reads as follows:

> *Above all, it must be stressed that the economic world is a creation of the personal initiative of each citizen, in his individual activity or in the bosom of various associations already established for the common good.*

This basic statement radically excludes abolition of private property as the means of production in which, according to Marx, all Communism consists; on the contrary, it includes a most wide diffusion of private property, contracts, associations, and, most generally, free economic activity regulated by the political power, which is the representative of the common welfare, to which the economy must be subordinated.

Father Arrupe and the Jesuits

Such is the Church's social doctrine. Only it can insure justice, freedom, and prosperity, to the extent said goods are attainable. What is left of it, or what is rediscovered of it, explains why the Western countries, despite their vices, are able to provide their people a less unjust, tyrannical, and miserable life than that prevailing in nations submitted to the Communist yoke.

Is the Church's social doctrine endangered? One has to avow it is, according to the French episcopate. But even yesterday it was ratified by John XXIII, and professed today by R. F. Calvez, the eminent Jesuit who knows Marx perfectly and is a French expert in economic affairs.

I cannot understand Mr. Salleron's regret and astonishment at the materialistic and Communistic tendencies of Cardinal Daniélou's words. The latter's very name is suspect, his pre- and post-Conciliar activities are even more suspect, but there is no doubt that His Eminence faithfully follows the supreme directions that inspire and guide his Superior General in the Society of Jesus.

As Provost General of the Society of Jesus, Father Arrupe carries his premises up to their ultimate consequences. In his above-mentioned letter, he decides and proclaims the Society of Jesus' *social reformation*, which purports not only a shameful denial of the Society's entire past, but of the very spirit and constitutions with which Saint Ignatius endowed his sons.

One of the commentators on the Father General's letter said: "To acknowledge that man is no isolated being, but lives within a society, is the necessary basis for the change in structure and mentality which Fr. Arrupe mentions in his letter." That is true, but such doctrine is completely antagonistic with what Saint Ignatius teaches us and upon which Fr. Arrupe and I meditated so many times during the Holy Exercises:

> Man has been created to praise, revere and serve Our Lord God and, through this, save his soul. All other things on earth have been created for man to help him reach his ultimate end. It follows that man has to use these things so far as they help him attain his ultimate end. Therefore it is necessary that we become indifferent to all created things so far as it is permitted and not prohibited to the liberty of our free will, in a manner that we do not want health rather than disease, wealth rather than poverty, honor rather than dishonor, long life rather than short life, and so forth. We must long for and choose only what is more able to lead us to the end for which we have been created.

This is indeed a full concept of life that does not deny the social reality surrounding us, nor the urgent problems our earthly life poses for us, but which puts man, each and every one of us, at the very center of our existence, and lets us see things according to the perfect hierarchy of life's values as ordained by God Himself. What the commentator on Fr. Arrupe's letter affirms is absolutely false: "The more the Christian enters into and commits himself to the socializing needs of the *social body* to which he belongs, the more he becomes perfect." And this commentator adds: "Only this perspective of a 'growing socialization' can help understand the contents of Fr. Arrupe's thought." The commentator is right, but this perspective is neither the perspective of the *principle and fundamental*, nor the Gospel's perspective. Everlasting salvation is the personal end that, above all, man has to pursue in this life. Such is the supreme goal of his existence. Everything else, including his relationship with people surrounding him, no matter the circumstances and his obligations towards them, is subordinated to this ultimate end. Salvation and personal perfection are not a collective, but a very personal business. God did not create us as a heap, but individually. The Provost General, Fr. Arrupe, also says:

> It is undeniable that change of secular structures, as such, belongs to lay people, while our task is rather concentrated in changing mentalities.

The above sentence is ambiguous. It leaves the door open for an eventual intercommunication: Change of structures belongs to lay people; our task is rather concentrated in changing mentalities. "But," Fr. Arrupe wisely adds, "we cannot forget that secular activities themselves are not exclusive of lay people." This means that, whenever necessary or convenient, Jesuits can directly intervene in said "secular activities;" they can take part, for example, in strike committees during student conflicts, and discretely foster the establishment and diffusion of Christian democracy and the leading socialist groups. He also states that mentality and structure are not exclusive realities corresponding to absolutely different subjects, but that they have a point of relative convergence in the sincerely Christian conscience and task.

As a matter of fact, the change of mentality that Fr. Arrupe proclaims concerning Jesuits, if not exclusive of them, has to be reflected into action. Ideas are just like clouds which are condensed above our heads, but finally come down upon earth as a storm. The structure is the fruit and consequence of a mentality, and the mentality gives birth to a structure. Such is the most serious danger of this new theology of revolution and the masses, preached and defined by the Society of Jesus' modern theologians, who, at the cathedras of their universities and schools, have infected the fresh and unprepared minds of youth with destructive principles that are presented to them as the infallible opinions of John XXIII, Paul VI, and Vatican II. Since Jesuits are in charge of the leading educational centers for tomorrow's priests, it is easy to forecast the deviation of the mentality of the new ministers of the Lord and the young

Father Arrupe and the Jesuits

bishops who will progressively occupy vacant sees. In reality we can see it right now: the new mentality has had astonishing manifestations even at the top levels of the ecclesiastical hierarchy, not only among young priests who are unable to preach any other way, but also among bishops, who frequently talk about change of structure and social justice.

In his letter, the Father General also said the following:

> Therefore I encourage the Provincial Fathers to meditate once again on this duty of humanizing and personalizing society and have it clearly understood, even by those of us who do not belong to the C.R.S.A., so that no one may hinder this *apparently less sacerdotal* [italics added] effort, but cooperate with it as much as possible.

Here we have the secret of these spectacular changes we all have seen, not only in the mentalities, but in the baffling activity of modern Jesuits. Ill-understood obedience makes them see God's most holy Will in everything their superiors say. Then many but not all Jesuits received these strange directions that contradict the old principles of the Ignatian ascetics and the Society's theological science as if they were the new doctrine of God's Church. This basic idea of the Father General is to be found in a definitively bold phrase of his: "*My wish is to set up a center for world social promotion beside me.*" [italics added]. For the sake of the Society, the world, and the Church, I hope that Fr. Arrupe's wish never turns out to be a reality.

Father Arrupe's letter is melodramatic in some respects:

> We must avow we have not done our utmost to grant the social the place it deserves in the Society's scale of values. I cannot help recalling Fr. Janssens' eloquent firmness in calling for the Society's *social conscience,* to quote:
>
>> Most of us have been educated in high class families ... only a few have been able to directly know the actual life of workers, laborers, clerks, and low-rank employees hired by private persons or the government. We must get to understand lifelong humiliation, how one feels when finding oneself in the lowest possible condition, ignored or condemned by many, unable to show up publicly because of lack of decent clothing and social education, how it feels to be an instrument of others' wealth while one's daily bread is scarce and one's future never turns out to be safe, how one has to risk one's health, dignity, and honesty in a job that either surpasses or is very much beneath one's strength, what it is like to find oneself unemployed day-after-day and month-after-month, tormented by inactivity and need, unable to educate one's children adequately, but instead, to have them exposed to the dangers of disease, misery and the

street. How one has to weep over many of them who die in childhood due to lack of adequate care, never to enjoy physical or psychical rest worthy of man, when, at the same time, one sees that those who enjoy wealth and even superfluous luxury are able to engage in liberal studies and noble arts, gather honors, and succeed.... Let our brethren discover how many privileged and how many unfortunate people there are in their countries.

Inspired by Fr. Janssens phrases depicting the present inhuman social inequality, as well as by other similar texts of his, I encourage the Provincial Fathers and their advisors to check whether in fact they have objectively hierarchized the urgency of the various apostolic activities in their provinces.

The above absolutely demagogic and incendiary paragraph of the Black Pope's encyclical letter seems to be an attempt to readjust not only the Society but the very order of Providence and man's nature. Maybe the Jesuits feel that they are the trustees of divine Providence to remedy all physical and moral world needs? Have Fr. Arrupe and his predecessor in the administration of the order forgotten these words of the Gospel:

No man can serve two masters: for either he will hate the one, and love the other; or else he will hold to the one, and despise the other. Ye cannot serve God and mammon.

Therefore I say unto you, Take no thought for your life, what ye shall eat, or what ye shall drink; nor yet for your body, what ye shall put on. Is not the life more than meat, and the body than raiment?

Behold the fowls of the air: for they sow not, neither do they reap, nor gather into barns; yet your Heavenly Father feedeth them. Are ye not much better than they?

Which of you by taking thought can add one cubit unto his stature?

And why take ye thought for raiment? Consider the lilies of the field, how they grow; they toil not, neither do they spin.

And yet I say unto you that even Solomon in all his glory was not arrayed like one of these.

Wherefore, if God so clothe the grass of the field, which today is, and tomorrow is cast into the oven, shall He not much more clothe you, O ye of little faith?

Therefore take no thought, saying, "What shall we eat?" or, "What shall we drink?" or, "Wherewith shall we be clothed?"

(For after all these things do the Gentiles seek); for your Heavenly Father knoweth that ye have need for all these things.

But seek ye first the kingdom of God, and His righteousness; and all these things shall be added unto you.

Father Arrupe and the Jesuits

Take therefore no thought for the morrow: for the morrow shall take thought for the things of itself. Sufficient unto the day is the evil thereof. (Matt. 6:24-34).

In the above words of the Gospel, as in many others, we find that God's inscrutable providence has wanted this inequality among men, the way He has also wanted us to use our intelligence to earn our bread through the sweat of our brow. Such inequality would perhaps be meaningless to us were this life the only real one. Even so should we have the right to call God to account? Should we have the right to demand equal distribution of the goods He gives us free? But as Saint Ignatius, perfectly consistent with the Gospel, teaches, all things other than man have been created for man, so that they help him attain his ultimate end. Moreover in the order of divine Providence, one's generous disinterest in material things for charity's sake, and his willing renunciation are more helpful than Fr. Arrupe's material security. That is why Jesus Christ began His beatitudes, which we could call the code of true happiness, with the following words: *"Blessed are the poor in spirit* [not *all* poor; only the 'poor in spirit'] *for theirs is the kingdom of heaven."*

Tell us, Father General, would the charity or justice you seek as the most apostolic and urgent task of the modern Society of Jesus be possible, were it not for the social inequality you condemn? Please also tell us if in the Communized masses, where equality of slavery prevails, have they eliminated poverty, suffering, cold, hardship, tears, injustice, and the privileged classes who oppress those who are below them? Cubans would give up everything, despite what the Papal Nuncio says, to live again in the times of Batista's so-called hateful tyranny!

Were both latest Generals of the Society of Jesus sincere and their accusations accurate, I guess the holy Society's priests and hierarchs ought to give us the example, selling something of what they have (and it is not little!), to give to the poor. Some millions of dollars, not pesos, would help remedy some of the world needs, at least for some time!

The commentator of Fr. Arrupe's letter says:

> Reading the analysis of the situation made by Fr. John Baptist Janssens, we become assailed with doubt concerning the efficacy of texts and directions issued by some ecclesiastical institutions [the Society of Jesus, for instance?]. Perhaps too many recommendations that have had no practical answers have accustomed us to read reform documents coming out of the Church meditatively, but with a good dose of internal inhibition. Presently, in post-Conciliar times, we risk incurring the sin of self-satisfaction, that is, becoming satisfied with a theoretical elaboration of the Conciliar Utopia without checking, as Fr. Arrupe indicates, "whether in fact we have objectively hierarchized the urgency of the various apostolic activities." In this respect, the urgency, insistence, and

reformist orientation of this document by Fr. Arrupe are meaningful.

> I feel the activity of the Jesuit Fathers, objectively hierarchized, ought to begin with suppression of good meals, fashionable clothing, cars, frequent apostolic or recreational trips, luxurious universities and not a few colleges, high tuition fees they charge their numerous pupils, as well as the usual trick of charging their benefactors for these "apostolic works" for which they say they do not collect anything, but which are supported by abundant alms they receive monthly from countless benefactors registered in their records.

Father Arrupe has not distributed the Society's property, for he knows he is not the owner, but only the administrator thereof and that, according to the spirit of the constitutions and taking into account the dispensations they have received from the Holy See, said property can be used only for the indispensable support of priests and colleges, as well as students and novices who do not belong to the Society's body, though they have taken the vows of poverty, chastity, and obedience. But the Father General wanted to be practical, and, therefore, established a new Latin American Council of the C.R.S.A. (Centers for Research and Social Action). Thus the complete name for the new secretariat (remembering that these are post-Conciliar times, the times of secretariats!) is L.A.C.C.R.S.A. Somewhat long, but meaningful, like the "elimination of social classes!"

> With respect to the new Latin American Council of the C.R.S.A., the Provincials were right in asking for an explanation of the future faculties of said council, which everybody accepted *prima facie* as most useful. As contained in the statutes, the function of the L.A.C.C.R.S.A. consists of reporting to the Provincials and the Father General (or the latter's social aid advisors) the needs, feasible remedies, *conflicts,* etc., concerning the social apostolate of the C.R.S.A., coordinating the C.R.S.A's joint activities, organizing mutual information and aid, harmonizing their various specializations, and so on. But since the reporting activity is an official one, the members of the L.A.C.C.R.S.A., each of them in his own region, are authorized to ask and receive all kinds of information they need to perform their tasks or which are conducive thereto.... Their functions will require the executive secretariat to devote practically all its time, and the regional coordinators to devote most of it, to such duties.

This is, indeed, efficacy! The Society has set up a whole apparatus to perform this new apostolate of social justice. The lucky members who will occupy the leading positions are full-time workers, whom the Provincials must efficiently aid. There are "technical advisors," "regional coordinators," a whole "ministry" with subordinate departments, so that the Father General and the Jesuits may be able to develop an intense apostolate of social justice. But the Father General wants to be realistic and, against his wishes, avows that "the C.R.S.A., as a whole, have been unable to attain the results that could be expected in accordance with Fr. Janssens' plans." We quote:

> These motives can be basically reduced to three: first, the social apostolate is the most complicated one, and, due to pressing reasons of conscience and humanitarism, it has to solve more undeferrable realities, while other apostolates, including the scientific and educational ones, no doubt pose transcendental problems that are, in a way, within reach of the ways and means we have. Second, the Society is not oriented toward the social justice apostolate; it has been focused, according to a strategy determined basically by historical circumstances, to influence the ruling social classes and the education of the leaders thereof, instead of *the factors of evolution which today compel social transformation*. Third, lack of men and indispensable means: the men who, with great effort, have been appointed and formed, are somewhat isolated, not fully understood, and deprived of able means of performing this new *apostolic venture*. Perhaps not all of them were strong enough to overcome the extraordinary difficulties inherent and consequent to the swift course of the social forms.

It is worthwhile to study the three causes to which Fr. Arrupe attributes the slow pace of the new apostolate in which the Jesuit Fathers who faithfully obey their General's and the Pope's directions are engaged. The first cause is inherent to the apostolate of social justice, which is the most complicated and also the most pressing one, due to reasons of conscience and social justice. The wider the field one is trying to cover—"consciencizing" of the working classes, leader formation, union activity planning, demand for urgent and undeferrable structure change and, if necessary, strike, student conflict, urban and rural guerilla organization—the more evident this reason becomes. We mentioned before that institutional violence can be overcome only by unlawful violence, and that the wider the socializing or Communizing program of the Jesuit Fathers' social justice apostolate, the more urgent that violence. Other apostolates, including the scientific and educational ones, entail transcendental problems, but are, however, within reach of the Jesuit Fathers' ways and means.

The second reason stated by Fr. Arrupe, refers to a 90-degree turnabout that abandons the ruling classes to which, due to historical circumstances, the Jesuit Fathers had been linked. Now it is the proletarian classes who are the present evolutionary factors that today "compel" social transformation, the new goal of the modern apostolate. In the presence of Communism's unavoidable success, it would have been preposterous and harmful to God's greater glory to remain attached to the former ruling classes that fate has called to disappear.

The Montinian Church

The social origin of the Church's priests and religious is enormously important. Our everyday experience of former excessively spiritual positions that absolutely segregated minister and ministry, gives many examples of *"spiritual colonization."* That is why it becomes important to remember Cardjin's initial motto: *"The workers' salvation will come through the workers themselves,"* and the memorandum of Fr. Díez Alegría S.J., to the National Congress for Perfection and Apostolate (Madrid, Sept., 1956), in which, in stating the principle, *"There is no redemption without incarnation,"* he examined Spain's specific problems of religious disincarnation: "Since the institutes, institutionally and as a state, profess poverty in the Church, doesn't it behoove them to carry on, in an institutional and stable way, the process of incarnation of the Church in the world of the poor?"

The comparison of divine work and human work is, indeed, bold and disrespectful. But let us take it as a metaphor. I agree with Fr. Díez Alegría when he affirms that it is the religious who, because of their very status, must give the example of disinterest in and renunciation of earthly things in this new, so-called Church of the "poor." But we cannot agree, for it could be interpreted in an entirely Communistic way, with Cardjin's affirmation that "The workers' salvation will come through the workers themselves." What salvation is he referring to? How will the workers work it out? Hands and feet cannot lead the head. To speak like that is plain demogoguery.

Finally, Fr. Arrupe's third reason for the turtle-like pace of social justice is the lack of men and means. According to the commentator:

> This is a fundamental problem in which we find the drama of the "prophets of our times," who, to be faithful to the Church and pursue their apostolic vocation, have had to clash with ecclesiastical leaders who lacked the necessary sensibility to suffer along with the suffering, and were absent from their historical reality, because of the need of simplicity and dialogue with the believers.

This logic can lead to the conclusion that obedience, which Saint Ignatius so emphatically inculcated in his sons, and past sages have so much recommended, is a hateful hindrance to those "prophets of our times" who are anxious to overcome the barriers of rulings and obedience, and the sooner the better, establish the golden equality which Communist-dominated countries enjoy.

As to the lack of means the General mentions, I do believe it exists and will always exist, for this apostolate is very expensive despite so much preaching about poverty and social justice. It takes money to support so many secretariats, finance so many congresses, make so many trips, pay for propaganda and leader formation, and allow for all those not-small expenditures that have to be made in times of emergency or conflict, such as those of October, 1968.

Let us put an end to these comments in order to face what we consider to be the most important issue that the Father General stated in his letter. The following were his words:

> Finally there remains a subject that is not simple at all. I am referring to the *Society's approach to the Latin American social conflict.* This is a most delicate affair.
>
> On the one hand, I do not hesitate to accept the spirit of "taking sides" and even go beyond this in the sense that the Society has a definite moral obligation to visibly make amends for what we Jesuits have failed and are failing to do to aid social justice and equity. This spirit of reparation I would like to see more vividly in everybody, but first in the superiors, of course.
>
> On the other hand, I have thought it more suitable not to make any oral statement *to the outside,* but to start acting immediately to favor social justice with factual eloquence. Thus as soon as our activity of unmistakably fostering social justice requires and permits public justification, our position will have to be announced without hesitation.
>
> Meanwhile I have made up my mind to take an *internal* position within the Society which I now wish to put into practice at full speed. It is sad and grave that even today there are people in the Society who have not caught the urgency and priority of the social justice issue.

Fr. Arrupe's *mea culpa* is spectacular, and similar to Paul VI's *mea culpa* at the second meeting of Vatican II, when the Pope begged pardon for the mistakes of the Church of the past, due to which, he said, the "separated brothers" had left the way designed by Christ. Can the Father General cast such liability upon his Order, taking into account that the aim of the Society, according to Saint Ignatius, is not, indeed, to attain social justice for the indigent and needy? Has he forgotten that, throughout the history of the Society, there have been countless Jesuits who have not only given up whatever, much or little, they had, adopting the evangelical advice to follow poor Christ, but also abiding by the Order's rulings, have conducted an exemplary life of poverty? Doesn't Fr. Arrupe remember all those Jesuits who, in missions and leprosariums, performed their apostolic duties, silently endured the rigors of poverty, and tried to bring to the indigent comfort and aid to the extent of their possibilities? Doesn't he recall the trials of the novitiate, when the novices were trained to do the most humble and loathsome tasks, not only at the educational centers, but also at the hospitals, and the pilgrimages when we begged alms? Remember, Fr. Arrupe, the times we shared our dishes with the poor, eating the community's leftover food! How many exemplary saintly men have conducted worthy and unselfish lives of tireless charity quietly, unostentatiously, without boasting of having witnessed the first atomic bomb explosion In those times, lamented by Your Reverence, many people attended the Society's colleges free, or paid less than the regular pupils, but this was no hindrance to their passing the examinations or graduating, contrary to what is now the case in the Church of the poor and the Society, which has taken sides in the face of the Latin American social problem.

The commentator of Fr. Arrupe's letter says:

> Here rises the unbelievably vigorous spirit of prophetic denunciation.... This phrase, "I do not hesitate to accept the spirit of 'taking sides' and even go beyond this in the sense that the Society has a definite moral obligation to visibly make amends for what we Jesuits have failed and are failing to do to aid social justice and equity," is, in the letter's general context, something more than a rhetorical figure; it is the core of what Fr. Arrupe wishes and want to convey to us in the historical perspective in which his document stands. Father Arrupe's position overrides the regular approach of the social magisterial texts which have always striven to proclaim on the one hand, the theoretical defense of justice, while insisting on maintaining an ahistorical neutralism with respect to the social conflict, thus returning to the evangelical principles the strength they had lost. Fr. Arrupe breaks the "angelic tradition" that had delineated Christians from the revolutionary march of history in order to submerge them fully, boldly, and fearlessly. That is why he adds: "and [I] even go beyond this in the sense that *the Society has a definite moral obligation to visibly make amends...*."

The scope which the new historical revolutionaries attribute to these words of Fr. Arrupe can be inferred from the following words by the Spanish commentator we have been quoting:

> This affirmation "to visibly make amends" for our historical sins is particularly applicable to our [Spanish] Church's condition. Taking into account that the Spanish Church was a belligerent in a fratricidal conflict connected with this country's social conflicts, as I have pointed out before, our people, after several decades, are still expecting a sincere gesture, a collective *mea culpa,* as a point of departure for a new approach to the Spanish social conflict.
>
> The aforesaid belligerency is a heavy ballast that requires this preparation.

The Jesuit commentator thinks the "Spanish Crusade" that fought Communism and saved Spain from living enslaved under the Communist clutches, is a historical sin requiring a "collective *mea culpa*" from the Spanish

Church which refused to tolerate, not the Spanish social conflicts, as the commentator euphemistically says, but, I repeat, the unbearable slavery imposed by an atheistic, bloody, inhuman Communism that would have been the complete negation of Spain's history, heritage, and very essence. Should Fr. Pedro Arrupe's encyclical lead us thereto, we will fight it with the whole zeal of our Catholic Faith, for our love of Christ, the Church, and Mexico. The Spanish Church was not belligerent, but Spain as a whole was: the Spain of the Cid and Recaredo, the Spain of Lepanto and Trent, the Spain of Cortés and Pizarro.

It is very sad that the Father General's letter, which, since it was not an *internal* one, *(ad usum nostrorum tantum)* ("for our use only") as these documents used to be called, became widely known and gave further support to the bad reputation of the Ignatian Order. The Jesuits have been blamed for intruding in secular affairs in violation of their own constitutions and for provoking internal conflicts that seriously disrupt the peace of nations. This has been the excuse for the frequent expulsions of the Jesuits and Pope Clement XIV's suppression of the Order. A letter from the Society of Jesus' Provost General such as the one we are commenting on would have been an obviously strong argument for justifying the aforementioned drastic measures.

The texts of the Church's social magisterium cannot overstep a margin of orientation inferred from the immutable principles of the Gospel, the natural law and the Catholic conscience; and, when the Father General casts aside what the commentator called "angelic tradition," he is violating, as we have already said, the spirit and the literal meaning of Saint Ignatius' constitutions, gravely exposing his Order and even the apostolate and pastoral action of Christ's Church. These "marching revolutionary Christians" are disoriented infiltrators who have lost their religious spirit. If Fr. Arrupe has fully submerged himself into such a revolutionary march, he has betrayed the Society and endangered its very existence. Governments cannot tolerate this cassock revolution which, through a go-go liturgy, drugs, and sex explosion, is attempting to disrupt the social order, the pace of constructive work, and the real progress of the people under their charge.

> Father Arrupe's letter, *"Requiem for Constantinism,"* as its Jesuit commentators Comín, Manresa, García Nieto, González Ruiz, and Riera have called it, is a *requiem* where the bells all ring for a type of ecclesiastic Magisterium that, for centuries, in connivance with the money-power forces, had striven to rule and remotely control the march of God's people. The *requiem* of Fr. Arrupe announces the resurrection of a new face of Christianity in history.

The above words are a tremendous accusation against the Church: its Magisterium, despite its having been set up by Christ, "had striven to rule and

The Montinian Church

remotely control" the [revolutionary?] march of God's people. But, even more serious is that it has done so "in connivance with the money-power forces;" it has sold itself to and has become an accomplice of dictatorial power and ill-gotten money. But Fr. Arrupe has already recited the responsory, the last requiem for the dead. Now, let us wait for the resurrection of the new Marxist Christianity preached by Ignatius Loyola's sons. The Council, as a historical reality, is over. The breath of the Spirit is still giving vigor to the Church, but we are not satisfied with it. Nor could we be.... Comín says:

> Every Christian who feels obliged to follow the directions of Vatican II must accept this painful but unavoidable task of *exposing the facts*.

To complete in a more explicit way the progressivist thought, I should add, "And joining triumphalistic Communism's revolutionary march." Society of Jesus, Society of Love (as we were taught to call it), how far you are from Saint Ignatius!

Chapter XV

LETTERS SENT TO THE POPE BEFORE HIS ARRIVAL IN BOGOTÁ

We cannot devote any more time to the study of the orientation which the Provost General, the most Reverend Father Arrupe, has given to the Society of Jesus, its superiors, workers, brothers-scholars, and brothers-coadjutors. We have much material, but this would overstep our plan for this book. I believe I have already demonstrated the openly leftist and biased intervention of the "new wave" Jesuits, who believe themselves to be the chosen soldiers, headed by their most reverend Father General, and at the disposal of His Holiness Paul VI, according to the post-Conciliar mentality of Vatican II, not only in Bogotá, but also in the preparation and development of the 39th International Eucharistic Congress in Bogotá, during the socio-economic and socio-political LAMEC meeting in Medellín, and, afterwards, in all the countries of both Americas.

OPEN LETTER TO PAUL VI FROM COLOMBIAN PROGRESSIVISTS

We must go back to the Bogotá Eucharistic Congress, giving the reader some letters written to the Pope before he stepped on Latin American soil. We shall begin with the *open letter* written by Colombian progressivists intimately related to the National Liberation Communistic organizations that promote and lead guerilla warfare:

Brother Paul VI:

We Christians, aware of your coming to Colombia and other Indo-American countries to attend the International Eucharistic Congress, want to let you hear our voices, filled with the spirit of charity.

We do not at all object that homage be paid to the Divine Eucharist. If we are addressing you, it is by virtue of the right of poor people to speak to your heart as Father and Supreme Shepherd.

A congress devoted to honor Christ's poverty is going to be celebrated in a country where 30,000 children die from starvation and underfeeding yearly.

Tens of thousands have been spent in its preparation and celebration, to insure its external success, unusual pomp, and holy splendor. But the crowds will

The Montinian Church

remain hungry for justice and the goods that are essential for survival.

This will be a magnificent event, inspired by our Church, that is called *the Church of the poor*. But it will be no success for the poor, because in Colombia's and our continent's particular conditions, this Congress will be an insane expenditure and an insult to misery. How can a call be made to the faith of the exploited and dispossessed of America, the overwhelming majority of whom are Christian? This is no problem of faith, for they have enough faith, but a problem of food and shelter.

Brother, you will visit a continent where millions of men are the victims of misery, famine, and subhuman living conditions due to a social order that is neither human nor Christian.

You will see how wealthy people administer to the indigent a species of charity that defers their ascension to the dignity they deserve as men and children of God.

You will come to countries where violence has shed the blood of millions, for which hypocrites and egoistic people are responsible. And, you, Paul our Brother, will have to receive manifestations of loyalty and devotion to religious faith from those people who exploit it with hateful cynicism.

You will come to a country where wealthy people's unscrupulous conspiracy is responsible for the tragic sacrifice of priests such as Camilo Torres.

You will come to talk with those who imprison and persecute the annointed of the Lord, because the latter refuse to play the game of injustice and become rebels in order to help the poor.

You will be able to contemplate our Church's swaying and static structures constituted by calculating people who want to lose neither the material advantages of their present status nor their class privileges.

Brother Paul, we believe the magnates of economy and political opportunism play a very important part in this trip of yours.

At the Bogotá International Eucharistic Congress, an event that will not change their fate at all, people will crowd to attend the parade of shepherds and diplomats amidst rows of soldiers trained to murder poor people whenever the latter rebel against injustice.

Our zeal as believers is disturbed and our faith faints at the mere thought of our Brother Paul's presence and his silence authorizing the anti-Christian condition we are experiencing.

To come: This would be unconditional support for those who, in one way or another, keep us under their yoke.

To refuse to come: This would be a protest against an authority without parallel, against an order of things that have to change.

Acceptance would be dishonest and dishonorable, for it is not honest to take a seat beside wealthy people while humble people moan. Not to come would be to bear witness to the fact that our Brother Paul, the sovereign Pontiff, is

Christ's authentic spokesman, before the whole world.

To come and merely to utter formal statements would be of no use in case our Brother Paul is not able to expose exploitation and injustice, even on the part of those who enjoy ecclesiastical privileges.

The wish of seeing the Pope can provoke a humiliating mass mobilization goaded by curiosity or emotional stimulation, but not by an active faith that leads them to rebel against an oppressive and degrading economic, social, and political system.

Because, Brother Paul, if you come and our people remain in their present condition, this would be equal to legitimatizing, "sacralizing," and extending the life of conformism in Christ's name, but which could never really legitimatize the existence of those starved masses.

We firmly believe that the sovereign Pontiff is Christ's representative on earth, but the representative of a Christ who never pledged His person to the wealthy of this world. He did not establish a transitory Church, but an everlasting one; hence, just people are its prolongation and humble people its incarnation.

Your visit, Brother Paul, must not constitute an insult to our poverty.

Bogotá, April, 1968.

The above letter is an explosive mixture of evident deviation from Christ's faith, which becomes a stimulus and ally of Communist forces and the violent Marxist revolutionary design. It is a device for pressure upon the Pope, designed to make him definitely support revolution, violence, and the immediate change of structures; in other words to authorize guerilla warfare that had practically been "sacralized" by the immolation and blood of Camilo Torres, the guerilla-priest. In addition, the masterminds of the letter did know the contents of Paul VI's encyclical *Populorum Progressio*, in which His Holiness called for urgent, audacious, and decisive socio-economic and socio-political reforms in the countries already considered and cataloged by His Holiness as *"underdeveloped countries,"* the victims of *this new "colonialism"* which the odious and hated "imperialists" had imposed upon the starved countries of the *Third World*. Did not the Pope consider colonialism as "intrinsically perverse," even more perverse than Communism or at least *as* perverse, for it unmercifully exploits the colonized peoples' wealth by giving them nothing, or *almost* nothing in return, not even ready money?

The Pope, they believed, will certainly back us. A little more pressure will make him speak clearer than he has done so far, will justify our rebellion, our guerillas, and reduce the attacks which the hateful oligarchies have launched upon us. Who would be in a better position for this than Christ's Vicar, especially with respect to an almost unanimous Catholic population? On the other hand, to our credit, we have the fresh blood of the priest-guerilla leader, Camilo Torres Restrepo, as well as the most precious support of the post-

Conciliar Church.

Neither the guerillas nor the National Liberation forces ever thought their document would make the Pope relinquish his decision of coming to America. They knew that the Pontiff's decision was irrevocable, for he does not give up in the presence of hardship, nor does he faint before most hostile audiences. They remembered his behavior at the United Nations, where he bravely condemned war before the representatives of most countries of the world. On the other hand their secret allies at the Vatican had informed them that Paul VI had firmly decided to cast the whole prestige of his apostolic position, the whole weight of Vatican II, and the very Church of Christ to attain a quick, complete, and audacious solution to the Third World's afflictive problems. Is it not true that the unbelievable, continuous, and spectacular changes which, in such a little time, have "de-sacralized" the Church, removed its "triumphalism," and put it on a level with the sects in order to entertain salvational dialogue with them and bring about a beneficial "ecumenism," are evidence of an irrevocable decision? Indeed, neither the Colombian progressivists nor their Communist allies ever endeavored to prevent the Pope's coming to Latin America.

The program of the Eucharistic Congress, being so innovative and alien to Tradition, demonstrated that Paul VI, who no doubt knew the schedule and arrangements beforehand and had chosen as a legate the one of his cardinals whose thought and actions were the most progressive, wanted to take advantage of that extraordinary occasion. He may even have prepared it himself to shock the world, to take away misunderstanding from Latin American Catholics, and to set on fire the torch of liberation and equality in the Third World by himself. The Pope, then, *did* have to come to Colombia, and the above open letter from the Colombian liberators was but a pressure device designed to justify the Pope's activity before the whole world and his words of liberation before the people.

ANOTHER OPEN LETTER TO PAUL VI, FROM ARGENTINA

Another open letter, this one written by Juan García Elorrio on behalf of the Camilo Torres Movement in Buenos Aires, was written to Pope Paul VI before his visit to Bogotá. Its text follows:

Father,
   In the year 2,000, just 32 years from now, Msgr. Luis Concha, Cardinal and Archbishop of Bogotá, will occupy a dusty grave in the crypt of some temple. His memory will be recalled only by an epitaph written on his grave. Only this, and no one will think of him any longer.
   But by that time in Colombia and the whole of Latin America, avenues,

Letters Sent to the Pope

streets, squares, and monuments will carry a name that the history of social achievements, oppressed peoples' liberation, and men's brotherhood will record with glory. This name is that of *Camilo Torres Restrepo*, the guerilla priest who died February 15, 1966, in the Santander Mountains. Camilo gave up the ritualistic priesthood in order to experience prophetic priesthood to its ultimate consequences. He devoted himself to love and service to his neighbors and, above all, to the weak and oppressed according to the teachings of the Gospel.

This gun-and-cartridge-belt priest carried the censorship of the Archbishop of Bogotá upon him, because of "his having consciously parted from the Catholic Church's doctrine and directions."

Notice, Father, that according to the mentality of this and many other American bishops, *to die for one's poor and starved neighbor means to part from the Church's doctrine and directions.* Indeed, Father, though painful and shameful, such is the dreadful reality of Colombia and Latin America.

You know too, that with few exceptions *the Church's hierarchy stays consciously far from the people and allied to the more affluent classes.* The masses, that is to say 90% of Latin Americans, do not fail to notice this real problem: *The ecclesiastic hierarchy is pro-militarist, pro-oligarchic, and pro-imperialist.*

This notwithstanding, by the year 2,000, bishops, priests, and believers will boast about having had a Camilo Torres at the time of the Latin American social revolution, a Christian and revolutionary Camilo Torres, who shed his blood upon the Colombian and Latin American earth in the process of liberation.

Regarding you and ourselves, we must fulfill our main duty of being absolutely sincere. *We shall tell you what those who are exploiting your trip have not told and will not tell you.*

During your trip to Colombia to attend the Eucharistic Congress, if you are permitted to, enter into contact with the masses of workers and peasants, at least for an instant. You will hear but one clamor, the name of Camilo Torres, and but one demand, *social revolution.*

But in order to prevent the Pope from hearing these voices and witnessing what the Colombian people like all other people in this continent, have to bear and stand, imperialism with all its might, has already set up the necessary apparatus for the *kidnapping of the Pope.*

The Pope will be separated from the people. He will be prevented from contacting the people by the more affluent classes who will surround him constantly. When he has returned to the Vatican, the poor will be sure the Pope came to Bogotá in disguise as a Eucharistic pilgrim, *to play the game of the assassins of the workers and peasants, and the exploiters of the people.*

Father, we are not exaggerating. This is the truth which those who are preparing to exploit your coming to the Eucharistic Congress will never tell you. Whatever your intention may be, your presence in Bogotá, like in any other place in Latin America with the exception of heroic Cuba, will be used to *consolidate social injustice, oppress the destitute, and surrender the national wealth to imperialism.*

None of this will be said when the Pope delivers his vague and paternalistic sermons by means of which he will ward off the plot cooked up against him. The encyclical *Populorum Progressio* was published more than a year ago. But neither imperialism nor its puppet governments have ceased their ferocious negotiations, the idolatrous love for the right to private property, or their unbearable individualism in regard to business. Nothing has changed insofar as the flight abroad of earnings and capital, and the attack on the common welfare (with the poor becoming poorer and the rich becoming richer), are concerned. In brief, everything the encyclical condemns is still happening.

This is because imperialists, dictators, military men, and oligarchs have new tactics, namely to applaud, praise, and extol whatever the Pope says, while doing just the opposite and mocking what they consider naive statements of good will.

Father, accept this sincere and firm supplication of our Christian conscience. Do not come to Colombia.... Do not come for the love of the Eucharistic Christ and God's people, lest we scandalize the poor, the hungry, and the oppressed even more. Do not come, lest you become an accomplice of those who sell their fatherland and exploit and torture people.

WHY MUST THE POPE NOT COME TO COLOMBIA OR ANY OTHER LATIN AMERICAN COUNTRY?

1. The Pope must not come to Colombia, because Colombia is shattered by civil war. Through guerilla warfare, the people are striving to defend themselves against the mighty fifty-family minority that is strangling them with complicity of the Yankees. The Pope cannot be surrounded by murderers, by the murderers of Father Camilo Torres, and make any compromise with them, without making an immense mistake and outraging the poor.

As you too well know, to consolidate their privileges these murderers will not hesitate to turn the armed forces into occupational forces at the Pentagon's disposal, in order to smother the justified attempts of popular rebellion. They will not hesitate to bribe the high clergy with all kinds of flatteries, honors, sinecures, and economic inducements lest they fail to convince them to be their allies for the exploitation of the poor and the "defense of Western Christian civilization."

Do not let the Pope repeat Cardinal Spellman's Vietnam scandal.

Do not let him give rise to a wave of reprobation, such as the one his Christmas conference with Johnson produced.

The Colombian oligarchy knows very well that the Pope's mere

Letters Sent to the Pope

presence beside it will be interpreted by the people as a condemnation of guerilla and revolutionary violence, the oppressed people's only weapon against their oppressors and the prolonged tyranny that violates man's fundamental rights and damages the common welfare in Colombia and all of Latin America.

2. The Pope must not come to Colombia, because Colombia is a pilot plant of imperialist neo-colonialism in the Third World. Less than one-percent of Colombians own more than 75% of the land. Their feudal mentality conceives the right of ownership as a sacred right to use and abuse power without concern for the poor, whom they scoff at, exploit, and murder. It would be hard to find any other Latin American nation where the gravest condemnations of the encyclical *Populorum Progressio* could be so fully applied.

It is that minority who will approach the Pope to receive a sacrilegious Communion from his hands, thus permitting them to boast deliriously about their success, for they know that this is the best way of turning the Pope into an anti-Pope and to make him erase what his hand had written in the encyclical.

3. The Pope must not come to Colombia, because Colombia is the imperialists' most-dominated country. The Yankee monopolies own 96% of the oil. Yankee imperialism has appropriated 70% of the coffee, which is Colombia's monoculture. Imperialism fixes the price of the raw materials it imports and the manufactures it exports. As a result, the greater its earnings, the greater our peoples' misery and poverty.

Why is it that the highest percentage of illiteracy, 65%, belongs to this country, while Cuba, which is being boycotted by all America, has only a 3% rate? It is the fault of the liberal president Carlos Lleras Restrepo, who got 10% of the nation's votes in an electoral farce purporting 70% abstention. It is the fault of his ministers, of the fifty feudal families who enjoy all privileges, of the heads of the anti-national troops who fight the guerilla patriots, and of some representatives of the high clergy. These are liable for the shameful death rate for children, underfeeding, lack of necessary rest, and the resulting diseases, crime, and prostitution.

Behind the beautiful and hypocritical mask of smiles they will wear in the Pope's presence, people will recognize the face of those who are giving up their country and all the continent, those who murder captured guerillas, and those who exploit the poor and torture political prisoners.

How immensely painful and distressing for everybody, believers and unbelievers, to see the hangmen kiss the Pope's ring and wave small flags carrying the Pontifical colors which will seem to flutter as a signal of ignominy!

4. The Pope must not come to Colombia, because Yankee imperialism is planning to extend its advantages from this trip to the whole continent. Indeed, through the Organization of American States, its ministry of colonies, imperialism has already conveyed to the puppet presidents the order of meeting in Colombia to pay homage to the Pope. *As presidents, Christians, pilgrims,*

The Montinian Church

pygmies and servants of their master, all will carry their homage to you, believe they in God or the devil, in the Eucharist or the dollar. All of them will be there, to set up this farce against the American peoples.

As a matter of fact, this masquerade has been mounted by "pilgrim Johnson," who is responsible for the racial discrimination that is staining his own country with blood, for the aggression and permanent blockade of the Cuban revolution, for the criminal intervention in Santo Domingo, and for the slaughter of the heroic Vietnamese people, who have already won.

With this sacrilegious farce, imperialism endeavors to sound the mourning bell for violent revolution and condemnation of guerilla and armed warfare, as well as of popular revolution, that they expect the Pope will launch during the Congress, and the bishops during the LAMEC meeting.

With this sacrilegious farce, imperialism and its accomplices expect the Pope will practically condemn the social and economic revolution proclaimed in the encyclical *Populorum Progressio* and the Conciliar Constitution *The Church and the Modern World.*

With this sacrilegious farce, presenting him a crown of puppet presidents, imperialism seeks to have the Pope convinced that the masquerade of Bogotá and those of the other countries are singular homages and pledges of respect and love for the Holy See.

Even the most simple people, who are so deeply attached to the Church and the Pope, denounce such manifestation of servility, where the dignity of the American peoples will be publicly mocked. *Most of these presidents do not believe in God, but firmly believe in the Pope's influence over the people's gullibility and fetishism. They communicate with what they do not believe in, to take advantage of what they do believe in.*

This would be the last straw in the history of colonialism. The Pope must not lend himself to it. He must stay in Rome.

The behavior of the presidents will be the epilogue of the criminal history of slavery, be it white, black, or of entire peoples. The Pope's blessing will be used to sanctify economic exploitation, social injustice, and sale of national sovereignties.

We ask it again: Do not let the Pope lend himself to this hoax of the international imperialism of money, which undoubtedly will ignite the indignation of the peoples who have been fighting and perishing for their liberation for so many years.

If, in spite of all this that we have written you from the depth of our souls, you decide to come to Colombia, people will go out to meet you. Indeed, the crowds will welcome you, but with little religiosity, much superstition, and above all, great curiosity. *The Pope is not to be seen every day in America, and Rome is a tourist spot for the rich.*

But once the Pope returns to the Vatican, his trip will not be rewarded with a kingdom of faith, hope, and love, but with a kingdom of apostasy, disappointment, and frustration in Colombia and Latin America as a whole. In the circumstances this letter describes, actual circumstances of our continent today, the Pope's visit would be unable to produce results other than these.

Father, we are writing this to you with all possible respect and sincerity. We are doing only what our Catholic conscience, our duty as revolutionaries, and our commitment to the Church of the poor and the Gospel of those who hunger and thirst after righteousness, prompt us to do.

May God enlighten you and accompany you in your hard work of serving your people as they march towards justice and love.

      Juan García Elorrio
      General Secretary of the
      Camilo Torres Movement, Buenos Aires, June, 1968

MESSAGE FROM THE NATIONAL LIBERATION ARMY OF COLOMBIA TO PAUL VI

Printed below is a message from the National Liberation Army of Colombia (N.L.A.) to Pope Paul VI, regarding his visit to Bogotá:

To His Holiness Paul VI
Dear Sir,

The revolutionary forces of the Republic of Colombia consider that, in the present circumstances, your visit to our country will produce an irremediable social crisis in Colombia, because the monopolizing bourgeoisie is ready to exploit the popular masses unmercifully, conceal its attack on civil rights, praise the dictatorial regimes with the excuse of maintaining fictitious social peace in a country with no problems, where, in reality, only famine, ignorance, disease, injustice, persecution, and cruelty exist.

As standard-bearers of a just cause, we feel it is our duty to let His Holiness know that his presence in Colombia will facilitate the consolidation of autocracy and exploitation, which could only harm the Catholic world.

Thus, we declare:

That the National Liberation Army forces condemn the grotesque farce set up by the Colombian oligarchy, during which one of the main characters will be His Holiness, Paul VI, whose presence, maybe unconsciously, will favor the exploitation of the less affluent classes.

That they will fulfill their duty of defending the natural and civil rights of their fellow countrymen, and will use all possible means to prevent the visit of His Holiness, Paul VI, to Colombia.

The Montinian Church

The National Liberation Army will respect the person of His Holiness, but does not promise his stay in Colombia will be a happy one, in case circumstances determine a general mobilization of our forces. In consequence, if there is fighting against the National Transformation Front (President Carlos Lleras Restrepo's electoral party), we shall not be liable for the resulting occurrences, but the Colombian clergy will.

Long live the Colombian revolution!
The National Liberation Army

The above documents are revealing and give us a clear idea of the underground agitation prevailing in Colombia before the Pontiff's arrival and during his stay in Bogotá. I could go on quoting other documents whose openly revolutionary nature consists of bold opposition to Paul VI's trip to attend the International Eucharistic Congress. In spite of his evident and widely-known turn toward the Communist left wing, determined by pastoral reasons it has been said many times, despite his *Populorum Progressio* and his meddlesome relations with Communist countries, neither the guerillas nor the followers of the Communist parties welcomed Pope Montini.

These documents show the discrete intervention of the progressivist priests who gave the theological and canonical bent to them. Such documents, on the other hand, did not cause much disgust to the Pontiff and the heirarchy, which was anxious to adopt the new pastoral of revolution and audacious change of structures.

But it was feared, in fact groundlessly, that the Pope's mere visit could be diabolically exploited by the hateful oligarchy and cause the decisive defeat of the revolutionary movements which heroically seek Colombia's liberation as well as that of all the Latin American peoples. Since power was still in the hands of the oligarchies, which kept their money, social status, and influence, the Pontiff was supposed to be received, entertained, and constantly accompanied and controlled by them. The Pope's very safety called for and justified such solicitous and constant surveillance on the part of the oligarchs, in whose hands the power lay. Even if the Pope were very much decided to apply the doctrine and tactics of the *Populorum Progressio* in America, he could not say anything that those entertaining him could interpret as justification of guerila warfare and Pontifical authorization of *terrorist violence* against *institutional and legalized violence.*

Obviously the Communist and militant leftist groups did not approve of the Eucharistic Congress and the Pope's visit. Their letters are sincere. They were not just trying to pressure him. To them, the Congress was a useless and showy waste. Like Judas, they would say they could use this money for the benefit of the poor and the guerillas. Moreover, despite the Pope's goodwill, his presence and commitment could be of no use to the National Liberation armies.

Letters Sent to the Pope

This suspicion of mine seems to have been confirmed by the sacrilege in Manila when a Bolivian attempted to kill Pope Montini with a dagger. This aggression was not the act of a lunatic, but a prearranged plot. Taking into account who performed it (a Bolivian, a Latin American), we could wonder whether this was a revenge of the National Liberation armies, as they call themselves, or of the guerilla movements, as everybody calls them, against Paul VI who, disregarding the petitions addressed to him, came to America to attend the Congress and the ceremonies which had been scheduled for his arrival.

Chapter XVI

THE POPE COMES TO AMERICA

On Thursday, August 21, 1968, the Pope was still at his summer palace in Castelgandolfo. United Press International let us know His Holiness' latest pronouncements:

> Pope Paul VI formulated an energetic call for Czechoslovakia's freedom, saying he was "greatly anxious." He asked the Latin American clergy and believers not to resort to violence and revolution to solve social problems.
>
> The septuagenarian Pontiff made that call during the last general audience he granted at this apostolic summer dwelling before his trip at daybreak tomorrow to Bogotá, to attend the International Eucharistic Congress and open the second Latin American Episcopal Conference.
>
> The Holy Father also intoned a fervent prayer for Czechoslovakia's freedom, saying again that he was "greatly anxious" due to the use of force in this central European country occupied by army units of the Soviet Union and its Communist allies.
>
> The Pope pointed out clearly that his chief concern in his trip to Colombia would be the great poverty and social injustice borne by millions of human beings in Latin America, as well as the resulting revolutionary movements occasionally supported by priests, which have arisen in that region.
>
> Paul VI announced that his wish was to personify *"the Christ of the poor and hungry"* in his pilgrimage, adding that "With this prospect in our heart, we shall carry humble joy and much hope" to Latin America.
>
> "It has been said that there we shall find *ferments of impatience and rebellion,* even among the ranks of the clergy and the believers," remarked the Pope. "We believe the solution to these sad, in some places *very* sad, situations lies not in revolutionary action nor the use of force, but in love."
>
> The sovereign Pontiff dramatically remarked that revolution would bring about "an oppressive dictatorial regime" as well as damage, crime, ruin, and civil and religious decadence.
>
> "To us, the times of sword and force, even though supported by just and progressive goals, are over," said the Pope. "This is the right moment for Christian love among men."
>
> Before the beginning of his sixth and longest trip abroad, the Holy See

made public that occurrences in Czechoslovakia would not alter the Holy Father's travel schedule, but remarked that during his stay in Colombia, he would keep on praying "for the restoration of peace in freedom, dignity, independence, and self-determination" for the Czech people.

Paul VI spoke to the Czech pilgrims present at his audience without mentioning the Soviets or their allies directly. But he expressed his hope that "violent and bloody conflicts could be avoided, and the dignity and freedom of a people who are zealous for their independence not be violated.

"We hope that wisdom may prevail upon any motive for conflict and that peace may be assured to the peoples involved."

A cloud had darkened the optimistic sky under which the papal trip to Colombia was being prepared; using full force and might, the Soviet Army had invaded the enslaved country of Czechoslovakia. The case of Hungary repeated itself, and no adequate human power protested against this bloody aggression. Paul VI himself did not do anything, except to pray and hope that human wisdom would solve the conflict and grant peace to the peoples involved. The Pontiff's anxiety was very great, but not great enough to mention "the Soviets or their allies directly." Paul VI just hoped that "wisdom" could avoid "violent and bloody conflicts ... and the dignity and freedom of a people who are zealous for their independence not be violated."

A remarkable feature in Pope Montini's political activity is his deference, exquisite prudence, and indulgent understanding toward Communist governments. He has always avoided censoring them, even when they have shown inhuman cruelty against traditionally Catholic peoples who were faithful and devoted children of the Holy Church. Such policies are not contradictory to the active Pontiff's not always wise or opportune moves, warnings, diplomatic and pastoral audiences granted to people financed and led by international Communism to fight against the energetic Catholic governments which, within the law and justice of their courts, try to curb the Communist assault. Even the new Secretariat for Justice and Peace Paul VI set up at the Vatican as a *"supreme court of justice"* to hear claims and to protest against the excesses of tyrannies, keeps silent when the subject concerns terrorist acts, kidnappings, and Communist slaughter of unarmed and slave peoples. On the other hand, the Secretariat issues bold statements against repression carried on by governments which, in the performance of their constitutional duties, endeavor to establish order and peace to enforce their citizens' rights and legitimate interests. Such have been the cases of Brazil and Mexico during the painful student conflicts.

Moreover, these *remote-controlled* policies have been and are being occasionally conducted by the episcopal conferences, either collectively or individually. A recent case occurred in Guipuzcoa when a group of terrorists, among whom were two "new wave" priests, were about to be tried by a military court according to the emergency conditions prevailing in that Basque province. Even before the trial had begun, the bishops unduly intervened and asked that the court be changed and the defendants acquitted, thus dictating to the authorities the way to be followed.

The press told us that the Vatican, that is the Pope, had also sought to influence the judges and prevent the sentence they had to render according to justice and law. This was before the sentence of the Burgos court had been passed. I quote what follows from *Sun of Mexico (Sol de Mexico)*, noon edition for Tuesday, December 15, 1970:

> Vatican City, December 15 (AP).—The Vatican announced it had asked the government of Generalissimo Francisco Franco to save the life of the Basques being tried in Burgos.
>
> The newspaper *L'Osservatore Romano* organ of the Vatican, made public said statement. This is the first public intervention of the Holy See in the explosive trial being conducted in Spain.
>
> There is an opportune and rapid exchange of notes between the Apostolic Nuncio to Madrid and the Spanish Minister of Foreign Affairs, says *L'Osservatore Romano.*
>
> The Holy See's intervention was conducted in accordance with its high "religious and humanitarian mission."

It is a pity that this "high religious and humanitarian mission" interferes in the proper administration of justice, and jeopardizes the sovereignty of a country which defends itself from the clutches of Communism, whose ferocity it knows only too well. Why is it that the Vatican intervenes in a trial whose final sentence has not yet been pronounced? Why does it publicly boast of seeking mercy for criminals who did not show any when they cowardly and vilely murdered a representative of authority? Did Paul VI by chance protest in the cases of Hungary, Czechoslovakia, or the kidnapping and dreadful murder of the German ambassador by the Guatemalan guerillas? Did he mention the kidnapping of Consul Eugen Beilh, which aggravated the collective and individual liability of those who, through terror and crime, sought to disturb order and force governments to surrender?

The bloody invasion of Czechoslovakia by the Russian Communists and their henchmen, which took place on the eve of his trip to Colombia, in a way justified the "chief concern" of this apostolic trip, namely, "the great poverty and social injustice borne by millions of human beings in Latin America."

The reference to "the resulting revolutionary movements, occasionally supported by priests, which have arisen in that region," has a secondary place in the context of the Pontiff's speech. In fact, these revolutionary movements seem to have been justified beforehand by the poverty and social injustice which Paul VI denounced.

The Pope, however, does not want to be the standard-bearer of revolution and violence. He will not support the progressivist priests and skillful agitators of the illustrious Society of Jesus. It was necessary and urgent to make an audacious change of structures and react with "Christian love" against institutional violence, oppression, and plunder; but "Paul VI announced that his wish was to personify *'the Christ of the poor and hungry'* in his pilgrimage...."

I am tempted to repeat here the previously-cited words of the apostate Roca, applying them to this evidently demagogic phrase that mixes up Christ's person and message with the present Pontiff's progressive politics: *This class Christ is not the Christ of the Gospel.*

Considering the circumstances of Latin America, the Pope's announcement of personifying *the Christ of the poor and hungry* in his pilgrimage signified an implicit and cautious acceptance of the Castroite Communist revolution that was in the process of liberating the despoiled and the oppressed who were enslaved by odious oligarchies. Following his ambiguous way of affirming and denying at the same time, condemning and skillfully justifying what he condemns, Paul VI adds: "It has been said that there we shall find *ferments of impatience and rebellion*, even among the ranks of the clergy and the believers." Those existing in Latin America are not ferments of impatience and rebellion, but the *ferments of a Communist revolution* that has been introduced and imported by international agents of subversion, among whom there are not a few foreign priests who, under the guise of the apostolate, have sown uneasiness, demagoguery, class hatred, and violent revolution throughout the continent. These are ferments of bloody struggles, intolerable dictatorships, and of permanent and hopeless slavery for our underdeveloped people who believe, if not in their leaders, at least in the "little Fathers."

With his imprecise style, the Pope adds: "We believe the solution to these sad, in some places *very* sad, situations lies not in revolutionary action nor the use of force, but in love." This Paul VI believes, but perhaps the agitated ferments of impatience and rebellion do not agree with him. In the presence of unjust conditions, the new apostles of social justice have depicted these conditions with exaggerated strokes, and seem able to react only with submachine guns and rifles. If love does not come *from* God and does not lead us *to* God, it becomes a meaningless word, a sophisticated selfishness, a sex explosion, and the "fraternity and equality" of the revolution, which guillotines the opposers or those merely suspected of opposition.

The Pontiff gave warning that a violent revolution would bring about "an oppressive dictatorial regime," but discretely avoided saying what kind of dictatorship this would be. "To us, the times of sword and force, even though supported by just and progressive goals, are over," said the Pope. "This is the right moment for Christian love among men."

In all these words of the Pontiff, in which we cannot find the accuracy, clearness, or immutability of the Magisterium, there is the evident purpose of covering the reformist activity that characterized the Bogotá Eucharistic Congress and the subsequent LAMEC meeting with Christian love. When is the right moment for Christian love among men of which Paul VI speaks? Has not this right moment existed from the time of Christ? Perhaps we must conclude that the commandment of the divine Master has not found the right moment to be fulfilled during these past 2000 years. Was it by chance Vatican II which brought us the actual fulfillment of the commandment of love among men? In reality, ideological confusion has sown the most profound divisions in all fields of human life.

THE JOURNEY OF PAUL VI

Following is a quotation taken from the newspaper *El Espectador* from Bogotá, for Thursday, August 22, 1970:

> In order to get continuous information about the development of the papal flight, the airline Avianca set up a modern direct communication system last night to connect the international airport of El Dorado with the aircraft *Marshal Sucre*.
>
> At 10:30 p.m., priests, religious, pilgrims, and agents of the armed forces awaited the news of the pilot of the 707-320B aircraft with expectation.
>
> Captain Enrique Fajardo, the pilot of the plane that brought the Holy Father to Bogotá, contacted the Avianca maintenance office at 10:56 p.m. and from his aircraft compartment, announced to the whole world:
>
> > The Holy Father got on the 707-320B Avianca aircraft at 5:05 a.m., Italian time. At Fiumicino airport many people movingly saw him off on his journey. I expect to fly over Fatima at 5:40 a.m. I will be in touch with the airports of Spain, Portugal, the French islands, and Venezuela as the trip develops. I will call later on with a new report.
>
> At 11:40 p.m. Captain Enrique Fajardo Boada released his second report from the aircraft that brought the sovereign Pontiff to the capital of this republic, and said: "QSO Bogotá. Avianca papal aircraft here. We expect to be in Madrid at 5:04. Flight continues to be normal. The Holy Father is resting by now. Over."
>
> One of the Avianca operators called Captain Bardo, another member of the crew of *Marshal Sucre*. Captain Fajardo answered: "Understood. Now we have flown over Barcelona. We have your message for Captain Bardo. This

The Montinian Church

frequency is bad. Do you have the control over there?"

"Understood, Captain. Then we shall turn to AM. Ready, Captain. Go ahead."

"Message received. Captain Bardo will pass on later. For now we shall remain QAP at 5:05."

At 0:05 a.m. (Colombian time) the third contact with the Avianca 1402 flight was made. On this occasion it was not Captain Fajardo, but the assistant captain, Jaime Nieto, who said:

> Papal flight over Madrid at 5:04, at a 33,100 level. Fatima estimated at 5:41. For your information, a message was received from the Spanish head of government, Generalissimo Francisco Franco, to His Holiness and, in turn, the Holy Father sent a message to the Spanish people, from the aircraft.

The Avianca operator answered: "Understood, Captain of the 1402, papal flight. Over."

At 12:41, on passing over Fatima, there was a new communication. Captain Ruiz said:

> We are passing over Fatima at 5:40 at a flight level of 35,000 feet. We expect to be at 39.40 North 13 West at 6:08. The Holy Father is sleeping at this moment. The flight is normal in accordance with the flight plan. The messages received from Spain and Portugal have been answered.

While a message was being prepared to inform him that there were representatives of all radio networks in the country at the control offices of Avianca waiting to broadcast the course of the flight, Captain Ruiz said:

> The panorama over here is wonderful. The sun is rising on the horizon right now. We are making for the Atlantic Ocean, over which we shall fly for more than 8 hours.

After 2 hours and 37 minutes of flight from the *Marshal Sucre,* Captain Ruiz announced:

> We shall be QAP. Let us know whether you are not too sleepy. The sun is already on our back, and we expect to arrive at the Bogotá airport at 10:15 a.m. The communications with the Avianca station at El Dorado, where our press friends find themselves, have been perfect. Greetings to all of them over there, and to our relatives.

The Pope Comes to America

At 1:55 a.m. Bogotá time, the aircraft commander, Captain Fajardo, made a new contact from the Atlantic Ocean with El Dorado airport, and said:

> The temperature is about -47° centigrade, wind 110°, diagonal 40. The sky is a most beautiful blue all around. Captain Jaime Nieto paid a visit to the Holy Father, who was reading. The Holy Father received him enthusiastically and blessed the medals and shields of the pilots, as well as each one of them.

He related that all the passengers had already had breakfast by that time and that during the flight they had not noticed even the slightest turbulence, despite the fact that by then they were flying over a vast layer of cumulus and stratus clouds.

To avoid problems for the sovereign Pontiff, passengers and aircraft crew, due to atmospheric changes from Rome to Bogotá, the altitude of the aircraft was changed to 6,000 feet 7 hours and 45 minutes prior to its arrival in the republic's capital.

Then Fajardo entered the Pope's room in order to talk with the sovereign Pontiff and get to know his opinion concerning the flight and his attitude regarding the trip to Latin America.

At 2:03 a.m., after a flight of 4 hours and 5 minutes, Captain William Medina, who was in charge of the aircraft while Captain Fajardo visited the Holy Father, sent another report, stating that the weather and communication conditions were fine and that the flight continued to be normal.

At three a.m., Captain Enrique Fajardo issued a new report to say that the Holy Father and the other passengers were either reading or resting. The weather remained wonderful, the sky cloudless and the outer temperature -47°, with a 50 mile wind.

At 3:30 a.m. (10 a.m., Italian time) the commander of the jet *Sucre,* Captain Fajardo, read the answer by the Avianca president, Dr. Juan Pablo Ortega, to a request made by the ANDI to the Vatican, entreating an audience with the Holy Father. The message read as follows:

> Regarding question on board the *Sucre,* I was told your petition for an audience with the Pope will be taken into account and decided jointly with His Excellency Muñoz Duque, it being possible on Saturday afternoon. A small group of undersigners of the manifesto would be admitted to the audience.

Later on, Captain Fajardo reported that the Holy Father had left his chamber and by then was handing personal gifts to the special guests who were on board the aircraft in the rear chamber. The chief papal presents consisted of photographic cameras.

At 4:20 a.m., Captain Barbo, the Avianca technical vice-president, asked the latest news about the crisis produced by the invasion of Czechoslovakia by the member countries of the Warsaw Pact. A radio network issued a long report on that subject, the news being received in the papal aircraft through the Avianca system.

At 5:00 a.m. (11:00 a.m. Italian time), Captain Fajardo reported that the Holy Father was having lunch, the flight remained normal, but the weather conditions were hindering communications, and that he expected to land at El Dorado at the scheduled time of 10:15 a.m.

At 5:30 a.m., the pilot of the papal aircraft reported they found themselves to the east of San Juan, Puerto Rico, making for Curaçao, the wind calm, visibility 30-40 kilometers, and he announced the route to be followed over Colombian territory, 4 hours and 25 minutes prior to their arrival in Bogotá.

During the Holy Father's flight to Bogotá, Don Juan Pablo Ortega, the president of Avianca, gave the Pope a white ruana, a heavy square poncho made of virgin wool in Lenguazaque. In accepting the gift, the sovereign Pontiff conveyed his delight and said he would use it at his private apartment in the Vatican.

At 6 a.m., Captain Fajardo said he was changing the original route and reported the papal plane would follow the "Kilo Route" at a height of 30,000 feet, from Curaçao to Tibu, and then to Barrancabermeja, Velázquez and Bogotá, in order to avoid turns. In consequence he asked the Civil Aeronautical Agency to get permission from Maiquetia, for him to follow the new itinerary while in Venezuela.

At 6:10 a.m., Captain Enrique Fajardo reported that the flight was still normal and that they were approaching Curaçao to enter the route he had mentioned a few minutes before, thus being able to arrive at Bogotá directly through Barrancabermeja. By then the Avianca jet had made most of the journey from Rome to Bogotá.

Chapter XVII

THE NEW THEOLOGY OF THE BOGOTÁ INTERNATIONAL CONGRESS

Let the Pope's airplane follow its way, while we attend one of the meetings of the "new wave" theologians, who pompously call themselves the "experts" of the new Church.

At the international theology meeting the possibility that the quality of the Eucharistic bread be modified was considered. According to the new theologians, the Eucharistic bread will no longer necessarily be made from wheat, but from yucca, corn, barley, or other cereals. It was also said that there is the possibility that the host shape may be modified, and that it may not be obligatory that it be round. It is these theologians' opinion that, through these changes, without changing Christ's institution, the Church could adapt its administration to our times.

Father Luis Alonso Schokel, S.J., a professor of the Rome Bible Institute and one of the most renowned theologians in the world, spoke at the gathering yesterday, on the subject, "The Eucharist: Blessing to the Father through Creation and Salvation." His whole address was focused on the bread's *symbolism*, and stressed the possibility of the previously-mentioned changes taking place.

Father Schokel spoke in Spanish, and embellished his peculiar brand of theology with poetry and some humorous sallies. After having spoken about biblical subjects, he entered the field of literature, read a beautiful poem of *"The Love of His Youth,"* as he called it, and quoted verses by Gabriela Mistral in order to stress the bread's symbolism: "Bread of love and justice—Bread of rye and good fellowship."

Father Schokel totally rebelled against the theology which he had studied 25 years ago. He declared with malice that this theology posed two superfluous problems which he thought were not worthwhile: one of them was how to explain Transubstantiation metaphysically, the accidents and substances; the other was a quantity problem, how Jesus Christ, being approximately 1.75 meters tall, could fit into a fragment of bread. "These questions," he said, "are superflous." He then affirmed: "I revolt against this old theology."

Later on in his address, Fr. Schokel said:

Man blesses God, that is, thanks Him, because He has blessed him with gifts, and so that He will bless him again. This is the meaning, the basis, the dialectics of blessing. Man expresses this blessing or thanksgiving by word, rite, or a combination of both elements. The rite consists of offering God something that is ours. The thanksgiving can be either general for all gifts received, or individual for a particular gift. Our offering can include a series of gifts or limit itself to one. . . .

God's gifts can be divided into nature and history, or creation and salvation. Human gifts are those which man owns and creates, those which express his skill, work, social being, etc. If we find an object that symbolically concentrates many of God's gifts, that symbolically expresses a human fullness and plurality, we shall offer it to God in a rite of benediction, and we shall interpret the symbolism in words.

This object can be bread. The Old Testament gives us some data concerning its symbolism in various stages of its existence. We find: (a) An oral blessing or thanksgiving, which is an organized series of memorials of creation and history, and leads to the gift of our daily bread, which summarizes what precedes. (b) The rite of the weekly presentation of loaves of bread on behalf of Israel without uttered words. (c) The rite of offering the first fruits which represent the whole crop. The words accompanying this rite are replete with the history of salvation. (d) Some historical occurrences in which the daily bread assumes a historical role. Descent into Egypt, manna in the desert, and exile, are examples. (e) Finally, definite data that point to the bread's cosmic symbolism: rain, fecundity, etc.

In the New Testament, the bread's symbolism is stated, mainly by Saint John, as being food, an apportioned gift, a gift of life linked to Israel's history, and as a symbol of fertility in the dying grain. The bread is loaded with this symbolism to perform its function of sacramental meaning.

Christ, who is present under the figure of bread which represents the gifts of nature and history as well as those of ownership and work, is our blessing to the Father through creation and salvation.

All these heresies were stated at an International Eucharistic Congress, at a Congress of Theology attended by cardinals and "new wave" "experts," and at a Congress enhanced by the presence not only of the papal legate, but of the sovereign Pontiff himself.

When they say that the most Sacred Mysteries of our Catholic Faith, the dogmatic doctrines of Catholic Faith defined infallibly at the Council of Trent, are superfluous, they reject the *inerrancy of the Church,* they avow the failure of Jesus Christ's promises, they deny His divinity, and they seek the self-

The New Theology

demolition of our very holy religion. In endeavoring to reform the Church and accommodate it to the modern world, they deny the reality and very existence of the Church, the fundamentals of Peter's primacy and the hierarchy, the hierarchical priesthood, the Word's Incarnation, the supernatural order, and the life of grace. In summary, by denying a single dogma as revealed by God and defined by the authentic and infallible Magisterium, they overthrow all the other pieces of truth of our religion.

The two problems stated by the wise theologian of the Rome Bible Institute, the nest where the present subversion of the Church has been hatched, namely, *Transubstantiation* and *Christ's real presence in the consecrated Bread, in the tiniest piece of this consecrated Bread*, are two dogmas of Catholic Faith that progressivism says should be declared superfluous, but which, in fact, it has denied with *nationalistic* and *impious* criteria. Our Catholic Faith, our Eucharistic Faith proclaims, along with Saint Thomas of Aquinas:

> *Quod non capis, quod vides*
> *Animosa praestat fides . . .*
> *Credo quidquid dixit Dei Filius,*
> *Nihil hoc Verbo veritatis verius.*

(What you cannot understand, what you cannot see, the spirited faith teaches you . . . I believe in what the Son of God has said. Nothing is more truthful than this word of truth.)

Let us remember some of the canons of Session XXIII of the Tridentine Ecumenical Council, which was not merely a pastoral, but a definitively dogmatic and infallible Council, provided that the Church's Magisterium is infallible:

Canon 1. Should anyone deny that the body and blood, along with the soul and divinity of our Lord Jesus Christ, and, in consequence, Christ as a whole, is actually, really, and substantially present in the Sacrament of the most Holy Eucharist but, instead, say that He is there figuratively or virtually, let him be anathema.

Canon 2. Should anyone say that in the most Holy Sacrament of the Eucharist the substance of the bread and wine persists together with the body and blood of our Lord Jesus Christ, thus denying the wonderful and unique transformation of all of the substance of the bread into the body, and all of the substance of the wine into the blood, leaving only the accidents of bread and wine, a process which the Catholic Church appropriately calls *Transubstantiation*, let him be anathema.

Canon 3. Should anyone deny that in the venerable Sacrament of the *species,* once the separation is made, Christ is not present as a whole, let him be anathema.

Canon 4. Should anyone contend that after the Consecration in the wonderful Sacrament of the Eucharist, there is not present the body and blood of our Lord Jesus Christ, but just the use thereof, as one is receiving, but not before or after, and that in the *consecrated Hosts* or *Particles* which are left or gathered after Communion, there is not the body of the Lord, let him be anathema.

Canon 5. Should anyone contend that the main fruit of the most Holy Eucharist is the remission of sins, or that no other effects come from it let him be anathema.

Canon 6. Should anyone contend that, in the Holy Sacrament of the Eucharist, Christ, God's only-begotten Son, must not be worshipped with external devotion, venerated *with special joyful celebrations,* and according to the Holy Church's universal rite and praiseworthy custom, *carried in processions* and shown for the people's public adoration, or that His adorers are idolaters, let him be anathema.

Canon 7. Should anyone contend that it is not legitimate to gather the Sacred Eucharist in the ciborium, but that, after the Consecration, it must necessarily be distributed among those present or that it is not legitimate to carry it honorably to the sick, let him be anathema.

Canon 8. Should anyone contend that in the Eucharist Christ is received in just a spiritual, but not in an actual and true way, let him be anathema.

Canon 9. Should anyone deny that each and all of the male and female Christian believers, after arriving at the age of discretion, are obliged to receive Holy Communion at least once a year, during the Easter season according to the law of Holy Mother Church, let him be anathema.

Canon 10. Should anyone contend that it is not legitimate that the celebrating priest give himself Communion, let him be anathema.

Canon 11. Should anyone contend that faith alone is preparation enough to receive the Sacrament of the most Holy Eucharist, let him be anathema. And so that this great Sacrament be not worthlessly received, therefore for ruin and condemnation, this holy synod establishes and states that, provided there be confessors, the sacramental confession must be made necessarily before communing when there is awareness of mortal sin, despite the fact that those who intend to commune feel that they have perfect contrition for their sins. If anyone should presume to teach, preach, or pertinaciously affirm the opposite or defend it publicly, let him be anathema.

This is the dogmatic, infallible doctrine of the Council of Trent, which, as was said in Bogotá, was overridden by the "experts" in the new theology. That doctrine does not pose just *two* problems, but entails many deep Mysteries that the finite and limited human intelligence cannot understand. We accept them, however, because the arguments of credibility have proven to us that these are Mysteries revealed by God, who cannot err or deceive us. These are not opinions, but Catholic truths. Father Schokel, like many other Jesuits and not a few bishops, have lost their faith, provided they are not infiltrators who have never *had* our Catholic Faith. Deprived of faith, reason will become lost when attempting to rationalize the revealed truth.

Inexplicably Father Schokel confuses the symbol with what the symbol means. The law of symbolism presides over all the divine messages from God to man, both in the order of nature and in that of grace. In His infinite wisdom, God lowers Himself to our smallness and speaks the narrow and limited language of men. But to confuse the symbol with what the symbol means, to rationalize the symbol to construe and define what we think instead of what God wanted to tell us, is plain denial of revealed truth that only the authentic, living, and infallible Magisterium of the Church can express. And when the latter has already spoken and dogmatically defined the only authentic meaning of God's Word, any attempt to surpass the definitions of a dogmatic council by the absurd fictions of faithless theologians is unbearable conceit and presumption.

These theological meetings carried on during the Bogotá Eucharistic Congress, were just scandalous expressions of the sacrilegious feelings of heresy which, with nobody objecting and the Pope being present, insinuated that Catholic doctrine had definitively and irreversibly changed, and the Council of Trent had finally been overthrown by the advancement of the new theology under the inspiration of the "separated brothers" in ecumenical alliance with Vatican II.

OTHER WORDS BY THE PAPAL LEGATE, CARDINAL LERCARO

Taking into account what Cardinal Lercaro represented at that time, President Lleras of Colombia in a gentlemanly and noble gesture, awarded him the high decoration of the Cross of Boyacá. Forgetting his present commitment, the socialist Cardinal had to answer that ruler's diplomatic gesture by delivering a speech:

Most Excellent Mr. President:
 ... From the first moment I got the impression ... that those were honest, open people with smiling, good-natured faces. I saw numerous crowds of applauding youngsters lining the streets. Their genuine and hopeful enthusiasm has touched my soul.... I knew Colombia's bosom conceals gold, silver, and emeralds and that it is rich in natural resources, but I am not wrong in affirming that an incomparably greater wealth is its young people, who are full of

enthusiasm, hope, and deep-rooted feelings of faith, honesty, and integrity.

Today all over the world, there is manifested in many different and sometimes strangely contradictory ways, the spirit of nonconformity, the will for further development, and the hope for deeper justice and true peace.

Mister President, I dare say this country has the basic resources and forces it needs to start a process of continuous and successful progress that includes cultural, economic, and social development, and it would be a mistake to waste precious energies protesting with the sole and unavoidable result of opening new and deeper trenches among brethren.

This step forward can and must be made without sacrificing the spiritual and human wealth of this country. Moreover, the way must be illuminated by the torch of its traditional faith, moral customs, integrity, and the tight links uniting the country.

The task which Providence has entrusted to you, Mr. President, due to your sensibility, and that of those who share the responsibility of government with Your Excellency, is just truly exhilarating, and I am glad to think that, in this historical moment, the Eucharistic Congress has helped to fully reveal the greatness of that task with its wonderful and fruitful possibilities.

In consequence, most excellent sir, permit me most fervently to forecast that you, not in a single journey but after hard years of noble and intense work, will be able to see the Colombian people, the people of the future, enjoy a climate of freedom, justice, fraternity, and peace, and in God's welfare and with God's blessing, achieve the fruits of their honest and intelligent work and civic life . . . .

The above is a classic progressivist speech, where isolated references and light strokes of affected spirituality tint integral humanism, the earthly paradise of which it dreams. The "diplomatic" eulogy about the Colombian people's human virtues does not seem to be sincere: ". . . honest, open people with smiling, good-natured faces." So indeed are the Colombian people, but they were not the only ones to be seen and heard at Bogotá during the time of the Congress, for a large contingent of agitators had attended the Congress and was boldly sowing the nonconformity and discontent to which Cardinal Lercaro cautiously referred.

The former Archbishop of Bologna dared to say that the American country into which he was welcomed so triumphantly, has the basic resources and forces it needs to start a process of continuous and successful progress, and that it would be a mistake to "waste precious energies protesting" (His Eminence carefully avoids mentioning *guerilla warfare* and *subversion*, which are being fostered and blessed by the apostles of social justice, the loyal Jesuit followers of His Holiness), *protesting* (I repeat this equivocal and ambiguous word), "with the sole and unavoidable result of opening new and deeper trenches among brethren." This eloquent paragraph discretely alludes to *trenches*, thus appeasing the followers of Camilo Torres. The sole and unavoidable result of protestation, and the waste of the precious energies of the Colombian people, were the guerilla bands of the militia-priest who exchanged his cassock for a machine gun and a rifle. The climate of freedom, justice, fraternity, and peace, which the Cardinal forecast for Colombia and Latin America is that of the Communizing socialism of Cuba and Fidel Castro.

THE NEW COMMUNAL CEREMONIES OF PENANCE

The post-Conciliar mentality that is trying to change the whole doctrine and heritage of the Constantinian Church and above all the Conciliar definitions of Trent, is also trying to eliminate the Sacrament of Penance, stressing the communal aspects of sin, and seeking remission of personal sins through the generic and ambiguous confession of the ecclesiastical assembly. Progressivists could not possibly spare us this public act of collective repentance in Bogotá, where, to please the "separated brothers," the Catholic Church was burdened with the responsibility for all the schisms, heresies, and crimes of the past.

On the fourth day of the Congress, a public act of collective repentance took place.

First, it was Cardinal Lercaro who came to the pulpit and begged pardon for mankind because of their sins. He said: "God has revealed to us His design of love and meekness. Let us acknowledge our sins most consciously and faithfully. We humbly beg pardon of God and our brethren for our guilt in the long series of dissents and separations that have delayed the unity of the Church."

Monsignor Ruben Icaza, Coadjutor from Cartagena, in turn said: "We humbly beg pardon of God and our brethren because we have failed to care for the sheep of our dioceses as good shepherds, because we have not always been examples of love and diligence as real fathers are, and because we have not fully oriented our lives according to the needs of the times."

Father Bernardo Sánchez, as a representative of the priesthood, stated: "As priests we humbly beg pardon of God and our brethren because many times we have ignored the living conditions of the people, because we have failed to serve everybody with humanitarianism, following the example of the Lord, and because we have frequently disregarded the poor and indigent."

A father of a family, Jorge Rubiano, came to the center of the shrine and also begged pardon, using the following words: "We humbly beg pardon of God and our brethren, because our homes have not always been the Church's domestic sanctuaries where there could be the same faith and common prayers, because of the mutual sins of our spouses, parents, and children, because of our

The Montinian Church

disregarding the sanctity of holy days, because we have not generously practiced hospitality, and because we have not promoted justice and other good works for the service of our brethren who are in need."

Two youngsters, Mario Humberto and Gloria Cuella, in turn begged pardon, on behalf of the youth, as follows:

The boy said: "Being responsible for the future of the Church and builders of its present, as youngsters we humbly beg pardon of God and our brethren, because we have failed to apply all of our energies to ripen the consciousness of our own personalities."

The girl stated: "We beg pardon because of our haste, our lack of understanding of our elders, our faint interest in getting to know the Christian revelation in depth, for not always having oriented our juvenile ardor to goals of justice and fraternity, and for not having assumed our responsibility in the development of social and conjugal welfare."

On behalf of the country's political leaders, Minister Miguel Pastrana Borrero said: "As political leaders we humbly beg pardon of God and our brethren, because we have failed to promote the common welfare unselfishly, because we have not endeavored to perfect social and public institutions according to the spirit of the Gospel for the people's benefit, because we have violated the rights of God, Church, and man in society, and because we have failed to act always with a spirit of solidarity."

Doctor Eduardo Arias Robledo performed the penitential act on behalf of businessmen. He acknowledged his offenses against justice. "As businessmen we humbly beg pardon of God and our brethren for our offenses against social justice and workers' rights, because we have failed to improve the economic condition of the citizens belonging to the poorer classes, and because we have inflicted injustice in contracts and irregularities in transactions."

Mister Hernán Noriega, President of the Brotherhood of Labor from Peru, carried the voice of Latin American workers in a mood of penance: "As workers we humbly beg pardon of God and our brethren, because we have frequently felt mistrustful of the Church and failed to understand it, because we have failed to work for society's benefit with a dutiful conscience and the voice of justice, and because we have failed to defend and vindicate our rights using due charity."

These collective confessions remind us of the *psychological trick* of the "Short Courses in Christianity." They were one of the most preposterous, incomprehensible, and ridiculous ceremonies of the innovating Congress of the post-Conciliar Church. I have seen many penitential acts during the many missions and exercises I have given inside and outside Mexico. I have seen people weep humbly and sincerely when remembering their sins, and beg mercy of God. But I had never seen these communal confessions in which what was least important was said, and what ought to have been confessed was omitted.

The New Theology

Except for public sins which require public retraction, the Church has never demanded such public, ambiguous, and vague confessions, confessions which would suit a drama but not a liturgical, official act of the Church. The Sacrament of Penance, established by Christ, not by Cardinal Lercaro, in order to bestow the forgiveness of personal and especially mortal sins committed after Baptism, is a trial in which the judge, the hierarchical priest, not God's people, absolves or denies absolution according to the penitent's personal sincerity.

In one way or another, the great sin which everybody confessed in that penitential act at Bogotá, was the sin against *justice*, not any justice, but *social justice*. The bishops, as shepherds of the souls appointed by God to rule us through immutable truth, did not confess their really sinful silence in the presence of heresy, immorality, lack of discipline, scandalous and sacrilegious profanations of the Sacred Mysteries, seen and spread everywhere. They did not confess their having permitted the spiritual, intellectual, and even moral ruin of their seminaries where the workers of the Lord's vineyard are trained. They did not confess their having tolerated and even authorized the infected literature which pretends to be Catholic and in fact is anti-Catholic, or having given their *imprimatur* to literature which pollutes consciences and destroys the Faith.

They did not confess their permissiveness nor their endorsements of subversive priests and laymen who efficiently promote the self-demolition of the Church. They failed to confess their being unjust and unusually harsh in repressing priests and laymen who stand in defense of the Church and refuse to get involved in the tragic demolition of Jesus Christ's work. They did not confess their coveting collective administration or co-responsibility, which is depicted as obedience to Peter's primate but in reality denies it, and their refusal to abide by the Pope's legitimate promptings. They did not confess their treacherous ecumenism, through which they equate our religion with all other religions, in an unbearable syncretism, after having proclaimed freedom of conscience against which faith, reason, and the Magisterium's oldest documents had definitely taught.

They did not confess their having tolerated a most scandalous license in so-called Catholic colleges, which have become a highly profitable business. They did not confess their anti-Catholic *aggiornamento* through which they have subdued Christ's Church to the corrupt and corrupting world. They did not confess their having adulterated Holy Writ as well as the history and living Tradition of the Church, in order to exonerate the Jews from the collective responsibility which they knowingly and consciously assumed during Christ's Passion and death. They did not confess their having entered into secret arrangements with Masonic lodges and with destructive, intrinsically perverse Communism. In conclusion, our prelates did not confess to having attempted to eliminate God in order to elevate man.

The Montinian Church

The "penitent" priests, represented by Fr. Bernardo Sánchez (I am referring to the *aggiornated*, servile ones, those who fear to expose their privileges and their bishops' confidence and grace) confessed they had "ignored the living conditions of the people, ... failed to serve everybody with humanitarianism," and "frequently disregarded the poor and indigent." Church of the poor! Elitist Church! The priest's mission and pastoral work must not be the salvation of souls, but the apostolate of social justice, even though such an apostolate may entail grave sins against communal justice and the justice of God's kingdom. Poor priests, who are unconsciously helping to destroy and suppress their own priesthood! Why did they not confess their secularization, their willing "de-sacralization," their visits to cinemas, night clubs, and dancing places? Why did they not beg pardon for their lack of prayer, inner life, and the spirit of faith? Why did they not acknowledge their familiarity and lack of formality with young girls and mature women? Why did they not acknowledge their active participation in the subversive movements jeopardizing peace and stability of nations?

The most sincere and complete confession was that of the father of a family. To begin with, he acknowledged the fact that today's homes are no longer the Church's domestic sanctuaries, God's familiar shrine. He avowed that in Christian homes the sound of common prayer is being extinguished—that which used to bless the Lord at the beginning and end of the day, to praise the Most Holy Virgin perpetually with the family rosary, thus fulfilling the Marian prophecy, *"All generations will call me blessed;"* to bless the food and give thanks to God after meals, and to honor sacred images for what they represented, for they were permanent reminders of our relationship with the Church triumphant. Indeed that Christian life of fear of God, of austerity, sacrifice, and sanctified work is over. In spite of the Christian Family Movement, which has much movement, little family, and nothing Christian, we have lost unity of families, respect for elders, and solicitous dedication of parents to the difficult, self-denying, and continued work of educating and looking after their children. Is it not the progressivist priests who campaign for children's absolute freedom, and deny that they owe obedience and submission to their parents?

The youngsters also confessed. They who proclaim themselves "builders of [the] present" and "responsible for the future" did not confess their rebellion against authority and law, their unbearable presumption in knowing nothing but believing they know everything, their disdain of the lessons and experiences of the past, and their blindness in being used as tools of demagogues, the Communist revolution, and the hidden hand that rules or misgoverns the world. What did young Mario Humberto mean by that ambiguous, modern phrase: "... to ripen the consciousness of our own personalities?"

The girl regretted that youth had not always oriented their "juvenile ardor to goals of justice and fraternity," and had failed to assume their "responsibility in the development of social and conjugal welfare." What did this confession mean? Maybe they failed to avail themselves of pre-conjugal relations and the present-day experiences arising from them, to ripen conjugal life?

Nothing was said about sexual sin, which, should it be committed with love, is no sin at all, even though it be unnatural. Nothing was said about immodest fashions, mini-skirts, mixed bathing at the seashore or in pools, indecent and provocative dances, conjugal infidelity, lectures against natural law, sinful amusements, or alcoholism among both men and women. There was no reference to provocative conversations, corruption of minors, religious indifference and irreligiosity. How could these issues be debated, bearing in mind that the watchgirls wore mini-skirts, a sort of priest's hat, and a kind of cassock or half-cassock, in place of a blouse. Is this public repentance, or mockery of the most sacred things?

THE CARDINAL-LEGATE PAYS A VISIT TO BOGOTÁ'S MODEL PRISON

The visit to a jail was another demagogic feature of the Pontifical Legate's activity. There were speeches, and poems by an inmate, Oscar Uribe, who wrote them especially to honor the Cardinal. Unable to contain himself, the Cardinal went toward the inmate, embracing him and kissing his cheeks as a pledge of admiration and gratefulness. "I should like to do this with each and every one of you," he said, addressing the other inmates, "but it would take me all day."

Your Eminence, among us these kisses are not in style. Such warmth of manner is all right with one's mother or spouse, but not with men. That is why everyone was surprised at the kisses you bestowed upon the inmate-poet, as with the ones you bestowed with your hands on all those present at your visit to the model prison. But we forgot that in the post-Conciliar Church, the Church of the poor, "love" explains and justifies everything.

Chapter XVIII

THE ARRIVAL OF THE POPE IN COLOMBIA

Many people who up till now had seemed somewhat indifferent, were moved by their interest to meet the Holy Father, listen to him, and receive his blessing. To many Colombians, the Congress actually began on the day of Paul VI's arrival in Bogota.

In the newspapers of Bogotá, there appeared the text of the message sent by the Western Anti-Communist Mexican Federation (FEMACO) to His Holiness, Pope Paul VI. It read as follows:

Holy Father:

We strongly support any serious work designed to suppress famine and poverty both in the Communist world and the Free World; we endorse any attempt to raise the living standards of peasants, workers, and employees, and to establish social justice in Latin America. But we do not agree with the use of these noble aims by many priests and laymen as a hoax to yoke the popular masses to subversive movements whose real goal is to set up a totalitarian dictatorship of atheistic anti-Christian Communism, which, besides augmenting the misery of the working classes wherever it has been established, has subjected them to the most heavy yoke and tyranny in the history of mankind.

The regretful fact that some Catholic clergymen use their power over the masses to deceive them, affirming that Communism will take them out of their poverty and misery, and that Your Holiness endorses such affirmations, makes urgent an explanation of our concern. That is why we humbly supplicate Your Holiness to enlighten us with the light of truth in this respect in order to prevent the people from continuing to be deceived.

The case of Cuba cannot be forgotten. Fidel Castro has suppressed all liberties in Cuba; he has proclaimed himself a Marxist and, therefore, a materialist and atheist. But Fidel Castro would never have been able to enslave

The Montinian Church

Cuba's workers and peasants, if the Archbishop of Santiago and many other clergymen had not deceived the Catholic people, affirming that Fidel was no Communist, but a good freedom-loving Catholic. In Cuba, many shepherds, instead of preaching the truth and protecting the sheep from the wolf as our Lord Jesus Christ ordered them, deceived the sheep, giving them up to the wolf, betraying Christ and the people and adulterating their sacerdotal mission.

Among the hoaxes used in Cuba, the promise of suppression of poverty and raising the living standard of the working classes were two. The facts are plain to see: after the success of the tyrant Castro, attained with the aid of a large segment of the Catholic clergy, the wages of workers went down, and poverty increased instead of being suppressed. What is even worse, the workers who ask for wage increases are murdered, and there is mass-shooting of the peasants who attempt to strike and demand that the promises made prior to the revolution be fulfilled. Now, international Communism intends to reproduce this criminal hoax all over Latin America, and once again is using Catholic priests and bishops to exploit poverty and a desire for freedom. Some priests and bishops help to launch the people into subversive and revolutionary movements whose aim, sometimes openly, sometimes secretly, is to harness them to the yoke of Communism, the enemy of God and all liberty and, which, instead of suppressing famine and indigence, has catastrophically augmented them wherever it has been established. History reminds us that in Russia and China, after the Communist revolution, several million unfortunate peasants, clerks, and workers died from famine. Nothing of this nature has ever happened in Latin America, nor did it happen before Communism in Russia, which was known as the bread basket of Europe.

Their Holinesses Popes Leo XIII, Pius XI and Pius XII, in resolutely taking the side of social justice and fighting poverty, cried the alarm against the Communist danger and hoax, thus thwarting the kind of deceit we are depicting. That is why we humbly beg Your Holiness, now that you have honored us Latin Americans with your presence, that simultaneous with your reference to the Church's wish for social justice, you enlighten us, as did your above-mentioned predecessors, about the danger of materialistic atheistic Communism, thus preventing the bad shepherds from leading their sheep to the wolf's mouth, as in the case of Cuba. This is particularly urgent because some clergymen at various levels are acting as though His Holiness Pius XII's excommunication of Communists, clergymen, and laymen aiding them, has been overruled. Some clergymen even tell their believers that in reality, it has been overruled, which we all know is absolutely false.

The Communists who lie in ambush within the clergy have been able to skillfully deceive many prelates who acted in good faith, moving them to state that Latin America needs a change of structures, without the necessary condition of giving details as to what kinds of structures will replace those supposed to be eliminated. To destroy without building is absurd. In fact what the Communist clergymen who started this campaign want is to substitute present structures with those of totalitarian atheistic Communism; they talk about destruction and avoid mentioning the kind of structures that will replace those to be abolished. This favors the Communist deception, for Communism strives to cast people into destruction without their realizing where they are being led. To avoid the success of such tricks in fraudulently prejudicing the Catholic people, we humbly beg Your Holiness to prevent the clergy from speaking about change of structures without mentioning the new structures to be put into place, so that the people know where they are being led.

The hypocrisy of those Communists who have infiltrated the clergy can also be proven in a different way. In the cases of governments who are carrying out vast programs designed to improve the life conditions of the working classes as a whole, they refuse to participate in those grand designs; instead, they stand in their way and try to make them collapse, encouraging their parishioners to support the subversive Communist movements which disrupt the economy and sow anarchy and disorder. This leads the best projects of those governments to failure. They say the Church is not linked to any government, which is true, but they imply that the Church must be linked to *systematic* opposition to every government and is forbidden to cooperate with constructive plans worked out by some governments to suppress famine and indigence and to set up social justice. We humbly beg Your Holiness to prevent those clergymen from presenting the Holy Church as necessarily linked to opposition to every government, subversion, riot and disorder.

Summarizing, in Latin America there are two extremely grave problems which need urgent remedies. One is suppressing famine and poverty in many regions, raising the standard of living of the poor peasant and working classes, insuring social justice, and encouraging and supporting constructive plans drawn up by the governments, instead of fostering the subversion and chaos that could ruin such plans. Besides, the governments that have not yet acted, have to be called to action, giving them an opportunity *before* fostering chaos and anarchy, *not* vice versa, since, contrary to what the Communists-in-cassocks contend, the *Church is not linked to subversion, destruction, or chaos*. The second problem, as grave as the first, is the need of preventing the clergymen who serve Communism from deceiving their parishioners under the guise of suppressing poverty and famine and establishing social justice, deceiving them into supporting subversion and riots whose real aim is to introduce Communism, into Latin America. On the contrary, Communism, far from *eliminating* poverty and famine, would *augment* them and reduce the people to the most terrible sort of slavery in an officially materialistic and atheistic state.

We humbly beg His Holiness that, at the time he enlightens us with the principles of social justice inspiring the Holy Church, he put an end to the usage many clergymen are making of those noble aspirations to favor the propagation and triumph of anti-Christian, atheistic, and enslaving Communism.

Bogotá, August 20, 1968

WESTERN ANTI-COMMUNIST MEXICAN FEDERATION (FEMACO)

By:

Dr. Raymundo Guerrero
President

Dr. Rafael Rodríguez
Vice-President

Dr. Sergio Lastra
Secretary

SOME HISTORICAL BACKGROUND ON EUCHARISTIC CONGRESSES

In 87 years, 39 International Eucharistic Congresses have been celebrated in the Church. It was the faith and holy perseverance of a good woman that started these world expressions of Eucharistic faith which have contributed so much to our deeper knowledge of the Eucharistic Mysteries, the believers' more zealous participation in the Holy Sacrifice of the Mass, the reception of Holy Communion, and, above all, the public proclamation of Christ's kingdom. The Eucharist is the center of our religion, and it is at the Eucharistic table that the guests to the divine banquet must meet. Here they rise above material interests and learn to appreciate the interests of the divine life that was brought to us by Christ so that all of us may share in its abundance. But not all guests accept Christ's invitation. The Eucharist has been a source of scandal, due to human incredulity and haughtiness, ever since Jesus Christ issued the promise of its institution.

The first Eucharistic congress took place at Lille in June 1881 at the shrine of Our Lady of the Grapevine. It lasted three days and some 4,000 people from eight nations attended it. In its modest simplicity it was the beginning of those magnificent concentrations of genuine Catholicism, of enthusiastic response from those who believe in the divine gift wherein we receive Christ, the soul becomes filled with grace, and a pledge of everlasting happiness is given to us.

If two hundred French congressmen were able to consecrate France to the most Holy Heart of Jesus in the age of laicism and positivism when the Faith was fearfully concealed within temples and sacristies and this world's sages felt it was shameful to believe in the Eucharistic Mystery, why could not a great crusade of international meetings be undertaken to publicly proclaim a compendium of all the wonderful things God has done for man—the sacrificial

The Arrival of the Pope

Eucharist, the sacramental Eucharist, the Real and Permanent Presence of the Savior among us in the Eucharist.

At Bombay, as well as at Munich on the nights of closing earlier congresses, the huge squares—the Oval and the Theresenwiese respectively—were the stages for gatherings of more than a million persons each, *ex omni lingua, tribu et natione,* who in deep adoration received the *Eucharistic Bread* and praised the Lord's greatness. Lourdes, Rome, Budapest, Barcelona, Madrid, Vienna, Bombay, and Buenos Aires are places which have been blessed by these events of Catholic Faith and divine life. In Mexico we also had our memorable congress, if not international, at least national, and it was at the beginning of the tragic religious persecution during which blood bore witness to our parents' faith in the Divine Eucharist. The words of the anthem of that memorable Mexican congress, written by the great Jesuit, Fr. Julio Vértiz, resounded triumphally in all our Eucharistic processions until Vatican II killed the Constantinian Church to restore the restless and demagogic Church of the poor:

> Sing, sing, our fatherland kneels
> When Jesus Christ, the Redemptor, passes.
> A new sun shines for us,
> Sun of love, of love.

As in Bombay, Paul VI wanted to take part personally in the Congress of Bogotá. He had asked the Cardinal of Bombay to consider his trip a pilgrimage. His coming to Bogotá, however, would have a different meaning: He wanted to meet the poor and start the salvational program of *Populorum Progressio*, and it was only natural that the Eucharist be relegated to a secondary position. The new religion, accommodated to the ultra-modern world, had to be the religion of the assembly, of human solidarity, social equality, and repentant ecumenism which begs pardon for the aberrations of the ancient Church. This new religion accepts, respects, solemnly declares freedom of conscience, and permits worshipping God in the way that most conveniently suits each person's spiritual richness.

In analyzing Pope Montini's social pilgrimage to Colombia, the meddlesome Vatican journal writes:

> One would say that it is a verdict on political and social issues that is expected from the Pilgrim Pope before a Eucharistic altar.

This is probably correct, for more than being a Pope, John Baptist Montini is a politician who has bound himself to rebuild not only the Church, but the entire world, either for or against the institutional powers, for or against the prevailing ideologies, and for or against violence and revolution.

After having pointed out that the encyclicals *Mater et Magistra, Pacem in Terris,* and *Populorum Progressio,* as well as Paul VI's continued teaching, have already answered the questions of violence or nonviolence, evolution or revolution, *L'Osservatore Romano* says:

> What we mean is that regarding Paul VI's trip the error ought not to be repeated of those who consider the activity of the Church, not from a transcendental standpoint, but using criteria valid for political and social subjects, and not for faith and conscience.

The Vatican paper remarked that the welcome the Pope received from the peoples he visited in the past, Hindus, Christians, and non-Christians, wiped away all "malevolent forecasts."

The newspaper also stated:

> ...On the other hand it must be borne in mind that on each of his trips, the Holy Father maintained a polite and at the same time, independent attitude. The religious goal of the papal mission could never be denied, and the autonomy of the Pope's proposals can be inferred from their apostolic and pastoral nature.

We do not cease to be surprised at the insistence with which Pope Montini's trip has to be defended from any political aspect, to frame it within the new post-Conciliar pastorate. Taking into account the former Archbishop of Milan's political skill, diplomatic connections, and turn to the left, nobody could question his politeness toward the political authorities of the countries he visited nor his benevolent tolerance which permitted him to ecumenically embrace Hindus, Muslims, Jews, Masons, and Communists. What we can question is whether the multitudinous' of non-Christian or Protestant crowds was due to a healthy effect of Paul VI's visit, his warm greetings, his *ephod*[6] or *breastplate of judgment,* or his pastoral activity. The reasons more logical might have been a curiosity to see the Pope, who had never left Rome in the past nor traveled by airplane; the active propaganda and solicitous preparations by the members of the episcopate who did not want to lose the opportunity for future promotions in their ecclesiastical careers; or the political cunning of the civil authorities, who knew how to avail themselves of the opportunity for international propaganda and for winning the support of their Catholic subjects, even though only a few were present.

RETURNING TO THE POPE'S FLIGHT

The Avianca *Marshal Sucre* airplane is arriving at El Dorado airport. It

The Arrival of the Pope

was on Thursday, August 22, 1968, a few minutes after 10 a.m., that Pope Montini, for the first time as the sovereign Pontiff of the Catholic Church, stepped on the underdeveloped territory of Latin America which he called the Third World. A characteristically dramatic gesture impressed many people, although to tell the truth, it shocked many of us. The Pope, after having stepped on the earth, knelt to kiss it. This dramatic, spectacular gesture is contradictory to his subsequent suppression of genuflections at the Mass and the order that his progressivist fans try to impose upon all Catholics, of attending the Consecration of the Holy Sacrifice of the Mass and receiving Holy Communion standing. Was it perhaps the Teilhardian cosmogenesis, identified with the Christ-genesis, to confound itself at the omega point?

From the newspaper *El Espacio* we quote a demagogic chronicle showing the imprecision, lack of understanding, and lethargy noticed on that day in many Colombians and "pilgrims" regarding the unusual fact of the Pope's arrival:

> Here we have the august soul of Paul VI, the reigning Pontiff of Christ's Church, alighting on Colombian territory, the fatherland of a people who believe and practice the doctrines of the Son of God and who, perhaps because of their faith in the ineffable Martyr and His vivifying teaching, have obtained an invaluable grace, namely that Christ's visible head on earth extol and vivify them with his presence and his direct message of peace, understanding, and brotherhood.
>
> The present moment is the most convenient and adequate one for such a great ecumenical event, for presently all mankind is a flock not so much strayed as baffled, which, in its confusion, cannot find the doors of their sheepfold where they could receive loving shelter and warmth, protection from the furious elements, and radiant light amidst the darkness.
>
> It was at Jerusalem where, at the feast of unleavened bread, the Paschal Lamb had to be sacrificed, and where the Master wanted to take a seat at the table beside the twelve, to share with them the bread of life and the wine of the New Covenant. It is now at Bogotá, the capital of Colombia, where the beautiful old scene repeats itself, this time not on the eve of the grand deicide, but in expectance of the one who has to come, while the spirit of the Colombians is lifted up as a flag unfolded to the good wind and ready to approach the table of the mysterious banquet. Here one is invited to meditate, at least for a moment, on the dark meaning of hatred and the efforts for mutual destruction, in brief, the disarmament of the spirit.
>
> It all comes from the Second Vatican Council, this famous assembly of contemporary doctors of Christ's Church, on whom it can be said that the Holy Spirit came down a second time, at a new Pentecost to lead them along the right way sought and found by John XXIII, the Good Pope, and continued by our

The Montinian Church

illustrious visitor, Paul VI. This Council laid the basis for an essential and radical transformation in the Universal Church, which had possibly deviated from its primitive and eternal rules, this being the fault of those who mistook concepts and interpretations which led to disagreement and dispersion of the flock. This mistake has been obviated today by the efforts and goodwill displayed by the Vatican Council and its happy interpreters, who have planned the implementation of substantial reforms, as well as of understanding among all men.

The social doctrines proclaimed by the Church today clearly meet the need of the human genre, which so much lacks clear orientation. These doctrines, derived from truth, have permitted the rulers of Christendom to re-initiate the work of gathering imposed by the undeferrable necessity of having man understand that his way is not that of a beast. The privileged already find themselves staggering under the hard blows of the correctors of error who, in the name of Christ, are reviving and toning up His everlasting doctrines. These doctrines are the guiding norms of peaceful existence without discrimination and thus permit a definitive organization of men around the wonderful message of the Father and the message of peace entrusted to the Son.

The Vatican is no longer the household of reaction, a tame instrument of bold power used to attain its dark wishes. It has found its way, and Peter's heir will not be obliged again to hoist the flag of alien conquerors on Sant'Angelo.

To Colombia the presence of the sovereign Pontiff is a source of pride and grace, for with unbounding benevolence, he has come to our nation as a wonderful herald of a new spiritual order and the establishment and institution of ecumenical love.

With filial respect and admiration, we welcome the Holy Father, Paul VI, and convey to him our ardent wish that his visit to our fatherland will produce rich spiritual fruits not only for us, but also for the rest of the world. Let this visit of the supreme Shepherd of Christendom be an efficacious balm for all hearts of goodwill, and arouse all men's clear sense of peace and fraternity.

Such was the editorial, which in spite of its pretentious style, is impregnated with a rabid and heretical progressivism. It is unbelievable that these things could have been written and said at a Eucharistic congress in which so many cardinals, archbishops, bishops, and outstanding laymen gathered around Paul VI, to render a homage of faith, adoration, and praise to the Eucharistic Christ. And these heretical phrases circulated widely in Bogotá precisely on the day Paul VI performed the rite of kissing American soil. "Ecumenical event," ". . . mankind is a flock not so much strayed as baffled," "It all comes from the Second Vatican Council, . . ."—these were the words of Hernando Vega Escobar, the priest who wrote the above article. To progressivism, the Universal Church "had possibly deviated from its primitive and eternal rules, this being the fault of those who mistook concepts and interpretations which led to disagreement and dispersion of the flock." But this error or errors, have been "surpassed" today by the "famous assembly of contemporary doctors of Christ's Church, on whom it can be said that the Holy Spirit came down a second time, at a new Pentecost. . . ." It was Vatican II "and its happy interpreters" who have implemented "substantial reforms" in the Church and "understanding among all men." The new religion, the new, reformed Church that has accommodated itself to the modern world, is the new Whitsuntide, and the "contemporary doctors of the Church," the "experts" of the renowned pastoral council known as Vatican II, are the new apostles who, in denying the Church's infallibility for almost two thousand years, have come to mold a new religion which barely earns the name of Catholic and Christian. "This Council laid the basis for an essential and radical transformation in the Universal Church. . . ."

Indeed, this radical transformation is an auto-demolition of Christ's work and was not over with the Council, but has surpassed its author, inspirer, and ruler with unbelievable audacity, of which the Good Pope was just a docile and, perhaps, an unconscious tool.

The social doctrines proclaimed by the last two Pontiffs with the docile support of the Conciliar Fathers, have been inspired by the cabalistic signs of the times. These are doctrines produced by the ecclesiastical turnaround toward Communism which they want to Christianize if this is possible or, if not, to Communize Christianity. It is not the privileged who stagger "under the hard blows of the correctors of error . . .;" it is those dominated by error and their slaves who are demolishing the fundamental rights of man, his real liberties, his Catholic Faith, the immutable stability of the family, and everything pertaining to the rich heritage of our Western civilization, which germinated from the cross.

Discrimination and social inequality, so much hated by progressivists, have always existed and will as long as there are men in this world. Far from being eliminated by "the efforts and goodwill displayed by the Vatican Council and its happy interpreters," both discrimination and social inequality, as well as division and bloody fighting, have increased, particularly in our America despite Paul VI's ritual kiss. The social doctrines contained in *Mater et Magistra, Pacem in Terris,* and *Populorum Progressio* have parted from the traditional doctrine of the Church, the concrete application of Christ's Gospel, and have endeavored to merge Jewish, Masonic, and Communist premises with the genuine teaching of the Church's infallible Magisterium. The attempt has been to attain a utopia of mankind unified as to beliefs, government, social classes, and the just use of material goods, whose sole owners will be the descendants, *secundum carnem,* of materialistic Israel, the Israel which fought God and His Christ.

The Montinian Church

But let us go back to El Dorado, Bogotá's international airport to watch the thousands of persons who are warmly welcoming the Pontiff. "Three million people" said the journalists, but this is too large a number for the figure to be true. On such occasions, journalists are accustomed to exaggerate, for there is no risk they will be corrected. At any rate, there were a lot of people. This was something unusual that aroused curiosity although to tell the truth, one could not feel the religious fervor that we felt in Mexico when Cardinal Villanouvelle came as papal legate to attend the feasts of the semicentennial of the coronation of Saint Mary of Guadalupe.

When the airplane landed, the bells of the 105 temples of the city sounded and, from the peak of Monserrate, cannons fired 21 salutes to welcome the Pope of *Populorum Progressio*. At the airport, the President of the Republic of Colombia, Don Carlos Lleras Restrepo, his complete cabinet, the diplomatic body, the high officials of the sects, and the Jewish rabbis—all presided over by Cardinal Giacomo Lercaro—were waiting for the Pope. Pope Montini's golden dream was being fulfilled.

Upon appearing at the door of the aircraft, Paul VI received the first cheer of the people, who were finally seeing the Pope and who, if they did not receive his anachronistic blessings, *did* receive a victorious, open-armed salutation from the Pontiff. He went down to a red carpet which led him to a small platform on the central lane of the airport. There he listened to the welcome speech by President Lleras on behalf of Colombia's government and people. Paul VI answered with a brief allocution. Afterwards he received the military honors owed him as head of a government (which the Church still retains in this Church of the poor), honors presented with trumpets and shining sabers by the detachments of the military forces. What a contrast between this show, reminiscent of the Constantinian Church, and the entrance of John Baptist Montini as *primus inter pares* (without his tiara, which had been sent to the New York World's Fair to be publicly sold at auction) into Saint Peter's when he opened Vatican Council II!

After this first reception, Paul VI got into his Lincoln limousine and rode downtown. This was the same car he had used in New York in 1965, when he made his famous visit to the United Nations to deliver his deplorable speech, proclaiming that the hope of mankind was in the hands of that assembly dominated by international Jewry. It is an elegant, expensive car without a top and with a special compartment containing a throne that can be lifted 12 inches to give the crowd a better view of the supreme Shepherd of the Catholic Church. The Pope's car was the fourth one in a caravan of 14 automobiles. He was accompanied by his private secretary, Pasquale Macchi, and Cardinal Luis Concha Córdoba, the dethroned Archbishop of Bogotá. Eight motorcyclists of the presidential guard surrounded the papal car.

The Arrival of the Pope

PRESIDENT LLERAS' SPEECH

The text of the speech given by Don Carlos Lleras Restrepo, President of the Republic of Colombia to welcome Pope Paul VI to Colombia, is given below:

Most Pious Father:

Your Holiness is paying all Latin America a most high honor, coming here to participate in the 39th Eucharistic Congress. This land, crucible of so many races, entered modern civilization under the Sign of the Cross, and their peoples have remained almost unanimously Catholic. This common faith of ours is a strong factor of unity among our countries, despite the pluralism produced by geographic diversity and the different circumstances under which our peoples have evolved.

This is a link for which nothing could be substituted. It gives us a warm and deep feeling of brotherhood. That is why I believe that in paying filial homage to you, upon your setting foot on Colombian soil, I can speak, not only as a Colombian, to tell you that the whole continent from the Bravo River to the southern extreme, shares today in the same emotion, and that a feeling of veneration and gratefulness comes to Your Holiness from all the cities, valleys, mountains, jungles, and plains of America.

Colombia, most Pious Father, is a country which despite great hardship is bravely following the way of progress for all of its sons, seeking those conditions for human dignity that the illustrious word of Your Holiness has demanded on behalf of the Church. We have spent harsh hours of fighting, blinded by passions, but, fortunately, these hours are now over. A climate of political peace prevails among those who used to fight each other rudely. It is within this environment that we are trying to forge the structures of an egalitarian society, for we are sure that the spirit of the Gospel, more effectively than fear and more constructively than the spirit of rebellion, will inspire justice, curb egoism, appease ire, and eventually lead us to new plans of morality and welfare. Such efforts have received enormous support from the Vatican Council's Constitutions and papal encyclicals. The presence of Your Holiness and the environment of the Eucharistic Congress will no doubt greatly diffuse and create a deeper and more sincere evangelical spirit, without which all institutional reforms and material achievements would end by becoming altered by, or subordinated to, narrow selfishness.

Your coming, most Pious Father, moves us and, at the same time, fills us with hope. You are the symbol of our old faith, but your acts and words have also reminded us that more strongly than ever, the Church has resumed its work of charity and justice, and that, under your guidance, a revolution based upon Christian fraternity is firmly progressing and conquering souls more and more.

The Montinian Church

We turn our eyes toward Your Holiness, to the supreme Shepherd, who points out to us the right way to dignify the human race in its earthly life, to achieve peace in our days, and to attain everlasting happiness.

Through my humble voice, the people and government of Colombia merrily welcome Your Holiness, thank you for the gift of your presence, and beg your blessing for them and all of America.

This opening speech by President Lleras was that of a shrewd politician. He knew the though, leaning,and political activities of Pope Montini, and decorously stated the position of Colombia's government and people. He cautiously exposed the twisted deviations of progressivism, which is trying to divert the evangelical program through violence and Communizing socialism toward the absurd and unsubstantial program of so-called "social justice." The Colombian President, or the person who wrote his speech, no doubt had the ambiguous and revolutionary text of *Populorum Progressio* under his eyes. This encyclical states and summarizes the pastoral wishes and materialistic construction of the evangelical message now being preached by the post-Conciliar Church.

The greatness of Spanish America—or of Latin America, including Lusitanian Brazil—as President Lleras stated at the beginning of his speech, lies in the fact that "[t]his land, crucible of so many races, entered modern civilization under the Sign of the Cross, and their peoples have remained almost unanimously Catholic." The new theologians of progressivism question the Catholic Faith of our people; due to its expressions, they deem it reminiscent of superstition, idolatry, and degeneracy pertaining to the aboriginal tribes of our continent. However, I am sure our underdeveloped people's simple, ignorant, humble, and (in some people's minds), too-showy faith is more sincere, devout, and genuine than the rationalized faith of dialogue, pastoral *aggiornamento*, the post-Conciliar mind, and prevailing progressivism with its brainwashing, proselytizing dynamism, collective pressure and ecumenical pluralism. Our people do not *know*, but they *believe*. Many of them hardly know the essential dogmas of Salvation, but when the circumstances require it, they are ready to give their blood and their lives in the defense of their religion. On the other hand, the new Catholics are, or believe themselves to be, experts in theology; they feel competent to give their opinions and define even the most profound problems of our religion, but they do not believe, for they lack faith.

Faith, as we have explained, is an infused virtue which God conveys to us jointly with sanctifying grace on our justification through Jesus Christ. Through this virtue, as long as it is not lost, the Christian, even though he does not know or understand completely, accepts everything which God has revealed and which the authentic Magisterium of the Church teaches us. The Faith of the Church, the Faith of real believers, seeks and hopes in God, accurately projecting the secular onto the eternal. The faith of the post-Conciliar Church, of modern catechisms, of social justice, of mini- and maxi-doctors of prevailing progressivism, does not believe in God, but only in man, and seeks the fulfillment of the destiny of mankind in this world.

Undoubtedly the inveterate and living Catholic Faith of the Latin American peoples is the most conspicious wealth of these young countries. It is the cementing element of our nationalities, the "factor of unity," according to the Colombian President, that is stronger than "the different circumstances under which our peoples have evolved." Men can be united only by two factors: the material and the spiritual. The difference is that the unity arising out of the spiritual factor, the real faith, is deep, solid, and indestructible, while the unity arising out of the material factor of personal attractions or conveniences and of economic interests, is always ficticious and unstable, as it carried the seeds of disintegration and fratricidal battles within itself. That is why one of the darkest and least admissible issues in the docuoents of Vatican II, is the famous statement on religious liberty that seems to justify or enact not ethnic, social, or economic pluralism, but a pluralism of religion, creed, and faith which necessarily leads to indifferentism, atheism, and syncretism, in which our dogmas get mixed up and confounded with the most crass errors and even irreligiosity. To damage a people's religious unity and common faith is a criminal offense against its very nationality and foments bloody fighting, because a faithless man becomes a cruel and ferocious beast.

President Lleras was right in assuming the right of expressing the unanimous feeling of all Latin American Catholic countries, which, by the grace of God and despite the sects' and the lodges' nefarious activities, remain believing nations. The most dangerous enemy our countries' Faith has ever had is the de-sacralizing and blasphemous activity of progressivist priests and bishops such as Alvarez Icaza, Avilés, and other mini-pontiffs of the new Church.

"Colombia," said the President, "is a country which ... is ... following the way of progress. . . ." It appears that the President had intended to tell Paul VI that his country was not unaware of the innovating doctrine of *Populorum Progressio*, but that the Colombian people, not the guerillas nor the National Liberation militia, sought material improvement of the poor classes in different ways, within the immutable hierarchy of life's values. Peace, without which progress is impossible, has been enthroned in Colombia by the energetic attitude of the government which curbed the "Bogotazo" and guerila subversion within the framework of the law.

"It is within this environment [a climate of political peace made possible by repression of Communism], that we are trying to forge the structures of an egalitarian society, for we are sure that the spirit of the Gospel, more effectively than fear and more constructively than the spirit of rebellion, will inspire justice, curb egoism, appease ire, and eventually lead us to new plans of morality and welfare." These words by the President contain the wise answer of a prudent ruler who knew quite well the demagogic demands of the new apostles of social justice. A new plan of morality is the only way for the nations' genuine progress, for morality alone is the way of real progress and social welfare. It has been lost, and the Church's shepherds must seek it prior to any secular progress. Let us raise the morals of all citizens according to the immutability of God's law and the Gospel's doctrine, so that we will foster the constructive progress that so much concerns Paul VI. Without this deep and sincere evangelical spirit, "all institutional reforms and material achievements would end by becoming altered by, or subordinated to, narrow selfishness."

As praise to Paul VI and as acknowledgment of his reformist work, the Colombian ruler said: "... under your guidance, a revolution based upon Christian fraternity is firmly progressing and conquering souls more and more." Indeed Paul VI's integral humanism has been a *real revolution,* not only in the Church, but also in the nations which have been shattered by the agitation brought by the restless new apostles who have disregarded their transcendent and everlasting mission and seek "to dignify the human race in its earthly life, to achieve peace in our days, and to attain everlasting happiness" along new ways. The innovators seek the lost Eden now that the myth of "original sin" has been definitely surpassed by the astonishing progress of the new theology. Whether Christian brotherhood is the goal of the revolutionaries has yet to be proven. I believe that evangelical love does not organize revolutions, strikes, and socializing parties. Neither does it cover itself with the showy cloak of Christian democracy, which from the outside looks like a luminous advertisement for Christianity, while inside is Communism which boldly enslaves, divides, and kills without scruples.

THE POPE'S GREETING TO LATIN AMERICA

In answer to the President's speech, Paul VI voiced a greeting which used words I find somewhat similar to those of his legate, Cardinal Lercaro, at the beginning of the Congress. So it has to be, since the chief goal of the planning of this historical event was not so much the Eucharist as an audacious change of structures. According to the new pastoral sociologists, a change in the structure of a uniform socialistic system that destroys borders, eliminates prejudice, suppresses social inequality, and even accepts intercommunion among all religions, in other words, the pluralistic ecumenism of Vatican II was the only way for the Latin American nations to survive.

Below I quote Paul VI's first speech after having kissed the American earth:

The Arrival of the Pope

Mister President:

We greatly appreciate your politeness toward us, your presence here, and your hearty welcome from the Colombian nation.

We are deeply grateful to Your Excellency, the members of the government, the ecclesiastical, civil, and military officers, and all persons gathering here for your kind welcome to us at our arrival at this religious pilgrimage. We consider our trip a part of our world ministry and through it we want to unmistakably ratify our Faith, the Faith of all Catholicism in the Eucharistic Sacrifice and Sacrament, and to pray before the Prince of Peace for the world, which needs peace so much.

Our spirit is infused with inward joy and turbulent excitement at the thought that Providence has awarded us the privilege of being the first Pope to arrive in this most noble land on this Christian continent. Here, on a mysterious day, through God's predestined plan of salvation, the height of the cross was added to that of the Andean peaks, and the shadow of Christ was thrown upon the old paths of the Chibcha, Maya, Inca, Aztec, Tupí and Guaraní.

I greet all Latin American peoples, stirred by the same seas, among whose rivers and mountain ridges interweave communities of honest, patient, hard-working, and noble people; whose noble looks have the common feature of Christ's Faith, which has quickened centuries of history and given birth to countless moves promoting your culture and welfare. To each and every one of you, from Colombia's hospitable soil, our greeting, our love, our prayers. Our heart expands to thank God for the immense gift of your Catholic belief, and to beg Him that the dynamism of your traditional and renewed faith will arouse a feeling of fraternity and harmonious cooperation. We pray that you will foster and consolidate efforts toward an orderly progress which, through technical development and rational cultivation of the abundant wealth which the Lord has put into your soil, will equitably reach all families and classes in accordance with Christian principles.

Most beloved children from Colombia and all America: In the pleasant hope of putting all your intentions, needs, and wishes upon the altar of this Congress, our hands raise to bless you, ardently wishing that the Sign of the Cross will reach the whole word, as a testimony of our love and as a pledge of divine gifts.

Pope Montini calls his comfortable trip from Rome to Bogotá a religious pilgrimage which he considers to be a part of his world ministry. According to Paul VI, all of his spectacular trips, to the Holy Land, the United Nations in New York, India, Geneva, America, the Philippines, Australia, or Hong Kong, are religious pilgrimages. Since the Pope always moves in the religious field, these trips are parts of his world ministry. In the present circumstances, due to the hurricane that was blowing and in order to avoid suspicion and uneasiness, it was necessary to make restatement of his faith, of the faith of all Catholicism, in the Eucharistic Sacrifice and Sacrament.

The Pontiff, tremulously excited at the feeling of having been predestined by divine Providence to be the first Pope to step on Latin American soil (he had already been in the United States), cannot help contemplating Christ's cross which was raised by the children of Spain and Portugal not on the impressive peaks of the Andes, but in the Christianized hearts of people regenerated by Baptism, "Latin American peoples... communities of honest, patient, hard-working, and noble people; whose noble looks have the common feature of Christ's Faith."

But the Pontiff's lyricism, besides singing our peoples' Catholic Faith, does not and cannot forget *the new pastoral of Vatican II*, and the *Populorum Progressio*. Paul VI's heart expands to thank God for the immense gift of our Catholic belief. Despite his anti-colonialistic position, clearly stated in his social encyclical, the Pontiff acknowledges the fact that the works of Spain and Portugal, assuming divine intervention of course, were not absolutely negative in America. Our Catholicism, justly appreciated by Paul VI as an immense gift from God, derives from the titanic work of holy missionaries and the splendid collaboration of the crown of Spain. But he avowed it in order to prepare the new conquest, which, under the inspiration of Vatican II, was taking shape on those turbulent days of the International Eucharistic Congress under the leadership and guidelines of the Reformer Pope.

That is why Paul VI begged that the dynamism of our traditional and *renewed* faith would arouse a feeling of fraternity and harmonious cooperation, and would foster and consolidate efforts toward orderly progress, which, through technical development and rational cultivation of the abundant wealth which the Lord has put into our soil, may equitably reach all families and classes in accordance with Christian principles. We have "traditional faith" but also a "renewed faith." The traditional faith looked to *Heaven;* the new faith, renewed by Vatican II's pastoral documents and the most active solicitude of the current Pontiff, looks to the *earth*, to a material orderly progress, based on technical development and rational cultivation of the abundant wealth the Lord put into our soil. *Our faith has been renovated and reformed.* The ancient Faith, the one that exploited the precious lodes of revealed truth, the supernatural world, the everlasting perfect life, has been impotent to establish the most valuable order of "social justice" in our nations. Without this order there can be no Christian brotherhood, harmonious cooperation, or orderly progress. That is why the *aggiornamento*, the reformation, the new religion that more authentically expressed the evangelical sources, were urgently needed.

The ancient missionaries knew how to teach our religion's Mysteries through the eloquent language of our magnificent temples, our sacred images and our splendorous divine worship. People believed, people sang, and people

The Arrival of the Pope

put into practice the teaching of their priests. Today the reformed, abstract religion, deprived of saints, lights, bells, and organ, the religion that has exchanged the splendor of the ancient liturgy for the assembly and incomprehensible reading of Bible verses by the Protestant table, prefers that people think not so much about their future life, but translate their divine Faith into a material and technical progress.

So with words similar to those of his legate, Paul VI defined the real goal of the Congress, whose acts, according to a diligently masterminded plan, had to culminate in the revolutionary LAMEC meetings.

Chapter XIX

MONSIGNOR HELDER CAMARA ARRIVES IN COLOMBIA AND ISSUES STATEMENTS

Upon his arrival in Bogotá, Helder Camara, the controversial Archbishop of Olinda and Recife, Brazil, met his "alter ego," the no-less-controversial Bishop of Cuernavaca, Don Sergio Méndez Arceo, and granted an interview in which he told world press representatives that a bloody revolution in Latin America would give birth to an intervention of American imperialism that would "lead to the failure of the planned liberating revolution." He also stated that his theses were not new, for they had been inspired by the teaching of Vatican II. In his mind, young priests were longing for change and audacious amendments, indoctrinated as they had been by the activities and teachings of the post-Conciliar Jesuits. He felt that the new Church ought to be "a socialistic Christendom." Speaking about the forthcoming LAMEC meeting, he said:

> The Latin American Episcopal Conference will not have any special issues. There is a working document, prepared by a group of "experts." This is a preliminary paper which has been sent to all episcopal conferences on this continent. At the meeting a joint document will be presented; there will be no personal thesis . . .
>
> I am a supporter of nonviolence. I do not interpret this attitude as cowardice or pacifism. To me, nonviolence means nonconformity. I respect and will respect those who have chosen violence. I do want to state that the Latin American structures need change. The masses are marginal in their economic, social, political, religious, etc., lives, and it is necessary that they are integrated. . . . The masses are not prepared for revolution; this will take 15 to 20 years. The revolution is made not by intellectuals, politicians, clergy, nor students, but by the *oppressed masses*. . . ."

If the Archbishop could speak like this at a Eucharistic Congress some moments prior to Paul VI's arrival, it becomes evident what was projected for Latin America under the guise of a Eucharistic Congress. The program is clear: *they wanted and want now to socialize Latin America*, although to appease us, they tell us this socialization will not be carried on in the Russian way, but in our own way, respecting the dignity of the human personality. Revolution, in the post-Conciliar Church, is a Christian imperative designed to implement radical change of all structures. That it be violent or not is optional and secondary; it depends on the persons and the circumstances. In His Excellency's mind it is not the intellectuals, politicians, clergy, or students who will make the revolution. This is a cunning way of inviting all groups to join and lead the revolution. The oppressed masses cannot operate without a motor that sets them into motion.

In his statement, the revolutionary Archbishop pointed out that the post-Conciliar clergy was not out to make *little reforms* in Latin America, but *deep and positive changes of structures.* Analyzing Don Helder's thought, through these and many other statements of his, we feel that the Vatican's turnaround toward Communism, of which I have spoken before, is the goal sought by the post-Conciliar clergy in its reformist activity. All such activity is demagogic, compromising, nefarious and in contradiction to the supernatural mission which Christ assigned to His Church and His Church's apostles as the sole and supreme task to be accomplished. *It is evident that the Vatican approves and backs Don Helder's and Don Sergio's opinions and restless activity.* Without such aid, Their Excellencies would never have dared to promote subversion in Latin America so intensely.

To a question posed by journalists: "Would you raise Camilo's proselyting flag in Latin America?" the shrewd prelate answered as follows:

> If it is a question of mass liberation through nonviolent means, I would take the flag Camilo dropped when he died.... On the other hand, if it is a question of violence, I would not take it. One has to define the form of revolution.

Here we have the concrete and clear program: *One has to define the form of revolution.* In other words: the revolution has already been scheduled, blessed, and in fact, has begun all over Latin America. The orders come from above and have the inspiration of the Holy Spirit, who spoke through his Conciliar experts and the revolutionary encyclical *Populorum Progressio.* "As a rule, violence has to be discarded, for it is not constructive." In this vital issue, His Excellency Don Helder agrees with the Father General of the Jesuits. But when Christian democracy cannot be used as in Chile or Mexico under the nationalist name of *National Action,* when institutional violence fails to yield to the well-aimed blow of the elections, then ... well, then, let us have violence. But neither Don Helder, nor Don Sergio, nor the Pardinas, Mazas, Ertzes, Aviléses, nor all those *social justice* apostles and their satellites pertaining to the fake right wing, will take the flag Camilo Torres Restrepo dropped when he died, and head the guerilla movement. To do this, one needs special guts they do not have. But at the rear guard, they will keep on performing their specific tasks by sowing confusion, hatred, and rebellion among the poor, until the form of revolution becomes fully defined.

There is a point at which Don Helder's demagoguery identifies itself with that of the false prophets who are out to redeem us today. They all contend that the main enemy is American imperialism, of which the Latin American oligarchies are mere instruments. I do not intend to defend the American people here, for this is not the aim of my book, but I want to say that these people are accused of misbehaviors, abuses, and monstrous crimes which in reality are committed by a satanic mafia dominating and oppressing the American people. This mafia hides behind United States institutions and protects itself with the power and very blood of legitimate American citizens who do not have a double nationality. This imperialism, whose design is a world government and a religion of "world brotherhood," is not of the United States, but of the mafia. After having succeeded in imperceptibly enslaving, deceiving, and prostituting the American people, the mafia, using the huge resources of that mighty country, is carrying out its final conquest of enslaving the whole world.

But this cannot be said by those, who as useful tools, are engaged in this world conspiracy. Maybe they do not even *know* this. To them, the number one enemy is American imperialism or the United States government and people. They do not understand or even conceive of the fact that the American people are the prey of a secret power that controls and dominates all their institutions in the same way it controls England, France, and many other countries. World liberation will begin the day we open our eyes and acknowledge our enemy, the eternal enemy, the one who has plotted and keeps on plotting against all peoples' liberties.

There is another interesting point in Don Helder's statement on his arrival in Bogotá: "The masses," said the Archbishop, "are not prepared for revolution; this will take 15 to 20 years." What kind of preparation is His Excellency referring to? Military preparation? Political preparation? Demagogic preparation? Doctrinal preparation? All training takes time. In Mexico, after much civic education received from *National Action*, we have failed to learn the first lesson of real democracy. That is why I guess that, despite restless activity on the part of the new apostles of social justice (those who gave up the altar and the cassock to agitate the people), the time scheduled by Don Helder can be insufficient, unless they can count on the vigorous aid of intellectuals, politicians, high and low clergy, and students, who have proven to be good cannon fodder. But Don Helder *is* right: *Revolutions are made by the masses,* that is, by people unconsciously led by those who orient, control, and organize movements. Without the blood of such victims, the resistance of those who defend themselves or their rights cannot be crushed or broken down.

The Montinian Church

From the newspaper *El Tiempo* of Bogotá, Saturday, August 24, 1968, page 5, we quote the following information about Don Helder:

A nonviolent action project is to be presented by Msgr. Helder Camara at the Medellín Episcopal Assembly next week. In a 3,000-word paper, the Brazilian prelate sets the goals, mystique, and methods for a "positive, brave, dynamic, efficacious, and nonviolent action designed to free the Latin American continent from *institutional violence* without resorting to *armed violence.*"

This detailed plan most likely enjoys Pope Paul VI's approval, and *will be launched all over the continent, with precise goals, from 1968-1969. Its performers will be 15 percent of the Latin American bishops, priests and Christian laymen,* whom Don Helder calls *Abrahamic Minorities,* those who hope even in hopeless conditions. . . .

Well-informed sources estimate that the proposals for action presented to the bishops of the LAMEC Department for Social Action at Bahia, Brazil, will be ratified by Paul VI in his Bogotá speeches.

The document mentioned above examines the Christian attitude toward the already established violent groups in Latin America, and concludes: *"It is a question of justice and intelligence to honor the memory of those who sacrificed themselves as their consciences ordered them. They proved their sincerity by giving up their lives. God will accept all blood shed for thirst after righteousness."*

Don Helder Camara, who for health reasons will not be in Bogotá during the celebration of the IEC, will travel to Medellín next August 26, to attend the second general conference of LAMEC, as a representative of the Brazilian episcopate.

"Latin American Christians," Helder Camara proceeded to say, "have a triumphalistic approach in that we live in a Christian continent, and Latin America is a Christian creation. Today our approach is getting humbler and more realistic in that we admit our grave sins of omission. We are beginning to admit that we are very much responsible for the present underdeveloped condition of Latin America. We admit there is Indian slavery, national slavery, and internal colonialism."

From this point Don Helder proposes nonviolent action, for, "since abuse is structural, change must also be structural. *The Latin American condition is an invitation to violence. For violence against the weak is in process right now."* He adds, *"Above all, the impression of our youth is that violence is the only possible answer to violence."*

The Brazilian prelate pointed out that the roots of the new movement are to be found in the Gospel and in reality. *"Nothing is as deeply revolutionary as the Gospel,"* but this in no way means *violent* revolution. The revolution the Gospel demands works in us through divine grace and our cooperation. It consists of conversion, victory over selfishness and egoism, and for God and man.

Monsignor Helder Camara

"Though violence seems to be a solution, it is not; though it seems to belong to the Latin American scenario, in fact it does not. Anywhere in the world, especially in our continent, if violence were to burst forth, we would immediately have a new Vietnam. Even without a declaration of war, powerful forces would come to stimulate armed fighting with the aid of the most modern means of destruction."

Don Helder clearly defines the aims of nonviolence as follows: "Aid the Latin American masses to become a people and to get rid of underdevelopment without resorting to violence; give those who do not believe in anything or anybody a reason to believe, hope, and live; mobilize the youth around a cause which will arouse their hopes."

Using principles taken from the Christian message, the document defines the basis of a mystique: "Our condition as children of God implies fraternity among all men; our obligation to love our neighbor is as fundamental as that of loving God; our obligation to submit to the Will of God purports our mastery of nature and our perfecting of creation; our obligation to imitate the Son of God leads us to become incarnated in space and time, in order to bear our brothers' problems.

"Nonviolence may not be vague or romantic. It must aim high and keep its feet on earth. The more concretely it is able to act the better." emphasizes Don Helder in his blueprint, which delineates the 1968 to 1969 activity, established in the constitution of the *Abrahamic Minority's* working groups which seek to *take advantage of the commemoration of human rights.* "Nothing is as inspiring as what to do and how to do it, as reading the *Declaration of Human Rights* to find out which articles are the most disregarded and rejected.

"When it is proven that articles are *not* being applied, let this news be known to the population; at the same time it is indispensable to affirm the conviction that this disregard and contempt for human rights has to be fought and defeated. The most difficult, but most beautiful and efficient way of fighting abuse and injustice is nonviolent action. Nonviolence is believing that truth, justice, and love are stronger than lies, injustice, and hatred. It becomes uncomfortable and provokes reactions, and can be put into practice only when its supports are firm enough to answer violence with cries of faith, civic anthems, and acceptance of mass imprisonment."

This transcendental document ends by proposing a charter which is the same one used by Martin Luther King in the United States, and reads as follows:

> I give up my physical and spiritual person to nonviolent action. In consequence, I promise to fulfill the following ten commandments:
> 1. Meditate every day on Christ's preaching and life.
> 2. Remember that nonviolent action seeks achievement of justice and not victory.

The Montinian Church

3. Maintain an attitude of love in words and deeds, for God is love.
4. Pray every day to God for the grace to be an instrument of His, so that all men may be free.
5. Give up your personal interests in order that all men may be free.
6. Observe all rules of politeness with friends and enemies.
7. Devote yourself regularly to the service of other people and the world.
8. Avoid violence in heart, tongue, and hand.
9. Try hard to practice spiritual and physical hygiene.
10. At rallies, obey the orders of nonviolent action and the leaders thereof.

In the above statements by Don Helder, which are as smart as those of his colleague and comrade Don Sergio XII, we find the eternal trap of ambiguous, insidious and two-faced progressivism, which sometimes affirms, and then denies, sometimes simulates a dove-like simplicity and at other times may be as poisonous as the most dangerous of snakes. Let us remove the veil and see what he introduces as an up-to-date application of the evangelical program, *as a new redemption for us*.

Don Helder starts by saying that Latin America has to be liberated through "positive, brave, dynamic, efficacious, and nonviolent actions...." From whom must this poor victim be liberated? Is it violence against the weak, which is in process right now, or from violence institutionalized in the present structures? He seems to discard violence; it would have been dangerous to proclaim violence as the sole liberation device. Shrewd and skillful as he is, Don Helder knows how to engage other people without getting involved himself. He implicitly defends violence, however, when he speaks of "the memory of those who sacrificed themselves"—the guerillas, the red militiamen who have fallen in the battleground or are carrying out terrorism, ambush, kidnapping, air piracy, and all the other forms of struggle in the violent Latin American groups—and implies that we should honor their memory. *"It is a question of justice and intelligence...,"* says this prudent prelate. A question of justice, for they fight and die for a most noble cause, *the socialization of Latin America,* and a question of intelligence, for in this way we shall be able to aid them without becoming involved in civil or military courts. We are on their side; we perform our proper role, that of creating the environment, stirring nonconformity, cultivating demogoguery, and brainwashing those naive people who come to us or follow us. We will not condemn those who have shed their blood "for thirst after righteousness."

Ours was a triumphal approach of the Church and the world; but now, thanks to the preaching of progressivism, the ominous silence of the hierarchies, the Jesuitical demagoguery, and the new privileges supporting and enriching the promoters of subversion, "our approach is getting humbler and more realistic. . . . We are beginning to admit that we are very much responsible for the present underdeveloped condition of Latin America," says Camara.

Since Pope Montini begged pardon of the "separated brethren" at the beginning of the second session of Vatican II, everybody blames the Church for all the evils their people have suffered. "We admit," says the Archbishop, "there is Indian slavery, national slavery, and internal colonialism." In this accusatory sentence against the Church, its hierarchy of the past, and our very ancestors, several points should be cleared up, defined, and distinguished. Was there in America official, legal, and real slavery? Did the Church or Spain authorize such slavery? Were not there most wise laws protecting Indians and Negroes against the undoubtedly inadmissible human abuse on the part of the conquerors? Cannot His Excellency remember the speech Fr. Francisco Vieyra, S.J., delivered in his country against the slave trade's clandestine establishment in some regions of the New World in violation of statutes passed by the crowns of Spain and Portugal? Does not the Brazilian prelate know the wonderful work of Don Vasco de Quiroga, Fray Bartolomé de las Casas, and pious Sebastián de Aparicio, on behalf of the Indians? Even if there were no documents concerning these works, the stones of many hospitals, colleges, asylums, and temples, built by the Church of colonial times would bear silent but eloquent witness to the apostolic, civilizing, and extraordinarily beneficial activity of the wonderful saintly missionaries for the benefit of the natives and Africans. Mister Archbishop, how is it possible that you do not know this story, or adulterate it to serve the destructive and enslaving cause of international Communism?

Don Helder also implies an accusation against all the present Latin American régimes which do not belong to the Communist side. His Excellency says there is "national slavery and internal colonialism" and we "admit" it. Who is admitting it? The Church, the bishops, the clergymen, God's people? So it seems. We are all guilty, all of us except those who are Castroite militants and protect and encourage the guerillas. The Archbishop contends that all Latin American governments enslave the nations of the New World, with the consent, tolerance, and cooperation of the Church, save the progressivists, who are strenuously working to bring about Communism. And, without giving any evidence, he also says we are experiencing an internal colonialism. This demagogic phrase of Don Helder has evidently been taken out of *Populorum Progressio,* since this encyclical cursed all possible forms of colonialism, with the exception of red colonialism. I cannot agree with Don Helder, at least as far as Mexico is concerned, for I believe ours is a constitutional regime. Despite the defects and imperfections our constitution may have, it undoubtedly grants the country stability.

The Montinian Church

The chief sentence in the aforesaid statement, the one that synthesizes the thought and action of this Brazilian prelate and his progressivist brothers, reads as follows: *"[S]ince abuse is structural, change must also be structural."* [italics added]. That is why Don Helder discretely adds: "The Latin American condition *is an invitation to violence,* [italics added], for violence against the weak is in process right now." It is the violence of neo-colonialism, the law, and constitutional order, that invites another kind of violence, that of the guerilla, kidnapping, terrorist acts, air piracy, etc.

The prelate washes his hands as Pilate did, and confirms and ratifies his thesis using the witness of young people: "... the impression of our youth is that violence is the only possible answer to violence." To Don Helder, law is violence, order is violence, authority is violence, private property is violence, differences and inequality among men is violence, Christian civilization is violence, and there is no freedom outside the guillotine of the revolution, the shooting wall, the purges of Moscow and Cuba, and the sweet tyranny of international Communism. The youngsters, always the youngsters! Meanwhile, grown-ups deceive the youngsters, incite them, and skillfully avoid their own penal liability for their subversive work!

"Nothing is as deeply revolutionary as the Gospel," [italics added] Don Helder affirms subsequently. This phrase is dangerous, very dangerous, especially after what the prelate had said before about violence. Then the demagogic tone of his statements becomes the pastoral unction of a mystic: "The revolution the Gospel demands works in us through divine grace and our cooperation. It consists of conversion, victory over selfishness and egoism, and love for God and man," instead of the violent revolution which the young people long for and which we must respect.

Despite his nonviolent approach, this restless prelate proposes not a six-year or five-year, but a two-year plan to be carried out from 1968 to 1969. Those were years of turbulence and bloody fighting in all or almost all Latin American countries, including Mexico with its student conflicts, its Strike Committee in which some Jesuits, Marists, and perhaps some Lasallists were involved. These have the support of Brother Rafael Martínez, former director of the Benavente from Puebla, expert in guerilla art and invisible head of MURO,[7] and of Ramón Plata Moreno, an engineer who is no engineer, but an Israelite convert to our holy religion, as he vigorously swears. Brother Martínez is in Rome, where he holds an important position with the Superior General of the Brothers of Christian Schools. In times past these brothers were meritorious teachers of youth, but now they are cunning financiers and expert agitators leading secret groups.

The Brazilian Archbishop knew what he was talking about when he announced the *Abrahamic Minority* could rely upon 15 percent of the bishops, clergymen, and Catholic laymen to support his movement. The objectives, specifically defined by Don Helder, consist of aiding the Latin American masses, promoting development or, better said, raising from underdevelopment (thereby giving a reason to believe, hope, and live to those who do not believe in anything or anybody), and finally, mobilizing the youth. The apostles of social justice do not derive inspiration from the Gospel, however, although the prelate considers it to be "deeply revolutionary," but from the *Declaration of Human Rights* issued by the French Revolution. "Nothing is as inspiring," says the revolutionary Archbishop, "as what to do and how to do it, as reading the *Declaration of Human Rights*...."

It is no longer the Ten Commandments which show man the straight way of duty, but the commandments of Martin Luther King, approved and blessed by Don Helder Camara's episcopal authority.

The name which the Brazilian prelate gives the mafia devoted to the self-destruction of the Church of Christ is very meaningful and appropriate in that it points to the enemy masterminding this subversion, namely the ABRAHAMIC MINORITY who are the executors of International Jewry.

Chapter XX

PAUL VI IN BOGOTÁ, AND HIS RELATIONSHIP WITH THE HEBREWS

We have had enough of the Brazilian Archbishop, Don Helder Camara, and his subversive preaching. Let us go back to Paul VI's restless activity and the numerous elaborate and synchronized speeches he delivered during his brief stay at Bogotá. There is no room here even to quote all these speeches, and to analyze and comment on them would be even more difficult. We shall confine ourselves therefore, to the leading ones, in which we shall clearly find the Pontiff's thought and the *practical goals* of his trip to Latin America.

The chief event of the International Eucharistic Congress, the event which took the place of the triumphal procession closing the expressions of zeal, faith, love, and enthusiasm toward the Divine Eucharist at previous congresses, was the great *peasant rally,* through which Paul VI tried to enter into a dialogue of salvation with the poor classes of our underdeveloped countries. In Pope Montini's mind, that meeting would permit him to directly convey the constructive doctrine of *Populorum Progressio.*

Before attacking this subject, I feel it is necessary to study a most important point which perhaps may give us the key to the *disquieting enigma* of the present Pontiff. We shall analyze Paul VI's meeting with a Hebrew community at Bogotá, as reported by *El Espectador,* Saturday, August 24, 1968, page 1A, column 4:

> *At a Hebrew community. Fruitful collaboration.*
> We beg God to bless our efforts toward fruitful collaboration for the good of all mankind, so that there may come the day when all peoples will invoke the Lord with the same voice and serve Him under a single yoke.

The above brief words by Paul VI, bearing in mind who uttered them, what was said, and to whom they were addressed, are revealing. For some time frequent and no-longer-secret relations have been cultivated by the leaders of the great Jewish international agencies with the Holy See. On January 25, 1966, in the era of Vatican Council II, *Look,* a magazine published in the

United States by Jewish groups, featured a revealing article by Joseph Roddy, whose title shows us the importance of the bargaining being carried on at the top levels of the Vatican between the Hebrews and the ecclesiastical authorities: "How the Jews Changed Catholic Thought." It is a one-sided statement and as such, has exceptional value. Joseph Roddy, a Jew, writes:

> In the simplicity of their faith most Catholics rest their beliefs on the hard questions and not quite mature answers of the catechism... In the catechism they learn that *Catholic dogma cannot change* and, more importantly, that *the Jews killed Jesus Christ*."

The attack was launched against our catechisms. They had to be modified; their doctrine had to be a different one. Perhaps here we have the basic reason for the existence of new catechisms which today are circulating and adulterating Catholic doctrine. It is a mistake to believe and say that Catholic dogma cannot change, just as it is a mistake to keep on believing that the Jews were responsible for the death of Jesus Christ.

Previously, Hans Küng had written:

> As historical, human formulas, the definitions of the Church can be and must be improved. One of the features of dogma is its polemic perspective.
>
> In consequence, a polemically defined truth contains a peculiarly erroneous side. In its verbal formulation, every statement may be true and false. It is more difficult to discover how it has been thought than how it has been said. The "ecumenical" task of the theology of two sides consists of finding the truth contained in the error of others and the probable error found in one's own truth.

Such was the position the famous Conciliar "experts" succeeded in infiltrating most skillfully into the thought and deeds of the Vatican II Fathers. They admitted the possibility of amending and re-formulating the dogmatic definitions of the official, genuine, and infallible Magisterium of the Church. Without this fundamental attitude, Vatican II would not have been able to introduce its "reformation" into the Church. However, this attitude not only contradicts what Vatican I had dogmatically and immutably defined, but implicitly denies and destroys the Church's indefectibility and inerrancy.

Vatican I, which was a dogmatic and not merely a pastoral ecumenical council, said:

> The God-revealed doctrine of Faith cannot be considered as a doctrine propounded to the human intelligence in order that it perfect it, as if it were a philosophical system, but as a divine deposit entrusted to Christ's Spouse, that must be faithfully kept and infallibly taught. Hence, the same meaning of the

Paul VI in Bogotá

sacred dogmas Holy Mother Church defined must be perpetually conserved, and never, under the apparent pretext of finding a higher or deeper meaning, may one part from what the Church taught, not even verbally. (Vat. I, Sess. III; Densinger 3020).

In Canon 3, *"De Fide et Ratione,"* Vatican Council I defines:

> Should anyone contend that, at some time with the progress of science, it may be possible to give a higher (deeper) meaning (formulation) to the dogmas than the one the Church has always understood and understands, let him be anathema.

In fact, taking into account that dogma is the God-revealed word, and that when the Magisterium defines a dogma, it does not invent it, but merely tells us that this piece of truth has been revealed by God and belongs to the deposit of the divine redemption, and that its definition or statement is infallibly supported by Christ's promises, then it follows that said definitions are immutable and unreformable, which is the meaning of the Church's *inerrancy* and *indefectibility*.

The Jewish infiltrators who financed, led, and corrupted the faith of the "experts," had the necessary elements to provoke and lead the horrible revolution we are seeing in the Church. Under the guise of *aggiornamento* and adaptation, pieces of truth previously defined by the infallible Magisterium that we ought to have held as unchangeable were denied and muffled. That is why Roddy, in the euphoria of his success, laughs at the immutability of our dogmas. Here we have the fundamental explanation of the *auto-demolition* of the Church which has already caused the loss of countless souls. The basis of Vatican II was not a sincere, unreformable, infallible and safe acceptance of our dogmas, but an acceptance of the possibility and convenience of amending some dogmas already defined by the competent Magisterium. The monolithic immutability of the Catholic Faith had been dynamited by Jewish money. That is why Roddy boasts of "How the Jews Changed Catholic Thought." What kind of authority can the Magisterium of a Church have, if it avows its dogmas may change according to human circumstances or convenience?

It is not the Catholic catechism or the ecclesiastics who have invented the historical fact of the collective responsibility of the people of Israel in Christ's Passion and death. We would have to deny not only the Gospel's divine inspiration but even its historical accuracy if we were to affirm that it was not the Jews, but the Romans or *all men* who had the final responsibility in the crucifixion of the Savior. Of course Adam's sin and our personal sins make us responsible for the Sacrifice of the Cross; it is evident also that the Roman procurator, Pontius Pilate, and the executioners were guilty. The people of

Israel, however, through their leaders and representatives rejected the promised Messiah and asked that His blood fall upon them and their children, thus undoubtedly incurring collective liability which weighs upon those who, today like yesterday, continue to deny that Jesus Christ is the Son of the living God.

Roddy continues:

> This Christian idea has caused anti-Semitism to plague the entire human genre for twenty centuries following Christ's death. Sometimes its virulence has grown, and sometimes it has diminished, but anti-Semites have never ceased to exist. Sick mentalities, always ready to argue about anything, seem to have merged on all occasions to scorn and attack the Jews.

Poor little Jews, the victims of sick minds who have exposed their misdeeds! It is a fully proven historical fact that even before Christ, the Jews, not *all* Semites, have been and still are subject to periodic defensive actions on the part of peoples and governments within which they have established themselves as a minority always disposed toward conspiracy, smuggling, usury, and treason. It is not "anti-Semitism," but legitimate self-defense, which once again causes us to expose the Jewish-Masonic conspiracy which, after numerous infiltrations into the Church, has succeeded in perverting the immutable doctrine of truth to the extent of their being able to affirm that they, the Jews, have changed Catholic thought.

Going back to Bogotá, Paul VI's words to the Israelite community which went to greet him are indeed enigmatic:

> We pray to God that He may bless our efforts toward fruitful cooperation for the sake of all mankind, so that there may come the day when all peoples will invoke the *Lord* with the same voice and serve Him under a single yoke.

What *fruitful cooperation* is the Pontiff talking about? Though Paul VI seems to link it to "the sake of all mankind," his wish seems to indicate to us an "ecumenical" union, for he longs for the day when "all peoples will invoke the *Lord* with the same voice and serve Him under a single yoke." This is a wish Pope Montini has expressed several times as the only way through which mankind can attain harmony, unity, peace, and welfare. The barriers of races, social classes, nationalism, and religions that today separate us, have to be torn down in order to set up that *world government* which he proposed to the world in his speech at the United Nations. This is also the goal of the *materialistic Messianism* toward which all local and international activities of the Jewish mafia are moving. This goal seems to be the ultimate end to be affected through the *fruitful cooperation* of Paul VI and the Jewish international agencies.

"All peoples will invoke the *Lord* with the same voice..." Paul VI was addressing a Jewish community. He knows there is an abyss between religious Judaism and Catholicism, for the Jews deny the two fundamental Mysteries and dogmas of our religion, namely the mystery of the most Holy Trinity and the mystery of the Incarnation. However, he also failed to mention Christ, the Son of the Living God.

Chapter XXI

THE AMULET OF POPE MONTINI

In his *Counter-Reformation,* the illustrious Abbé de Nantes published an article which caused great impact all over Europe. It appeared in the November, 1970 issue under the title, "The Amulet of the Pope." May I quote from this article:

In *Paris Match* magazine, August 29, 1970, in an article by Robert Serrou, "The Next Pope Will Be a Frenchman," is an illustration of a large photograph of the Pope and Cardinal Villot. I looked upon those two hermetic countenances in which the Church's destiny was concealed. But, what is that which we discover on Paul VI's chest over his pectoral cross? It is a curious jewel that I don't seem to remember ever being worn by any Pope. The object must be made out of gold, square, decorated with twelve precious stones set in four rows of three each. It hangs, in a very peculiar way, from a gold cord which ties around his neck and is next to the Cross of Christ. They seem tied to each other.

I am almost afraid to find out, but without a doubt, this appears to be the object described in chapter 28 of the book of Exodus. There we read about the ephod and breastplate of judgment which Aaron, the Jewish high priest, and his successors must have carried as a ritual ornament. Over the 12 stones were inscribed the names of the 12 tribes of Israel as a "memorial before the Lord for ever." (Ex. 28:29). Paul VI was wearing the insignia of the Jewish high priest, Caiphas, the breastplate of judgment, around his neck and over his heart.

Who knows when and why and from whom he received this amulet? Is the Pope trying to imply that he is a direct descendant of the Levitical high priest? Is the Pontiff of the Catholic Church turning to the God of Israel? Or could he be preparing for the restoration of the Jewish religion as the religion of pure monotheism, of the most Holy Book, of the universal Covenant?

A Jewish sabbatical cult has developed this year in the Katholikentag, the annual German Catholic festival, and, in Brussels, Cardinal Suenens has announced a forthcoming Council of Reconciliation to be held in Jerusalem. We should also remember that the B'nai B'rith and the Freemasons dream of the construction of a "Temple of Understanding" in the Holy City similar to the one existing in New York. A model of this future temple was given to the Pope some time ago as a symbol of ecumenism. Everything is falling into place!

Who can tell us about this "pectoral" and other obscure signs? Do we have the right to know if the Pope, by wearing the breastplate of judgment of Caiphas, the Levitical high priest, is pretending to assume an old Jewish ritual without fear of Israel? Or is he going to try to conduct the Christian churches into "universal Judaism" and restore the Levitical priesthood to Jerusalem? What the amulet is telling us is ambiguous.

Up to now, the crucifix has never had to share its position with any other ritualistic symbol. Could it be that now, all of a sudden, the Pope has less regard for the crucifix? Could it be that it will soon be the last time that the cock crows in the Vatican? What do we know? We, the Catholic flock of Catholic sheep, know nothing of the long-range plans of our Shepherd, the Pope....

Georges de Nantes

The service the renowned Abbé of Nantes has rendered the Church in revealing what was being whispered within Church circles, amidst great scandal and astonishment, about the ritual pendant belonging to the Levitical high priest and appearing in almost all photographs of Paul VI after his trip to the Holy Land is doubtless an extraordinary one. We are unable to forecast or estimate its importance, but perhaps we have here the key to understand the current subversion in the Church of Christ, what Pope Montini himself called the "auto-demolition" of Christianity.

In Rome, on page 603 of the November 18, 1970 issue of *Il Borghese*, a widely circulated magazine, a sensational article was published under the following impressive headlines: "The Bronze Gate—Paul VI: Pope or 'High Priest'?" We quote from that article:

> The moral effect at the Vatican has been enormous, almost shocking. Rumors had been circulating for a long time in Vatican circles without anyone daring to expose the fact. It was only recently that Abbé Georges de Nantes disseminated the news that the sovereign Pontiff of the Apostolic Roman Catholic Church occasionally wears the insignia of the Hebrew high priest, Caiphas, along with his pectoral cross on his mozzetta. The echo of this news behind the Bronze Gate has been resounding.
>
> Nevertheless, there can be no doubt: the shape, color and embellishment of this badge corresponds to the description given in the Bible. No Pope in the preceding two thousand years had even worn a jewel like this, minutely described in chapter 28 of Exodus, one of the books of the Bible. John Baptist Montini most certainly wears it. Why? No one dares divulge the obscure motives for this decision of his, but everybody agrees about the possibility of intentional ambiguity on the part of the Pontiff. This object, made of pure gold, is square, enhanced by twelve precious stones arranged in four rows of three each, and

hangs from the neck by means of a golden cord made of interlaced rings ending in a tassel. All twelve precious stones have different colors.

This is the *ephod* of the Hebrew high priest, known as the *breastplate of judgment*. Aaron and his issue had to wear it as a ritual ornament, and its precious stones represent Israel's twelve tribes. The description of this peculiar thing is to be found in Exodus... exactly as it can be seen today in many photographs of Paul VI.... [*Editor's Note:* The ephod appears to have been a linen garment worn under the amulet spoken of by the author. The amulet is called the "breastpiece of decision" in Exodus 28:29 in the Saint Joseph Edition of The New American Bible (New York: Catholic Book Publishing, 1970. *Imprimatur*: Patrick Cardinal O'Boyle, Archbishop of Washington.); the jeweled amulet is called the "rational of judgment" in the Douay-Rheims version of the Bible (Rockford, Illinois: TAN Books and Publishers, from the 1899 edition. *Imprimatur*: James Cardinal Gibbons, Archbishop of Baltimore.); in the Revised Standard Version of The Oxford Annotated Bible with the Apocrypha (New York: Oxford University Press, 1965.), it is called the "breastpiece of judgment." Still another name, the "burse," is assigned to it in the Knox Bible (New York: Sheed and Ward, 1950. *Imprimatur*: Bernardus Cardinal Griffin.). The reader is urged to read the 28th chapter of the book of Exodus for a better explanation of the items spoken about in this section.]

How long is it since this unbelievable union of the pectoral cross and the badge of the Hebrew high priest took place? To answer this question, we have examined hundreds of photographs. In this way we are able to affirm that the first appearance of this strange amulet on the chest of the Roman Pope dates from at least 1964, some months after his visit to Palestine. It seems logical to deduce that this ritual ornament was given to him on that occasion, since Paul VI visited Israel also.

This is no isolated case or hallucination. The emblem of the Levitical high priest is clearly visible, especially when Paul VI wears his mozzetta, a red mantelet embroidered with white ermine. On such occasions the pectoral cross often cannot be seen in pictures, for the Pope's clasped hands may conceal it, but Aaron's device always appears, for it is connected by means of a large golden piece of cord. Only on one occasion did the strange emblem hang on the white robes of Paul VI without his mozzetta. This was when the Roman Pontiff paid a visit to India and the cameramen surprised him as he was being followed and surrounded by Hindu children.

In various photographs taken during Paul VI's visits to the holy places of Christendom and at the various sanctuaries, the breastplate of judgment is always visible. The jeweled breastpiece was conspicuous on many occasions, among them these: at Fumone, when the Pope visited the tomb of Pope Celestino V, the "great refugee;" at Saint Sabina on the Aventino on Ash Wednesday, when the litanies of the saints were sung as amended by the Bugninian liturgy, which now begins with a *Sancte Abraham* . . .; at the Piazza de Spagna, during the homage paid to the Immaculate Virgin; at Saint Agnes; and at Saint Mary of Trastévere. The Pope's wearing of this breastpiece is something at least strange, if not suspicious, and raises doubt requiring an answer different from the ambiguous silence we are accustomed to receive.

Is this, then, a Masonic deed or an obscure design? Someone must explain what this all means. . . . Indeed, it is disconcerting that beside or in place of the pectoral cross of Peter's successor (who still is Christ's Vicar, notwithstanding the contentions of the new theologians), on the chest of the Roman Pontiff, there appears a non-Christian emblem which, for its very richness, is opposite to the principles of the *Church of the Poor*.

We do not know what explanation could be given to Paul VI's wearing of this ritual device of the Levitical high priest. The first explanation suggested benevolently by Abbé de Nantes is not quite convincing and cannot be accepted.

Between Judaism, the religion of the promise, and Catholicism, the religion of the fulfillment of that promise, there is no real continuity, for present Judaism contumaciously denies that the divine promises of the coming Messiah have been fulfilled in Christ Jesus, the Son of God and the Son of Mary. Present religious Judaism rejects the two fundamental dogmas of our religion: the mystery of the Most Holy Trinity and the mystery of the Incarnation. How could anyone attempt to unite the Jewish religion with genuine Christianity, which is based on these fundamental dogmas? The promise and the preparation lost their reasons to exist when Christ came, and all of religious Judaism lost its legitimacy when Jesus Christ founded His Church, the new Israel, not the Israel according to the flesh, but the Israel according to the spirit.

Now then, the breastpiece was a prominent Jewish emblem. It symbolically represented the twelve tribes of carnal Israel at the ritual celebrations. Nothing, then, justifies the wearing of this ritual object by a Pope, the visible head of the new people of God, the children of the New Covenant. Even the fact that no previous Pope during the 2,000-year history of the Church has ever worn this ritualistic object of religious Judaism, seems to demonstrate that there is an absolute incompatibility between the profession of our Catholic Faith and the wearing of the ephod or "breastplate of judgment," thoroughly described in the Exodus as characteristic and exclusive of the Levitical high priest.

Since Paul VI wore it publicly, we have the right, and moveover, a grave obligation of conscience to investigate why the Pontiff did so. With good reason Abbé Georges de Nantes was afraid of understanding the only consistent explanation which, on the one hand, may be perfectly consistent and harmonic with other inexplicable deeds of Pope Montini, with his paradoxical Pontificate as a whole, and with all the subversion and auto-demolition inside the Church. *John Baptist Montini wears the breastpiece because in his heart, rather than a Pope, he is a Levitical high priest.* Consciously or unconsciously, only God knows, he seems to be associated with international Judaism, its mighty leaders, and its destructive tools of Communism and Masonry. On the other hand, in his genealogical line of ancestors we find actual roots of Jewish origin, just as in the cases of other cardinals, monsignors, and theologians who have masterminded this dreadful revolution in God's Church. Indeed I denounce *Judaism* as the active and most efficient force that, with its immense resources, has prepared this tragedy and harmed not only the Church and souls, but nations and peoples, sowing confusion, nonconformity, and class struggle, as well as civil and international wars which have bathed the whole world in blood and pain.

It is only too painful to conclude the above, but there is an unavoidable dilemma for us: either we save the Church, or we obstinately continue defending two Popes and a Council guilty of demolishing the unity of the Church.

In the previously-mentioned article in *Look* magazine, Joseph Roddy wrote: "When conservatives got to know about these secret conferences at the top, they began to point to the American Jews as the new power behind the Church." These conservatives were right in suspecting an *immense world infiltration of Jews, Masons, Communists, disloyal religious* who entered seminaries, novitiates, and all Catholic organizations with the assignment and orders to surreptitiously and discretely attain the leading positions from which they were to launch the internal revolution that had been planned in the dark dens of the Jewish-Masonic-Communist conspiracy. Facts? Evidence? There are more than enough, provided one is not obstinate in accepting them.

To begin with, we have the well-known case of Fr. Tondi, S.J., who, while an active member of the Italian Communist Party in his youth, was chosen by the party leaders to actively infiltrate the Society of Jesus. This crypto-Communist so successfully passed all the tests in his Jesuitic formation and was so clever in his studies, that at the end of his third probation (the finishing touch the Society gives its workers), the superiors appointed him to a position of utmost responsibility, that of *Prefect of Studies of the Gregorian Pontifical University,* the most important philosophical and theological center of the Jesuits and possibly of the whole Church. In his position, this hidden Communist faithfully followed the secret guidelines given by his real hierarch to launch and successfully develop the ideological revolution that later on corrupted the theological and philosophical thought of that most important university. Finally, this Jesuit's connections with the high leaders of Italian and international Communism were disclosed.

In another part of his article, Joseph Roddy wrote the following revealing words:

The Montinian Church

An advertising firm, close enough to the Vatican to be able to get the Roman addresses of the twenty-two cardinals and bishops coming from abroad to attend the Council, delivered each of them a copy of a 900-page book, *The Plot Against the Church (Il Complotto Contro La Chiesa)*. Among this book's slanderous pages *there were some traces of truth.* The affirmation contained in the book, that the Church had been infiltrated by Jews, was an efficacious intrigue of the anti-Semites; *but it is an undeniable fact that many Jews, ordained as priests, were in Rome working out a declaration in favor of the Jews.* Among them were Fr. Baum and Msgr. John Oesterreicher, both of whom were members of Cardinal Bea's secretariat. Cardinal Bea himself, according to the Cairo newspaper, *Al Gomhuria,* was a Jew named Bejar.

The facts being evident, international Jewry and its spokesman Roddy, could not deny the apparent fact of infiltration, although, as is natural, they take good care not to give us all the names of the infiltrators.

Sometime ago, Bea, Baum, and Oesterreicher (a few names to which we could add others of crypto-Jews, crypto-Masons, and crypto-Communists cunningly infiltrated into the Church), began to prepare the current subversion and were able to surreptitiously reach top positions so as to make themselves more effective. Using their personal skills, those chosen for this transcendental job had to have excellent capabilities and the influence of members of the hierarchy, who were no doubt impressed by the apparent zeal of the infiltrators, as well as by convenient flattery and gifts. Given great natural abilities, the chosen ones could not help inspiring confidence and gaining progressive promotions. In intrigue, hypocrisy, and skill, the infiltrator Jews are surpassed only by the devil. In addition, to conduct this intrigue, the Jewish mafia could rely on worthy non-Jewish, Catholic individuals, such as Fr. Timothy Fitzharris O'Boyle, S.J., who installed and protected them at the Bible Institute under the tutelage of the Most Eminent Cardinal Bea, who, as a member of the illustrious Society of Jesus, served as an information center for those engaged in the massive infiltration of the Church.

From Roddy's article, Jewry appears to have engaged all its tactical means, all its most valuable tools, and all its immense economic resources to deal a definitive blow to Christianity so that, without enemies worth mentioning, they could devote themselves to fulfilling their dream of a *materialistic Messianic world government* and a religious syncretism designed to eliminate any trace of Christ and His religion forever. The work was slow, discrete, and without a doubt, it attained a progressive and surprising success. I do not think non-Jews will ever be able to investigate all the secrets of this secular conspiracy; that is why Mr. Roddy's confession, though incomplete, is exceptionally valuable, for it seems to give us the reason why Paul VI wears the breastpiece of the Levitical high priest.

The Amulet of Pope Montini

Not only had the famous Pontiff of Tolerance permitted "salvific dialogue" with our "separated brethren" who never thought of converting to our religion, and with the Communists, with whom he dreamed of establishing "peaceful coexistence and mutual understanding," but also with the Jews, who *no longer so invisibly* were directing subversion without the big-hearted Pope realizing that there was a tremendous conspiracy jeopardizing the very life of the Church. John XXIII, the Pope of Tolerance, not only welcomed Khrushchev's son-in-law, but as Roddy writes, entered into extensive dialogue with the American Jewish Committee, the Anti-Defamation League of the B'nai B'rith, and other Jewish agencies. The conspiracy was on, and could rely upon prominent ecclesiastics opportunely infiltrated into the Catholic Church, among whom Cardinal Augustin Bea, S.J., stood out as the gray figure of the Vatican during the present age of transition.

"Though Matthew, Mark, Luke, and John were better evangelists than historians," writes Roddy, "their writings, according to Catholic dogma, were divinely inspired and to amend them, therefore, would be as impossible as changing the center of the sun." This Jewish writer is stupid enough to question the historical accuracy of the Holy Gospel, in order to eliminate its evidence about the collective liability of the people of Israel in Jesus' Passion and death. This notwithstanding, he quotes the Catholic doctrine which Cardinal Bea's "experts" forgot, namely that Holy Writ has divine inspiration, which guarantees the historical accuracy and faith of the evangelists. To change the Gospel, even under the guise of ecumenism, would indeed wreck the Faith. The inviolability of Holy Writ makes the famous declaration of Vatican II on the Jews inconsistent and ambiguous.

He who reads Roddy's article attentively will be very surprised at the large number of Jews who during the time of the Council, worked out that famous Conciliar statement exempting them from any liability for the Lord's Passion and death. This includes the American Jewish Committee, the B'nai B'rith, the Jewish World Congress, etc. Things did not seem to go very well at Rome, from where Max Schuster[g] filled the pages of *The New York Times,* the Jewish newspaper with the largest circulation in the world, in order to prepare public opinion. Fritz Becker of the Jewish World Congress wrote: "We do not have the same viewpoints Americans have about printing it." In other words: "Let us be more discrete." However, the Vatican approved these topics for publication, since the trip of Paul VI to the Holy Land had just taken place, and public opinion had to be diverted from the real goals of the Pontiff. Roddy wrote:

> An expert in public relations would have said that the Holy See [not the Holy See but Paul VI] had shown little skill while in the Holy Land. When Paul prayed beside the bearded Orthodox Patriarch, Athenagoras, at the Jordanian sector, everything was all right, but when he entered Israel, he had cutting words

for the author of *The Vicar* [a Jew's slanderous work against Pius XII] and gave a speech encouraging the Jews to convert. His visit was so short that he did not even make any public mention of the name of the young country he was visiting.

Paul VI's steps had to be diplomatically concealed under the veil of a pious pilgrimage, for the goals of that trip were not disclosed at the time. Only as time passed and further events took place could diligent observers progressively discover Pope Montini's secret aims in traveling to the Holy Land. That is why Paul VI spent more time in Jordan than in Israel and pretended to ignore the latter; that is why he spoke about conversion of the Jews, though in a superficial and delicate way. This was his elemental duty as a Pope, the successor of Peter. Nevertheless, after this visit, he started wearing the ephod and the breastpiece of judgment of the Levitical high priest on his chest. In his article Roddy completes the deceitful trick: "The Vatican observers who analyzed the activities of Paul VI while in the Holy Land considered there was less hope of a statement in favor of the Jews."

This phrase tries to convey the impression that there was a disagreement among the various elements of international Jewry engaged in the job of convincing the Conciliar Fathers as to the criteria and actions to be carried on. This, however, is but a typical astute Jewish maneuver showing various fronts to give us the impression there is division among their forces. This is why Roddy adds:

> There was a more optimistic mood at the New York Waldorf-Astoria. There, the guests celebrating the anniversary of Beth Israel Hospital, got to know that, years ago, Rabbi Abba Hillel Silver [the name Silver is characteristically Jewish and belongs to some of the most skillful initiates of the Jewish-Masonic conspiracy] had spoken with Francis Cardinal Spellman about Israel's efforts to get a seat at the United Nations. Spellman said that to aid this cause he would personally address the South American governments and invite them to support his deep wish that Israel be admitted into that world organization. By that time the "American Pope" (Spellman), at a meeting of the American Jewish Committee, said it was "absurd to maintain there is or could be any hereditary guilt."

This affirmation by the Cardinal from New York is false, of course, and shows a lack of theological and historical background. All men who through ordinary generation descend from Adam, come into this world with "hereditary guilt." *"In quo omnes peccaverunt"* says Saint Paul—in Adam we all sin. *Personal* guilt is not hereditary but, even among men, *collective* guilt is. In Germany the children of the so-called war criminals are still paying Israel for the damage the Jews claim they suffered from Hitler's regime.

The Amulet of Pope Montini

It was the Catholic Church in the United States which, acting in a pragmatic, rather than theological, way, most efficiently aided, fostered, and supported the Jewish claims to the extent of having the famous Conciliar statement passed. Monsignor Higgins, from the National Catholic Welfare Conference of Washington, D.C., obtained for the Jew, Arthur J. Goldberg, then a Justice of the Supreme Court, a personal appointment with Paul VI. And Rabbi Heschel[10], fostered by Cushing, the Boston Cardinal, got another personal audience for himself and Schuster. "The audience of the Rabbi with Paul at the Vatican, as well as the meeting of Bea with the members of the American Jewish Committee in New York, were granted on the condition that they would be kept secret. But when *conservatives* got to know about these secret conferences at the top *they began to point to the American Jews as the new power behind the Church.*"

At the Council the Cardinals from Saint Louis and Chicago, Joseph Ritter and Albert Meyer, demanded that the stronger scheme be restored, and Richard Cardinal Cushing demanded that the Council deny that the Jews had incurred the crime of deicide. The Auxiliary Bishop of San Antonio, Steven Leven, stated: "We must wipe out this word, deicide, from the Christian vocabulary, in order that it may never again be used against the Jews." But history and Holy Writ cannot be amended by the whim or compromises of men gathering at a pastoral council.

Following his well-known way of affirming verbally what he condemns in deeds, and vice versa, Paul VI, on Palm Sunday at an open air Mass in Rome, spoke about the crucifixion and said the Jews were the principal characters in Jesus' death. At Segni near Rome, Bishop Luigi Carli wrote two sound articles, published as booklets, with evidence taken from Scripture and theology, demonstrating that the Jews at the time of Christ, and their descendants up to our times, were *collectively* guilty of Jesus Christ's death. However, Bea, the Cardinal of Jewish descent, after affirming his secretariat had absolute control over the statement that was being prepared in favor of the Jews, said the Pope had spoken for simple and pious people, not for cultured persons, and the opinion of the Bishop of Segni was definitely not that of the secretariat he presided over and managed in secret connection with the Jewish agencies. In other words the preaching of the Pope was not to be taken very seriously, for he had not spoken to cultured people, but to ignorant people; there is one truth for cultured people and another for the simple and ignorant. As to what Msgr. Carli had written, it had to be rejected without refutation, because it was not consistent with the "infallible" thought of the Secretariat for Christian Unity and its supreme head, the German Augustin Cardinal Bea, S.J.

The World Council of Churches also agreed with this conspiracy, for later on Paul VI paid a scandalous visit to its headquarters and delivered an even more scandalous speech. At Geneva, Dr. Willem Visser't Hoff, the head of the

Council, told two American priests that, if the press reports on the famous statement in favor of the Jews were true, the ecumenical movement would be stopped. This was a way of pressuring the Conciliar Fathers. At Rome, Cardinal Cushing brought pressure to bear, while in Germany an anonymous group worked for Jewish-Christian friendship. "Now," these unknown persons said, "there is a crisis of confidence *vis-a-vis* the Catholic Church."

Another Jesuit, Fr. Gus Weigel, an old friend of Heschel, also worked in the dark to draw out the longed-for statement. Later on the Rabbi wrote, "I asked him whether he really thought that it were *ad maiorem Dei gloriam* that there be no more synagogues, seder meals, or prayers in Hebrew." Weigel is already in the grave, and Heschel took care not to give us his answer. In this affair, just as in the dialogue for reconciliation with the Masons, the Jesuits stood in a decisive position. A careful study of these occurrences poses a deep problem about the grave external and internal crises the Society of Jesus has undergone in its history.

Jewish lobbyists were very much interested in getting the famous Conciliar statement, and thought that the people of Israel had been sitting on the defendant's seat for four years, while the Conciliar Fathers were deeply divided as to opinions. Joseph Roddy makes this point:

> This delay was perfectly understandable on political grounds, but few people wanted to attribute it to religious motives. The current head of the Holy See, the Pope, was firmly convinced that a majority or unanimous vote had to be gotten every time an important issue was at stake. Due to the principle of collegiality, according to which all bishops help the Pope rule over the Church, any important issue divided the Episcopal College into two groups: the progressivists and the conservatives. The Pope's role consisted of reconciling both wings. To remedy these divisions in the Episcopal College, the Pope had to resort either to persuasion or to imposition, which upset the principle of contradiction. When one faction said that Holy Writ alone was the Church's source of teaching, the other contended there were two sources, Writ and Tradition. To bridge both positions, the statement in favor of the Jews was reworded to include some personal touches of Paul, including the affirmation that there are two sources of revelation, while it was suggested that the opposite approach is worth studying. When those who disagreed with the statement on religious freedom said it could contradict the doctrine that Catholicism is the sole and true Church, a similar solution came down from the fourth floor of the Vatican to the Conciliar room. Consequently, this statement on religious freedom begins with the doctrine of the one true Church which, in the conservatives' mind, preserves the Church's traditional doctrine. Then they are satisfied with this part of the statement, without realizing the rest of it contradicts or denies the opening affirmation.

Paul VI and Chaos

Here we have Paul VI: always ambiguous, always irresolute, trying to build a bridge between affirmation and denial, between being and non-being. Both of these statements of the Council evidence that the Holy Spirit was absent from the Conciliar room. When John XXIII said that the Council was barely pastoral, he closed the doors to the Holy Spirit. The post-Conciliar Church opposed the clear, immutable, infallible doctrine of the pre-Conciliar Church. Though Pope Montini is a skillful politician, he was not able to merge the opposite poles, and he caused a permanent schism in Christ's Church. Our very enemies, despite their own interests and the enormous advantages Paul's policies have given to them, avow that universal agreement about those famous statements of Bea and the Council has not been reached. Perhaps today when the majority of the episcopate has joined the openly progressivist party, when sound studies on theology have been replaced by pastoral concern, when through successive acts of surrender we have become more accepting of things that are absolutely opposite to revealed truth, the discussion at the Council would have been less violent and the vote more unanimous. Nevertheless, the Church should keep immutable the doctrine received from its apostolic sources.

The declaration promulgated on October 28, 1965, reads as follows:

> Although the Jewish authorities and those people who followed them pressed to have Christ killed (John 19:6), what Christ suffered in His Passion cannot be imputed to the then living Jews or to today's Jews without any distinction. Although the Church is the new people of God, the Jews may not be depicted as rejected by God or cursed, as if it followed from Holy Writ. Then take care that, in the catechistic work or the preaching of God's Word, nothing be taught that is inconsistent with the Gospel's truth and Christ's spirit.
>
> Moreover, the Church, which rejects any persecution against any human being, takes into account the heritage it shares with the Jews and, not inspired by political reasons but by the Gospel's spiritual love, regrets hatred, persecutions, and movements promoted by anti-Semitism against the Jews at any time and by any person.

Even disregarding the teachings of Holy Writ and the Church's Tradition, the above is a regretful statement! Fallacy was used to conceal the historical and theological reality, for it could not have been destroyed. We all know that God Himself established a certain solidarity in the Jewish people, the former people of the divine predilection in both divine blessings and curses. It is evident that not all Jews living at Christ's time were present in Pilate's courtroom, nor did they ask for our Lord's crucifixion and death. It is also evident that even the Jews who were present were not personally responsible to the same extent their leaders were, for the leaders not only pressed, but also made themselves and their people liable for the drama of Calvary. It was not they who physically whipped Christ or put a crown of thorns on His head and crucified Him, but they were the intellectual perpetrators of the deicide and principally responsible for all of the sufferings of the Lord in His Holy Passion. Finally, taking into account Israel's divine choice and the collective ingratitude of its people, it becomes evident that the liability, both jointly and severally, still falls upon those who, today as yesterday, would ask for His Passion and death again.

If the Church is the new Israel, as the Council avows, it follows that the old Israel has lost its privileges, and is now a people rejected by God. This is what follows from Holy Writ, unless we change its meaning. *Either we are with Christ or against Christ.*

Below are some passages from my book *With Christ or Against Christ:*

> It is convenient to stress a fundamental point on which basis some people are trying to exonerate the Jewish people of any liability for Christ's death. We shall begin by defining some ideas, even if this means we will have to repeat already stated thoughts. There are *personal* and *collective* guilts. There is *personal* responsibility only when there is personal sin or crime. On the other hand, there can be, and in fact is, *collective responsibility* when communities, through their leaders or representatives, gravely harm the inalienable rights of individuals or other communities. For instance, although not all Germans were personally guilty of the wartime atrocities imputed to Hitler, all Germans were held responsible, jointly and severally, to the extent that they had to indemnify in full those who claimed to have suffered damages, particularly the Jews. National solidarity caused all Germans and each one of them to be charged with *collective responsibility* for the crimes imputed to Hitler and his government, although it is evident that not all Germans living at that time, not to mention all Germans living today, can be held personally responsible for those apparent crimes. The *children* of that period have had to pay the tremendous penalty for the collective guilt of all Germans.
>
> In like manner, there is a twofold responsibility before God, namely, the personal responsibility each one of us assumes for his own or individual sins, and the collective responsibility belonging to human communities, especially when these communities are united according to a divine plan embracing and enclosing such communities. In biblical language, the chiefs of the race are identified with their respective descendants, which builds up a joint moral personality with these chiefs. As we have said, this solidarity is tighter and more universal when it has been established by God Himself to develop divine projects. This was the solidarity God established between Adam and all his descendants with respect to our rise to the divine life; such also is the solidarity God instituted for the Hebrew people who, as aforesaid, were collectively bound to prepare for Christ's advent.

Paul VI and Chaos

The Hebrews themselves have always avowed and most zealously defended the God-instituted racial solidarity existing among them. Any Jewish book, including the Talmud, makes reference to this racial solidarity. The great fallacy of Jewry and Vatican II, however, consists of defending this solidarity only as to the blessings, not the damnations and punishments the Lord inflicted upon them due to their infidelity.

Just as *Divine Messianism*, the redeeming plan and the divine choice to prepare the way for the coming Messiah, was the source of divine blessings for the Israelite people and the basis of all their greatness, so *Jewish Messianism*, a denial and attack upon divine rights, was, is, and will be the sign of disapproval and punishment of a betrayed and angry God for these people. The option cannot be avoided: Either Christ and His blessings, or the Antichrist and his curses.

The *solidarity of blessings* that according to the divine design were enjoyed by all Israelites . . . logically entails the *solidarity of divine punishment and curse* deserved by the Hebrew people due to the aggressive incredulity of their leaders. Those divine blessings or promises of divine love were conditional, not absolute. It was not God who failed to perform His part; it was Israel which, through its leaders, parted from God. Infidelity brought the divine curse.

God had promised His people His blessings, provided they fulfilled his commandments: "If thou shalt hearken diligently unto the voice of the Lord thy God, to observe and to do all His commandments which I command thee this day, then the Lord thy God will set thee on high above all nations of the earth . . . ." These divine blessings were conditional upon a rigid fulfillment of the divine law. If the people of Israel refused to accept God's precepts practically, if they attempted to throw off the yoke of His divine law, the Lord would also launch the fury and punishments of his infinite justice: "But it shall come to pass, if thou wilt not hearken unto the voice of the Lord thy God, to observe and to do all His commandments and His statutes which I command thee this day; that all these curses shall come upon thee, and overtake thee: Cursed shalt thou be in the city, and cursed shalt thou be in the field. Cursed shall be thy basket and thy store. Cursed shall be the fruit of thy body, and the fruit of thy land, the increase of thy cows and the flocks of thy sheep. Cursed shalt thou be when thou comest in, and cursed shalt thou be when thou goest out . . ." (Deut. 28:15-19).

God's Word has been written. "Heaven and earth will pass away, but this word will not pass away."

In the parable of the householder who let his vineyard to husbandmen, when the landlord sent his servants to receive the fruits, they killed them. When last of all he sent his own son, the husbandmen caught him, cast him out of the vineyard, and slew him also. Here the Divine Master makes a clear allusion to the ingratitude and perfidy the people of Israel returned to God for His *predilection. That is why Christ ends by saying: "Auferetur a vobis regnum, Dei, et debitur genti facienti fructus eius"* ("The kingdom of God shall be taken from you, and given to a nation bringing forth the fruits thereof.") (Matt. 21:43).

The Jewish masses, and especially its leaders, rejected Christ's invitations and resisted at the efforts of the apostles to convert them, so that they remained outside the Church, the vineyard and the kingdom of God, into which the Gentiles flowed from everywhere. A hundred times Jehovah had proclaimed Himself His people's liberator and Savior and the Messiah had to be, first of all, the Redeemer of the Jews, for Zion had been appointed beforehand as the center of the Messianic theocracy and converging point for the Gentile nations. But once the Jews rejected *divine Messianism*, proclaimed their *materialistic Messianism*, and slew the Savior, only the Gentiles, without passing through the synagogue, could enter the Church. They continue to do so almost alone, while the Jews are excluded, despite the fact that their rights seemed to be preponderant and, in their mind, exclusive.

Saint Paul devotes three chapters of his Epistle to the Romans to solve this enigma. Without denying the indisputable privileges with which God wanted to favor Israel, he affirms it was the Gentiles, who seemed to be nothing to God, and for whom God was nothing, who were called to the Faith, while the holy people, the sacerdotal race, the household of Jehovah were excluded. The legitimate heirs were disinherited and the legitimate children were replaced by intruders; God's promises seem to have been forgotten and the covenant broken. How can one reconcile all this with God's fidelity and divine justice?

Jewish claims are based upon their inveterate twisted interpretation of the Lord's promises. They invoke the name of Abraham as if it were an absolute safeguard against every evil, be their behavior what it may. They feel Israel's blood is sort of a sacrament that will save them *ex opere operato*, notwithstanding their personal mood. Here we find a certain parallel between Jewish claims and Lutheran claims. To the Hebrews, the blood of Abraham alone, and to the Protestants, faith alone, are pledges of salvation. The Hebrews forget there is an Israel according to the flesh, those who have Abraham's blood, and an Israel according to the spirit. Nothing is owed to the former; to the latter belong the promises. "For they are not all Israel, which are of Israel; neither, because they are the seed of Abraham, are they all children." (Rom. 9:6-7).

The unbelief of the Jews caused the Old Covenant to break and the New Covenant, the New Testament, to be born. This made the ancient blessings accrue to the Church founded by Jesus Christ, the new "people of God," *qui non ex sanguinibus, neque ex voluntate viri, sed ex Deo nati sunt* (which is not formed out of the blood or by the will of man, but by those who have been born out of God, that is, to the supernatural, divine life).

On the other hand, Jews have been traditionally acknowledged as disbelievers and callous-hearted. Even Isaiah regretted that callousness and said: "Behold me, behold me, unto a nation that was not called by my name. I have spread out my hands all the day unto a rebellious people, which walketh in a way that was not good, after their own thoughts." (Is. 65:2). Present unbelief, the object of so much amazement and scandal, is but an extra case in the records of the apostasy of the Jewish people.

After the above, Vatican II's famous statement becomes incomprehensible. It reads: "The Jews may not be depicted as rejected by God or cursed, as if it followed from Holy Writ." One would have to amend or suppress the holy books to be able to accept this pastoral approach of the Council which, disputing Scripture, dogma, Tradition, the writings of the Holy Fathers and Doctors of the Church, *and* historical truth, endeavors to exonerate the Jews from their guilt in order to please our deadly enemies who maintain a stand of rebellion and denial with regard to Christ and His Church.

On the other hand, we must bear in mind as Saint Paul affirms, that Israel's misfortune is neither total nor definitive. It is not *total,* for there have always been sincere converts from Judaism (we are not speaking about the "marranos," fake converts or crypto-Jews) who in acknowledging Christ as Messiah and His divinity, have entered the Church, joined spiritual Israel and turned back to be children of the predilection. It is not *definitive,* because as Saint Paul affirms, the conversion of the Jewish people will be one of the signs to appear before the Second Advent of the Redeemer, who will judge the living and the dead.

Just as it is absurd to affirm that every Jew, merely because he is a Jew, is a criminal, it is equally absurd to affirm that every Jew, merely because he is a Jew, is unable to commit any crime, including the crime of crimes, the crime of deicide.

To avoid the effect of fallacious propaganda designed to disorient public opinion and smash our defense of everything we are and believe in, we must be precise about the meanings of some ideas. On the one hand we have anti-Semitism, this crime against mankind (perhaps against Divinity also) that, as mentioned before, has never existed. In the presence of crimes apparently committed against Jews, the crimes of genocide of thousands or millions of people committed by the Jews are expunged or do not exist, since the victims are Christians. On the other hand, we have the reaction of the Free World against the atrocious secular misdeeds of cabalistic Talmudic Judaism. The racist, determinist, materialist type of anti-Semitism our enemies complain of has never been cultivated by Christians.

To the extent he was a man, Jesus Christ was a Jew. Not only were the apostles and the first believers of the Church Jews, but countless famous supporters of the Christian cause were also. The Jew, just by being a Jew, is not necessarily bound to do wrong; he can be, and in many cases is, a doer of good.

Christ also died for them, and they received the call to faith and salvation before we did. The Catholic Church condemns this so-called anti-Semitism, just as it condemns any racial discrimination, just as it condemns all the crimes of Judaism, Communism, and Masonry.

Christianity is the antithesis of cabalism and Talmudism. They struggle against Christ the Redeemer; they thirst for world domination over all peoples and nations; they perpetuate the synagogue of Satan, the Sanhedrin that condemned Jesus of Nazareth to death.

After the above comments, based on Roddy's article concerning the Jewish problem in God's Church, we believe the wearing of the ephod and the breastpiece of judgment of the Levitical high priest by Paul VI on his chest, as the photographs show, has exceptional and decisive importance, especially taking into account the secret relationship Pope Montini, personally and through his associates, has had with the leaders of the Jewish mafia right from the beginning of his Pontificate.

Chapter XXII

PAUL VI AND HIS RESPONSIBILITY FOR THE CURRENT CHAOS IN THE CHURCH

At the time of the Council, I delivered an address in the Holy Office in the presence of Cardinal Ottaviani, (formerly Msgr. Parente,) Msgr. Mazala, and another monsignor whose name I cannot remember. After having explained the written memorandum I had submitted to them on the revolution that under the guise of the Council and the Conciliar spirit was being hatched inside God's Church, I requested permission to openly put forth the contents of my heart, since my Catholic Faith was being shattered for the first time in my life. Permission was granted, and I spoke quite clearly in expressing my doubts about Paul VI's ideas and behavior, as well as the Council itself, for it was attempting to impose upon us the new theology that had been previously condemned by Pius XII.

Modernism, a doctrine and a party exposed and condemned by Saint Pius X, is resurging and imposing itself in our day with a power and might unparalleled in history. The Congress of Brussels, a recent consequence of the Council, speaks of "The Future World Church," prepared by the IDOC, that is, *Concilium* magazine and its international staff of widely-known theologians presided over by Cardinal Suenens, Fr. Schillebeeckx, Hans Küng, Congar, and superman Karl Rahner, S.J., who have either arbitrarily eliminated fundamental dogmas, silenced them, or interpreted them whimsically. It was during the turbulent days of Vatican II that Modernism obtained citizenship in the Catholic Church.

To me this Council is incomprehensible and unacceptable. Besides being ambiguous, some of its issues have revolutionized the doctrine of the Church and undeniably contradicted the definitions of former and recent councils, as well as the solemn documents of the Magisterium. May I ask: Did former definitions and documents have the inspiration of the Holy Spirit? Provided they did, how could one ignore or contradict them? The "experts" of Vatican II affirm that those definitions and documents had circumstantial value only, inconsistent with the progress of both theology and the world that is about to be born. The Church's *aggiornamento* to this new world demands that we revise our whole doctrine, all of our beliefs, our discipline, our morals, our liturgy and the laws of the Church. If these premises be accepted, nothing remains, and

Vatican Council II itself will pass through in history as a nightmare once the world's circumstances change. Between Vatican II, Vatican I and the Tridentine Council there is no continuity or progress, but instead, an antagonism and a complete change of mentality that, in my humble opinion, is a change of Faith. In addition, the *post-Conciliar age* was even worse than the pastoral council itself, for not only were the dogmatic definitions established by previous councils and all previous documents of the Magisterium disregarded, but even the contents of the documents released by Vatican II were surpassed and ignored.

Now, then, who are guilty of this *internal demolition* of the Church? Who have muffled the voices of orthodoxy which, supported by Tradition, strove to defend revealed truth? Why is it, if they were and are so sure of their most unusual demolishing reforms, that they have not granted others the "salvific dialogue," debate, or enlightening discussion which they have sought, with shameful servility, from all the enemies of the Catholic Faith? It is impossible to deny the personal and collective complicity of the Church's shepherds, especially the one who is Peter's successor.

When, at the beginning of this "auto-demolition" of the Church, I exposed the Head as the main cause of this tragedy, my words caused scandal; it was thought that I had lost my faith. But, little by little, things have been changing, and the cry of those who bravely voice an "I accuse" and point to *Montinism* as the root of the progressive destruction of the Church becomes more and more strident. Further occurrences have made not only trained observers, but even the believing masses examine the chaos more closely and less naively. The ruin of the Church coincides so exactly with the present Pontificate and its reformist and revolutionary changes that it has become impossible to close one's eyes and ignore that it is the shepherds, and most specifically Paul VI, who are responsible for this unique and unparalleled crisis of the Church. The Jewish-Masonic plot has been so successful *because it had the power in its hands.*

Several hypotheses have been advanced to explain the enigma of Paul VI. Among them, the principal ones are the following:

1. The Pope is a prisoner surrounded by mighty rampant enemies who oblige him to say and do what they want. Some people add that the enemy is blackmailing him; they know secret personal weaknesses of the Pontiff and will disclose them, thus gravely impairing his reputation, in case Paul VI fails to second their designs.

2. The Pope is sporadically or regularly drugged. The diabolical inventions of modern chemistry make this terrifying hypothesis very possible. Nowadays there actually exist drugs capable of nullifying one's will, causing it to waver and lead to contradictory decisions on vital issues. This nullification of the will can be intermittent, continuous, or permanent, depending upon the

Paul VI and Chaos

drugs and the dosage used. In one case, there is a certain duality in the deeds and statements of the drugged person, depending upon his being under the influence of the drug or not; in another case, the person is just a plaything in the hands of those who have drugged him.

3. After having been legitimately appointed, he incurred heresy and maybe apostasy. The privilege of infallibility Christ granted Peter's primate was, according to the definition of Vatican I, a privilege of the Church, not of the individuals who were to occupy Peter's See. It is not *personal,* but *didactical* infallibility. It does not make the Pope *infallible* as to all his judgments, opinions, and personal doctrines. It does not make him *impeccable* either, as the very history of the Church regretfully shows. Furthermore, didactical infallibility is present only when the four conditions stated by Conciliar definition according to the doctrine of Holy Writ and Tradition are fulfilled, namely: (a) that the Pope speak *ex cathedra,* with his supreme and universal authority; (b) that he speak about subjects of *faith or morals,* since his ministry covers just these two matters; (c) that he *define,* that is, that he tell us that the specific piece of truth he is stating belongs to the immutable deposit of the divine revelation. When the Pope defines he does not invent the truth; he does not adapt the Gospel to the world, but only tells us that a specific piece of truth was revealed by God and belongs to the immutable deposit of the divine revelation; (d) finally, that the Pope impose the obligation to accept his definition on us *on penalty of everlasting condemnation,* according to Jesus Christ's words: "Those who believe will be saved; those who do not believe will be damned." To deny a piece of truth defined by Peter's supreme Magisterium in the above circumstances is to surrender one's faith and deny Christ's doctrine.

As far as his regular Magisterium is concerned, the Pope is infallible only when he teaches us pieces of truth previously defined by other Popes or councils, or when he teaches a doctrine *quam semper et ubique tenuit Ecclesia,* that the Church has taught always and everywhere.

The famous definition of Vatican I would have no meaning if the Pope, just because he is a Pope, were personally infallible, unable to err and incur heresy. It is true that to perform his job, he can rely upon the assistance of the Holy Spirit, but this regular aid requires and is conditioned by the Pontiff's faithful consent, for the Pope is always free and subject to personal fluctuations according to his free will. It is no heresy then to affirm that the Pope is not always infallible and that, in consequence, he can err, willfully or not, and also incur heresy. What we may affirm is that, in those possible and regretful cases, the Pope will not define an error or heresy *ex cathedra,* for this would mean the ruin of the Church's "inerrancy."

In the regretful case that the Pope personally incurred heresy, many authors believe he would automatically cease to be a Pope: *non deponendus, sed iam depositus.* Others think that, though heretic or apostate, he remains a Pope. In their mind, only the Pontiff's death or resignation leaves the Pontificate vacant. To support their position, which is difficult to understand, they have to establish a real duality between two sorts of deeds and words of the Pope: if he speaks as a Catholic, then he is a Pope; if he does not speak as a Catholic, but as a heretic, then he is no Pope. His Pontificate would lack the stability and consistency Christ's words seem to require: "You are a rock, an immovable rock, and upon this rock I will build my Church. And the gates of Hell shall not prevail against it." What the foundation is for a building, Peter is for the Church: a principle of unity, cohesion, consistency, and permanence of all the elements of this building. How is it possible that Peter's representative could incur heresy and remain the foundation of the Church? Would not this be a violation of the Church's inerrancy?

Those who affirm that a heretical Pope *non est depositus, sed deponendus* (does not cease to be a Pope, but must be removed from office) seem to prefer *legal regulations* to the revealed truth. In my mind legal rules are *means,* not *goals,* while the *preservation of the revealed truth* is, no doubt, *the goal* of the Magisterium, the primate, and the episcopate, since faith is the root of justification, and without faith it is impossible to please God. There can be no real faith that is not founded upon revealed truth and upon acceptance of *everything* God has revealed to us.

On the other hand, the Shepherds have been instituted by Christ to graze their sheep in the truth, to lead them always along the safe way of salvation. When the Shepherds fail, when they personally incur mistakes, they cease to be real Shepherds, for they are no longer able to graze their sheep safely or lead them along the straight way of salvation.

4. The Pope is a real Pope; the Pope has not personally incurred heresy, but he is a weak Pope, who fails to perform his essential duty of curbing heresy and imposing suitable penalties against those who destroy unity, spread error, and have provoked the current doctrinal confusion in Christ's Church. Such was the case of Pope Honorius, who gravely neglected repressing heresy and was ecumenically complaisant with Monophysites and Monothelites, and finally after his death, was condemned as a heretic by a council.

5. The Pope is no real Pope: his election was not valid. Even though his election may have been legitimate *canonically,* to the extent we can know it, and the universal acceptance of his Pontificate within the Church seems to confirm it, nevertheless, if the subject were not *capax electionis* (able to be legitimately elected), his canonically legitimate election would actually be illegitimate. Several factors can *in radice* nullify an apparently legitimate election: if the elected is not a *real* Catholic or publicly professes anti-Catholic doctrines, or if the elected had been excommunicated and his excommunication has not been lifted by him who has the authority to do so. This supposes that the elected

completely recants his errors, for without sincere retraction the excommunication could not be validly lifted.

In brief, these are the various hypotheses put forth to explain the terrible enigma of the present Pontiff. They evidence a fearful reality, namely, that in the world many illustrious men are seeking the solution at the top and pointing to Paul VI as ultimately liable for what he himself called the "auto-demolition" of the Church. The opinions are at variance as to the solution, but not as to the diagnosis of the evil that is grieving us.

A Letter from Father Calmel

Now I shall quote two of the writers who have approached the problem precisely and bravely, before stating my own personal viewpoint on this conflicting and delicate problem. To begin with, I shall quote a letter written by the Reverend Father Th. Calmel, O.P.:

> The subject of this analysis on the revolution in the Church is a normal one, since the Lord appointed Peter as the supreme Shepherd in charge of the mission of confirming our faith. Then, in the present pitiful circumstances, it is normal that we address him, so that his Magisterium may dissipate every quibble and confusion, and return us our confidence and confirm our faith.
>
> *I unhesitantly acknowledge the Holy Father's authority. However, I affirm that any Pope, in the exercise of his authority, can abuse his authority. And I affirm that Pope Paul VI is incurring an exceptionally grave abuse of his authority in instituting a new rite of the Mass around a definition of the Mass that has ceased to be Catholic.*
>
> Rev. Fr. Th. Calmel, O.P.

A Letter from Father Barbara

The next quotation is that of an "Open Letter" by the French priest, Noel Barbara[10], to Paul VI:

> Most Pious Father:
> This letter is designed to convey to You the feelings of your children, who in You behold Peter's successor. On their knees they submit their broken hearts to You. Their faith and common sense have been tested to such an extent that they cannot keep silent any longer. They feel immensely willing to obey You, but this requires that their faith and common sense be no longer crushed.
> That is why they permit themselves to pose You some questions, I being their intermediary. Your answer will fill them with joy, for it will permit them to preserve their faith and accurate understanding, and obey You with a peaceful

The Montinian Church

conscience regarding what they now cannot comprehend.

Most Holy Father, has there always been a sole truth, an immutable dogma, an intangible Faith in the Holy Church?

Your wonderful *creed* has ratified it to us, but is adherence to this *creed* consistent with all those new catechisms that omit essential affirmations and question a large number of dogmas that they re-shape? Are You not the watchman and defender of our Faith? How can You then, tolerate the publication and spread of said catechisms, that adulterate the real meaning of the message of our Salvation as the Gospel and Tradition had always taught? May contradictory dogmas be accepted?

Most Holy Father, is your *creed* still admissible, taking into account that in the liturgy, in the Mass, and in the rites, every ascetic side of Christian life based on the reality of original sin and its consequences for mankind is willfully omitted, this omission being openly contradictory with the doctrine of the Gospel and Tradition? Why this constant contradiction between what You affirm and what You authorize with your signature? Has not such behavior been condemned by Jesus Christ Himself?

Most Holy Father, is your *creed* still true, after what your legate, Cardinal Willebrands, affirmed at Lutheran meetings, particularly the one at Evian, which You seem to have approved yourself? Can it be true, as he affirmed with your consent, for he spoke as a legate of yours, that there is a resemblance between Luther's orientation and that of Vatican II? Notice that this affirmation poses very grave problems of theology and conscience for us.

Please explain to us what we are not able to understand.

Most Holy Father, must this *creed* of yours still be believed by all Catholic believers, and defended up to the sacrifice of one's life, after your having received and shaken the bloody hands of the Communist hangmen of thousands or better said, millions of Catholics who want to remain faithful to your *creed* and the Roman Church, of which You are the supreme Shepherd? Must we confess your *creed* after your having prevented everybody in the Church from raising his voice to protest against and condemn those murderers and persecutors of Catholics? Five hundred forty bishops bear witness to the above, since they requested such condemnation at the Council without having been heard.

Please condescend to explain this contradiction to us.

Most Holy Father, we have hailed the defense of conjugal morality You have defended in your encyclical *Humanae Vitae*, but the episcopates from almost all countries have been able to contradict this encyclical without your raising your voice. Moreover, these episcopates harass priests and believers who have endeavored to make themselves heard, and You have permitted, if not secretly induced, them to do so; in Rome, those priests are considered to be "protestors."

What explanation can You give us about these incomprehensible facts?

Paul VI and Chaos

Most Holy Father, all of your priest-children, faithful to their vow at the sub-deaconate, have joyfully read your encyclical *Sacerdotalis Coelibatus* in which, once again, You affirm that *the Western Church may not abandon the old tradition, for it is its own Tradition.* Christian homes have also felt reassured and greatly aided to endure the yoke of conjugal fidelity by the example of the priests themselves who are faithful to their vow of chastity. How can one now explain to them that, in a letter to your Secretary of State You have questioned the subject of sacerdotal celibacy yourself, analyzing or insinuating the possibility of ordaining married men who would be able to combine their conjugal life with active performance of their priesthood?

How can one make the betrayed spouses understand the indissolubility of their marital bond, since it is yourself who so easily grants faithless priests dispensation from their holy engagements?

Most Holy Father, You have made an extraordinary eulogy of Saint Pius V's Mass, acknowledging that it contains precious documents going back to apostolic times, but nevertheless, You yourself have authorized it to be replaced. Moreover, either You have indulgently allowed the bishops to establish the new Mass as obligatory to all priests, or it was You who secretly issued this mandate for them. As a result, the continually-changing liturgy is subject to the whim of each celebrant as to its structure and its numerous different schemes and countless prefaces, which rapidly provokes indifference and abandonment among real believers.

How could we welcome a "reformation" in which six Protestant pastors have participated? At the end of the work, You received them and had yourself photographed with them as acknowledgment of their cooperation. So the heretics have been admitted to amend what the Church holds as most sacred and precious, the treasure which Jesus left it and which is none other than He Himself in His Holy Passion continued at the Altar.

How can he who has the real Faith conceive this? We beg You to condescend to explain it to us.

Most Holy Father, You praised Latin and Gregorian singing, and entrusted the Gregorian monks to preserve this treasure of the Church. How is it possible, then, that just a month later You authorized those very monks to suppress Latin and Gregorian singing?

Most Holy Father, You begged the bishops to preserve the custom of giving Holy Communion on the tongue, but, adducing numerous unusual reasons, it was You yourself who finally authorized the distribution of Communion in the hand. What does all this mean? Explain it to us.

Most Holy Father, You have frequently regretted that your authority is less and less respected in the Church, but please tell us, who took off your tiara, the symbol of your authority, to be sold at public auction amid the astonishment of many Conciliar Fathers who were not involved in the conspiracy of your

The Montinian Church

"uncrowning?"

Most Holy Father, You have deplored—at least You have not sanctioned—the "inter-Communions" of Holland, Paris (Rue de Vaugirard), and Medellín, but who allowed the sacramental Communion of Christ's body to be administered to Barbarino Olson, a stubborn Presbyterian, and during the Bogotá Eucharistic Congress, to the heretic ministers?

How can it be explained that You have practically acknowledged the episcopal dignity of Michael Ramsey, president of Anglicanism, on whose finger You publicly put your own ring and whom You asked to bless the crowd, taking into account that, according to Leo XIII's bull *Apostolicae Curae,* a bull which he confirmed as "irrevocable" *(perpetuo ratam, firmam, irrevocabilem),* the ordinations conferred according to the Anglican rite are absolutely null and void?

Indeed, we cannot understand this and beg that You condescend to explain to us what we have reason to deem a scandal.

Most Holy Father, You regret atheism and growing irreligiosity, but who has made all the crucifixes disappear from the offices and rooms of your Secretary of State, thus laicizing the Vatican?

Who obliged You to enter the place of Masonic worship at the United Nations in New York, and bow in a religious posture?

Who has created countless problems for the few Catholic governments? Who has openly fostered "protests" and revolution against said governments, either appointing bishops whose ideas and leaning are Marxist, or openly expressing your sympathy for all rebels, whether they be clergymen or laymen, now when all smiles are addressed to the Communist governments and those who lean in that direction?

Would You like to explain it to us?

Is this a result of the "Statement on Religious Freedom" by Vatican II? But, then, what must we think about this Council?

Most Holy Father, You unceasingly affirm the Church is undergoing a hard and painful crisis, but whose friends are the leading provokers of this crisis? Who appointed Cardinals Suenens, Döpfner, and Lercaro as moderators of the Council? Who appointed all the people surrounding You who are paving the way for the enemies of the Church? Who removed the saintly men, who had worked so much for the Church and were its real supporters and defenders, from their important positions in the curia?

Who asked the president of the most important episcopal conference to resign his presidency? [He refers to Cardinal Siri, former president of the Italian Episcopal Conference.]

Who has done his utmost, although this maneuvering has not succeeded at all, to prevent the only secretary of the Council who had never been a cardinal [Msgr. Morcillo, Archbishop of Madrid and Alcalá] from being appointed president of his episcopal conference?

Why do You regret this crisis You refuse to remedy, taking into account You are the only one in a position to apply a suitable remedy?

All these are mysteries we are not able to clear up. Please help us to shed light over them, we beg of You.

Most Holy Father, You have affirmed your adherence to the Tradition and the Faith of the Church, but You are ruining the Church and its Tradition. You open your arms to all those who, always in the past and today more determinedly than ever before, fight this Faith and Tradition: heretics, Freemasons, Communists, Jews, and all those who in the Church commit adultery and live in concubinage with such doctrines, while You close those very arms to all faithful servants of the Church.

Most Holy Father, it is with the greatest anguish that we say what follows. Your behavior reminds us of that of Solomon, who, having received the inheritance of his father David, did not hesitate to establish intimacy with foreign women, along with their gods and beliefs. And, just as he did, You will ruin the kingdom of the real Israel, the Holy Church. We cannot help noticing it.

As disciples of Jesus, we prefer the truth of *acts* to the truth of *words*. That is why we feel tempted to ask You: *Quid dicis de te ipso? Quis es tu?* What do You say about yourself? Who are You?

Noel Barbara, Priest.

Chapter XXIII

PAUL VI—
A LEGITIMATE POPE?

Various cardinals and writers have voiced differing points of view about John Baptist Montini's Pontificate and its legitimacy. This chapter will quote from some of those scholars and give the author's point of view as well.

AN ARTICLE BY DR. CARLOS A. DISANDRO

From *La Hosteria Volante,* an Argentinian magazine, we quote the following article by Dr. Carlos A. Disandro:

Pontificate and Pontiff—A brief theological question.
In the brief pages of *Church and Pontificate* (Montone, ed., Mar del Plata, 1969) I have explained the doctrinal circumstances that appear in the present dramatic moments of the world. Here I shall try to complete the picture of a Pontiff—to me, a *false Pope*—whose figure seems to summarize the mystic history of the Pontificate, although, in fact, he erodes, enslaves, and debases it and, as a result, erodes, debases and enslaves the entire Church, *Sacramentum Trinitatis.*

Through a thorough analysis of the doctrinal points regarding the divine form of the Church, we get to know that the Pontificate is a necessary element of the concrete historical link between the heavenly and the terrestrial levels. We know his is a *personal* Magisterium and jurisdiction whose continuity is irrefutable. Finally, we know that the Pontiff's personal errors in the general ethical-religious order do not imply the frailty of his Magisterium (such as in the cases of simony, concubinage, Caesaro-Papism, etc.) but that, regarding the link with the theological level connecting faith and authority, it could happen that the Pontiff could sever himself from the Church or, in other words, that the Pontificate could become vacant, not only by physical death, but also by theological death (heresy and schism).

This clear position of ours is different from that of those who enthusiastically defend Paul VI but attack the inviolable basis of his Pontificate (Cardinal Suenens, for instance, and a great many other people), and also from those who subvert the dogmatic, Hellenic formula of our Faith (Councils of

The Montinian Church

Nicea, Chalcedon, and Ephesus) and try to save both Pontificate and Pontiff according to a theological nominalism that bases everything upon an incomplete or false notion of authority. This applies, for instance, to Cardinal Danielou and almost all so-called "traditionalist groups," at least here in Argentina. In this doctrinal and practical field then, we are fighting a nefarious and destructive Jewish progressivism as well as the no-less nefarious design of a false tradition *which subverts the link between faith and authority.*

It is convenient then, to concretely state the principal positions being maintained in the world, and to provisionally outline our own approach to the problem. Those who accuse us of pride and exaggeration will be able to notice these ideas have complicated features. It should stand out more clearly that, without condemning passionate tones, legitimate as any other, we acknowledge this as a *quaestio disputata* and consciously choose a solution, perhaps the most delicate and compromising one, but nonetheless lucid.

To begin with, these are two important points of view: first, the one that avows the legitimacy of the election of John B. Montini to Paul VI, a legitimate successor of the Popes preceding him. Second, one that maintains he is a false Pope *ab initio,* since he became a Pope as a result of a conclave that was void because of reasons different people explain in various ways. The first position is supported by an overwhelming majority of persons and seems to have gained the universal agreement of the Church forever. The second position is maintained by a small number of interpreters, theologians, and canonists. Nevertheless, it does not lack surprising features that are not convenient to disregard, for they somehow concern the *quaestio disputata.* Since this concerns an opinion that can be quickly examined, let us describe it minutely.

According to the interpreters, three causes could be distinguished that establish the nullity of Cardinal Montini's election and consequently, the nullity of Paul VI's Pontificate, namely: (a) Before and after his becoming a Cardinal, Montini has furthered *heretical opinions.* Since he has not abjured such doctrines, the conclave's election is not legitimate. (b) The *bio-spiritual condition* of the appointee to be elevated to the supreme Magisterium of the Church, must indicate a certain degree of normality (for instance, a blind, mentally deranged, or a homosexual cardinal could not be elected). (c) The *formal procedure of the election* and the authenticity and normality of the circumstances surrounding the conclave, should not be altered to impose a false, demolishing Pope upon the Church.

Now then, the three synthetically essential possibilities regarding the basic nullity of the current Pontificate stated above, would require a thorough investigation. This is practically impossible today, with the exception perhaps, of the first item, Cardinal Montini's heretical doctrines. Even this investigation would be hampered by a general assent which has been maintained for seven years without change. However, in this vast enthusiastic world, there are some

Paul VI—A Legitimate Pope?

people who, for the sake of total doctrinal coherence and lucid defense of *faith* and *authority*, hold up such interpretations bravely and with good evidence. Here in Argentina just to mention this subject arouses howls, contortions, pseudo-doctrinal tearing of vestments, gibes, and insults. The questions at stake belong to the intelligence of the Faith, however, not to the criteria of theological *gendarmerie*, which uses the banner of authority to disrupt the real life of the Church. Faith is not a bandage; it is an act of possessing the *Theandrical Mystery*,[11] including a chiaroscuro margin of intelligibility and a zone of totally inaccessible penumbra. The work of the great theological centuries has consisted of moving within this deep dimension with a certain degree of fundamental coherence and constructive design. Let us put aside howls and gibes then, and let us face the present dramatic circumstances of the life of the *Faith* and the *Church* resolutely.

Now let us scrutinize the aspects of that position which maintains the legitimacy of Montini's election to the Pontificate and, as a result, the initial legitimacy of Paul VI, as the 262nd successor of Peter to the Roman See.

Here we shall distinguish three fundamental interpretations which in reality, comprise the most important tendencies existing in today's Church. First, some people think Montini's initial legitimacy and uninterrupted continuity of Pontifical jurisdiction are absolutely and solidly united and therefore could not cease. According to these authors, only death leaves the Pontificate vacant. Traditionalist Danielou and progressivist Suenens support this position, which comprises all conceivable hues.

Second, there are some people who distinguish between the legitimate and illegitimate, or void, deeds of Paul VI. They maintain his personal jurisdictional legitimacy, but nullify it in concrete circumstances. When these are present, it would not be the Pontiff, but John Baptist Montini who acted. Legitimate (Pontifical) and illegitimate (Montinian) acts would coexist in a single individual. The classical formula, *Papa haereticus est deponendus,* could be applied to this interpretation.

Third, some people acknowledge Paul VI's initial legitimacy, but contend it has lapsed or has been lost along with all the privileges pertaining to Peter's successors, including infallibility, because of formal, continued and explicit heresy. Thus the Pontificate would be vacant from a given moment on, and, as a result, the classical formula, *Papa haereticus est depositus,* could be applied to Paul VI.

We could give examples of all the above opinions, along with suitable reasoning and objections, without shedding much light on the problem itself. Among those who believe Paul VI was, *ab initio,* a legitimate Pope, are almost all traditionalists and progressivists. They are caught at the apex of an ambiguous authority, and this favors Paul VI's dialectical moves and skillful leadership as an heresiarch. The Church is being destroyed while the cardinals, the bishops, and even Montini weep. Who is destroying it? *Mysterium iniquitatis,* say the more

The Montinian Church

audacious ones.

Among the supporters of the opinion that Montini was a validly elected Pope and remains a true Pope, is Father De Pauw (United States Catholic Traditionalist Movement) and Abbé Georges de Nantes *(Contre-Reforme Catholique au XXe. Siècle)* in France. Father De Pauw rejects the *new Mass* openly and totally, but exonerates Paul VI of formal and explicit responsibility for its heretical contents. He does not allow the valid continuity of Paul VI's Pontificate to be questioned, although he avows the falsity of apparent Pontifical acts of his to be argued about. He speaks, then, about *"our unaltered belief in the continuity of papal authority,"* and says: *"This concept of the continuity of papal authority appears to me, at least from a pragmatic viewpoint, to provide us even more spiritual strength and justification for our NO to the new Mass than all the juridical, moral, and dogmatic reasons we will discuss later in this newsletter."* (Cf. *Letter*, Spring 1970, p. 9).

Father De Pauw maintains that the Church is a ship that has been captured and whose captain, Paul VI, *"is held captive by a mutinous crew issuing false orders in his name."* (Cf. statements to the *St. Louis Globe Democrat*, June 10, 1970). Rome's orders concerning numerous and delicate subjects are false, but the Pontiff has been, is, and will be a legitimate and true Pope up until his death. His orders must be resisted, but Paul VI's legitimacy must also be defended.

Abbé Georges de Nantes stresses the difference between *Paulian* acts (for instance, the encyclical *Mysterium Fidei*) and *Montinian* acts (for instance, *meeting with the World Council of Churches at Geneva*). He seems to support the formula, *Papa haereticus non est depositus, sed deponendus*, and ultimately defends the legitimacy of Paul VI, who remains a real Pope. However, he seems to be increasingly prone to affirm the heretical nature of Montini-Paul VI, judging by his conclusive statements contained in his analysis of the Dutch Catechism *(Contre-Reforme*, No. 35, August, 1970):

> Le silence de l'Autorité suprême de l'Eglise est à lui seul une complicité avec l'Hérésie, et il porte un coup mortel à la foi... En face de cette conjuration de l'Hérésie moderniste et des Pouvoirs Suprêmes de l'Eglise, que pouvons-nous, que devons-nous faire? Ou bien perdre la foi, en maudissant les Papes et Evêques des siècles passés, qui ont preché et imposé comme vrai ce qui est maintenant tenu pour des opinions déspassés et des fables inconsistantes... Ou bien tenir cette immuable et sainte foi catholique, et persister à l'opposer fermement aux nouveautés pernicieuses du Modernisme, non pas au nom de nos misérables personnes, mais au nom de l'Eglise, et ce, nonobstant le silence criminel du Pape et des Evêques. Est-ce à dire que nous condamnions ceux-ci par notre jugement propre? Non, ce n'est pas nous qui les condamnons, mais en nous la foi de l'Eglise qui ne s'affirme et resiste, qui ne trouve de passage et d'issue en nous qu'a travers l'Anathème. Ce que notre foi effectue spontanément, il faudra que l'Eglise

Paul VI—A Legitimate Pope?

future décide de faire infailliblement quand elle voudra restaurer dans le monde l'unique et immuable sécurité de sa foi catholique.

(The silence of the supreme authority of the Church is in itself complicity with the heresy and a lethal blow against the Faith.... In the presence of this conspiracy of the Modernist heresy and the supreme powers of the Church, what can we do? what must we do?... Either we lose our faith, cursing former Popes and bishops who preached and imposed as divine truth what is now held as surpassed opinions and inconsistent fables... [o]r we stick to the holy immutable Catholic Faith and firmly fight Modernism's noxious innovations, not indeed in the name of our wretched persons, but in the name of the Church, this notwithstanding the Pope's and bishops' criminal silence. Does it mean that we, following our own judgment, condemn them? No. It is not we who condemn them, *but the Faith in us, the Faith of the Church that steadies and makes itself firm, and finds no way out through us but via the anathema.* This is done spontaneously by our faith, but the Church of the future must make up its mind to do it infallibly once it wants to restore the unique immutable certainty of its Catholic Faith.)

It is difficult to reconcile "the Pope's... criminal silence" and his apparent present legitimacy, since this silence regards the *essence* of the Faith, and not an accidental or complementary detail thereof. It is difficult to understand, then, what limit the doctrine would have to impose in order that this crime might cease and the Church recover its real life.

With respect to this abstruse doctrinal subject, we have endorsed the formula *Papa haereticus est depositus* right from the beginning. Without our being aware of it at first, our opinions have coincided with those of the publishers of *Trumpets of Jericho (Trompettes de Jericho)* in France, of whom we have let you know through various references. The proofs of Paul VI's formal and apparent heresy are numerous; they can be found in Abbé de Nantes' and Fr. De Pauw's writings, in *Trompettes de Jericho,* in *Das Zeichen Mariens,* etc. Thus we affirm that Paul VI was legitimately elected and remained a legitimate Pope up until he approved what the heretical Vatican Council II had done. Though a pastoral council, it introduced the Modernist heresy implicitly, via *theological nominalism*. This was the beginning of the Church's historical, if not mystical, drama.

In effect, when John XXIII died, the Council automatically ceased. About John XXIII we can say that he tolerated and fostered heresy, although, at least so it seems, he did not undersign and ratify it. Legitimately elected, Paul VI reopened the Council and, using the pseudo-law which we call *implicit heresy* as well as *Modernist heretical nominalism,* he unchained an *explicit heresy* and started to lead it through his personal authority, which lapsed from that very moment. The examples of explicit heresies incurred by Paul VI are so numerous and grave as to be able to convince anyone who honestly analyzes the present situation, especially after the suppression of the Catholic Mass, the Eucharist, which Paul VI defended in an apparently traditionalist document.

Simply speaking, the Church considers all this void. Paul VI has ceased to be a Pontiff, and, from the date of his undersigning Vatican II up to now, is *a false Pope, and therefore all his acts, decrees and documents lack jurisdictional, canonical, religious, or ecclesiastical force.* In other words: *Papa haereticus est depositus.* The Church is submitted to the power of a tyrant who is exercising the powers of the theological monarchy to *subvert the Faith and destroy the Church.*

This approach is basically endorsed, as mentioned before, by the French *Trumpets of Jericho* which, in affirming Paul VI's heresy and schism, maintains the Pontificate is vacant and is using opportune and definitive reasoning, which the parody of the *"new Mass"* has confirmed.

I have attempted to objectively get down to the really dense and complicated core of a problem which, in spite of its being painful, belongs to the dearest part of the Faith. I have also detailed the various approaches and hues of the problems that are circulating in the world today. Moreover I have stated what is and has been my position with complete frankness. Although my person is a very humble one, my opinion does have importance and doctrinal value, for *it is a matter of doctrine, not of persons.*

What we are facing is tremendous, and even more tremendous is what can be inferred from the various enumerated and described opinions. However, I feel that in establishing the possibility of the "vacancy of the Pontificate" with supporting evidence, and estimating this possibility as a *probability*, we place ourselves in the light of utmost historical clarity. In effect, beyond the catastrophe that seems to be moving toward us, the exit can also be discovered provided the Church becomes conscious that in the future, the doctrinal authority of a legitimate and really "Catholic" Pontiff has to be rebuilt. Solutions other than this would contradict the real Tradition.

Carlos A. Disandro

AN ARTICLE BY ABBÉ GEORGES DE NANTES—SOME OPINIONS

In his *Contre-Reforme Catholique* of November, 1970, Abbé Georges de Nantes quoted several opinions concerning this subject which has been stirring up the Catholic world around the enigma of Paul VI. The first one was an article by M. Feuillet:

Paul VI—A Legitimate Pope?

From M. Feuillet

1. "The Privileges of Peter and His Successors according to the Gospel," published in *The New Man (L'Homme Nouveau)* on October 4, 1970:

What makes Saint Matthew's text so valuable is that it contains two violently antagonistic scenes: Simon Peter, rock of the Church (Matt. 16:13-20), and Simon Peter, rock of scandal, a hindrance in the way leading to God. (Matt. 16:21-23).

This passage stresses Peter's personal privilege and most energetically rejects any *unconditional* praise of Peter or his successors which would be *popelatry,* the illegitimate worship of the Pope's person. It decisively discards the frequent error of confusing *didactical infallibility* with *impeccability.* Peter, insofar as he, enlightened by the Father, professes faith in Christ, the living Son of God, is the rock upon which Christ wanted to build His Church. But this same Peter, laying aside the abstraction of divine aid, is but a poor human being like all men; far from being a rock, he can be a stone for scandal and have Satan's thoughts: "Go behind me, Satan, thou art a scandal unto me: for thou savourest not the things that are of God, but the things that are of men." (Matt. 16:23).

From Civis Romanus

2. An article by Civis Romanus, in *Rivarol*, October 29, 1970:

Our abidance by the hierarchy is absolute, and our obedience to what it commands includes no reservations ... But the depositaries of such a high, sacred authority are men; they exercise their authority as men and, in these conditions many times act imperfectly, undergoing the risk of mistakes, connivance, weakness, cowardice, partisanship, and prejudice. In consequence, they do harm to the Church, the Faith entrusted to it and, finally, to its souls. That is why, outside *well-specified circumstances,* no Pope, no bishop, and, *a fortiori,* no priest, may claim he is impeccable or infallible in any realm. If any of these clergymen, whatever his position be, behaves scandalously, teaches and fosters erroneous doctrines, or plans and implements innovations that damage, for instance, the dignity of divine worship, it is evident that every believer has the right, and perhaps the duty, to express his opposition, which will be more or less strong according to the gravity of the faults and the various circumstances surrounding them. I acknowledge it to be a delicate question of sound judgment, insight, information, prudence and perhaps justice. Once all precautions have been taken, however, lest one cause a disorder worse than the one which one intends to expose, the hierarchy cannot complain of lack of respect or lack of submission to what it has no right to command.

The Montinian Church

From the Abbé Dulac

3. The Abbé Dulac, in the September 30 issue of the *Rome Post (Courrier de Rome)*, wonders: "No doubt, the unity of Catholics has to be made over ... But of which Catholicism? ... and of which Pope?"

These are horrible questions, but it would be hypocritical to conceal them ... Which Pope will be granted submission, and deemed to be of true Catholicism, on that day when, due to a dreadful tragedy, *it may seem* that there are several Catholicisms fighting each other?

The hypothesis of a Pope who goes out of his mind or is imprisoned, has never existed in history, but undoubtedly, both hypotheses are possible. One might add another possibility: that of a *drugged* Pope, which the satanic inventions of modern chemistry have made much more possible than what is usually thought. Now there are drugs capable of nullifying one's will, making it intermittent or contradictory as to the most important decisions. In that case, we should have a man who would be unable to perform really human acts except, and this would be even more fearful, in an *intermittent* way. Thus we would have hesitancy when it would be criminal to hesitate, and contradictions as to what he would say from one week to another and from one year to the next. He might say something and his *deeds* might contradict it. People could think he is playing a double game, but, in reality, it would be a duality rather than duplicity.

> ... [T]he perplexity of this subject is even more dramatic should the oscillation of the will and mind become more and more imperceptible and progressive, and the change with respect to the center of gravity remain unnoticed except at a distance. Besides, one might hesitate to acknowledge such a change and attribute it to a single cause, jeopardizing the mind's moral responsibility, and disturbing its functioning. In consequence, a drug may destroy the psychosomatic faculties that rule the psychological or moral conscience, and cause the mind to unconsciously and innocently betray....

To tell the truth, these atrocious hypotheses cannot be excluded with respect to a Pope. Christ promised Peter that his faith would not wither, but he did not promise him that his reason and his prudence would never suffer such defaults. The same is the case for his virtue. During the night of the Passion, Peter denied his Master three times. According to Paul, later on he succumbed to weakness and "walked not uprightly according to the truth of the Gospel." In consequence, Paul "withstood him" face to face (Gal. 2:11-14). We do not know whether we are back again to the times of the fall of Honorius I, but we cannot remove from our mind that painful occurrence in the Church's history.

In the hypothesis of a Pope who under the influence of drugs

Paul VI—A Legitimate Pope?

becomes irresponsible, what must a Catholic's position be? . . . We have to say that this hypothesis supposes a single Pope, but a Pope with a double personality. In this hypothesis, the Catholic's drama will no doubt be more painful than in the event of two Pontiffs, each of whom gained possession of the Papacy for himself. It would not be a question of deciding who is the Pope, but who is the *real* Celestinus VI (we simulate this name to facilitate our reasoning).

The *real* Celestinus VI would be the one who intermittently has the *conscience* of his function and exercises it *consciously*. The *real* Celestinus VI would be the *real Pope* not the one who, under the influence of drugs, is a puppet, a mere semblance of truth.

A swaying rock is no longer a rock from the moment it moves and reels, but there is no authority in the Church empowered to remove it. This rock will remain where Christ put it until He Himself removes it.

Abbé Dulac remains faithful to his position, that a Pope cannot be a heretic, and under no circumstances may a Pope be overthrown. This is not possible. . . . The drug solution is an ingenuous way of avoiding the theological difficulty, supposing an unconscious, irresponsible Pope when he scandalizes us, and conscious only when he acts according to his own convictions and our own beliefs. To me, Paul VI has never appeared more conscious and acted more freely; he has never appeared more himself than at the implementation of liturgical subversion and the revolutionary preaching he introduced as divinely inspired during the Council and his Pontificate. Where then are the drugs?

Concerning the Pope's Intention to Abdicate

4. The Pope intends to abdicate. Alarming news concerning his health reinforces the gossip about his resignation. Will Cardinal Villot be his successor? Does a progressivist plot to maneuver the next conclave exist? This is the reason why the rumor about a drugged Pope spread.

The Vatican physicians (we are not saying the *Pope's* physicians) explain that to be able to keep up with his overwhelming tasks, spending all his time without respite, Paul VI, uses and abuses medicines. Thus it might be said that he is physically drugged. This sounds like burning the candle at both ends, but it is evidently the only way for the Pope to endure the fatigue of the long trip to Australia and the Philippines and the many activities he attended there.

The many grave problems he has to deal with aggravate the Pope's condition to such an extent that he disregards his state of health and torments his mind. On the one hand, he is extremely worried by his duties and concerned about their nature. On the other hand, new grounds for uneasiness come out continually. As a matter of fact his daily life is a long martyrdom, and the

The Montinian Church

hellishness of his continuous medicines helps turn Paul VI into a man literally undermined by anguish and hesitation.

Even though this were true, evidence is only circumstantial. We know that for six years the progressive preaching of a heretical ideology has been going forward and that during this period, Paul VI's design for subversion in the Church has been executed. Undoubtedly, he has gone far outside his Magisterium and, in a confusing number of fields. Paul VI and the theologians distinguish very well between his speeches as an infallible doctor (which he practically never gives, and then only with a set of reservations) and his prophecies as a disciple of Lammenais and Maritain. He seems to prefer the Christian-democrat prophecies to doctrinal teaching, but sometimes he does the reverse. How could a drugged man effect this skillful strategy with perpetual equilibrium and cunning, if he has no consciousness of what he says, does, or intends to do?

Let us abandon this easy hypothesis which permits integralists to keep intact their worship of the Pope and their certainty about his infallibility, notwithstanding their growing uneasiness and passive resistance to Paul VI's doctrines and resolutions. We prefer to see him as one of those "two ambiguous, changing and dubious Popes" the La Sallete prophecy mentions, one of whom was his predecessor or, perhaps, his successor. But in the Church, nothing seems to contradict the equal tyranny of an apostate or drugged man. Two opinions prolong this intolerable crisis. On one hand, the progressivist clan is suggesting in an increasingly aggressive way as the year 1972 approaches, the Pope's *resignation,* of which the case of Celestinus V is the only example. This "solution" would solve nothing. We, on the other hand, propose the urgent *dismissal* or *deposition* of Paul VI, which is a reasonable and convenient solution. Its procedure is not complicated, nor is its realization impossible, as some people say.

From Herald Zimmermann

5. In *Papstabetzungen des Mittelalters* (Vienna, 1968), a work that became known in France through an extensive comment by Robert Folz in *Erasmus* (1970, col. 508-511), the Austrian historian Herald Zimmermann studied dismissals of Popes in the Middle Ages.

Zimmermann examines a series of facts which apparently contradict the maxim, *"Prima sedes a nemine iudicatur"* (Nobody can judge the First See), which was drawn after the Pontificate of Symmaque.... Despite this principle, there have been dismissals of Pontiffs John II, Leo VIII, and Boniface VI.... After the presentation of historical facts, he systematically analyzes the principles and methods applied to the dismissal of Popes during the Middle Ages ... from about the middle of the seventh century to the enthronement of

Paul VI—A Legitimate Pope?

Gregory VII.

Principles: Among the grounds given to attempt the deposition of a Pope, the gravest one was the charge of heresy. This charge was examined by Isidor from Seville for the first time and according to the false decretals, was brought by Pope Symmaque himself, who, making reference to his own trial and several trials concerning his predecessors, stated that "the sheep entrusted to a shepherd have no right to censor him, unless they feel he is diverting them from the right Faith." This was a terrible accusation. It was brought against John XII in 963 and against John Philagotos in 998. Both of them were charged with apostasy. Another ground was simony, either specifically named as such, as in the case of Formosus and the dismissal of three Popes in 1046, or under the name of spiritual adultery which was brought against Leo III in 799. . . . Even more often than simony, the charge of "invasion" is recorded. This word meant usurpation of the Apostolic See. . . . Constantine II was condemned for his having risen to the Pontificate while a layman, since the particulars of his ordination were irregular; Formosus was convicted for his having violated the rule prohibiting transfers from one see to another. Still another charge was perjury, which meant: (a) one Pope's testifying against another, as in the case of Leo VIII against John XII, (b) denying an agreement, (c) changing one's mind, as in the case of Boniface VI, who belonged to the Reformation party before being elected.

Procedure: Zimmermann demonstrates that the requirement of a *libellus acusatorius* was not always observed as in the case of John XII, against whom, according to Liutprand de Crémone, a cardinal brought a long list of charges before the council presided over by Otto I in 963. It was preferred that a high-ranking ecclesiastic, acting as a probator or *testis legitimus* bring the accusation. When it was not brought (for instance, in Rome in 800 or in Montue in 1064) the decision was that the accusation was slanderous, and the defendant was restored to his former dignified position. Previous investigation was always required, and the defendant was summoned to defend himself. Disregard of the summons was considered as contempt of court. The complexity of these procedures caused the secular power to become gradually involved in all of them. . . . Since the emperor was frequently involved in these charges and, in fact, the dismissal trials were frequently provoked by political reasons or personal feuds, the supreme appeal was to be brought before the council, and no verdict of guilty was ever passed outside an ecclesiastical assembly. Historical sources show that the questioning of the legitimacy of a Pope provoked enormous difficulties and occasionally schisms. The council had to be basically a Roman one, but since a Pope's condemnation concerned the whole Church, the subject sometimes became universal. Etienne III, for instance, had Constantine II's condemnation ratified by the Frankish bishops. The process of rehabilitation of Formosus began in Rome and ended in Ravenna with the participation of the

The Montinian Church

Lombard bishops. In exchange, strong complaints were heard in France in 1046, against Henry III's intervention in Roman affairs, because the episcopate of the Gauls had not been consulted.

Judgment: We can get a glimpse of what happened in a council summoned to try a Pope. The defendant was able to justify himself through a purgative oath; *Leo III* accepted this solution, which was offered in vain to John XII. When the guilt was apparent, it was frequently preferred that the person involved avow it and beg pardon; in such cases, the assembly's judgment just confirmed what the Pope himself had stated. The penalties imposed on the guilty individuals were dismissal and degradation to the lay status. Sometimes these measures were accompanied by excommunication. The mutilations of which John Philagotos was the last victim in 998 were essentially aimed at preventing any further restoration of the Pontiff.

What becomes clear in Zimmermann's writings is that *"The men who tried such-and-such a Pope for heresy or usurpation shared the common belief that 'nobody may judge the primary See' and that their proceedings were aimed solely at saving the Church from a pseudo-Pontiff."*

It is then, firmly witnessed by history, that the dismissal of a notoriously heretical, apostate, simoniacal (or drugged?) Pope can be legitimately requested and even demanded. It is also true that a trial is absolutely necessary, and that it must be conducted by an ecclesiastical assembly, preferably of a Roman majority. Such an assembly would not intend to stand over the Pope or settle any doctrinal question against his will, but would be designed only to force the Pope himself to openly and clearly explain whether he is a loyal Catholic or a heretic, schismatic, or apostate. The Pope, in stating his personal opinions or beliefs, would pass his *own* judgment, and the assembly would then receive the Pontiff's testimony and enforce the very sentence that the Pope's confession had passed in advance.

What is our condition in this autumn of 1970? We have come to the sad conclusion that the Pope no longer accepts any rule or authority arising out of Tradition or law. He revolutionizes the rites, lets morality be trampled and his teachings scorned. He endorses the most notorious heretics of our time and pursues chimerical political-religious policies, despite the fact that such tactics were condemned by the Church long ago. Moreover, his sole answer to the charge of heresy is to lift up his arms to the sky, an unworthy, insufficient, and immoral answer.

The time has come, then, (a) to teach all Catholics that the Pope is not always infallible, and even less impeccable, (b) to explain to the sophisticated the errors and public faults of Paul VI which are compromising the very existence of the Church, the unity of the Faith, and the everlasting Salvation of souls, (c) to remind the Roman clergy, and above all the cardinals, of their prerogatives of admonishing and even coercing Paul VI to stop his doctrinal and pastoral overflowing, and (d) to encourage the most solid defenders of the Faith to threaten the Pope with the convocation of a legitimately convened and integrated assembly designed to demand that he answer the charges brought against him.

If not even a single cardinal, priest, or high-ranking minister of God appears before such an assembly *to sustain these charges* as a *probator et testis legitimus,* the Abbé de Nantes, who for six years has been saying and publishing that this is a *heretical Pope,* though unworthy, would appear to sustain his accusation of heresy and apostasy against Paul VI, in order that the Roman clergy demand that the Pope answer said charges in a clear and definitive way, under penalty of dismissal and excommunication.

To provoke the dismissal of an "incompetent and unworthy" Pope, to use the words Paul VI himself employed to qualify himself, would render a service to the Church and above all, do honor to the Papacy itself.

From Brazil

6. *Brazil.* "The Pope's heresy will provoke a schism," (*La Croix,* November 4.)

We are about to witness the first hints of a schism. A group of young men and adults who used to belong to a Marian fraternity and have now joined a Tradition, Family, and Property group (abbreviated T.F.P.), have rejected the new *Ordo* of the Mass and stated that this order is unacceptable for Catholics. They have gone even farther than that. Through Dom Castro Mayer, Bishop of Campos, in the state of Rio de Janeiro, they have distributed a tract in which they demonstrate, based on the teachings of the Church Fathers, that a Pope who has incurred heresy no longer deserves obedience on the part of believers, and ceases to be a Pope. Then they accuse Paul VI of having prescribed the heretical contents of the new *Ordo* of the Mass. "I believe," says the *La Croix* commentator, "that, if a schism is coming, it will come from the integralists."

From Monsignor Spadafora

7. *Italy.* Theologian Msgr. Spadafora charges Cardinal Willebrands with heresy. (*La Croix,* Nov. 4, 1970).

In its issue of October 25, the ultra-rightist *The Mirror (Lo Specchio)* magazine published a violent attack against Cardinal Willebrands, president of the Secretariat for Christian Unity, by Msgr. Spadafora, a prelate and professor of exegesis. Commenting on the Cardinal's involvement in the World Lutheran Assembly, he affirms that his speech "abuses the Catholic Church and historical Truth, and is objectively heretical." He writes, "One thing is clear, that only a heretic can pay homage to Luther on behalf of a gospel defined as heretical by the infallible Magisterium of Trent."

The Montinian Church

From the Abbé Georges de Nantes Himself

8. Now it is Abbé Georges de Nantes who speaks. "Is Paul an Apostate?"

My God! My God! Give me the courage I need to get to the end. Give Your Church saintly Doctors and Pontiffs who realize the need and have the determination required to dismiss Pope Paul! *Why is the Pope's dismissal the urgent and only way of coping with the current crisis?* Because good Catholics (there are many of them at all levels of the hierarchy, as well as among the simple believers) are in danger of succumbing to either of two temptations which they must resist: (a) *accepting everything,* disorder and corruption of worship, faith, customs and of everything commanded or authorized by a seemingly unanimous hierarchy whose head and chief is the Pope, or (b) *rejecting everything* as a whole, for everything is really inadmissible, very sad, impudent, and perverse, thus abandoning a Church which provokes them to rebel and seems to wish that it be abandoned. *These two, very easy solutions are sins.* On no grounds must we abandon Jesus Christ's Church. We must adhere to neither the Modernist reformation not to the integralist revolution.

Then what *is* the solution? The solution is to reject the reformation while remaining within the Church. There seems to be no way to dissociate the Church from the reformation, however, other than accusing the present Pontiff himself, since it is he, and *only* he, who links two worlds: that of order and disorder, of Tradition and subversion, of Christ's work and Belial's schemes. Only Paul VI is able to combine these two opposite and antagonistic spirits within himself, forcing us to accept one of them in the name of the other. The aim is not to disobey a progressivist priest who goes against the Church's Faith which the bishop is supposed to represent, but one is *obliged* to expose heretical or apostate priests to their bishops. If, however, the bishop defends his heretical subordinates, the treacherous bishop must be resisted in the name of Faith and discipline of the Roman Church, incarnated in the Pope, and an appeal made to Rome. Should one appeal to Rome in vain, should the Pope scorn our anguish and just anger, should his absolute, stubborn, and fearful will support the Church's "demolition" and the murderers of the Faith, then the will of the Pope, Christ's Vicar, would be opposite to the truth. It would be as though God were against God Himself, and our Faith would be at its end.

The only way out of this dreadful doubt, the sole possibility of dissolving the enigma, points to the Pope's person. His will seems to be the will of an apostate Pope. Let him define his position in a precise and decisive way. Then and only then, will we be able to get out of our most serious anguish. If the Pope is unworthy, if in one way or another it is proved that he supports subversion, our condemnation will be justified; our Faith, resting on the Church's "inerrancy" and strong enough to confound the apostates who want to throw it down, will finally recover its immovable certainty.

Paul VI—A Legitimate Pope?

For it is written *"Auferte malum ex vobis ipsis"* ("Put away the evil one from among yourselves") (I Cor. 5:13), and: *Episcopatum eius accipiat alter* ("And his bishopric let another take") (Acts 1:20).

> SHOULD THE POPE BE A HERETIC
> THERE IS NO NEED TO QUIT THE CHURCH,
> WHICH IS NOT HIS WORK, OR ANY MAN'S WORK.
> IT IS NECESSARY TO REMOVE HIM.

Paul VI flagrante delicto. Any accusation against Paul VI will of course begin with a public, undeniable, permanent crime, namely that this Pope has not only sanctioned, but obstinately refused to combat heresy and schism, and has boldly performed sacrilege, perpetrated and professed by numerous members of the hierarchy. Simultaneously he permits himself and his direct subordinates to be treated as heretics without doing anything save lifting his arms to the sky, seeking only that his accusers in their desperation abandon the Church that puts them in perilous anguish. Not even one of the principles of modern theology that he invokes or could invoke, might excuse his ignoring the essential duties pertaining to his sovereign authority. The fact that Paul VI never pronounces "anathema" on the most monstrous heresies or an "interdiction" on the temples where invalid or sacrilegious masses are celebrated, and that he never excommunicates priests and laymen participating in those ecumenical services and scandalous "inter-Communions," suffices to support the accusation of *treason* against the present Pope. There can be no immutable Faith, safe worship, or real justice in the Church as long as the Roman Pontiff refuses to exercise his triple magistracy as a prelate in charge. The Church has the right and obligation to remedy the disordinate fact that such a "striker" continues to occupy the Apostolic See. Peter's See is not vacant; it is occupied by an individual who refuses to fulfill his functions, and this is even worse. The remedy to this inadmissible inertia of power consists of the Roman clergy's intimidating Paul VI to act as a Pope on penalty of being declared inactive and deposed.

Three leading charges in the pastoral field: simony, usurpation, and perjury. Paul VI's pure, abstract, religion is not at stake. In the realms of faith, transcendental Mysteries, and private worship, his religion is the same as ours. Notwithstanding his incense burning, it does not seem that Paul VI has a true piety or, if so, he conceals it well. What is true and can be proven is that, in the daily universal life of the Church, he hides this pure religion under deadly indifference. His feverish concerns, his passion, his grand projects follow other ways. In this field he delivers very traditional, though inexpressive speeches; ...he even publishes encyclicals containing good doctrine... provided he is demanded or forced to do so, but he will immediately afterwards authorize and praise the opposite, and even lie to save the reformation party that is in danger, as he did with respect to Latin and the Mass in November of 1969. This feature is, to us, the most grave, but to him the least important. Catholic Mass or Protestant Last Supper? He celebrates the Catholic Mass in the right manner no doubt, but he gets involved in false masses celebrated because of his negligence, irresponsibility, and complicity in Holland, and sometimes even in his own diocese of Rome. Thus, all the liturgy finds itself systematically altered by the replacement of God by man, apparently without his paying attention to anything except increasing his glory as a world reformer. Likewise we behold his being absolutely indifferent to the subversion of the Faith contrary to his intimate beliefs, when innovations are introduced under the guise of *aggiornamento* and the Council's ambiguity. Souls perish, but he does not seem to be concerned. He believes in Hell, but theoretically, not practically.

This neglect of the *essential,* to use the ancient vocabulary, might substantiate three basic charges:

Simony: This is the price he has to pay to conserve his popularity in progressivist circles and among the enemies of the Church. An instance is his proclamation before the United Nations of religious freedom as a universally accepted dogma even before the Council had discussed it. On that day, the Pope's faith was his token to gain admission to that Jewish-Masonic Manhattan assembly. That was, indeed, a simoniacal contract.

Usurpation or Inaction: The inviolable realm of religion is being invaded and ruined more and more by absolutely human diplomatic and political concerns to such an extent that to please heretics and schismatics, the *Pater Noster* and the Eucharistic words of Consecration have been changed.

Perjury: The cardinals who appointed him, the clergy and the Roman people who cheered him, and the whole Church which received him as a legitimate Pope, have been able to hear his private and public protests and oaths of fidelity to the steadfast discipline and traditional Faith of the Church, but such promises have never been fulfilled. We all know that the Pope, in the foreword of his *Creed,* stated that he would apply all his energies to defend the Catholic Faith he was proclaiming to the world; not only has he failed to defend it but hundreds of times he has practically contradicted and overruled himself.

This *Adultery,* to use the old biblical expression, according to which any treason to divine Faith is adultery and prostitution to idols, is to be felt in the Church's daily life, especially in Rome. It is the heretics from the inside and the outside who get in, while faithful Catholics remain outside. It is the North Vietnamese Buddhists who have secret conventicles with the Vatican hierarchies, while the southern Catholics do not. As to the Jews, their power is immensely superior to ours. Terrorist murderers are very kindly received by the Pope, while the gates are closed to the supplicant defenders of Saint Pius X's Mass and the real catechism. This Pontificate has been the Kingdom of Outsiders, and legitimate children have not only been cast into oblivion, but

Paul VI—A Legitimate Pope?

abhorred.

The chief charge is *Apostasy*. The reason for all this disorder, to follow the central theme of prophetical teaching, is the idolatry provoking this spiritual adultery, which is not to be found in Paul VI's pure, speculative religion, but in his applied religion, namely, *his political Messianism, his Masdu*. Apart from his intimate faith and zeal, which we hypothetically suppose, we can say that in the more tangible realm of the secular life of modern mankind, the Pope has built an ideology, an extraordinarily sophisticated, powerful, and absorbing "mystique." His is a project for total renovation of the human condition, which includes a new and definitive stage of salvation, a liberation that is a hundred times more real and radical than the Church-implemented two-thousand-year-old Christ's Redemption. *"Paulus extra muros"* ("Paul outside the walls"), an undeniably forceful expression by Fr. Congar, has gradually become overpowered by this dream, this *Utopia* outside the walls of ancient Christianity. To this Tower of Babel, which he places in Manhattan, Jerusalem, or Peking, he sacrifices *all* in an implacable way except when the Holy Spirit decisively intervenes. Catholic Faith, morality, and worship must adapt to this humanitarian, cosmopolitan, and futuristic "mysticism," as means to their end, just as the Church must put itself at the service of this world, whose material and cultural development will provide men *peace, the supreme good.*

Evidently it cannot be admitted that the Pope, Christ's Vicar, may be completely absorbed and devoured by chimerical *politics,* to which he sacrifices all his thoughts, speeches, and major decisions, while abandoning God's *religion,* of which he is the supreme and absolute earthly representative. We have already reached the stage where his "mystic" policies appear to have replaced the "mysticism of the everlasting truth." We are at the stage where this heresy is ousting and passionately profaning the vital and sovereign place belonging to *divine Faith.*

Thus I have summarized and given a brief demonstration of the apostasy of Pope Paul VI. When tomorrow Paul VI is tried for heresy, his message on the 25th anniversary of the United Nations in which he repeats and aggravates to the point of blasphemy the errors contained in his speech concerning his encyclicals *Ecclesiam Suam* and *Populorum Progressio*, will suffice to accuse him. Should Paul VI's *Creed* be true and sincere, the Church will have to pronounce the anathema. As for me, I want to avoid the divine curse, but his Masdu message is a work of the Antichrist.

Are you astonished at my audacity? This is because you have not realized the terrible danger that all of the members of the Church (not *all* of them, because this could not happen, but *almost* all of them, as past experience and even current experience evidence) may follow their Head in this *"course toward Mao,"* with their eyes focused on an illusion. Should the majority of the members of the Church follow the apostate Pope, it would be the world's worst punishment.

MY OPINION ABOUT THESE OPINIONS

Obviously, the above quotations by several eminent men from various parts of the world show convincingly, as I have indicated many times throughout this book, that the crisis of the Church is most grave everywhere, and that confusion is becoming more terrifying every day.

As time passes and events occur, all forecasts agree as to the principal evil forces behind it, namely, the deviation and manifest turnabout of the hierarchy and the ambiguous Vatican Council II, which intended to create a *new pastoralism* without firmly resting it on the immutable dogmas of our Catholic Faith. Both of the last two Pontiffs have indisputably interrupted the harmonious unity of the *Church's Tradition and Magisterium*. That is why I have always maintained that as long as we keep on trying to save John XXIII, Paul VI, and their pastoral council, we shall find ourselves in a blind alley. This is not the first time it has become necessary to put the mistakes of Popes, pseudo-Popes, and councils between parentheses when they did not rest upon revealed truth, for those parentheses were necessary to save the Church's *inerrancy* and *equilibrium*.

I realize, foresee, and am already seeing that, moved by self-esteem, personal interest, and human, not divine, fears, the accused ones try to defend themselves using the same revealed truth they boldly violated before in order to proclaim, establish, and carry on their reformation. The blackmail of obedience is in the cards. "We are the Church," say the current innovators, "we are the sole authentic successors of the apostles, we are God's representatives, we have divine assistance, we are infallible, we are the authority, and we have the power to destroy the opposition." They forget, however, that despite the privileges they have which we do not argue about, the *Faith, the Church's inerrancy,* and *God's authority* are on top. They forget that the Church's doctrine is immutable. They forget that the legitimate development of the Church, which Jesus Christ designed and announced, cannot be ignored or suppressed, even under the guise of returning to the purity and sincerity of the primitive Church. They forget that among Catholics it is not possible to accept the pretended change of mentality that they are now asking in order to adjust ourselves to the new ecumenical and post-Conciliar Church, for, I have said many times that *this change of mentality is a change of Faith*.

Even the most cursory analysis of the Vatican II pastoral reformations, the innovative teaching of the encyclicals *Mater et Magistra* and *Pacem in Terris* by John XXIII and the encyclicals *Ecclesiam Suam* and *Populorum Progressio* by Paul VI would show that the post-Conciliar Church has definitively overridden the solemn teachings and condemnations of Pius IX (his Syllabus),

Paul VI—A Legitimate Pope?

those of Leo XIII, Pius X (his encyclical *Pascendi* and his condemnation of Modernist errors), and Pius XII (especially the *Humani Generis* and *Mediator Dei*), as well as the solemn definitions of the Tridentine and Vatican I Councils.

This poses such a big problem, that the very top of the new Magisterium has to be questioned. Neither God nor His revealed truth may change. *If both latest Pontiffs and their pastoral councils have revolutionized the whole Church, we are right in questioning their legitimacy.* Above the organs of the Magisterium is the holy untouchable deposit of the divine revelation. That is why we question the reforms introduced by this council and both latest Popes. Our question is not rebellion against the authority, but against *abuse* on the part of this authority. Let us remember that obedience to any human authority is meritorious, Christian, and worthy only when the people who exercise such authority do not exceed the limits imposed by reason and Faith, and when they do not attack divine rights. The principle is clear and unreformable: *"We must obey God before we obey men."*

"I am the Pope; I am the bishop." Right, but this does not mean you are God, *impeccable,* or *personally infallible.* The juridical fact of your supposedly legitimate election does not authorize you to do whatever you want with the Church, or to nullify any definition or teaching of the also authentic and legitimate organs of the Church's Magisterium, by means of a *Motu Proprio,* Conciliar statement or any other document you sign. If we find any discrepancy, we have the right to doubt you and your innovative teachings.

Of the opinions about Pope Montini quoted above, I believe only two are worth studying. These are (a) the one that denies the legitimacy of the election of John Baptist Montini, and (b) the one that, while accepting his legitimate election, affirms that Paul VI has incurred heresy and apostasy and because of his permanent omission in the performance of his most high duties, has ceased to be the immovable foundation, the firm rock upon which Christ built His Church.

If the Pontiff's heresy were proven, any further discussion about whether he is automatically dismissed or whether a juridical dismissal (pronounced by the Roman clergy, among whom the cardinals are *ex jure*) is necessary, would be of secondary importance, for it would be difficult in either case, to implement an efficacious action, to make him quit his position. Personally speaking, I prefer the first thesis which states that once the Pope has incurred heresy, he automatically ceases to be *Peter,* the immovable rock, the principle of unity, cohesion, and stability upon which Christ's Church stands. The Roman See can become vacant not only due to physical death, but also due to heretical theological death, but this does not mean that the Church, or the Papacy, perishes. As said before, the vacancy of the see can last months and even years, without this vacancy altering the existence or the stability of the One, True Church founded by Jesus Christ.

The Montinian Church

Otherwise, we would have to join the unsafe position many leaders of the resistance have adopted with respect to this matter and the vital problem of the *Ordo* of the Mass, that the new Mass is unacceptable and ambiguous, but remains Catholic, valid, and legitimate. The present Pontiff is a heretic and an apostate but nevertheless is the real Pope, to whom we owe complete obedience. What then? May we associate affirmation and denial? May we accept that a heretic Pope continues to be the supreme Master of the Church? I cannot accept this ambiguous approach as Catholic, for it gives allegiance both to heresy and Catholic truth. To me, a heretic Pope loses all authority. If the premises are proven, do not let us be afraid of the consequences that will most clearly arise.

Taking this still as a thesis, not a hypothesis, it is possible that a Pope can be no Pope, provided his election was not valid and was void from the beginning. The history of the Church proves it. I feel this is the first research made to clear up Pope Montini's enigmatic personality. Was John Baptist Montini legitimately elected as a pope? Was his election void *in radice?* Were his election null, it is evident that the enigma of his personality resolves itself. In such a case, his Pontificate and his council, whose reformist activity has almost turned our Church into a new Protestant sect or a constantly evolving dialectic religion, have to be put between parentheses as a period of punishment for mankind. Thus we could put our Catholic Faith into a monolithic position again.

To investigate the legitimacy of the election of John Baptist Montini, checking whether all canonical requirements for a papal election were complied with is not enough. If we discover that his connections, doctrines, and activities show contradictory and meaningful signs, I believe that a thorough analysis of his personality must be carried out before going ahead with other possible hypotheses.

STATEMENTS BY ALFRED CARDINAL OTTAVIANI

Even before this, however, another meaningful occurrence which might be very useful for the research I have suggested, should be mentioned. I quote from the Spanish *What's Up (Qué Pasa?)* magazine, Vol. VII, No. 363, of December 12, 1970:

> *The famous and "regretfully" octogenarian Cardinal Ottaviani does not conceal his bitterness.*
>
> In its issue of Thursday, November 26, in three columns on the first and second pages, *The Messenger (Il Messagero)* from Rome, published a sensational interview with His Eminence Alfred Cardinal Ottaviani. The report is accompanied by a large photograph of this venerable prince of the Church....

Paul VI—A Legitimate Pope?

According to the Pope's November 24 *Motu Proprio,* beginning next January no eighty-year-old cardinal will be able to participate in the election of the Pontiff. Presently, these persons amount to twenty-five. Among them is saintly Cardinal Ottaviani, who celebrated his eightieth birthday on October 29, 1970.

Question: What does His Eminence think about this decision of Paul VI?

Answer: More important than my personal opinion, which could be deemed biased because of my age, I should like to convey the feelings of canons, prelates, and even renowned hierarchs who are unaware of the current problems of the Church. Undoubtedly they all are impressd by this unusual and expeditious way of enacting this grave disruption in the high ecclesiastical hierarchy. This radical change was implemented without previous consultation with experts and specialists, at least to observe the formalities to a certain extent.

Question: Why did Your Eminence say *"unusual?"* Perhaps because no one expected such a big upsetting decision?

Answer: It is unusual that, through a *Motu Proprio,* without previous advice, the pages of the constitution *Vacante Sede Apostolica* and those of the *Code of Canonical Law,* which regulated the position of the cardinals, both as to the cooperation they owe the Pontiff for the rule of the world Church, and as to their most important ministry as top electors of the Head of the Universal Church, are suppressed. This *Motu Proprio* then, is an act of abolition of a multicentennial tradition. It rejects the practice followed by all ecumenical councils. Regarding the age limit [the Most Eminent Cardinal spoke calmly and composedly, without any sign of uneasiness], should old age be respected, we would be able to sow the seed whose fruits you yourselves would harvest. But here respect was laid aside.... It is precisely the motivation of age which the *Motu Proprio* invokes to justify such a grave regulation. In fact, along the centuries, a principle was always deemed immutable, namely, that old people are a firm safeguard of the Church and its best advisors, for they are rich in experience, wisdom, and doctrine. If, in a given case, these gifts were not present, it sufficed to examine the circumstances concerning this particular person to determine whether disease or mental disturbance made him inept, this check belonging to skillful experts. In Holy Writ," [the Most Eminent Cardinal was astonishingly bright], "the *value of age* and *the aged* are often mentioned. This shows how constructive are the cooperation and guarantee of advanced age in the administration of holy things and in right and efficient pastoral administration. In addition, let us not forget the glory of Pontiffs, who, in their old age, enlightened the Church with their wisdom and sanctity. Finally, when we cardinals are in our eighties, to our credit is a *curriculum vitae* full of merits, experience, and doctrines at the service of the Church. The Church cannot afford to lose these advantages by accepting only the cooperation of younger and less-experienced people.

Question: Eminence, could not this discrimination of octogenarian cardinals by chance affect the Pontiff himself someday?

Answer: Certainly, for the same criterion must be analogically applied to the case of the sovereign Pontiff, be he an octogenarian or be his acts questioned due to age.

Question: Finally, Eminence: What was your impression about this decision of the Pope?

Answer: You will see. I felt flattered each time Paul VI, verbally or in writing, called me *"il mio maestro"* ("my master"), but now this act of laying me aside completely is openly contradictory with his autographed letter of October 29. In that, he congratulated me for my eightieth birthday, using affectionate phrases and flattering felicitations for my long, faithful, everyday services to the Church.

STATEMENTS BY CARDINAL TISSERANT

According to the November 27, 1970 issue of *La Croix,* 86-year-old Cardinal Tisserant, who enjoys full mental clarity and excellent physical health, answered questions on Italian Television (First Network). I quote *La Croix:*

Rarely had an interview attained such importance and contained such interesting information. In just three minutes, the audience was informed about the Pope's critical health condition ("he had to be held up on the way out of his Wednesday audience"), about the Cardinal's excellent state of health, about Christ having founded His Church under the form of a *monarchic state,* and about the collegiality of the bishopric about which we have heard so much ("The more it is mentioned, the less it is exercised").

Apropos of Paul VI's decision to keep the election of the Pope in the hands of less-than-80-year-old cardinals, Cardinal Tisserant said he did not know the grounds thereof (though the Pontifical document stated them clearly), and that, undoubtedly, the Pope *wanted to please young people,* since *"now, everybody wants old people to disappear."*

Wednesday afternoon, Professor Alessandrini categorically denied the Cardinal's words regarding the Pope's health condition.

Paul VI—A Legitimate Pope?

SOME COMMENTS BY FATHER RAYMOND DULAC

When Fr. Raymond Dulac was asked his opinion of Paul VI's decision to take away the right of voting in papal elections from cardinals 80 years and older, he made these statements:

This decision taking away the *right* of voting in the papal election from a whole category of cardinals, is an enormous decision. Until now, the most important part of their function was this right. It commands and effects their *beheading* in the most accurate sense of this word; they keep their hats, but their heads are chopped off. This is what the ancient Romans called *diminutio capitis*, a lessening or amputation of their civil rights and, of course, of their personality.

Let us not forget that the statute creating the cardinals' right to elect the Pope dates back to the year 1059; that during the arduous course of this thousand-year period of history this rule was never questioned; that the "impediment" of advanced age has never prevented the creation of a cardinal or the continuing of a Pope once he became 80 years old, that it is contrary to the Catholic spirit and the Roman Tradition to suspend a law supported by such a time-honored custom without most grave reasons; and that this type of change, affected by the Pope in 1970 in such a sudden, personal, and suspicious way, will increase most people's feelings of insecurity, instability, and the alienation which has contributed to de-sacralizing the Church and loosening its customs.

Let us forget the inhuman, vain, vile aspects of this decision concerning the age of men whose sacerdotal ordination had separated them from mortal mankind as far as powers and dignities are concerned.

After this blow and all the others of the past five years designed to naturalize and laicize the clergy, how could one have the heart to keep on telling the ordained young priests: *"Tu es sacerdos in aeternum secundum ordinem Melchisedech?"* Priest for all eternity? Of what order? Not of the carnal Levitical tribe, but of the order of that astonishing, unique, *ageless* personage, Melchisedech, whose mystery is revealed in the Epistle to the Hebrews, verse 3 of Chapter 7: "Without father, without mother, without genealogy, having neither beginning of days nor end of life, but likened unto the Son of God, continueth a priest forever."

This all being over, today's priest is just like an *official* who, in due course, is "retired," with a life pension, like a Swiss guard.

Since Paul VI, without much of a preamble, has nullified a millenary legislation, it is important to know whether his *Motu Proprio* was not in fact, a *Motu alieno*.

This most unusual act is an act of *personal* might on the part of a Pontiff who, so far as others are concerned, keeps on covering himself with the curtain of collegiality. We are sure this act *has not been free*. Should it be proven that it *was* free, there will be no need to nullify this act; as a matter of right, it will be null and void....

"For behold... the Lord of hosts shall take away from Jerusalem, and from Juda... the strong man, and the man of war, the judge, and the prophet, and the cunning... and the *ancient*. The captain over fifty, and *the honourable... and the counsellor*... And I will give *children* to be their princes, and... the *child* shall make a tumult against the *ancient,* and the *base* against the *honourable*." (Is. 3:1-5). *He who is able to understand, let him understand* [italics added].

This is Paul VI, living contradiction. On the one hand, he affirms; on the other, he denies. Many times, without even preserving appearances, he destroys with facts what he has built with words. Let the reader remember what the Pontiff wrote in his brief to Cardinal Lercaro when the Cardinal was almost eighty years old, wishing him a long life in the service of the Church. Then let him read the *Motu Proprio,* whereby he deprives octogenarian cardinals of their legitimate rights on grounds of age, not because of incapacity. Paul's dialectics are incomprehensible and plainly destructive.

Applying these dialectics, regulating our criteria by the principles of this *Motu Proprio,* we must conclude that the octogenarian Pontiff, John XXIII, was an inept pope, and his council was no real council, because, according to Pope Montini, one's reason quits functioning when one is eighty years old, and one is no longer able to receive the light of the Holy Ghost.

THE ARCHBISHOP OF GENOA, CARDINAL SIRI, SPEAKS

In order to decipher the enigma of the current Pontiff, I believe it to be extremely important to quote the courageous statements of Cardinal Siri, Archbishop of Genoa. He did not speak directly about Paul VI, but I believe that what he said can be applied to Pope Montini:

1. *Opinions Replace Truth.*

In this world the first and fundamental doctrine of power consists of an affirmation that there is no truth. Saint Augustine said that the difference between the city of this world and the city of God consists of the former having a thousand opinions, while the latter has only one truth. The basic difference between both cities, therefore, is not based on the content, but on the very existence of truth. It suffices to remember the dramatic dialogue between Jesus and Pilate.

What is most grave is that there is a *technique* to replace truth by opinions. This technique exists and is very useful. It suffices to look at present religious, literary, and philosophical productions. Opinions can be so cautiously expressed that it is impossible to get to know what the author's thesis is, or even more paradoxical, doctrines that are mutually contradictory are juxtaposed as if they were consistent.

Let us look at the words, "God is dead." If the slogan were *denial*, everybody would be able to understand. However, here we have a subtly sophisticated idea through which "theologians" want to convey the deceitful impression they are preserving the most assayed and chemically pure idea of God . . . through its "identification" with the most profound reality of man.

Even the ambiguous terms "conservative" and "progressive" conceal the relativistic technique, which leads every doctrinal issue in the direction of right wing and left wing. Thus *everything becomes relative;* everything becomes a matter of opinions and an instrument of power. Relativity of truth and doctrine is the actual goal of these arbitrary developments of the Church's present problems.

Is not this measure, proclaimed even by bishops and cardinals among us, absurd and most unjust, as if it were an ideal to place us halfway between truth and error?

2. *Is Gnosis Reappearing?*

[To name the current errors in the Church, one speaks about a new *Modernism* and also the *Protestantization* of the Church, but the Archbishop of Genoa prefers to use the term *Gnosis*.]

Let it be remembered that *Gnosis*, with its appeal to science and higher speculation, with its eagerness to understand mystery and to naturalize the Faith, was, during the second century, perhaps the worst danger in all the history of the Church. I believe that the complex of errors circulating today can be called *Gnosis*, systematically speaking. But . . . do many people know what they are talking about? This is terrible, but they do not!

One does not act on rational grounds, but on one's excessive desire to adapt oneself to the world. Worldly power, however, has its own philosophy, and fashionable theologians translate fashionable opinions into theological language, not because they accept a doctrine as such, but because they accept these doctrines that flatter the powers of this world.

The present times are grave, not because it is no longer a question of opposition or contrast between truth and error, but between truth and non-truth, between the order of truth and the *dictatorship of public opinion.* People believe they are free because this appears in juridical texts; as a matter of fact, this deceiving belief is evidence of their servitude.

Is the Church also under the despotism of public opinion? Perhaps not the Church, but certainly many people within the Church are. The Church could not be deprived of its freedom without the Holy Spirit's provoking powerful reactions. . . .

The altercation around the Council was not intended by John XXIII, who suffered profoundly as a result of it; of this I am a personal witness. The real

Christian greatness of John XXIII consisted of the serene Christian manner by which he humbly accepted his cross up until his death, fully realizing the tremendous gravity of the problems.

3. *What is Most Urgent?*

The most urgent work is to restore the distinction between truth and error in the Church. We have reached a point where any exercise of ecclesiastical authority is considered an abuse of freedom, as if authority were a denial of freedom! A thousand illegitimate powers severely and systematically curtail the conscience and liberty of people at a superficial level, while at the deepest level they detach them from the truth contained in the sources of revelation and Magisterium. I hope that just and authorized distinctions will be forthcoming. *Pastoral authority is no art of compromise and concession, but the art of saving souls through the truth.*

This truth is many times obscured by abusive liturgical deformations. Today dangerous losses are discovered in the essential. Not only is the rite sacred, but also the presence in the rite of the meaningful reality. Once the rite is mythologized the meaning of its contents is lost. No wonder that the Eucharist becomes for some a mere feast of human unity where God is just a spectator. *This is no longer heresy, but apostasy.*

Right. The present situation in the Church is one of the most grave in its history, for this time the challenge does not come from outer persecution, but from inner perversion. This is very grave. *But the gates of Hell will not prevail.*

Chapter XXIV

IS JOHN BAPTIST MONTINI A TRUE POPE?

Jesus Christ, the divine Founder who chose and appointed "the twelve" to be His apostles, His witnesses, and the continuators of His divine work, compared His Church with a flock ruled and led by a single shepherd, the divine Redeemer Himself: *"I am the good shepherd"* (John 10:11). The apostles were His representatives, His lieutenants on earth, and, among these, Peter was the Shepherd of shepherds: "Feed my lambs. Feed my sheep." The divine Master admonished us, using precise and indisputable words, to beware of false prophets, who will come to us wearing sheepskins, but, inside, are rapacious wolves. *Ex fructibus eorum cognoscetis eos* (by their fruits you shall know them). Jesus Christ Himself then, granted us the obligation to beware of false prophets and saboteurs who pretend to do good but do evil; not only is this an obligation, but it is also a most grave duty of conscience which our fidelity to God and our own salvation demands.

In terms of the current catastrophe, I do not know whether the acts and words of the present Pontiff have been used to efficiently and rapidly resolve the condition of anguish in the Church. At any rate I want to formalize some charges which my priestly conscience tells me are indisputable:

1. In re-opening the Council which John XXIII's death had interrupted, Paul VI abruptly turned this ecclesiastical assembly around and designed its future ambiguous way when he showed up without his Pontifical mitre. This showy gesture was his implicit acceptance of the bewildered voices of progressivism which, condemning the triumphalism of the Constantinian Church, wanted to put the responsibility for all heresies and schisms upon it. I remember my awful feelings in hearing Pope Montini's words when he begged pardon of the "separated brethren," the victims of the sole Church founded by Jesus Christ. Paul VI's words and deeds meant the definitive breaking away from the pre-Conciliar Church. It was then that the *reformation of the Church* actually began.

2. Since the Roman curia was the prop and human bulwark of the Magisterium and the jurisdiction of Peter's primacy, it was natural that the Conciliar attacks were decisively launched against its structures, beginning with the hateful and hated Holy Office, a reminiscence of the flames of the

The Montinian Church

Inquisition, and a hindrance for the progress of more liberal and human theology which would be more appropriate to our world's requirements. Given the democratic slant the Pope wanted to implant in the pastoral council, he knew how to second the reformist projects with millimetrical accuracy, so as to practically demolish those old-fashioned structures. What is left now of the Roman curia?

3. To carry out the experts' *reformation,* the first goal to be attained in the dogmatic field at the Council was democratic "collegiality." The bishops attempted to introduce it as a way of making the Pope less of a Pope and the bishops more bishops. A marginal remark, written by the Pope as an appendix to the scheme written out by the committee, saved the dogmatic definitions of Vatican I on the *primacy of jurisdiction* and the *didactic infallibility* of Christ's Vicar. However, the Pope wanted to show the bishops his goodwill and his wish for reforms, so, opening his generous hands, he awarded them extraordinary faculties that the Church had once reserved for the Roman Pontiff for most serious reasons of prudence and justice. A new national or territorial organization, which would give the bishops larger representation (or *co-responsibility,* as the Belgian primate would say) in the administration of the Church, was set up with legal and definitive status. These were the episcopal conferences, designed to make the powers of the Pope and the bishops more even. According to this change, the bishops would not have a personal and independent power in their dioceses (I am not speaking about their dependence upon the Pope), but they would be ruled by those democratic episcopal conferences. As for the Pope and his judgments and decisions, he would not be able to divorce himself from the feelings of the Church he rules. Finally, as extra evidence of Paul VI's unlimited generosity and desire to please the bishops, the Pontiff created some democratic "synods" in order to discuss the most grave problems of the Church with the bishops attending them. The spirit of the Council would thus give the Church a permanent mood of reform and change.

Undoubtedly Paul VI not only put off his mitre, suppressed the Pontifical court, and got down from his august throne, but, perhaps unintentionally, curtailed his own authority to the extent of becoming *de facto,* if not *de jure,* the first among his equals, *primus inter pares.* This is why the episcopal conferences, for they are the majority, can afford the luxury of interpreting and even challenging papal orders and teachings, as in the case, already well-known, of *Humanae Vitae.*

4. The progressivist attacks were skillfully aimed at the fundamental dogmas of our Catholic Faith. The voices of the anti-Church began to deny the Mystery of Faith and the Transubstantiation, using an innovative word the modern world was able to understand: *trans-meaning.* Then Paul VI published another encyclical, *Mysterium Fidei,* in which he seemed to ratify the

traditional, Tridentine faith, the only Catholic Faith. However, there were new, more-or-less apparent, attacks against the sacrificial Eucharist, the sacramental Eucharist, and the real Eucharistic Presence of Christ. These attacks culminated in the revolutionary *Novus Ordo Missae,* which was preceded by an *Institutio Generalis,* a real summary of the Lutheran and Anglican heresies. How could it have been otherwise, taking into account that six Protestant ministers had taken part in the restructuring of the new *Ordo Missae?* The *Novus Ordo Missae* was enacted by the present Pontiff's Apostolic Constitution, *Missale Romanum.* The Mass, according to this first version of the *Novus Ordo Missae,* is *"the assembly or meeting of God's people, gathering under the chairmanship of the priest to celebrate the Lord's Memorial. That is why, speaking about the local meeting of the Holy Church, the promise of Christ is eminently valid: 'For where there are two or three gathered together in my name, there am I in the midst of them.'* (Matt. 18:20)." This definition, be it essential or descriptive, can be applied to the Protestant Lord's Supper, but not at all to the holy, true, and real Sacrifice, where, in a bloodless way, Christ as Priest and Victim offers up Himself on the altar to convey to us the fruits of His redemption.

Priests and believers showed their nonconformity through so many protests and eloquent theological analyses that it became necessary to introduce new changes to the *Institutio Generalis,* but the quibble, if not the heresy, of the new Mass remained. As mentioned before, it attempts to identify the dogma of *Redemption* (for all men) with the dogma of personal *Salvation,* which depends upon our acceptance of God's grace (not for *everybody,* but for *many,*). All this came because of the tricks of translations into vernacular languages.

Who can enumerate all the sacrileges committed within and without temples under the guise of liturgical reforms? Under disguise of a lack of priests, the divine Eucharist has been put into the hands of all the faithful, men and women, married or unmarried, to be distributed among those who come to commune. In order to make the drama of the Lord's Last Supper more realistic, and to break a multicentennial tradition, in many countries, Holy Communion is no longer given on the tongue, but in the hand. This of course leaves the door open to the episcopal conferences to spread this innovative way of giving Communion. And what about the consecrated particles? The new guidelines seem to have forgotten the third canon of Session XIII of the Tridentine Council: *"Si quis negaverit, in venerabili sacramento Eucharistiae sub unaquaque specie, et sub singularis cuiusque specifi partibus, separatione facta, totum Christum contineri, anathema sit."* ("Should anyone deny that, in the venerable Sacrament of the Eucharist, Christ is contained under each one of the species or in each part, or particle, of each of the species, once the separation is made, let him be anathema.") Then it is a matter of faith that Christ is in the consecrated particles. How can we compare this faith with those innovative practices, whereby neither the celebrant nor the faithful are concerned about the particles that could remain among one's fingers or fall down to the floor?

Studying the liturgical reforms and comparing them with Trent's dogmatic doctrine, I have begun to realize that, with unbelievable skill, and ignoring the Tridentine definitions, the Protestant doctrine was accepted, despite the fact that it had been condemned by the Church as contrary to revealed truth. To give extra examples, let us quote canon four of Session XIII of the Tridentine Ecumenical Council: *"Si quis dixerit, peracta consecratione, in admirabili Eucharistiae Sacramento, non esse corpus et sanguinem Domini nostri Iesu Christi, sed tantum in usu, dum, sumitur, non autem ante vel post, et in hostiis seu particulis consecratis, quae post communionem reservatur vel supersunt, non remanere Corpus Domini, anathema sit."* ("Should anyone contend that, after the consecration, in the wonderful Sacrament of the Eucharist, the body and the blood of our Lord Jesus Christ are present only when they are received, neither before nor after, and that, therefore, in the hosts and consecrated particles that remain after Communion and which are reserved in the ciborium, the body of the Lord does not remain, let him be anathema.") Is not this denial in the very placement of the ciborium, which no longer occupies the central position now reserved for the priest or chairman of the ecclesiastical assembly, but occupies a corner beside a column in a secondary position in the Church? A Jesuit at the College of the Ladies of the Sacred Heart of Sarria in Barcelona told the astonished nuns: "Christ is, indeed, on the altar at the hour of Communion, but is not, as if preserved, in this box." Even in temples where the tabernacle still occupies a central position, the priest, president of the assembly, performs the new Mass with his back to the ciborium. Would we dare to do this if we could see Christ standing there?

Canon 11 of Session XIII of the Tridentine Council reads: *"Si quis dixerit, solam fidem esse sufficientem praeparationem ad sumendum Sanctissimae Eucharistiae Sacramentum, anathema sit. Et, ne tantum Sacramentum indigne atque ideo in mortem et condemnationem sumatur, statuit atque declarat ipsa Sancta Synodus, illis, quos conscientia peccati mortalis gravat, quantumcunque etiam se contritos existiment, habita copia confessoris, necesario praetermitendam esse confessionem sacramentalem. Si quis autem contrarium docere, praedicare, vel pertinaciter asserere, seu etiam publice disputandum defendere praesumpserit, eo ipso excommunicatus existat."* ("Should anyone contend that faith alone is enough preparation to receive the Sacrament of the most Holy Eucharist, let him be anathema. And, so that this great Sacrament be not unworthily received, and therefore received for death and condemnation, this holy synod establishes and states that those who are conscious of grave sins, even though they feel very much repented (with contrition, not with attrition), and have a confessor, are not to come to commune without making confession. Should anyone teach, preach, or pertinaciously say or dare to contend the opposite publicly, let him incur the penalty of excommunication *ipso facto,* as a result.")

In spite of this, here in Mexico Méndez Arceo and several Jesuits have not only maintained, but *performed,* these sacrilegious practices. Even more surprising, newspapers have recently given us sensational news. Below is a quote from the paper *El Universal* from Mexico, D.F., for Sunday, January 10, 1971:

> "The Vatican is Considering the Possibility of Authorizing Collective Confessions." Vatican City, January 9 (United Press International):
> This evening the Vatican announced that it is considering the possibility of authorizing collective confessions and the absolution of sins in a series of "special cases." This statement was released by the Vatican Press Office more than 24 hours after *United Press International* (UPI) announced that Pope Paul VI had asked the 3,199 bishops of the world to study a recommendation to make private confession optional for everybody, with the exception of a small number of grave sins. This statement says there have been no changes in the confessional rules, but confirmed that some changes are being considered. "At the request of many bishops of missionary countries, the Holy See is considering the possibility of applying the directions given by the *Apostolic Penance* of March 25, 1970 to some special well-defined cases. These guidelines regard the sacramental absolution imparted in a general way to a series of persons," says the statement.

Such have been the tactics used to introduce these reforms that appear to be in contradiction to the infallible and immutable doctrine of the Council of Trent. First, in the style of sounding gongs, the vanguard theologians spread the species, while progressive bishops put it into practice; then comes the cautious, deceitful Vatican news, and finally *the reform.*

One cannot think the news is false or has been misconstrued, for several of the leading newspapers of this capital published it as a report from the Vatican Press Office. What we can say is that this is not only surprising, but really scandalous news. Apart from the cases where to make a personal confession is impossible, the power of forgiving sins supposes a trial, for according to Christ's Will, the priest is the judge, and the sinner himself is both defendant and prosecutor. These were Christ's words: *"All the sins you shall forgive on earth shall be forgiven in heaven; and all the sins you withhold on earth will be withheld in heaven."* We do have the really divine privilege of forgiving sins, but not whimsically or in heaps. To render our judgment of acquitting or withholding, we must get to know the personal attitude of each penitent; we must reach a decision by listening to each one in Confession. To accept the Pope-suggested collective confessions now being imposed upon us one would have to challenge the whole dogmatic doctrine of the Tridentine Council.

The Montinian Church

5. Other dogmas the progressivist reformation fights are the Marian dogmas and generally speaking, the Christian people's zealous and overwhelming devotion to the heavenly Mother, the Immaculate Virgin, this devotion fulfilling her prophecy, *"Beatam me dicent omnes generationes"* ("All generations shall call me blessed.") To these innovators, who repeat the heresies of yore, this "exaggerated" devotion for the Mother is detrimental to the Son. Dialectical Paul VI played his regular game: at the Council, he proclaimed Mary as *Mother of the Church,* but permitted the others to fight not only the devotions to Our Lady, especially the holy Rosary, but even the very untouchable Virginity of our Blessed Mother, more or less furiously, more or less boldly. The feasts of the most Holy Virgin, which so much enhanced Christian life, were suppressed or merged. In the meantime, the Pope weeps and keeps quiet.

6. I remember that, at the opening of the second session of Vatican II, the then recently appointed and enthroned Paul VI solemnly recited the Tridentine Profession of Faith, and the anti-Modernist oath prescribed by Saint Pius X. My soul was greatly touched as I listened to his Catholic Profession of Faith, including the veneration of the sacred images the Catholic Church has consistently professed and defended. Who could have foretold that a little later, even before the Council was over, the reformers, like new vandals, would loot the temples and destroy those very sacred images, as though their veneration in our temples were one of the biggest mistakes of our pre-Conciliar Church. Even the crucifixes required by the liturgy for the performance of the holy Sacrifice were eliminated from the altars and the offices of the Vatican State Department. In some places, such as Cuernavaca, all sacred images were either destroyed or put away. The new iconoclasts believe the images are reminiscent of idolatry and, therefore, must disappear from the home of God's people. Does the Pope ignore these facts, this "de-sacralization" of the Church and all the things consecrated to divine service and worship?

7. Later on an even graver compromise was effected, something that will necessarily affect future generations. Vatican II, which was no dogmatic council but merely a pastoral council, wanted to have its own catechism, a different, absolutely different one from Saint Pius V's Catechism, also known as the Catechism of the Council of Trent (an eminently dogmatic council) or the Roman Catechism. Thus there appeared the famous Dutch Catechism, plagued by heresy and most serious omissions. In previous ages, it would have been solemnly condemned by the Pope; but in these ecumenical times of religious freedom, the sole obligation of its editors was to add an appendix with explanations, which would establish a bridge between heresy and truth. With this slight change, the Dutch Catechism began to be disseminated throughout the Church by the progressivist clergymen and bishops, who found that it perfectly stated their new gospel. Then we had catechisms for the United States,

Is Paul VI a True Pope?

France, and Italy, all of which included the same slant, the same ideas, the same vocabulary. A catechism for each nation! Perhaps we had not yet wiped off Rome's hateful centralization? The *aggiornamento* had to liberalize the statements of doctrine to ease their adaptation to the mentality and customs of each people, race, and nation. (Centuries ago Jesuits sought to do this through the acceptance of Chinese rites.) Meanwhile the Pope, at his weekly audiences, keeps on weeping and proclaiming the truth.

8. Apparently the problem that caused the Protestant revolution in Germany to explode was that of the indulgences. This problem continued to be a hindrance for our merger with the "separated brethren." That was why Paul VI, still at the Council, attempted a total review of the concept of the use and granting of indulgences. The Pontifical reformation achieved the result it was intended to, for it imperceptibly diluted and eliminated the notion and use of indulgences as a fanaticism of the past without any solid theological basis. Who speaks about indulgences today? Even jubilees have been forgotten. Suppressing the controversial issues opened us wider to heresy, thus making the Christian unity of which we dreamed easier. Forgetting indulgences and ceasing to mention them caused the suppression of one of the most consoling inducements to the devotions of Christian life. Paul VI however, keeps on telling us that nothing essential has been eliminated in the doctrine and practice of our religion.

9. The idea of *ecumenism,* evidenced by the presence of "observers" from other religions at the Council, including, of course the "non-official observers" of Judaism, was the most briliant innovation of Vatican II. The Church not only had to confess all its past injustices, but suppress all censorship and canonical penalties against the adventurers in theology or religion. All former heretics or schismatics, all members of other religions, all the enemies of God or the Church, including Lucifer himself, had to be attracted through the most sweet name of "separated brethren." There was just one exception: that of the stubborn traditionalists, who persisted in defending the Faith of twenty centuries. They were punished with "disqualification," "episcopal excommunication," and "suspension by the ordinary." Our ancestors were wrong; perhaps they died obdurate, for they did not accept this evangelical "opening" to the heretics and schismatics. If to bring about pastoral ecumenism, it becomes necessary to amend the New Testament, let it be done for the sake of human peace and welfare. Paul VI, at Colombia, Geneva, Rome, and in all his apostolic trips, gave us constructive examples of this practical ecumenism *that invokes the Lord in unison,* although to some of the brethren, it was an immanent God, to others a transcendental God, to some a Triune and single God, to others, a single God in a single person, to some the Creator of the universe, and to others, the great Architect of the universe.

10. In this universal reformation of the Church, the orders and religious

congregations could not be spared. A total revision of all the religious families was necessary in order to adapt them to the spirit of the Council, even if this means they had to give up the specific spirit their founders had given to their own institutions. The illustrious militia of Saint Ignatius Loyola had to march in front, and with its influence on the religious communities, especially on the feminine orders and congregations, had to totally change the ascetic and mystic mentality, on very short notice, into an "up-to-date" mentality, including TV, radio, freedom to come and go, suppression of the cloister, loosening of constitutions and regulations, new "Christ experiences" and elimination of any "paternalism" or "maternalism," in order that members might develop with total liberty and independence. Moreover, since the Council's pastoral spirit demanded a constant dynamism, even the static communities devoted to contemplative life changed their medieval robes for fashionable clothes, miniskirts, gogo blouses, masculine hairdos, and other novelties of modern life; above all, they had to devote themselves to do something worthwhile, not to be idle but to develop an active life without the inner life of devotions, choirs, or the absurd pious practices they used to perform, even though obliged by statutes.

What is left of religious life? What is left of regular observance, poverty, obedience, and even chastity? There is division within almost all communities; there is loss of spirit and hundreds of claudications. Many people, following the advice and example of Teilhard de Chardin, continue to live in religious houses and pretend to be religious, although they live a life not only alien to, but *opposite* to, the religious life and religion itself, thus fighting the Church of Christ from within. A most excellent prelate, complaining of the madness of the "new wave" Jesuits, was right in telling me: "They are the worst ones; *corruptio optimi pessima"*—the corruption of the best is the worst thing. One of these Jesuits, whose name I do not want to remember, dared to celebrate the Mass in a bathing suit before male and female bathers in Acapulco. Oh, Society of Jesus! Oh, Jesus, what a Society!

What about the old "good press?" The various magazines used to spread the doctrine of truth, favor piety and form healthy and accurate criteria to rule customs. Now our literature, through which the Mazas, Guineas, and Pardinases disseminate errors, irreligion, and lies, is good only for enhancing the "business" and justifying the demolishing work of these treacherous sons of the holy Society. Should the old people rise from the dead, and should Fr. Romero, saintly Joseph Anthony, come back to their offices, just to glance at the illustrations of the *Messenger, Christus, Union,* etc., I am sure they would feel just as angry as I am at the revolutionary writings which adulterate the spirit and letter of the very Gospel.

Now, the religious go to the movies, attend night clubs, and enjoy freedom and mutual familiarities with young girls. Not long ago, at the novitiate and juniorate of Puente Grande, S.J., a priest, accompanied by young boys and girls, experienced "living together" in which, during the night, one of those angelic girls rushed into the room of the "Padrecito," took off his blanket and ran away, followed by the Father, who repeated such an angelic and "progressivist" joke. The superiors know this, or ought to know, but they tolerate it or keep quiet, and do not punish the impudent profaners of the religious life.

It is interesting to read what Fr. R. Dulac, under the impressive heading, "Toward Spiritual Genocide," has published in *The Rome Post (Courrier de Rome)*, about the planned liquidation of priests and monasteries devoted to the contemplative life. This is a plan, not just a blueprint, but a well-organized plan being carried out by a minority of plotters with countless accomplices and useful idiots. Father Dulac studied the "euthanasia" of monasteries and seminaries, and states that the French Seminary at Rome, which used to have 220 students, now has less than forty.

Who is ultimately responsible for this wreckage of the religious life, the life of perfection, in which, according to its rules, the religious must seek after their own perfection? *Paul VI and his Council's reformation.*

11. The Council of Trent, endeavoring to remedy the moral corruption which had regretfully plagued the clergy, paid particular attention to the seminaries, where future priests and future bishops, must be properly trained in virtue and knowledge. Our old seminaries were proud of being called *Tridentine,* so as to explain to candidates for the priesthood the reason for the austerity, thorough care, and solicitous surveillance displayed in the training of seminarians. Now after Vatican II, which seems to have, *a priori,* stamped out everything Trent decreed, everything has changed in the seminaries. Young people are granted complete freedom in order that they get no impression of paternalism, discipline, or inhibition. Attend Mass? Only if they want to; otherwise, they may stay in bed or spend their time in the urgent socio-economic or socio-political research required by their future apostolate of social justice. Let them be free to go out, even during the night, go to movies, treat girls and (why not?) have a girl friend. This way, this broad criterion, (to me, pure licentiousness) will help future priests to feel surer about their vocations, riper, less childish, less prone to be scandalized, and more able to cooperate in the urgent adaptation of the Church to the new world that is being born.

Latin, Greek, humanities, rhetoric? They are no longer of any use. Scholastic philosophy and theology have lost their reputations, and are obsolete and out of style. Logic and metaphysics? Barren and useless speculation. Let Marx, Lenin, Teilhard, and the Conciliar "experts" be studied, in order to delve deeply into the *Conciliar reformation.* Let the theological texts of the "separated brethren" be studied in order to acquire the ecumenical spirit, and,

The Montinian Church

if possible, let Holy Writ be construed, explained, and taught by rabbis, just as is being done in many seminaries, for, as experts in exegesis, they are able to disclose hidden meanings that the Magisterium had not even suspected.

These innovative reformations are accompanied by copious "ultra-Modernist and progressivist" literature, which has the *nihil obstat* of censors and the *imprimatur* of bishops or cardinals (such as Cardinal Lienard, Cardinal Miranda, and Don Marcelo, the Bishop of Barcelona). This literature is free to enter and circulate profusely in the post-Conciliar seminaries, to intoxicate (I mean, to "shape") the minds of the ill-prepared seminarians who are not able to distinguish between truth and sophistry, between heresy under the cover of new theology and progress, and immutable theology founded on revealed truth. In addition to such readings, one has to take into account the teaching and explanations of the post-Conciliar professors, who laugh at the scruples and theological censorship of ancient textbooks. As an unavoidable and logical result, we have an accelerated pace of loss of vocations and loss of faith on the part of the few priests who are ordained. Seminaries are empty; there is a lack of vocations, and, out of the few who enter the seminaries, many quit. The new priests, especially those coming from Rome, with very few exceptions, are already infected with an unbearable self-sufficiency, twisted views, and a lack of piety and spirit. These young priests feel they are the reformers of the Church; it is out of their company that our bishops will come!

I believe this revolution inside our seminaries and houses of formation where the new workers of the Lord's vineyard are being trained, is one of the most grievous and symptomatic expressions of the "auto-demolition" of the Church that Paul VI himself exposed. Those who knew the Gregorian University of yore and compare it with the modern one are astonished at what is to be seen, said, and taught under the guise of the new theology. Even divorce is defended by the skilled professors of this top center of theological knowledge, which is ruled by the Fathers of the Society of Jesus as reformed by Fr. Arrupe.

Does the Pope not know what is going on in the seminaries? Does His Holiness not investigate the causes of the growing desertion of seminarians and priests? Why do we oblige ourselves to look outside for the destructive force, when it is within, *very much within,* the Church? I am convinced that most desertions are not due to *want of vocations,* but to lack of formation, to basic disorientation in the minds of those youngsters who entered the seminaries seeking God, but instead found only the world, a bare, unconscious, and unscrupulous world.

12. As to the appointment of bishops, illegitimate, especially adulterous, children used to be excluded. The Church's point was that this prophylactic measure helped preserve morality; experience had taught that illegitimate children frequently inherit their progenitors' vices. Today, instead of this, we can see several prelates whose illegitimate background is well-known, who do

Is Paul VI a True Pope?

not have a mitre, but occupy leading positions in that most active movement of episcopal conferences. Today attention is not focused so much on the candidates' backgrounds but on their flexibility and steadfast adherence to the post-Conciliar reformation. In a certain diocese in Spain there is a bishop who belonged to an obstinate Protestant family (in Spain, this is almost unbelievable), was "converted" and entered a seminary from which he was ousted, after having been found performing an immoral act with another pupil. He was fired, but powerful influences were exerted and he was accepted again. He was ordained, and now he is the bishop of . . . . How many cases could I mention here, possibly not so regretful but equally revealing, as a confirmation of what we have said before! The appointment of the "new prelates," those who zealously carry on the post-Conciliar reformation, is one of the leading causes of the Church's present crisis. Who appoints the bishops? Who awards them their positions in the Church?

13. During the reforming Council an attempt was made to amend conjugal morality, particularly with respect to the new birth control pills. The Pope kept this issue for himself, imposing his supreme authority and appointing a special committee to study and resolve this most grave problem which had been definitively and unequivocally solved previously by two of his predecessors, Pius XI and Pius XII. A divine law is involved, and no human power may contradict it. Paul VI, however, in his usual dialectical way, set up the committee to establish the antithesis, in order that he himself could make the synthesis in his *Humanae Vitae* which, as Fr. Arrupe pointed out, must not be read in a light or cursory manner. Four long years passed in which Paul VI spoke only occasionally, and not magisterially, about this vital problem upon which the very morality of the conjugal life depended.

Meanwhile, the progressive theologians such as Fr. Alfredo Mondria, S.J., of Spain, began to authorize the use of pills. If the Pope appointed a committe to study the matter, it was because he saw very serious reasons *for* and *against* contraceptives. The law was doubtful, and a doubtful law does not oblige as a matter of conscience. Pills could be used at ease, then, with daily Communion and without scruples of conscience. Moreover the new theology contended that the primary and essential goal of marriage was not, as taught before, procreation and education of children, but love, the mutual love of spouses, which is translated into sexual satisfaction. Children are the consequence of such love. This loose doctrine led to widespread use of contraceptives among Catholic couples. It is not surprising, therefore, that when the Pope finally published his encyclical after a four-year *vacatio legis,* voices of protest rose everywhere, not only from individual priests, laymen, or bishops, but from the mighty episcopal conferences. They fought the Pope or at least gave an explanation designed to find a milder solution taking into account the requirements of the present world and permitting spouses to avoid children

The Montinian Church

and receive Communion and the other Sacraments without uneasiness. *Non sunt inquietandi.*

14. The law of retirement, which imposes on bishops the obligation to resign at a certain age at which they are no longer capable of ruling their dioceses, gave Paul VI a powerful instrument to select bishops, eliminate conservatives, but, whenever convenient, to maintain docile aides who were unconditionally addicted to papal directive. Thus, though over eighty years old, the old Secretary of State, Cardinal Cicogniani, remained in his position, while Cardinal Ottaviani, the illustrious and meritorious Secretary of the Holy Office, was the first one to be politely dismissed and made to give up his position to another cardinal whose leaning was similar to that of the Pontiff. We have been able to observe cases like these everywhere, including here in Mexico, where our primate, who has already had his 75th birthday, still rules the largest archdiocese in the whole world. This innovative criterion was also implemented by Paul VI by means of a *Motu Proprio*, through which he barred octogenarian cardinals from the Conclave. Obviously among these cardinals were the most conservative ones, those who, at an election, might have overthrown the whole post-Conciliar reformation.

I have already expounded upon the calm and energetic criticism given by Cardinal Ottaviani against this new regulation enacted by Paul VI, but there is an extra feature worth considering. It is very meaningful that the *Motu Proprio* was passed on the eve of the Pontiff's trip to Australia and the Philippines. It appeared as though he wanted to make sure that the vote would be controlled by his unconditional supporters, so that the reformation might go on irreversibly.

15. There is still another one of Pope Montini's moves that certainly deserves comment. I am referring to the suppression of countless saints from the calendar and liturgy of the Church, saints whose devotions were discontinued, notwithstanding the attachment the Christian people had for them, as well as the official support the Church had bestowed upon them. This purge, so to speak, provoked an enormous scandal and roaring protests on the part of many Catholics. Even the "separated brethren" themselves smiled scornfully at the lack of solidity and value of the old devotions. Then, as a soothing solution, it was said Catholics might keep their old devotions privately, though the world Church ignored them.

Some saints had enjoyed the privilege of being the patrons of certain churches, such as Saint George of England, or Saint Gennaro of Naples. Others, such as Saint Christopher, had been proclaimed special patrons by previous Popes (in the case of Saint Christopher, he was the patron of car-drivers). In the mind of the "expert" advisors of Paul VI, however, these devotions were remnants of superstition and legend, unacceptable to modern critique. Thus our liturgical calendar was simplified and noticeably deprived of

Is Paul VI a True Pope?

the local feasts that so much contributed to enhancing popular devotion. As things are going, it would not be surprising if even the remaining saints were cast into oblivion in the new liturgy of *aggiornamento* and ecumenism, leaving their positions to Luther and other reformers. But this issue is worth an independent chapter.

16. In his "Open Letter to the Pope," Abbé Barbara mentions the unbelievable speech by Cardinal Willebrands, the successor of Cardinal Bea, at the meetings of the World Lutheran Federation. His Eminence spoke as the President of the Vatican Secretariat for Christian Unity and as a representative and legate of Paul VI. From *Lutheran World,* a magazine of the World Lutheran Federation, we quote some of the most unacceptable concepts for the Catholic conscience stated by the Cardinal:

> Today it is an accepted fact that no church can be indifferent to what happens in another church.

The phrase is so bold that it almost appears to me as meaning that diversity of beliefs, morality, sacraments, discipline, or hierarchy is no hindrance for our Church's getting interested in the welfare and growth of the other, so-called Christian churches. Is this not an *Irenic,* surrendering ecumenism, designed to establish a certain equality between truth and error? Perhaps as Catholics we should be concerned about the spread of the so-called Lutheran Churches? The Cardinal continues:

> ... [B]ut if I am right, you [the Lutheran churches] are not so emphatic about the idea of universalism as you are about the belief that the Church has been sent to the world, to the world as it is today, and even more to the *man* of today's world. As a result of his having an inner life, man rises above all things. At the same time, by virtue of his bodily being, he belongs to the material world. Has the Church understood this dignity of the human being? Has it avowed it? Has it served the human's dignity?
>
> Man's dignity can be particularly distinguished by his freedom. This essential element of his dignity is considered by modern man as a real characteristic of the human personality. (Vatican II, *De libertate Religiosa,* para. 1; *Gaudium et Spes,* 12-12, particularly 17).

Here we have the perfect agreement between the Catholic Church and the Lutheran sects, not so much as to the universality of their mission, but as to the adaptability of the Church to the human being and the modern world, and to the human and today's world including all its miseries, madness, license, vices, and disregard for and contempt of God's things. The Cardinal asks: *"Has the Church [avowed] this dignity of the human being? ... Has it served man in*

The Montinian Church

his dignity?" This is what matters to the Protestants and this is also what must matter to us Catholics, that the Church serve man in his dignity, man who, in his freedom, as His Eminence points out in quoting Vatican II, is the supreme authority and the ultimate source of truth. This, then, is the religion of the post-Conciliar Church which considers man and his world to be the center of the universe. The Church's transcendental mission must be aimed at today's man and the world in general. Is this what the signs of the times announce?

The dignity of the human personality, which certainly includes his freedom, lies in his natural and supernatural relationship with God. The *real* dignity of man consists of his being justified by sanctifying grace, his being the adopted son of God, and his having the beatific vision as an ultimate goal. This is the real dignity of man. His freedom is a condition of his dignity, for if man uses his freedom according to God's Will, he expresses this noble dignity; if he abuses his freedom, he vilifies that dignity.

Cardinal Willebrands continues:

> Man's dignity and freedom relate to his bodily and spiritual dimensions, since both are inseparably united in his personality.
>
> To our common aims the decisive question is: Specifically, what is the nature of the Church's mission in today's world? The Church has not been sent to the world with empty hands but is, on the contrary, the bearer of Christ's Gospel. This priority of the Gospel has been given particular emphasis in this assembly within the subject of the first session entitled: "Sent with the Gospel." Vatican Council II found it convenient to complete this heading with the following words: *"ad universum mundum missa"* ("sent to the universal world") *"ut mundus ad Evangelium convertatur"* ("so that the world is converted to the Gospel").

Cardinal Willebrands—I do not know if with good or bad intentions—wants to equalize Lutheran theology and the theology of Vatican II. Although both are ecumenical and "sent with the Gospel" to the universal world so that it could be converted *to* the Gospel, they are not equal. In the first place, the Catholic Church, but only the Catholic Church, was sent by Christ. Lutherans, who started to exist in the sixteenth century, were not sent by the divine Master, who did not set up *many* churches but a *single* Church which goes back to apostolic times. The Church was sent to evangelize the world (not specifically with a *written* Gospel), so that the world would be converted to the living Gospel which the teaching Church conveys to all nations up to the consummation of the centuries, according to the words of Jesus Christ Himself, *"Euntes in mundum universum, praedicate Evangelium omni creature"* ("Go all over the world and *preach* [He does not say, *write*] the Gospel to every creature"). With their free inquiry, Lutherans carry a Gospel in their hands, but

Is Paul VI a True Pope?

their own Gospel, not that of Christ. The Catholic Church was sent to the world to convert it, not to accommodate itself to it, as His Eminence seems to feel, since his view is consistent with the Lutheran view. That is why he asks himself:

> Do the Catholic Church and the World Lutheran Federation agree about conceiving their missions in this way, taking the same source as a basis? Four hundred and fifty years ago, our ancestors thought they had to part company in the name of the real Gospel. Today we are confident in our hope to be able to overcome this separation (that, even at the time of its origin, was not considered good, but was accepted by both parties as unavoidable), in the name of the real Gospel.

The Cardinal's question is cunning and insincere, not only from the Catholic point of view, but also from the Protestant. He does know that, although we appear to have the same Bibles, they are not identical, due to the suppressions, interpretations, and interpolations Protestants have made in the holy Text. We shall never be able to base our beliefs on the same source, because we have received ours immediately and directly from Christ and the apostles, while they received theirs adulterated from Luther and the followers of his religious Reformation. If, 450 years ago, we, or rather our ancestors, tore off these withered and lifeless branches from the millenary trunk of the real Church, now we, on behalf of this same Gospel, should keep on rejecting them as long as they do not acknowledge their mistakes and change their Gospel. Our ancestors did not want it, but, in the presence of the rebellious Lutheran revolution, there was no choice. Today the ecumenical solution of His Eminence will not be feasible, unless Lutherans sincerely accept all dogmas of our Catholic Faith, including the dogmas of Peter's primacy, Pontifical infallibility, Mary's Immaculate Conception, Our Lady's glorious Assumption into Heaven in body and soul, Transubstantiation, the bloodless, yet actual and true Sacrifice of the Mass, the Real Presence of Christ in the divine Eucharist, etc. Is that not so, Eminence?

With his ambiguous vocabulary, the Prefect of the Secretariat for Christian Unity, trying to unite two contradictory statements, goes on by saying:

> When referring to the Church and its mission, we are very much exposed to the danger of limiting our discussion to abstract terms. Are not we ourselves the Church? How does a Christian conceive his mission? Let us remember the Church lives in every Christian individual. Let us listen to Apostle Paul's answer: "... a servant of Jesus Christ ... separated unto the gospel of God." (Rom. 1:1). I feel this answer of his can be divided into two fundamental principles. The first principle can be found in his famous expression: *"For whereas I was free as to all, I made myself the servant of all ... I became all things to all men, that I might save*

The Montinian Church

all." (I Cor. 9:19-22).

The second principle and the corresponding attitude are expressed by Saint Paul many times in different ways. We find an example in the phrase where he defines the subject of his Letter to the Romans:*"For I am not ashamed of the gospel. For it is the power of God unto salvation to very one that believeth..."* (Rom. 1:16). Again we find the same idea in the following phrases: *"For the Jews require signs, and the Greeks seek after wisdom: But we preach Christ crucified, unto the Jews indeed a stumbling block, and unto the Gentiles foolishness: But unto them that are called, both Jews and Greeks, Christ the power of God, and the wisdom of God."* (I Cor. 1:22-24). Both attitudes, service of man up to extremism and the madness of the cross, are thus completely justified and an essential part of the attitude of the Church *vis a vis* the world.

Expressed above is the innovative idea of the Church which the post-Conciliar Church presents to us in complete opposition to Tradition. Ecumenical Vatican Council I did not use abstract terms in stating: "... the shepherd and bishop of your souls (I Pet. 2:25), in order that the healthy work of His redemption would be perennial, decided to build His Holy Church where, as if in the house of the living God, all believers were united by the bond of the same Faith and charity." Nor are the words which Leo XIII used in his encyclical *Satis Cognitum* of June 29, 1896, abstract:

"... That the legitimate, Christ-founded Church be one [Church] is recorded in so many brilliant and numerous passages of Holy Writ, that no Christian may dare deny it. But several mistakes have separated many from the straight way in judging and determining the nature of this unity. Not only the origin of the Church, but its whole constitution, belong to the realm of things made with free will. As a result, to determine the nature of that unity, our research must not be aimed at finding out how the Church can be one, *but how He who founded it wanted it to be one.* Now then, concerning what has been done, Jesus Christ did not model or form his Church so that it comprised various similar communities that were different, though united by links that turned them into a single, undivided Church. For, as we confess it in the symbol of faith, *Credo... Unam Ecclesiam,* when Jesus Christ speaks to us about this mystical building, He mentions but a sole Church He calls His: *"aedificabo Ecclesiam meam"* ("I will build my Church") (Matt. 16:18). Should anyone think of another Church which Jesus Christ has not built, he is not thinking of Christ's Church.... Then the Church must propagate to all men and in all ages the salvation coming from Christ as well as all the benefits arising therefrom. In consequence, it is the will of its divine Founder that there be only one Church in the whole world through all ages.... The Church of Christ is one and perpetual, and those who part from it, part from the will and orders of Christ Our Lord.

Once they lose the way to salvation, they throw themselves headlong into their loss. And He who built a single Church wanted it to be one, that is, the same one, so that all those who in the future entered it were united by most tight links, to become one people, one kingdom, one single body: *"Unum corpus et unus spiritus, sicut vocati estis in una spe vocationis vestrae."* ("One body, and one Spirit; as you are called in one hope of your calling.") (Eph. 4:4).

The mission of the Church is not, as Cardinal Willebrands says, *to serve man,* but *to serve God* through the salvation of men. Saint Paul was made all things to all men to save us all and thus give God the glory owed Him. *We are not the Church;* we are *members* of the Church. The Church is a divine institution or work. We have profited from the divine work for, regenerated by Baptism, we have Christ's full Faith, are united to Him by sanctifying grace and form part of the membership of the sole Church He founded. The equivocation of the head of the Secretariat for Christian Unity is an unforgivable one, for he seems to endeavor to identify Protestant doctrine with Catholic doctrine, as though our Gospel could be interpreted in the heretical way Luther's followers do. Only *one,* says the Church's Magisterium, is the Church founded by Christ. It is *one* because of its origin, and *one* because of its constitution. Taking into account the doctrine of Tradition, this attempt to associate us with that absurd organization called "Church Unity" becomes unbearable.

Neither can I understand the words cited by His Eminence, Cardinal Willebrands, concerning the Ecumenism of Vatican II:

> Vatican Council II recommended to all Christians that the main goal of their collaboration should be a "cooperation for a right estimate of the dignity of the human personality, promotion of peace, application of the Gospel's sociology, fostering of the progress of science and arts amid Christian spirit, and supplying all sorts of remedies to the suffering of our times—famine, disasters, illiteracy, grievances, lack of accommodation, and unfair allocation of goods." (*De Ecumenismo,* para. 12).

This cooperation which Vatican II asked all so-called Christian churches, which are not the real and sole Church Christ founded, has a nature and a tendency that can hardly be called religious. This is not an invitation to seek after truth, to seek after righteousness through the fulfillment of the divine law, and to seek after God *in* all and *above* all. It is a call to serve the human being, to satisfy the earthly needs of man, to turn this life of testing and pilgrimage into the longed-for lost Eden. If this is the main goal of ecumenical cooperation with the so-called Christian sects, I believe that, besides changing the aim Christ designed for His Church, the relationship required by such collaboration cannot be beneficial for us, since it will only ease our "separated

The Montinian Church

brethren's" proselytism, scandalize our simple believers with good reason, and oblige us to yield with respect to issues on which we may not give up. To me, ecumenism is one of the most nebulous and impugnable subjects in the presence of traditional theology! We have changed apostolic zeal and restless work for the salvation of souls through the only truth of the Gospel, for hypocritical feigning. It appears that we intend to tell our "separated brethren" that our separation is the result of old-fashioned feuds which today have no importance to us.

Let us quote another passage from Cardinal Willebrands' speech, in which His Eminence delved not only into servility but also into historical falsehood:

> As said before, the Lutheran-Catholic dialogue cannot forget the 16th century quarrels. This is also true with respect to the person and the work of *Martin Luther,* from whom your large family has taken its name.
>
> I want to follow in Cardinal Bea's footsteps and emphasize that what I am about to say is no attempt to allot the guilt in this regretful division. [This refers to a letter from Cardinal Bea to President Schiots, in 1967, with respect to the 20th birthday of the foundation of the Lutheran World Federation and the 450th birthday of the Reformation.] We should rather jointly seek after the ways and means of reconstructing our lost unity. Who would fail to avow that a correct appraisal of Luther and his work is necessary on our part to bring about this common ideal? [On this very thesis, the sadly famous Fr. Ives M. J. Congar wrote an article entitled *"Expérience et conversion oecumeniques," Témoignage:* "Je sais, hélas! que Luther a encore aujourd'hui un trés mauvais renom chez les catholiques, sauf peut-être en Allemagne. Je sais qu'il y a en lui de quoit justifier se renom. Je sais aussi qu'on ne rend justice, ainsi, ni à son intention foncière, ni même a sa pensée religieuse. Je sais enfin quote rien de tout sérieux ne sera fait de notre part vers le protéstantism, tant qu'on n'aura pas accompli la démarche de comprendre vraiment Luther et de lui rendre historiquement justice, au lieu de simplement le condamner. Pour cette conviction, qui est mienne, je serais prêt à donner joyeusement ma vie." ("I know that Luther, unfortunately, still has a bad reputation among Catholics, except perhaps in Germany. I know there are some things in him that seem to justify such a reputation. I know justice has not been rendered either to his fundamental intention or to his religious thought. I know, finally, that nothing serious will be done towards rapprochement with Protestantism as long as we refuse to make a step to really understand Luther and render him the justice historically due to him, instead of simply condemning him. For the sake of this conviction, which is my own conviction, I would willingly give up my life.")
>
> During the past centuries Catholics have not always correctly appraised Martin Luther's person, and his theology has not always been correctly presented

either. This has not contributed either to truth or love, and therefore, has not helped achieve unity between you and the Catholic Church, as we have bound ourselves to re-establish. On the other hand, we must joyfully notice that during the last decades a more correct understanding of the Reformation, and consequently of Martin Luther and his theology, has been growing scientifically among Catholic intellectuals.

If today, 450 years after that critical year, 1520, I speak this way, it is because I am fully conscious of the many inhibitions still existing between you and us as a result of the mighty personality of Martin Luther and his work. These inhibitions have always led the Catholic Church to maintain certain reservations, but love wipes off fear of being ill-understood, and long-lasting dialogue has effaced much misunderstanding.

Who, and I am speaking to the Catholics, would still deny that Martin Luther was a deeply religious person who sincerely and with dedication always sought after the evangelical message? Who would deny that despite his having fought the Roman Catholic Church and the Apostolic See and, for love of truth we cannot deny it, he kept a considerable amount of his old Catholic Faith? Is it perhaps true that Vatican Council II has used demands originally expressed by Martin Luther among others, the results of which are that many aspects of Christian Faith and life have been stated in a better way than before? To be able to affirm this, despite the differences existing between you and us, is a motive of great joy and much hope.

In a certainly extraordinary way for those times, Martin Luther turned the Bible into a point of departure of Christian theology and life. From then on, in all your churches, the Bible has been treated as a particular treasure and studied with the utmost zeal. In turn, Vatican Council II has inserted Holy Writ so deeply into the life of the Church and its members, that the Bible has become more fruitful and rich for them. In such a mood the Council said: "Holy Writ itself is a precious instrument of dialogue to achieve the unity the Savior proposes for all humans." (*De Ecumenismo*, para. 21).

There is a word we find over and over again in Martin Luther's writings, namely the most important word, *"Faith."* Luther understood its value, and many people, in your churches and beyond your churches, have learned to live this faith. Perhaps some people who are not familiar with this subject and notice Martin Luther uses such a word too emphatically might think his idea of faith is different from ours, and be apparently right. However, joint research by Catholic and Protestant theologians has demonstrated that, in Luther's use, the word "faith" does not at all exclude works, love, or hope. We should have many good reasons to say that Luther's approach to faith, taken in its full meaning, does not mean anything except what we in the Catholic Church, call love.

It is neither necessary nor possible to state the highlights of Luther's theology here. Much could be said about his theology of the cross, his

Christology, his emphasis on Jesus Christ's Divinity, a subject on which we feel particularly close to him. On the other hand, many intellectuals, both Catholic and Protestant, have pointed out that it is very difficult to restate Luther's thoughts in a precise, exhaustive and, above all, really balanced way. In other words: it is difficult to precisely state his thoughts in a way that renders justice to his numerous formulations which ultimately he never unfolded or developed systematically.

It is comforting to me to think you share in the same painful thoughts with me, if in these common reflections I prefer not to mention certain fierce attacks Martin Luther launched against the Roman Pontiff. These outrages sadden my heart and surely also yours, for you must consider them to be a regrettable thing.

Since we are speaking at an assembly where the issue is: "Mission toward the world," it is undoubtedly good to mention the man to whom the doctrine of justification was *"articulus stantis et cadentis Ecclesiae"* ("article of the standing and the falling Church"). From this we can learn that God must always remain the Lord, and our chief human answer must always be our absolute confidence in God and our adoration of Him.

Everything we have quoted from Willebrands' unbearable speech demonstrates the gravity of the Church's present circumstances. This Cardinal, a Secretary of the Vatican Secretariat for Christian Unity, a legate and representative of the Pope, did not speak in Catholic, but in heretical language. Only a heretic can use this language and maintain these concepts. This is no place to introduce the most grave problem, the Reformation. A dogmatic and ecumenical council has judged, defined and condemned all of Martin Luther's most grave errors.

That a prince of the Church and representative of Paul should defend a heresiarch, should introduce him as a "deeply religious man," as an idealist reformer of the Church, "who sincerely and with dedication always sought after the evangelical message," is just unbearable for Catholics, for this implies, in substance, a condemnation of the Ecumenical Council of Trent, which was not pastoral, but dogmatic, and which defined the Catholic doctrine on justification against the Lutheran errors.

This *convergence of Luther and Vatican II* that the Secretary for Christian Unity tries to achieve is not too complimentary for the Council, for, besides implying it is openly contradictory to the Tridentine Council, it also casts the responsibility for the "Protestantization" of the post-Conciliar Church upon Vatican II. "Who would deny," His Eminence asks naively, "that despite his [Luther's] having fought the Roman Catholic Church and the Apostolic See... he kept a considerable amount of his old Catholic Faith?" This means we may divide the Faith at whim, choosing what we find convenient and rejecting what we do not!

Luther wanted to shelter his heresies through a twisted interpretation of the Holy Writ, and this attachment of the sects to the letter of the Bible has nothing to do with Catholic truth, which avows that these holy Books are one of the sources of divine revelation, not as construed by our judgment, but according to the interpretation of the Magisterium and the Tradition of the Church. As long as this interpretation is not accepted, the "dialogue," the "salvific dialogue" with the "separated brethren" will hardly be a precious instrument to attain the unity the Savior wanted for us. It is impossible that two different and opposite interpretations of Holy Writ may serve as a basis for a loving "dialogue" between sincere Catholics and sincere Protestants. I see the most real danger that our theologians, in case they are not very firm in their convictions, may become infected by heresy as, unfortunately, is the case of so many so-called "new wave" theologians, whose chosen authors are the so-called "Protestant theologians."

His Eminence's bad faith is especially apparent when he wants to convince us (I assume he is not trying to deceive the Lutherans) that Luther's concept of *"Faith"* includes and covers good works and, in consequence, is a perfectly Catholic concept. Maybe Luther, says the Cardinal, called "faith" what the Catholic Church calls "love." In this concern I want to quote some paragraphs from a book, *Rebuilding a Lost Faith* by the well-known playwright John L. Stoddard, who was a Protestant intellectual who converted to Catholicism. Chapter X, devoted to Luther, shows us the lack of sincerity (I do not want to assume ignorance) of the Secretary of the Secretariat for Christian Unity:

MEN MUST BE CHANGED AND REFORMED BY RELIGION, NOT RELIGION BY MEN.

Egidio Canisio de Viterbo.

The scandalous and harmful revolution against Catholicism and the Pontificate engineered by the apostate monk Martin Luther, has given this sad historical character exaggerated and undeserved importance.

It is indeed very doubtful that, at the beginning of his apostasy, Luther intended to reach the point to which his violent passions and the selfish patronage of the princes of the Empire propelled him. On the contrary, it seems more probable that this poor apostate friar who lived in the bosom of the Catholic Church until he was 35, started the Reformation the way an unconscious individual sets fire to some powder without realizing that this powder is near a huge powder magazine which, with the fire, soon bursts with irretrievable damage.

When Luther affixed his theses to the doors of the church of Wittenberg, he was fighting the *abuses* involving indulgences, not the *doctrine* of indulgences itself. Moreover, before the argument and his own stubbornness had dragged him beyond the limit he had imagined and from which it was not easy to go back, Luther wrote to Pope Leo X: "Most Holy Father, I am throwing myself at your feet with everything I am and have. Render me my life or take it away from me. Call me or push me back; approve or disapprove of me. Your voice is that of Christ, who commands and speaks through you." Thus Luther reasoned at the beginning of his apostasy. When he abandoned himself completely and with all the violence of his passionate soul to the revolutionary movement, when he understood he was the spokesman and the standard, so to speak, of a powerful political faction supported and incited by several princes, he could not find enough blunt, vulgar, coarse, and mean words to expose and rebuke the Holy Father, the same one he had venerated and revered with so profound and filial a humility, and to condemn the doctrine and practices of the Faith he had been professing for so many years, and, at whose altars he had served with the truth and sincerity of his heart . . . .

Of course, as I had not carried on unbiased and serious studies on this nefarious man, I used to consider him as the national hero of Protestant Germany, as the author of the anthem, *Eine Feste Burg ist unser Gott,* and as the intrepid brave monk who publicly challenged the Pope at Worms.

But the time had come to see the other side of the coin. To begin externally, Luther's looks could not have been more repelling or unpleasant than they were. All the features of his face show such a vulgar and apparent brutal sensuality that I do not recall having seen anything of the like in any other human countenance. Nothing is spiritual or appealing in this face; nothing reveals supernaturalness, virtue, or self-control. Behold his looks: tell me whether a man with a head such as his, with such a large and grotesque mouth, with cheeks such as his, with a red, swollen nose owing to his excessive fondness of wine, can be held as a really and deeply religious man, a spiritual *leader,* a shepherd of souls, a reformer of customs and license, as the founder of a religion that proclaims the purity and sincerity of the Gospel. One would rather say this is the face of a sensual, selfish, and licentious man, whose malignity goes so far as real and cruel bigotry, and whose character was just as his portraits show.

Eating and drinking were two of the most important concerns in the Protestant reformer's daily life. His biographical data and particularly his letters to his dear "Katie," supply a lot of evidence. A couple of them will give us an idea.

On the 29th of July, 1534, for instance, he wrote to the person he called his wife (as a matter of fact, his mistress) that he did not have anything good to drink and he added: "Pray send me lots of wine and some casks of beer as often as you can." Moreover, during his last weeks at Eisleben, he wrote to Katherine as follows: "We have more than enough to eat and get drunk." (February 6, 1546).

Is Paul VI a True Pope?

(See also *Grisar*, Vol. II, p. 305.)

Among his statements the following words can be read: "If God the Lord, accepts my excuses for having vexed Him for about twenty years celebrating the Mass, He will certainly excuse my occasional excesses in drinking to His honor. May God grant it to me, and let the world judge it as it may."

Everybody knows that the fast and abstinence which the Catholic Church prescribes on certain days are penitential practices which the Bible very much commends and Jesus Himself praised and recommended. Saint Paul admonishes the Christian Corinthians to give themselves to fasting and prayer (I Cor. 7:5) and Christ, in the Sermon on the Mount recommends to His disciples that, when fasting, they do not do it ostentatiously, but before their Father, who sees the secret and the concealed ....

Now then Luther, despite all these unequivocal attestations, condemning ecclesiastical Tradition and ignoring the express admonitions of the Bible and the words and examples of Our Savior, fully condemns this custom, which evidently was very disagreeable for him. "This doctrine," he says, "it so perverse and shameful before God, that no orgy or drunkenness, no gluttony, no intemperance as to drinking could be worse, and it would be better to be completely drunk day and night than to fast." (*Luther, Works*, vol. II, p. 730).

His famous marriage, due to the special circumstances in which it was celebrated with a nun who, just like him, had violated her solemn vow of chastity contracted with God, was one of the most meaningful acts in the life of the Protestant reformer. One Leonard Koppe, along with two other fellows, following Luther's orders and the arrangements made with him, kidnapped twelve nuns from the Cistercian monastery of Nimpsch, Silesia, on Easter Eve (April 5, 1532), during the night, and, in connivance with Luther, carried them to Wittenberg.

A little while after this vile deed, Luther wrote a letter calling Koppe a "blessed thief" and impiously compared him with our resurrected Savior. "Just as Christ," he said, "by Easter redeemed everybody through His Resurrection, Koppe, through his brave and intrepid exploit, redeemed these nuns on Holy Saturday." (Luther, *Works*, vol. II, page 40).

It has been said that among those runaways was Katherine Bora, with whom Luther united in an apparent sacrilegious marriage two years later, when the former friar approached his 42nd birthday and Katherine was about 26. The ceremony was performed by another apostate priest by the name of Bugenhagen, who in turn had wedded a little time before.

Much has been written and said about the love relationship between Luther and the nun before that final scandalous union was completed. Bugenhagen himself, some time after this took place, said: "Slanderous gossip caused Dr. Martin to marry so unexpectedly." (Grisar, vol. II, page 175).

On this particular matter the famous Erasmus wrote from Rotterdam: "It

The Montinian Church

is believed that Luther was the hero of a tragedy, but I rather believe he played the leading character in a comedy which, like all comedies, ended by marriage." Somewhere else Erasmus wrote: "It does not seem that the Reformation had had any other aim but to turn friars and nuns into husbands and wives." [This is the case with the present Montinian Church.]

Melanchton was tougher and more severe in his comments on this subject. In a confidential letter to Camerario, dated June 18, 1535, he blames the runaway nun for the disgusting event. "Luther," says Melanchton, "is extremely hare-brained and frivolous. The nuns have convinced him by means of cunning and shrewdness, and they got what they wanted. Perhaps his conduct with them has made him somewhat weak and effeminate or swollen his passions, notwithstanding his noble and sublime views." (Grisar, *Luther*, vol. II, page 145). The same Melanchton adds that he feels Luther has "changed his life inopportunely, but he expects marriage will make him enter the track of morality." Taking into account that the author of so severe a criticism was one of the closest friends and leading aides of Luther, we shall not question the accuracy of his remarks and conclusions.

But the effect of his immorality and unlawful marriage with a nun was very insignificant in comparison with his licentious preaching and his crude and dissolute writings on moral subjects. To him it was not enough to have sinned himself. Pressed by the accusing voice of his conscience, which continually called him to account for his behavior, he sought a way to defend himself or justify his deeds, inciting others, as many as possible, to follow his steps along the road of iniquity.

If it is true that misery does not want to be alone, it is also true that sin looks for mates. Luther, using many vulgar, crude, and vile words, challenges celibacy, ridicules religious vows, particularly that of chastity, and incites friars and nuns to follow his example, evading their sacred obligations and deserting their cloisters. (Luther, *Works*, vol. XII, page 1796). As it was only too normal, the results of all this was regrettable. Eberlin from Gunzberg, among others, wrote: "As soon as a friar or a nun spends two or three days outside the convent, he or she hastens to get married, he with the first woman and she with the first man he or she encounters on the street." (Grisar, *Luther*, vol. II, page 124).

Supported by Luther's authority and deceitful speeches, many friars and nuns who so far had led virtuous and moderate lives, considered themselves to be free of all the sacred obligations of their vows, and their scandalous behavior not only harmed their souls very much, but also induced countless people to pick ways of a most dreadful moral license, thus weakening the faith and morality of the crowds.... Chastity was declared as contrary to nature and totally impossible; celibacy was held to be a sin; the Sacraments, things completely useless and secondary; the Mass, a real idolatry; examination of conscience, a foolishness; confession, a crazy deed; and the Roman Pontiff, the Antichrist. So spoke Luther in his sermons and writings. There was only one thing he believed to be indispensable and sufficient for salvation, *"Faith,"* but a faith without works, a sentimental faith, a sort of blind and daring confidence . . .

One of the Luther-spread doctrines which exerted a most harmful effect upon the masses, was the one that denied man's freedom: "Human will," said Luther, "is just like a beast of burden. If God rides on it, it goes where God wants to go, but if the devil rides on it, it does and wants just what Satan wants to. Neither can the will choose its rider nor make this or that one come to it; it is the riders who fight for its possession." (*De servo arbitrio*). This is just like saying everything man makes, says, thinks, or does, be it good or evil, is the work of God or Satan, not of man.

In this concern Melanchton also wrote: "Just like Saint Paul's calling, as well as David's adultery and Judas' betrayal of Christ, all this was the work of God." (See Sezozis: *Church History,* vol. XVIII, pp. 270-279).

To Luther the most important and essential thing was faith, as defined above. As long as there was blind and trusting faith, a man's deeds had no importance at all. Thus he wrote to Melanchton: "Be a sinner: *pecca fortiter sed crede firmiter,* but believe firmly. Sin cannot root us out of Him, even if we commit thousands of acts of formication and murder every day." (Luther's letter of August 1, 1521).

The Ten Commandments were so unbearably absurd to Luther that he wrote: "We must remove the whole Decalogue from our eyes and our hearts. In case Moses scares you *with his ten stupid commandments,* tell him at once: "Take this away from us and carry it to your Jews." Hang Moses . . . .

The flaming Protestant reformer incited the people repeatedly and used typical terms of his to commit acts of violence against the members of the Catholic hierarchy. Thus in 1545 he wrote: "The Pope and the cardinals must be exterminated and, blasphemous as they are, their tongues ought to be torn out through their napes and nailed to the gallows." (Wieder: *Das Papsthum za Rom.,* 1545, 130).

In 1522, a compact and undisciplined mob furiously entered the Church of Wittenberg, on whose doors Luther had affixed his famous theses and, breathing anger and fury, destroyed all the altars and statues and, after throwing all the fragments into the street, expelled the clergy. In Rothenburg the image of Christ was beheaded and its arms severed. This happened in 1525. On February 9, 1529, the beautiful and rich cathedral of Basle, Switzerland, was looted and robbed by a mob. An old chronicle describes the occurrences of this sacrilegious offense as follows: "They tied some long, thick ropes to a monumental and venerable crucifix, and a throng of eight-, ten-, and twelve-year-old children began to pull it and drag it to the public market place, all the time singing, 'Oh poor, old-fashioned Jesus, if you are God, defend yourself; if not, you are just a man, then, die!' The Protestant reformer Ecolampadio (John Hauschein,

1462-1531) rejoiced exultantly at this sacrilege and, bursting from joy, wrote to Capito: 'That was a real show for the superstitious people; the Catholics would have liked to weep bloody tears!'...." (Tanssen, III, 96).

Erasmus wrote: "What could be more harmful than permitting words such as the following to reach the people: the Pope is the Antichrist; bishops and priests are parasites; human laws are barren; Confession is harmful; works, merits, and efforts to attain everlasting salvation are heretical words, too; there is no freedom; all happens fatefully and necessarily ... I see that, under the guise of the Gospel, a new bold, impudent, and unruly race is rising and growing. At the proper time it will become unbearable for Luther himself." (*Epistolae*, book XIX, p. 601, and book XVIII, p. 593). "Common sense and right reason teach me that a man who has provoked such a big conflagration in the world, who enjoys abuse and sarcasm and seems not to be satisfied with the work done so far, is in no way working to enhance the cause of God. It is absolutely impossible that such a big and extraordinary haughtiness as we have never seen to be matched, is not mixed up with a sort of insanity or madness; and such a turbulent individual cannot be in perfect hamony with an authentically evangelical spirit...." (Erasmus, *Works,* vol. IX, p. 1026).

On a certain occasion, when Luther appealed to Europe's universities to judge his doctrines, when his dogmas were condemned, the reformer became full of anger and, overflowing with coarse fury, broke out into a tirade of outrage and insult against the venerable centers of knowledge. For instance, speaking of the University of Paris, he termed it: "Mother of errors, daughter of the Antichrist, gate of Hell." The right to private interpretation, hoisted by Luther as his rebellion banner, was no doubt considered by him as an exclusive privilege of his own. It is often said that it was Luther who restored the right to free research, which had been curtailed, in the world. Nothing, however, is further from the historical truth. It is true that he spoke about this right to justify his apostasy from the Church's traditions, but he also engaged all his efforts to the end of submitting the minds of all his followers to absolute serfdom, to an inexpugnable and closed Bible ... as interpreted by him.... Since he had become the sole authoritative interpreter of Holy Writ, the case was, practically speaking, that paradoxically, Luther vindicated for himself that very privilege of infallibility which he had denied the Pope and the Council.

This long quotation was designed to show the opinion about Luther of even a sincere Protestant who sought after the light of truth and found God in the real and sole Church Christ founded. How is it possible, then, that Cardinal Willebrands, a papal legate and head of the Secretariat for Christian Unity, dare proclaim man's freedom as the characteristic feature of human dignity, later on establishing a flattering parallel between Luther's and Vatican II's theology as a device to attract the "separated brethren?" Luther and his supporters denied free will, imputing all of man's deeds to the devil or God.

It is true that this heresiarch, like his predecessors in heresy, wanted to lay the basis of his errors upon the Holy Bible, whimsically construed and mutilated. Luther's Bible, however, is not God's Word, but the word of free examination, the word of heresy which adulterates the texts of Holy Writ, saying and affirming just the opposite to what God revealed to us.

His Eminence's boldness reaches its utmost when he affirms that the Lutheran *"Faith"* is just the Catholic *"Faith"* enhanced by "love" with a stroke of sentiment and heart. According to this Cardinal, Luther's faith does not exclude good works, love, or hope. Are these words consistent with the reformer's words to Melanchton: "Be a sinner, *pecca fortiter, sed crede firmiter?*" "Sin" Luther emphasizes, "cannot root us out of God, even if we commit thousands of acts of fornication and murder every day."

The central issues of Lutheran theology, those which the Cardinal, on ecumenical grounds, refuses to state for his "separated brethren," are to be found in the documents of the Tridentine Council, since this Council, with supporting evidence, not only stated and condemned them but, with divine inspiration, also defined the doctrine of our Catholic Faith which is absolutely opposite to the innovators' pseudo-theology.

If Vatican II converges, as Willebrands boldly says or hints, with Luther's thought and Reformation, then *iam iudicatum est,* we know what to think about this pastoral council which revolutionized the teaching, Tradition, and the whole life of the Church. Luther did not give better formulations to the Faith and Christian life, as the Cardinal naively affirmed. On the contrary, Luther destroyed faith and Christian life down to their roots. Denying human freedom, affirming that good works are not worthwhile, and giving us an absolutely false notion of *"Faith,"* this former friar set up a Christianity which is totally opposite to that of the Gospel. As a matter of fact, in many respects, Vatican II not only contradicts or seems to contradict the dogmatic doctrine of Trent's and Vatican I, but, ambiguous as it is, conveys to us the impression that it seeks to compromise with and follow Luther's *Reformation* in all aspects.

The Protestant reformers' chief error consisted of confusing the Church with its members and launching their attacks on the immovable truths of the Faith instead of against human abuse. This is also the mistake I have noticed in Vatican Council II and the post-Conciliar Church. The metaphor of "God's people" never ceases to be beautiful, for it has its basis in revelation. It is, nonetheless, somewhat ambiguous also, for God's people are not the Church's *people;* they *belong* to God's Church. We are not the Church; we are members *of* the Church. In past centuries, when man's weakness provoked internal reforms in the Church, if the saints who conducted these reforms had followed Luther's technique right from the beginning, would the Church have undergone the dreadful evils the German reformer bred? Far from defeating error, they would have been the victims of it. Egidio Canisio de Viterbo was right in saying: *"Men must be changed and reformed by religion, not religion by men."*

Pope John's Conciliar *aggiornamento*, in trying to adapt the Church to the new world being born, endeavored, at least so I believe, to follow in the steps of Luther and his followers and not to reform the life of man but to "reform" the life of the divine institution, the Church. This is not just a fancy of mine, for I shall quote the blueprint for the "renewal" of the Roman Catholic Church handed around to the theologians gathered together in small seminaries to prepare for the Council convoked by John XXIII in 1958:

> *Suppression of the following:* Fasting, abstinence, holy water and holy water basins, incense, kneeling and praying desks, altars and Communion altars, the Sign of the Cross, the lamp of the Holy Sacrament, days of precept, Holy Friday, blessing with the Holy Sacrament, the law that stipulates that women wear a covering on their heads, the Legion of Decency, votive offerings, processions, the Forty Hours Devotion, the Blessing of Throats, Ash Wednesday, bells, candles, images, novenas, the Index of Forbidden Books, litanies, tabernacles, crucifixes, the obligation of attending Mass, the mentioning of the name of the Trinity, Gothic architecture, large windows, clerical robes, sacraments, precepts, monasteries, sanctuaries, scapulars, medals and monstrances for the exposition of the Eucharist.
>
> *Change of names.* The Mass will be called liturgy; instead of Catholic, use the name Christian; let the Catholic Church be called the Universal Church; the parish will be the community; the priest, minister; baptism, initiation; the Gospel, the reading; the offertory, the preparation; the Consecration, the blessing of the Memorial; Extreme Unction, prayer of the living; and the Pope, Head of the Church.
>
> *Other changes.* The societies of the Holy Name and the altar societies must be called fraternities or corporations. The Ten Commandments shall be replaced by phrases of love and peace. Instead of confessing before a priest, one has to confess with one's neighbor. Statues must be replaced by revolutionary badges. The adoration has to be changed for fraternity and the genuflexions for kisses. Teilhard's *Phenomenon* has to be substituted for Saint Thomas' *Summa.* The parish temples will become community centers. Instead of birth control one will speak about family planning. Strict moral codes will become democratically flexible, according to the requirements of each individual. Religious and nuns will no longer teach religion; they will secularize and get married or live outside convents. Catholic schools and academies will become centers for political and social action.
>
> *The Mass has to evolve gradually.* Of course, prayers at the foot of the altar, prayers after Mass, and all mention of the saints will be eliminated. Latin must be

suppressed little by little, with the suppression of the *Canon* being the last one. Vernacular versions will be gradually adopted so that, finally, the entire Mass will be said in the various national languages. None will object to the first change, since the name of Saint Joseph will be added to the prayer *Supplices*. The immutability of the *Canon* will be suppressed using various Eucharistic prayers. Priests will progressively be suppressed through the admission of married priests and part-time priests, who, little by little, will be replaced by laymen (deacons, etc.). The participation of laymen in the liturgical ceremonies will cause them to gradually concelebrate the religious ceremonies, singing, reading the lectures, serving, preaching, playing instruments, with all of this finally leading to the liturgical services being carried to their homes to be celebrated at the dining room table, as in the Jewish Passover. Traditional Catholic music will be substituted by Protestant hymns, jazz, or mariachi orchestras, according to the culture and preference of the audience. To implement these changes, the youth must be conquered first. The catechism must be constantly changed, issuing different editions by different authors, in order that there be no time to object to this continued changing. The books will have an innovative presentation, with modern style, art, and methodology. Our people will be trained to organize and lead secular affairs. Unions must be promoted in all fields such as social service, life insurance, free schools, etc., in order to attain a socio-economic revolution or development. The liberalized hierarchy must become involved in all political movements of the government, in national or world councils of churches, in order to merge all governments into a world government, with one religion and one people. Make the seminary a preparation for *future socialism*. The bishops, who ought to be called "executives," will lead their dioceses' political and social activities. They will have information agencies, work agencies, and teams for various activities, financed by collections and alms which used to be raised for schools. Vatican City will be ruled by the bishops, and will be liquidated as a pattern of imperialism. The sessions of the future world ecumenical council will be held at Jerusalem, Israel.

> Distributed by
> CATHOLICS AGAINST HERESY
> P.O. Box 932
> Fall River, Mass. 02720
> U.S.A.

I have compared Cardinal Willebrands' speech with what a Protestant intellectual thought and wrote about Luther. This Protestant writer, John L. Stoddard, after having realized that the sects' rationalism, free examination, and license lead to internal destruction and growing atheism, dropped into agnosticism, but was able to get out of that abyss by converting to Catholicism and embracing Christ's real Faith sincerely and zealously. After this comparison, I repeat my opinion on His Eminence's speech: Only a faithless or lowly abject man can speak like this!

I still wish to quote another part of the speech given by Cardinal Willebrands as the head of the Secretariat for Christian Unity. It is about the Holy Sacrifice of the Mass:

Prospects of Larger Communion (between Lutherans and Catholics)

> Let me finish my remarks by suggesting an outlook for the immediate future. What concrete steps can be taken in the coming years to attain a more intimate Communion? The course that our discussions have had so far, and the Vatican Council II can give us some ideas. Though Vatican Council II frequently spoke about dialogue, it never did supply any concrete suggestion as to what the chief subject of dialogue should be, with one exception. In connection with its statements on Baptism and the Eucharist, the Council had this to say: "Hence, the teaching about the *Lord's Supper,* the other Sacraments, the worship, and the ministry of the Church should constitute the main subject of dialogue." (*Unitatis Redintegratio,* para. 22). Moreover, the same document also speaks about ecumenical dialogue with respect to the application of the Gospel to the world's moral questions. (*Unitatis Redintegratio,* para. 23). This means certain directions were given as far back as 1964 for the subsequent Lutheran-Catholic dialogue, which has turned out to be both central and essential. In fact, the discussion has evolved in such a way that the problems concerning the ministry and the Eucharist have come to be the center of reflection as to both national and international dialogue. All results have led us to a larger understanding of these subjects and will advance the moment when we will together be able to celebrate the Lord's Supper, which creates unity.

Indeed His Eminence is right. As things are going, all of us will soon be able to gather together to celebrate the Lord's Supper, all, including non-Christians. The Sacrifice eliminated and the Eucharist turned into an assembly, as proclaimed by the formula that Christ's blood was shed *for all men,* what might the hindrance be for all of us, without distinction as to belief, race, or color, to be able to celebrate, not the Mass, for *the Mass no longer exists,* but the memorial of the Lord's Supper? The Eucharistic banquet, like a new Jewish Passover, will find us sitting at our tables in fraternal unity, eating and drinking, singing and dancing, thus commemorating the Lord's Last Supper.

This heretical speech by the head of the Secretariat for Christian Unity (I cannot conceal the truth with regard to the ill-gotten purple) encompasses such grave affirmations that, should we accept them, we should not only fall into Protestantism, but deny revealed truth. If Vatican Council II, though merely pastoral, coincides with Luther's central ideas, if "ecumenical dialogue" leads us to compromise with the "separated brethren" to the extent of telling them Trent's condemnations were just intemperances—this is what Willebrands seems to hint—then a dilemma is posed for our consciences, namely, that either Luther, Protestantism, and its doctrines are the genuine expression of the Gospel, in which case the Council of Trent and the Catholic Church have incurred error and the truth is to be found only in Protestantism, or it is Vatican II and its faithful spokesman Cardinal Willebrands, who have erred as far as their faith is concerned. After reading the Cardinal's speech, we face an unavoidable option. It was not I (poor outcast priest of Christ!) who proclaimed the incompatibility of our Faith with the Lutheran doctrine, but the violent anathema of the Council of Trent, a dogmatic council which infallibly stated the unblemished Faith of the sole Church Christ founded. How is it possible that the dialogue of Vatican II and Paul VI are able to perform the "metaphysical" miracle, the ontological contradiction, that error ceases to be error, and truth, without ceasing to be truth, is coated with the heresy that has been drastically condemned by the authentic, living, unfailing Magisterium of the Church? Moreover, since Willebrands is a cardinal, the head of an official Secretariat of the Roman curia, and a proxy of Paul VI for those meetings, he did not speak as a private person. He appeared to have been absolutely backed by the Pontiff's supreme authority. If this is so, the responsibility for this speech devolves upon Pope Montini, too. Paul VI could and ought to have discredited his legate, condemning his mistakes and proclaiming the Church's unblemished truth once again. Because he keeps silent, as usual, the anathema against heresy transfers to his person. Nevertheless, the program goes on.

17. From Vatican City, AFP and AP cabled one of those sensational pieces of news to which we are becoming accustomed, by which the world is informed of other Montinian reforms, one of which is dialectically destroying the life of the Church or rather, the Faith of countless Catholics. It reads as follows:

Vatican City (March 2, 1971).

The new code of Canon Law, which has been under formulation for ten years, is aimed at "healing," rather than "punishing," since "more apparent Christian charity will lead to greater respect for the dignity and rights of personality." Excommunication, which *ipso facto* dishonored bigamists, homosexuals, duelists, profanators of the Sacrament, people who attack the Pope, bishops, or cardinals, renegades, heretics, and schismatics, will disappear and will be applied only through a special process. It will never be automatic again.

From now on, excommunicants will be able to receive the lesser sacraments and absolution in case of death, as well as ecclesiastical burial.

Priests who get married, and those believers who marry persons belonging to other religions will not be excommunicated automatically. Neither will those who read works by renegades, heretics, or schismatics, or those who join Masonic societies or summon a bishop, cardinal or officer of the Roman curia before a secular court.

On the other hand, it was reported that the Vatican sees no reason for not increasing its relations with the Communist nations, to the end of improving international conditions and consolidating world peace. (*Novedades*, March 3, 1971).

It is a long time since the Church's penal code was practically discontinued. A few Pope-approved "disqualifications" were launched against stubborn priests who bound themselves to the old "mentality" which the post-Conciliar Church had irreversibly overridden. Now, finally, after this long-lasting *vacatio legis,* the Vatican, or rather Paul VI, faithful to his absolute respect for the dignity of a human being, announced the definitive suppression of already-incurred censorships. There will be no excommunication, even for the greatest crimes, without a previous trial. It is evident that excommunication will not prevent people who have been excommunicated by a court's sentence from receiving the lesser sacraments, and, when dead, from being buried in holy places.

The change has to be total. The post-Conciliar Church has to accept what the pre-Conciliar Church had rejected, and suppress everything that had been standing for centuries. The dignity of the human personality is above any other consideration, no matter how grave such considerations may be.

I thought that every crime, but especially certain *kinds* of crimes, had twofold aspects with a twofold liability: *personal offenses* which are inflicted by the criminal upon the offended person, and *social offenses,* outrages which the criminal commits against society. Personal offenses can be forgiven, not out of respect for the dignity of the human personality but for other higher and nobler reasons, such as evangelical advice. The social feature of the public crime, however, cannot and may not be forgiven, on pain of grieving society and endangering the very existence of society, especially when it is a question of very grave crimes. Justice may not be flexed for the sake of sentimentality which takes the place of reason. Any society without criminal statutes drops into anarchy.

Canon 2214 of the agonizing code of Canon Law passed by Benedict XV, reads: "Due to its own constitution, the Church has the right of punishing its subjects, both with spiritual and secular penalties, independently of any human authority." Paragraph 2 of the same canon reads:

Bear in mind the advice of the Council of Trent, sess. XIII, *de ref.,* chapter I: "Remind the bishops and the other ordinaries that they are shepherds, not

Is Paul VI a True Pope?

satraps, and, as to the rule of their subjects, it is convenient that they do not brag about their authority but instead, love their subjects as children and brethren, form them, and draw them away from illicit things through exhortations and admonitions, so that, in case they commit crimes, they will be properly punished. If anyone does commit crime due to human frailty, the shepherds must adhere to the apostle's commandment to warn them and, most kindly and patiently, beg them to stop it, for frequently, kindness is more efficacious than authority, supplication than peremptory order, and mercy than might. If punishment *is* necessary due to the seriousness of the crime, it should be enforced; judgment should be merciful; severity should be accompanied by kindness, so that a healthy discipline, so necessary for society, may be a means by which the castigated mend their ways, and in case they refuse to change, seeing the healthy example of the punishment inflicted upon guilty ones, may withdraw from vice."

Once more, the Vatican through Paul VI tells us it "sees no reason for not increasing its relations with Communist nations, to the end of improving international conditions and consolidating world peace." It seems evident that Pius XI was wrong when he told us Communism is intrinsically evil, and no Catholic, no one who loves Christian principles, may cooperate with it. Pius XII was also wrong in abusing his power when he hurled excommunication against those who joined the Communist Party or cooperated with it. Paul VI, following the directions he receives from the power behind the throne, not only accepts intense cooperation with Communism to spread the latter's tyranny all over the world, but rejects the bourgeois scruples of previous Pontiffs. Tomorrow's Church must be Communist.

Chapter XXV

IS JOHN MONTINI A TRUE POPE? THE AUTHOR'S AND OTHER OPINIONS

The problem posed to the Catholic conscience under the grieving circumstances cited so far in this book, is so big that I believe Catholics have never found themselves in such a difficult condition of anguish in all history. *We are and want to be Catholics,* in the full sense of the word, and we want to be Catholics at the supreme hour of our lives when we appear before the tribunal of divine justice. Since we are Catholics and know what this profession of faith means, we do not and cannot accept a *change of mentality* which is opposed to the Church's traditional apostolic doctrine, even if it is imposed on us in the name of a pastoral council. To this, those who are scandalized by our immutable position, answer: "It is the Pope who commands it. Above all, we must support the Pope." To this I reply: Saint Pius V and his predecessors Paul III, Julius III, and Pius IV, during whose Pontificates the Tridentine Ecumenical Council took place, were Popes, as was Pius IX, who solemnly and infallibly ratified Vatican I. In the presence of the evident contradiction between the *pre-Conciliar* and the *post-Conciliar* Church, in the presence of what they call a change of mentality, which in conscience I see to be a change of Faith, and before the disconcerting silence of the hierarchy and the inexplicable attitude of Paul VI, we necessarily have to focus our attention to Pope Montini's very personality, *to Montinism, its dialectics, and to the Montinian Church,* which is absolutely different from the Church of the Tridentine Council and Vatican I, both of which kept the apostolic Tradition infallibly.

Let us not forget it! We believe in the Pope and in the bishops because we believe in God, in Jesus Christ, true God and true man, and in divine revelation. We believe in our traditional Catechisms, in the Church of all the Councils, and in all that our dogmatic theology taught us as the theses of divine and ecclesiastical faith. *In the presence of contradiction there is doubt, precisely because there is faith.*

MY PERSONAL OPINION OF POPE PAUL VI

Which of the two opinions, then, is correct with respect to Paul VI: Is he a legitimate Pope, or is he not? As mentioned before, the first hypothesis to me is indefensible and unsatisfactory because it tries to explain the present Pontiff's anomalies by a dualism of thoughts and actions. Some people suggest that he may be a captive and would have to act against his conscience to save his life; others say that he may be intermittently drugged; still others maintain that, even after having personally incurred heresy, he would still retain his supreme authority. In all these cases, the rock, the foundation of the Church would lack the necessary immovable stability that guarantees the Church its very existence.

As to the second hypothesis, opinions are also divided. Some think John B. Montini was legitimately elected a Pope but after his election dropped into personal heresy and, in consequence, automatically ceased to be a Pope and lost all his privileges and powers. To others, this heresy became apparent when Paul VI signed the ambiguous documents of Vatican II or when he approved and enforced the *Novus Ordo Missae* which, after having been published under his authority, apparently had to be substantially amended to save what was essential. Still others maintain that John B. Montini was not validly elected, because his election was void *in radice,* either because he did not belong to the Church, or because on other grounds he was not only unworthy, but incapable of being validly elected.

This case that we are studying is so grave that, just as it would be bold and scandalous to judge a thesis affirmatively without a solid basis, it would also be bold to deny it *a priori,* especially taking into account the present condition of the world and the Church. We must not close this important door in our research.

Paul VI's dialectical activity is well known, and this requires a thorough investigation of his doctrine before and after his election, his personality, his life, his acquaintances, and his reformist activity before, during, and after the Council. One day, when there is no *reverential fear* left, when his death may have paralyzed his influence and power, an unbiased and objective verdict will have to be given, just as it has been done with other Pontiffs in past centuries. We want to advance the verdict of history because we find ourselves in a crisis whose urgent and pressing solution implies and requires dissolving Pope Montini's disquieting enigma, thus saving our Catholic Faith.

It is probable that Paul VI's pictures bearing the breastplate of judgment and the ephod of the Levitical Jewish high priest have given us the decisive key. Let us look at this unbecoming ritualistic badge on the Pope's breast, at the current subversion in the Church, at the self-confessed infiltrations of Jews, Masons, and Communists into the clergy, and the secret but apparent relationships of Pope Montini with the most stern enemies of the Church, even though we know little about the whole scope and reality of those relationships. Let us analyze the Montinian steps toward the reformation of the Church, the destruction of its structures and the changes in Catholicism so that we would become similar to other religions. Do you remember his visit to, and speeches before, the United Nations and the World Council of Churches at Geneva, his surrendering ecumenism, and his humanistic dialogue which lacked supernatural spirituality? I believe we have the right and obligation to ask: Is John B. Montini a real Catholic or an infiltrate, a Jew who is being remotely controlled by the mafia? In the beginning this was only suspicion; now there is almost evidence that Paul VI is no legitimate Pope, but an anti-Pope, a Jew trained by the mafia to climb, using despicable means as well as time, money, and evident cunning, for the benefit of those who have always dreamed of dominating the world.

Who could have foreseen that after so many years of continued struggle against secularization, anti-clericalism, and militant atheism, after bloody religious persecutions as in Spain and Mexico, and after the Calvary of the Church of the Silence, that the Vatican would again become the center of convergence of all the great statesmen especially those from the Communist world, those controlled by Masonry, and the international leaders of Jewry. Who could have foreseen that the previous Pontiffs' tough anti-Communist line would become a loving "dialogue" in the comings and goings of Cardinals Bea, Willebrands, Suenens, and König?[12] The persecutions against the Church in Yugoslavia, Hungary, and Cuba have ended with the establishment of most hearty diplomatic relations, whereby the Vatican seems to have undertaken not only to respect the governments' atheism, their aggressive statutes, and their dictatorial systems, but to cooperate, through a real progressive *integration* (such were the words used by the Nuncio to Cuba) with the establishment of Communism which, in turn, is an indispensable requisite for world domination by Judaism. Cardinals Mindszenty and Stepinac's glorious martyrdom was the price paid to attain coexistence and cooperation of both rivals.

Jewry dreamed of its *materialistic Messianism,* or world government, in which they would command and we would be their slaves. Through experience, they knew that there was an insurmountable wall against their attaining this supreme goal of their program. a religious wall, and particularly, the wall of the Catholic Church. They also knew that slander, imprisonment and even death would not crush the Faith, but only revive it. They had no way, then, except through infiltration, to destroy Christ's Church. The case of Anacletus II is repeating itself; the infiltrations exposed by St. Pius X have plagued the hierarchy and reached Peter's See.

To establish a world government it was also urgent to establish universal religion: the religion of *world brotherhood, ecumenism,* and *dialogue,* a sort of religious *syncretism* in which dogmas would be eliminated or muffled, morality corrupted, and discipline suppressed, and all religions would be merged into a single religion, the basis and complement of *world government.* Was there any more intelligent way of carrying out this program, than forming a Council where the prelates, skillfully led by Pope Montini, enacted ecumenism, *aggiornamento,* religious freedom, and a *total reform* of its liturgy, morality, discipline, law, and even dogmas? All this had to be done cunningly, dialectically, and with the skill of professionals who promised a spring in the Church, a new Pentecost. In this mass movement, false rights, brainwashing, numerous national and international associations (such as the Short Courses in Christianity and the Christian Family Movement), the continuous conferences of clergymen and laymen to indoctrinate neophytes of the new religion, the "experiences," the post-Conciliar terminology (*authenticity, engagement, conscientization, relativization, de-sacralization,* etc.), all were able means to bring about the necessary confusion, the elimination of old prejudices and beliefs, and the scruples of conscience which necessarily had to appear with the creation of the new religion of world brotherhood.

All this could be done only by putting the power of the Church into the hands of those that the mafia could rely on. *Jewry was playing its decisive card and to attain its ambition, engaged all its resources to infiltrate the Vatican.*

Many thought that Pope Montini, even with all his weaknesses and oscillations, his equivocal manner of doing one thing while saying another, his double-cross, his friendship and relationship with enemies of the Church, was still a legitimate Pope, but because of his heresy and the nonfulfillment of his principal duties, had to be dismissed. Although everybody fears that the future Pontiff might be a false Pope or an anti-Pope, nevertheless, those who think the present Pope should be dismissed still maintain his legitimacy. They become terrified at the possibility of an anti-Pope in the Church, contrary to what history and theology teach us.

The denunciation of Paul VI's wearing of the ephod and breastplate as shown in almost all of his pictures, and as blasted by Abbé Georges de Nantes in his *Counter-Reformation,* turned suspicion into fear, for many people felt that John Baptist Montini had mounted to the Pontificate in an invalid way and as a result was not a real Pope. The ceremonial Jewish necklace which Paul VI wore allows us to suspect that Paul VI may not only be the most efficient tool of the Jewish mafia, but also a *member* of this mafia, for which reason, besides the pectoral cross and the fisherman's ring, he wears the breastplate of judgment and the ephod of the Levitical high priest, the descendant of Caiphas.

The *Encyclopedia of Freemasonry,* published at San Antonio, Texas, by Albert Gallatin Mackey, M.D. 33°, the author of the *Lexicon of Freemasonry* and a textbook on Masonic jurisprudence, gives us interesting data on the *breastplate of judgment* belonging to the Levitical high priest, and the use which this badge presently has in the lodges:

> In Hebrew, this is called *chosen, selected* or *preferred,* because through this Breastplate of Judgment the high priest receives divine answers, and states his decisions on all things regarding the welfare of the people. It was a piece of cloth

enbroidered in gold, purple, and scarlet, and made from fine white linen of twisted thread. It was folded about nine inches square in size, and was strong enough to bear the precious stones that were put onto it. In each of its corners was a golden ring. Golden chains were affixed to the one at the top edge, through which it was fastened to the cord of the ephod in such a way that it could remain in position. On the breastplate there were twelve precious stones, on each of which the name of one of the twelve tribes was engraved. The stones were arranged in four rows, three by three. As to the order of their arrangement and the names of the stones, there have always been different opinions.... The translation of the Vulgate version is probably the best as far as authenticity is concerned, since it was made in the fifth century when the ancient Hebrew names of the precious stones were better known than in our days. The order to be found in this version was as follows: emerald, topaz, sardonyx; jasper, sapphire, ruby; amethyst, agate, ligur; beryllium, onyx, chrysolite. The order of arrangement, according to the Jewish targum, was as follows (it refers to the ages of the twelve sons of Jacob): Levi, Simeon, Ruben, Zebulon, Issachar, Juda, Gad, Nephtali, Dan, Benjamin, Joseph, Aser. The twelve original names (of the stones) are specified in the 28th chapter of Exodus.... The breastplate used in the first temple does not seem to have been returned after the captivity, for it is not mentioned in the list of objects returned by Cyrus. Due to their great beauty and worth, the stones were probably taken off the original framework and put into various ornaments of their seizers. A second one was made for the service of the second temple. According to Josephus, when the high priest wore it, it radiated strong beams of fire, thus revealing the presence of Jehovah. But he adds that, two hundred years before his age, its miraculous power had begun to extinguish itself due to the nation's impiety. As a result, it was carried to Rome, along with all the spoils of the temple. As to the fate of these treasures, including the breastplate, there are two versions: one, that they were carried to Carthage by Genserico, after plundering Rome, and the vessel that carried them became lost during the journey; and the other one, which is King's (*Ant. Beems.* 137), and the more probable one, that they had been carried to Byzantium a long time before, and deposited by Justinian in St. Sophia's treasury.

The breastplate is worn in the [Masonic] American Chapters of the Royal Arch, by the high priest, as an official part of his official ornaments. According to Webb, the symbolical meaning is to remind him of his responsibility before the laws and regulations of the institution, and that the honor and interests of his chapter are always the tenderest affections of his heart. This is not materially different from the ancient symbolism, since one of the names of the Jewish breastplate was that of "reminder," for it was designed to remind the high priest of the love he owed to the tribes whose names were written on it....

This is what the *Encyclopedia of Freemasonry* tells us. Then, when we see this strange amulet on the present Pontiff's breast, we can boldly suspect a Jewish influence or a Masonic influence, or both, on Pope Montini, since this badge has been worn only by the Levitical or the Masonic high priest. Our suspicion increases when we realize that never before had a Pope worn this jewel on his breast. Paul VI well knows what this breastplate of judgment and this ephod mean. He knows the origin is to be found in the ritual vestments of the Old Covenant. He knows that the Masons use it as a distinctive emblem of their high priest. Can we accept that he naively put on this amulet to please those who gave it to him, without realizing the responsibility this entails? He who disposed of the Pontifical tiara to auction it at the New York World's Fair because the Council had proclaimed the end of the triumphal Constantinian Church and the beginning of the Church of the poor, banishes all scruples and wears this highly esteemed amulet, and shows up before the initiates, not as the Pope of the Catholic Church, the successor of Peter, the Vicar of Christ, but as the Levitical high priest, the successor and representative of Caiphas.

The Pope's pectoral cross and this strange amulet are so incompatible that, if in the Old Covenant, in the religion of the promise and the preparation, it was a ritualistic symbol of the high priest, conferred by God Himself to signify a divine predilection, then in the New Covenant, on the breast of Christ's Vicar, it almost means a denial of Christ and His religion, for Christ is no longer a promise, but a wonderful reality. This is as if Paul VI, in wearing this ritualistic emblem of the Levitical high priest, wanted it to mean that he does not accept the reality that has been substituted for the image, the figure, and the promise made by God. Connecting the breastplate of judgment and the ephod to Christ's cross, Pope Montini seems to give us the impression that he intends to unite Christ and the Antichrist. "It is characteristic of the evil Angel," said Saint Ignatius, "to transform himself *sub Angelo lucis* (with the appearance of the Angel of light) so as to enter into the pious soul and live with it."

It is important to remark that what we have quoted from the *Encyclopedia of Freemasonry* demonstrates the existing links between the Jewish mafia and the Masonic lodges. Jewry engendered Masonry to make use of it as a most valuable tool of its satanic work of destroying Christ and His Church. Using the breastplate of judgment and the ephod, Pope Montini is telling us that he is a docile instrument, a sympathizer and a friend of both Judaism and Masonry. These coincidences might perhaps prove that John Baptist Montini, a Jew by familial descent, was an instrument prepared by the mafia to infiltrate and dominate the Church. The holy Priest of Ars wrote: "We cannot analyze the behavior of the Hebrews without becoming astounded." The role these people have had in the course of history is unbelievable. Formerly they were predestined by God, but, due to their iniquities, they became the permanent enemies of God and Christ. Taking into account such firm grounds to suspect

Paul VI, we should do some research on John Baptist Montini's person, deeds, and statements.

What is the Montini family's background? The 1965-1968 edition of the *Golden Book of Italian Nobility* does not mention the name *Montini*. In the *Golden Book* for the period 1962-1968, on page 994, we find *Montini* for the first time:

> A branch of the homonymous noble family from Brescia, originally from Val Sabbia, wherefrom their noble blazon comes and which avows as its sure trunk and founder, a Bartholomew (Bartolino) de Benedictis, said Montini being of Hebrew origin. The family spread itself throughout Lumezzano, Sarezzo, Nave, Concesio, and Brescia. The family name appears repeatedly in the *Rural Noblemen* registry, between 1946 and 1948. In Sarezzo, in the gallery of the Montini family, there is a genealogical tree prepared by Angelo Bosio (deceased 1795), alderman of the community of Sarezzo, who documents the inclination of the Montini family to be notary publics, physicians, jurists, religious and ecclesiastics, some of whom became very famous. By virtue of the apostolic constitution *Urbem Romam,* of January 4, 1746, the family became a member of Roman nobility.

The Montini family's heraldry is three mounts topped by three French lilies which are surmounted by three faces, among which the figure of Paul VI in profile stands out. He is looking at the six-summit mountain, his head surrounded by three disarranged lilies on a silver background.

Paul VI's parents were George Montini and Judith Alghisi. George was born in 1861 and died in 1943. Ludovico, a brother of the Pope and a senator of the republic, was born on May 8, 1896. John Baptist, now Paul VI, was born at Concesio (Brescia), on September 26, 1897.

On December 14, 1969, the Spanish journalist and progressivist priest Martin Descalzo, published a document in the *ABC* from Madrid, which was attributed to the Vatican Secretariat for Christian Unity, according to its bold headlines. Later on it was discovered to be a document issued by an American Secretariat for Relations between Catholics and Jews, sponsored by a cardinal. The document read as follows:

> 1. Judaism is the depository of freedom, dignity, and human values, toward which the Church is moving after having carefully considered the aspirations of mankind.
>
> 2. The Church, after two thousand years, has avowed its mistakes, begs pardon of the Jews, and wants to initiate a dialogue with them.
>
> 3. The Jewish people, the only ones with whom God established and maintains an indestructible link and tie, have been permanently elected and are

The Montinian Church

God's chosen ones.

4. This religious bond is connected [here the goal of the document becomes visible] to the possession of the Promised Land and the constitution of the state of Israel, which must be recognized by all Christians.

5. The Church owes Judaism its doctrine, institutions, beliefs, worship and even its liturgy.

6. The Old Testament has its own validity, autonomy, and independence, which must not be understood or explained in the light of the New Testament.

7. In the reading of the Bible, the Church must avoid any unfavorable interpretation of the Jewish people, especially with respect to the death of Jesus.

8. Jesus Himself was a product of the Jewish people who identified Himself with His people in almost every respect. When He opposed them, He did so within the Jewish framework and as an internal thing, within His race, just as the prophets who preceded Him.

This document, which denies the divinity of Jesus Christ and the divine institution of the Church, is attributed to the Vatican Secretariat for Unity, published in the pages of a pro-monarchic Spanish newspaper *ABC* and reprinted with a cardinal's consent, by the American Secretariat for Jewish-Christian Relations. It is too symptomatic for anyone who objectively studies the present condition of the Church. At one time this document could not have been published in Spain, for both the official and the ecclesiastical censorship would have prevented such a monstrosity. This time nobody objected; nobody said anything. The document passed without raising a protest. This is the Spain that overthrew the Decree of Expulsion of the Jews by the Catholic kings. This is the *aggiornated* Spain which, to increase its holdings, denies its history and traditions.

A PLOT AGAINST THE CHURCH

God, in His infinite mercy, in the way He always offers us the inexhaustible help of His divine grace to attain our everlasting salvation, also gives us enough light so that we are not deceived by the enemy or, due to the shrewdness of the Tempter, lose the safe way of our salvation. Under the inspiration of the Holy Spirit, the high Pontiffs, in an uninterrupted way, warned us about the most grave prelude to the indescribable tragedy we are beholding, whose origins go back to past centuries. Many Popes had sounded the alarm and pointed to the appropriate means of defending ourselves from the Hidden Power: Pius VI, in his allocution on the martyrdom of Louis XVI, Gregory XVI, in his frequent and most grave admonitions; Pius IX, in the encyclical *Quanta Cura* and his *Syllabus;* Leo XIII in his most wise encyclicals, especially *Humanum Genus;* Pius X, in the *Pascendi,* his new *Syllabus,* and in

The Author's and Other Opinions

his condemnation of *Le Sillón*, founded by Marc Sagnier; and Pius XII, in his encyclical *Humani Generis* and on his brilliant instructions of May 31 and November 2, 1954 to the bishops of the whole world.

Following the Pontifical teaching, prominent prelates such as Msgr. Delassus and Msgr. Jouin, as well as brave writers such as Leon de Poncins, Pierre Virion, and Maurice Pinay, had exposed *the tremendous reality of a Luciferian project for world domination by the counter-Church*. Satan's agents, who already considered themselves victorious, did not hesitate to print such expositions and issue statements referring to them. Let us mention Stanislas de Guaita, the former Canon Roca, Saint Yves d'Alveydre, and the Synarchy. The details of a plot are widely confirmed by the *Protocols of the Elders of Zion*, stolen at the end of the last century, for evidently the Hidden Power would never have made the mistake of voluntarily publishing a document that, due to its contents, had to be kept in the utmost secrecy.

Unfortunately, admonitions, condemnations, and revealing denunciations were not adequately heeded by the ecclesiastics or the laity, who did not pay attention to them or, with unbelievable levity, denied their authenticity. We are beholding the storm and the wreckage, but neverthless, we keep on disbelieving the existence of that infernal Jewish-Masonic conspiracy, which is beginning to clamorously celebrate its success. Because the Pontifical teachings were not followed and the theologians and historians who announced the danger were not believed, the Church is now undergoing the most grave crisis in its history. To find out the causes of this crisis we must remember the program of the Luciferian Hidden Power and the lodges' secret instructions. The Holy See got to know about these instructions and had them published by Crétineau-Joly in his works, *The Roman Church in Face of the Revolution* and *The Jewish-Masonic Plot Against the Church*.

In the 18th century, the head of the Illuminati, the Jew Weishaupt, wrote:

> Freemasons must impose their might upon the men of all states, nations, and religions, dominate them without visible coercion, keep them united by stable links, inspire the same spirit in all of them, spread the same ideas, and, with utmost secrecy and activity, lead them all throughout the world to the same goal. It is in the intimacy of the secret societies that public opinion must be formed (original writings of the Order and Lodges of the Illuminati, 1765, Munich, as quoted by Barruel in his *Mémoires pour servir à l'histoire du Jacobinisme*).

To create public opinion, this is the aim. In his booklet, *How To Form Public Opinion*, Maurice Talmeyer depicts this hoax and its terrible efficacy:

> Until people decisively join a sect or a school, and until they become

convinced party members, public opinion progressively develops this solidarity in them and puts them on guard. These men, even though not united among themselves and without any consciousness of what they are, still think and judge alike, and they constitute what is being attempted, namely, a "consensus," an artificial, external "consensus" but one which appears spontaneous and is vividly impressive.

Weishaupt issues the order:

> Let Christians believe that our Lord Jesus Christ was the great inventor of the Masonic trinomial, *"liberty, equality, and fraternity,"* that this is the doctrine He taught, but that it must be understood in accordance with the teachings of the sects. Our doctrine is the very divine doctrine Jesus Christ taught His disciples and whose intimate and real meaning belongs to the secret discourses of the lodges.... [Here we have the cabala.] This doctrine gives the whole human race the means to attain complete freedom.... Nobody has opened ways so safe to freedom as our great Jesus of Nazareth.

At Florence on August 5, 1806, Simonini disclosed to Abbé Barruel the program of the Hidden Power, as one of his high officers had explained it to him. This Abbé communicated it immediately to Pope Pius VII, who affirms that it is authentic and quotes the essential passages:

> 4. That, on our Italian soil, they had already recruited as members more than 800 ecclesiastics, both secular and regular, among whom there were many parsons, professors, prelates, and some bishops and cardinals; and that, as a result, they did not relinquish their hope of having a Pope of their own party.
> 5. That they also had many members among the clergy in Spain.
> 6. That the family of the Bourbons was their biggest enemy, but they intended to eliminate it in just a few years.

Shortly after, the heads of the Supreme Venta summarized their ideas in like manner, teaching the Christians that *"Christianity is an essentially democratic doctrine,"* and inculcating them with *equality and humanitarism.* A secret direction dated 1819, states:

> There is an idea that has always concerned the men who strive for world regeneration; it is the thought of the liberation of Italy, which will one day achieve the liberation of the whole world, the federal republic, the harmony of mankind. But there is a hindrance, namely the Church, and this is a tremendous obstacle. Our goal is that of Voltaire and of the French Revolution: *the total annihilation of Catholicism and of the Christian idea itself....* The Pope,

whoever he may be, will never come to the secret societies; it is the secret societies who must make the first step toward the Church with the aim of defeating it. Then they will give the following instructions: all the dangers of fanaticism have to be made known. The happiness that social equality and the great principles of religious freedom provide us have to be praised, against intolerance and persecution. They end by saying: "This, and only this, is the law of social progress; do not take the trouble to search for it elsewhere."

Above all, that which we must request and seek as anxiously as the Jews expected their Messiah, is a Pope who will meet our requirements ... so that, for the purpose of *destroying the rock upon which God built His Church*, we will have the small finger of a successor of Peter committed to our plot; this small finger will permit us to organize this crusade against all the Saint Bernards and all the Urban II's of Christianity ....

This supreme goal of our efforts has to be attained. But how? The unknown cannot be seen yet, but nothing will make us relinquish the scheduled plan; on the contrary, all must push us toward it ... That is why we want to give you the advice given by the Supreme Venta ... [This advice is really devilish.]

Crush the enemy, whoever he may be; crush his might through calumny and slander, but, above all, crush him while he is still an egg. *It is to the youth that we must pay attention;* it is the youth who must be seduced and prepared without their realizing it, under the banner of the secret societies. To attain this, you have to be as simple as doves, but as wise as snakes ....

According to these directions, in order to exercise more control over people, some details are revealed on condition of:

maintaining absolute secrecy [especially with respect to the Supreme Venta], for he who voluntarily or involuntarily reveals these secrets would sign his own death sentence.

Hence, to secure a Pope with the required qualities, *this Pope has to be prepared a generation before the kingdom* we long for. Ignore old and grown-up people. Take the youth and, if possible, the children .... Once you have obtained a stable reputation in the schools, the high schools, universities, and seminaries, once you have won the confidence of teachers and pupils, work primarily on those who will embrace the clerical state and give you support. This reputation will pave the way for our doctrines among the young clergy and in the intimacy of the convents. In a few years this young clergy, under the weight of events, will have invaded all positions; it will be these young clergymen who will rule, administer, judge, and form the Sovereign's council; it is they who will be called upon to elect the Pontiff who will reign, a Pontiff like his contemporaries, imbued with the Italian humanitarian principles we have begun to put into circulation ...

The Montinian Church

> *Search for the Pope whose features we have given you...;* let the clergy march under your banner in the belief that they march under the flag of the apostolic keys...; cast your nets... in the intimacy of the sacristies, seminaries, and convents...; gain friends around the Apostolic See. *Then you will have preached a sacerdotal and Papal revolution..., a revolution that with little effort, will set fire to the four corners of the world.*

Another instruction read:

> Flatter all passions, both the most perverse as well as the most generous.... The Church's education has to become immoral *to attain the success of the revolution through a Pope*.... Give the torch to anyone who wishes to carry it.... Infiltrate the germs of our dogmas into their spirits subtly..., so that clergymen and laymen become persuaded that Christianity is an essentially democratic doctrine. (Writings published in Munich, 1765, quoted by Barruel in his *Mémoires pour servir à l'histoire du Jacobinisme*).

On August 9, 1839, Vindice wrote Nubius to tell him he condemned individual murders, for which the Carbonari were held responsible, and with hateful cynicism, he added:

> Let not crime be individualized; to spread it to the scale of patriotism and hatred of the Church, *let it be general*. Catholicism does not have the same fear of a steel or dagger as the monarchy, but these two bases of the social order can collapse through moral corruption. Let us corrupt unceasingly... let us not make martyrs, but *popularize vice amid the crowds*. Let everyone breathe vice through the five senses; let him become saturated with it... Make vicious hearts, and Catholicism will cease to exist. It is a universal corruption which we must propagate, a corruption of the people and the clergy, a corruption which will finally carry the Church to its grave.

What results did the Hidden Power attain? On April 3, 1824, after two months of his having assumed the leadership of the Supreme Venta, Nubius wrote: "Especially in Rome, part of the clergy has swallowed the bait with marvelous vigor." On April 3, 1843, he wrote: "These lesser means, which have been used properly, though ill-defined at times, will bring about the success of the *revolution through a Pope*."

In 1845 another leader of the Supreme Venta wrote with regard to the priest Gioberti:

> The priest Gioberti speaks to the priests in their own language, and I want to tell you that everywhere the doctrines of Italian freedom and independence,

headed by the Pope, are accepted. These doctrines seduce many to such a degree that they become convinced Catholicism is essentially a democratic doctrine. This party attracts more and more followers among the clergy every day. The new work by Gioberti, mainly written for priests, is expected anxiously.

Thus the leaders of the anti-Christian plot boast about the success of their execrable activities. Credence is given to this boast by the Secretary of State of the Holy See who conveys his fear in a letter dated August 8, 1845:

> *Our young clergy is already imbued with liberal ideas* .... They have abandoned serious studies. Most of the priests who will succeed us in the leading positions are a thousand times more plagued by the liberal vice ... ; most of them do not know the nature of the things that are taking place and let themselves be influenced by suggestions from which spring forth the great crises of the Church. The same spirit of discord is to be found everywhere among the priests .... *They have broken with the past to become new men.* The spirit of the sect replaces the true love of neighbor, and individual pride is growing in the dark.

This Luciferian program is the one we can see everywhere in the Church, under the names of *aggiornamento, ecumenism, dialogue, religious freedom, Conciliar spirit,* or *reformation of the Church.* Stanislas de Guaita wanted "to reveal to Christian theology the esoteric magnificence with which, without realizing it, [the Church] will progressively become enriched and transformed." (*Essai de Sciences Maudites,* I, p. 159). The former Canon Roca, answered de Guaita:

> Beloved brother in Jesus Christ, I do not deny any of the principles of your teaching, which is also mine. We agree completely as to all the points of the esoteric doctrine, which, as I wrote to Papus, is the real initiation Christ gave the twelve after the teachings given to the seventy-two. We do not have any problem to solve with the Protestant churches, just as there is none with Masonry and the synagogue, either. The only difficulties we have are the ones which the Church of Rome poses us. (Fr. Marsoudon, *Le Temple,* Sept.-Oct. 1946, p. 34).

We have already seen how Roca announced liturgical anarchy under the guise of primitive purity:

> I believe that divine worship, as regulated by the liturgy, ceremonies, rites, and precepts of *the Roman Church, will soon undergo a transformation at an ecumenical council, and return to the simplicity of an apostolic golden age* and adapt itself to the state of modern conscience and civilization. An immolation is

The Montinian Church

being prepared.... *The Papacy will succumb; it will die under the sacred knife of the Fathers of the last council.* The Papal Caesar is a host crowned for the sacrifice. Scientific theology will succeed mystic theology, as the grown-up nations are roaringly demanding. They will hurry to destroy the *Summa Teologica* and replace it by a scientific Summa. A new, sublime, tolerant, deep, really universal, absolutely encyclopedic Christianity ... a universal worship, in which all worships will identify themselves and *in which God will be mankind* ... [is coming].

Pignatelli, on page 29 of his *Batailles Maconniques,* wrote:

Only in a theocratic society that has the universal nature of Masonry, will Islam and Christianity, the Jews and the Buddhists, Europe and Asia be able to join together in the same ideal and a common hope.

In an article entitled *"Politique et Maconnerie"* in number 37 of the *Bulletin du Grand Orient,* the Grand Orient affirms:

Masonry will be the super-church, the Church that will unite all religions. The worship that will replace the Christian one will be a worship in which all worships will merge. We aspire that there will be no intermediary between us and God. It is, then, probable that the religion of the time to come will burn each believer into his own priest.... In this way, *initiation* will be the great religious school, and *symbolism* will help thinkers to discover the truth that lies at the bottom of the human spirit. The future world will believe anew, after having assimilated Christianity and other present forms of spirituality, and perhaps will bring about a rebirth of *pantheism* through analogy with physical phenomena and total collectivization. In this pantheism, all the forms of current thought will be amalgamated with a new, unbelievable dynamism to attain their goals.

Roca also gives us a synthesis of this new Christianity:

Then there will be a *new dogma, a new religion, a new rite, and a new priesthood* whose resemblance with the dying Church will be exactly that which the Catholic Church has with the Mosaic Church, its late mother. Faith will disappear in the presence of science, which will illuminate everything...; science is the king of the world because *it is God Himself in mankind*.... Everyone's duty in the present hour is to foster evolution, designed to *transform the Papacy and to harmonize it with the new spirit of the world and the natural sciences.* Above the various religions there is a world church, comprised of all dogmatically-free believers, who unite their beliefs regarding the existence of a supreme being, a future life, the immortality of the soul, and the duty of human love, proclaimed by all the religions as the first of all commandments. (*Congrès Spiritualiste Mondial,* Brussels, 1946).

The impersonal and divine kingdom of truth in freedom, justice in equality and social economy in fraternity is the sacred trinomial of the evangelical synarchy.

To us, this is Lucifer's kingdom.

Roca also announces the "conversion" of the Pope to the world's new spirit after an ecumenical council has returned the Church to the simplicity of the apostolic golden age:

> The old Papacy will break the silence at the time this totally evangelical work, this glorious polygenesis, is finished. Then it will go back to its grave. Peter will fulfill Christ's oracle. He "will confirm his brethren," . . . all Christian people. . . . *He will consecrate science as the queen of the modern civilized world and will proclaim it daughter of the Church,* heiress of the Lord's promises, and the real spirit of the parables . . . Once the Roman Papacy has proclaimed its own overthrow, it will *Urbi et Orbi* state that its mission and function as an initiator being at an end, it will voluntarily dissolve and abandon its primitive form leaving the field open for the superior operations of the new Pontificate, the new Church, and the new priesthood, which it will set up itself before breathing its last. . . . For it will become evident to everyone that the new order will logically issue from the ancient order . . . The old Papacy and the old priesthood will voluntarily abdicate before the Pontificate and before the future priests, who will be the same converted and transfigurated ones of the past, in view of the new organization of this plant in the light of the Gospel. . . . Though this new Church will keep nothing of the scholastic discipline and the rudimentary form of the old Church, it will receive its ordination and canonical jurisdiction from Rome. . . . It is necessary that this liberation be attained and the law of evolution follow its divine course in a cycle opened by the Holy Gospel following the steps of the new man.

According to Roca, the Pope, whom he mentions as the head of the ecumenical council that will reform the whole Church,

> . . . is not for us a Pontiff of faith or piety, but a Pontiff of gnosis and esoteric science. . . . Something will happen that will strike the world with wonder and make the world kneel before its Redeemer. This thing will be the demonstration of the perfect consistency between the ideology of modern civilization and the ideology of Christ and His Gospel. This will be the consecration of the new social order and the solemn baptism of modern civilization.

The Montinian Church

According to these revelations of the initiates, if we study Vatican Council II and the post-Conciliar times, we will be obliged to acknowledge that the plan drawn up in the dens of the mafia has already been implemented and is in the process of complete fulfillment. Pope Montini's behavior seems to us to be totally consistent with this program of the anti-Church. We are right in suspecting that Paul VI might be the Pope of *Revolution*.

Chapter XXVI

POPE PAUL VI SEEKS ALLIANCES WITH COMMUNIST COUNTRIES

Before returning to Bogotá to study Paul VI's activity, I feel it pertinent to mention the Vatican's diplomatic activity with regard to the Communist countries. This turnabout is being accelerated. Appearances indicate that we are turning toward Communism fearlessly and without suspicion, for Communism cannot be avoided, and we must assume our positions before it dominates and enslaves us. This seems to be the program and historical mission of Pope Montini, who is consciously or unconsciously being remotely controlled by the secret forces of world revolution. I have interrupted my comments on the Montinian activities in Colombia because I believe it is necessary to bring the light that will subsequently help me explain what I saw and heard at the post-Conciliar Eucharistic Congress after Paul VI's coming to Bogotá.

LOYAL TO HIS PROGRAM, PAUL VI SEEKS ALLIANCES WITH COMMUNIST COUNTRIES

For many years, Msgr. Agostino Casaroli, Archbishop of Carthage and Secretary of the Council for Public Affairs of the Church had been carrying on a positive work of understanding and intercommunication between the Holy See and the Eastern European Communist countries. This pastoral activity by Msgr. Casaroli was preceded by that of the Cardinal-Archbishop of Vienna, Msgr. König. Feeling safe about the faithfulness of the Catholic states such as Spain, Portugal, and the South American countries, the Vatican not only forgets them, but pretends to be in "opposition" to them, trying to break, or at least to loosen the links it maintained with these governments through concordats. Simultaneously, with the mighty Jewish-Masonic help of the United Nations, it makes strong efforts to establish and widen its diplomatic relations with the countries that are publicly or secretly dominated by the "Star of David." As far back as 1967, Msgr. Casaroli carried on conversations with the Polish government to the effect of establishing relations between it and the Vatican. In the summer of 1970, he also went to Belgrade to talk with Tito, thus preparing for the subsequent audience with Paul VI granted Tito in Rome.

The Montinian Church

Later on, as part of this process of defrosting, Msgr. Casaroli flew to Moscow on a Russian Aeroflot aircraft. He was accompanied by Msgr. Silvestrino, from the Church's Council for Public Affairs, and John Kwaku Nimo, a member of the lay council.

Monsignor Casaroli had already made several visits to Russia and some satellite countries, although, according to Vatican sources, those were private trips. On this occasion, his visit to the Kremlin was official. This was a high honor for His Excellency and the person he represented, Pope Paul VI. The aim of this unexplained visit, which neither Pius XI nor Pius XII would have tolerated, was to sign the Treaty of Non-Proliferation of Nuclear Weapons on Thursday, February 25, 1971. A copy thereof was also signed at Washington and London by the apostolic delegates, Msgr. Raimundi and Msgr. Enrici. The Vatican, anxious to attain world peace, wanted to commit itself not to make any nuclear bombs in the hope of engaging other governments with the moral weight of its example, to stop the arms race which jeopardizes world peace. The aim of the Holy See was, as always, to promote peace and concord among all men on earth. Monsignor Casaroli was also desirous of easing the living condition of Catholics living in those countries. This skilled Vatican diplomat conversed with high officials of the Soviet government. He had an interview with the president of the Council for Religious Affairs of the Soviet Union, Vladimir Kuroyedov, who endorses a policy of "softening" with respect to the Russian Orthodox Church (officially authorized within the Soviet Union territories) and the granting of certain privileges to Catholics on a controlled basis. Monsignor Casaroli also spoke with Kosures about the necessity of a careful preparation for the Conference of European Security, the Middle East and Vietnamese situations, and the disarmament issue. The Secretary for Public Affairs of the Vatican also had a meeting with the leaders of the Orthodox Church and particularly with the primate, Pimen, who has administered the Patriarchate of Moscow since the death of Patriarch Alexis.

Then with the aid of its allies, the Jews and the Masons, the Vatican is on the eve of realizing its golden dream: establishing relations with enemy number one of church, civilization, mankind, and (why not say it?) God Himself. A Catholic Archbishop, a Secretary of one of the many new secretariats that in the Vatican have replaced the obsolete Roman curia, a person who is almost a papal legate, travels to Moscow, not on an Alitalia, but a Russian Aeroflot, aircraft. He is received at the Kremlin, just as the Communist leaders had been received at the Vatican. He then has meetings with the supreme heads of Communism in hopes of smoothing the condition of the few Catholics who live in Russia and the many who live in the satellite countries, while keeping those Catholics under control. The pretext of signing the Treaty of Non-Proliferation of Nuclear Weapons was a good one. Only God knows what was said over there at the secret meetings.

Meanwhile, the Communists won the game. All the previous Pontifical condemnations have been disregarded; naive Catholics can be told that the Church, our Church, is already united with Communism and is disposed to accept and impose upon us, in the name of the Gospel, the yoke of slavery, the dread of tyranny of the godless. Pope Montini continues his program inch by inch; he knows where he is going, and what he wants, for he has the international support of his powerful allies who already consider themselves to be rulers of the world.

Communism is still intrinsically perverse, and all those who cooperate with it are cooperating with the anti-Church and the anti-fatherland, even though cooperation is made on the humanitarian pretext of treaties (worth as little as the paper on which they are written). *The Church is beholding its own "auto-demolition," while widening its diplomatic relations with the Communist countries.*

A MESSAGE FROM THE WORLD CONFERENCE ON RELIGION AND PEACE

Still, as extra evidence of the ecumenical flexibility which the Church has adopted under the pastoral administration of Paul VI, I shall quote a message from the 22 main religions of the world, sent from Kyoto, Japan, after the World Conference on Religion and Peace, in which 1,600 delegates and observers (among whom were Dr. Eugene Carson Blake and Don Hélder Cámara) took part. The chairman of this unique and strange conference was Msgr. Fernández, the Catholic Archbishop of Delhi, India. The message that came out of this conference reads as follows:

1. The Conference on Religion and Peace is an attempt to induce all men and women belonging to the great religions to discuss the urgent problem of peace together.

2. This is a crucial age. In this very moment we behold cruel and inhuman wars, as well as racial, social, and economic violence. Man's survival on our planet is jeopardized by nuclear destruction. Man has never experienced such a deep despair.

3. Since we are deeply convinced that the world religions must render a real and important service to the cause of peace, we have gathered together at Kyoto. This includes Bahaists, Buddhists, Confucians, Christians, Hindus, Jains, Jews, Muslims, Shintoists, Shiks, Zoroastrists, and others. We have gathered together in peace, moved by the same concern over peace.

4. In jointly conversing to face the problems of peace, which prevail upon all others, we have discovered that what unites us is more important than what separates us.

The Montinian Church

The Common Heritage of all Religions

5. We have realized we have the following in common:

   a. Our conviction of the fundamental unity of the human family, and the equality and dignity of all human beings.

   b. The feeling about the sacred nature of the individual and his conscience.

   c. The belief that force cannot substitute for law, that the power of man is not self-sufficient or absolute, and the conviction that love, piety, selflessness, and the force of inner loyalty and spirit are superior to hatred, enmity, and egoistic interest.

   d. The feeling that we have the obligation to take the side of the poor and the oppressed against the rich and the oppressors.

   e. The intimate hope that good will prevail in the end.

6. By virtue of the above convictions that are common to us, we believe that a peculiar mission has been entrusted to all religious men and women, so that, engaging their hearts and intelligences, they become concerned about peace and pacification and become the servants of peace.

7. By virtue of our nature as religious men and women, we humbly and penitently confess that we have too frequently betrayed our religious principles and our engagement with peace. It is not religion which has failed to join the cause of peace, but religious men. This treason of religion can and must be corrected.

8. In accepting the urgent challenges which peace poses to us in the second half of the 20th century, we have decided to study the problems of disarmament, development, and human rights. It is absolutely evident that peace is endangered by the growing abyss between rich and poor within the nations and among the nations, and by the tragic violation of human rights all over the world.

9. In studying the problems of disarmament, we have become convinced that peace cannot be achieved through the accumulation of weapons. Consequently, we demand immediate steps to foster disarmament, covering all destructive weapons: conventional, chemical, and bacteriological.

The Scandal of the Arms Race

10. We have discovered that disarmament problems have grown worse, because the amounts devoted to research, fabrication, and accumulation of such weapons constitute a scandalously high percentage of the resources of mankind. We are fully convinced that, on the contrary, these resources are urgently required to fight injustice, which, in turn, favors war and other forms of social violence .... Any society where one child out of four dies is in a state of war. Though development alone is not able to achieve peace, there can be no lasting

peace without it. That is the reason why we have committed ourselves to second the efforts of the United Nations to turn the seventies into a decade of development for all nations.

11. Social upheavals, which are so evident in today's world, demonstrate that peace depends upon recognition, promotion, and protection of human rights. Racial discrimination, repression of ethnic and religious minorities, torture of political and other prisoners, legalized and *de facto* denial of political freedom and equality of opportunities, the various forms of colonial oppression, and all sorts of violations of human rights, are responsible for the growth of violence presently debasing human civilization.

12. In this conference we are speaking on our own, as people who are members of numerous religions gathered by our deep concern in favor of peace, and also on behalf of the immense majority of the human family which is deprived of power and whose voice can rarely be heard—the poor, the exploited, the refugees, all those who have no lodgings, and whose life, goods, and liberty have been ruined by war.

13. We address our religions, the ecumenical councils, and all interconfessional organisms struggling for peace, the nations, beginning with ours, the United Nations, and the men and women who, without religions, are concerned about the welfare of man.

14. To each and all, beginning with ourselves, we state that the starting point for any serious effort in the human enterprise—at the educational, cultural, scientific, social, and religious levels—is the solemn acceptance of the reality that men and all their activities are from now on united by the same fate: we shall live or die together; we shall be able to follow the present course toward joint destruction, or jointly commit ourselves to the struggle for peace.

We may not honestly expose war and whatever favors it, if our lives are not totally committed to peace and we are not ready to make the necessary sacrifices to attain such an end. We must do whatever is in our reach to educate public opinion, so that people rise strongly against war and against the deceitful hope of peace attained through military success.

All Religions Must Unite for the Sake of Peace

We are convinced that religions, despite the historically-provoked differences, must presently strive to unite all men around projects that foster real peace. We believe we have the obligation, above any sectarian boundaries, to cooperate with those who, outside the historical religions, share our wish for peace.

We commit ourselves to warn the nations of which we are citizens, that the efforts to create and maintain a military power lead to disaster. Such efforts create a climate of fear and distrust; they require assets that are essential to meet the needs of health, lodging, and welfare; they increase inequality among nations, building military and economic blocks; they lead man to consider peace as an armed truce or a balance of terror, and to censure the really universal concern about the welfare of all mankind as a utopia. To all this we say: "NO."

We expect the United Nations will share our concern for peace. Peace and its maintenance require not only that the existence of the United Nations be acknowledged, but moreover, that they be given full support to implement their resolutions. We are issuing an urgent call for world representation at the United Nations in favor of a more equitable apportionment of power and responsibility in their activities. We are calling upon the member nations to accept a solution to the problems that have led or might lead to conflicts, under the rule of the organization.

We hope that this conference will help us see and accept the responsibility belonging to us, as religious men and women, to achieve a lasting and real peace. (*La Documentation Catholique*, Feb. 7, 1971.)

Here we have an imitation, a world ecumenical adaptation of the *Populorum Progressio*, the document which Pope Montini considers to be the chief work of his Pontificate, and which we deem a cunning and apparent statement of the Communist demagogical utopia, sprinkled with holy water. The bare fact that the Catholic Church had attended this conference of all religions on an equality basis was an implicit act of surrendering our Catholic Faith, the acknowledgment that all religions are the same. The temporal goal of peace, which might be appealing for many, cannot be the element to unite all religions, for religion must basically and essentially aim at the fulfillment of our primordial obligations toward God, and the attainment, after this life, of the only true happiness for which we were created. "Peace," says Saint Augustine, "is quietness in order." There can be no order when values have been overthrown.

This document, in which we find all the features of Pope Montini's mentality and wishes, states the elements belonging to all religions, but does not mention God even once. God is no longer important, and man appears to be the very center and common denominator of all religions. The document states that one of the leading principles of any religion is the *obligation* we have to *take the side of the oppressed against the rich*. Is not this a declaration of war against anyone owning private property? Is not this an attempt (against natural and eternal law) to merge all religions with the debasing slavery of Communism? The disarmament which occupies Paul VI, is the disarmament of the Free World, so that, without any resistance, all people will become identical and equal as slaves under the world government of Communism and international Jewry.

Once more, human rights as summarized by the famous words of the French Revolution, "Liberty, Equality, and Fraternity," are being proclaimed

Paul VI Seeks Alliances

as a guarantee for peaceful human existence under the just regime of the United Nations. The commandments of God no longer matter; they have been abandoned; they have proven to be of no use. Now, as Paul VI said at the United Nations, mankind is turning its hopeful eyes to the paternalistic and fair ruling of this international organism, led and controlled by the Jewish mafia. That is why the message said:

> To each and all, beginning with ourselves, we state that the starting point for any serious effort in the human enterprise—at the educational, cultural, scientific, social and religious levels [notice that religion is the last of the life values]—is the solemn acceptance of the reality that men and all their activities are from now on united by a common destiny.

To complete the Montinian thought, I shall add: Under one government and one religion. "We are convinced that religions, despite the historically provoked differences [not of ontological antagonism between truth and error], must presently strive to unite all men around projects that foster real peace." Let us suppress dogmas; let us muffle beliefs; let us loose the promptings of Catholic morality and of discipline; let us make some rites that will be acceptable to all; let us bow, with religious reverence, before the Montinian idol of peace. But let us not forget that: "Peace and its maintenance require not only that the existence of the United Nations be acknowledged, but moreover, that they be given full support to implement their resolutions." That is why Cardinal Villot, Secretary of State for Paul VI, in a telegram sent to the Pontiff on the occasion of the attempt on his life at Manila, called him "the pilgrim and messenger of peace and world brotherhood."

In the January, 1971, issue of his *Contre-Reforme*, Abbé Georges de Nantes is right in calling our attention to the fact that:

> In the last few months, the Pope has uttered or written an impressive series of speeches and highly important messages which Christian people, who cannot spend their time reading the Pontifical texts, could not possibly have commented on, nor even remembered. All these texts have the same goal: expounding and incessantly repeating the paragraphs of the other creed of Paul VI regarding the present world and the earthly fate of mankind. No doubt this historical and planetary vision is a personal view of the Pontiff, an opinion of his, and, to use the language of theology, his thought as a private theologian. In no way is this an act of the solemn and infallible Magisterium. Neither is it an act of the regular Magisterium, since it does not express a defined doctrine or a doctrine that *semper et ubique docuit Ecclesia*. But this is not merely a political or economic doctrine of Paul VI; it is a specifically religious view, designed to impose a series of moral obligations. This vision fully enters the realm of faith and morality,

The Montinian Church

since the Pope invokes the Gospel and Christian Faith to impose his way of thinking upon the attention and submission of believers. Thus a serious and calm study by theologians is absolutely necessary.

Even though impossible to repeat here the study by the meritorious Abbé de Nantes, I shall at least mention the points which this analytical work covers:

1. The ultimate goal of history is the integral and joint development of mankind.

2. The fundamental thesis is the declaration of the rights of man: liberty, equality, and fraternity.

3. Previous conditions must be a radical change, and a complete shift of mankind.

4. The providential tools of salvation are the United Nations and its special agencies.

5. Today's Christ is at the service of those who rebel against hypocrisy and injustice.

Chapter XXVII

POPE PAUL VI AND THE PEASANTS

After having studied Paul VI's enigmatic personality, it is time to go back to the International Eucharistic Congress in Colombia.

DEVELOPMENT DAY AT BOGOTÁ— PAUL VI'S SPEECH TO THE PEASANTS OF AMERICA

This is Development Day, or the Day of the *Populorum Progressio*. Who, except the Pope, could give shape and orientation to the innovations of this Eucharistic Congress? From the August 24, 1968, edition of *El Espectador* from Bogotá, I quote as follows:

> The morning is cold, intensely cold, zero degrees. The morning light rises slowly, just creeping up amid the fog that is vanishing in pockets and lingers in the trees. An immense parade begins along the network of side streets. The peasants from all the towns set out from Funza, the old dwelling of the *zipa*, from the mounts of Bosa, the wheat fields of Mosquera and Madrid, the paths coming down from La Mesa de Juan Díaz, and from the farm lands of Subachoque and Tenjo. Most of them have not slept, expecting their grand day. All these pilgrims merge at a field which bears the name of Saint Joseph, as a memorial to Jesus' putative father, as though it would have been predicted that one day, His Vicar on earth would arrive at this spot.
>
> In this field, beside the symbolic cross that points to the way which the Pontiff will traverse, stands a tree, a gift of the earth from which symbolically hang all the fruits of the tropics. On its branches merge the mandarin orange and the lemon, the apple and the pineapple, the custard apple and the tassel of corn, everything that feeds and sweetens life.
>
> The field, green under the sunlight, has now turned into a sea, a huge human sea. These are the Lord's sheep ... a sea where the sucklings are the foam. This immense carpet of human heads is adorned with all the joyful colors. And the green has faded before the multi-colored festive clothing. A huge helicopter can be seen at the horizon. As it comes nearer, the sea becomes white. Handkerchiefs are waved just like the foam of the sea. The Pontiff gets down,

The Montinian Church

welcomed by the unanimous emotion revealed by the handkerchiefs and the thousands of hailing arms.

So was this unique meeting planned with the peasants of America. They had expected millions, but only a few thousand showed up. Besides the peasants, and in larger numbers, were the "pilgrims," as we foreigners were called at Bogotá. We had gone to honor Christ in the divine Eucharist, but were faced with a show that looked like a mass meeting.

The speech which the Pope gave began as follows:

> Hail, Colombian peasants! Hail, workers of the Latin American land! Peace and blessing to all, in the name of Jesus Christ, our Lord and Savior!
> This meeting with you is one of the *most longed-for and beautiful events of our trip, one of the most intimate and meaningful occurrences of our apostolic and Pontifical ministry.*

This introductory salutation, a really unusual one to be uttered by a Pontiff, reveals to us the true aims of Pope Montini in his trip to Latin America. This is the top event of his journey, which is evidently full of shades of demagoguery. He stands before all Colombian and Latin American peasants. His apostolic imagination saw it so and felt that the moment had come to raise the banner of redemption among them. As a matter of fact, it was not so. Generously stretching figures, less than fifty thousand peasants gathered together at St. Joseph's field, for we "pilgrims," the mere spectators who did not number even a hundred and fifty thousand people, were by then the majority.

To Paul VI, that meeting with the peasants was one of the "most intimate and meaningful" of his apostolic and Pontifical ministry. Why? Because he was opening a program worked out at the Vatican laboratories, with the advice of the Conciliar "experts," the "new wave" theologians, the Jesuits, and the Jews. He was fulfilling the specific goal of his Pontificate, overthrowing the old structures, awakening the lethargic crowds, changing the old mentality and the preposterous triumphalism of the pre-Conciliar Church in the immense territories of Latin America and the Third World and among the underdeveloped peoples who are called to be the future of the world and the Church. Yes, that was not *one* of the most beautiful moments, but *the* most beautiful moment of Paul VI's journey, the most intimate and significant moment of his apostolic and Pontifical ministry. He was fulfilling the directives of the mafia, breeding the ambitions of the working classes, and paving the way for the guerilla militiamen to assault the pinnacles of power. In those moments, Paul VI was about to state the revolutionary doctrine of the *Populorum Progressio* through a harangue.

The Pope continued:

Pope Paul VI and the Peasants

We have come to Bogotá to honor Jesus in the Eucharistic Mystery, and feel fully joyful to have had the chance to do so. Now we are celebrating the presence of the Lord among us, amid the Church and the world, in you. You are a sign, an image, a mystery of Christ's presence. The Sacrament of the Eucharist gives us His hidden presence as alive and real. You too are a sacrament, in other words, a holy image of the Lord in the world, a reflection that represents and does not conceal His human and divine face. We remind you what a great and wise bishop, Bossuet, said about "the eminent dignity of the poor" (Cf. Bossuet: *De l'éminente dignité des pauvres*). The whole Tradition of the Church acknowledges Christ's sacrament in the poor, not as identical to the essence of the Eucharist, but in perfect analogical and mystical coincidence with it. In addition, Jesus Himself told it to us in a solemn page of the Gospel, where He proclaims that each suffering, hungry, sick, unfortunate person, anyone who needs understanding and help, is He, as though He Himself were this wretch, in accordance with Christ's mysterious and mighty sociology and humanism (Cf. Matt. 25:35 ff).

The pretext of the Paulian journey was the International Eucharistic Congress, but the goal was to get to Saint Joseph's field to joyfully celebrate the Lord's presence among the Latin American peasants, "amid the Church and the world...." The Latin American peasants are "a sign, an image, a mystery of Christ's presence." Why a "sign," "an image," "a mystery of Christ's presence?" Why the peasants and only the peasants? Paul VI's dialectics find the analogy and seek to establish his thought upon Holy Writ, the divine Master's very words. The Eucharist shows us Christ's hidden presence. We do not see Him with the body's eyes, though we do believe in His divine words: "*Quod non capis, quod non vides—animosa praestat fides, praeter rerum ordinem*" ("What you do not understand, what you do not see, the spirited faith causes you to accept, against the very laws of nature."). But there is another presence of Christ—in the assembly, in the people, in the American peasants. It is this peculiar presence that the Pontiff wants to celebrate, amid the Church and the world. In a way, this visible and apparent "presence" overrules the hidden, disguised Eucharistic "presence." That is why Bossuet devotes a paper to praise "the eminent dignity of the poor."

To repeat from Paul VI's words, the Church's Tradition "acknowledges Christ's sacrament in the poor [and only in the poor], not as identical to the essence of the Eucharist, but in perfect analogical and mystical coincidence with it." This means, according to the Pontiff, that there is a perfect analogical and mystical coincidence between the Eucharist and the poor. From this, two consequences arise: first, that the poor, just because they are poor, even though they may have all sorts of vices, represent Christ and are a sign, an image, and a mystery of Christ's presence. Hence poverty is, in itself, a manifestation of the presence of Christ. The second logical consequence of this affirmation is that we, far from fighting poverty, must foster it, just as we foster the Eucharistic life, Christ's real presence in the Eucharist. Though the program change of structures and fair distribution of wealth might have entailed great inconvenience and great danger on other grounds, it must not be rejected because of this, but because it comes to eliminate poverty among us, which is the "analogical and mystical" correspondence of the Eucharist, a sign, an image, a mystery of the Lord's presence among us.

Saint Matthew as quoted by Paul VI, does not say that Christ will say on the last day that each suffering, hungry, sick, unfortunate person or anyone who needs understanding and help, is Christ, but that He will receive the works of mercy which anyone does for the poor because of love for Him, as if made to Christ Himself. If this is Jesus Christ's "mysterious and mighty sociology," if this is His humanism of which the Pontiff speaks, let it be, but these phrases are not too accurate or Christian. We must not forget that Jesus Christ is neither a sociologist or a humanist, that His kingdom does not belong to this world, and that the divine Master came to teach us, with His life and example, the voluntary giving up of earthly goods, both with respect to the rich and to the poor. Were the Gospel merely sociology and integral humanism, it would be powerless in the Communist paradise.

The Pope continued:

> Most beloved children, you are Christ to us, and we, who are formidably lucky to be His Vicar in the Magisterium of the truth revealed by Him and the ministry of the whole Catholic Church, want to discover Christ as revived and suffering in you. We have not come to receive your filial acclamations, though they are always pleasing and moving, but to honor the Lord in your persons. [We have come] to bow before you and tell you that the love which the risen Christ demanded three times from Peter (John 21:15 ff) . . . we render to Him in you yourselves.

The Pope confessed, before that heterogeneous crowd, the goal of his trip, which was not exactly the Eucharist: "We have . . . come . . . to honor the Lord in your persons." This is John Baptist Montini's religion: integral humanism, social integration, and the equalizing of the underdeveloped countries with the rich and mighty nations. Thus does the Pontiff honor the Lord. The love which Christ demanded from Peter before making him the promised primate, he renders to the Latin American peasants, because to Paul VI, they are Christ.

The Pope said further:

> We love you as a shepherd, sharing your indigence, being responsible for your guidance and looking after your welfare and salvation. We love you with a

Pope Paul VI and the Peasants

feeling of predilection, and along with us—remember it well and bear it always in mind—the holy Catholic Church loves you.

What kind of welfare and salvation is it that Paul VI seeks and wants for the poor, the indigent, and the suffering? The goal of Jesus Christ, in setting up His Church, was in no way intended to establish the equality of the revolution, the equality of the guillotine, or the brotherhood of the encyclopedia[13] and the synagogue. He established His kingdom to seek His Father's glory and the salvation of souls through it. He instituted Peter's primacy so that it might be the foundation of His Church, but neither the Church nor the primate should have earthly things as an aim. Neither the Pope nor the Church must have predilections based upon the larger or smaller amount of goods which various men or people have, but upon the larger or smaller fidelity with which they respond to God's call. Paul VI reached the height of his demagoguery and provoked fratricidal fighting when he showed nonconformity in formally denouncing those who have something, as shown in the following portion of his speech:

> We know that, for many of you, the conditions of your existence are conditions of misery, and at times, insufficient to meet the regular needs of human life. You are listening to us quietly, but we can hear the cry of your suffering and that of the largest segment of mankind (Vatican Council II, Const.; *Gaudium et Spes*, No. 88). We cannot ignore you; we want to make common cause with you, the lowly, poor people, for this is the good cause. We know that economic and social development has been unfair in this large continent of Latin America, and that, while it has benefited those who fostered it in the beginning, the bulk of the native population has almost always been abandoned to an ignoble standard of living, and sometimes exploited and harshly treated. We know that today you realize the inferiority of your social and cultural condition, and are impatient to attain a fairer distribution of goods and a more proper recognition of the importance you deserve (for you are so numerous) and the position that belongs to you in society. We do believe you have some knowledge of how the Church has supported you: the Popes, our predecessors, with their social encyclicals, have vindicated your cause (Cf. *Mater et Magistra*, A.A.S., 1961, pp. 422 ff), and the ecumenical council has defended it (*Lumen Gentium*, No. 8; *Gaudium et Spes*, No. 88). We ourselves have sponsored your cause in the encyclical, *On the Peoples' Progress*.

U ndoubtedly, the standard of living is not the same for all the inhabitants of Latin America, for as said before, neither their ethnic conditions, their cultures, nor their ways of life are the same. To speak as Paul VI did, however, is to ignore the real condition of our young people, to judge and interpret Latin

America with European criteria, and above all, with Communist criteria. Even if the demagogical work of the bishops, priests, and progressivist laymen engaged in subversion were extremely successful, the only results we could expect would be bloodshed, destruction, paralysis, and ruin of enterprise, sources of production, and work. The social evolution of our people requires more time, more silent and self-denying work, more preparation, better knowledge of our environment, more sincerity, and less demagoguery. By stirring the passions of our underdeveloped people, or better said, of the classes in the process of progressive development, we will just provoke a violent crisis which will make us retreat on the road of real progress.

It is not true, as Paul VI says, that in Latin America economic and social development has profited only those who promoted it. Neither is it true that this development has ignored the bulk of the native population, almost always abandoned to an ignoble living standard and sometimes exploited and harshly treated. It is obvious that the civilizing, Christianizing process has been slow, for as said before, it necessarily takes time. In Mexico, to give a specific example, the process of improvement and recovery of the condition of the Indian and poor classes has never been interrupted. If there were no documents, and there are many eloquent ones, the buildings alone would give evidence of the civilizing work of Spain and the Church in our fatherland. Not everywhere were the same results achieved, because the condition of the natives was not the same. Never could we compare the Tarahumara Indians, a nomadic tribe addicted to hereditary vices, with other tribes living in our territory before the conquest. However, even these Tarahumara Indians are slowly, but continually and unceasingly, developing.

Misery is not always a result of oppression and plunder, as modern demagogues believe. Work is the law of life. When an individual does not work because his laziness, vice, or own will opposes work, he has no right to complain about his misery or seek his personal or familial progress through guerilla warfare, mugging, robbery, or crime. There are poor people who become rich through work, and there are rich people who become beggars through the madness of their dishonesty, extravagance, and useless lives. In the countries enslaved by Communism, the law of work is rigid, inhuman, and often cruel.

Paul VI is fervently devout to democracy. To him it is quantity, not quality, that counts. That is why he told the peasants that they were the majority and therefore deserved a better position in society. According to this principle, it is the majority which has to get its way and rule the minority, even though the latter may be the most skilled and capable individuals. In a factory, the workers outnumber the bosses; thus, it is they, the workers, who should rule the enterprise.

It is not the peasants who have realized the inferiority of their social and cultural condition. It is not they who are eager to attain a fairer allocation of material goods. From the very moment an individual wants to progress—through legitimate means, of course—he has advanced a step toward the improvement of his condition. What is evil is to agitate those poor, naive people who lack human roots, and use them as easy tools of the guerilla movements.

Then the Pontiff went on to say:

> But today, the problem has become more serious, for you have become conscious of your needs and suffering, and, like many other people in the world, you cannot tolerate that these conditions last forever, without applying a valuable remedy. We wonder: what can we do for you, after having spoken on your behalf? You know we do not have direct jurisdiction in these secular affairs, neither do we have the means and enough authority to act in this field.

Indeed the problem has become more serious, but this is not precisely because the peasants had become more conscious of their needs and suffering, but because all over the world, the apostolate of social justice has been intensified. The "new wave" priests have turned the chair of God's word into a tribune for agitation, demagoguery, and subversion. The Jesuits, betraying the spirit of their Society and the letter of their constitution, have forsaken the old ruling classes to devote themselves to the spread of this new gospel, aiding the wretched to become conscious of their economic, social, and cultural inferiority, thus fostering nonconformity and discontentedness, as a necessary prelude for the complete change of all structures, so designed as to expedite the happy coming of Communizing socialism. But without violence . . . understood?

Paul VI realizes it is not his business to act in the field of secular affairs or economic subjects, nor to apply a valuable remedy to the many individual, familial, and social problems afflicting this poor segment of mankind. He has no jurisdiction, but he has displayed so much activity in these subjects that it appears he is more concerned about earthly things than he is about the eternal. The friends of this Pontiff have availed themselves of his papal authority to succeed, on behalf of *aggiornamento*, "progress," "peace," and "integral humanism" in bringing about the necessary "change of structures," in order to quickly establish Communism in all countries, through socialization, absorbing statism, and dictatorship under cover of democracy, as a necessary step to impose a world government. By abandoning the ruling classes, private enterprise, capitalism, and all those who have some private property; by joining the party of the disinherited, arousing their eagerness, and letting them realize they are the victims of oppression and exploitation; and by turning Christ's Gospel into the new gospel of revolution, Paul VI has most efficiently contributed to the spread and consolidation of Communizing socialism all over the world. Rather than religious meaning, his trips have had an obvious political message. They are aimed at accelerating world socialization.

The Montinian Church

Now let us see what he promises the Latin American peasants:

1. We will go on defending your cause. We are able to affirm and confirm the principles upon which practical solutions depend. We will continue to proclaim your human and Christian dignity. Your existence is of first-rate value. Your persons are sacred. Your pertinence to the human family must be recognized without discrimination on a basis of brotherhood. Even accepting the existence of a hierarchical and organic order in the social system, this brotherhood must be recognized as a matter of fact, both in the economic field, with particular attention to fair payment, convenient lodging, basic education and health services, and in the field of civil rights and a progressive share of the benefits and responsibilities of the social order.

The Pontiff, notwithstanding his lack of means and authority to effectively intervene in this field, engages himself publicly and solemnly to defend the Latin American peasants and their cause against the so-called exploitation and nefarious oppression of which they are victims. By saying this, he poses the problem on the basis of struggle between antagonistic fields. "We will go on defending your cause." Since there is defense, there must be oppression and exploitation. On whose part? Of those who have: the businessmen, the landlords, the rich. Our peasants and poor classes, who are not too sophisticated, in listening to the Pope who proclaims himself as their defender, feel that they are victims of cruelty and injustice. As a practical result, they realize they have to deprive those who have, of their property. Private property is theft. Institutional violence can be defeated only by guerilla violence. It is not the principles, but the consequences of these principles, which will bring about mass liberation. The masses will become owners and rulers while the rich and mighty people will either be carried to their graves or become wretches and slaves.

It surprises me, that in these times of de-sacralization of all persons and things that we used to deem holy, the Pontiff sacralizes the peasants and the poor, just because they are not rich. "Your persons are sacred." I believe that, to Catholicism, the person of both the poor and the rich is sacred, for both are God's creatures, God's children, and both are destined for the same goal. Neither the nature nor the rights and obligations of man are modified by his having or not having earthly goods. In the Church's history we find rich saints, as well as very saintly or perverse poor.

The achievements which the civil authorites and social aid have facilitated for those who work are good. It would be ideal that such achievements not hurt other people's legitimate interests or become a pretext to curtail businessmen's legitimate rights. As often happens in human affairs, some government officers in charge of administering such benefits for the poor classes abuse their positions and profit from the aid which the government provides the workers. However, abuse on the part of private persons is unable to corrupt the good intentions of those who enacted good statutes.

The Pope continues:

> 2. We will go on exposing unjust economic inequality between rich and poor, as well as governmental and administrative abuse against you and the community. We will go on encouraging the moves and projects of responsible agencies, international entities, and affluent countries on behalf of countries in the process of development. In this concern, we are happy that, in lucky coincidence with the grand Eucharistic Congress, new and organic projects are being studied, for the sake of the working classes, especially for you rural peasants! And as far as this is concerned, we encourage all governments of Latin America and other continents, as well as the ruling and affluent classes, to go on using wide and brave perspectives to face the necessary reforms that ensure a fairer and more efficient social order, involving progressive advantages for the less privileged classes, and fairer taxation for the affluent classes, particularly those people who, owning plantations, are unable to make them more fruitful and productive or, being able to do so, enjoy the fruits for their exclusive benefit, and for those persons who, with little or no effort, realize excessive profits or collect considerable fees.

The first sentence of this second point of Pope Montini's social program is a real declaration of war: "We will go on exposing unjust economic inequality between rich and poor . . . ." Does Paul VI believe that all economic inequality is unjust? Or what are, in his mind, those inequalities that deserve the epithet *malignatis naturae*? Is his ambiguous denunciation an efficient way to attain equilibrium? Or on the contrary, would it not rather be self-defeating and increase nonconformity, thus provoking the conditions for violent and destructive reactions? Can we achieve social justice while ignoring and violating commutative justice?

Paul VI feels he is the judge of every public administrative authority: "We will go on exposing . . . governmental and administrative abuse against you and the community." A power within another power. "We will go on encouraging the moves and projects of responsible agencies, international entities, and affluent countries on behalf of countries in the process of development." Here we find the Pope and the Vatican, who absolutely disregard the most grave problems that the convenient administration of the Church requires, totally devoted to judging governments; and to encouraging international entities (even though they are managed by stubborn enemies of the Church) and affluent countries, in accordance with the proclamations of *Populorum Progressio*, to share their huge resources with the underdeveloped countries, not as loans, but as generous gifts. Furthermore, since Pontifical authority no longer has the power and influence of yore, Paul VI feels he needs to be backed by the international power of the traditional enemies of the Church. Paul VI has pledged the freedom of the Church, the authenticity of its Magisterium, the Catholic liturgy, the very revealed truth and the immutable and universal morality of the natural law, in exchange for his being accepted in the group of those who seek to rule the world.

The Pope continues:

> 3. Likewise, we will go on sponsoring the cause of those people who need fraternal help, in order that other peoples, who have larger wealth they do not always use properly, be generous in their gifts, do not hurt the dignity and liberty of the beneficiaries, and open easier ways to trade, on behalf of nations who still lack adequate development. As far as we are concerned, we shall engage the means at our disposal to support this effort designed to give wealth its primary function, namely: to serve man, not only in a private and local level, but in a wider, international field, thus stopping the easy and selfish enjoyment thereof or its being devoted to superfluous expenditures or exaggerated and dangerous armaments.

What will the nature be of these generous gifts which Paul VI demands from the rich on behalf of the poor? Will they be interest loans or accommodations without interest? Will they be gifts? Will they consist of technical assistance? In his *Populorum Progressio*, the Pontiff included the same ambiguous, unrealizable statement. The fact that some nations have plenty of wealth or use it improperly does not mean they should feel like divine Providence or a charitable institution. Why is it that the Pontiff fails to expose the international octopus that has impoverished the people and paralyzed their progress? Why does he not speak about the deceitful economic system that, based on pieces of paper, has drained all the resources of many countries and appropriated all their sources of production? Paul VI's good wishes and the means at his disposal will be of little use, particularly at the international level, in relieving the indigence of the underdeveloped Third World people, as long as the Jewish mafia continues to impoverish the world.

We come back to Pope Paul VI:

> 4. To the extent we are able to, we will try to set the example and revive the Church's best tradition of disinterestedness, generosity, and service, calling more and more each time upon that spirit of poverty which the divine Master preached to us and of which the ecumenical council has reminded us in an authoritative manner (*Lumen Gentium*, No. 8; *Gaudium et Spes*, No. 88).

Pope Paul VI and the Peasants

The post-Conciliar Church, or rather the people of the post-Conciliar Church, boast of their being "the Church of the poor." However, I believe there have been few times when so much money has been spent in the Church. Money is spent for many things: the adaptation of the temples to the new liturgy; the replacement of our altars by the Anglican table; the destruction of many artistic treasures; the frequent journeys of lecturers, leaders, and prelates who meet at episcopal conferences; the establishment of many new bureaus which each day the new and more numerous agencies and secretariats require; the upkeep of the growing bureaucracy that keeps the Conciliar spirit standing with its style of secularized clothing, private cars, leisure-time spent at cinemas, nightclubs, and holiday trips to tourist spots; the propaganda, mail, and secret missions. All of these take money, much money, which is drawn out of tithes, special collections, gifts from rich people and plentiful aid from *Misereor, Caritas*, and other remote-controlled agencies which dispense money that Germany, the United States, and other wealthy countries generously send us.

Just think of the money spent in the papal trips of pastoral solicitude! This will help us realize that within the limits of his economic means, Paul VI has revived the Church's best traditions of disinterestedness, generosity, service, and poverty! The total transformation of the Church demands huge expenditures which have to be taken from gullible believers, the treasures of the temples, and the secret aid of those who used to be our enemies and are now our most faithful friends: the Jews and their banks.

Some bishops and priests have taken the term, "the Church of the poor," very seriously. They have taken off their pastoral rings, which normally did not cost too much; they have given up their episcopal vestments, which, no doubt, helped them preserve their authority among the believers; they have relinquished their so-called "episcopal palaces," which were just decent accommodations for those who, due to their positions, were heads and chiefs of the Church. Others, on the contrary, do not seem to have taken the mandate too seriously, for they are still exhibiting their purple, their precious pastoral rings, and their impeccable vestments, designed abroad or by the best tailors in the country. Neither do they quit their palaces, but enrich them with new gifts which they get from those who want to keep their protection and aid.

On the other hand, one has to bear in mind what the evangelical doctrine says about poverty, so as not to confound appearances with reality. The reality of poverty does not consist of not having, but of not sticking to what one has. Though it appears to be contradictory, there are rich, very rich poor people, and also very poor rich people. There are poor people who spend their lives feeding their ambitions and their unlimited covetousness. The more they have, the more they want. Likewise there are rich people who, being in a position to enjoy the luxury and the pleasure which richness can provide, nevertheless, live modestly, do good liberally and unostentatiously, and are the unknown providers for all the good which the people of the Church do.

The Society of Jesus had sumptuous colleges, magnificent and very rich temples, superb libraries, modern research laboratories, astronomical and seismological observatories, but nevertheless, the Society of Jesus (I can say this accurately) definitely lived in the spirit of poverty. This was a personal, silent, and concealed poverty, which counts in God's eyes. What is the use of living in a golden cage, when nothing of what surrounds them belongs to them, when secretly they sacrifice even what their superiors give them, in order to imitate Christ, who lived as a pauper and died in utmost poverty? Now in exchange, the Jesuits quit their splendid colleges, their apparently ostentatious lodgings, to hire apartments (as we say in Mexico) or "flats" (as Spaniards would say), where they live without the restrictions and surveillance of the communal life. They have private cars, they spend money on countless trips, go to the movies and places of secular entertainment, and wear different clothes, so as to appear, as it suits them, either as potentates and bankers, or as laborers and office clerks. This is the Church of the poor!

The Pope continued:

> 5. Most beloved children, allow us to also announce to you the beatitude that belongs to you, the beatitude of evangelical poverty. Let us remind you that, although we strive by all means to alleviate your suffering and to provide more abundant and easier bread, we remind you that "Man does not live by bread alone" (Matt. 4:4), and that we all need another bread, that of the soul, which is to say, that of religion and faith, that of the divine Word and grace. And let us tell you something else: your condition as humble people is more efficacious for attaining the kingdom of Heaven, in other words, the supreme and everlasting good of life, if it is borne with the patience and hope of Christ.

Finally the Church's indefectible voice spoke! The demagoguery finally subsided, and in its place the Word of God resounds: "Blessed are the poor in spirit, for theirs is the kingdom of heaven." The Church cannot do anything better or more efficient to remedy the misery of the world, of those who suffer and weep and lack earthly goods, than to remind them that "the sufferings of the present life cannot be compared with the everlasting glory that has been promised to us."

Do we or do we not believe in the words revealed by God? Christian charity for love of Christ would be able to relieve some of these sufferings, but would never be able to eliminate them. Paul VI's speech at this memorable meeting with the peasants and his elaborate words were but beautiful promises, flattering meaningless words. The sole constructive thing Paul VI included in this demagogic speech of his was his warning to the poor that undergoing poverty is the greatest treasure, for it allows them to buy the kingdom of

Heaven. This does not mean we believe one must not work for the secular improvement of the condition of the poor classes. That *has* to be done, but without demagoguery and realistically, without rushing. It *has* to be done, but without thinking we shall be able to suppress poverty in the world completely, without aiming at plundering those who are not poor, without reversing life's values, and without turning the Gospel of the justice of God's kingdom into the gospel of social justice.

The Pontiff concludes:

> Finally, let us encourage you not to trust violence or revolution. Such an approach is opposite to the Christian spirit and can also delay, instead of foster, the social level to which you legitimately aspire. Endeavor instead to second the moves that favor your education, for instance, that of the Popular Cultural Action. Try to be united and organized under the Christian sign, and trained to modernize the methods of your rural work, love your fields and appraise the human, economic, and civil functions you exercise as laborers of the land.
>
> Receive our apostolic blessing! It is for you, peasants of Colombia, of Latin America, for all of you workers of the field in the whole world. May it descend upon your persons, upon your families, upon your children, your young, your old, and your sick. May it descend upon your houses, upon your crops, and upon all those who love and aid you. May it descend full of consolation and grace, by virtue of Jesus, whom we represent here in the name of the Father, and the Son, and the Holy Spirit.

I think Paul VI's final admonition was amended or added to at Bogotá, right on the eve of the meeting. According to some people, the manifesto of the Mexican delegation, undersigned by Dr. Guerrero, Dr. Rodríguez, and Dr. Gasca, deeply impressed the Pontiff, who is sensitive and knows perfectly how to moderate his words. He did not advocate violence or revolution, for this approach is anti-Christian, but rather, he advocated education, training, and organization. Don Helder Cámara had said it before: the preparation of a people for a revolution takes some fifteen or twenty years. On the other hand, one must not be disappointed. Let us remember Paul VI's dialectical spirit: on this occasion, he set the thesis. LAMEC will cautiously establish the antithesis, and the synthesis will be made by the Jesuits and the leaders of the eminent and indispensable subversion.

This speech by Paul VI within the framework of an International Eucharistic Congress has no meaning. It is the indisputable evidence of that for which the Congress was the *pretext*, but the *goal* was the canonization, and the public and solemn ratification, of the revolutionary doctrine of the *Populorum Progressio* which alludes, albeit discreetly, to violence and revolution as the indispensable means for the "changes of structures." Paul VI lit the fuse of

The Montinian Church

the powder keg of Latin America. His Apostolic Blessings were also extended to the guerrillas.

(Due to a printer's error, page 422 was omitted from the book.)

Chapter XXVIII

POPE PAUL VI, HERESY, AND PAPAL SUCCESSION AND INFALLIBILITY

We had stopped at the point progressivism was enjoying its success at that meeting where Paul VI, making a public and solemn profession of his proletarian and classic faith, started the structural change in all of Latin America. From then on, those who opposed it would commit the crime of insubordination to Pontifical authority.

ABBÉ DULAC EXPOSES POPE MONTINI

Now I will quote a recent opinion *on the Pope of the revolution* by the Abbé Raymond Dulac, an illustrious French theologian who attended the Council where, using his indisputable wisdom and ardent zeal for the Church, he tried to stop the successful subversion. In the *Courrier de Rome* (France), Fr. Dulac wrote as follows:

> *The Pope-Decreed Exile of the old Cardinals is the Culminating Point of a Disastrous Pontificate.* The proscription of 25 cardinals, who were suddenly excluded from any future conclave by a personal *Moto Proprio* by Paul VI, will be recorded by Catholicism as the culmination of a disastrous Pontificate. Catholic historians will divide this period of the Church into two parts: "before" and "after" Paul VI's *Moto Proprio*. No doubt acts more serious than this one have taken place during his reign, but no other act has matched it as to violence, cynicism, and cruelty. We have seen the Holy See's scandalous inertia in the presence of the Dutch schism, the demolition of the Holy Office, the guardian of orthodoxy, the abolution of the anti-Modernist oath, the authorization of an Italian edition of the heretical Dutch Catechism, the Pope's visit to the congress of the World Council of Churches, the destruction of liturgical treasures, the Lutheranization of the Mass, the public homage to Luther, the destruction of religious and clerical life, and the continued appointment of liberal or progressivist bishops to sees forced into vacancy by the maneuvering of the Holy See. Any of these acts would suffice to dishonor a Pontificate. We, the most tenacious defenders and loyal supporters of Rome's authority, could not help closing our eyes each time one of these unjustified acts occurred. All of them

were made under cover of "episcopal collegiality," but any of these facts would have sufficed to show us the existence of a wisely masterminded *plan* which has been carefully worked out with admirable persistence.

What is this plan? It is that of setting up the Church of man, the one that can be adapted to what the Superior General of the Brothers of Christian Schools dares to call, *"the post-Christian age,"* a Church without defined dogmas, a mixed religion whose morality will be debased into anthropology, whose authority will be "service," and whose clergymen will be a society of cultural activists.... The Pope has no constitutional power to deprive the prelates over eighty *of their right of being the electors of the new Pontiff*.... Why is it that this *Moto Proprio* is applicable only to future cardinals? Why does it not have a retroactive effect? Because what was endeavored with this document was to prevent just such cardinals as Ottaviani, Tisserant, Arriba y Castro, and a dozen others from entering the new conclave. It was against these cardinals and their weight in a future conclave that the document created the category of the "octogenarians." Through it, Paul VI practically suppressed the people involved. Why? Just a few weeks before, Paul VI had promised venerable Cardinal Arriba that he would remain in the rule of his see, and the same certainty had been given to Cardinal Ottaviani. What was the cause for that sudden contradiction? It was that Montini wants to perpetuate himself through his successor. Who will he be? Will he be the vicious Alfrink, the egoist Suenens, the tireless revolutionary Helder Cámara, or the radical Villot? Whoever he may be, from now on we know that the new Pope will be elected by the cardinals and conclave dominated by Paul VI.

THE VATICAN SUPPRESSES THE CONCEPT OF HERESY

We offer a new light to convince those who persist in believing in the person, the doctrine, and the deeds of the present Pontiff. The word "heresy" must no longer be used in the Catholic Church. Any assassin of the Faith may now destroy it safely, without any censorship. This new audacity is based on the principle that the most efficient way of preventing crime is to make all crimes legal. The term "heresy," says Msgr. G. Tomko, a member of the Congregation for the Doctrine of the Faith (the former Holy Office), will no longer be used. He affirmed that his Congregation will no longer excommunicate anyone who is found to be in error. The worst penalty will be to bar the guilty ones from teaching positions, as well as a statement by the Vatican that the one who has so deviated is "mistaken."

Such is the pattern for stubborn heretics who may continue to remain within the bosom of the Church and receive the Sacraments and a Christian burial in Catholic churchyards. From now on, it will be said just that they are wrong, and, if they are stubborn, they will be prevented from teaching but not from writing. Their books will go on circulating in Catholic circles, seminaries, and convents, surrounded by the magic propaganda of their having been censored by the Vatican. To what have we come?

CARDINAL WILLEBRANDS AND PONTIFICAL INFALLIBILITY

Cardinal Willebrands, whom our readers already know, has just come to Houston to attend the opening of a center for ecumenical worship, the Rothko Chapel of the Institute of Religion and Human Development. In his statements to the press (*The Houston Post*, Feb. 28, 1971), the Secretary of the Vatican Secretariat for Unity said that "the doctrine of the infallibility is a subject that must be analyzed again in the light of the dialogue for Church unity. The claim that the Pope cannot err in certain definite statements was officially approved at Vatican Council I in 1869. The present ecumenical discussions may submit the Council's phraseology to a more careful study." He refused to comment, however, on a recent book by the controversial Catholic intellectual, Hans Küng, who pointed out that the doctrine of infallibility is the biggest obstacle for the Protestants, who otherwise might seek more unity with Rome. Hans Küng says that papal infallibility "cannot be directly proven from Holy Writ, and, in the past, has often been badly misunderstood." His recent paper on this doctrine aroused serious criticism on the part of many Catholic intellectuals. Willebrands, however, refused to make any comment because, as he said, Küng is a personal friend of his.

Willebrands showed an optimistic mood regarding progress in dialogue with groups of people of different religions who were represented in record numbers at Vatican Council II, which started in 1962. Willebrands said:

> The problem consisted in how to continue the good relationships which the Council had started, since the representatives of other religions to the Council did not come from the same place.
>
> But it was easier than I thought. We are on the eve of harvesting the first fruits of the dialogue being carried on in several nations.... Besides the problems of authority which papal infallibility involves, there remain the doctrines on the Church and the Sacraments as subjects for discussion and dialogue between Catholics and Protestants. The position of the Roman Catholic Church has traditionally put too much emphasis on the role of the clergy. Recent discussions on the priesthood and a growing emphasis on the importance of the laity will be the climax next fall, during the synod of bishops in Rome.

This is Bea's and Willebrands' "ecumenism," endorsed by Paul VI's silence and authority, for Bea was, and Willebrands is, a head of a Vatican

The Montinian Church

Secretariat, that is, a new congregation of the Roman curia. We shall debate all the dogmas of the Church and we shall deny them, silence them, and disguise them, in order to please the "separated brethren." And to facilitate ecumenical unity, we shall gradually eliminate the Catholic priesthood, up to the top, in Paul VI's next synod, which will take place in the fall of this year. Paul VI is aware, and cannot ignore what is being said in the Church, especially when it is cardinals and heads of Vatican Secretariats who speak. Paul VI, then, knows that the dogmas on the primate and Pontifical infallibility have to be reformulated, and that the "full-time workers," the old priests of the Church, have to be suppressed in order to put laymen in their places.

Chapter XXIX

PAUL VI, LAMEC, AND THE NEW THEOLOGIANS

Expecting a homily rather than a speech, we found ourselves not at the field of San José de Mosquera, at the political-religious event of Pope Paul VI's meeting with the representatives of the peasants, but at the Eucharistic shrine, at a Mass the Pope was about to celebrate.

DISCOURSE OF THE POPE AT THE SHRINE OF THE CONGRESS

Paul VI did not want to lose the opportunity to insist, *oportune et importune* as Saint Paul would say, on the issue of structural change in Latin America, the fulfillment of his program as stated in *Populorum Progressio*.

I will not quote the Pope's whole speech, but just some important parts, the ones that serve particularly to cast some light on the Pontiff's behavior in Colombia:

Latin America's Problems

We ... know that human and secular realities, at the moment that the Pope has come to visit Latin America for the first time, have undergone profound and truly historical crises involving many aspects of grave concern.

May the Pope ignore this ferment? Would not one of the goals of this journey have failed, should he have returned to Rome without having faced the central issue of the problem that aroused so much uneasiness?

Many, particularly young people, insist on the need for urgent change of social structures, which, in their mind, are in the way of implementation of truly just conditions for individuals and communities. And some people find that Latin America's essential problem cannot be solved except with violence.

Using the same loyalty that makes us feel that these theories and practices are frequently caused by noble impulses of justice and solidarity, we must stress that violence is neither evangelical nor Christian, and brisk or violent structural changes would be deceitful, ineffectual in themselves, and certainly not consistent with man's dignity. The dignity of man demands that the necessary transformations in social structures be carried on from within society through adequate conscientization, preparation, and effective participation of everyone in the society. Today's ignorance and life conditions, at times sub-human, may make this very difficult.

Here we have the Pontiff again, striving to change the structures in all of Latin America. One of the goals of his journey, he confesses, and perhaps the main goal, was that of facing the central issue of the social problem arousing so much uneasiness in Latin America. But I wonder, who has sown discontentedness and nonconformity? Masonry and Communism are not aboriginal Latin American plants. They were imported by their creators to imperceptibly destroy the very essence of our nationality.

Recently (who could have forecast it?) the agitation caused by Fr. Lombardini, S.J., Fr. Arrupe, and the Provincial Fathers of the Latin American Assistances have been most efficient subversive factors, not only due to the personal efforts of the above-named persons and the impulse they gave the members of that Order, but due to their example and their advice to other religious, even the most pious nuns, especially those devoted to teaching. Do we have a better example of activism than that set by the Ladies of the Sacred Heart and the Daughters of the Incarnate Word? They are already projecting the establishment of mixed high schools for students of both sexes; they go out freely, go to dinner with their families and friends, and have dropped all cautiousness as to their religious vows. They accept all kinds of pupils without restrictions, though, as far as I know, they still charge high tuition fees, since the "new wave" has enormously increased their expenditures, as the *aggiornamento* clothing has logically awakened their feminine vanity.

" . . . [T]he youth," said Paul VI, "find that Latin America's . . . problem cannot be solved except with violence." The Pontiff also feels that "these theories and practices are frequently caused by noble impulses of justice and solidarity. . . ." What he adds, as usual, is the counterweight, the antithesis of Montinian tactics and dialectics: "We must stress that violence is neither evangelical nor Christian. . . ." But who would be barred by this? If the ultimate cause is a noble impulse of justice and solidarity and if institutional violence can be defeated only by armed violence, it follows that the Gospel and Christianity have been "overruled" by a more human approach to society and the world. "Conscientization, preparation, and effective participation of everyone" are far-off things, unable to remedy the urgent and undeferrable needs of the people. A six-year program has to be implemented in a semester!

Pope Paul VI continues:

> As a result, in our mind, the key to solving the fundamental problem of Latin America consists of a twofold, simultaneous, harmonic, and mutually

beneficial effort: to reform social structures, but in a gradual way so that everybody can assimilate it and in such a way that, so to speak, it will be a result of the vast and patient work designed to foster the rise of the "human way" of the large majority of those who live today in Latin America. [We must] help everyone to become fully conscious of his own dignity, to develop his own responsibility within the community to which he belongs, and to become a valid element of economic, civic, and moral progress by his own will, without which any sudden social structural change would be a futile, ephemeral, and dangerous artifice.

This venture, as you well know, concretely consists of every activity able to promote the human being integrally and introduce him actively into the community—alphabetization, basic education, permanent education, professional training, formation of the civic and political conscience, and the methodical organization of the material services essential for the regular development of the individual and collective life in the modern age.

What can we think about the above ideas, stated by a Pope, included in the homily of a Mass during the celebration of a Eucharistic Congress? Not even a word about God, not a single idea about what constitutes the Christian life in its transcendence toward the everlasting. The Pontiff's isolated references to the Eucharist are good only to enhance his integral humanism, but alphabetization, basic education, permanent education, professional training, and the formation of a civic and political conscience by themselves do not help the elevation of the style of mankind for "the large majority of those who live today in Latin America" unless there is re-Christianization of society, family, and individuals. For man is a real man, not when he is highly educated or cultured, or has a high civic and political consciousness, but only when he walks along the path of the law of conscience, when, be he poor or rich, he knows how to give his life a *transcendental aim*.

Paul VI went on:

> Can we expect that this grave problem will also be adequately examined and understood by the light of the charity we are celebrating? Will you, dear children from Latin America, be able to draw the necessary and efficient force out of this Mystery, in order to give each one his due and urgent lot, so as to solve it? Yes, the Pope hopes so. The Pope has confidence in you.

Here you have one of the allusions which Paul VI made to the Congress and the Eucharistic Mystery, linked, of course, to the grand problem he intended to solve in Latin America. The Pope hopes and asks that the fruit of the Congress be the beginning of a complete transformation of structures, so as to solve the pressing social problem. Then the Pontiff gives special directions to the authorized representatives of all Latin American social categories:

> Continue with renewed enthusiasm and with all the means at our disposal in the struggle to realize and bring about all the goals mentioned before, goals and purposes we have already proclaimed to the world through the encyclical *Populorum Progressio*.

To the intellectuals, the Pope said:

> Now, let us say a special word to you students, scholars, and men of culture. It is necessary that your charity engage itself especially through thought, and that it have the thirst, humility, and bravery of truth. It is your special obligation to free yourselves and your intellectual world from unconditional support of commonplace phrases, mass culture, ideologies that fashion, or propaganda made easy or irresistible, and it is you who have to find the freedom to act as men and Christians in the truth, the sole thing that has the right to engage our minds. It belongs to you, of all people, to be apostles of truth.

In different circumstances, this message to the students and the intellectuals would have been a call to preserve the precious heritage of our Hispanic, Catholic, and Roman culture and civilization, the essence of our nationality, a condition of our progress, and a guarantee of our independence amid free peoples. Indisputably, Paul VI is right in warning our students and scholars not to let themselves be dominated by mass culture and fashionable ideology that, without our noticing it, enslaves us and makes us like lambs in a sheepfold. Only the truth has the right to engage our minds, and only the truth opens up the way to act freely as men and Christians. I cannot understand how Pope Montini, who proclaims these principles of everlasting life, has become the prey of the prevailing currents of progressivism and the mafia.

Should our intellectuals and our students proclaim themselves apostles of the truth, they do not need to look for it; I am speaking of the transcendental and eternal truth, since we have Christ, who is the Way, the Truth, and the Life.

To the workers, the Pope said:

> We want to tell you too, workers, what we feel is the way for you to display your charity, fed by the Faith and by Communion in Christ, the way that leads to an encounter with your companions in toil and in hope. This way is that of unity, that is, of association, not as a mere organizational structure or an instrument for collective submission in the hands of a few despotic, unappealing chiefs, but as a school of social conscience, and as a profession of solidarity, brotherhood, and a defense of common interests and a pledge to perform common duties. Your charity, therefore, must include force, the force of numbers and of social

dynamism, not the subversive force of revolution and violence. It must be the constructive force of a new, more human, order, wherein your legitimate wishes come true, and every economic and social factor merges into the justice of the common welfare. You should know that, in your effort toward this new and better order, the Church is, particularly for you workmen, Teacher and Mother.

Paul VI advises workers to display their charity "fed by the Faith and by Communion in Christ." This way leads to "an encounter with your companions in toil and in hope ..., unity, ... [and] association" (we should say *union*, not as an organizational structure or as "an instrument for collective submission in the hands of a few despotic, unappealing chiefs, but as a school of social conscience, and as a profession of solidarity, brotherhood, and a defense of common interests and a pledge to perform common duties"). It may be true that the labor organizations, the unions, the agrarian communities, the *ejidos* (common public lands) have, no doubt, the advantage and necessity of protecting the workers' legitimate rights, both in the field and in industry, but they are also dangerous. They are dangerous not only for society, when they become organisms of agitation and demagoguery as well as pawns in the contest of political strife, but also for the workers and peasants themselves in the internal quarrels that can arise among them. In this case, as the Pontiff says, they become instruments of collective submission in the hands of a few despotic, unappealing chiefs.

What can and must the Church do with respect to these labor problems? I feel that, besides the religious work itself, that of cultivating the workers and businessmen, the peasants and landlords, besides the spread of the social doctrine, which contains the basic principles based on the natural law, the Church and the ecclesiastics must avoid abandoning their transcendental mission to become apostles of social justice or propagandists of subversion. "[A] school of social conscience" is the term Paul VI uses. I believe that such a term is ambiguous and requires many distinctions and sub-distinctions to deserve being accepted. To begin with, the classification contained in the adjective "social," referring to the human conscience, is as equivocal as that of social "justice." No social justice exists without distributive justice, and no social conscience without moral conscience. Solidarity, union, brotherhood, the force of the number deprived of moral and religious principles, of clear consciousness of one's duties as well as one's rights, may exert a dangerous force that can seriously jeopardize social and national equilibrium.

The "new order" and the "new structures" are obsessing Paul VI and the post-Conciliar Church. How, when, and by whom will this transformation be implemented? They do not say it, but they hint it; it will be the beneficiaries of such changes: "the force of numbers and of social dynamism . . . ." Do not forget that " . . . in your effort toward this new and better order, the Church is, particularly for you workmen, Teacher and Mother." The allusion to John XXIII's encyclical is very meaningful, for it was this encyclical that paved the way for the post-Conciliar reformation. It was the first one to Christianize socialism and socialization, which the Magisterium used to condemn.

To the ruling classes, the Pope said:

> And to you, men of the ruling classes, what can we say? In what direction must the charity you also want to derive from the Eucharistic source stretch itself? Do not reject our word, though it seem paradoxical and hostile. It is the Lord's word, and we solicit your generosity. In other words, we ask you to withdraw yourselves from the immovability of your status, which can be or appear to be a privileged one, in order to serve those who need your wealth, your culture, and your authority. We might remind you of the spirit of evangelical poverty which breaks the ties of selfish ownership of earthly goods and encourages Christianity to arrange the economy and the power for the benefit of the community. You, lords of the world and children of the Church, must have the instinctive spirit of good that society needs so much. Let your ears and hearts be sensitive to the voices of those who ask for bread, attention, justice, more active participation in the ruling of society, and the attainment of the common welfare. Leaders, receive and undertake bravely to bring about the necessary changes in the world surrounding you. Let the less affluent, the subordinates, and the needy see solicitude, equilibrium, and prudence in your authority, which in consequence will deserve respect and benefit everybody. Let promotion of justice and defense of human dignity be your charity; do not forget that certain crises of history could have had different results, if the necessary reforms through brave sacrifices, had prevented explosive revolutions borne out of desperation.

The Pontiff defines the position of the ruling classes as one of "immovability" that "can be or appear to be a privileged one." This privilege of those who have something must be put into motion to "serve those who need . . . wealth, . . . culture, and . . . authority." This Montinian program, basically identical to the one stated by *Populorum Progressio*, seems to overflow the social function of capital, enterprise, and the sources of production that the previous Popes had proclaimed, thus openly sticking to the natural law. Paul VI incites activism very similar to that of Marxism-Leninism. Paul VI's mention of the spirit of evangelical poverty does not seem to be very convenient or able to encourage the ruling classes to arrange the economy and the power for the benefit of the community, as the Pontiff wants. The spirit of evangelical poverty *advises* but does not *command* those who seek perfection to lay aside all earthly goods to follow poor Christ: *"si vis perfectus esse"* ("If you want to be perfect") *"vade, vende quod habes"* ("go and sell what you have, and give it to the poor").

"If you want"—this is no obligation, no regulation. In this sense of total renunciation, evangelical poverty is not even an indispensable condition for perfection. The history of the Church shows us there have been saints who lived in palaces. The doctrine of evangelical poverty teaches us about the danger of wealth, not because of its possession, but because of its abuse in attempting to attain salvation. But at the same time, this doctrine teaches us that these material goods may help those who have them to do good and increase their merits for eternal life. The doctrine of evangelical poverty teaches us all, rich and poor, disinterest in earthly goods, that is, not to let our hearts adhere inordinately to wealth. It is evident that ownership of private property demands the fulfillment of duties that, both in the realm of justice and in that of charity, arise from the social function this property has. If it be this that Paul VI means when he encourages those who have, to serve those who do *not* have, his approach is similar to those of Leo XIII, Pius IX, and Pius XII.

On the other hand, if, in demanding that the ruling classes break the links of selfish ownership of secular goods, in stimulating Catholics to "arrange the economy and the power for the benefit of the community," the Pontiff seeks the socialization of Latin American countries, then we Catholics and Latin Americans must oppose him, for the right to private property is a natural right, and we do not want to be enslaved by a tyrannical regime.

As said before with respect to the social problem of our Latin American nations (totally different from that of the European nations), it would be unrealistic and suicidal to give the economy and power to people who do not have the same degree of training and education, the same abilities of managing their own economy, or of assuming the tremendous responsibility that the administration of public affairs entails. The crisis of history we are presently undergoing cannot be solved by surrender, compromise, or sacrifice of our liberty and legitimate rights.

This homily was delivered by Paul VI on the sixth day of the Congress, "Development Day." The *Populorum Progressio*, written by the Pontiff as he thought of problematical Latin America, had its ratification before the whole world at the Mass in the shrine. In addition, Paul VI made another classic gesture on behalf of the dispossessed on that day, when he visited not only Saint Cecilia's parish in the Venetian quarter, but also two homes of poor people, chosen and prepared in advance. In this way, the Congress became extremely useful to this most active Pontiff as a historical frame for the Pope to enhance his *Populorum Progressio* progressivist thesis.

THE PONTIFF ALSO INAUGURATED THE NEW SEAT OF LAMEC

Everything was arranged, organized, and set at Bogotá, so that the event

The Montinian Church

of the Eucharistic Congress would be influential to the utmost on the planned transformation of Latin America. LAMEC (the Latin American Episcopal Council) would celebrate its second general meeting at the Colombian city of Medellín after the Eucharistic Congress. The sovereign Pontiff had opened that meeting at the Cathedral of Bogotá prior to his return to Rome, but the official headquarters of LAMEC, built mostly with the economic aid of Germany and other rich countries, were also established at Bogotá.

On this occasion, the Pope delivered the following speech:

Most beloved brethren and children:

In these moments of the inauguration of the new headquarters of the Latin American Episcopal Council, our spirit becomes crowded by a set of feelings, whose brief description will be set off by the intensity of our affection.

We congratulate you for this opportune work, which is added to the numerous and praiseworthy moves carried on by LAMEC during its fruitful existence. They have providentially contributed to the growth of the Church in this continent.

The present occasion is quite convenient for us to thank you for the efforts having been made, to bless the Lord for the attained success, and to remember, with praise and acknowledgment, the precious cooperation the episcopal conferences, the religious congregations, and many believers from other parts of the world have developed and are developing on behalf of the Latin American Church, through economic aid and the remittance of priests and vocationally-consecrated personnel.

And finally, a wish: May this see always be a center of spiritual zeal, the soul of any efficacious ministry, a living witness of loyalty to Peter's chair and the teaching of the recent council, a point of mutual understanding unifying the actions in those projects that require confluence of wills to be more efficient, and a center for active service and continued aid to the national episcopates. And may the often tiresome and concealed work of these agencies have the spirit and supernatural worth of the apostolate for those who perform it.

Along with these wishes, we bestow upon you, most beloved brethren and children, and also to all of you at LAMEC, its various departments and aides, a special apostolic blessing, which is a pledge of the divine gifts we make for their huge and arduous work of aiding *in aedificationem Corporis Christi.*

LAMEC is one of the new structures of the post-Conciliar Church. It is an episcopal council that intends to unify all the pastoral efforts of the Catholic Church in Latin America. The goal was summarized by Paul VI in his last words: "*in aedificationem Corporis Christi*" (in the building up of Christ's Body), and the spread of revealed truth. This would cause an increase in the sanctity of the members of the Church, particularly the bishops and priests; the

Paul VI and the New Theologians

encouragement of the religious life; the austerity of customs, according to the immutable codes of Catholic morality; the unity and fidelity of spouses, children's obedience, the chastity of youth and the loftiness of their ideals, and the piety of the home; the sanctification of the Lord's Day; and the cultivation of solid virtues, sincere zeal, and the renunciations necessary to Christian life. From the standpoint of these goals, may we say the existence and work of LAMEC have been really fruitful? Have they contributed, as Paul VI affirms, providentially to the growth of the Church in this continent?

We must not live with illusions or conceal reality by using nice words. Consciously speaking before God, we cannot say that this entire movement nor the Council nor the post-Conciliar period, has been beneficial, fruitful, or convenient for the Church in Latin America. We know of bishops and provincials of religious orders who get married, abbés who are psychoanalyzed to justify sexual freedom, priests, religious, and seculars who become secularized to such an extent that they dance, drink, or solicit their female students, nuns who wear miniskirts and male hair styles, the destruction of altars and images, sacrilegious desecration in the temples. What is the use of going on? Everywhere we see desolation in the house of God and profanation of holy things. Consciously speaking, I do not think Paul VI may affirm that LAMEC has contributed much to the growth of the Church on this continent.

On the other hand, the Pontiff certainly can thank the episcopal conferences for their loyal fulfillment of his directions. He can thank the religious congregations, especially the Jesuits, for their most active cooperation with the Vatican's ambitious projects; he can also thank the American and German bishops for their economic aid in helping with the huge expenditures which the building of the new Church entailed. But we cannot agree with him as to his feeling content and thankful for the *"remittance of priests and vocationally-consecrated personnel,"* for this means lots of "new wave" activists who came to brainwash our people, to transport them ideologically from one mentality to another, and from one Faith to the new Conciliar faith. These Conciliar "experts," these pastoral pseudo-theologians, these organizers and lecturers from abroad who unceasingly visit us, are responsible, before God and history, for our Catholics' apparent acceptance of the change in Faith.

Among these activists, a very remarkable place is held by certain communitary movements which, under the banner of Redemption and re-Christianization, have expedited the spectacular changes we are experiencing. For instance, I refer to the Christian Family Movement and the Short Courses in Christianity (Cursillos), which include an appendix with "working days" for youngsters. Neither of these movements is indigenous; they were imported. Both have been nefarious, for our people are always ready to welcome anything coming from abroad.

THE CHRISTIAN FAMILY MOVEMENT

The Christian Family Movement, which, thank God, has lost much of its original enthusiasm and proselyting efficacy, was introduced to the Latin American countries under the attractive program of renovation and Christianization of families, and the haunt of its "fraternal" familiarity and frequent meetings, with intimate affairs being commented on and discussed at its gatherings, and the "national and international meetings," which provided the occasion for trips and unexpected feasts. Who could have told Pepe Alvarez Icaza, who used to live so poorly sometime ago, that, using the Christian Family Movement's communitary funds, he was going to be able to travel so much, and rent a mansion or small palace in Rome to entertain monsignors, bishops, and cardinals, spending 500,000 pesos (40,000 U.S. dollars) during the turbulent days of the Council?

This novel organization, which has much "movement," very little "family," and nothing "Christian" at all, has been the mighty tool through which new ideas have been incorporated into our families, thus overthrowing the walls that had protected our genuine Catholic heritage for centuries. It has not only efficiently served to "de-sacralize" the clergy, letting all the members of such groups familiarly address, criticize, and condemn priests and bishops, but it has rendered valuable services for the acceptance of the new rites and for the theological and moral training of the laity, the eventual replacements of the ecclesiastics in the very liturgical services, the administration of Church properties, and the most modern activities of the current post-Conciliar pastoral work in the Church.

THE CURSILLO MOVEMENT

The Cursillo Movement (short courses in Christianity) is even more dangerous. It is a psychological trick, where everything has been prepared in advance to move and deceive their previously selected followers, thus achieving unconditional support from the "converts" for the future Cursillo work. It is just a sect, a colorful permanent plot designed to prepare Christianity for the success of Communism. What is most regretful is that the initiates are not able to understand that they are pawns in the game of a hidden hand, secretly led by the Jewish mafia. We must not forget it was a *chueta* Jew (a descendant of converted Jews), a doctor and psychologist, who was the author of this movement which has invaded all America. In the United States, the Cursillo Movement has been an efficacious means of spreading Chicano subversion.

The Pope's wishes for the future consist of consolidating progressivists' ambitious projects with a certain spiritual zeal as a living witness of loyalty to

Peter's chair and "the teaching of the recent Council." Why not the teaching of *all* the Councils? The insistence with respect to Vatican II, without even quoting what it said, is one of the most remarkable things for those of us who are desperately sticking to the 20 centuries of heritage in the Church. "Peter's chair" meant also the documents of previous Popes, especially those who condemned many of the errors now being imposed upon us under the name of a post-Conciliar change of mentality.

Finally, Paul VI entrusts this integrally reformist program to collegial work, mutual understanding, unified action, confluence of wills, and constant aid of national episcopates and their corresponding conferences. LAMEC and its headquarters will be a focus of unceasing change, continuous evolution, and secret dynamism which will facilitate the coming of this so-much-publicized "Spring of the Church," or "Second Pentecost" that will regenerate and save the world.

THE INAUGURATION OF THE SECOND ASSEMBLY OF LAMEC AND THE SPEECH OF PAUL VI

The Eucharistic Congress was ending without those expressions of faith, zeal, and spiritual renovation that had enhanced the previous congresses, such as those of Madrid, Budapest, and Buenos Aires. The triumphal procession that had been suppressed even for Corpus Christi holidays, would not take place. Now speeches replace sermons, and social programs replace the old-fashioned issues concerning the dogmatic Mysteries of the Faith.

The top event of that turbulent Congress had to be the opening of the second general meeting of the Latin American episcopate, at the Cathedral of Bogotá. Paul VI personally opened the meeting and gave directions to our most faithful prelates as to the way to be followed to carry on the urgent work of changing the social, economic, political, and religious structures in all Latin American countries at an accelerated pace. So spoke Paul VI:

Venerable, dear, most dear Brethren,
    Benedicamus Domino!
We bless and thank the Lord, who provides us this fraternal meeting. We hail each and every one of you with the veneration, love, depth, and richness of feelings that our Lord's charity and the common election for pastoral ruling and the unselfish service of the Church can arouse in the heart of Peter's mean successor. And, along with you, we greet and bless all the bishops and ordinaries of Latin America who are represented here by you, as well as the priests, male and female religious, all the faithful, and the entire Holy Catholic Church in this great continent.

The Montinian Church

The Pope's greeting was extremely hearty, flattering, pre-Conciliar, and triumphal. Paul VI introduces himself as "Peter's mean successor," so as to back his words with all the weight of his Pontifical authority. It was as though he had said: "With the depth and richness of feelings, the veneration and love owed to your pastoral status, it is Peter who is speaking to you; it is Peter who will set the line for the complete transformation you must carry out in all the nations of your continent."

Venerable Brethren! We cannot conceal the fact that our spirit is being invaded by an intense emotion in these moments. We ourselves are amazed at finding ourselves amidst you. The Pope's first personal visit to his brethren and children from Latin America is not, indeed, just a simple and unusual piece of press news. In our mind it is a historical fact included in the long, complicated, and tiresome evangelizing activity being carried on in these huge territories. It acknowledges such work, ratifies, celebrates, and, at the same time, concludes it as to its first secular age. And, through a convergence of prophetic circumstances, *this visit opens a new period of ecclesiastical life*. Let us try to become fully conscious of this happy moment which, owing to divine Providence, seems to be a conclusive and decisive one.

Here we have, amid the exuberance of feelings that characterize Paul VI's speeches, the real goal of the Congress of Bogotá and the Pontiff's visit to our nations. "*...[T]his visit opens a new period of ecclesiastical life.*" The Constantinian age is over; the paternalism of the Church and its shepherds is over; the dogmatic period is over. The transformation of the structures is beginning; the age of socialization on behalf of the Gospel has begun. The moment has come for the revolution to give a kiss of peace to the hierarchic apostolate, for the sake of underdeveloped peoples' redemption. That is why one has to become fully conscious of this happy moment. What does this "consciencizing" of the prelates mean and imply, save to accurately interpret signs of the times?

We should like to tell you so many things about your missionary and pastoral past, and do honor to all those who have plowed the furrows of the Gospel in these so wide, so inaccessible, so open and, at the same time, so difficult fields, in order to spread the Faith, and for the sake of sincere religious and social vitality. Christ's cross has been set up; the Catholic name has been given; super-human efforts have been made to evangelize this area; big and countless works have been made; despite scarcity of men and means, results worth admiring have been attained. In summary, the name of the sole Savior, Jesus Christ, has been spread throughout the whole continent; the Church has been built; the Spirit has been propagated, whose warmth and impulse we are feeling right now.

Paul VI and the New Theologians

God bless this grand work! God bless those who have spent their lives! God bless you, most beloved brethren, who are consecrated to this huge enterprise!

The Pontiff could not ignore the wonderful Christianization of Latin America, so heroically brought about by the missionaries, holy missionaries, who came mostly from Spain and who, with the generous aid of the Spanish crown (this the Pope omits), were able to make the Catholic Faith and Christian civilization take root among our people in just three centuries, as said before. This real miracle can be explained only through the supernatural intervention of God and the most holy Virgin, and our missionaries' absolute commitment. We must not forget that Paul VI avows that the Church, right from the beginning of the evangelization of America, had and displayed sincere religious and social vitality. Then it is not true, as it is said now in order to justify the progressivist and Communistic activities of many clergymen and bishops, that the Church ever disregarded our peoples' social problems, or that Spain did, as far as its colonial administration was concerned. In fact, the social problem was focused then, just as it must be focused now, on the task of civilizing and educating the natives and the poor, so that they, through their personal work and efforts, might progress and increase their means.

As we all know, this work is unfinished. Moreover, the work already done shows its limits, evidences new needs, and demands something new and big. The future requires an effort, an audacity, and a sacrifice that introduce a deep wish into the Church. *This is a moment of total reflection.* We are being invaded, just as if by an overflowing wave, by the typical uneasiness of our age, especially of these countries which have been thrown forth to their complete development and stirred by the conscience of their economically, socially, politically, and morally unbalanced condition.

The work is unfinished because, short of a miracle, it could not be finished. It takes time, as I said before, to grow a child in a mother's womb, just as it does to grow one to its full extent in Christian civilization. The work already done which, no doubt, has rendered best fruits, certainly requires new efforts and continued fruitful activity which will always have to push forth, but without any jeopardizing audacity, destructive haste, or dangerous demagoguery, toward the conscious progress of a marching people. To Paul VI, this is a moment of *total reflection*. This means breaking with the past, that we are no longer sure of anything, and that we are going to start again what has already been done. This overflowing wave of uneasiness began to asphyxiate us when we began to realize everything was shattering, everything was being overthrown, and everything had to be reviewed and reflected upon.

The Montinian Church

The Church's shepherds also assume the peoples' wish at this stage of the history of civilization, do they not? And they also, the leaders, the masters, the prophets of faith and grace, warn of this instability jeopardizing us all. Brethren, we share your sorrow and your fear. From the helm of the holy bark of the Church, we also feel the storm surrounding and assaulting us, and this to a not lesser extent than you do. But you, brethren, who are personally stronger and braver than ourselves, listen to Jesus' words coming out of our mouth. During a dangerous night, He appeared to His disciples amid the tempestuous waves and cried to them who were sailing: "It is I, be not afraid" (Matt. 14:27). Indeed, we want to repeat this exhortation by the Master: "Fear not!" (Luke 12:32). This is for the Church a time of courage and confidence in the Lord.

Paul VI avows there is a most grave storm shattering the bark of the Church, which seems to be about to capsize it at any moment. Then it is not our imagination or our futile fear that makes us cry from the bottom of our believing souls: *"Save us, O Lord, for we shall perish!"* The shepherds of your Church, who now prefer to be called "prophets of faith and grace," keep quiet, and leave the whole responsibility for solving the present crisis to the eager peoples existing at this stage of civilization. Indeed, we know the bark will not sink, for the Church of Christ cannot perish. But we are also seeing not only the growing fury of the tempest, but also the fact that immortal souls are becoming lost. Our Church, the sole Christ-erected Church, on the dock, or beside the heretics, disbelievers, and schismatics! And we can also hear the hideous mockery of our eternal enemies who, just as at Pilate's court, keep on asking for their victim's blood and boast of having changed Catholic thought, that is, the Catholic Faith. Before, our shepherds led and grazed us with the plentiful grass of truth and love. *Now we poor strayed sheep, who lack a shepherd, risk perishing in the gullet of the rapacious wolves.* Indeed, this is the time for us to confide in the Lord, but not in the men who no longer seem to represent the Lord.

Let us devote some paragraphs to a brief summary of the many things we have in our heart for your present and near future. Do not expect complete treatises from us; your problems will be considered in depth at the sessions of your second general meeting of the Latin American episcopate, which we know have been prepared thoroughly and skillfully. We will just give a threefold direction to your activity as bishops, successors of the apostles, trustees and masters of the Faith, and shepherds of God's people.

The Pope says he intends to give a threefold direction to the Latin American bishops, successors of the apostles, trustees and masters of the Faith, and shepherds of God's people. We have always considered them as such; we have always beheld them performing their holy ministry. But now many of them speak a language we are not accustomed to hear. Now they seem to sleep or have made a deal with the enemies of the flock.

A spiritual direction first. We feel that, above all, this must be the main concern of the sovereign Pontiff as to a thorough ruling of the Church. Paul VI is quite able to perform this side of his most serious pastoral duties. A religious, due to his vocation, is always obliged to seek the perfection of the Christian and evangelical life. But the bishops are supposed to have reached that very evangelical perfection to a certain degree, so as to be able to tell their sheep, as Saint Paul did: *"Imitatores mei estote, sicut et ego Christi"* ("Be my imitators, just as I imitate Christ"). Paul VI certainly knows what the Church, from the apostolic age, has demanded of those to whom the Holy Ghost entrusted the administration of God's Church. That is why he said:

> A spiritual direction first. I mean, above all, a *personal* spiritual direction. Certainly none will dispute that we bishops, who are called to perfect and sanctify others, have the imminent and permanent duty of seeking perfection and sanctification for ourselves. We cannot forget the solemn exhortations that were addressed to us at the act of our episcopal consecration. We cannot avoid practicing an intense inner life. We cannot announce God's Word without having meditated on it first amid the soul's silence. We cannot deal out the Divine Mysteries faithfully without having first attained their wealth ourselves. We must not dedicate ourselves to the apostolate unless we are able to fortify it with the example of Christian and sacerdotal virtues. We are being very much looked upon: *Spectaculum facti sumus* (I Cor. 4:9); the world looks upon us today in a particular way, as to our poverty, simplicity of life, and the degree of confidence we have in using secular goods. The angels look upon us in the transparent purity of our love for Christ that manifests itself so brightly in the firm and joyful observance of our sacerdotal celibacy; the Church looks upon our loyalty to Communion, which makes us all one, and to the laws, whose visible and organic frame we must always bear in mind. Happy is our tormented and paradoxical age, which almost obliges us to be saints, as it belongs to our profession, representative and full of responsibilities as it is. It obliges us to recover that intimate treasure of personality, beyond which our commitment to our extremely pressing profession almost projects us through the asceticism of the ministers of the Holy Spirit.

The above words of the Pope's speech summarize what the bishops must be, as far as their persons and private lives are concerned. They are the successors of the apostles, but "if the salt corrupts itself," said the divine Master, "it is of no use; it must be thrown away to be trodden on by men." This is one of the many passages of Paul VI's speeches that could be depicted as the genuine voice of the Magisterium. Regarding these words as a rule, we could well call our post-Conciliar prelates to a serious examination of conscience. *"We are... very much looked upon,"* said Paul VI to our bishops, and he is right. We look upon his unexplainable silence in the presence of the denial or adulteration of our dogmas, in the presence of our Bugninian liturgy's continued irreverence, in the presence of the growing surrender of our priests who quit the altar to enjoy the pleasure of the bride-chamber, of the fugitives of faith, of what is being written in Catholic magazines, and of the immorality which has been accepted in our very temples. We look upon the contradiction between his words and his works, following the rule of the divine Master, as we must: *ex fructibus eorum cognoscetis eos*—by their fruits you will know them.

We look upon the frequent episcopal meetings, the subjects treated by them, and upon the many national and international lecturers being used to brainwash us and convince us that black is white and white is black. We look upon those who allow what they previously condemned, such as *co-education* in Catholic schools as well as *sexual education* being implemented by the "new wave" priests with so much display of anatomy. We look upon the selection of the new bishops who are called to succeed the venerable saintly men who gave up their lives to serve the Church. We look upon the appointment of their auxiliaries in this huge post-Conciliar work, and the appointment of chiefs and assistant chiefs of the agencies required to implement the directives of Rome, LAMEC, and the episcopal conferences. Indeed the Pope is right; those of us who are neither asleep nor compromised, those of us who are not concerned for privileges or the title of monsignor, are paying utmost attention to our bishops, our shepherds and those who boast of being the apostles' successors but who might, perhaps, betray the apostolic heritage in many respects. Just as Luther and his accomplices intended to reform the Church to return to the Gospel's purity, our prelates intend to reform the Church a second time, in order to go back to the primitive Church's mentality and way of life. That is why they demand that we change our mentality, which is a change of Faith, despite the fact they must know they are wrong.

To prove the post-Conciliar Church is the Church of the poor, they took off their pastoral rings and now wear the simple golden rings without any stones or ostentation, that Paul VI gave them at the end of Vatican II. They have also exchanged their pectoral crosses for a cross which is no cross at all and which hangs from a steel chain. But they keep on traveling frequently, administering their properties or those of their dioceses, and making gifts to their friends and aides. Without giving any names, we do know that some of them, during the time of the Council, were not guests of any seminary or religious house, but of the luxurious Continental Hilton of Rome. We also know that some of them sell their parishes to those priests who are ready to pay the best prices.

I will stop saying what else I know, lest I scandalize naive Catholics. In spite of what the new "apostles of social justice" say and preach, several dioceses of the post-Conciliar Church have been mortgaged, so as to raise funds to afford the expenditures of their shepherds' trips to Rome, the transformation of the temples, and the upkeeping of the agencies, the new bureaucracy and their aides, the activists. It would be interesting and revealing to draw up a thorough balance of the outlays of the pre-Conciliar, Conciliar, and post-Conciliar movements, including the Pope's trips and those of the bishops and leaders, the temple reforms, the adaptation of the seminaries, etc., so as to prove the "poverty" of the post-Conciliar Church through the irrefutable argument of figures

We can compare the real poverty of the saintly Archbishop of Sonora—by now a *former* Archbishop—who had built the church of Sonora almost from its cornerstone, his apostolate being fertile and self-denying, with the "simple life" of the present Archbishop, who boasts of being poor but does not know how to live as such or want to. I will stop giving examples, lest I scandalize naive people who might fail to tell the difference between men and institutions.

The Pope avows that this tormented and paradoxical age obliges the shepherds to live saintly lives corresponding to their representative and responsible offices. People are fed up with demagoguery; they seek the truth through works. A friend of mine, a Protestant, a sincere lover of the truth and Christ, was about to convert to Catholicism, but what he saw at the Council and during the post-Conciliar age forced him to relinquish his intention. Conversions have ceased, and the number of desertions has increased, for our prelates' "ecumenism" has made many people believe everything is the same thing and that it does not matter whether one is a Catholic or remains within other religions. What matters is to be genuine.

The Pope went on by saying:

> Let me be a bridge between us and our flock. [May I make a remark: it seems that Paul VI accepts the principle of corresponsive collegialism, thus becoming the first one among his equals (*primus inter pares*) with respect to his brethren, the bishops.] The theological virtues become of utmost importance both for our soul and those of our neighbors. We called on the Church to celebrate a "Year of the Faith" as a memorial and homage to the centennial of the martyrdom of the holy apostles Peter and Paul, and the echo of our solemn Profession of Faith reached you too. We know well that faith is the basis, the root, the source, and the primary cause of the Church. We also know that faith is being polluted by the most subversive currents of modern thought. Even in Catholic circles there is widespread distrust about the standing of the fundamental principles of reason, that is, of our *philosophia perennis*, and this has disarmed us against the often radical and artful attacks of fashionable thinkers. The vacuum produced in our philosophical schools by lack of confidence in the great masters of Christian thought is frequently invaded by a

superficial and almost servile acceptance of fashionable philosophies which are often both simple and confusing. And these have shattered our regular, human, and wise way of approaching the truth. We are being tempted by historicism, relativism, subjectivism, and neo-positivism which, in the realm of faith, engender a spirit of subversive criticism and the false conviction that, in order to attract and evangelize modern men, we have to give up the doctrinal heritage the Magisterium of the Church has been gathering for centuries, and that we are able to model a new Christianity to meet the whim of man instead of God's genuine word. And all this not for the sake of clarifying thought, but to change its dogmatic contents. Unfortunately, some theologians go off the straight path, even among us.

We quite appreciate and need good and dedicated theologians. They can become providential scholars and brave expounders of the Faith, provided they remain intelligent disciples of the ecclesiastical Magisterium which Christ, through the Holy Spirit, set up as guardian and interpreter of His message of everlasting truth. But today some people use ambiguous doctrinal expressions and feel free to expound their own doctrines while imputing them to the authority they more or less openly question and which, by divine right, has such a tremendous and zealously kept charisma. They even let everyone think and believe one's own way, thus incurring free examination, which has torn the unity of the Church itself, and mistaken the legitimate freedom of moral conscience for so-called freedom of thought, which often leads to error due to insufficient knowledge of the religious truth.

Venerable Brethren who are teachers and shepherds of God's people: Do not get angry at us if we, by virtue of the prompting given by Christ to Peter, "Strengthen thy brethren" (Luke 22:32), repeat our admonition using the apostle's very own words: *"Resistite fortes in fide"* (I Pet. 5:9).

These words by Paul VI are undoubtedly not only realistic, but perfectly consistent with the 20-centuries-old traditional doctrine of Christ's Church. But on the other hand, they contradict other deeds and words by the Pontiff. They contradict what was said and done at Bogotá during the turbulent days of the Eucharistic Congress. The theological meeting, which was attended by cardinals, archbishops and bishops from different parts on those very days at Colombia's capital, was the triumphalistic expression and profession of faith of the Modernist heresy, progressivism, and the new post-Conciliar Church, which pretends to be faithful to the heritage while destroying it on behalf of the new theology, on behalf of *aggiornamento* to the world of today, on behalf of the Council-proclaimed ecumenism and freedom of conscience, on behalf of *better expression of the dogmatic truth* the Magisterium of the Church had defined as immutable prior to Vatican II.

We have a new, custom-made Christianity, based upon man instead of

Paul VI and the New Theologians

God's genuine Word. That is what we are seeing in the new post-Conciliar Church presided over by Paul VI. He tolerates and skillfully fosters it with the most efficient aid of a compromising or cowardly hierarchy and the irrevocable obedience of the Fathers of the Society of Jesus, his loyal aides. It was not a personal profession of faith by Paul VI which the most grave evils of the Church required. In addition, we know that the Pope who took the oath of fidelity to the Tridentine Faith and the anti-Modernist oath at the beginning of the second session of Vatican Council II, was the same one that suppressed said oaths, so as to channel his reformation freely and give his aides the necessary freedom of conscience for them to rejuvenate the Church, thus making it attractive to the disbelieving, materialistic, corrupt, and corrupting world in which we live. Not "frequently," but "always," the vacuum left by our abandonment of the "everlasting philosophy" has been filled by the madness of contemporary philosophy, including psychoanalysis and psychiatry, of course. To the "new wave" Jesuits, these are the utmost of wisdom, the loving encounter with the "unknown man," the man who has not been made in God's image, but the man who has become God, the man who is sex and love.

Paul VI backs his authority with the privileges which Christ granted Peter and Peter his successors. This is undoubtedly the Catholic truth, the revealed truth. But the problem arises when Paul VI's voice is not consistent with those of his predecessors, with those of the previous councils, and when his deeds contradict his words. Why did he not expose the heresy proclaimed at the theological meeting on the very days of the Congress, when he spoke at Bogotá's cathedral? Was not his silence a tacit acceptance? Would that not have been a magnificent occasion to condemn modern errors, not vaguely and ambiguously, but concretely, since that official speech seemed to cover all the ceremonies and acts of the Congress?

I do not think Paul VI intended to proclaim his personal infallibility when he spoke about "... the authority they more or less openly question and which, by divine right, has such a tremendous and zealously kept charisma." As said before, the privilege of infallibility according to Vatican I and traditional theology, does not mean *personal* infallibility, but *didactical* infallibility, and applies only under the circumstances Vatican I stated. Then, even conceding the hypothesis that Paul VI is a true Pope, he is not always infallible, and as said before, he can incur even personal heresy. Almighty God could prevent it, but He did not reveal to us that He was always going to do so.

Paul VI does know and say that "faith is the basis, the root, the source, and the primary cause of the Church." But amid the present confusion, how has Paul VI defended the holy deposit of our Catholic Faith? Is what he calls a solemn Profession of Faith, his creed, the urgent, undeferrable, and decisive remedy against the heresies arising from Modernism and progressivism and spread by the bishops themselves, such as Don Sergio VII from Cuernavaca,

The Montinian Church

Don Helder from Brazil, Suenens from Belgium, Alfrink from Holland, Lercaro from Bologna, Willebrands, the Secretary of the Secretariat for Christian Unity, etc.? Has Paul VI fulfilled his chief goal of strengthening his brethren in the Faith? The judgment of God and history will decide this point. Now let us continue to study Paul VI's speech:

> You may understand how this principle gives birth to several other criteria of spiritual vitality both for us and the flock that has been entrusted to us. The principal of them are the following ones. The Acts of the Apostles reminds us of them, namely, prayer and the ministry of the Word. (Acts 6:4). In this connection, you already know many things, but let us recommend the implementation of the liturgical reform as to prayer, with its beautiful innovations and disciplinary rules. Above all we must consider the primary goal and spirit of prayer, to purify real Catholic worship and render it genuine according to the Paschal Mystery, which involves, renews, and conveys. One of our aims is to associate God's people to the hierarchic and communal celebration of the Church's holy rites, to that of the Mass within a familiar, deep, simple, and beautiful environment (we particularly recommend the holy, liturgical, and collective singing), so as to exercise fraternal charity, not only formally, but sincerely and heartily. As to the ministry of the Word, everything that can be done for the benefit of the religious education of all the believers will be well-done. This education must be cultural and popular, organic and tireless. Religious illiteracy must no longer exist among Catholics.

Paul VI recommends prayer and the ministry of the Word to the Latin American bishops. His admonitions have been expressed in post-Conciliar language which is not the traditional language, the one the pre-Conciliar Popes and the saints used, the one used in teaching ascetic and mystic theology. It appears there are no prayers save the liturgical and communal ones. Personal prayer, that meditation wherein souls met God, spoke with Him, humbled themselves, and repented, mourned, and asked with hope; that concentration, external modesty, and approach to the divine Presence that prevented absent-mindedness and associated the imagination with quiet prayer; all this no longer means anything and must no longer be taught or practiced. The modern liturgical movement has destroyed solid piety. The Mass used to be an actual and true Sacrifice, wherein Christ, Priest and Victim, immolated Himself for a second time, through the ministry of His hierarchical priests. The believers attended and participated in the fruits of the Lord's Passion and death, but not today. Today, Catholic worship, as purified and authenticated by Lercaro's and Bugnini's imagination, is a "meeting" presided over by the priest, where it is the Paschal Mystery, not Christ's Passion and death, that is commemorated. What sort of Easter is this? The Jewish or the Catholic one? The Jewish Passover was the legal dinner the Jews celebrated as a memorial of their liberation from the slavery of Egypt. The Catholic Easter is the victorious Resurrection of the Savior, who defeats sin, the Devil, and death, for us and to us. The Mass does not represent and bloodlessly repeat the Paschal Mystery, but Jesus' Passion and death. The Mass is no hierarchic and communal celebration, but, according to Trent's doctrine, a Sacrifice where only the hierarchical priest acts on behalf of, and with the power of Christ. The people attend the Sacrifice and attain the fruits of the Sacrifice, but are not actively associated with the Sacrifice. Remember what Pius XII taught us some years ago, in his wonderful encyclical, *Mediator Dei:*

> This ransom [that of Christ at the cross] did not reach its full effect immediately. It is necessary that Christ, after having redeemed the world with the most copious price of Himself, *take real and effective possession of souls . . . ; in order that all of the sinners become purified by the blood of the Lamb, their own cooperation is necessary.* Even though Christ, generally speaking, has reconciled man, it was necessary that people approach Him and be carried to the cross through the Sacraments and the Eucharistic Sacrifice, so as to obtain the fruits of Salvation He had gathered at the very cross itself.

Unfortunately, not everybody approaches the cross or accepts the Sacraments and the Eucharistic Sacrifice, the only way through which Christ's redemption reaches us. Then, *though Christ died for everybody*—this is the dogma of Redemption—the fruits of Redemption do not benefit everybody through the Eucharistic Sacrifice and the Sacraments—this is the dogma of Salvation or justification. Pius XII goes on to say:

> And this, far from eroding the dignity of the bloody Sacrifice, enhances its greatness and *proclaims its necessity,* as the Council of Trent affirms. Its daily renewal warns us there is no salvation without the cross of our Lord Jesus Christ, who wants the repetition of this Sacrifice from East to West, so that the hymn of glorification and thanksgiving men owe their Creator never stops, since they need continued aid and the Redeemer's blood to efface the sins which offend His justice.

The participation of the believers in the holy Sacrifice has given birth to a grave mistake that Pius XII had condemned. Many people think all believers enjoy the sacerdotal power, but Pius XII does not agree:

> Then, Venerable Brethren, there are now some people who, adhering to already condemned errors (Conc. Trid., Sess. XXIII, c. 4th), contend that, in the New Testament, the word priesthood includes all baptized people, and that the

rule Jesus Christ gave the apostles at his Last Supper, of doing what He had done Himself, directly affects the whole body of believers, and only later was the hierarchical priesthood introduced. That is why they believe the people have real sacerdotal power, and the priest acts only as the community's proxy. That is why they claim the Eucharistic Sacrifice is, strictly speaking, a concelebration, and believe it is more convenient that the priest concelebrate surrounded by the believers; that is why they do not celebrate the Sacrifice privately, without the attendance of people.

What a contrast between Pius XII's doctrine and Paul VI's ideas on liturgical reformation! Paul VI affirms his liturgy is a purified liturgy that gives authenticity to Catholic worship. In his mind, the pre-Paulian worship was impure and lacked authenticity; thus, the aid of the "separated brethren" was necessary to purify and give authenticity to the Mass. This may be the case according to Lutheran doctrine, but it is not according to the doctrine of Trent.

Speaking about the ministry of the Word, the Pontiff uses a bold statement: "Religious illiteracy must no longer exist among Catholics." Unfortunately this evil does not exclusively pertain to Latin America or the underdeveloped classes. Religious illiterates are to be found in Italy, France, Belgium, and almost all European countries. There are many of them among graduates and university students.

Many factors have helped spread religious illiteracy, among them these: (a) At home, de-Christianization of the family has grown for many reasons. Frivolity of life, irresponsibility on the part of parents, an all-consuming hunger for amusements, the corrupt and corrupting environment in which children grow, and even the active Christian Family Movement, whose meetings, numerous social gatherings and tireless zeal, leave Christian spouses no time to educate their children and give them convenient religious training—all these influences have helped to de-Christianize the family. (b) In schools, where religious and moral training and formation ought to be the primary concern of the teachers who almost always are or ought to be religious, religious education has been disregarded for a long time. I am not speaking about government-managed schools which, in many cases, are laical and irreligious, but about so-called Catholic schools. Individuals who are not only *not* religious, but are *irreligious,* bad people, and real corrupters of youth, are accepted as assistant teachers. This is a trick used to multiply the number of schools without the necessary personnel by replacing male or female religious teachers with lay male or female teachers who do not always meet the minimal personal requirements to be serious and healthy teachers. In addition, in some schools, religious training (*in some Catholic schools it no longer exists*) has been entrusted to ill-prepared male or female religious who are not prepared to teach other subjects. As a result, these classes may be considered secondary, unimportant, and uninteresting by the pupils. (c) Textbooks for religious training adapted to the various ages and cultural levels of pupils are not available. Even the catechists improvise their own catechisms, not always exempt from errors and inaccuracies. The new catechisms, such as the Dutch, French, Italian, and American ones, are unable to nourish a simple and firm faith, but, instead rationalize the Faith, engender doubt, foster free-examination and create free thinkers. (d) Even the preaching of God's Word has been amended so that it is no longer the religious teaching, solid catechesis, homilies, and panegyrics, which had always promoted the increase of truth in souls. Now almost all of the new apostles of social justice make efforts to pose scandalous problems and sensational issues which shock the ill-prepared faith of the audiences. Fashionable preaching is quite similar to the demagogical speeches of political parties. The language and the doctrine of the "new wave" preachers is very different from the solid, deep, and constructive preaching based on Holy Writ as construed by the Holy Fathers, theology, and genuine ecclesiastical sciences.

Still other influences, perhaps even more universal and nefarious, have undermined the faith of our Catholic people. The continuous changes which the liturgy has experienced in a few years and the subversive doctrines that circulate today under the title of "spirit of the Council," are important ones. Some religious and Catholic magazines, such as *Christus, Union,* and *Exemplary Lives (Vidas Ejemplares)* cover subjects and use language which spread the works of Teilhard de Chardin and other ultra-progressivist propaganda. These absolutely anti-Catholic opinions heard and read everywhere, and all this religious subversion we are beholding increase not religious illiteracy (this would be preferable) but *irreligion, atheism,* and the *Satanic thesis* of *the death of God.* Holy Father, this religious illiteracy, this faith of the collier which our poor people have (since they know and believe the truth essential for salvation and accept the teaching of the eternal Church without any objection) is preferable to the rational religion that discusses everything, gives its opinions on everything, and willingly separates itself from the doctrines of Tradition. Such is the cause of the dreadful confusion in which we live.

Pope Pius XII went on to say:

> Any direct exercise of preaching and teaching will be all right, and your bishops, singularly or as canonically organized groups, must care to do so among God's people. Speak, speak, preach, write, take sides, as it is said, about the truths of faith. Defend and give examples of them with harmonic intentions and plans. Also do this as to the actuality of the Gospel, the questions concerning the life of believers and the care of Christian customs, the ways leading to dialogue with the "separated brethren," [and] the dramas of current civilization, that are either grand and beautiful, or sad and dangerous.

The Montinian Church

In this passage the Pontiff points out the personal and inalienable obligations the bishops have, as Doctors and Masters of the Church. Sometimes they will have to speak individually, at others, collectively, but their chief mission consists of teaching. *"Docete,"* said the divine Master. When the bishops fail to expose errors against the Faith, they are, as a Holy Father said, *"sicut canes muti,"* like dumb dogs. The bishops do not have to take sides; this phrase is not convenient and seems to be a political one. We as Catholics have already taken sides, or rather, we know what we must do according to the immutable doctrine of the everlasting Gospel. In what respects must the bishop take sides? He must take sides respecting the truths of faith, the actuality of the Gospel, (which must not be adapted to the requirements of the times), the question concerning the supernatural life of believers, the preservation of Christian customs, the ways leading to "dialogue," and the dramas of contemporary civilization. Of these episcopal subjects, I think the most important are those which pertain to the defense of faith and morality. The rest will come in addition: *"Quaerite primum regnum dei et iustitiam eius et haec omnia adiicientur vobis."* "First," said Christ, "seek after God's kingdom and its righteousness, and everything else will be given to you in addition."

So far the Pope had given personal directions. Then the pastoral directions were stated:

> The pastoral constitution of the Council, *Gaudium et Spes,* includes rich teachings and stimuli of high value. Thus we have reached the point of stating our pastoral directions. We are in the field of charity. What we have said so far helps us draw the basic lines in this concern, which, according to the demands of charity, must develop itself along many practical lines.
>
> We deem it convenient to call your attention to two doctrinal points. First, charity toward our neighbor depends upon charity toward God. You know about the assaults which this most clear and irrefutable evangelical doctrine suffers in our day. Some are trying to secularize Christianity, disregarding its essential relation with religious truth and its supernatural communion with ineffable and overflowing charity of God toward men. Man's response is to love Him, call Him Father, and consequently, to call all men brethren. Christianity is thus freed from "religion, that form of neurosis" (Cox), thereby avoiding theological concern and offering Christianity a new pragmatic efficacy, the sole one able to give it its real dimensions and render it acceptable and active within our modern profane and technological civilization.

We find ourselves in the field of charity. This is the chief argument used to justify the turnabout of the post-Conciliar Church, which used to be "theocentric" and now is "homocentric." Paul VI acknowledges such a turnabout and, apparently, censors it:

Paul VI and the New Theologians

Some [people] are trying to secularize Christianity, disregarding its essential relation with religious truth and its supernatural communion with the ineffable and overflowing charity of God toward men.

Then, Paul VI skillfully turns around to orient his speech toward his *social creed,* in which God Himself and the love we owe Him serve as a basis for the Pope's socializing program! Instead of telling us "[s]ome people are trying to secularize Christianity, disregarding its essential relation with religious truth and its supernatural communion with the ineffable and overflowing charity of God toward men. Man's response is to love Him, call Him Father and consequently to fulfill His divine precepts, devote our lives to His service and avoid any offense to our Creator, our Lord and Master," Paul VI said, "and consequently, to call all men brethren." Is he saying that the acknowledgment of our divine relationship must be love for all men as brethren, without even mentioning our duties toward God? Since it allows us to call God our Father, there cannot be any relationship except the one we acquire through our justification through Christ. It permits us to participate analogically in the divine life and, through it we are God's "adoptive children," God's heirs, and Christ's coheirs. Those who have not been regenerated by Christ do not enjoy such a relationship. Not all men have this divine relationship and not everybody may call God his Father.

From this love for Christ arises our love for our neighbors. Indeed, love for God moves us to love men, for they are God's creatures. Because they, just like us, have been called to participate in the divine heritage, if we serve our fellow human beings, we are serving God and obeying His most holy Will.

I cannot understand what Paul VI meant with the following words: "Christianity is thus freed from 'religion, that form of neurosis' . . . thereby . . . offering Christianity a new pragmatic efficacy, the sole one able to give it its real dimensions and render it acceptable and active within our modern profane and technological civilization." To me, these words are incomprehensible. Is religion a form of neurosis? May we offer Christianity a new efficacy? Just to suggest this is absolutely opposite to revealed truth. Christianity is not a pragmatic religion; it does *not* seek acceptance through compromise, reticence, and concessions. Saint Paul's words are applicable quoted here: *"Nos autem praedicamus Iesum Christum et hunc crucifixum: iudeis quidem scandalum, gentibus autem stultitia"*—"we preach Christ, but a crucified Christ, a scandal for the Jews, and foolishness for the Gentiles, but for the chosen ones, the divine wisdom!" These words also apply: *"Animalis homo non percipit ea quae sunt spiritus"*—"the animal man cannot perceive the things of the spirit."

Let us continue quoting Paul VI's speech:

The Montinian Church

THE INSTITUTIONAL CHURCH AND THE CHARISMATIC CHURCH

The other *doctrinal* point refers to the so-called institutional Church as opposed to the present charismatic Church. It is contended that the [institutional Church], communal and responsible, organized and disciplined, apostolic and sacramental, was an outdated expression of Christianity, while the [present charismatic Church], spontaneous and spiritual, would be capable of interpreting Christianity for grown-up people within contemporary civilization, and meeting the needs of the urgent and real problems of our times. We do not have to preach the eulogy of the Church to you, whom *Spiritus Sanctus posuit episcopos regere Ecclesiam Dei* (Acts 20:28). Christ erected it and the faithful and coherent Tradition delivers it to us in its constitutional lines, which frame the real mystical body of Christ, as vivified by the spirit of Jesus. It will suffice us to ratify our confidence in the authenticity and vitality of our *One, Holy, Catholic and Apostolic Church,* and its ability to accommodate its Faith, its spirituality, its fitness to approach and save mankind (which is so various and changing nowadays), its charity that comprises and stands everything, with the saving mission Christ entrusted it. We will make an effort of loving intelligence to understand what is good and acceptable in these restless and often wrong forms of interpretation of the Christian message, to purify our Christian profession more and more, and to carry these spiritual experiences, both the secular and charismatic ones, to the basis of real ecclesiastical rule.

In this passage, Paul VI considered another very grave subject which, in the post-Conciliar Church, has given birth to a world organization devoted to destroying the very structure Christ gave His Church. I am referring to IDOC,[14] the charismatic and prophetic Church which, as the Pontiff himself says, intends to become the spontaneous and spiritual expression of the new Christianity that has surpassed the institutional Church. Unfortunately these prophetic groups swarm in Latin America. They are managed by bishops, clergymen, and laymen, who feel impelled by the Spirit who has come down upon them, just as if in a new Pentecost. In the presence of this most dangerous reality, I do not think the Pope's ratification of confidence in the genuineness and vitality of the One, Holy, Catholic, and Apostolic Church is enough. They say they are the rejuvenated and new Church which the Holy Spirit and the spirit of Vatican II has strengthened and made malleable. The Pontiff said: "We will make an effort of loving intelligence to understand what is good and acceptable in these restless and often wrong forms of interpretation of the Christian message...."

Paul VI and the New Theologians

HANS KUNG, BOLD THEOLOGIAN

One of the boldest theologians of the charismatic and prophetic Church is the Swiss, Hans Küng. Tanneguy de Quenetain (*Réalités*, Sept., 1963) writes:

> He incarnates the most audacious and deep reformist tendencies that are shattering the Catholic Church nowadays.... Last spring, Hans Küng made a tour of the United States and delivered a series of lectures in the large Catholic universities of Boston, San Francisco, Los Angeles, etc., as well as at Yale University. The subject was: *"Church and Freedom."* Before his astonished and enthusiastic audience, he spoke, on behalf of the New Testament Christian liberty, against *"the spirit of inquisition" and intolerance, which are still leaving traces in the Church.* He stated the Church had to publicly proclaim the right of every man to practice religion according to his own conscience, and this doctrine had to be implemented in countries such as Spain, too. He spoke against the suppressiveness of the Index and the previous censorship of books.

After this, the newspapers delivered some regretful, shameful, and humiliating news of "a cardinal's attack against the Holy Office," that is, against the guardian and defender of the Vatican and the whole Church. "There was a vigorous applause at the Conciliar room of Saint Peter's Basilica, although the regulations of the grand assembly forbid it." That was why the most meritorious Cardinal Alfred Ottaviani, the Secretary of the Holy Office, rose, in a sublime and honor-giving gesture, to say: *"I must protest most vigorously against the condemnation we have just heard!"* Hans Küng's propositions succeeded, however, because they were backed by an authority higher than his. Religious freedom was proclaimed at the Council, the Holy Office and censorship were suppressed, and salvific dialogue was established, so as to have us united with people from other religions.

He published two books on the Council by the time it was being convened, and they aroused enormous amazement in Catholic and Protestant circles: *Council and Return to Unity (Concile et Retour a L'Unite)*, and *The Council, a Challenge for the Church (Le Concile, Epreuve de L'Eglise)*. With utmost sincerity, and unbearable conceit and presumptuousness, this theologian from Tübingen impugned all traditions, all dogmas, everything our religion deems as most precious and sacred:

> Every institution, even the most holy ones [for instance, the celebration of the Eucharist], every constitution [for example, the Pope's preeminence], can, through the process of historical formation and deformation, attain such a state that they need renewal and, as a result, reform and renovation.

The Montinian Church

So that the Council might be successful, Küng asked it to become *"radically* conscious of only the Gospel, in its practical perspective of and for our age." He further continues:

> The Council must take into account the legitimate claims of Protestants, Orthodox Christians, Anglicans, and liberals.... John XXIII, for the first time after four hundred years, had definitively overthrown the barriers of misunderstanding, inertia, isolationism, merely defensive attitudes, and reaction, and had inaugurated an active and strong spirit of understanding toward our "separated brethren.".... [The Church has the right to demand] big sacrifices from Peter's ministry, provided it wants to recover its unity.

He wants the Pope's duties, rather than his rights, to be stressed; he also wants the bishops' rights, rather than their duties, to be emphasized. "The apostolic of the bishops' ministry," he says, "must recover the spirit of the New Testament.... The Pope's infallibility gets naturally integrated into the Church's structure.... Today's Church," he affirmed, "needs integrity above all."

He also spoke about improvement of the dogmas:

> Since they are human-historical formulas, the Church's definitions are, in themselves, capable of improvement and must be improved. One of the features of dogma is its polemical perspective. Hence a polemically-defined truth includes a peculiarly erroneous side. Every statement verbally stated, may be true and false. It is more difficult to find out how it has been thought than how it has been said. The ecumenical task of the theology of both sides consists of discovering the truth contained in the errors of others, and the probable error found in one's own truth.

WHAT I THINK OF HANS KUNG'S THEOLOGY

The above was a summary of the thought of the famous Swiss theologian Hans Küng, who is one of the founders of the charismatic and prophetic Church which is aimed at supplanting the institutional Church, the Church founded by Jesus Christ. Around 1963 I wrote: "He greatly scandalized the Catholics (priests and laymen) of the United States, who are not too prone to be scandalized." He was one of the leaders of the deep and nefarious revolution that, bearing the attractive name of progressivism, grew within God's Church and, seemingly, cropped out within the Vatican Council II. Since Küng boasts of his frankness, I will not let him surpass me as to frankness. It is urgent to call a spade a spade. It is necessary to unmask heresy, which is using sophisms under the cover of theological reasoning. It is absolutely vital for the Church's

Paul VI and the New Theologians

future that the wolves in sheep's clothing be exposed. Everything Küng wrote and included in his book on the Church appears to me to be not only scandalous, *piis auribus offensivum,* but in many passages, openly heretical, destructive, and perverse. Hans Küng's doctrine is aimed at shaking, splitting, and destroying the whole Church. The *Nihil obstat* and the *Imprimatur* which precede and sponsor the Rhenish theologian's doctrines are not able to change the doctrine this writer teaches, but only demonstrate that the plague has reached the highest circles.

1. Küng, with intolerable arrogance, dares condemn the whole Lateran Council V, which he calls a failure and a catastrophe for the Church, suggesting this council was the cause of the Protestant Reformation. *"Post hoc, ergo propter hoc."* The Protestant movement burst six months after the Lateran Council V, hence, it is logical to affirm that it was the cause of that catastrophe.

2. This Swiss theologian does not realize that his complete condemnation of a council (that was not merely *pastoral*) logically and unavoidably entails the condemnation of all of the councils and, moreover, the condemnation of the living, genuine, and infallible Magisterium of the Church! Cannot he understand that, by removing the cornerstone, he causes the entire edifice to fall to the ground?

3. What does this bold theologian mean when he asks Vatican II to become radically conscious of only the Gospel in its practical perspective of and for our age? Does he mean that the future of the Church belongs to the *audacious people,* and that it is necessary to rediscover the primitive Tradition of Catholicism again, under the dust and ruins of almost two thousand years, as the writer of *Le Monde* affirms?

If this is the case, then the Church in which we were born and baptized, in which we have believed, for which we have given up our lives, is *not* the real Church of Christ. This is a man-made Church, and now it is necessary to go back to the real evangelical spirit, to the genuine doctrine of Jesus Christ, which was darkened, concealed, and buried by the nefarious work of the councils and the Popes. Who could convince us that the work of the last two Popes and the last Council is no trick, no new hoax? What is the immutable rule and the safe criterion of truth?

4. With almost dogmatic authority, Küng pointed out the way to be followed by the Council. Of course the legitimate claims of Protestants, Orthodox Christians, Anglicans, and liberals have to be taken into account. This is the basis of post-Conciliar ecumenism. What legitimate claims does the theologian speak of? I guess the *doctrinal* ones, since he writes and speaks about doctrine. Does he mean that some errors professed by our "separated brethren" and condemned by the Magisterium of the Church are legitimate claims that Popes and councils unduly dismissed and condemned? Cannot Küng understand that he is jeopardizing his own position? Cannot he understand he is

stating that the Popes of yesterday and today, as well as Vatican II and the previous councils were mutually opposite? What is left of the Magisterium's infallibility and the Church's *inerrancy?*

5. "Today's Church," he affirms categorically, "needs integrity above all." Need implies lack. Does the theologian from Tübingen imply that the Church, prior to Vatican II and for who-knows-how-many years, has not had any integrity? Has it been an imposter; has it deceived the believers? Has it been obstinate about dismissing the just and rightful claims of our "separated brethren?"

6. According to Küng, Vatican II will be successful only if it becomes "radically conscious of only the Gospel, in its practical perspective of and for our age." Away with Tradition, away with the opinions of the Fathers and Doctors of the Church, away with the previous ecumenical councils, their dogmatic definitions and those of the sovereign Pontiffs! The Gospel, only the Gospel! But a freely interpreted Gospel. Christianity has to be rediscovered, since the Church has adulterated it for almost 20 centuries. On the other hand, this very Gospel has to be interpreted and accommodated to the "practical perspective of and for our age."

7. According to the theologian from Tübingen, *both Catholics and Protestants are responsible for today's division of the Church.* This is a subtle sophism since it cleverly confuses men with institutions. Baseness and sin have always been found among Catholics, even among the members of the clergy and the top hierarchy. Such has also been the case with the "separated brethren" and the apostates who founded their sects, even to a more scandalous and hateful extent. But, Mr. Küng, these human sins are not the Church, although at times they may be Protestantism. The Church has never taught or authorized evil, while Protestantism, by mutilating and adulterating Christ's doctrine, did justify, legalize, and spread such abuse. The evidence? What is the use of mentioning it, since we already know it?

8. In your laudatory phrase to the lamented Pontiff of Tolerance, John XXIII, you affirm he came to overthrow "the barriers of misunderstanding, inertia, isolationism, merely defensive attitudes, and reaction," in a decisive way, thus implicitly condemning the Popes and Councils of Trent and Vatican I who had sustained a different position for four hundred years. You deem this attitude to be wrong, if not false, heretical, and contrary to the Gospel. We must not forget that such a long spell of error, obstinance, or institutional malice, Mr. Küng, would be a proof of the Church's *fallibility* and deny its divine origin and Jesus Christ's promises. A spirit of understanding toward our "separated brethren" is fine, provided we do not give up the immutable doctrines of revealed truth or charge Jesus Christ's Church with responsibility for the religious revolutions some of its children have conducted during its 20 centuries of existence.

9. How subtle, sophistic, and dangerous is what this theologian from Tübingen insinuates about the relationship between Peter and the apostles, between the Pope and the bishops! Once again, he resorts to the spirit of the New Testament, as if the work of the Church throughout the centuries had adulterated the divine institution. *Question:* What is Hans Küng up to? *Answer:* To have the Pope be less of a Pope and the bishops more powerful as bishops. He says: "The apostolic ministry of the bishops must recover the spirit of the New Testament . . . ." One recovers what one has lost. The Church's dynamics had lost the spirit of the New Testament. The whole theological doctrine of "Roman Pontiff" is thus overthrown. Everything Vatican I analyzed, cleared up, and defined under the inspiration of the Holy Spirit needs review and amendment.

Let us look at two principles Küng has either disregarded or maliciously forgotten:

a. Christ made Peter the Head and Cornerstone of His Church and to him was given the keys of the kingdom of Heaven; he, *separately from the other apostles,* was given the power of binding and loosing, whereas the other apostles were given such power only with Peter, in communion with Peter, and dependent upon Peter. In other words, Christ gave only him the primacy of jurisdiction and the full Magisterium of the Church.

b. The bishops share the privileges of the apostolic college insofar as they are united with Peter, since the apostolic college does not exist without Peter.

If, within the spirit of the New Testament, as Küng hints, the divine origin of the Church's episcopate were the reason for comparing the bishops with the Pope, thus disregarding Peter's primacy, then the divine origin of the priesthood could also be the basis for establishing equality of simple priests with the bishops. Is it not true that the sacerdotal order has divine origin? Then away with the hierarchy! Let us proclaim the *égalité*, the democracy of the revolution.

10. Much has been said about the Roman curia's centralization and decentralization, and of its Italianization and internationalization. I feel two ideas must be distinguished in this concern. The Church cannot become *decentralized* without losing its organic constitution, as set up by its divine Founder. *Ubi Petrus, ubi Ecclesia.* It is impossible that the building not rest upon the one Cornerstone which Christ wanted to give it. A very different and less important aspect is that of the *internationalization* of the Roman curia. This is a subordinate subject where convenience and wisdom must be taken into account. Strictly speaking, there are no nationalities within the Church. Italians and French, Spaniards and Germans, Mexicans and Colombians, we are all the same. Fairness demands, however, that the members of the curia not be chosen according to their nationalities, but according to their skill, background, and

spirit, since the management of the Church includes many sensitive positions. Given the same qualities, it would be worthwhile to choose officers from different nationalities, so as to make the Church's catholicity concretely visible, but I believe it would be wrong to overstress this factor of nationality, to the extent of sacrificing the Church's interests. In order that the most important functions of the Roman curia be efficiently performed, the persons in charge must be well trained and the best ones chosen, even though all of them are Italians. To confer positions on foreigners just because they are foreigners and not Italians, when they are not well trained or have wisdom and experience enough, is, in fact, to jeopardize the Church's management.

11. Another remark on a chief subject: the Pope's inerrancy or infallibility does not belong to the structure of the Church, as Hans Küng says. It depends upon the Holy Spirit's aid and the promises of the divine Founder. That is why the *ex cathedra* definitions, as Vatican I says, are *infallible* in themselves, not because of the Church's consent.

12. Now we reach the very center of the ecumenical theology which, to be consistent, must necessarily flow into the charismatic and prophetic Church. Küng says that *the dogmas and definitions of the Church, are in themselves subject to improvement "since they are human-historical formulas . . . ."* Why? *Because any "polemically-defined truth includes a peculiarly erroneous side." In its verbal expression any statement "may be true and false."* Hence, this sharp theologian says, *"it is more difficult to find out" how a truth "has been thought than how it has been said. The ecumenical task of the theology of both sides consists of discovering the truth contained in the error of others and the probable error found in one's own truth."*

    a. If this luminous principle of Küng, which to tell the truth, smells of free "Protestant examination" and philosophical skepticism, were to be implemented, we should have to distrust everything and everybody. Who could tell me what the real thought was of anyone who spoke or wrote, since the verbal expression can be interpreted in different ways and be simultaneously right and wrong? The Gospel's very words, taken as human-historical formulas, are, according to Küng's ideas, subject to different interpretations. Since Holy Writ's words cannot tell us what Jesus Christ's thought was, who could do so, and with what authority?

    b. Mr. Küng, in your mind, the Church's definitions are *merely human-historical formulas.* You ignore their essential and typical elements, their divine inspiration and support, and their *infallibility.* You ignore the fact that there is a living, genuine, and infallible Magisterium of the Church, the only one that, in case of doubt, can give us the meaning of the words of Holy Writ or of the expressions that state dogmatic definitions. Any argument that might arise in unusual cases, ceases when the authoritative voice of the Roman Pontiff or the councils say their final word. However, we must bear in mind that such councils must be *real* councils and not contradict the teachings of other ecumenical councils, and that the Popes be *real* Popes, and not contradict what other Popes or ecumenical councils have previously defined as Church doctrine in accordance with revealed truth. In other words, there must be no gap between the definitions and definitive teachings of a council and another council, or of a Pope and another Pope.

c. Provided that the principle of contradiction is right and logic exists, we cannot accept Fr. Küng's destructive description of theology's ecumenical task, as he terms the fraternal compromise between orthodox and heterodox. He affirms that such a task consists of *"discovering the truth contained in the errors of others, and the probable error found in one's own truth."* There is no error at all in truth, although any error may have a true side, as Pascal said; in every error it is possible to find a part of truth, even though deformed by falsehood and sophisms.

I am convinced that for many of us priests in this world's hour of transition, it is a terrible thing for us to have to change and destroy the safe, deeply-rooted beliefs we all had. To hear that we were wrong, that our secular interpretation of theology was not correct, and that we must rediscover an authentic Christianity in which all religions and separated brethren are to be accommodated, is very difficult medicine to take.

ABOUT JACOB MARITAIN

Before ending this section in which I point out and refute the basis of the charismatic and prophetic Church, I must mention the French Jew Jacob Maritain, a baptized Catholic whose bold theses (close to heresy in some respects, if not *plainly* heretical) make him important to be included among the forefathers of *progressivism*. As is the case with Felicitas de Lammenais, he advances some schemes to unify the world, taking into account the various religious beliefs and the new age the world is entering. He defines private and public worship, even though it be false, as a natural right of the human person. He is the father of modern pluralism, which can also be derived from the famous "Statement on Religious Freedom" by Vatican II. I feel that Maritain's theses, which Paul VI has widely accepted and even spread, have been accepted by the progressivisits who, through their aspiring and hopeful dialogue, seek to unify the world and build a more human, more comprehensible, less rigid, and less inflexible Christendom. What matters to them is unity even though the truth be distorted!

The Montinian Church

A FURTHER CRITIQUE OF POPE PAUL VI'S SPEECH

The Most Eminent Cardinal Siri, the Archbishop of Genoa, wrote a letter addressed to his priests and dated August 1, 1959, entitled "Orthodoxy, Errors, and Dangers." The letter tells us about "certain intellectual and practical courses which either violate the sacred welfare of Catholic orthodoxy, or carry within themselves the germs from which, sooner or later, contradiction, or at the least inconsistencies, arise . . ." His Eminence said that "there are some people who caress the secret idea of a *world change* of affairs from which none will be able to escape. To them, the problem of orthodoxy consists of becoming adapted or interpreting, not of defending and conveying unchanged the truth received from the apostles." This most worthy Archbishop acknowledges the duty we have of loving our Protestant brethren and praying for them, "so that the adequate conditions for their return to unity may become true . . . . [W]e are not speaking about them . . . , but about a climate that, from Luther's times, has impregnated modern history and consists of cultural forms and feelings instead of proselytism. . . ." This climate has been called Jansenism, Illuminism, Modernism, and Progressivism.

The authors of these philosophies, along with Congar, Bea, Rahner, etc., are the forefathers of present progressivism, which of course leads to the charismatic and prophetic Church that Paul VI mentioned in the speech upon which we are commenting. The Pontiff said:

> Toward this Church we will make an effort of loving intelligence, so as to understand the good and acceptable things these restless and frequently wrong forms of interpreting the Christian message contain, to purify our Christian profession, and carry these spiritual experiences, be they secular or charismatic, to the seat of the true ecclesiastical rule.

In this regard, Rahner wrote:

> I have had the *sudden* idea that it is within the Church where radical opposition arises . . . . It is within the Church where struggle against secularization, de-sacralization, and so on, is necessary. In the coming years, it will be in the very Church where the non-Christian heresies will arise. These heretics will not seek to make us abandon the Church, but nevertheless, we must strongly defend Tradition and face them with absolutely clear disapproval and true condemnation . . . because, on behalf of the progress of the Church, our times, and its tasks, they are attacking the essence of Christianity and intend to acclimatize themselves to the Church." (*Ecclesia*, 29, 1969, no. 1471).

Paul VI and the New Theologians

Rahner condemns something and, on the other hand, accepts the same thing he has condemned, just like Pope Montini: "We will ... carry these spiritual experiences, be they secular or charismatic, to the seat of true ecclesiastical rule." Then Paul VI studies the problems of particular groups, and attacks the chief issue of his speech and the LAMEC meeting, the social problem. I continue to quote from Pope Paul's speech:

Groups Deserving Particular Attention

These remarks lead us to recommend to your pastoral charity some categories of persons which deserve our most affectionate thoughts. We shall mention them briefly, for the common apostolic interest demands it. We shall not be able to say everything they deserve, but we know their condition will be considered by this meeting, so we shall confine ourselves to stimulating your study.

THE PRIESTS

The first category is that of priests. We send them a most affectionate greeting from this see and in these moments. Priests are always in our spirit and mind and they also enjoy our appreciation and confidence. They are in the focus of the concrete activities of the Church. They are our first and indispensable co-workers; they are the most direct and dedicated "dispensers of the mysteries of God" (I Cor. 4:1), that is, of the Word, the grace, and the pastoral charity; they are living patterns of the imitation of Christ; they are, along with us, the first to participate in the Lord's Sacrifice. They are our brethren, our friends. We must love them very much, more and more each time. Any bishop who devotes his most dedicated, intelligent, patient, and hearty efforts to form, aid, and encourage his clergy will spend his time, heart, and activity in the proper way.

Try to give the presbyterial and pastoral councils the consistency and efficacy required by the council. Prudently advise them with paternal understanding and charity, as far as it is possible, in the event of irregular or undisciplined clerical attitudes. Try to call their attention to the affairs of the diocesan ministry and meet their needs. Be extremely careful in recruiting and training seminarians. Let male and female religious become involved in pastoral activities. In this way, by focusing our attention on the clergy, we will be sure to harvest the fruit we long for, that of a living, holy, orderly, and flourishing Church all over Latin America.

The sacerdotal problem is undoubtedly the principal problem that the bishops are facing. However, painful as it is to say, this is the problem bishops regularly disregard the most, concerned as they are with keeping their authority. They feel their authority is impaired by dialogue with their priests, although they do not hesitate to chatter with lay people. Between many bishops and their priests there is no other communication except the impersonal, cold, and official contacts they have as officials of the diocesan curia. Of course you find the chosen ones, the friends, the privileged ones, those who enjoy the "charity," the confidence, the overflowing generosity of the masters whom they serve with servility, adulation, and filial surrender. But these are a minority and perhaps have less merit. The way of party politics is, unfortunately, that of Church politics, which are not sincere, convenient, or profitable, as far as the bishops themselves are concerned. Many times those who flatter people to their faces are the same ones who censor them most severely among groups of clergy and laity!

I am convinced that many priests lose the wonderful ideals of their sacerdotal vocation when they experience and are the victims of misunderstanding, intrigue, and lack of charity on the part of their superiors and brothers in the priesthood. Nevertheless, it is priests who bear the *pondus diei et aestus*, the weight of the heat and work. It is priests who have to spend many hours in their confessionals, listening to the sorrowed souls who seek relief, pity, advice, and hope in religion. It is priests who, in the middle of the night, get up to aid the dying. It is priests who regularly baptize and teach religion to the ignorant. What would happen to the Church without its priests? What would happen to the bishops themselves?

From the Council, it appears that our prelates are more concerned for lay cooperation than for the unselfish, silent, though efficient, work of the priests, the "full-time workers," as the infiltrated Jew, Ivan Illich, called them. What should we say about the poverty amid which many of these priests live? If it were not for the charity of their believers whose private gifts help them, the majority of the priests in Mexico would not be able to live as human beings. I am not referring to the monsignors, or to those who have command in the post-Conciliar Church agencies. These have more than necessary to buy cars, spend their holidays at tourist spots, dress gorgeously and fashionably, and to attend cinemas, nightclubs, and other improper amusements not suited to their priestly role. Let us not forget it: this is the Church of the poor!

Pope Montini continues with his speech, mentioning another group deserving his thoughts and affection:

THE YOUTH AND THE STUDENTS

Then, Venerable Brethren, we present the youth and the students to your charitable wisdom. Our speech would never end if we were to cover this field. It suffices for you to know that we consider it to be worthy of the utmost interest and frightfully up-to-date. Of this you are all perfectly convinced....

Paul VI and the New Theologians

Indeed, the subject Paul VI mentions is extremely important. All of the big struggles are taking place in the field of the youth and students, which he poses and commits to the pastoral concern of our bishops. Some time ago, the agitator Bishop of Cuernavaca delivered a lecture (if this is the right name,) at the University of Puebla, where he unloaded all his revolutionary ideology, so as to give students the brainwashing they need to perform their future activities, which Sergio VII and the members of the underground National Liberation Army are preparing.

Two archbishops and a bishop challenged the subversive ideas the lord of Cuernavaca uttered, but he forged ahead, supported as he is by his colleagues, the former Benedictine Abbé Lemercier and the infiltrated Illich.[15] Not long ago the Archbishop paid a visit to the University of Guanajuato, where he suggested, as always, a "change of structures." He presented Communism as the way to implement Christ's redemption, suggested optional sacerdotal celibacy if the Fathers have "good taste when choosing wives." He asked for saints to be banned from the temples, for it is "idolatry to keep on revering images," and he called worship of the Church's "grandmother," as he impiously called the most Holy Mary, improper. In spite of all of this, another lecture by the indefatigable activist has been scheduled at Queretaro University.

Certainly the youth problem is very interesting and up-to-date, particularly as far as students are concerned. In almost every country, including Italy and Rome itself, we have seen Maoist, Trotskyite and Leninist youth: young people who are being encouraged to assault, raise barricades, commit terrorist acts, plunder, bring wild anarchy to the cities, and haughtily defy the police and the army when they try to restore order. Marcuse's destructive ideas are being spread within the pseudo-religious centers, as in the so-called university parishes where naive youths are being indoctrinated according to the *new* gospel. There is almost no school or university, even Catholic ones, where drugs are not used, pre-marital intercourse is not justified, and lectures designed to spread leftist ideologies are not sponsored. At the Universidad Iberoamericana of the Jesuits, lectures were given by Lombardo Toledano, Sergio VII of Cuernavaca, and the super-Communist Jesuit, Joseph Porfirio Miranda y de la Parra. The latter went so far as to affirm that private property, *any* private property, is the result of oppression or exploitation.

Let us quote again from Pope Montini's speech:

THE WORKERS

This idea leads us to remind you without less fervor, of another category of men: the peasants, the industrial workers, and others, be they believers or not. Thus we have reached the third issue that we wanted to submit for your consideration, namely, the *social* one. Do not expect a discourse, as this would be endless, particularly in Latin America. We shall confine ourselves to making some remarks which follow those we have made in our previous days' speeches.

Social Guidelines

ENCYCLICALS AND TEACHINGS OF THE EPISCOPATE

Above all, we remind you that, in the latest days of its centennial life devoted to promote civilization, the Church has elaborated a social doctrine of its own which has been stated on memorable documents worth studying and being disseminated. We must not forget or fail to put into practice the encyclicals of the Roman episcopate and the teachings of the world episcopate. Our counsel would be incomplete if we were not to remind you of the most recent social encyclical, *Populorum Progressio*. Many other documents deserve special mentioning too: the "Statement by the Bolivian Church" of last February, that of the Brazilian episcopate of November, 1967, which bears the title "Mission of the Hierarchy in Today's World," the findings of the sacerdotal seminary carried on in Chile from October to November, 1967, the pastoral letter by the Mexican episcopate on the nation's development and integration, published on the first birthday of the encyclical *Populorum Progressio,* the long letter by the Provincial Fathers of the Society of Jesus gathering with its Provost General Fr. Arrupe at Rio de Janeiro in May of this year (1968), and the document by the Latin American Salesian Fathers who recently met at Caracas. Many times the Church has borne witness in the social field. *Let us try to follow words with deeds.*

After having spoken as a Pope, Paul VI entered his favorite field. Now it is the statesman, the politician who speaks. He seeks not only peaceful coexistence with atheistic Communism, but also allegiance and cooperation with it, always preserving religious principles, even though these be relegated. The basis for his projects is his favorite encyclical, *Populorum Progressio,* and the episcopal documents that supported his directions. Evidently, when Paul VI wrote the encyclical, he first aimed at solving the problems of aching Latin America and its underdeveloped peoples. Now, he expects his words and those of his venerable brothers in the episcopate to be turned into a dynamic transforming action, which is why he says: "Let us try to follow words with deeds."

We return to Pope Montini's speech:

PASTORAL TECHNIQUE

We are not technicians. However, we are pastors who must promote good for our believers and stimulate renewal of the countries where our missions take

Paul VI and the New Theologians

place.

In this regard, our main duty is to state and affirm basic principles, discover and point to needs, support the social and technical programs that are truly useful, just, and lead to a new order and the common welfare, organize priests and laymen who know the social problems, and encourage trained laymen to work to solve them in the light of Christian principles. These will let us discover man at the top, and other values subordinated to man's complete earthly advancement and his everlasting salvation.

What does the Pope ask of the bishops? Let us divide his words into different parts. First, he demands that they state and affirm basic principles. Life's supreme values certainly belong to the spirit, not to man's material welfare, so this duty belongs to the sacerdotal and episcopal ministry, provided that the principles to be affirmed remain in the religious field, and not in the merely human scientific field. In this field, we have no jurisdiction, since human scientific thought is not the goal of our vocation or the Church's specific goal. Second, he asks us to point to the needs. Perhaps in this realm our lack of jurisdiction begins; in order to point to needs, we should have sufficient data at our disposal, and we do not. Next the Pontiff advises the bishops, and consequently the priests, to "support the social and technical programs that are truly useful, just, and lead to a new order and the common welfare . . . ." In spite of the respect which the Pontiff deserves from me, I believe this would overstep our mission and usurp a task belonging to the government. How could we and the bishops possibly support such social projects? With money? With personal activity? By devoting ourselves to the apostolate of social justice? Paul VI tells us: organize priests and laymen who know the social problems, in other words, form leaders. Here we have the reason for so many priest-activists who have put aside theology, prayer, inner life, study, and their sacerdotal duties. Trained lay people, such as the Avilés, the Alvarez Icaza's, and the leading members of National Action (*Acción Nacional*), *a priori* condemn everything the government does, with demagogical harangues which surpass those of the most radical members of the government. All these activists feel they are the elements their prelates have chosen to carry on programs of justice that establish world equality.

But Paul VI asks even more than this. He wants the bishops to bring all laymen to this grand task through which we will discover man at the top, although I fear we will forget God. It is man's development that matters.

The Latin American bishops are right in complaining of the scarcity of priests in their dioceses. How then could the bishops afford to have so many of their full-time workers engage in this new apostolate whose goal is the advancement of man? Besides, the sole force we can resort to in order to carry on any work of social apostolate in charge of lay people is, or at least should be,

The Montinian Church

a spiritual mission and an intensely Christian life which will necessarily then flow without alien pressure, and be turned into truth, unselfishness, sacrifice, and true love for others. Unfortunately experience has shown us this is not always the case. Sometimes, lay people (I am using this qualification with reservation) who work in these projects of the modern apostolate may do so because such is their *modus vivendi*, their way of travelling at other people's expense. Indeed it is not all gold that glitters; nor is it the *real* apostolate if it is not aimed completely toward God.

Again we go back to Pope Paul VI's speech:

WITNESS OF POVERTY

We have still other duties to fulfill. We have been informed of some generous projects being carried on in some parishes, which have put properties at the disposal of the people who needed them, thus effecting programs of thorough agrarian reform. This is an example worth praising and imitating wherever it is wise and possible. The Church is being appealed to by Christ's poverty. In the Church some people are right now experiencing the want of poverty, sometimes in lack of bread, and frequently of resources. Let these people be comforted and aided by their brethren and good believers, and be blessed. The Church's indigence, along with decorous simplicity, witnesses our loyalty to the Gospel. Sometimes it is the condition necessary for us to believe in our own mission. It may be an almost superhuman exercise of spiritual freedom, in face of the ties of wealth, to strengthen the apostles' force to perform its mission. Force? Yes, because *love is our force,* while selfishness, administrative decisions deprived of religious and benevolent goals, avarice, longing for possession as an end in itself, and luxurious welfare are *hindrances* to love. Ultimately, they are weaknesses, and they prevent one's commitment to sacrifice. Let us conquer these hindrances and let love rule our comforting and renovating mission.

The post-Conciliar Church has definitively contracted the vow of poverty which, according to evangelical advice, used to bind only the religious. At least that is what those who want us to give up everything, are continually telling us. This way we shall be able to devote ourselves to the apostolic work without any hindrance. Some objections come to mind. Would the bishops' renunciations really relieve (I am not speaking about eliminating) poverty, suffering, and indigence in the world? In stripping themselves of everything, are they not augmenting the number of the needy? In addition, with what right do they give away what, strictly speaking, is not theirs but the Church's, that which belongs to the dioceses they rule and administer, and possibly against the will of the people who gave them such goods. Perhaps they do not even need the minimal economic resources to feed their poor priests? There is indigence in the Church, too. Unfortunately, even to do good, earthly goods are necessary. Have we not noticed that the post-Conciliar Church, the Church of evolution, makes large expenditures to bring about its program of total renewal?

Today, like yesterday and tomorrow, the Church finds itself face-to-face with Christ's poverty, because the "evangelical advice" has always stood for those who hear the Master's unmistakable voice inside themselves: "Come and follow me!" The Church is always confronted by Christ's poverty because the *spiritual poverty* the Lord proclaimed in the first blessing is a most efficient way of reaching the kingdom of Heaven. I do not think the vocation of Christ's poverty, however, obliges the prelates to strip their dioceses of the gifts they received from the believers, gifts necessary for the fulfillment of the duties of their pastoral charge. Are we going to despoil the temples of the treasures our ancestors' faith and zeal gave them, to enhance divine worship and provide for the support of the shepherds?

On the other hand, as mentioned before, the Gospel does not require that those who have much, strip themselves of what they have as a condition for salvation or sanctification. "There will always be poor among you," said Jesus Christ. This means there will always be wealthy too.

The Pontiff praises the *"generous projects being carried on in some parishes, which have put properties at the disposal of the people who needed them...."* To Paul VI this is an example worth praising and imitating. These properties, gifts made to the Church for the upkeep of its prelates and priests, the support of seminaries, and the execution of all works of the apostolate and charity the Church unfailingly used to make, were the necessary means for the Church to pursue the task entrusted to it. By stripping the Church of those properties, they killed the hen that laid the golden eggs. They may have crippled the Church and prevented it from pursuing its mission of salvation. They rely on new gifts, which according to the signs of the times will no doubt decrease, since the socializing trends today ruling the world, tend to run through such reserves. On the other hand, when impious governments stripped the Church of its properties, such as in Italy (of the Pontifical states), Spain (through the Mendizábal Act), and Mexico (through the reform statutes), the Popes and the bishops protested on behalf of the Church. They did so legitimately, since these plunders were sacrilegious; they were not made against the prelates as men, but against God's Church. The Church is a visible society and therefore needs visible means to subsist and spread its redeeming work.

In this concern there is another point worth studying. I am referring to the *agrarian reform,* which is also mentioned by Paul VI as one of the basic issues of the reform he promotes. From the time of the Alliance for Progress which United States President Kennedy proclaimed, much has been said by Figueras, Betancourt, and other well-known politicians, about the *five basic reforms* necessary for the salvation of Latin America: *agrarian* reform, *urban* reform, *tax* reform, *educational* reform, and *political* reform. This was a cunning plan aimed at ruining our countries, thus preparing for the world government of which Paul VI spoke in his speech at the United Nations. I will not stop to comment on each one of these reforms, but I think it convenient to say something about the *agrarian reform* Paul VI canonized at the Cathedral of Bogotá. In fact, the Alliance for Progress and its five reforms were just a means of expediting the enslavement of our peoples to the mafia's designs.

Let us speak first about what *agrarian reform* means. It is the concrete solution to a perennial problem which has existed and exists now in Latin America, the *agrarian problem*. By agrarian reform, I mean there are social, economic, and political reasons for progressively increasing the ownership of small farms. The agricultural problem consists of many factors that intervene in land production: weather conditions, irrigation, cultivation, fertilizers, money, human minds, and labor. Under agrarian or agricultural reform, hasty and radical solutions may be necessary to handle these problems, some of which may be due to some governments' impatient attitudes, possibly inspired by poor advice.

The land problem has always existed in our countries right from the days of the conquest. Spain did not disregard it. Only through ignorance or evil intentions could one ignore the wonderful codes, the statutes of the Indians which the crown decreed in order to efficiently and progressively solve the problems or lack of expertise and scarcity of a population who could exploit the enormous possibilities these virgin lands offered the conquerors and the conquered. The solution was not definitive, nor could it have been otherwise. It was a temporary solution whose terms would change as the natives became more civilized. This process is still continuing; the full integration of the natives and the *mestizos* takes time, as mentioned before, and haste does not benefit those people one is trying to help. Radical land reforms carried out in Latin America, in Mexico for example, have jeopardized the country's peace and economy and failed to solve the problem. Instead they created the problems of "wet backs," the *braceros,* and the *bandoleros,* which have spoiled our national economy through unceasing emigration. Those people have formed an important minority with a feeling of inferiority in the United States. Only demagoguery, compromise, and political interests can continue to defend and foster the famous land reform among us.

What did those bishops who deprived their dioceses of the properties the believers had given them, intend to do? Did they believe those properties would suffice to solve all of the economic problems of the poor? No, they did not. What appears to be clear is that such demagogical examples would help unchain the longed-for land reform that *Populorum Progressio* proclaimed, but they failed to realize that such a hasty solution would ruin the national economy, harming those peoples they intended to benefit. Remember that to create land-owners it does not suffice to give land to people who cannot save, foresee, organize their work, or even conveniently invest the transistory income that the distribution of land gives them. Without knowledge, labor is not enough, insofar as lasting and fruitful exploitation is concerned. How much land has been impoverished by monoculture, since the people in charge of the *ejidos* are not able to conveniently exploit the land they have been nominally given, which, in reality is not theirs!

Let us continue with Paul VI's speech:

CHRISTIANITY AND VIOLENCE

Although we must encourage every sincere effort intended to promote renewal and elevation of the poor and all those who live in inferior human and social conditions, and although we cannot support systems and structures that conceal and foster grave and oppressing inequality among the classes and the citizens of a given country without putting an effective plan into action to remedy the unbearable conditions of inferiority that the less affluent population frequently experiences, once more we repeat ourselves: Neither hatred nor violence is the force behind our charity. Among the various ways leading to social justice, we cannot choose either atheistic Marxism, systematic rebellion, or even less, bloodshed and anarchy. Let us part from those who depict violence as a noble ideal, a glorious heroism, and pleasant theology. In order to correct errors of the past and banish today's evils, we must not commit new offenses, for this would be contrary to the Gospel and the spirit of the Church. To commit new offenses would be contrary to the very interests of the people and the happy sign of our present age, which is that of justice marching toward brotherhood and peace.

An open letter that a Mexican anti-Communist organization published in the newspapers of Bogotá on the days of the Eucharistic Congress, is credited with having made Paul VI amend this part of his speech. At first sight, he seems to condemn *violence* as anti-Christian and anti-evangelical. This issue was an essential one, taking into account the intense turmoil all the countries of South America were experiencing. Camilo Torres and "Ché" Guevara were considered two saints of the new post-Conciliar Church. The Jesuits, Don Helder and Don Serge from Cuernavaca, spoke about violence, though with reserve and reticence, so as not to get engaged themselves. Perhaps at one time they may have aspired to personally lead the guerillas, but they did not do so, although they did spread subversion everywhere.

Paul VI's eye for politics could not ignore the anti-Communist trend trying to stop the alien wave designed to establish Fidel Castro's and the Soviet's regime of slavery among us. That was why he skillfully amended his speech, stressing his condemnation of violence. As usual, however, he left the door open for the guerilla to enter the post-Conciliar Church. He said: "We cannot choose [the way of] systematic . . . violence . . . ." Not *systematically,* but *occasionally,* when the circumstances make it necessary, may we use guerilla violence, sabotage, kidnapping, and terrorist acts, in order to defeat institutional violence backed by the law and protected by the police and the army, who are bound to defend, unreasonably and unlawfully, what they feel to be theirs but which, in fact, according to the new post-Conciliar doctrine, belongs to the poor? In fact, taking into account the poor classes' unpreparedness by destroying wealth that belongs to private people, we enable poverty to spread and harm everyone and suppress the sources of production. Otherwise we have the government assume control of everything and imperceptibly establish a new slavery of terror and blood such as the one prevailing in Cuba.

Certainly the Pope condemns atheistic Marxism (this was one of the few times he did so), but with moderate terms: ". . . we cannot choose [the way of] atheistic Marxism. . . ." He failed, however, to point to a definite way to counter-attack Communism which, all over America, is spreading its tentacles in order to dominate us.

The second American Episcopal Convention, inaugurated by Paul VI, also spoke about another delicate subject, talk of which floated around Bogotá during Paul VI's stay. We continue with more of Paul VI's speech:

PEACE

Peace! You remember that the Church is most interested in it, and that we have personally made it, along with the Faith, into one of the most outstanding issues of our Pontificate. Now then, here at the celebration of the Eucharistic Sacrifice, symbol and source of unity and peace, we repeat our wishes for peace, the real peace arising from believing and fraternal hearts, peace among social classes in justice and cooperation, peace among people through humanism enlightened by the Gospel, and peace for Latin America.

While the Pontiff delivered the above flattering words, bloody programs for new guerilas, acts of terrorism, and contests were fermenting amid the young clergy, students and workers, which would soon leave the Latin American countries in bloody ruins. Peace cannot be achieved through demagoguery.

Pope Paul VI continues with his speech:

Paul VI and the New Theologians

LOVE AND TRANSFORMATIONS

In many circumstances, society needs deep and far-reaching transformations, which will promote by loving more intensely, and teaching to love with energy, wisdom, perseverance, practical deeds, confidence in man, confidence in God's fatherly aid, and the innate force of goodness. The clergy understands us by now, The youth will follow us. The poor will willingly accept the good news. We can expect that economists and politicians, who are already foreseeing the right way, will be no hindrance, but a stimulus at the vanguard.

Paul VI feels he is an enlightened commander in this transformation of the world and society. "... [A]t the celebration of the Eucharistic Sacrifice, symbol and source of unity ..., we repeat our wishes for peace...." This phrase by the Pontiff clashes with what the Bishop of Minorca, Dr. Michael Moncada, said last January. Part of what he said is worth quoting here:

> Nowadays we have a sociological Christianity, an underdeveloped Catholicism, a secular Mass.

In the opinion of the chronicler, Don Valentin Arteaga, the overwhelming majority of believers are not so because they have personally chosen and committed themselves or because they freely and deeply "live" their faith, but only because of sociological, environmental or hereditary reasons, as the Bishop of Minorca hinted. What does this mean? Plainly speaking, that the people, the laity, have always believed and still believe that salvation takes place, according to the Bishop, in a magic way, and, since this power, the liturgical rites, is in the hands of the clergy, "salvation is expected from those holy hands." Thus it can be explained that the laymen pay no attention to, part from, and dare not lend a hand to, the most urgent chore of living the Faith and committing themselves as a community. However, lay people should not seclude themselves, and they must become involved in the political-social action. This brave diocesan Bishop stated that he was committed because the Gospel demands and imposes it. Moreover, the Eucharist itself, aside from the fact that it is the Redeeming Sacrifice of Jesus, can be said, without circumlocutions, to be a *plot*, a *scheme*. It is a plot intended to perform a common task. If we really lived the Eucharist, the two barriers that prevent laymen from becoming involved would be overthrown: *passivism* and *individualism*. The Bishop of Minorca said to his audience:

> You enjoy freedom of culture, science, and political options, because Christianity is like salt, and salt can season many soups.

The Montinian Church

(Including, we might add, the soup of Communism.)

Let us go back to the Pope's speech. That society needs a deep transformation has been the constant claim of the Conciliar reformers. We shall implement this transformation through love. Fine! The clergy understands what the Pontiff meant. The youth, yes, the youth, will follow him. The old, marginal ones cannot follow him, for Paul VI's program no longer is, to us, the evangelical program. The poor will willingly accept the cry of freedom and independence the post-Conciliar leader proclaims. The Pontiff expects that the heads of government will not hinder, but encourage the brave ones. The meaning of this can be found in the documents of the second meeting of the LAMEC.

ON THE *HUMANAE VITAE*

Through our recent encyclical we have had to deliver a good, though grave, word in defense of the decency of love and the dignity of the family. The vast majority of the Church has welcomed it with confident obedience, though they understand that the rule we have reaffirmed carries a strong moral message and a brave spirit of sacrifice. God will bless this decent Christian move. It does not purport a blind course toward overpopulation, nor does it diminish the responsibility and freedom of the spouses. It does not prohibit honest or reasonable birth control, legitimate therapeutics, or the progress of scientific research. Our attitude encourages an ethical, spiritual, coherent, and profound education; it bans the use of those means that violate the conjugal relationship and tend to solve the big problems of overpopulation through excessively simple expedients. Ultimately this attitude of ours is a eulogy of life, which is a gift from God, glory for the family, and the strength of the people. Brethren, we exhort you to try to understand well the importance of the difficult and delicate approach which, as homage to God's law, we have deemed to be our duty to reaffirm. We pray that you will employ all possible pastoral and social solicitude so that this position be maintained, as it corresponds to people guided by a true human understanding. God grant that the lively discussion which our encyclical has aroused may lead us to better understand God's Will, to behave without reservations, and to make us serve souls, amid these pastoral and human difficulties, with the heart of a good shepherd.

Faced with any spiritual, pastoral or social problem, the Latin American episcopate, from the position it holds, will render a service of real truth and love, to the effect of building a new, modern, and Christian civilization.

At the end of his speech, the Pontiff touched upon the problem of the fiery argument his recent encyclical on birth control, *Humanae Vitae,* had stirred. Few times, if any at all, had the Church beheld such a reaction as the one this papal document provoked, despite the fact it had merely ratified what Pius XI and Pius XII had peremptorily said. Considering that more than four years of actual *vacatio legis* has transpired, the fact of Paul VI's having convened a committee of "experts" to study the problem of birth control pills gave the vanguard theologians the occasion of affirming that the natural law that forbids the use of any chemical or mechanical device to prevent pregnancy was a *doubtful* law. Since the Pontiff had been obligated to convene such a committee to study and weigh the arguments for and against the new contraceptive methods, these theologians maintained that this law could not be obligatory. Priests, bishops, and even cardinals authorized and privately defended not only the use of pills but of *all* contraceptive devices, now that the new theology had discovered that the primary and essential goal of marriage was not as had been taught up to this time, the procreation and education of children, but love and the legitimate satisfaction of sex.

In Latin America, the problem was very grave, because in these countries demographic explosion is more impressive and overwhelming. Lives had to be suppressed, so that these underdeveloped countries could survive. The American government (that of the United States), deeply concerned for this problem, organized and financed "health" brigades to spread and facilitate the use of birth control pills among our people, with the result that even thirteen- and fourteen-year-old girls started to carry them in their handbags in order to avoid disagreeable eventualities.

Paul VI, then, could not ignore this problem on an occasion such as the one during which he was speaking particularly to the Latin American episcopate. In spite of his saying that "the vast majority of the Church" had favorably received this encyclical with confident obedience," they had not. As we mentioned before, not only private people, priests, and laymen, but even episcopal conferences had frowned upon this Pontifical document. They opened a way out that Paul VI failed to close; on the contrary, he recommends to the prelates that "these pastoral and human difficulties" be faced "with the heart of a good shepherd." This might be interpreted to mean that we are to be complacent about human weaknesses.

A SPEECH BY JOHN CARDINAL RICKETTS, ARCHBISHOP OF LIMA

Here I terminate my brief commentary on the Pope's speech at the opening of the second Latin American Episcopal Conference. I believe it interesting to now reproduce the speech by His Eminence John Cardinal Landazuri Ricketts, Archbishop of Lima and primate of Peru, co-chairman of the second general conference of the Latin American episcopate. His text follows:

The Montinian Church

Most Holy Father,

America, a land where the people are brotherly and linked by close ties of blood, religion, language, and culture even though divided by unjust social, economic, and cultural differences, welcomes you with much hope.

America, the land of Rose of Lima and Marianne of Jesus, of Toribio of Mogrovejo and Francis Solano, of Peter Claver and Martin of Porres, welcomes you, convinced that the spirit that inspired them will give birth to many real Christians who will search for new ways of serving their brethren. [Vatican II says: "Let it be clear to everybody that all believers, whatever their state or condition, are called to the fullness of Christian life and to the perfection of charity, and that this sanctity fosters a more human way of life, even in this earthly society."]

America, the land that honors Christ's Mother in Tepeyac and Chiquinquirá, in Aparecida and Coromoto, in Copacabana and Luján, reaffirms in your presence the need for a poor Church devoted to the service of its Lord.

The Pilgrim of Peace

We welcome you with thankfulness in our souls and joy in our hearts. We joyfully greet the Pilgrim of Peace, for we know this is the sign of your presence among us. You are a pilgrim whose light is gleaming in the present age on the critical stage of Latin American history. Well do we know that today, in America and throughout the world, peace is featuring a new aim: "The development of every human being and of all human beings." Permit me to state then, my great joy in welcoming the pilgrim of this development of suffering peoples. Welcome among us, Pilgrim of Peace. [This was the title Paul VI awarded himself before the Conciliar Fathers upon his return from his trip to the United Nations. *AAS*, 57, 1965. 895.]

Latin American Collegiality

The Latin American bishops gathering for our second general meeting presided over by Your Holiness, affirm episcopal collegiality, and participate in the hope and concern of our people. This is the hope of almost 270 million men and women, most of whom are young. They are concerned about the present economic, social, cultural, political, and religious situation.

Deep Transformations

For the people in charge of this historical moment there is no choice between maintaining the present conditions and changing them. To maintain the present conditions is old-fashioned. We all agree about the need for profound

Paul VI and the New Theologians

and rapid transformations; what concerns us is the *method* of accomplishing such an urgent task. An abnormal situation exists in Latin America, where the dignity of the human person is ignored, and where large masses are still waiting for the sign of their Redemption.

Rapprochement with Man

Taking this disquieting reality into account, and following outstanding examples set by Your Holiness, we cannot help avowing that our attitudes have not always encompassed a total picture of the situation. It is certain that, imitating the Lord, we have been concerned for the poor and the needy, thus being faithful to our mission, but we believe we need a work of purification that, like an encouraging impulse, will carry us to much-longed-for reform. We must bring ourselves closer to man, for by leaning toward him and the earth we go deep into the kingdom of God. [So also said Paul VI at the last session of Vatican Council II.]

Latin American Liberation

In Latin America, salvation, which is the fulfillment of the kingdom of God, embraces the liberation of man as a whole, and the change for each and all, from less human to more human conditions of life *(Populorum Progressio)*. That is what we anxiously desire and are bound to fulfill. To do so, we must be deeply and fully immersed in Christ's message in order to understand that God's kingdom will not reach its maturity where it does not find complete development. Therefore, in our pastoral service we will seek the ways of incarnating the Lord's love in the Church today.

Task of the Meeting

Our task in this conference, where the Latin American Episcopal Council and the Pontifical committee for Latin America have worked harmoniously and joined their best efforts, consists of introducing the Church to the present transformation of Latin America, according to Vatican Council II.

This work which we undertake with humility, obliges us first to become more consciously aware of our destiny. Where are we going? What are we bringing to the people who are waiting for us?

The Signs of the Times

In a decided effort for continued conversion and to live according to evangelical love, we cannot help acknowledging that it is the Church, our

The Montinian Church

Church in Latin America, that is being challenged to deepen the consciousness it has of itself (*Ecclesiam Suam*).

Each one of us sincerely wonders about the meaning of our presence and action in these changing moments and this difficult state of search. At this crossroad, the Church of Latin America is not searching after prestige or privilege. God's people, who are living and suffering in these lands, want to be faithful to the Lord in saying of themselves that they want to serve humanity. "All this doctrinal richness of the Council points one way: to serve man in all his circumstances, weaknesses, and needs..., in which the idea of service has occupied a central position." (Homily of Paul VI, at the last public session of Vatican Council II).

In the light of Vatican II, we want to see whether we have put its central, deeply Christian idea of service *(Lumen Gentium)*, into practice, and want to understand to what point this service to man must carry us.

Need for a New Order

Because we are concerned for man as a whole, in the process of transformation and development of our peoples, we want to help them be the authors and makers of their progress *(Populorum Progressio)*. Let them be the ones who freely undertake the tasks and obligations given by the Creator. On our part, we must offer them the spontaneous and audacious engagement arising from the Eucharistic brotherhood. It is an invitation to rectify inequality among persons and sectors of people. Let, then, solidarity and a fairer distribution of earthly goods among the members of human communities accompany the conveyance of the supernatural wealth of Christ, our Savior and Brother (Paul VIth's radio broadcast message to the Peruvian National Eucharistic Congress. AAS, 57, 1965).

To effect this, we need an urgent, deep change, one that does not replace a minority by another one, and that does not implant hatred where only brotherhood should reign. We need a new, more human, more Christian, and more Eucharistic order.

Not in vain did this 39th International Eucharistic Congress, with its motto, *"Love Bond,"* signify hope, struggle, and a dream turned into reality. It means serving a society in the process of changing, not to dominate, but to cooperate, not to compromise, but to inspire, not to hinder progress, but to promote it. It is the Eucharist, a gift of the Holy Spirit, who strengthens it. It is the Spirit of Jesus who will enable all men to have more, to *be* more.

We know that this action of ours is difficult and full of risks and incomprehension, but it will be the sign that the transformation, progress, and development of Latin America will not be ambiguous *(Populorum Progressio)*. Our goal on behalf of the Lord will turn it into a completely human goal, for it will be rooted in Jesus Christ.

Most Holy Father: Before the fear and uneasiness entailed by this task which we share with men from all continents, we conceive this visit paid to us in this noble, generous, and hospitable land of Colombia as a most assuring sign of hope.

We expect that your advice will guide us safely in our task. We heartily thank you for your presence in Latin America, at the same time that we renew our firm adherence and filial affection.

Pray bless us all: our peoples and this second general conference of the Latin American episcopate. Your blessing as a Pilgrim of Peace will be a promising sign for the whole Church and for all men.

Here we have the speech of a person compromised, one who seeks to please his master so as to keep his privileged position. Excuse me if I tell you frankly what I thought and felt when I heard the above words at the Cathedral of Bogotá. The Cardinal-Archbishop of Lima, ignoring or concealing the portentous work of the Church in all Latin American countries, seems to support the charges the *Populorum Progressio* brings openly against the colonial countries, among which we must obviously include Spain. Pope Montini has never been friendly to Spain, as we Spaniards and Spanish-Americans well know. To him the astonishing richness of pre-Columbian culture which the conquest buried, is a plunder not compensated by religion, language, Christian civilization, or the blood which Spain bequeathed to us. The Latin American people, although united through the close links of blood, religion, language, and culture, are, however, divided by "unjust social, economic and cultural differences." Who, may I ask, is to be blamed for these differences and divisions? Spain? The Church? The ecclesiastics of the past? The Peruvian Cardinal-Archbishop did not say that, but he hints it. This is the *mea culpa* of the post-Conciliar Church, which attributes to the pre-Conciliar Church all the horrors, injustices, and calamities of this poor and suffering humanity.

The title which Pope Montini uses in order to justify and explain his frequent lightning trips which he has already made in his Pontificate is certainly a novel one. "Pilgrim of Peace": this is the sign of his presence in Bogotá, "a pilgrim whose light is gleaming in the present age on the critical stage of Latin American history." The gleam and glitter we saw at the Colombian capital was sinister and announced grave storms that are to cover almost all of the peoples in this continent with blood. The directive was "a bold change of structures." The Pontiff's presence was not designed to enliven our faith, to renew our behavior according to the rules of the eternal Gospel, or to confirm us in the immutable principles of Christian life, aimed at the everlasting. Rather, his goal was that his encyclical, *Populorum Progressio*, would have all the efficacy necessary to effect a complete transformation among us. That was why the

The Montinian Church

Peruvian Cardinal calls him "Pilgrim of Peace," since "peace is featuring a new aim: 'The development of every human being and of all human beings.'" Peace is no longer, according to Saint Augustine's definition, "orderly tranquillity," the peace that "comes from God," the "quality of God," or "God Himself living within us" *(Pax Dei, Deus pacis, et Ipse est pax nostra)*. Now peace is the development of man as a whole and of all human beings.

The Pontiff is welcomed and greeted, then, as the pilgrim for development of the suffering peoples. Little does it matter in Europe, America, and the whole world that Catholic ideals are not only trampled, but forgotten and rejected and that the Faith has undergone a serious crisis among the believers themselves. Paul VI boasts of being "the pilgrim of material development in the poor stricken countries." Will Paul VI be able to even relieve, not to speak about cure, the poverty of individuals and countries, despite his goodwill and the utopia described in his encyclical?

The reference to "collegiality," of which our venerable post-Conciliar prelates feel so proud, as if Vatican II had defined something new on this subject, could not be absent. Actually collegiality is not to be found in a regional or national group of bishops, but in the gathering or communion of all the bishops of the Catholic Church with the sovereign Pontiff, with *Peter,* as long as he is *Peter.* But the Cardinal wanted to remind Paul VI of the communion of all the bishops of our peoples, who share the hopes and concerns that stimulate the Pontiff's tireless activity, and which are common to almost 270 million human beings living in this continent. So what are our hopes? What are our preoccupations? Our concern arises from our present economic, social, cultural, political and religious inequality in which we unhappy Latin Americans find ourselves. We hope that the application of the *Populorum Progressio* may resolve these enormous and long-standing problems, through a complete change of stiff, old-fashioned, and decadent structures.

No one argues about change itself, for this has already been decided, but disagreement arises as to the way it has to be accomplished. Through new laws, revolutions, or guerilla warfare? *Intelligenti pauca:* to him who has intelligence, it is enough to hint at the solutions. In Latin America—horror of horrors!—the dignity of the human personality is not only not respected, but ignored. In Latin America large masses are still waiting for the sign of their Redemption, which is not that of Christ, since most of the natives had already received this, but the Redemption Pope Montini now offers us through his *Populorum Progressio.* To attain this, *we must approach the human being.* ". . . [W]e need a work of purification that, like an encouraging impulse, will carry us to much-longed-for reform." The way the Jews had their purifications prior to the celebration of Passover, our bishops must purify themselves prior to the longed-for reform, or at least this appears to be the Cardinal's advice. The bold phrase, the one I deem unbearable, states that by leaning more toward man we enter deeper into the kingdom of God. I would say it is the reverse: the more we approach God, the more we do or can do for man, but the more we approach man, the more we forget God.

The liberation which the Cardinal-Archbishop seeks implies slavery, which I do not believe exists in our countries. There is inequality among us, the way there is inequality in almost all countries. There are indigenous people like the Tarahumaras and the Huicholes, who, despite the efforts made by heroic missionaries, still live a nomadic life. There is ignorance; there is poverty; there are degenerating vices. As I mentioned before, when we consider the social problems in Latin America, it is not possible in a short time to bring about the basic education and the necessary prophylaxis to permit our poor people to live a more human life. It is a work of much time, sacrifice, and intelligent efforts. However, this does not mean we must oblige those who are living a more human life, those who are more educated, developed, or well-bred, to live under the same conditions as the indigent. The ripeness of the kingdom of God does not mean material development or that the Lord's love incarnates itself in earthly benefits. Christ wanted to be born and live in poverty in order to sanctify our poverty and teach us how to resign ourselves to what God has given us, while looking forward to the gifts of everlasting life.

In Latin America, besides these earthly problems, there are some other most grave problems which must have greatly preoccupied our prelates, the episcopal council, and the Pontifical commission for our continent. We are experiencing a progressive de-Christianization of our peoples, a lack of religious training, and a religious illiteracy that is to be found not only among the uneducated who at least have the collier's faith, but also among people who call themselves cultured and whose religion consists mainly of sophisms and inconsistent objections they find in the many books circulating today. There is open immorality that tolerates the most provocative excesses in feminine and masculine fashions. Unbridled passions look for satisfaction in continuous, morbid amusements in the most illicit freedom.

Vocations are lacking, and those who enter the vocations do not receive a solid, austere, and truly pious education that guarantees perseverance and the correct exercise of the sacerdotal ministry. Catholic schools, having lost the reason for their existence, have been converted into very productive businesses which make the male and female religious who work there lose their spirits. Day after day the infidelity of priests and even some bishops grows, causing them to leave their holy ministries and look for the satisfaction of their insatiable appetites in marriage or licentious places.

What is the goal of this foolish and crazy race? Do our pastors ignore these most grave evils? Can they not see the wolves cutting the sheep into pieces? Can they not see that the only thing that ecumenical dialogue has achieved is to facilitate the proselytism by the sects of our poor and ignorant people? Notwithstanding these pertinent questions, the task of the second conference of the Latin American episcopate consisted of "introducing the Church to the present transformation of Latin America."

Who will establish this new order among us? The same people who have failed to defend and preserve the traditional Faith in Europe? Those who have incurred irreligiosity in the most regretful and painful way? What is left of Catholic life in Holland, Belgium, France, and even in Italy? Were statistics to speak, we would have to confess that the European panorama is not more flattering than that of our poor underdeveloped peoples, as far as religion is concerned.

What can we give, asks the Cardinal, to the people who are waiting for us? I would answer what Saint Peter told the poor sick man: We have no gold nor the power to give you the technological, economic, political, and social transformation you ask of us, but we do have something worth more than all that, the traditional Faith of the apostles and the immutable Faith of our ancestors who brought about the amazing miracle of carrying civilization to the Latin American countries. We have this heritage we received from God through the ministry of Mother Spain. If our peoples have become stagnant along the road of true progress, it is because we have abandoned the Catholic way of life, the very essence of our nationality, and because we have allowed the Masonic lodges, then the Protestant sects, and finally Communism, to divide us and provoke barren fratricidal struggles among us while making us consciously or unconsciously join the parties of the real enemies of our countries.

These are the actual signs of the times. We have abandoned God, in order to stupidly convert ourselves into creatures. In these present moments, when everyone is talking about earthly redemption, a peace without God, material progress and a process of developing what we have and we are in this world, it is unbelievable that our pastors should abandon their transcendental and basic mission in order to become reformers of the conditions of this transient world and apostles of social justice. This is no investment, but a waste of life's values, according to the immutable hierarchy God Himself gave them. Such is the cause of the confusion, uncertainty, nonconformity, and the growing disquietude in which we live. Through the magic of the pastors themselves, the Church's monolithic stability has become part of the world of permanent change and instability in which we now live.

This is the famous *aggiornamento*, this is ecumenism, this is the dialogue of Vatican II! And who are the beneficiaries of this subversion? The mafia, that Jewish-Masonic conspiracy which is already planning the establishment of a world government and a single homocentric religion of universal brotherhood.

Chapter XXX

LAMEC DOCUMENTS, RESULTS, AND THE TRUTH ABOUT PAUL VI

The Bible speaks of the eschatological signs which will announce the end of the times, and in verse three of the 16th chapter of the book of Matthew in the Douay Rheims Version (TAN Books and Publishers, Rockford, IL, reproduction of the 1899 edition of the John Murphy Company, Baltimore, *Imprimatur*, James Cardinal Gibbons), the phrase, "signs of the times," is used by Christ while talking to His apostles.

It was John XXIII who first used this term in an encyclical or document he delivered to all "men of goodwill," Catholics and non-Catholics.

Consistent with its reformist terminology, Vatican Council II definitively consecrated the phrase, "signs of the times" in its Constitution, *The Church in Today's World*. Chénu[16] wrote an article in *Nouvelle Révue Théologique*, explaining the meaning of *"Les signes des Temps."* According to *Gaudium et Spes*, they are those great events, facts, attitudes, and relations that typify a given era.

SOME DOCUMENTS OF THE SECOND LATIN AMERICAN EPISCOPAL CONFERENCE

In Medellín, at the LAMEC meeting, we have our prelates thoroughly scrutinizing the signs of the times in Latin America in order to mathematically arrive at an exact diagnosis of the unrest, inner struggle, and huge problems of these underdeveloped countries in the process of development and integration under the bright light of the *Populorum Progressio*. Here we have God's Church, the work of Christ, subject to fluctuations in order to "get to see, through these signs and transient currents that reveal God's Spirit" acting in "the world in which we live, with its hopes, aspirations and the dramatic bias that frequently characterize it." This language is most certainly unknown to us, and, in our ignorance, seems to be more adequate for demagogical conferences than for the serene exposition of Catholic theology. Here we have the Church as a function of the world and man, not man and the world as functions of the Church's salvific task.

The Montinian Church

A Document by Monsignor Mark McGrath, Bishop of Santiago de Varaguas, Panama

The Most Excellent Msgr. Mark McGrath, Bishop of Santiago de Varaguas in Panama and second vice-president of LAMEC, delivered one of the first speeches about "The Signs of the Times in Today's Latin America" at the LAMEC meeting in Medellín. The Bishop explained the meaning of this cabalistic or Talmudic term for us, according to post-Conciliar vocabulary, and said that the signs of the times disclose to the scholar the underground currents, the causes and effects of events, as well as the hopes and concerns of men. The person who understands them is able to intuitively know and spiritually feel the dynamic currents of his times in living history. Thus he becomes better able to influence history.

What did our skilled prelates discover on the misty horizon of our continent's current times? Monsignor McGrath gives us three main signs: (a) change, (b) appraisal of the temporal and the spiritual, and (c) world approach. He discusses *change* first:

> Today man is going through a new historical age whose features are deep and swift changes progressively spreading throughout the whole world. They are provoked by man with his intelligence and creative dynamism, but then they affect man, his ways of thinking, and his behavior as to reality and the men with whom he lives. This is so to such an extent that one may speak about a real social and cultural metamorphosis which affects religious life, too. (*Gaudium et Spes*, 4).

Paul VI, in his apostolic exhortation to the Latin American episcopate on November 24, 1965, said:

> Latin America presents a society in movement, subject to rapid and profound changes. These transformations are evidenced first by the rapidly expanding population, which at the present pace, according to the experts, will increase the Latin American population to more than 500 million by the end of this century. This single phenomenon reverberates with grave consequences in all the segments of life and, in a special way, alarms the Shepherd, who asks himself what the Church can do to shelter and lead to a really Christian life the new children that each year are added by the millions to its already plentiful flock. The Shepherd first thinks of defending the existing conditions, but this attitude is not enough, either because existing things do not suffice for the whole population and all its needs, or because even what exists is intermixed and dragged by movement and transformation.
>
> The changing conditions we are going through demand new

approaches to an urgent, global, and profound structural reform. The presence of new problems and the resolution of old problems constituted a real challenge, but in the realm of Providence, they stand as signs of the times requiring imagination, audacity, and joint work in order to find an adequate solution. (*Working Document,* Second General Meeting of the Latin American Episcopal Conference, Latin American Reality).

Unquestionably, to the post-Conciliar Church, *change* is not only an impressive fact, but also an expression of God's salvific design that exists to save the world through change. "There is always change," affirms Msgr. McGrath. "Living is changing," said Newman,[17] who also said: "To live much is to have changed often." The spectacular changes we are experiencing now, however, have already brought man into a new period of history. The question is whether this new period of change is one of progress, stagnation, regression, or a tragic decline for humanity. Has man unconsciously fallen into the deadly traps set by its enemies in order to dominate, enslave, and subdue him? To me the metamorphosis is so destructive that it has begun to invade the *Sancta Sanctorum*. It is not a sign of progress or stagnation, but evident proof of a dangerous regression by which human folly is trying to merge the opposite poles of affirmation and denial, and of being and non-being according to Hegelian and Marxist philosophies.

As Msgr. McGrath points out, large segments of our population used to live outside of the surprising changes that take place daily in the more developed countries, where madness has succeeded in imposing itself up to the limits of the most inconceivable and inadmissible excesses. It was the post-Conciliar ecclesiastics (I publicly denounce them here) who, by introducing these continued changes in liturgy, theology, morality, and discipline, gave us a terrible feeling of instability, insecurity, and constant change that made us accept these absurdities pre-fabricated by the mafia. These changes have been disseminated, accepted, and even legalized in the materially rich and developed, but spiritually poor and degenerate countries, and gradually have been spread among us, too, thanks to the compliance of the ecclesiastics and the silence of the shepherds. That is why mistrust of traditional things and institutions of the past grows among some unknowing or corrupt people. That is why there is now a deep division between children and parents, and subjects and the authorities and their laws. Bishops rise against bishops, priests against priests, and members of religious orders against those who do not think as *aggiornated* people and refuse to change what their saintly founders taught and bequeathed to them. The *change,* the *signs of the times* are also the *signs of a permanent revolution.* When everything changes within a society, a family, or an individual, its ruin and disintegration begin.

Let us briefly analyze Msgr. McGrath's ideas on the second sign of the times in Latin America, *the appraisal of the temporal and the spiritual*:

Gaudium et Spes (34) says: "One thing is certain for believers: Human activity, individual and collective, and the prodigious efforts realized by man throughout the centuries in order to achieve better life conditions, are, considered in themselves, consistent with God's Will. Once man was created in God's image, he received the order to rule the world according to justice and sanctity, thus subduing the earth and whatever it contains, and leading it to God, as Creator of all, in such a way that, all things being subdued to man, God's name be revered in the world."

Paul VI, in closing Vatican Council II in December of 1965 said: "Has all this and whatever we might still say about the human value of the Council, perhaps bent the mind of the Church to the anthropocentric direction of modern culture? Bent, no, but turned, yes. Anyone who observes this prevailing interest of the Council for human and temporal values cannot deny that such concern is due to the pastoral nature of the Council's program, and will have to acknowledge that this interest is never separated from the most authentic religious interest due to charity. Charity is its sole source of inspiration—'where there is charity, there is God'—and the union of human and earthly values with those specifically spiritual, religious, and eternal values that the Council has consistently affirmed and promoted, may lean first, toward man and the earth, but also rise toward the kingdom of God."

The above-described secularization of culture has influenced faith and beliefs, thus provoking a crisis, which has been logically followed by positive and negative consequences. (*Working Document,* Second General Meeting of the Latin American Episcopate, *Religious Situation*, 8).

If we agree that change is an expression of God's Will and providence, we must logically accept the second sign of the times that was cautiously studied by our prelates at their Medellín observatory. I am referring to the appraisal of the temporal and the spiritual. According to apostolic tradition, the pre-Conciliar Church which had certainly noticed great and profound transformations in society and the world but had never thought of adapting the Church to those changes, did not ignore or disregard the value of the temporal or the dignity of the human being. Today, from an opposite point of view, the post-Conciliar Church in viewing the terroristic signs of the times, is leaning more toward man, thinking that by so doing it will more closely approach God's kingdom. Is this right?

Secularization, concentration on the values of this world with the consequent de-Christianization, de-sacralization, de-mythification, and irreligiosity on the part of the pseudo-intellectuals and those who have been infected by the satanic ferments of the mafia, are fruits of free thought and the encyclopedia of revolution and Masonry. Vatican II wanted to baptize the term, to place a bridge between the two seemingly irreconcilable positions of spirituality and secularization. We cannot accept secularization as long as it means indifference to or rejection or exclusion of religion and religious considerations, but only as long as it signifies the intrinsic value of creation, or the emancipation of man from other men and nature. "The aforesaid scientific and technological advances, along with the progressive mentality and the stress on the development that accompanies them," says Msgr. McGrath, "puts us face-to-face with the necessity for revaluation. This planned approach (science and religion, progress and salvation, etc.) is one of the great signs of the last few centuries."

Prior to Vatican II, the problem was to show that there is and there can be no antagonism between faith and reason. Not now. Notice this bold statement: "The limited hope that religious preoccupation for unearthly things arises in man's imagination is pale for many people and a hindrance to others for the real task of man right here and now." (*Gaudium et Spes*). In other words religion, and its hope in life everlasting, turns pale in face of the great reality that man has in this world right here and now before death. In fact, religion may even become an obstacle for man's progress on earth.

Monsignor McGrath has this to say about secularization:

> This sign of so-called secularization has been studied a great deal in all its aspects. Just to mention some interesting points regarding its interpretation, may I say that, starting with some sociological data, some theologians have reached the so-called theology of the death of God. Some sociologists blame this theology for its having exaggerated or misunderstood the real basis of their lucubrations. They affirm that secularization might in many circumstances mean a search for God instead of a rejection of Him. It may mean an effort to find God in things and events, in creation or, at least with regard to creation, to give it its *real* meaning instead of the idea of an abstract God who has no meaning for man.

The God which Christianity has consistently depicted is no abstract God deprived of human meaning, as implied by this *secularization*, a term which to us is devoid of any religious meaning. Our God is our Creator, from whom we have received all that we are and have and through whom we maintain our existence. Our God is the ultimate goal toward which we direct our steps in all the acts of our lives, provided we walk along the safe path of His divine precepts and always try to obey His most holy Will. Our God is a provident God who foresees and arranges (or at least *permits*) everything, for "neither does a leaf of a tree move nor a hair fall from our heads without the intervention of the Will of our Heavenly Father."

Our God has ennobled and sanctified our sufferings, our privations, our needs. "Take no thought for what ye shall eat, or what ye shall drink. Behold the fowls of the air: for they sow not, neither do they reap, nor gather into barns; yet your Heavenly Father feedeth them. Consider the lilies of the field, how they grow; they toil not, neither do they spin. And yet I say unto you, That even Solomon in all his glory was not arrayed like one of these." *"Quaerite primum Regnum Dei et iustitiam eius et haec omnia adiicientur vobis."* ("Seek ye first the kingdom of God, and his righteousness; and all these things shall be added unto you.")

The creatures speak to us about God and reveal God's infinite perfection to us, according to what the apostle says: *"Invisibilia enim Ipsius, per ae quae facta sunt conspiciuntur."* ("God's invisible things become apparent to us in the visible.") This is the real value of earthly goods which to us are a means, not an end, and through which we reach God, at times through use, and at others through renunciation. When man loses this clear idea of creation, when, like Teilhard, he wants to identify the universe with God or Christ, he denies God and parts from Him.

This is the only real and intrinsic value of the things God has put to man's use, namely, that of being a means of serving God, aiding one's neighbor, and working for his own salvation and sanctification. At this point it is worthwhile to continue quoting Msgr. McGrath's discourse:

> In the positive sense, one insists upon the real and intrinsic value of things which are at the service of man, and upon man's domination of them to serve him, both individually and collectively (Paul VI's speech of August 24, 1968). This insistence is greatly important for pastoral and Christian asceticism. It urges that each Christian thoroughly fulfill his technical or professional earthly task so as to honor God and benefit men and cooperate with all men of goodwill so that the world progresses and men are served. In the way of asceticism, it entails a revaluation of earthly things, in all their aspects, from the intellectual and scientific to the beautiful and pleasant, with special emphasis on interpersonal relations, that is, human love. This has provoked a crisis in the prayer life of many, including priests and religious who have rejected devotions as routine and abstract. They are searching for a kind of spirituality that, more "incarnated" in earthly problems and more "horizontal," expresses itself through personal and social love. God is sought in the love of one's neighbor; this is a legitimate trend and must be respected. Criticism of the so-called "traditional devotions" (rosary, office, examination of conscience, systematic meditation) is not groundless. This danger is common to any transition. People reject the traditional devotions, but they cannot find any to replace them. Even meditation on the Bible itself may end in discussing the Bible.

According to this new statement of our Catholic religion, man has not been created to love, praise, and serve the Lord our God as the famous Ignatian meditation on the principle and fundamental taught us, but rather to serve man individually and socially. Only by thoroughly fulfilling this earthly task will he be able to serve God, benefit others, and save and sanctify his own soul. The poor hermits were just fools who neither served God, did anything for their neighbors, nor did they save themselves. The contemplative orders are not only anti-Conciliary, but anti-Christian. That is why they are being pressed to give up their contemplative lives and devote themselves to an active one! We are witnessing heresy in action! This is *naturalism,* which is intended to become the religion of man.

Our prelates feel Latin America is in urgent need of secularization in order to uproot our peoples' "superstition." "Many peasants rely on prayers, blessings, and *mandas* [promises to God or the saints] to get better crops, etc., and that is why, to an extent, they are distrustful of technical means (fertilizers, insecticides, etc.)." I cannot agree with this new theology, which seems to condemn the old blessings of the Roman ritual, the simple faith of our people, and even God's power. Technocracy has corrupted the Faith and challenged the power of which the Gospel gives us numerous proofs.

I feel that what the Panamanian Bishop calls "crisis in the prayer life of many" is but a crisis of faith or a new proof of the crisis of faith originated by Vatican II, progressivism, and the very shepherds of the Church. They reject the traditional devotions not because they are routine and abstract, but because they have lost the basis of real prayer, the conviction of God's infinite greatness, and man's utmost indigence. This new, more "incarnated" and "horizontal" spirituality, which Msgr. McGrath finds understandable, is but a humanism or activism that can be classed only as a denial of the true teachings of the Gospel and the life and doctrine of the Catholic Church.

Finally the third sign of the times discovered by the bishops at their Medellín observatory is the *world approach.*

> While the world feels strongly its own unity, mutual interdependence, and unavoidable solidarity, it finds itself, nevertheless, gravely divided by the presence of antagonistic forces. (*Gaudium et Spes*, 4).
>
> In these recent years, sorrow and anguish caused by war or threat of war have surrounded the world human family, whose process of ripening has reached a moment of supreme crisis. Little by little, people have become more conscious of their unity and solidarity everywhere, but they will not be able to perform their task of building a more human world for everyone unless we all orient ourselves with a renewed spirit toward a real peace. (*Gaudium et Spes*, 77).
>
> Your statute goes even further, and our message accompanies it. You exist and work to unite nations so as to make them partners. Let us adopt the formula: to unite them with each other. You are an association, a bridge between people.

The Montinian Church

You are a network of relations among the governments. We would almost be tempted to affirm that you reflect, in the secular order, what our Catholic church wants to be in the spiritual order: one and universal. Nothing can be loftier at the worldly level, as far as the ideological building of mankind is concerned. Your vocation consists of leading all countries, not just a few, to fraternize. Is this a difficult task? No doubt it is, but this is your noble task. Who could fail to notice the need of progressively *setting up a world authority* so that it will be in a position to act effectively at the juridical and political levels? (Paul VI's speech at the United Nations).

This economic situation is also characterized by submission to foreign investors, who in many cases tend to be more powerful and master everything without any control, being very little interested in remaining within the countries in which they operate. In addition, Latin American trade is threatened by submission to the developed countries which buy raw materials from Latin America at low prices and sell it the manufactured goods necessary for its development at higher prices. Lack of continental integration and a joint approach to face the developed world make the social and economic processes of our nations even more difficult. (*Working Document,* Second General Meeting of the Latin American Episcopate, *Economical Situation,* 3). [The meeting of lay representatives of Latin America which took place at Lima in July of 1968, criticized this working paper for its not having stressed the "world approach" for all of our problems.]

The most interesting point which came out of the discussions on the signs of the times by our expert prelates at their Medellín observatory, was the *world approach* which we must apply to our problems in order to find convenient solutions. I agree; moreover, the huge religious problems the Council and the post-Conciliar period presented to this agitated and convulsive world are not local problems, but international problems to which we will not be able to find any human solution until we unite, lay aside our selfishness, our superiority or inferiority complexes, and make a supreme effort to save ourselves. Unfortunately there are people who believe we Latin Americans still live naked or wear feathers, or that God reserved the gift of intelligence for the Europeans or those people living north of the Bravo River. In the past Latin Americans have accepted this false and denigrating judgment with humility that borders on servility. Even in Spain, where people are supposed to value and respect us very much, we find prejudice, and this is unjustifiable, since they know, or should know us very well, for we have inherited everything good and evil that we have from them.

The communications media, which have shortened and almost eliminated distances, have been convincing everyone that no nation, no matter how rich and powerful it may be, can do without the other nations in their own and other continents. In fact many times things can be more clearly seen from the outside, from a distance, rather than at home, under the pressure of unsound and subjective opinions. In Rome, for example, some think our poor underdeveloped people do not appreciate or even notice what is going on at the top levels and that we accept with Christian submission the spectacular changes we have witnessed in the entire history of the Church. This is not so; even the humblest of our people are surprised and scandalized at what they are beholding and, above all, at the attitude of the Vatican, which they find incomprehensible.

Another, even more important point in this *world approach* refers to the unity and catholicity of the Church. In Europe, little more than a century ago, there was a tendency to break this unity and build "national" churches. The same trend appeared in the United States. So were born Gallicism, Febronianism, Josephinism, and Americanism. In reality, Spain and the peoples born out of it have been the most loyal defenders of the unity of the Church and the primacy of the Roman Pontiff. Not a few are the writers who have endorsed the absurd principle: "Europe is the Faith, and the Faith is Europe." Poor Faith, if that were so!

In the so-called "Dogmatic Constitution on The Church" (*Lumen Gentium*), we read:

> Since Christ is the people's light, this sacred Council, gathering under the inspiration of the Holy Ghost, vehemently wants to illuminate *all men* with His light, which glitters on the Church's face, announcing the Gospel to every creature ... Since the Church, in Christ, is a sort of sacrament or signal and instrument of its intimate unity with God and *the unity of the whole human race*, it endeavors to clearly state to its believers and the world its nature and *its worldwide mission*. (*LG,* 1).

One of the features of the real Church Christ founded is certainly that of being *one*. The Council said later:

> All men are called to join God's people. Consequently, these people, for they are one and sole, must embrace the whole world all the time, so as to fulfill the design of the Will of God, who, from the beginning, created one human nature and decided to gather all his scattered children together. To this effect God sent His Son, whom He made His universal Heir, to be our Master, King and Priest, the head of the new and universal people of the children of God. (*LG,* 13).

These are the reasons why I find these new national and regional agencies to be dangerous and somewhat incomprehensible. Moreover, as I said before, they impair the authority of the Pope in the world Church, and also that of the bishops in their own dioceses. The so-called episcopal conferences seem to be prone to give birth to the "national" or "regional" churches which the Church with good cause, used to disapprove of. Even the ritual divisions of the Eastern churches which the Church respects, fail to meet the ideal pattern of unity Christ wanted for His flock.

The spiritual unity which the Church must have according to the Will of its divine Founder, does not prevent a fair nationalism, which has also been respected and fostered by the Church in all countries. The goal Paul VI mentioned in his speech at the United Nations is neither Christian nor human. World government—a dream cherished by Judaism and its materialistic Messianism—could not be set up or last without a slave regime such as the Communist one, including concentration camps, execution walls, and lethal gas chambers.

The political unity established and backed by the United Nations, which, according to Paul VI, is the hope of the world, is anti-human, anti-patriotic, surrendering and cowardly. This artificial organism, established by International Jewry, claims to represent the whole world, but in reality does not represent anyone. The acceptance of Pope Montini's proposal at the United Nations, the installation of "a world authority," would betray our own fatherland and the sovereignty of our country.

We are a human genre, but God Himself wanted to divide us into various races, peoples, and nations. I do not believe that the widespread intercommunications we are seeing, is good at all, but rather a great evil whose nefarious results we are already feeling in this contagious wave of immorality flooding the world. Through its fantastic tourism, Spain has experienced the consequences of this exchange in the progressive loss of the robust features of its glorious race.

To think that the unity of all peoples and nations could be achieved with justice, fundamental equality, and respect for the proper autonomy of each people and culture, as Msgr. McGrath maintains and our prelates foresaw at their Medellín observatory, is, in my mind, a sweet but unrealistic utopian thought. (Let us not forget the fable of Febro.[18]) Since there is no equality among the children of the same parents or among the members of the same people or race, it is utopian and demagogic to talk about equality among rich and poor countries or among the technological nations and those in the process of development. It is also utopian to expect that rich nations should give up their wealth in order to relieve the poverty of those who do not work or care about coping with their own indigence, illiteracy, and underdevelopment. These peoples, like small children, must be skillfully and wisely led, without hurting their feelings or curtailing their freedom and sovereignty in such a way that they improve their condition by themselves and become masters of their own fate.

This is not, however, the specific work of the Church. We bishops, priests, and Catholic laymen must all work within the framework of our own capabilities and duties in order to improve the spiritual condition of our poor people, so as to educate them *completely*. We must cooperate with our governments in the constructive work to lead us out of our poverty or, at least, train the youth that will carry on such a huge task. Demagoguery will not redeem any people!

"A more human world." "A better world." These were the demagogic mottoes Fr. Lombardi, S.J., spread all over Latin America. Instead of improving our condition, they aggravated our evils. They brought us guerilla warfare, *coups d'état,* kidnappings, bank robberies, loss of religion, ever-increasing strikes, formation of fake right-wing movements, stagnation of trade and industry, and all the other evils that affect our continent. Mexico itself suffered, especially in 1968, the disastrous effects of this clerical demagoguery that brought the regretful turmoils of the actual urban guerillas to the universities and centers of education.

We shall finish this section by quoting some other words given by Paul VI on November 24, 1965 to the Latin American episcopate:

> To carry on this kind of activity, it would be harmful to be fearful or distrustful, which disarms and deprives even the best men of the necessary impetus for an arduous constructive task. The Church must trust itself and inspire its children with bravery and confidence, reminding both God's ministers and believers that *arma militiae nostrae non carnalia sunt, sed potentia Dei.* (Our militia receive their power not from the flesh, but from God.) The moment is propitious; the ecumenical council has aroused a strong awakening of energies that have to be stimulated and set into motion. It has produced an ardent hope among the people who must in no way be deceived.

What sort of work is Paul VI talking about? What kind of militia does he lead? He quoted Saint Peter who speaks about our battle against the enemies of our souls and says: "Though we walk in the flesh, we do not war according to the flesh, for the weapons of our warfare are not carnal, but of the power of God" (II Cor. 10:3-4). Driven by his dominating ideas of change and worldly transformation, Paul VI uses these words which the apostle certainly did not say with reference to struggle for earthly things. The council *did* arouse "a strong awakening of energies," a sort of psychosis of change which the restless work of the progressivists continues to foster. They are strongly backed by the owners of all the communications media and have the necessary means to carry on their destructive work, which has succeeded in gravely jeopardizing the faith of countless souls. Apparently the Latin American prelates have not frustrated the ardent hope of the Pontiff, who, in reforming the Church, wants to set up a worldly order of peace and brotherhood; in fact, they have helped bring about the spiritual ruin we are beholding.

A Document by Monsignor Samuel Ruiz, Bishop of San Cristobal de las Casas, Chiapas

It would be impossible to study all the discoveries of our prelates congregated in the episcopal meeting at their observation center in Medellín. This is not the place nor the proper occasion to do so. However, we cannot disregard some things which are most revealing.

We shall continue with what a Mexican bishop, Msgr. Samuel Ruiz, Bishop of San Cristobal de las Casas, Chiapas, said. After having proved that the Church is basically missionary, and he did not need to quote Vatican II to demonstrate it, he turned to tell us that evangelization is a necessity in changing Latin America. These are his words:

> *Latin America was incompletely evangelized.* None may deny that the 16th century was a strongly evangelizing century, and left a deep track in our continent. The roots of our religious way, I would rather say our Catholicism, are in the style of preaching, the type of catechesis, and in the contents of the message then presented.

According to our prelate, there are several ways of being religious and a Catholic, since there are several styles of preaching, of catechesis, and even contents of the evangelical message. Certainly our missionaries, who were mostly, and in some cases exclusively, Spaniards, taught us a mutilated Catholicism, a Catholicism of meaningless "devotions," of "offerings," "blessings," "images," "religious feasts," "Baptism," "Confirmation," "Extreme Unction," "Matrimony," and sometimes, of "Ash Wednesday" and "Holy Week." Were our people fervent or not?

The prelate continued:

> Notwithstanding all the defects for which the first evangelization of our continent might be blamed, *it had a charisma* that made people convert and support Christ. . . .
>
> It is necessary to acknowledge, nevertheless, that these efforts were, unfortunately, not general, and that, although sometimes native languages were used to convey the message, it was more common that indigenous translators were used, upon whom were imposed new religious ideas which sometimes conflicted with their own concepts. Furthermore, the work of evangelization was finished at the beginning of the 17th century. Thus the second and third generations of missionaries, finding already baptized Indians, devoted

themselves to moralistic teaching by rote. In addition it should be noted that baptized people wanted to enter the civil community in order to enjoy the social and economic advantages belonging to Indians and *mestizos*. There were also not enough catechumens, and the catechesis provided mostly disconnected doctrinal subjects to be learned by heart. Summarizing, it is no exaggeration to affirm that generally speaking, in Latin America, evangelization was incomplete.

I do not know how to qualify this disconcerting exposition by a Mexican bishop who apparently has failed to grasp not only the *historical* reality but also the *present* reality of Mexico and the rest of the Latin American countries. As far as I know, the Spanish evangelizing work is unparalleled, at least in comparison with contemporary colonialism. There is an abyss between an almost savage paganism that includes human sacrifices and cannibalism, and the simple but persevering faith of our sincere, humble, and fervent people that I myself have seen among our natives and *mestizos*. Only the tenacious heroic missionaries, the generous aid of the crown, and, above all, the divine aid we received through the most Holy Virgin could have bridged this abyss. It is false to affirm that in order to teach the neophytes, missionaries had resorted exclusively to native translators who were infused with new religious ideas which may have conflicted with their own beliefs. How many books those genuine apostles left, from which we can see how conscientiously they tried to learn the dialects, so as to be able to convey the message of Salvation without mistake! It is also false that evangelization had ended in our nations! How many missions do we still have, in which this slow, difficult, and silent work of evangelizing our Indians and our poor people is being carried on?

The new masters condemn the method of learning by memory, as if it were a method that paralyzed the proper use of intelligence. They forget the saying: *"Tantum scimus, quantum memoria retinemus"* ("We know as much as we keep in our memory"). Any catechesis without memorization fails to give permanent fruits. That is why, as I said before, there is so much religious illiteracy, as Paul VI lamented. This affects not only the poor Indians or lowly people who, due to the "backward" methods the parsons and missionaries use, still continue to memorize their catechism, but also to an even more alarming extent those who attend so-called Catholic schools. In many of these schools, no religion is taught, but instead, frequent, disconcerting lectures are delivered on sex, development, social justice, and other subjects belonging to the wide range of amazing themes that progressivism offers.

Old Ripalda[19] summarized the catechetical program in the following four words: *belief, commandments, prayer* and *Sacraments*. These are not disconnected doctrinal subjects, but the wonderful synthesis of our religion. On the other hand, His Excellency forgot there are pieces of truth that are essential for our salvation, as well as other pieces of truth that illiterate and uncultivated people implicitly accept, which are not essential for our salvation. In other words a soul can be saved without specifically knowing some pieces of truth.

Certainly the evangelization of Latin America was incomplete, for the simple reason that the work of salvation has never ended nor can ever end. In our countries, as in old Europe, evangelization is unfinished and, pray God, will never end as long as the Church lasts. Let it also be said that it is easier to teach catechism to the ignorant than to the atheistic, irreligious, Voltairian, or progressivist people of our time.

His Excellency, the Bishop of San Cristobal, made an even ghastlier affirmation, that catechesis presently disregards evangelization. The Prelate begins by giving us an ultramodern definition of evangelization. His complicated and intricate definition has nothing to do with Saint Paul's synthesis: *"Nos autem praedicamus Iesus Christum et hunc crucifixum"* ("We preach a Christ, and a crucified Christ").

The Bishop said:

> Evangelization is the ministry which displays God's Word in a dynamic way, like a mighty saving word. It arouses faith and personal attachment in a nuclear and global way. The evangelized man becomes, first, a believer, who breaks his relationship with the human world and concentrates on God personally and totally. Evangelization announces the Gospel of Jesus Christ as saving *good news*, aimed at founding a Christian community through conversion which leads to Baptism. It is addressed to non-practicing baptized people, to those who have ceased to believe, to the practicing non-initiated adults, and to the baptized children and adolescents who must ratify their adult faith.

Nowhere in the above statement can we find any reference to the supernatural gift, the infused virtues of faith and sanctifying grace that we receive in our justification through Jesus Christ, even though our religious knowledge comes from the pages of an abridged catechism. If, however, through our own guilt or sins against faith we lose this supernatural gift, it is very difficult and morally impossible that we recover it, for these sins are against the Holy Spirit. To me this rationalized faith which the modern pastoral care wants to impose upon our people, is more dangerous than the blind faith of him who believes without arguing about what he believes, for he knows that it is God who has revealed our beliefs to us.

The Bishop continued as follows:

> Our pastoral concern for the Word in Latin America supposes that most people in this continent are baptized. This granted, we ordinarily believe that an adequate catechistic teaching will automatically raise the baptized to an adult faith. We do not realize that a *body* grows and develops automatically following

biological laws, but that a *person* is made by a series of free decisions. Thus no adult becomes a Christian without his knowledge or will. Hence, when a child grows and becomes able to shape his own destiny, he has to ratify the promises delivered by his godfather in his name at the time of his Baptism, uttering an irreplaceable personal vow. Nothing exempts the baptized person from converting.

Here we have a phrase that seems to include an innovation but to me embraces heresy. According to the Bishop of San Cristobal, "Nothing exempts the baptized person from converting." We are speaking about conversion to faith. What does His Excellency mean? Does he mean that as long as man does not freely and personally accept revealed truth, he has no faith and is not a real Catholic? Then baptized children have no faith and are not real Catholics. Then children do not have to be baptized, but should wait until they are mature, and freely choose their religion. This is what the progressivists preach. We have heard such heresies in Mexico; the Bishop of Cuernavaca, scandalizing Mexico, said it in one of his endless chats. In opposition to what the Bishops of both Cuernavaca and San Cristobal say is the infallible dogmatic doctrine of the Council of Trent, which today like yesterday continues to be the basis of our Catholic Faith. I have been a convert since the happy day of my holy Baptism; I have not had to convert to my religion again. I was born into the bosom of a Christian family and my beliefs were formed in really Catholic schools. Never, thanks be to God, have I had any doubt about my religion, which, through the grace of God and His instruments—my parents, my masters, and the priests who have formed me—has been ever growing. God bless them! My decision to preserve my faith has been, and, I hope, will always be, unchanging. The renewal of the promises of Baptism is not aimed at "converting" us, but at increasing our faith.

In the third point of his lecture, Msgr. Samuel Ruiz talked about the Latin American dichotomy. To those who do not understand, let me explain that by this technical term the Bishop meant a split or division of Latin American Catholicism into two parts, namely, official and elite Christianity, that of the lay movements and Vatican II on one side, and on the other an "illiterate" and popular, culturally-underdeveloped Christianity which embraces 80% of the continent. "It can be said," stated His Excellency, "that there are two religious worlds, a Western and an underdeveloped one." (Good Heavens! I confess to belonging to the second group; I join myself with those of my brethren whom post-Conciliar progressivism calls "underdeveloped." Among the select laity of the first group I guess I can find some well-known faces, such as those of the Avilés, the Alvarez Icaza, the Sahagúns, the editors of *Guia* and *Senal,* and many other ridiculous figures conspiring against our Faith.)

We must not blame the lack of evangelization for this process of

The Montinian Church

secularization and de-sacralization ending in de-mythification and, in the long run, in an "ersatz" religion which, as the Prelate said, degenerates into atheism, irreligiosity, anticlericalism, and satanic hatred against God. It was this pseudo-preaching of progressivism which created the chaos threatening us with humanly irreparable ruin. It is this sort of evangelization which the Bishop of San Cristobal mentions, that is devoted to actively evangelizing the illiterate and syncretist Christianity that loves rites and processions. Come on, Mr. Bishop! Neither the saints nor the great Doctors of the Church used to speak like that! You and your venerable brothers have imagined a world where the only people who know anything are those who have the new mentality. Those who firmly adhere to the Faith of Trent and Vatican I, to the 20-centuries-old Faith of the Church of Christ, form a Church that Their Excellencies feel has been surpassed by the new post-Conciliar Church.

In his definitively vanguard speech, Msgr. Samuel Ruiz expounded on another very interesting subject. To quote in his own words:

> *Ecumenical Climate.* While a swarm of pseudo-Christian ideologies are entering our continent and finding a particularly favorable culture in the context of the crisis which our people are undergoing, there exists, on the other hand, a new environment of mutual respect, acknowledgment, and dialogue between Catholics and Protestants which is surging out of the current ecumenical spirit. This then, is a new phase of the evangelization of Latin America, particularly because the Catholic *charisma*[20] is not essentially different from the Protestant to the extent that one cannot say that a real Protestant who joins Catholicism goes through an actual *metanoia* but instead, through a maturation of faith through catechesis.
>
> No one fails to see the favorable consequences that a joint work of evangelization by Protestants and Catholics would yield as far as unity is concerned. We cannot help mentioning and praising the movement of the Protestant community of Taizé, which has put the ecumenical New Testament at the disposal of Catholics, so as to aid the task of evangelizing our continent.

These are the words of a heretic, not of a real Catholic. They resemble those of Cardinal Willebrands at the Protestant meetings in Germany, which we quoted before. They mean that Catholics and Protestants are more or less the same thing; it's just a question of how ripe one's faith is. The *charisma* is the same. We can then amicably divide the work of evangelizing Latin America into equal parts without resentment, mutual attacks, or groundless mistrust. In this way we will quickly achieve a rapid Catholicization or Protestantization of all Latin America; either way is all right! Have not our venerable pastors already proclaimed a "religious pluralism?" As long as we persist in keeping our dogmas, our rites, our morality, and our discipline, the world cannot be united or have peace. *Ecumenism* is the only remedy for the grave evils of the world. Now I understand why those "separated brethren" of Taizé have put the ecumenical New Testament at our disposal, and also cooperated by making an ecumenical Mass, with the compliments and blessings of His Holiness.

In speaking about the indigenous people, the learned Prelate acknowledges that their regretful condition deserves particular consideration:

> In Latin America, there are 30 million of them. Though this is a remarkable figure, they, up to now, remain socially, economically, politically, and even worse, "pastorally marginated" human beings, with the exception of the few who are taken care of with genuinely pastoral zeal. Otherwise the attention of the missionaries at the parish headquarters is concentrated in the white and *mestizo* centers.

This is a terrible accusation from a bishop to all bishops, all provincials, and to all religious communities in Latin America! It is they who have pushed aside these 30 million wretched Indians so as to devote themselves to the more profitable job of attending whites and *mestizos* in the parish headquarters. Why had not Their Excellencies noticed such a grave omission? The responsibility for this rests on their consciences. But there is even more:

> The native is not always acknowledged the right of receiving the message in his own language or in terms consistent with his own mentality and peculiar views, for oral communication is different from mental and cultural communication.
>
> The evangelical message is generally conveyed by using translations of pre-Conciliar textbooks. One needs programs covering the diocesan and national level that are the fruit of a profound knowledge of indigenous cultures, instead of improvisations "for Latin America." There does not exist a solid, collective, and effective responsibility to undertake the task, in each nation, of solving the problem of totally integrating the natives. Generally speaking, many workers do not know what this integration is all about, and frequently this is thought of as murder of native cultures.
>
> Some people believe that the mere multiplication of educational personnel will resolve the problem. Sometimes people go to the extreme of devoting themselves to philanthropic charities without any clear picture of the difficulties of the incorporation of the habits and values of divergent cultures, their underdevelopment, or a method for promotion, apart from themselves and their own values and cultures.
>
> The practical criterion that seems to prevail in the episcopal conferences is this: the indigenous problem is not the most urgent and consequently, not the most important. We strongly urge that we must know precisely how to distinguish

between the urgent and transcendent, though less urgent, areas of our pastoral care. Without this approach, more centuries will pass on this shameful problem that might be called the "methodological failure of the evangelizing action of the Church in Latin America."

Thus did Msgr. Samuel Ruiz end his demagogic and, in several points, heretical speech. Formerly, at the time of the Inquisition, this speech would have sufficed to prosecute His Excellency, who so clearly spoke against Catholic truth. Not now, however, for our prelates have become used to hearing gross things without getting upset at all. Monsignor Ruiz not only stated that the catechesis of our indigenous people must be addressed in their dialects, but be consistent with their mentality and culture. I would appreciate His Excellency's letting us know of what our Indians' present culture consists, for they are backward, use rudimentary hermetic dialects, and live amid half-savage customs and ancestral vices. Practically all the natives who had some degree of culture or traces of civilization are incorporated into our Christian civilization. They speak our language, have our mentality to a large extent, and as far as religion is concerned, not a few of them have attained a profound theological knowledge, as proven by, among others, the case of the Archbishop of Mexico, Don Pascual Díaz Barreto, S.J.

Monsignor Ruiz blames the pre-Conciliar textbooks for their being obscurantist, dogmatically false, or unfit to be understood by the indigenous mentality. Now with the post-Conciliar textbooks, whose terms not even the "experts" themselves understand, the poor Indians will be in a better position to grasp the message of Salvation, especially if they behold the *padrecitos* (little Fathers) amidst the glitter of the Bugninian liturgy or wearing carnival costumes.

The solution is not to multiply the educational personnel or to remedy the indigence of our poor Indians; this would turn the Church into a philanthropic institution. What matters is to get a picture of the difficulties of the incorporation of the habits and values of divergent cultures and their underdevelopment, so as to create a method arising out of the indigenous people themselves, with their own values and cultures. Mr. Bishop, remember *"nemo dat quod non habet,"* ("none can give what he does not have"). Since they have no values or culture, let us start by carrying the Gospel to them.

The Prelate of San Cristobal made a sharp point when he told the other bishops: first, the transcendent, then, the urgent. To which, perhaps, they may answer: "The latter is necessary, but do not omit the former."

Monsignor Samuel Ruiz's speech did not finish with that. There is a second part, in which he tells us how the evangelization of Latin America must be achieved. Latin America, said he with a prophetic air, is in a missionary state. Neither secularism nor Communism is dangerous, but our permanent attachment to patterns of life or activity (educational politics, parish views, the role of the laity in the world and the apostolate, the Church as a "mission" or conversion) is. Though created by the Church, all these patterns must be transformed by the Church, in order that it remain a sign of light among the peoples and an evangelizing ferment among the masses. From all that Msgr. Ruiz says, all Latin America, just like the rest of the world, is in a permanent missionary state, and a state of change in which a deep work of evangelization must be carried on.

Monsignor Ruiz says we must begin by distinguishing between the ministry of evangelization and that of catechesis. According to him, faith has two aspects, that of the emotions and that of the mind. The first aspect is called "conversion" by the Prelate; evangelization brings about conversion, a submissive support of God and His plan of Salvation which entails a change of thought and deeds. Catechesis reveals the meaning of the facts and words of the message of our Salvation; it makes us delve deeply into them. Theoretical, theological, and practical moral or pastoral consequences arise from the above wise distinction.

I believe His Excellency's thinking is based on a naturalistic basis. He dispenses with the intrinsic supernatural fertility of divine grace and the infused virtue of faith. This shows his pastoral experience was very limited. He was never faced with the wonderful, frequent cases of our humble and unlearned people, who, though being illiterate, speak about God and God's things with such accuracy, certainty, and conviction, that our modern theologians should envy them.

What did the Bishop mean by firmly stating that our task today consists of converting the baptized people? Baptism gives us the *custom of faith,* not just the capability, but the proneness and virtue of making acts of faith. Unconsciously a baptized person begins to make these almost from the very moment he hears the first Word of God from his parents' mouths. The supernatural faith we receive at our Baptism cannot be lost except through a complete and conscious denial of what God revealed to us. It is active in itself; its intrinsic activity comes from God, not from our reason and not from human science. The life of faith that silently and fruitfully develops in souls, enlivens our whole religious life from the beginning to the end. Faith is the root of our whole supernatural life. I turn to challenge what the Bishop of San Cristobal said—that real faith entails conversion—unless he meant the spiritual "resurrection" we had to the divine life, to the life of grace through Baptism. I am a convert right from the day I was baptized, for I am a regenerate, a justified one. The preaching of the *charisma* might be necessary for those who, unfortunately, were born in paganism or other religions, but not for us who, through God's grace, were born into Catholic families, no matter how ignorant or indifferent the parents of the newly born baptized children.

The Montinian Church

Of course I do not deny the need of religious teaching. Above all, I consider it to be indispensable for those people who, due to the pressing circumstances of modern life, grow up in an environment hostile to religion or at least a secular environment. I maintain, however, that in really Christian families, such as our families of yesteryear, such education and training took place slowly and progressively, within the family and the really Catholic schools, in which parents and teachers were clearly conscious of their highest duties, and without putting us into a state of mission. Moreover, without this home and school education, there is the danger that modern catechesis, the catechesis that uses tools adequate for our specific realities, achieve not an authentic Catholicism, but a *religious typology*, exclusively adapted to Latin America. This easily degenerates not only into religious indifference, which is bad enough, but also into complete irreligiosity. If anything, the post-Conciliar pastoralism has augmented, not a religious illiteracy, but a religious insecurity and a continued loss of faith, not only among the laity, but even among the religious, priests, and bishops. The current crisis is a crisis of faith!

How could the *charisma* lead us, as the Bishop says, to a personal decision without intellectual adhesion? *"Rationabile obsequium vestrum,"* a rational gift, as Saint Paul calls faith, which is not founded on the evidence of the truths accepted and the dogmas believed, but on the evidence that it is God who has revealed to us these truths. Such is the supernatural certainty of faith, the precious gift of faith which we receive at Baptism.

In explaining the *charisma*, the Bishop of San Cristobal made another mistake. He said that Jesus Christ sends to those who repent and accept the Faith, the Holy Spirit, who renews hearts through Baptism for the forgiveness of sins, with salvation as an aim and with the hope of participating in the resurrection of the kingdom of God, when He comes as Judge. This definition of the *charisma*, which as the learned Prelate from Chiapas said before, is the preamble of justification at Baptism through Jesus Christ, again excludes the newly born and baptized children, for they have no sins, except for "original sin," for which they are not capable of repentance, since they lack the use of reason. As said before, however, we find justification through Jesus Christ and also sanctifying grace, the infused virtues of faith, hope, and charity, adoptive filiation, the right of inheritance, and effusion of the Holy Spirit at those children's baptism. What the Bishop called *conversion* through Baptism, I would rather call *justification,* which turns the baptized person into a member of the Church and, if you, Mr. Bishop, like metaphors, also a member of God's people and God's family.

The problem of modern incredulity or the spread of atheism is due to the lack of care to avoid pollution and the fact that all passionate excesses that corrupt hearts and ruin the Faith are welcome. *Either we live the way we believe, or we end by believing the way we live.* That is why the post-Conciliar movement, which has welcomed passionate excesses, has efficaciously fostered a loss of faith, despite all the favorable *charisma* it wishes to present.

According to the Prelate upon whose speech we are commenting, our fight against incredulity or the errors of the disbelievers must not be apologetical; it is not a matter of silencing foes or proving Christianity convincingly. The great apologists of the Church were wrong. Today according to Msgr. Ruiz, the most persuasive, effective, meaningful, concrete, existential, and historical reasoning must lead non-believers to the light of faith. Evidently it is not a question of refuting objections, but of creating an environment of understanding and truth, from which an opening for the evangelical message can arise. Will there be any environment of understanding as long as the obstacles of error are not removed from the minds of the incredulous? Will there be any opening as long as the doors are closed, and there is prejudice, stubborn denial, and a bandage covering the eyes? Evidently the arguments concerning an imminent and personal order may be used by efficacious apologetics, not as definitive, but at least as auxiliary tools. However, solid and permanent conviction, sincere and active faith, cannot be founded on existential or historic arguments, but on arguments based on Holy Writ, Tradition, and theology, presupposing the credentials of faith, the arguments for belief, and, above all, God's grace.

Then Bishop Ruiz spoke about the communitary touch Vatican II wanted to give the Faith. The Prelate said:

> The Christian community, the fermenting apostolic groups, must speak the language of the "signs" the Lord left in order that His Church be known and acknowledged, namely, *charity* and *unity,* with all that it purports in our Latin American world.

Theology taught us that the four criteria or typical features that permit us to recognize the One, True Church, founded by Jesus Christ, not Vatican II, were *unity, sanctity, catholicity and apostolicity.* *"Et unam, sanctam, catholicam et apostolicam Ecclesiam."* We used to proclaim this as the symbol of our faith, but now our prelates from their Medellín observatory, on beholding the signs of the times, say that the Lord left two signs (just two), *charity* and *unity,* so that His Church may be known and acknowledged. Sanctity and apostolicity have little importance. The counter-signs have to be eliminated, for they are insurmountable hindrances to evangelization. They state that the poor will not be evangelized as long as we are latifundists. The weak and the oppressed will move away from Christ if we appear to be allies of the mighty ones. The uneducated will not be evangelized if our religious institutions continue to search after the earthly paradise of the big cities instead of the towns and suburbs. The Gospel will not fully shine if those of us who are responsible for local churches prove to be reluctant to the new mentality demanded by Vatican Council II.

We must certainly give up the rich, the mighty, the learned, the pre-Conciliar ones, so as to belong to this new Church, the Church of the poor, the post-Conciliar Church, the Church of John XXIII and Paul VI. This new Church, despite its internal divisions, is one, with its formal and apparent unity, wherein the most varied rites, subjective types of morality, and personal beliefs are compatible. It is the Church of charity for everybody except the stubborn traditionalists.

We return to Msgr. Samuel Ruiz:

> We must find new types of presence, new forms of evangelization, and a better use of what already exists. We must appreciate popular religiosity in order to purge it and turn it into a "sign" and an instrument of evangelization. Evangelization must be the goal of education in Catholic schools. We must give an evangelizing dimension to the pilgrim-attracting sanctuaries. The mass evangelization media must be omnipresent. We must create a theology and a sense of poverty in the countries in the process of development.

This is decidedly the psychosis of "change." Up to now popular religiosity was wrong and, therefore, needed a purge. Away with rosaries, holy works, Spiritual Exercises, old-style missions, devotions, novenas, and exaggerated Marianism. In the schools, permanent evangelization, not through religious instruction or acts of piety, but through the witness, the omnipresence, not of God, but of the mass evangelization media. So far, there has been no theology or sense of poverty in the Church of those countries in the process of development. This is the immense task of the post-Conciliar people under the light of Vatican II, not necessarily that of the Gospel.

Among these changes, one of the most important ones is to fight the *parish approach,* because, the Bishop said, "How can we build a Christian community where there is no human community?" The Prelate posed several possible solutions. His words are worth quoting:

> Are the basic worship-decentralizing communities or subcommunities the way of turning the parish into a centrifugal and irradiating entity that has and develops its own leaders? As far as big cities are concerned, should not evangelization be made within circles: students, professionals, artists, and so on? Should the cities have elites, or must we create communities based on secondary relationships, such as the evangelization of the 6:30 bus people? Can evangelization be conveyed through mass communications media? Can a real witness be conveyed through a tape recorder? What must the witness consist of so that the depersonalization of the city does not depersonalize Christ too? The

city goads us to multiply the non-ecclesiastical agencies. *Will the Church be better established on man-made societies?* The question can build an impressive list that must be completed, and to which answers must be supplied.

Once the way is lost, digressions are possible and multiply themselves. At Medellín, our prelates seemed to lose the way of the everlasting Gospel, the 20-century Tradition and experience of the Church, and devote themselves to the search of solutions for an already-solved problem. Neither imagination nor human views will show us the way we have been following and testing for centuries. It is absurd and criminal to destroy the existing things to build what is not even blueprinted. That is why, after several years of continued experiments, surveys, polls, and changes, only the disastrous ruins of the past are to be seen. We keep on waiting for a miracle from the Conciliar Fathers.

VIOLENCE

As I said before, I cannot study all the moves of our prelates at the second LAMEC meeting and their documents. The above are just samples. I cannot help mentioning, however, a very challenging point. Using the style of Paul VI with fashionable shrewdness and dialectics, the prelates left the gate open for possible solutions to the complex Latin American problems. To quote:

> Violence is one of the most grave problems in Latin America. A decision on which the whole future of the continent's nations depends cannot be entrusted to the impulses of emotions and passions. We would fail to fulfill a grave pastoral duty if we did not remind our consciences of the criteria arising from the Christian doctrine and the love of the Gospel.
>
> No one will be surprised if we strongly reaffirm our faith in the fruitfulness of peace. This is our Christian ideal. "Violence is neither Christian nor evangelical." Christianity is pacifistic and not ashamed of this. "It is not just pacifist, for it is capable of fighting." (Paul VI, Message of Jan. 1, 1968). It prefers peace rather than war, however. It knows that brusque or violent changes of structure are treacherous, useless, and definitely inconsistent with people's dignity, which requires that the necessary transformations be made from within, that is, through a convenient examination of conscience, an adequate preparation, and an effective participation of everyone, which ignorance and sometimes subhuman life conditions prevent. (*Populorum Progressio*, no. 30; Allocution of Paul VI, at the Mass of Development Day).
>
> If Christianity believes in the fruitfulness of peace to attain justice, it also believes that justice is an essential condition for peace. It does not fail to notice that, in many places, Latin America finds itself in an unjust situation that can be called *institutional violence*. As a result of structural defects in the industrial and

agrarian sectors of national and international economic systems, of cultural and political life, "whole populations lack necessary things and endure a dependence that prevents self-determination and responsibility as well as possibilities for cultural development and participation in social and political life, in such a way that fundamental rights are violated." (*Populorum Progressio*, no. 30). This condition requires audacious, urgent, profoundly renovating, global transformations. Then it cannot surprise us that "the temptation of violence" arises in Latin America. *One must not abuse the patience of people who, for years, have been enduring a condition that would hardly be accepted by those who have a higher degree of consciousness of human rights.*

Here we have a statement of the moral, social, economic, and political problems, but above all, of the religious problem regarding the legitimacy of guerilla warfare, revolution, and violence. Our prelates are extremely cautious not to incur moral or legal responsibility through a revolutionary harangue. The way is shown by Paul's school of dialectics, as shown by these points:

1. A categorical affirmation of our faith in the fruitfulness of peace is the Christian ideal. Moreover, in a vague and general way, violence is apparently condemned, for it is "neither Christian nor evangelical." Then a discrete distinction is made for the necessary change: Christians are pacifistic, not pacifists. Then they point out the inconveniences of violence.

2. Latin America's condition is unbearable: Whole peoples lack necessary things, and are in a situation of impotence unworthy of the dignity of men.

3. The entire liability rests on the industrial and agricultural corporations. The structures are unfair, and fundamental rights are being violated.

4. This situation demands *global, audacious, urgent, and deeply renewing transformations.*

5. "The temptation of violence" is logical, comprehensible, and in my mind, justifiable. Against the unjust violence of the establishment, the only solution is armed guerilla warfare.

The pastors added:

> Before this situation that so gravely attacks the dignity of man and, consequently, peace, we pastors encourage all the members of the Christian world to assume their serious responsibility of promoting peace for Latin America.

They did not talk about solving the problem, but of promoting peace. Since there can be no peace in this condition, Christians are obliged to fight the unjust violence of the establishment with guerilla violence, terrorism, kidnapping and air piracy. It is the principle of the lesser evil that has to regulate Catholic criteria. This "temptation of violence" can no longer be resisted.

The document continues as follows:

> First, we address this call to those who have a larger share of wealth, culture, or power. We know there are Latin American leaders who sympathize with the needy and try to help them. These people acknowledge that on the whole, the privileged often press the government with all the means at their disposal, thus preventing necessary changes from being implemented. Sometimes this resistance is violent, including destruction of lives and good.
>
> Consequently, we encourage them not to profit from the Church's pacifistic attitude to actively or passively fight the deep necessary transformations. If they jealously keep their privileges and, above all, defend them by using violent means themselves, they become responsible before history for provoking "desperate explosive revolutions" (Allocution of Paul VI, at the Mass of Development Day). To a large extent then, the peaceful future of Latin America depends upon their behavior.

In their constructive dialogue, the prelates face the "privileged" with anguish. They ask those who have something or are somebody in Latin American society to give up their privileges, their goods and their power so as to expedite a bold and urgent "change of structures."

They must not pressure governments or use their constitutional rights to defend themselves or what is theirs. They must not repel force with force, even though their very lives be endangered. They must not abuse the Church's pacifistic mood in order to jealously keep their privileges, that is, what they have and are. This passive attitude of the ecclesiastics may change. Then it is those privileged ones who defend themselves and defend what is theirs who will be responsible for the "desperate explosive revolutions." The last sentence is a challenge and an ultimatum: "To a large extent, then, the peaceful future of Latin America depends upon their behavior." Your purse or your life! Is that not so, venerable pastors?

Let us go on:

> Responsible for injustice also are all those who fail to act to endorse justice with the means at their disposal, and remain passive for fear of personal sacrifice and risk implicit in any audacious and really efficient action. Justice, and consequently peace, are attained through a dynamic process of consciousness and organization of the popular sector that urges changes by the public powers, who are often incapable of carrying on social projects without popular support.

The Montinian Church

If this is not politics, then what is? This is a revolutionary harangue addressed to all citizens, including the *padrecitos* and nuns, of course. We must not be afraid of sacrifices or risks, including life itself. We must first consciously prepare and then organize the popular masses, so that they support the government's social and political projects, in other words, the progressive but quick "socialization" of all the sources of production in Latin American countries. Without this dynamic action there will be no justice or peace. Let those who have something or are somebody, sacrifice themselves and strip themselves of their "privileges;" those who do not have anything should sacrifice themselves by organizing themselves and exposing their own lives, if necessary.

We continue:

> Finally, we address those who, before this grave situation and legitimate resistance to change, place their hopes in violence. Along with Paul VI, we avow that their attitude "frequently finds its ultimate motivation in noble impulses of justice and solidarity." We do not speak here of empty verbalism that does not imply personal responsibility and departs from peaceful, fruitful, and immediately realizable actions.
>
> If it be true that revolutionary violence can be legitimate in fighting "an apparent and prolonged tyranny that attacks the country's common welfare" (*Populorum Progressio*, no. 31), be it the tyranny of an individual or of seemingly unfair structures, it is also true that violence or "armed revolt" generally "engenders new injustices, ruins, and instability. . . . The price for fighting a real evil cannot be a worse evil" (*Populorum Progressio*, no. 31).

Here we have our venerable pastors' full justification of violence from their observatory and command post at Medellín, using Paul's dialectics and language without euphemisms, circumlocutions, or dissimulation:

1. With Paul, they avow that violence "frequently finds its ultimate motivation in noble impulses of justice and solidarity." The end justifies the means.

2. Violence and revolutionary insurrection may be legitimate, not always, but when an apparent and prolonged tyranny severely attacks man's fundamental rights and the country's common welfare.

3. This tyranny can be that of a person or of structures.

Such is the case in the Latin American countries. As the prelates said before, they find themselves in a condition that gravely impairs man's dignity and, consequently, peace. Father Arrupe had said it, too. The conclusion then, is quite clear that guerilla warfare, kidnapping, terrorism, and crimes are legitimate since through them, all inequality will disappear, for we will all become equal slaves of those who retain power. This is the theology of violence which Don Helder, Don Sergio, and other pacifists endorsed at Medellín, where, according to Antonio Cardinal Samoré, not even a word about violence was uttered by anyone.

THE RESULTS OF THE ASSEMBLY IN MEDELLÍN

The beneficial results of the Eucharistic assembly, the pastoral visit of Paul VI, and the second general meeting of the Latin American episcopate at Medellín were soon apparent. Only a few months elapsed before almost all of the countries in this continent were shattered by violence. Our underdeveloped countries became powder magazines. For the sake of brevity I will limit the evidence to Mexico. One of our best writers, if not *the* best, wrote a book whose very title portrays the theatening and dangerous reality in which we live, despite the fact that our country is, no doubt, one of the most tranquil on this continent. I am referring to the recent work by Dr. René Capistrán Garza, a beloved friend of mine and a celebrated champion of the Catholic cause from the bitter days of religious persecution. The book is called *Chaos in the Church and Betrayal of the Government*. Let us read from the chapter entitled "Before and After Bogotá:"

From Bogotá, the voice of Paul VI resounded worldwide. To Catholics and non-Catholics, his historical speeches, one of which was addressed to the Latin American bishops and the other to a huge gathering of peasants coming from all over South America and Mexico, appear as the top of an imposing mountain, one of whose slopes was enveloped in the shade of a most painful and upsetting confusion, while the other shows a sunny panorama under the unquenchable light of perennial truth. The former was before Bogotá, and the latter, after Bogotá. The contrast was only too startling between the tone of voice in speaking to these two groups. I shall limit myself then, to quoting both of those two most eloquent positive and negative voices, adding some brief comments of my own.

"There is no way back. The Church has finally acknowledged its errors, its ancient haughtiness. It has realized it is not the sole depository of the Truth . . . There will no longer be tiaras in the Church." These are words delivered by the Most Excellent Don Sergio Méndez Arceo, Bishop of Cuernavaca, at Cautla, April 9, 1965, at a dinner of Lions and Rotarians. There he announced the end of the tiaras, while quite selfishly forgetting the mitres.

The words that follow were spoken on August 13, 1967, at Querétaro, by Fr. Ramón de Ertze Garamendi, a Spanish priest, now a prebendary canon of our holy cathedral, during a lecture entitled "Communism and Christianity are Two Big Human Hopes" at the university of that state. Among other things, he said:

The Montinian Church

Communism is a big human hope ... and, along with Christianity, is one of the big hopes of mankind; ... from a Christian viewpoint, Communism will not strive for class struggle but will become a great human aspiration for the liberation of man and the dignity of work. ... (*El Sol de Mexico*, Mar. 14, 1967, noon edition, front page).

The Most Illustrious Spanish canon of our cathedral is devoted to correcting the errors of the ill-focused Franciscan evangelization in Mexico.

"In front we find the *healthy* youth that matured first ... that impatiently demand brusque and violent changes.... These youth are better attended and encouraged by Marx's materialistic world and the big dictators. These youth ... [are] the force of the future Church ..." (Rev. Fr. Xavier Escalada, S.J., *El Sol de Mexico*, Aug. 20, 1968). "There are some people who are frightened of these new and nonconforming ways of the Church." (Rev. Fr. Xavier Escalada, S.J., *El Sol de Mexico*, Aug. 27, 1968).

Under the headline: "Presence," *El Dia* featured a front-page article on August 7, concerning the so-called *student conflict* of Mexico. It read as follows: "We Jesuits deeply sympathize with the demands for fairer structures and freedom of speech presented to the government by students and teachers." The undersigned, who simultaneously ratify their "presence," are the Reverends S. Carlos Palomar, M.A. Salvatori, Javier Palencia, and Enrique Brito. (It is known that no one acts on his own account in the Society of Jesus, but only with the consent or command of his superiors.)

Commenting on the student turmoil in Paris in May, 1968, Fr. Enrique Maza, S.J., wrote an article entitled "World Stage" which was featured in *Union (Unión)* weekly magazine on June 9, 1968. Following are some of the things he wrote: "The Latin Quarter was left in chaos: burned cars, fallen trees, broken windows, heaped up pavements, fires, and paroxysmal violence.... The police stormed in and the battle lasted five hours." Did this, perhaps, merit His Reverence's disapproval? Not at all, for he went on as follows: "Generally speaking, France sympathized with the students. They saw adolescents being injured by the merciless Republican Division of Safety.... The dwellers of the Latin Quarter cast their lot with the students.... The trade unions, the workers, the teachers, intellectuals, and even school children took sides with the bloodstained students." Two days later, General De Gaulle received a landslide victory in France's general elections. His Reverence is as bad a prophet as he is a reporter.

"The Bishop of Recife, Msgr. Helder Cámara, affirmed he will follow the ideological revolution of the guerilla priest, Fr. Camilo Torres, without resorting to violence." (A.P., Bogotá, Aug. 23, 1968). Of course, we all know that Fr. Camilo Torres' ideological revolution turned into armed violence. The famous Bishop and pacifist guerilla follows the doctrine but impedes the way of implementation. He thinks like Don Camilo, but he does not act like him. This is the concealing magic of ambiguous words.

At Bogotá, the most authoritative voice after that of Paul VI was that of Cardinal Lercaro, the Pontiff's Legate, who, due to "his Communist leaning" was nicknamed the "Red Cardinal." Among other things, he said: "There were no conservatives or liberals at the Council. Councils are meetings of free men who profess a common faith." So the "Red Cardinal" showed his true colors, much to the sorrow of those who trusted him so much.

The Pope, in turn, proclaimed the unity of the Church, the traditional fidelity to the Faith, the authority of all of the councils, the explicit condemnation of violence as a means of transforming useless structures (for this must be evolutionary and peaceful) and, above all, the clear, definitive and firm rule that any action of Catholics, clergy and laity, individuals and institutions, must be inspired and supported by the spirit of righteousness and charity drawn from the Gospel. He categorically affirmed: "The Church may not endorse systematic revolution or atheistic Communism."

During those days, the newspaper headlines summarized the essence of the Pontiff's thoughts: "Paul VI Condemned Violence as a Way of Fighting Poverty" [*The Pr3ss (La Prensa)*], "Violent Change is Contrary to the Christian Faith" [*Mexican Sun (El Sol de Mexico)*], "Paul VI Told Youth: Violence is Not the Way" [*News (Novedades)*], and "Neither Systematic Revolution nor Atheistic Marxism" [*Mexican Sun (El Sol de Mexico)* and *The Herald (El Heraldo)*]. So read other newspapers, including *The Day (El Dia)*, which I cannot quote for the sake of brevity. All this, however, was sort of a blow to the Rev. Fr. Maza.

But no one is as stubborn as a proud and haughty man. On August 27, the [Telex] Agency issued a report from Bogotá announcing that Fr. Albert Gómez S.J., director of the Movement for a Better World, had stated that "for the time being" the Pope and the Church's leaders are right. He affirmed, however, that "the end is not far-off . . . that *now* violence would be self-defeating. . . ." Also, although he did not justify the decisions "of Camilo Torres, the guerilla priest who was a close friend of his, he did explain them thoroughly."

The governments of the world should be too wise to embrace a bold and excessive confidence. Catholics also should be too wise to part from doctrine and support violence, claiming to be persecuted and demanding "religious freedom" from governments that defend themselves, which they have the right and duty of doing.

So my dear, brave friend and famous journalist, Dr. René Capistrán Garza wrote on September 16, 1968. His good faith and sincere Catholic way prevented him from becoming aware of the world's dreadful reality. This is the sad case of many Catholics who, while being aware of the tremendous reality we are facing, would like to save Paul VI, the hierarchy, and the Vatican's official agencies, even though these are *actually responsible for the present crisis and destruction of the Church*. They see the shadow of a most painful and upsetting confusion, and they hear the ghastly howls of the "new wave" Jesuits, the leaders of the pseudo-redeeming movement "For a Better World," the work of the revolutionaries, Fr. Lombardo, S.J., Sergio VII, Don Helder, Camilo, and "Ché." Still, they believe Paul VI, and his Legate, Lercaro, are masters in that they know how to say "no" while skillfully leaving the door open for the initiates, who catching the Pontiff's idea, can say no "for the time being." "The end is not far-off," however. When the long-suffering patience of people ends, and they break the chains of slavery and proclaim their liberty, people will open fire against the institutionalized violence of governments and laws. This will be the fire-and-sword violence of guerilla warfare in the countryside, the cities, and the *aggiornated* temples.

At Bogotá, Paul VI, inconsistent with his own line as stated clearly in the *Populorum Progressio,* said: "Violence is neither Christian nor evangelical." At Medellín, his skillful and obedient interpreters quoted him:

> Guilty of injustice are also all those who fail to back justice with all means at their disposal and remain passive for fear of sacrifices and personal risks implicit in any audacious and really efficacious action. Justice and, consequently peace, can be achieved through a dynamic action of consciousness and organization of the popular masses. . . .

Then those who fail to work for social justice are liable for injustice. Hence we must employ all means at our disposal, guerilla warfare, terrorism, kidnapping, air piracy, etc. We must be ready to face any sacrifice and personal risk. We must follow a dynamic course, closing the schools for wealthy children, using the money we get from the sale of the sumptuous buildings for subversion, organization, and training of the masses. It is the popular masses that concerns us. The Church, or rather the Vatican, has turned left toward Communism, which is the contemporary way of implementing Christ's redemption today.

. Meanwhile, *we respect* those people who, before the seriousness of injustice and the illegitimate resistance of governments to Communist changes, *are already using violence* because, as Paul VI said, "they find their ultimate motivation in noble impulses of justice and solidarity." (Allocution of Paul VI, at the Mass of Development Day).

THE TRUTH ABOUT THE PONTIFF

Those of you who have read this book from its beginning certainly know the process that Pope Montini followed from the beginning of his Pontificate, in carrying on a definite program of compromise, collaboration, and complete surrender to the unmistakably clear projects of the Jewish-Masonic mafia. Their aim is to destroy the Church, eliminate Catholic governments, and brainwash Catholics and "men of goodwill" of other religions, so as to paralyze and eliminate their legitimate and necessary defenses. With his dialectics of affirmation and denial, wholesome doctrine and dark deeds, Pope Montini, in but a short time, has been able to outdo the revolution of Vatican II. He has been active in many of the transformations necessary to carry on the program of slavery of a world government and a common world religion, and has become the key man for the success of subversion. Through apostolic blessings and the promotion of surrendering or compromising bishops, the world plot has been developing for a long time, as proclaimed by the *Protocols of the Elders of Zion, The Plot Against the Church,* and many other books that disclosed the secret designs of the satanic conspiracy.

According to this secret design, the rousing of the consciousness and the organization of the popular masses must be continued. Nonconformity, discontent, hatred, and thirst for blood must be provoked in them so that, in a short time, once mankind has plunged into chaos, the new Messiahs and the new Christs can impose Communism upon us without any resistance. Communism will then no longer be a theory or the subject of a redeeming sermon, but sorrow, misery, plunder, and firing walls. This may give us the chance to be able to relive the Church of the poor, the "primitive Church," and the "Church of the New Testament."

Chapter XXXI

TITO'S VISIT

Recent evidence of Pope Montini's design is given by a visit by Marshal Tito of Yugoslavia to Rome. The Jew, Tito,[21] the tyrant of Yugoslavia, the persecutor of the Church, the hangman of Cardinal Stepinac, was fraternally and ecumenically welcomed in an embrace by Paul VI at the Vatican.

From page one of the Mexican newspaper *El Universal* we quote the following:

France Press, Vatican City, March 29, 1971.

For the first time in history, a Pope addressed an official allocution to a Communist head of state. This morning Paul VI told Marshal Tito here that Yugoslavia is "a friend of peace" and its "international prestige is growing."

The Pope had had a one-hour meeting with Marshal Tito before his speech. In his allocution, the sovereign Pontiff spoke in Italian in order to stress "the promising rapprochement between the Vatican and Yugoslavia." He said the relations between both countries are excellent and will prove useful "to analyze problems that are especially grave and upsetting," such as those of Indochina and the Middle East, where "adequate solutions" are needed, and will be found through a joint effort of men of goodwill.

In his allocution, the Pope paid homage to Yugoslavia and its government. He also stressed the existence of cultural and spiritual links between the various Yugoslavian peoples (Croatians, Serbians, Montenegrins, Herzegovinians) and the Apostolic See, and the "pages of prosperity" of its history, where "grave hours of misfortune" are recorded. "The Yugoslavian people," said Paul VI, "seem to have been called by Providence to find a common ground for meeting and understanding in order that the continent can spare itself new conflicts and find the way to international cooperation. Through it," he added, "greater progress and a more fraternal civilization will be achieved.

"To this task," continued the Pope before Marshal Tito, "Yugoslavia is being led under the impulse and leadership of Your Excellency. This is an international task that goes beyond European borders to a world that, in fact, has become smaller and more consolidated, as much in its positive as its negative aspects."

President Tito and his wife had arrived shortly after 9:00 a.m., through the

The Montinian Church

Door of Bells on the south side of Saint Peter's Basilica, where a detachment of Swiss guards paid them homage. The long, official Vatican car that brought them, bore the Yugoslavian and Pontifical banners, and, surrounded by 15 motorcyclists, had gone through the Eternal City. Tito was wearing a tuxedo, and his wife a long black dress with a veil of black lace.

Tito had delivered an allocution before the Pope had uttered his. Tito promised to make the utmost effort to find a peaceful solution to the Middle East conflict, and said he was deeply concerned about the latest events in Southeast Asia. He affirmed, "I am glad to see that the Holy See and Yugoslavia have similar or identical views on the big international problems and the necessity of solving them through peaceful coexistence."

In all, Tito and his wife's visit to the Vatican lasted two hours and a half.

One of the newspapers in Yugoslovia's capital city also covered the news event of Marshal Tito's visit to Rome:

> March 29. Communist President Tito is back today from a state visit to Italy, and said he was "extremely happy" with the conversations he had with Italian leaders and Pope Paul VI. This was the first time a Yugoslavian head of state met a Catholic Pontiff. His visit to the Vatican was additionally peculiar because Paul seemed to grant his approval to a speech which Tito had given denouncing Israel's "aggression." Yugoslavia's official news agency, *Tanjug*, reported the Chairman as stating, on his return here, that he was "certainly extremely happy with the results" of his visit.

Before commenting on the press reports about the speeches of Paul VI and Tito, I feel it important to translate here Pope Montini's address to some delegates of the American Jewish Committee. These delegates, under the leadership of their president, Bernard Abrams, were confidentially and cordially received by Paul VI on March 31, 1971, two days after the visit of Tito, the Communist Jew who has shed so much blood, especially in Croatia. This new Pontifical audience enlightens us completely about the Pontiff's enigma and his national and international political activities which he has perseveringly and tenaciously carried out as part of his program for peace and human progress. Pope Montini's address follows:

> Dear friends:
>
> We are very happy to welcome you at the Vatican as representatives of the American Jewish Committee.
>
> In promulgating its declaration on relations between the Catholic Church and other religions of the world, Vatican Council II sought to lay the basis for an improvement of relations between Catholics and people of other religions. There

Tito's Visit

is a special link between Catholics and Jews. God Himself united us through His revelation. His first commandment asks us to love Him with all our hearts, with all our souls and with all our might, and to love our neighbors as ourselves. (Deut. 6:5; Lev. 19:18; Mat. 22: 37-39).

That is why we seriously wish that the directions of the Vatican Council be put into practice so that the development of a better understanding and deeper respect between Christians and Jews may permit them to work together for the sake of peace and human welfare.

We know that the American Jewish Committee is actively cooperating, and we ask the Lord that He bless our joint common efforts, made through His inspiration.

Here we most certainly have the very links that permit us to unravel the mystery and discover the secret schemes skillfully devised and fulfilled by the Jewish-Masonic mafia. Marshal Tito, who not only has long been enslaving Yugoslavia and the neighboring countries but is a key figure in the world plot, was received by Paul VI on March 29, 1971. Two days later, the Pope welcomed the president and other representatives of the American Jewish Committee. Was this just a coincidence or rather a precisely implemented program by which Pope Montini is putting the Vatican at the service of a design for world domination demanded by the materialistic messianism of those who fight Christ?

Now let us quote an accusation recently released in Rome by the International Committee for the Defense of Christian Civilization - Italian Section *(Comitato Internazionale per la Difesa de la Civiltà Cristiana - Sezione Italiana)*:

Catholics and Romans:

A visitor has come to Italy, an honored guest of the Italian government and the Vatican, but one who has been despicable to, and despised by the Italian people and real Catholics. The celebrated Josip Broz, known as Tito, Communist dictator of Yugoslavia and "Trojan Horse" of International Communism within the Free World, is in Rome.

We cannot remain quiet and indifferent before this profanation and betrayal of our blood brothers who were brutally assassinated by Tito and his accomplices during the hateful massacres of Istria and Carso. This innocent blood deserves at least a little respect and gratitude from the living, but instead, it receives contempt and mockery from those who ought to be its guardians and avengers. Today the assassin is being welcomed with full honors.

We cannot and *must not* forget the sacrifice of the most noble Italian land and the cultural European heritage represented at a geographical area that was destined to be the meeting place for different peoples and cultures. This has all

The Montinian Church

been destroyed by Tito, the very Tito our irresolute government and Machiavellian Vatican welcome with the honors that ought to be reserved for decent people.

Catholics and Romans: If we cannot impede this loathsome political farce, let this despicable guest feel we do not want him to stay amid us, for we have not forgotten his crimes, and we condemn this outrage against our most holy national and Christian feelings. When the dictator from Belgrade passes by, let us loudly cry together: *"Tito, go home! We do not want to shake hands with him who is guilty of the martyrdom of our Catholic Croatian brethren! Tito, we have not forgotten the heroic Archbishop Stepinac! Tito, do not profane Italy's holy soil which you have already mutilated! Go back to your cave in Belgrade! Tito, the Italian people condemn you as a tyrant and oppressor of the Yugoslavian people!"*

Then let the Vatican feel our bitterness as Catholics whose most holy feelings of solidarity with our brethren of the *Church of the Silence* have been hurt. Their humiliation and desperation is ours and reaches its maximum height with this meeting of Herod's spiritual heir and him who represents Christ and Peter. The Church used to honor the martyrs and condemn persecutors. What now?

Christ, have mercy on us!

The members of the Yugoslavian people who are living as exiles also released propaganda in Rome speaking on behalf of themselves and their brethren who are being oppressed by the unmerciful tyranny of Communism:

To the Italian People:

The Multinational Council of the Political Democratic Organization of the Croatians, Serbians, Macedonians, Slavs, Albanians, and Hungarians living in the fatherland and abroad, petitions your civic and democratic conscience to show to the world your disapproval and condemnation of the indecorous and humiliating state visit of Josip Broz, Tito, the dictator of Yugoslavia, one of the worst tyrants in our times and murderer of tens of thousands of our Italian brethren. In fact one cannot seek one's own political and economic welfare by welcoming a tyrant and willfully ignoring the sorrow, tears, and slavery of a nation subject to tyranny.

The representatives of the religious creeds of the Multinational Council (Catholic, Orthodox, and Muslim), appealing to the conscience of the Catholic world, solemnly protest and morally condemn the upsetting decision by Vatican officials to welcome and honor Tito, persecutor and enemy of every religion.

No political, diplomatic, economic, or even ecumenical consideration may in our mind justify this humiliating debasement of the Italian government and the Catholic Church.

Above all, we call the attention of those who are responsible for Vatican policies to the diabolical scheme concocted by Tito and world Communism to make use of the position of Christ's Vicar on earth who, willingly or not, by the mere fact of receiving this vulgar and fatuous tyrant before his august person, automatically rehabilitates him and gives him moral support. We cannot help remembering how much more wise and coherent was the attitude of the great Pius XI, when another dictator came to Rome.

Vatican diplomacy believes this is the way of saving the Church, but it cannot see that it "saves" only its doubtful and controversial diplomatic apparatus, while Catholics are lost and non-Catholic believers are disgusted and estranged. The desperation of humble, oppressed, and persecuted people calls for vengeance before man and God. We remind those who hate civil and ecclesiastical power of just this!

Italians, join us for the triumph of
Human dignity, trampled by Tito.
Civil and religious liberty, oppressed by Tito.
The national liberty of the Yugoslavian people, enslaved and tyrannized by Tito.

The documents quoted above eloquently and publicly expose the Vatican's policies which are no longer those of peaceful coexistence, but of cooperation with international Communism and the Jewish-Masonic conspiracy. After having read them, we easily find an explanation for the disconcerting speech that Paul VI delivered, much to the scandal of those who read it and do not support the modern ideology that tries to Christianize atheistic Communism. Pope Montini says the rapprochement between the Vatican and Yugoslavia is "promising." Before such an affirmation, we may ask the same question we asked before: Has the Vatican or atheistic Communism changed? Tito and the Yugoslavian government are Communistic; they may have changed their tactics but not their ideology or goals. To believe that these diplomatic encounters, these vague and commonplace speeches, show that Communism has relinquished its irreligiousness and its militant atheism, is to believe that not-being is being. The tolerant paternalism which the Communist governments have recently simulated in the satellite countries enslaved by godless conquerors, is just a tactic designed to paralyze our resistance, keep the opposition quiet, and encourage the ecclesiastical authorities, duped by this apparent mollification of diplomatic relations, to persuade their parishioners to maintain the same kind of relations. It is neither Tito nor Communism which has changed; it is the Vatican's unbearable policies which have changed and seem to have finally acknowledged the world success of Communism.

"The relations between both countries," said Paul VI, "are excellent, and will be useful to analyze problems that are especially grave and upsetting" such as those which Tito mentioned. Perhaps the Yugoslavian dictator mentioned the tremendous religious problems the Church of Silence has been undergoing for such a long time? Maybe the Pontiff was offered reparations for the outrages inflicted upon Catholics, the bishops, the seminaries, and the religious schools? Was Christ's Church promised and guaranteed absolute freedom for the future? What a difficult task it is to convert people like Tito, who do not believe in anything and only wish to comply with the directions the mafia has given them! Had Tito sincerely converted to our faith or had he made personal independent decisions, he would have long ago ceased to be President of Yugoslavia or even be alive by now.

At the time, the Pope, just like Tito, was concerned only for political problems, particularly those of Vietnam and the Middle East. Of course both statesmen's concern was brought about by the interests and strategy of international Jewry. The Tito-Montini meeting was aimed at facilitating the plans of the mafia. Tito's allusion to Israel's stubbornness was designed only to dupe naive people into believing that there are opposite antagonistic fronts among the militants and servants of the Israeli power. This is an old, well-known tactic of the synagogue!

Paul VI tried to soothe the oppressed peoples when he said: "The Yugoslavian people seem to have been called by Providence to find a common ground for meeting and understanding in order that the continent can spare itself new conflicts and find the way to international cooperation." In other words, the providential vocation of those oppressed peoples consists of being patient and enduring Communist tyranny, and becoming the meeting place for the Free World and the Communist world, for Catholics and atheists. This mutual understanding, which is but longsuffering, will spare us conflicts and enable all of us to willingly cooperate in the coming complete success of atheistic Communism, which will be the salvation of the world. "Through ... [this mutual understanding]" said Paul VI, "greater progress and a more fraternal civilization will be achieved." Once Communism had united all men and deprived them of any possibility of resistance or response, the United Nations' international apparatus will be able to set up a world government, the longed-for "messianic materialism" of international Jewry.

Under the impulse and leadership of His Excellency, Marshal Tito, Paul VI believes that an internationalized Yugoslavia expanded beyond its European borders in a world that has become smaller and more consolidated, can be (it is not the Pontiff, but we who say this) the starting point for the peaceful conquest of the world by international Communism and the mafia.

Tito had stated before, in his speech before the Pontiff, that he was ready to engage his best efforts to obtain a peaceful solution to the Middle East conflict and the problem of Southeast Asia. "I am glad to see," he affirmed, "that the Holy See and Yugoslavia have similar or identical views on the big international problems...." Does not this similarity and this identity as to international policies prove that both the Holy See or the Vatican and the Yugoslavian government receive their inspiration *from the same source,* have *the same secret leaders,* and that the subsequent audience with the American Jewish Committee let us know who those leaders are? Coincidences and bold statements, perhaps, but the fraud is apparent: "the necessity of solving [big international problems] through peaceful coexistence." Maybe the Vatican quieted down with the alluring prospect of peaceful coexistence, but Tito and those who back him know quite well that this coexistence is not only unacceptable for them, but impossible, since a strong, healthy organism cannot coexist with germs.

As a last remark on the visit of the tyrant of Yugoslavia to the Vatican, we must note that, despite the voluntary renunciations of the Papal court, the protocol was invested with all the magnificence of Constantinian triumphalism. The Church of the poor went back to its times of grandeur and splendor to urbanely welcome Marshal Tito, Josip Broz, persecutor of Catholics.

Chapter XXXII

PRIESTS' MOVEMENT FOR THE THIRD WORLD

It was Pope Montini and Vatican Council II who classed us Latin Americans as *"underdeveloped peoples," "hungry peoples,"* and the *"Third World,"* a world between capitalism and Communism. The upsurge of the *Priests' Movement for the Third World* is one of the explosive features of the post-Conciliar Church, which many call "the grown-up Church." John XXIII set the Church's social line in his *Mater et Magistra.* Paul VI went further with his *Populorum Progressio,* and the bishops, at their level, echoed it. No wonder then that the most bold statements, the most aggressive movements and the most impudent subversion arise from so many priests in this vast area of the Third World, that feels more and more oppressed by the growing expansion of the United States and the Union of Soviet Socialist Republics. That is why a famous statement by 18 bishops from Asia, Africa, and Latin America and the concluding speeches of Paul VI to these countries ended with these words: *"We exhort you to remain firm and brave, as an evangelical ferment in the world of work, trusting Christ's words, 'Stand up and raise your heads, for your liberation is at hand.'"*

This message was published in mid-1967. The newly-born movement was joined by 270 priests. Of these 23 were Argentinians, among whom were Frs. Masciliano, Mayol (now former priests), Mugica, and Carbone, a scholar of Fr. Tello's humanistic teachings. Communities of town and worker priests, and priests from the Catholic University Movement, led by Fr. Anthony Paoli, the forerunner of dialogue between Catholics and Marxists in Argentina, also joined this movement.

The Third World Movement proclaims that it *"formally rejects the current capitalistic system and its logical consequence of economic and cultural imperialism."* Then, without any inhibitions, it endorses *"Latin American socialism,"* which will *"socialize the means of production and the economic, political, and cultural power."* The secretary general, Fr. Michael Ramondetti, affirmed that socialism is the most "evangelical system, though not the most perfect." "Anyhow," he said to defend himself, "capitalism is certainly not Christian." The other reporters, Fr. Oswald Catena, Fr. Reuben Dri, Fr. Joseph Nasser, and Fr. Ronald Concatti, emphatically justified a reference to a document on Peronism (the 1945-1955 experience), which, in their mind, "was a key element in the incorporation of our people into the revolutionary movement;" however, they did not concern themselves with "the temple burning and the persecution of the Church." The movement grew rapidly in Argentina; by the end of 1970 it consisted of almost 400 priests, among whom the Jesuits, with their Universities of Buenos Aires and Córdoba, stood out.

Following the well-known trick of Marxist dialectics, the permanent committee of the Argentinian episcopate launched a manifesto on August 12, 1970, in which they seemed to condemn the Third World Movement. We quote: "To join a revolutionary process... choosing a Latin American way of socializing the economic, political, and cultural power does not belong to any group of priests, nor is it legitimate, because of their sacerdotal status, the Church's social doctrine, to which it is opposed, nor by the character of the social revolution which implies the acceptance of violence as a means of achieving the liberation of the oppressed." (*Statement*, Third National Meeting of the Priests' Movement for the Third World, Santa Fe, May 2, 1970).

The Movement had emphatically declared: "We have stated before what the mission of the priest as such is in the Church, namely: '*There will be no real socialism in Latin America without the takeover by real revolutionaries* who come from the people and be faithful to them.'" The very statement of the third meeting is to conciliate the *social revolution* with all its inherent *violence*. Such is the real line of the progressivist priests who are the allies of Marxism right now, without fear of their prelates' criticism. They issue incendiary statements, lead bloody outbreaks, and support and preach subversion as the newest edition of Christ's Gospel. Why should they be afraid, since they know the Pope endorses them, blesses them, and thinks the way they do? The press had let us know on August 18, 1971, in the morning issue of the *Mexican Sun (Sol de Mexico)*, that Paul VI had sent a telegram to Msgr. Adolph Tortolo in which he blessed the Third World priests.

The dialectical movement, typical of the whole process of spectacular changes in the language, ideology, liturgy, discipline, and the post-Conciliar pastoral, makes the documents contradict each other. As a result, the bishops become paralyzed and impotent to react when the ecclesiastical activists draw logical conclusions from their discourses and acts. That is why Frs. Alberto Carbone and Carlos Mugica, in examining the ecclesiastical prospects of Argentina, said:

> Today, unlike in previous times, the Lord poses a way, namely: *the people in command*. The human process changes the political process; today it is the people who have priority to decide. The liberation has been decided by God, and faith has to echo God's voice. We assume this liberation has to take place through a socialistic process, starting from Argentinian reality, but we cannot,

nor must we, give concrete guidelines for this program to be implanted.

This is also why the Third World people would invoke the statement of the Argentinian episcopate issued at the end of the meeting at San Miguel to justify their subversive activities. The prelates had written:

> The need for a quick and deep transformation of the present structure obliges us all to seek after a new, human, and efficient way of liberation. This will overcome barren resistance to change and ban radical approaches, particularly the Marxist ones, which are alien, not only to Christian views, but to the feelings of our people, too.

Just read Fr. Carbone's and Fr. Mugica's statements and you will notice that demagoguery and conceptual falsehood are their leading features. They also incur "prophetism," which is typical of the new redeemers. Who has revealed to them that "the Lord poses" the way of *"the people in command?"* What God has told them He has decided the "liberation?" They claim theirs is no *political* movement, but their and the Argentinian episcopate prelates' statements use the terms, "a socialistic process," different from "the Marxist one . . . ," "change" of "process," etc.

The Third World people's pastoral zeal is not limited to demagogic agitation and revolutionary harangues. Sometimes they become activists, militia men, terrorists, and assassins. I am not referring only to the case of Camilo Torres Restrepo, but also to the kidnapping and slaughter of the former Argentinian President, Peter Eugene Aramburu. The July 12, 1970 *Confirmed (Confirmado)* magazine, Number 265, gives us an example. An article by André Rouquine Laplume reads:

> You are looking for an Algerian priest that could be involved in the kidnapping, and I know who he is. . . . This priest is *Raoul Guillet,* who fled to Peru after the kidnapping of Aramburu and was a collaborator of the Nazis during the occupation of Paris in World War II. After the liberation he fled to Spain. Afterwards he moved to Algeria and cooperated with the Organization of American States and General Raoul Salan. There is a priest by the name of Guillet, not an aide, but a confessor of Salan, who lived in Buenos Aires for a time and evolved toward the so-called Third World political line. Guillet, who is credited with having excellent contacts with the French mafioso Francois Chiappe and the Spaniard Rafael García (a mercenary who operated in the Congo and Indochina), was actively involved in the organization of the Cursillo Movement led by another Frenchman, Father George Grasset, linked to the Organization de l'Armée Secrète of Raoul Salan.
>
> It is not difficult at all to prove Carbone's links with the Third World

priests. He is the editor of *Connection (Enlace)* magazine, the bulletin of the Third World priests, a group founded October 15, 1967 in Tucumán, Córdoba, Rosario and Mendoza. It was the Third World priests who conducted political courses under the leadership of the Jesuits, at a villa of a Los Naranjos neighborhood, Córdoba, where some people were arrested, and later found guilty of the robbery of La Calera.

Be it true or not, the Catholic hierarchy decided to tolerate the discrediting campaign in order not to aggravate Carbone's position. That was the reason why they advised the Third World priests not to issue any statement. Obviously the Church is not involved in the Priests' Movement for the Third World, but it responds as a body instead. [This could have been said in good faith some time ago, but not now, after the "blessing" Pope Montini sent the Third World movement and priests, according to recent press reports.]

So it had to be: the movement was created as a concrete and active answer to the Pontiff's social line, as expressed in his *Populorum Progressio,* his Bogotá speeches, and the Medellín documents he knew, approved, and blessed. [We must by all means open our eyes and become aware of the dreadful situation in which we are living.]

But the advice of the hierarchy, do not aggravate Carbone's position, was of little use. During the night of Sunday, June 12, 1970, the police found imperfect evidence of his involvement in some obscure events at a religious institution in the federal capital, which Carbone used to visit. There they found the typewriter used by the kidnappers to write down the communiques issued by a group called the "Montoneros."

Other evidence worsened the position of some Third World priests. At the Los Naranjos (Córdoba) villa, a file was requisitioned that widened the field of the inquiry and paved the way for another police investigation on the weekend at Fr. Moyano's dwelling in Villa Allende (Córdoba). In his possession was found a notebook which permitted the police to detect the existence of 170 cells involved in the kidnapping of Peter Eugene Aramburu and the subversive activities launched in the previous months.

The assassination of August T. Vandor, the kidnapping of the Paraguayan Consul Waldeman Sánchez, the storming of barrack 7 of Campo de Mayo, and some robberies in the quarters of security agencies, police detachments, and the Tigre Prefecture, show the agitation which the Third World movement of committed priests has been producing in the nation.

On August 15, 1967, 18 bishops (nine of them from Brazil, one from Algeria, and one each from Oceania, Egypt, Colombia, Yugoslavia, Lebanon, China, and Indonesia) headed by Don Helder Camara, started the work of putting the directions of *Populorum Progressio* into practice. To this effect they created the Third World Priest Movement.

Priests' Movement

These 18 bishops wrote:

> Christians are obligated to demonstrate that *real socialism is but integral Christianity*, including the actual allotment of goods and real fundamental equality. Far from fighting this new system, we must get to know how to join it with a spirit of joy, discovering in its structure a pattern of social life better adapted to our times and more consistent with the evangelical spirit.

Approximately four months later the Priests' Movement for the Third World was born in Argentina. Presently it includes more than 400 priests. One hundred and twenty-four of these issued a paper that, to many officials of the security agencies, shows clearly the links of its members with the radical underground groups involved in operations of urban guerilla warfare beginning in 1969.

One of the important thoughts contained in the paper issued by the 124 Argentinian priests mentioned above is given in this quotation:

> The movement is no political party, nor wants or is able to be one. As such, it does not give any opinion or take sides as to tactics, strategy, or trends of groups or organizations, *thus respecting its own members' freedom of choice.*

Two months later, a quiet and far-off suburb of Córdoba named LaCalera was transitorily occupied. Primary research showed that some lads of well-known Christian beliefs and even a priest belonging to the Buenos Aires branch of the Priests' Movement, Albert Carbone, were involved. Carbone, who was born in Berlin but brought up and ordained in Buenos Aires, was, up to the time of his arrest, the spiritual advisor of the Catholic Student Youth (CSY), a branch of Catholic Action. He shared with Fr. Charles Mugica the responsibility for the spread of the Third World ideas. In addition, along with Mario Edward Firmenich and Ferdinand Louis Abal Medina, the whole staff of the juvenile Argentinian Catholic Action was involved in the kidnapping of General Peter Eugene Aramburu, although they claimed it was the Communists who brought this charge against them.

To the Catholic right wing, the progressivist, not necessarily Third World, movement was introduced into the nation by Gilbert Rufenach, a priest and a member of the Mission de France, the ideological source of the worker-priests. Charles A. Sacheri, on page 92 of his book, *The Underground Church*, says that Rufenach was a captain and chaplain of the French Army who, "from the time of his ordination as a priest, was associated with the NLF, the National Liberation Front. When the French Army got to know it, Fr. Rufenach fled to Argentina." The same sources call Fr. Rufenach an "active indoctrinator of Fr. Ramondetti," and affirm that "the leaders of the Villa Crespo cell of the

The Montinian Church

Communist Party say Ramondetti was an active member of the Party."

Bearing in mind the ideology, the dynamics, and the program of the Priests' Movement for the Third World, we find no ground for surprise at the involvement of several priests in the violent events that have taken place throughout Argentina. As a prelude to the *"Cordobazo,"* rallies of workers and students were headed by several priests, notably, Frs. Milán Viscovich, Gustav Ortíz, and Nelson Delaferra. The same thing happened at Tucumán, Corrientes, Rosario, Santa Fe, and also Buenos Aires, where the lay militant, Juan García Elorrio, the late editor of the newspaper, *Christianity and Revolution,* instigated a riot at the cathedral to let his views be known. In fact, 24 dioceses included Third World militants, determined to fulfill the original commitment:

> Convinced as we are, that *liberation will be made by the poor and of the poor,* and that we shall get to know the right way through permanent contact with the people, we commit ourselves to the task of getting in touch with the people, amid the poor, and assuming human attitudes that show and, verify our commitment.

In the July 7, 1970 afternoon newspaper *Córdoba*, the Priests' Movement claims:

> ... [I]t cannot be held responsible for the various options of its members as far as the revolutionary struggle is concerned. The Movement respects those who, believing all possibilities are exhausted, feel armed struggle to be the only way, but the Movement has chosen the way of the Word and seeks to awaken consciences to the service of the people and the poor.

These are the well-known tactics of Helder Cámara, Paul VI, and our clerical Mexican agitators. In the words of Fr. Arrupe, they are laying the tracks for their rapid violent trains to run wild. They do not want to assume any liability, but they verbally encourage subversion and violence, notwithstanding their having condemned them before. Thus when the militants are punished by the authorities, they can claim that those violent deeds *are not the work of the Movement, but of its members, who have freely chosen*. This is like casting a stone and hiding one's hand. Is that not so, Father Miranda y de la Parra?

Father Charles Mugica is the author of "The Death of God," an article I shall quote shortly, for it is very important for us to realize the threat of destruction of the Catholic religion caused by the priests' betrayal of the divine mission of the Christ-instituted priesthood. Mugica is a priest who entered the priesthood later in life than most priests, a restless man who did not hesitate to read all the subversive literature circulating in ecclesiastical circles today.

Priests' Movement

"Indefatigable curiosity," said *Extra* magazine, "caused him to read eagerly every single book he could. He traversed the streets of Paris amid the student riots, along with the rebels who hated the structuralists and let only Jean Paul Sartre speak." He and the regular leaders of the shanty towns before Puerto Nuevo, managed the concrete problems of the dwellers. "For," as Abbe Pierre, the inspirer of the Third World priests, put it, "you cannot talk about God to a man who has no home. First, give him a home, which actually is a way of talking to him about God."

Below I quote a dialogue between Fr. Mugica and a journalist:

Newsman: What is a Third World priest?

Fr. Mugica: He is a priest of the Catholic Church who tries to take seriously the Church's directions as stated in *Populorum Progressio,* at Medellín, and at San Miguel. He assumes the defense of the oppressed and tries, as Helder Cámara said, to be "the voice of voiceless people."

Newsman: Does it cause many priests to have problems with the hierarchy in our country?

Fr. Mugica: Yes, indeed. In our country, the episcopate as a whole is far from fulfilling the demands of today's *pastoral of the Church.*

Newsman: At the beginning of this chat, we said some members of the hierarchy were turning from statements to facts, and we mentioned the actual case of Msgr. de Nevares, and the cases of Devoto and Di Stéfano. Are these still incipient attitudes bound to provoke a crisis between the Church and the government?

Fr. Mugica: I feel that, if the Church is faithful to its mission, the crisis will necessarily occur. In fact it already has. It can be avoided only to the extent that our rulers, who claim to be Catholics, put the teachings of the Church into practice. These have been clearly stated in the *Populorum Progressio* and the prophetic paper our bishops released shortly before the "Cordobazo," where they warned about the danger of not rapidly seeking the substantial changes our nation needs. Then, if once and for all, they understand the current condition and take steps to transform it, I feel that there can be a dialogue between the Church and the government. At any rate, our movement and many other segments of the Church (lay and priest movements not of the Third World) are exerting stringent efforts to assure that the Church is fully independent of the government, not linked to any earthly power, and free to express itself even though it loses some properties. I feel the revolution *has* to be carried on within the Church too, since the Church remains a propertyholder, although less and less so.

On the other hand, if the responsible authorities and rulers do *not* take this into account, they will be ultimately and definitely liable for the potentially tremendous *violence* that can be unleashed in our fatherland. They will be the ones guilty of subversion.

The Montinian Church

Through Fr. Mugica's statements, we become aware of the effects of the Montinian encyclical, *Populorum Progressio,* upon the priests' mentalities and attitudes. Father Mugica himself says a Third World priest is one who ". . . tries to take seriously the Church's directions as stated in *Populorum Progressio,* at Medellín, and at San Miguel." Once the premises have been laid, the consequences follow, though they be terrible. Father Mugica does not discard the use of violence. On the contrary, he foresees it, and says: ". . . [I]f the . . . authorities and rulers do *not* take this into account, *they will be ultimately and definitely liable for the potentially tremendous violence that can be unleashed* in our fatherland" [italics ours].

Chapter XXXIII

THE DEATH OF GOD

Below I quote from an article written by Fr. Carlos Mugica published in the *Panorama* magazine of July 21, 1971. The article is entitled "The Death of God:"

Is God dead? Is there any future for the Church? Twenty years ago these questions would have been scandalous. The fact that today, although hesitantly and without getting any answers, we may pose them, shows we are undergoing a condition of insecurity and crisis to such an extent that the Dutch Augustinian monk, Robert Adolfs, published a book called *God's Grave*.

According to Marx, Christianity never considered the salvation of the community. He is referring to the salvational individualism which expresses a Manichaean mentality inherited from Plato which the Church has endorsed so many times. Why should I save my soul and not my life, my history, *our* history, that of *all* human beings? The Bible does not define the human being as body and soul, but as breathing dust. When God addresses man, He does not speak with the individual, but with the community, and Israel, God's friend, is not an individual, but a people.

Marx's ideas were endorsed by Lenin, who, in *Socialism and Religion*, wrote:

Religion is one of the aspects of spiritual oppression resting everywhere on the popular masses who are continually being crushed by work for the benefit of others, and by misery and abjection. The exploited classes' weakness unavoidably engenders their belief in a better life beyond the grave, the way that the weakness of the savage, in his fight against nature, engenders a belief in gods, devils, miracles, etc. Religion preaches humility and resignation in this world to those who spend their lives in work and misery, consoling them with the hope of a celestial life. Conversely, to those who live off the work of others, religion teaches the benefits of this world, thus offering them an easy justification for their needs as exploiters, and selling them cheap tickets to heavenly happiness. Religion is the opiate of the people.

The Montinian Church

We Christians must acknowledge that this is a tremendous objection. However, it is not aimed at Christianity, but at the formulation which we have made of it in the last few centuries. The early Christians lived in a community of goods and life. When the Industrial Revolution came, the Church cast its lot with liberal capitalism and failed to assume the condition of the exploited masses. That was why Marx proposed the replacement of Christian humanism by Communistic humanism. Today Christians understand that they cannot continue to conceal Christ's face, and really feel the words Saint Paul addressed to the early believers: "For your cause God's name is blasphemous among the pagans." Thus the prophets of our age appear: Helder Cámara, Martin Luther King, Camilo Torres. I am sure that the Christianity of these men would have modified Marx's and Lenin's ideas of religion. To them Christ's faith is not just an opiate for the people, but the deepest impulse of their revolutionary commitment.

WHAT IS "THE DEATH OF GOD?"

We call "the death of God" the widespread conviction that God is no longer necessary for the building of the secular city, and that matter and its determinism suffice. Religion and God have become superfluous as far as the development of science and technique, philosophy and the arts, and work and rest are concerned. Modern cosmovision tends to think more and more of man as an end in himself. Rational man, that of Aristotle's four causes, is dead; he has been replaced by existential man. Hence God belongs to metaphysics, abstraction, and ideas. Present man is a realist, and what is real can be explained without recourse to God.

THE SECULAR LIFE

This is the normal consequence of God's death. Sacred things are being de-sacralized for the above reasons and also as a result of the following: (a) world congestion, (b) urban pluralism, and (c) ideological chaos. The Church has always been largely responsible for this process. It has not always been able to distinguish between the God of natural reason (of whom Vatican Council I speaks, saying He is within reach of any honest intelligence) and the God of revelation, Jesus Christ's Father, who cannot be reached by our reason, and gives Himself up to the world as an immense supernatural gift. Many times, the Church has insinuated that without it as a revealed and supernatural religion, man would not be able to build the secular city. It hinted it was intrinsically essential for the building of the world. Now the Church portrays itself as a co-worker, and Paul VI called it the "servant of mankind," just as Christ was, since He "came to serve, not to be served by men." The Church now acknowledges that atheism can be lived by people in good faith. It also avows that it has projected a certain image of God so as to conceal His real face, as proven by its wealth, its allegiance to capitalistic and imperialist power, and its past inquisitorial preeminence. It has exploited God as a solution to problems that concern science, progress, and man. Remember recent statements by the Pope exonerating Galileo? He acknowledges the historic meaning of all religions, particularly the Jewish and Muhammadan, and declares that it is not the individual, but mankind that needs a witness of faith, hope, and love, as Christ demands. To this effect, not only persons, but also structures must be changed, be it to love or destroy them. He also emphasizes psychological characteristics of faith: the confidence in Christ as a revolutionary leader, and the belief that His principles will bring justice to the world, a justice that will be complete only if it is transcendent and ends in eternal life.

PRIESTS BEFORE THE VATICAN

People talk about a sacerdotal crisis everywhere. In fact this is the crisis of the clerical priest who lives in an ecclesiastical way and according to an obsolete Canon Law. Today many priests' loyalty to anachronistic legal rules estranges them from life and the world which is the field in which they must announce Christ. That is the root of the celibacy problem. Theirs is not just a sentimental loneliness, but a consciousness of their uselessness, the fruit of a life castrated of its creative possibilities. To this add the fact that many priests, full of evangelical enthusiasm, are scandalized by their hierarchies' partnerships with the ruling classes, with the oppressive system Helder Cámara calls "established lawlessness." The above is confirmed by a recent survey in Brazil.

The mere existence of the Vatican is already a source of conflict for many Christians. They see it as an ally of capitalistic imperialism, and notice that its anti-Communist preaching fails to defend the human person, but instead is aimed at the Vatican's survival as a power factor, with its ambassadors, wealth, and influence. The Conciliar Fathers clearly saw the difficulty that the ecclesiastical apparatus entails for the message of God and the evangelization of the poor. To the Brazilian Catholics, it was very painful that Cardinal Barros Cámara congratulated the "gallant Brazilian armed forces" when they overthrew Joao Goulart to save the nation from Communism and cast it into the hands of imperialism. When popular reaction burst out, the gallant armed forces' response was persecution and tortures even against the priests and nuns who serve the people.

A few years ago, Antonio Cardinal Caggiano determined that the Colombian priest, Camilo Torres, had deserted his vocation. No doubt he was sincere, but he could not understand that Torres's brave love of the humble and the exploited could have caused him to immolate himself for their benefit, painfully giving up the Mass in order to assume the prophetic dimension of his ministry. This sternness is disappearing now, as the Church's hierarchs begin to echo Paul VI in his *Populorum Progressio*.

MISSION OF THE CHURCHES

A look at the "Death of God" theology permits one to draw some conclusions:

1. The Protestant theologians, and then the Catholic ones, have studied the many aspects of modern life, using the methods of the social and cultural sciences. This analysis is causing the Church to progressively abandon its triumphalistic attitude towards the world, with a corresponding, progressive diminution of its influence.

2. The churches' alternative is to renew themselves or disappear. They must acknowledge they are no longer nursemaids or owners of adult men. If they fail to give mankind something creative, they lose their reason to exist. The Vatican Council grasped this. In Colombia, Paul VI said that "the poor have become conscious of their oppressed condition." Afterwards Helder Cámara affirmed that in Latin America the revolutionary process will be carried on with the Christians, without the Christians, or eventually, against the Christians.

3. No longer can the churches be conceived as institutions living off the government and society, and linked to the power factors, or even less, a function of a cultural priesthood for the benefit of select minorities. To prove the weakness of the religiosity of such minorities, just weigh the fruits of their renunciation, humility, and love of neighbor. Unless the churches embrace the cause of righteousness, they will disappear.

4. The above causes me to proclaim the churches' revolutionary mission. Harvey Cox (whom Paul VI mentioned, too) has the unique merit of having acknowledged the fact that, in the United States (the seat of liberal individualism) today's Church is either social-revolutionary or nothing.

5. Today the sole possible apologetics for the churches is to embrace the cause of man's liberation, international social justice, brotherhood, and peace. The theologians and the Council believe that bishops, priests, and believers will be able to carry on such a revolution only through poverty, simplicity, and loyal service to their neighbors. On the other hand, experience shows that wealth and connivance with power lead to prostration and not to people's liberation.

But the activity of the Church, however, cannot be reduced to launching a deep change of the structures that oppress people. The existence of concupiscence and sin shows that, even though the Church assumes the cause of justice, development and brotherhood, it will have to undertake the hard and tremendous task of converting each man under the influence of Christ.

As long as in official Church circles only the pill, the rites, the cardinals' apparel, and the marriage of priests are the subjects of discussion, the Church will be separated from the course of history, which is certainly above the confessional.

ARGENTINIAN CATHOLICISM

An old missionary who used to live among humble people, affirms that, "To the poor, God is a neighbor. They mention Him frequently in ordinary conversation, and resort to Him faithfully; at the same time, however, He is a far-away being from whom they expect to receive something, and who is feared more than loved, a God who does miracles and punishes."

However, Argentinian prayers are more frequently addressed to the Virgin Mary (especially the Virgin of Luján) or to the saints, above all, Cayetano and Anthony. This is a religiosity of votive offerings, promises, and pilgrimages in which the memory and worship of the dead have great importance. It includes Baptism, First Communion, sometimes the Last Sacraments, less frequently, Confession and Marriage. People believe that anyone who has not been baptized has not reached the human dimension, hence the expression, "He is like a little animal." These Sacraments have social consequences (in humble families, the *godfather* is a real institution), but they do not carry much weight in Christian life. To have received them is often very little related to a deep life of faith. The moral conduct of Catholics leaves much to be desired insofar as alcoholism and sex are concerned.

Until just before the last Council, the Argentinian Church was basically sacramentalist. It counted its children through the number of baptized people. Today Baptism and First Communion are stagnant rites and shining patterns of collective behavior all over the country. According to the evaluation of the bishops at Medellín, Colombia, in 1968, this affirmation was also true for Latin America as a whole, where said rites set the religious behavior of society. Ninety percent of Argentinians have been baptized, 70 percent have made their First Communion, and 60 percent have been married in the Church.

The sacramentalist attitude has in turn fostered a formalistic and superficial religion. To many people, to be a good Catholic means to accept a series of external rulings (to fast in Lent, to confess and receive Communion once a year, to give alms, etc.) instead of accepting a new way of life and thought according to the example of Christ.

THE POST-CONCILIAR CHURCH

The changes within the Church in the past 10 years are irreversible. This period can be divided into two definite parts following the Council. The Council was a blessing from God to His Church, and permitted the Church to confront its own deep being. On the one hand it allowed it to recover a de-alienated vision of

The Montinian Church

God, the living God of the Bible so different from the cold and abstract one of the Scholastic. On the other hand, it became decentralized as to men, communities, and people as a whole, who began to see it closer to them. Thus the Council was a twofold movement: a re-encounter of the Church with its roots, and a horizontal opening of the Church to all men.

In Latin America and particularly in Argentina, the process began with the charismatic influence of Abbé Pierre, the French priest who, with the simplicity of the prophets, said: "Before talking of God to homeless people, you have to give them a roof," thus pointing the way which today's Church has adopted. Afterwards Helder Câmara summarized the post-Conciliar task with the formula, "We must help man to stand up." The Argentinian episcopate joined this line through a document released at San Miguel in April of 1969, in which they affirmed that "[e]vangelization covers the entire field of human promotion." To help man grow as a man, teaching him to read, and helping him to become politically aware, are ways of announcing Christ to him and initiating him in the way of his liberation.

In Argentina an important part of this evolution of the Church was due to the guilt feeling of many priests who appeared to be linked to the oligarchy and elements which oppressed the people. After Peron was overthrown, the clergy felt the Church had been involved in contributing to his fall, and afterwards, many priests became aware of their being divorced from the people. Then they understood they had to seek their sacerdotal fulfillment from and with the people. Later on, the bishops ratified this view through their Popular Pastoral Document of 1969. The process was accentuated in shanty towns and working places by the presence of priests who realized that man can be evangelized only through his concrete and real problems. The roles of the laity became more and more that of main characters in the drama of life. Another important factor was the contact of Marxist university students with Christians, particularly those belonging to the university Catholic Action groups. Contact with the people created a revolutionary consciousness in segments of the Church which were growing more numerous each day. To this must be added the enlightened testimony of those two prophets of our age, Helder Câmara and Camilo Torres.

Each day Christians are becoming more acutely aware of what has been called the Third World, the world of the exploited and the oppressed. The Vietnam War has had an enormous influence upon the evolution of ideas; without it, there would have been no French rebellion in May of 1968. The Vietnamese people who have been at war for more than twenty years (fifteen of which have been spent in fighting the most powerful adversary in the world) are seen by the youth as undergoing a great injustice. Latin American events such as the Cuban revolution and the invasion of the Dominican Republic by American Marines, have been instrumental in the building of political consciousness. As a result there is a new fact, not yet analyzed but highly influential and of great future importance, namely, a certain degree of conversion to socialism. In the last century Pius IX said it was absolutely impossible to be a socialist and a Christian at the same time. Today on the contrary, we can affirm, along with the Third World bishops, that "Socialism is less estranged from the Gospel and the prophets than oppressive capitalism." Many youngsters are already disposed to give up their lives, maybe not for socialism, but for the revolution, and they identify this commitment with their fidelity to Christ.

Camilo Torres said that the best way to love your neighbor is to make revolution. Today the number of people who die from hunger or are marginal in their dignity and culture are legion; among them are certain minorities that are increasingly influential with the masses, since they express the people's deep hopes. In this respect I can give a very concrete example. I have been surprised by the comments of Argentinians and Bolivians on "Ché" Guevara. In the beginning he was admired by the bourgeoisie and constituted a myth for college students throughout the world, but now, he has entered the people, and is a standard-bearer of the humble classes.

You can see a similar attitude in many priests, for instance those from Tucumán who are the natural leaders of the impoverished people; those from Northern Chaco, Santa Fe, who accompanied unemployed peasants and workers marching from Villa Ocampo to Santa Fe; those who are active in shanty towns and who, at the end of 1968, made a silent rally before the *Pink House* [the Argentinian equivalent of the White House] to protest against an eradication project that does not solve, but aggravates, a problem. Prophetic deeds such as these are to be seen everywhere, even among bishops, such as Msgr. Devoto (Goya), Msgr. Distéfano (Chaco), Msgr. Angeleli (La Rioja), Msgr. Caferata (San Luis), and, most recently, Msgr. Nevares, who made an evangelical defense for the workers of El Chacón.

THE ORIGINALITY OF CHRIST'S MESSAGE

As a reaction to all this transcendental and spiritualistic Christianity, there is a tendency to limit Christ's word to a message of human redemption. This is not fair to Jesus Christ. Although Christian commitment includes a revolutionary commitment, including even the radical transformation of the social, political, economic, and cultural structures, Christ is far more ambitious than a revolutionary. What Christ seeks is not simply a more just and fraternal order; even if all human needs were satisfied and even if there were no social injustice, exploitation, disease, or neurosis, Christ would still offer His original message, namely, the possibility of rising to divinity, and entering a dimension man would not have been able to reach by himself. God had to reveal Himself through His son, Christ, who is a complete man, the God-man. This is the essential mystery of resurrection. That is why Paul says: "If Christ did not rise from the dead, we

Christians are the most foolish of men, since we believe in one who has deceived us." It is here where the dimension of faith enters. If Christ did not rise, if Christ is not the God-man, He, frankly speaking, does not interest me. He would be an important man such as Gandhi, Muhammad, or "Ché," but He would not be the man who solves man's basic problem, death. Only He can respond affirmatively to my thirst for divinity.

The title alone of the above article shows us the satanic boldness of the progressivist priests. Following the doctrines of Marx, Lenin, "Ché," and Camilo, in their own way they want to solve the social problems they have aggravated themselves, or have even provoked. The article "The Death of God," is an Argentinian version of the Mexican text written by José Porfirio Miranda y de la Parra, S.J., whose title was: "Marx and the Bible." So many and so grave are the errors which this article contains, that it would be tedious not only to refute them, but even to enumerate them. These are the extremes to which the integral humanism of Paul VI, John XXIII, and Vatican II have carried us.

Let me enumerate at least some of the most outstanding heresies of this devilish article, in which the writer seems to confront, judge, and condemn God as a myth, a nefarious deception that has served only to impede human development and progress. We must take into account that the author is a priest who invokes the authority of Vatican II, of *Populorum Progressio,* of Helder Cámara, and the 1969 pastoral document of the Argentinian episcopal conference.

1. Father Mugica seems to approve and endorse the thesis of the Dutch Augustinian, Robert Adolfs: *God is dead.*

2. Christian *salvationistic individualism* never aimed at the salvation of the community; it is the result of a Manichaean mentality inherited from Plato. In other words, the problem of salvation, according to the doctrine of the Gospel, Scripture, Tradition, etc., is a *personal affair.* God did not create us in series or in a heap, so He will not save us collectively. Salvation to Marx, Fr. Mugica, and current progressivism seems to be a mass communal problem.

3. Father Mugica justifies, or seems to justify, Marx's principles: "Religion is one of the aspects of spiritual oppression; . . . [r]eligion is the opiate of the people."

4. The Church made common cause with liberal capitalism. Christian humanism must be replaced by Communistic humanism.

5. These are the prophets of our time: Helder Cámara, Martin Luther King, and Camilo Torres, as well as "Ché," Méndez Arceo, Felipe Pardinas, Ertze Garamendi, Enrique Maza, and José Porfirio Miranda y de la Parra.

6. *God's death* consists of the widespread idea that God is no longer necessary for the building of the secular city. Religion and God have become

The Death of God

superfluous.

7. The man of reason is dead. He has been replaced by existential man.

8. De-sacralization of everything that is sacred seems to be suggested.

9. The Church is largely responsible for this process. It failed to distinguish the God of the natural reason from the God of revelation. [Is this not by chance the innovating thesis of José Porfirio Miranda y de la Parra: "The God of the Bible is not the Christian God!"]

10. Many times the Church hinted that without it, man would not be able to build the secular city. Now, after the two latest Popes and Vatican II, the Church is content with being *a servant and a co-worker.*

11. The Church with its wealth and its allegiance to capitalism and imperialism has defaced the image of God.

12. The Church acknowledges the historic meaning of all religions, especially the Jewish and the Muhammadan. It also emphasizes its confidence in Christ as a revolutionary leader.

13. The sacerdotal crisis is due to living according to obsolete canonical rules. The celibate is conscious of his uselessness and his life castrated of its creative possibilities.

14. The hierarchies associate themselves with power and the established disorder.

15. The mere existence of the Vatican (that is, the primacy and Magisterium of Peter) is a ground for conflict, since the Vatican is an ally of capitalistic imperialism.

16. The Conciliar Fathers clearly saw the difficulties provoked by the ecclesiastical apparatus, that is, the established Church.

These theses of Fr. Carlos Mugica can be frequently heard or read in similar terms, in the extensive progressivist literature being spread without any restriction throughout the world. The consequences of these theses are clear: the Church must progressively abandon its triumphalistic attitude, accept the continued diminution of its influence in the modern world without any objection, and be renewed unless we want it to disappear. Adult humanity no longer needs nursemaids or owners. Vatican II embraced it, Paul VI acknowledges it, and Helder Cámara puts it this way: *"The poor have become conscious of their oppressed condition."* That is why the revolutionary process in Latin America will be carried out *with Christians, without Christians* or, ultimately, *against Christians.* Consequently, unless the churches, all the churches, do not embrace the cause of justice, they have to disappear. Either the Church is a social revolutionary, or it is nothing. All the activity of the Church must be put at the service of the indigent.

This ideology is very much like that of Pope Montini. The Church's sole ground for existing, acting, and fulfilling its mission is social justice, defense of the poor, plunder of the rich, and service to man, but man of the humble classes.

The Montinian Church

Analyzing the *Populorum Progressio,* we notice that many of these destructive theses are based upon John Baptist Montini's social program.

Chapter XXXIV

SOCIALIZATION IN MEXICO

In Mexico also, our prelates, eager to fulfill Rome's directions and echo the *Populorum Progressio,* released a message on October 10, 1968, through the chairman of the Mexican episcopal committee, wherein they spoke about "The Opening of the Neo-Modernist Church to the Left." Following are the highlights of the episcopal message:

Much is still to be done in order that social justice be the norm of life for everyone.... [W]e draw your attention to the necessity for a change of mentality, attitudes, and structures, and emphasize the urgency of these changes as an indispensable condition of unity and peace.... [W]e must be conscious that we are living in a society which, like any developing society, is many times affected by unjust structures....

[W]e must define the contents of the kind of society we want to build as an answer to the existing one.... We do not support any one-way dialogue, or rather monologue, but a sort of dialogue that obliges one to acknowledge that the other party is right and free, and that at the social level, the parties in dialogue must consolidate their efforts to build something better than their private views....

Under this light we focus on the student problem, which is not privy to Mexico.... [We must] build the necessary bridges for dialogue with youth ... and ... insistently seek after this dialogue.... [Y]outh and adults want to be more and more free and responsible as they keep on progressing....

If we, the most responsible segments of civic and social life, refuse to make a self-examination and revise our values and ways, there is the imminent danger that the hopeless people will resort to violence, which is opposite to peace.... Still there is time for all of us Mexicans to retrieve the practice of justice under the dynamism of fraternal love....

Peace entails and demands the establishment of a just order; ... wherever there is unjust inequality among men and nations, there is a disruption of peace.... Peace [according to the Medellín International Congress] can be achieved by creating more perfect justice among men....

The human community develops itself as time passes, and is subject to a movement which implies a constant change of structures, transformation of new attitudes and change of hearts.... [T]ranquillity... is the result of a continued effort of adaptation to new circumstances, demands, and challenges of a changing history..., the practice of justice under the dynamism of fraternal love.

The Mexican Traditionalist Front wrote to the bishops of the Mexican episcopal committee:

> Anyone who reads your message, particularly the above-quoted outstanding phrases, will understand it is inspired by a *dialectical philosophy* according to which there are no everlasting or even perennial values. Values change along with various historic ages according to the demands and challenges of history, as your evangelical message from the episcopate expresses.
>
> The philosophy of perpetual transformation of the world and its values, of the eternal flux and reflux of history, was born in Greece. Heraclitus taught: "Never will your body touch the same water of the river for a second time, for once you turn to plunge, the water will have passed away..." It is necessary to go to the mid-19th century to hear Hegel (1779-1871) expound his *"dialectical idealism,"* based on the theory of the logical development of the idea. His work was completed by his disciples, Fichte, Schelling, and Feuerbach, who were the masters of Rabbi Mordechai Marx, today known as Karl Marx, the author of dialectical materialism, otherwise known as historic materialism. In his *Communist Manifesto,* published in 1847, Marx teaches: "... *[L]aws, morality, and religion are just bourgeois prejudices, the ideology of the prevailing social class."*
>
> The language of dialectical philosophy, the perpetual transformation of the world and life, is the language of the Mexican episcopate: "The human community develops itself as time passes, and is subject to a movement which implies a constant change of structures, transformation of new attitudes... a continued effort of adaptation to new circumstances, demands, and challenges of a changing history...."
>
> Your episcopal message includes words whose connotation is exclusively Marxist: *"self-examination," "change of structures," "adaptation to new circumstances," "changing history,"* etc. We must conclude then with deep immense sorrow, that the Catholic Church *"has drunk the hemlock,"* has been brainwashed, and "changing history" has caused it to abandon Christian philosophy based on perennial axiological and social values. The Church is openly proclaiming the theory of dialectical, economic, or materialistic dynamism as a reflection of the views stated at the second international meeting of LAMEC at Medellín, inaugurated by Paul VI.

Socialization in Mexico

This document by the Mexican Traditionalist Front shows some parallels between the venerable episcopate's ideas, programs, and words, and those of the most radical Mexican leftists. It is worthwhile to show here with seven different examples, some of the parallels between Communism and the dialectical philosophy of the Mexican episcopate.

1. General Lázaro Cárdenas, in a statement regarding the so-called "Mexican student conflict," (better called "student *rebellion*") which was published in the November 2, 1968 edition of *Excélsior*, affirmed that it is not the youth that is endangered by the changes taking place, but the "rigid and old-fashioned structures, based on the exploitation of man."

2. The "Oaxtepec Letter" was signed by Russians, Cubans, and Communist youths from Mexico and other countries after a meeting held at the Sport Center at the end of the 19th Olympic Games. Some of the views expressed in this letter are these:

> We, the youth, want to change society. We have been repressed, accused, forgotten ... [W]e are a dynamic force ..., [which] is why we accuse those who oppose our just wishes.... [W]e socialist youths of the U.S.S.R. support the Oaxtepec Youth Statement, and endorse all its social issues....

Thus does this letter continue to clamor for a change of structures.

3. According to statements published in the September 20, 1968, issue of *Excélsior*, the presidium of the Communist Party in Mexico was sealed with the motto, "Proletarians of All Countries, Unite!" The party backs the student movement, condemns arbitrary government, and defends the democratic rights of students and a "change of structures."

4. Journalist Bernhard Ponce, in an article published in the November 20, 1968 edition of *Excélsior* concerning the death of Vincent Lombardo Toledano, a luminary of world Communism, said:

> ... [A]long with other Marxists, he sought to impose *historic materialism* as the only official doctrine of Mexican universities and as a result, he had a heated discussion with his former master, Don Antonio Caso, who defended the freedom of the chair. Lombardo, the top leader of Communism in Latin America for many years, always demanded *change of the constitutional structures of Mexico.*

5. The September 24, 1968 edition of *Excélsior* contained an article about a manifesto issued by the New Fatherland political party ("Patria Nueva") and sponsored by its coordinator, Frank Joseph Paoli. Parts of it read as follows:

The Montinian Church

> Hail, Party of the Youth! ... People long for a deep transformation of the paralyzing system oppressing them. This party will accept any citizen, whatever his age, who is disposed to *transform our structures*, ... [to] proclaim his *fight against paternalism*, and [to] *support people's awareness*.

These words, coined by international clerical progressivism, expose the origin of the New Fatherland party.

6. An article in the November 22, 1968 edition of *Excélsior* was written by the Jesuit Henry Maza and bore the titles, "Sacerdotal Agitation" and "Before This Changing World." After a comment on the unfrocked priests who got married and those who refuse to obey the encyclical *Humanae Vitae*, the author said:

> Others look for a government job to earn a living. Others are becoming priest-workers. Others *fight wholeheartedly for social justice and assume the cause of the poor. Others join the student movement.* Others speak about dogmas in a way many find scandalous. Others perform strange Masses, and so on.

It is known publicly that many priests, mainly Jesuits as Maza confesses, took part in the student conflicts of 1968.

7. The progressivist Bishop of San Cristobal de las Casas, Chiapas, a member of the department for social action of LAMEC, delivered a statement to *Excélsior* on September 19, 1968. Part of what he says follows:

> *This continent is urgently in need of changes of structures* .... [T]he cause of student unrest in Mexico and other nations is that youth is a most important factor for development.... We face not only the *demand for quantitative changes, but for profound global structural changes ... What matters is not to preserve what exists, but to seek the forms of a new society.* In order that there be deep global changes, there must be a process of awareness by those who belong to the oligarchy.

As we can see, the progressivist Mexican clergy, following Rome's directions after Vatican II, have adopted a deeply revolutionary attitude. They demand the demise of present society and deep "changes of structures." My charges against LAMEC and the documents of Medellín, which to the progressivists are a new gospel, are therefore fully based on evidence.

Chapter XXXV

THE NEW THEOLOGY OF THE POST-CONCILIAR CHURCH

The Most Excellent and Reverend Don Joseph Melgoza Osorio is the new Bishop of Ciudad Vallés, San Luis Potosí, Mexico. He is also the president of the episcopal committee for promotion of the clergy and a renowned lecturer who has gone to several cities in the nation in order to fulfill his most high mission, namely, to infuse all the priests with the new mentality that will promote them to leading positions provided they docilely follow the new theology formulated by Vatican II and the two latest Pontiffs. He also published a paper on the occasion of the silver anniversary of the great Bishop of Veracruz, the Most Excellent Don Guadalupe Padilla Lozano, which is scheduled to be pompously celebrated on April 20, 1971. This paper by the Bishop of Ciudad Vallés is worth quoting, I feel, in order to compare it with a document by Don Manuel Talamás Camandari, Bishop of Juárez and delegate of the Mexican episcopal conference to the coming synod of bishops of the world Church to be celebrated in Rome next October. The synod's issues include these two vital points: (a) The role of the priest of tomorrow, and (b) the urgent problem of social justice.

Let us begin by quoting both documents faithfully:

I — CRISIS OF VALUES: AUTHORITY - OBEDIENCE

1. *Authority, its origin*

   a. The Father's love expressed itself in the fact that "He sent His only begotten Son into the world, that we might live through Him;" He sent Him "as Savior of the world." (I John 4:9, 14). In order that this salvific task might be accomplished, the Father awards the Son power over the whole human race (John 17:2) and introduces Him with the following words: "This is my beloved Son, in whom I am well pleased; hear ye Him." (Matt. 17:5).

Maybe His Excellency could have been more accurate, since his paper was addressed to priests who, having been formed in the old theology, still can cross the *t*'s and dot the *i*'s. By virtue of the hypostatic union, two natures can be distinguished in Christ, despite the unity of the divine Person. As far as He is

God, He is equal to the Father and has complete and absolute power over the world. As far as He is man, He is awarded every power in Heaven, earth, and Hell itself. In these times of confusion, it is worth remarking that Jesus Christ's divinity is not merely analogical, but real, actual, and identical to that of the Father.

    b. Christ appeals to the authority He received from the Father when He sent His apostles to announce and fulfill the task of Redemption. "Just as the Father sent me, I am sending you" (John 20:21). "All power is given unto me in heaven and in earth" (Matt. 28:18). "He that heareth you heareth me; and he that despiseth you despiseth me; and he that despiseth me despiseth Him that sent me" (Luke 10:16). "Verily I say unto you, Whatsoever ye shall bind on earth shall be bound in heaven: and whatsoever ye shall loose on earth shall be loosed in heaven." (Matt. 18:18).

None of the texts quoted by the Bishop of Vallés proves that Christ resorted to the authority He received from the Father when He sent His apostles. Christ has His authority because He is God; and His power because He is man, through the hypostatic union. Saint Hieronimus put it this way: *"Ex verbis inordinate prolatis incurritur haeresim"* ("inordinate words cause you to incur heresy"). In speaking about the relationship of the members of the Trinity and Christ's authority and power, Saint Thomas said this:

    In speaking about divine deeds we must avoid two opposite errors: that of Arius who affirmed that the Trinity of Persons presupposed a Trinity of substance, and that of Sabelius, who contended that the unity of the divine essence demanded the unity of the divine Person. Then, in speaking about divine things, we must avoid any diversity or difference that denies the unity of the divine essence. However, we may use different names to express the relative opposition. Hence, if in any part of holy Scripture we find texts indicating diversity or difference among the three divine Persons, we must see such diversity or difference as *distinction*. The Father is not the Son, nor is He the Holy Spirit; the Son is neither the Father nor the Holy Spirit; the Holy Spirit is neither the Father nor the Son. But this does not mean there can be any diversity or difference in the unity of the divine essence. Thus, when we speak about Christ, we must distinguish the twofold nature and the unity of His Person. Christ is God, because, although there are two natures in Him, it does not mean there be two Persons in Him. By "authority received from the Father" we mean Christ's human nature, Christ as a man. Otherwise we risk denying Christ's divinity.

Undoubtedly Christ gave the apostles and their legitimate successors a

The New Theology Continued

triple privilege: magisterium, jurisdiction, and priesthood. This privilege of jurisdiction is not, however, an absolute or independent one. It depends upon God's exclusive and absolute power, is backed by divine authority, and cannot surmount the limits God Himself has set. Above human authority is divine authority; above legal rules is the revealed truth; above human jurisdiction, whatever it may be, is God's law. These privileges Christ granted His apostles and their legitimate successors, not for their benefit, but *in aedificationem Corporis Christi* (for the building up of Christ's body). These ideas should be borne in mind and defined, since His Excellency, in advancing his views, seems to mean: "If you do not accept what I am going to say, you do not accept Christ's word." It all depends, Your Excellency, it all depends!

When the word of human authority, whatever this may be, clearly contradicts God's Word, we must not listen to human authority, thus following Christ's teaching and what Saint Paul of Tarsus teaches us: *Sed licet nos, aut angelus de caelo evangelizet vobis praeteruquam quod evangelizavimus vobis, anathema sit. Sicut praediximus et nunc iterum dico: Si quis vobis evangelizaverit praeter id quod accepistis, anathema sit. Modo enim hominibus suadeo, an Deo? Aut quarero hominubus placere? Si adhuc hominibus placerem, Christi servus non essem.* ("For, if we ourselves or a heavenly angel announced to you a gospel different from the one we have announced to you, let him be anathema. As said before, we repeat it now, if anyone announce to you a gospel other than the one you have received, let him be anathema. Am I, by chance, trying to persuade men, or God? Am I trying to please men? No doubt that if I were still trying to please men, I would not be a servant of Christ.") If we accept His Excellency's premise, we should have to conclude that we, as Catholics, are obliged to docilely accept what Cardinal Suenens, Cardinal Alfrink, and our Sergio VII have told us.

In returning to the Bishop of Vallés, we read his third point under *authority*:

> c. Among other Church ministries, there is that of authority. The bishops, "along with Peter's successor, Christ's Vicar and visible Head of the whole Church, rule the house of the living God." (*Lumen Gentium*, 18). "... [T]he bishops, along with the presbyters and deacons, receive the ministry from the community, in order that they may preside over the flock in the name of God." (*L.G.*, 20). "The bishops rule the various churches as vicars and legates of Christ." (*L.G.*, 27). The presbyters, "under the bishop's authority ... rule the portions of the Church entrusted to them." (*L.G.*, 28). No doubt in Christ's Church there is a legitimate authority that is essentially connected with the salvific mission entrusted to it.

To His Excellency and the progressivists, there is no source of doctrine

The Montinian Church

except the pastoral documents of Vatican II. Before Vatican II, we knew that Christ built His Church and gave Peter the power of jurisdiction independently, and the other apostles were dependent on Peter. Therefore, the Roman Pontiff's power is like that of Peter, while the power of the bishops as successors of the apostles, is like theirs. The hierarchic priests, but not all the faithful Christians, have their power dependent on both the bishops and the Roman Pontiff. Above the *jurisdictional* power is the *sacramental* power. Since jurisdictional power does not bestow an indelible nature, it can be removed, while the sacramental power, besides its being the base of jurisdictional power, cannot be removed by anyone, for it stamps on one an indelible character.

No doubt there exists in the Church founded by Christ an authority essentially connected with its salvific mission. On the other hand, there is also no doubt that the men who have received this power can abuse it and erode the Church's very salvific mission. The history of the Church has many examples of this. Then, Your Excellency, you must make many distinctions and subdistinctions in order that the premises of the frail reasoning contained in your pastoral directions to the clergy can produce clear results with no place for sophisms.

We now come back to the Bishop of Vallés for his discussion on *obedience*:

2. *Obedience.*

   a. The relationship between authority and obedience is so close that one cannot exist without the other. He who institutes authority institutes obedience.

   b. Christ stressed the importance of obedience to the Father: "Not every one that saith unto me, Lord, Lord, shall enter into the kingdom of heaven; but he that doeth the will of my Father which is in heaven." (Matt. 27:21).

   Redemption is intimately connected with obedience. Saint Paul encourages us to have the same feelings Jesus Christ had. For He "took the form of a servant, and was made in the likeness of men. And being found in fashion as a man, He humbled Himself, and became obedient unto death, even the death of the cross." (Phil. 2:5-8).

   c. Jesus is our model. In His words one finds a revelatory insistence of His pedagogy. He said to His disciples: "My food is to do the will of Him who sent me, and to accomplish His work." (John 4:34). "I seek not mine own will, but the will of the Father which hath sent me." (John 5:30). "Father, I have glorified thee on earth: I have finished the work which thou gavest me to do." (John 17:4).

   In the apostles' writings we find the relationship between obedience and redemption: "... by the obedience of one [Christ] shall many be made righteous" (Rom. 5:19); between preaching and obedience (Acts 4:19); between obedience and salvation: The Son became the author of eternal salvation unto all them that obey him " (Heb. 5:9). "Ye have purified your souls in obeying the truth" (I Pet. 1:22).

Before accepting the moral, not the mathematical, binomial relationship established by His Excellency between "authority" and "obedience," some other fundamental principles are worth bearing in mind. Perhaps the Bishop of Vallés omitted them for the sake of brevity, but I feel they are essential if we are to understand both the concepts between which we want to establish a basic relationship. We should remember what authority is, the various kinds of authorities, and the hierarchy existing among them, which causes all human authority to be ultimately dependent upon and subordinated to God and forbidden to go beyond the limits which God Himself has established.

Human authority is dependent upon, analogical to, and non-identical with divine authority. God, as Creator, Keeper and Supreme Being, has an absolute and unlimited dominion over man, His creature. Human authority, a reflection of and analogical participation in God's authority, is, so to speak, the instrument by which God leads the human will to the fulfillment of the divine will. Human authority is neither absolute nor unlimited, but conditioned and limited, because of God's inalienable rights and the inviolable rights which God has given to man.

Blind, mute, passive obedience, considered by some people as heroic and necessary, cannot be accepted in an absolute and unconditional way. Only moles move blindly. When God gave man intelligence, He obviously intended that he use it in everything, including obedience. Since God gave us law and doctrine, His purpose is that we adjust our behavior to it. When an order must not be complied with, human dignity, conscience, and faith itself advise and even impose the most grave duty of disobeying and fully accepting all the responsibility arising from this misnamed *disobedience.* Of course there are small spirits incapable of understanding what I have just written. Countless small people justify and conceal their infidelity to God with their ill-understood obedience to men, but every sincere man who verily seeks after God, must always act the way his intelligence, his conscience, and his faith point out to him, come what may. In such circumstances, disobedience to men is a sublime and heroic virtue, because it places obedience to God before obedience to men, reprisals from abusive power notwithstanding.

Obedience is practical acknowledgment of authority by virtue of our freedom or free will, because it seeks to do the Will of God. It is a moral, not a theological virtue; hence it is not the supreme virtue. When obedience reflects God's authority directly and immediately, then it is a religiously virtuous act; when it submits to the will of man, to human authority representing God and proceeding from God, it is a moral virtue. In either case, in order that obedience be a worthy and ennobling virtue, it must be based on faith and supported by faith. Submission to man, for any other reason, is unworthy and meaningless in the supernatural order. That is why Saint Gregory said: *"Obedientia, non servili metu, sed caritatis affectu servanda est; non timore poenae, sed amore iustitiae"* ("Obedience is not based on abject fear, but on the effect of charity, not for fear of punishment, but for love of justice").

"It can happen," says Saint Thomas, "that an inferior may not be obliged to obey his superior, whoever he may be, as in the following two cases: *When there is a rule issued by a superior authority* that forbids obedience, or *when the authority* commands what it has no jurisdiction to command." In the words of Christ, quoted by His Excellency from the Gospel according to Saint Matthew: *"Not every one that saith unto me, Lord, Lord, shall enter into the kingdom of heaven; but he that doeth the will of my Father which is in heaven."* The Savior did not mean obedience to men, but the obedience we owe God. Faith is not enough for us to save ourselves; good works are necessary, too. Redemption is connected to the obedience of Christ's most Holy Humanity to the command of His Father; and Christ's obedience must be an example for us to comply with God's Will and obey human authority, when this is not opposed to the divine will.

Your Excellency, great is the power, no doubt, which God has given you to bind or loose our consciences, but do not think that, because of this, you are somewhat like God, or that your authority permits you to impose on us anything contrary to our Faith and our submission to God's Will.

II—FURTHER CRITIQUE OF THE CRISIS OF VALUES

1. What *crisis* means.

This term can have two meanings, as a negative phenomenon or as an ordinary phenomenon.

a. As a negative phenomenon, crisis means deprivation or need.

b. As an ordinary phenomenon, it is a feature of dynamic realities which are subject to progress, evolution, and change.

2. Necessity of paying due attention to a crisis.

Any kind of crisis must be heeded, for it affects institutions and people. In any crisis situation a step can be taken toward the loss of a value, toward the gain of another value, or even toward a greater firmness or purification.

In neither case are repressive measures justified. Fidelity to Christ obliges one to save the values affected by crisis. Charity indicates the means of helping those who are in a crisis.

It is not easy to understand all this progressivist terminology. In this respect progressivists are just like Communists; they have words of their own whose meanings are always changing, some of the same words which we have always used, but with definite meanings. I must praise His Excellency for his beginning his reasoning with definitions of the ideas he was about to explain, even though they are vague definitions. He spoke about the "crisis" we are witnessing in the Church which the whole world is talking about, albeit in different ways. In traditional language, crisis means a considerable change, an apparent and symptomatic alteration. As examples, in an illness, business, or affairs of state, crises affect life, the success of the business, or the fate of a government. The present crisis that everyone sees in the Church today is, then, a symptomatic and most serious modification that has compromised and continues to compromise, *not the permanence and inerrancy of the Church,* for these are guaranteed by Christ's promises, but the *faith of countless souls and their eternal salvation.* The Church is a divine institution and, as such, is not subject to change affecting its dogmas and morality, and all that has been established by its living, authentic, and infallible Magisterium concerning liturgy and discipline. Mr. Bishop, this tremendous crisis of the Church has been caused by those who have dared to reform the Church radically, ignoring the doctrine and canons of Trent and Vatican I. These new reformers accept the presence, opinions, and activity of even those who do not belong to the Church but are its enemies, disregarding the definitive teaching of other Popes, and letting the "new wave" experts introduce and spread their monstrous errors. This crisis cannot be progress or natural evolution, but *"auto-demolition"* of the Church, just as Paul VI himself has acknowledged.

This crisis does not purport the loss of *one* value, but of *all* values, because once any dogma is denied or ignored, all of them may be denied or ignored. What progressivism contends and His Excellency cautiously hints, is that this crisis leads to more firmness and to a purification of the Church. This, however, is simply inadmissible, for the implication of this premise is that the Church has not been firm or pure for two thousand years; it is the present bishops who, with their modern ideology will amend Christ's work. So far as the crisis affects one person or all Catholics, guilt can be imputed principally upon those who were appointed by the Holy Ghost to rule God's Church.

3. *Crisis of authority*

"Fashionable deeds, trends, theories, and words contest not only this or that authority, but the very principle of authority itself. We all know that this wind contrary to authority, however sacred and legitimate it may be, has invaded, here and there, even the ecclesiastical environment." (Allocution of Paul VI to the Italian episcopate, Dec. 6, 1965).

These words by Pope Montini are ambiguous and imprecise, as they can have a given meaning or an opposite one. The Bishop of Vallés uses them to establish the fact of the crisis of authority. Though the crisis involves both members of a binomial, there is a crisis for those who hold the power and a resulting crisis for those who must obey. The words by Paul VI quoted, however, refer to those who contest the very principle of authority, that is, the jurisdiction which Christ gave to the shepherds of His Church. This principle has already been accepted and explained.

    a. In the negative sense, authority is in a crisis due to the evils of the past, which to a large extent, have deprived it [the Church] of its evangelical character. Every form of authoritarianism, privilege, mastery, domination, haughtiness, and princely attitudes or behavior, can imply a crisis of authority. We said *in the negative sense*, because this indicates deprivation, and reveals an authority that is not the one delegated by Christ and awarded to His Church.

    b. Crisis is an ordinary phenomenon. The Church is going through a period of growth and purification. It knows that "even today there is much distance between the message it announces and the human frailty of its messengers" and, therefore, wants to be aware of the deficiencies and "fight them with utmost energy, lest they impair the spreading of the Gospel.... Led by the Holy Spirit, ... [i]t never ceases to encourage its children to purify and renovate themselves, in order that Christ's signal may gleam more clearly on the Church's face." (*Gaudium et Spes,* 43).

    The review of the present condition is the point of departure for purification. This review puts authority into a state of crisis, revision and purification to attain a greater evangelical solidity as a response of fidelity.

Your Excellency, the Church is not going through any period of growth and purification. The Church has always been growing and developing, in accordance with the words of the divine Master: "The kingdom of Heaven is like a mustard seed." Growth does not mean a negation or break with the past, but, on the contrary, real growth is based upon the past and backed by it. Is that not so, Excellency? You are a bishop because you were a priest and before this, a Catholic. The impressive epithets progressivism uses to debase the authority of the past—*authoritarianism, mastery, haughtiness, paternalism,* etc.—were the decisive arguments used to destroy authority, under the pretext of purifying the Church and of making it more evangelically authentic. Besides, this criticism cannot be sincere, as the bishops who excel in their demand for evangelical purification through an ostentatious triumphalistic renunciation of their Christ-given legitimate rights, are those who most zealously enforce their commands with an abuse of authority. He who keeps the position God awarded to him and who does not renounce the external signs which authority has always had among men, is not acting with authoritarianism, mastery, or behaving in a haughty way.

    The progressivist review of the history and institutions of the Church and the powers of the Roman Pontiff and bishops of Vatican II, was not a good

The New Theology Continued

point of departure for a purification, but for a collapse of the Church. The history of the post-Conciliar age is one of the saddest pages in the Church's history.

4. *Crisis of obedience*

a. Unjustified revolt and negative nonconformity, of which there are so many examples nowadays, are manifestations of a crisis of obedience. We also see a negative crisis in the attitude of those who try to demonstrate the incompatibility of obedience with freedom and human dignity.

b. Not everything is negative insofar as the problem of authority and obedience is concerned. We see the wish for purification of obedience, a purification strongly related to the renewal of authority in its existential form. Salvific obedience is sought. This kind of obedience is consistent with conscience, freedom, dignity, and co-responsibility. At any rate, we are not discussing an easier, but a more responsible obedience.

The above was the synthetic enlightened analysis of His Excellency of the phenomenon of disobedience prevailing among God's people today. I think that this phenomenon is not so simple nor so easily solved. The widespread crisis of obedience presupposes a crisis of authority which His Excellency has not clearly defined. When authority begins by denying all the past, when it accepts, tolerates, and fosters a total reform that ignores what previous authorities had definitively affirmed, when it establishes principles that have already been refuted and condemned, when it dissimulates or tolerates evil and persecutes and attacks legitimate defense, then the authority that boasts of having descended from its throne to seek democratic approval by the majority, and accepts compromise and settlements, is lost. It no longer is legitimate, but unbearably abusive. Paternalism, authoritarianism, haughtiness, domination, and privilege, as His Excellency calls all this external appearance of the authority of the past, are a thousand times preferable to this new dissimulating comradeship, with which the *aggiornated* authorities zealously guard *their* privileges, while boasting of democratic equality. They tolerate their brethren's suppression of the titles befitting and owing their dignity, and they tolerate speaking familiarly, if the situation warrants it. They movingly shake hands with hippies and, if necessary, they glory in a classist, revolutionary, and seditious sort of Christianity. Why not?

The crisis of power is always sinister. Any authority that fails to respect itself or make itself respected, any authority that suppresses punishment for violators of the law, any authority that compromises with rebels, is an authority that betrays its duties and the most fundamental rights of the society over which it presides. Peace was made with subversion in order to suppress all nonconformity and "purify" the Church (as the Bishop of Vallés affirmed); the

The Montinian Church

result was disobedience, revolt, and practical disregard for authority. Authority was challenged because it stripped itself of its dignity. "In other times," said His Excellency, quoting the words of Paul VI, "people enjoyed admiring the bishops adorned with grandeur, power, pomp, and majesty. But it is not so today, nor can it be so. Far from giving admiration, people become astonished and scandalized if a bishop appears dressed with the superb anachronistic signs of his dignity, and appeals to the Gospel for support." (Allocution of Paul VI, to the Italian episcopate, Dec. 6, 1965). It was this very sophism that was used to suppress authority, so as to destroy the basic structure of Christ's Church!

Bishop Melagoza, who is in charge of the promotion of the clergy, makes every possible objection against Christian obedience derived from the Gospel. To him, any external sign of authority is improper, and all authority is temptation for power. Twisting of authority makes some people servile and other people rebellious. Obedience blindly confuses a monstrous anti-social conception for the responsibility that each Christian has within the Church. This innovative and revolutionary doctrine ultimately denies the evangelical doctrine, condemns the history of the Church, and pitilessly attacks Peter's primacy, which is the sole foundation of the Church and the bishops' jurisdiction. Real obedience, Christian obedience, is never servile, for, being based on faith, it is not subordinated to man as man, nor for fear of man's lawless abusive reprisals; on the contrary, if man's heart is inclined toward the Will of God, he obeys his superior, whoever he may be, because he sees him as a representative of God.

His Excellency is right in affirming that the crisis of authority and obedience, the binomial which the Bishop of Vallés' sharp insight discovered, is a crisis of faith, mind, and will. In rejecting God, man logically and unavoidably rejects all human authority, for this cannot be based on force, prejudice, or the goodwill of subjects, but on the very authority of God, from whom all human authority is derived. As I said before, progressivism wants to change our religion from *theocentric* to *anthropocentric*, inasmuch as this new integral humanism that bases every authority and law on "the dignity of man," essentially destroys the binomial of "authority and obedience."

I will not detain the reader any longer by analyzing the paper by the "Clergy Promoter." I do not wish to lengthen this book too much, and His Excellency's theses are ultimately those of charismatic and prophetic progressivism, which are well summarized in IDOC. It is distressing that the episcopal conference had not conscientiously studied this paper thoroughly before assuming the responsibility of supporting the ideology of Mr. Joseph Melgoza Osorio, the Most Excellent Bishop of Vallés, and chairman of the episcopal committee for the promotion of the clergy.

Chapter XXXVI

THE PRIESTHOOD, THE NEXT SYNOD, AND THE PREPARATORY INQUESTS

In a persevering and open way, the leaders of progressivism who are anxious to purify the Church, have been making frequent demands for change of the *hierarchical priesthood*, "the full-time workers," as Ivan Illich called them. This difficult subject is the primary one on the agenda of the coming Roman synod. The Vatican committee responsible for arranging this meeting, scheduled for September 30, 1971, has sent secret instructions to the episcopal conferences, in order that they may take surveys among the priests concerning the "problems of the clergy." I feel it is highly important to report on one of the surveys, which was undersigned by the Most Excellent Don Manuel Talamás Camandari, Bishop of Juárez, and delegate of the Mexican episcopal conference to the synod of bishops of the world Church. I have read the surveys of the episcopal conferences of Central America, Argentina, and Spain, but I believe this sample will suffice. Below is a survey made among Mexican priests, which was most certainly distributed only among progressivist, or at least, docile priests, in order to assure the "unanimous" response desired.

This survey ought to make all priests realize the true danger to our very priesthood, our vocation, and the basic ideals of our lives for which we have sacrificed everything.

The survey report of the Bishop of Juárez reads as follows:

Dear priest,

During these changing times, in which we are conscious of the common duty of *preserving the permanent values of the Catholic priesthood*, we also acknowledge the necessity of adequately responding to what is *reasonable* in the new attitudes and mentality of the world. The fulfillment of this wise purpose requires that we detect beforehand, among all the *changing* elements of yesterday's priest, those which in fact should be changed, and the new ones that will replace them, so as to mold the priest of the *immediate* future. This task is really difficult and concerns us all. That is why we need everybody's loyal, sincere, and dispassionate help. To this effect, pray answer the following questions in a clear, reasonable, and concise way:

1. In your mind:

The Montinian Church

　　a. Has anything that just a few years ago shaped the image of the *exemplary* priest ceased to be a feature of the *exemplary* priest of our age and the immediate future?

　　In case of an affirmative answer, show it clearly, and explain the reason.

　　b. Does anything belonging to the ministry of the *exemplary* priest some years ago no longer belong to the ministry of an *exemplary* priest today?

　　In case of an affirmative answer, give specific reasons.

　　c. Is there anything pertaining to the life habits of an *exemplary* priest some years ago no longer *exemplary* in a priest today?

　　In case of an affirmative answer, point it out and say why.

2. In your mind:

　　a. What are the *new* features that must shape the personality of the *exemplary* priest of the immediate future?

　　b. What are the *new* ministries the *exemplary* priest will have to perform in the immediate future?

　　c. What are the *new* life habits the *exemplary* priest will have to adopt in the immediate future?

The above was the document that *mutatis mutandis,* secretly circulated throughout the world as a preparation for the next synod of bishops of the world Church. *Change* is presumed as a fact. Even the text of the document insinuates the urgent need for changing the conception of our priesthood, so as to fully enter the Council's *aggiornamento.* The *exemplary* priest of yesteryear cannot be the *exemplary* priest of this epoch, just as the ministries, habits, or sacerdotal virtues of the past cannot be advisable or desirable for the modern, post-Conciliar priests. I am really pained and saddened to read this document, which was officially drawn up by a representative of the Mexican episcopate to the episcopal synod, a democratic appendix of Vatican II intended to keep the *sacred fire* of reformation and change burning in God's Church.

The survey's aim is clear: *secularization and de-sacralization.* The *exemplary* priests of the past, those who built the Lord's Church using their virtue, wisdom, and apostolic zeal, are already obsolete, just like the cars of the past. Now they are not only useless, but real obstacles to the *progress of the people.* The questions themselves show what the Most Excellent S. Talamás and the Pontifical preparatory committee expect from those priests who wish to be included on the "payroll" of the Montinian Church.

Our prelates addressed this survey to priests who do not always have the necessary wisdom to defend themselves, the necessary shrewdness to understand the twisted answers encompassed by the questions, or the necessary courage to confront their shepherds' concealed seductions. Here, then, Most Excellent Prelates, is this document which history will judge. It was drawn up by "new wave" theologians (?), undersigned by one of you, but sponsored by all of you with your acquiescence or tolerance. You invited, requested, ordered, or demanded your frightened and scandalized priests to meditate on it and give quick answers. Your priests will compromise with your post-Conciliar pastoralism and their status and privileges, once again, so as not to lose your confidence.

This survey is not about various *theological schools* in conflict, but about *different creeds,* namely, that of the survey and that of the twenty-centuries-old Church. Do you think, perhaps, Mr. Bishop, that the ideas of the survey are optional for the priests? In conscience, do you really believe that your priests must shape a new life and lay aside the asceticism, mysticism, and perennial sanctity of the Church?

You have had the time to study this Machiavellian survey before giving it to your clergy. If you did not find it acceptable, it is the bishop in each diocese who is responsible before God, not the episcopal conference or the synod committee. If a diocesan bishop failed to notice the poison contained in the survey, he must resign, for he is inept and ignorant; if he *did* notice it, he must resign, for he is a traitor. These are very serious and important matters! Do not tell me you don't impose upon your priests the obligation of following the ideological way that your document openly insinuates. How absurd! You convey the impression that this new way is not only optional, but the most suitable to the whole world's demands. "When the bishops do not say anything" is a phrase repeated by not a few confused priests. Do you think your silence and tolerance have caused only a little damage?

Just the simple fact of having seen this survey gives one the impression that the priesthood is merely human, flexible, changing. What in the past was "exemplary" is now unbearable. We used to seek the salvation of souls, and above all, our own salvation, but now we must seek social justice, the material and human welfare of the poor, and the "progress of the people." Previously the priest had to pray, watch his feelings, and avoid the occasion of sin. Now, on the contrary, he must adapt to the world through "normal" living and secularization. We have to say it clearly, that this survey, these showy changes, congresses, conferences, documents, etc., are disrespectful, in that we priests have been treated as guinea pigs in a progressivist laboratory that has abused our virtues of reverence, respect, and obedience to our bishops.

I will now quote another letter from a Spanish priest addressed to the bishops of Spain:

> Now young shepherds are beginning to cry out against the wolves and against the old, sleepy, fainthearted shepherds. The Spanish priests are regularly submissive to their hierarchy, but since they are crying now, they obviously have most grave reasons to do so. This is a clash between the Spanish clergy and a given ideology. This is a struggle, a painful, and soon angry, complaint against

the bishops who have paved the way for this ideology. Unless you stop this process in time, the wave will turn against you. You will be pressed in such a way, and with so many means (this is happening right now), that it will be difficult and almost impossible for you to keep the firm position faith demands from you.

THIRTY-NINE SPANISH BISHOPS DENY THEIR SUPPOSED UNANIMITY

Thank God, 39 Spanish bishops proved that they were not unanimous in desiring the changes in the Church pushed by their progressivist leaders when they addressed the 13th plenary assembly of the 1970 episcopal conference. We quote below parts of their address:

... [W]e are concerned that questions referring to secular subjects continue to occupy first place in our agenda and to absorb most of the energies and time of our meetings, while many ecclesiastical problems are not seriously and thoroughly studied. ...

... [E]ven more than the disproportionate time and exaggerated attention, we are concerned for the criteria used to handle such affairs. On the one hand, ecclesiastical pluralism is praised, and all sorts of dogmatic relativisms and indeterminism are tolerated in schools and publications. [Certainly, the episcopate could not be blamed for doctrinal integrity. Pray God it does not deserve to be blamed for not fulfilling its task of safeguarding the deposit of faith!] On the other hand, people dogmatize in fields where the indeterminate and the disputable prevail. There is much pressure to make us compromise in the socio-political area. It is painful to us that we may give the impression that, faced with great intra-ecclesiastical problems, we appear to be hesitant and incompetent, while at the same time, we present ourselves as being quite resolute before the problems that are outside our jurisdiction, as though we had magic formulas to solve them. Are we not on the verge of falling into a paradoxical socio-political integrality?

We agree with all our brothers that the Church must impregnate and perfect the whole secular order with the spirit of the Gospel, and this must be done through its own religious mission (which is not political, economic, or social), that is, as a sacrament of God's love for men (cf. *Gaudium et Spes*, 42, 45; *Apost. Actuositatem*, 5). The limitless requirements of charity must inspire all human life and social progress. Christians must strive for a society that will become an authentic community of brothers, in which goods are distributed fairly to all (*GS*, 23, 24, 64, 69). This demands a constant renewal of man's spiritual life, as well as social reforms (*GS*, 26, 63).

... [T]he planning and management of the social order belong to the citizens and civil authorities. The Church can enlighten and encourage, but this does not authorize it to dominate in areas that are not included in its jurisdiction. The Spanish episcopate has said on two occasions: "Though the hierarchy must enlighten the believers' consciences in the fulfillment of their civic-social duties, it must not invade the field of civil authority through attitudes or statements regarding the choice of contingent means in the secular realm, which belongs to political wisdom."

The orientation and stimulation of the ecclesiastical authorities must not degenerate into party politics. There is a real danger of this, for sometimes due to an ambiguous enunciation of certain principles, some citizens not only draw the conclusions they logically think to be correct, but also identify the principles with their own particular points of view. Other citizens make the same mistake due to a real intrusion into the field of controversial subjects, something which can easily happen when issuing moral opinions on civil accomplishments.

No doubt the episcopate can, and sometimes must, "pass judgment on the conformity of secular works and institutions with moral principles" (*AA,* 24). However, since excesses and the imposition of new bonds of conscience must be avoided where no problems exist, it must be done only "after mature consideration" and, as the Spanish episcopate explained, "only in the event that the fundamental rights of man and the family, or the salvation of souls apparently demand it because of their very nature or their general way of working...."

We are sad because some people believe that latent political reasons influence the bishops' pastoral decisions. Many people suspect a scheme is afoot about which the conference has no information, or that the hierarchy is looking for a new "secular arm," choosing a segment of the Catholic people to the exclusion of the rest. Numerous Spaniards devoted to cultural, social, and political activities (who are no less Catholic than those who claim to be) are beginning to feel hurt.

... [W]e are alarmed more and more each day by the growing tension that all this is producing within the conference to the detriment of its effective capability for ecclesiastical work and effective charity.

The frequent interventions into secular and controversial subjects erode the authority of the ecclesiastic Magisterium and exacerbate clerical and anticlerical attitudes.

Finally, we cannot omit a very important consideration. To effectively serve men, the Church needs healthy cooperation with the government (*GS,* 76). To this end, dialogue is essential, and in July, 1969, the plenary assembly acknowledged the need for discreet and cordial talks in many cases. On these talks depends the fate of decisive areas for the future of the Church, such as in education, whose status may be decided in the coming months. Along with several most grave problems of mixed jurisdictions, we must mention the possibility and need for finding a fair and efficacious solution to economic problems. For some time however, several obscure factors have merged to block the way of negotiations and understanding. Will the episcopate be called to account someday for wasting its historic possibilities?

To us who are not Spaniards, the above document signed by 39 Spanish bishops and addressed to the episcopal conference, is symptomatic and somewhat encouraging. Perhaps this is the only document the Spanish bishops have delivered as a reaction against the Modernist trend dominating almost all ecclesiastical areas in these times of post-Conciliar renewal. The signing prelates confess that human and secular subjects have been consuming the time and energies of the episcopal meeting, which disregards ecclesiastical problems even though these should officially be the principal preoccupation of the bishops. Is this the bishops' fault or that of Rome, whence pressure and directions are continually coming? The phenomenon is the same everywhere, hence the cause must also be the same. Neither the Spanish episcopate nor any other in the world can be accused of doctrinal integrality. Rather, one might well censor the ease of acceptance of today's pluralism, which impairs the unit of Catholicism and which is not only to be noticed in schools and publications, but also in fashionable heresies that are undermining people's faith. The fact that 39 bishops acknowledge this and decide to protest soothes us who still believe that Spain has the providential mission of saving the Church in our tragic times.

Chapter XXXVII

FATHER ARRUPE VISITS THE UNION OF SOVIET SOCIALIST REPUBLICS

The morning edition of the August 26, 1971 *Mexican Sun (El Sol de Mexico)*, gave a sensational piece of news regarding a proposed trip to the U.S.S.R. and the Far East by Fr. Peter Arrupe, Father General of the Jesuits, at the request of Pope Paul VI. The text of the article follows:

Vatican City, August 25, 1971 (FPA). At the end of the month, the Father General of the Jesuits will travel to the U.S.S.R. and the Far East for the first time as a messenger of Pope Paul VI. He "will carry a Christian greeting to our brethren in Christ."

The Reverend Fr. Peter Arrupe, Father General of the Jesuits, was received August 8 by Paul VI at Castelgandolfo. He mentioned the tasks of his militia, which has traditionally been at the service of the Pope. Among such tasks are those of helping the Pope in promoting contacts between Orthodox and Apostolic Roman Catholics, and to open Europe to the Third World.

After staying in Moscow and Leningrad, Fr. Arrupe will visit the institutions of the Society in Japan, Hong Kong, and Macao. It is not yet known if China is included in the schedule of the trip. Only 125 Chinese Jesuits survive; a dozen of them, among whom one is a bishop, are still in prison, and several of them live in forced residences.

It is worth mentioning that contacts between the Vatican and the U.S.S.R. have been intense lately. Jan Cardinal Willebrands, President of the Secretariat for Christian Unity, was the first member of the Sacred College to visit the U.S.S.R., to attend the burial of the Orthodox Patriarch, Alexis. He went back to the U.S.S.R. last June, when Alexis' successor was elected.

Some months before, Msgr. Serge Pignedoli, the Pope's Secretary for Foreign Affairs had stayed in Moscow from February 23 to March 1, conducting conversations with the Kremlin.

In turn, Andrei Gromyko, the Soviet Chancellor, was received by Paul VI for the third time last November 12, and President Nicolai Podgorny himself came to the Vatican on January 30, 1967.

According to experts, these interviews have led to the finding of a field of understanding for Soviet policies and Vatican diplomacy regarding certain subjects, especially in respect to peace, *but the basic situation has in no way been modified.*

Father Arrupe is a famous Orientalist and an enthusiastic traveler. He has written several books about the Far East. The Society of Jesus has historic links with Russia; when Clemens XIV dissolved the Society in 1773, its members found shelter in Russia until its reestablishment in 1814. After the 1917 Revolution, Pius XI entrusted them with the management of the Pontifical college *"Russicum"* designed to evangelize Russia when the time was right, but Stalin considered it to be a nest of spies. The policies and politics of appeasement of Pope John XXIII paved the way for Paul VI to diminish distrust. The way to Christian unity goes through the Soviet Union and the Far East.

As I mentioned before, this piece of news is certainly sensational and, above all, symptomatic. Father Arrupe is going to visit Russia, Japan, and maybe China "as a messenger of Pope Paul VI," carrying "a Christian greeting to our brethren in Christ." Amid sinister lightning that forecasts a coming storm, the Father General of the Jesuits will tighten diplomatic links with the hierarchs of international Communism, links that have already been cultivated by Cardinal Willebrands, Msgr. Pignedoli, Msgr. Casaroli, and even Paul VI, who granted three personal audiences to Chancellor Gromyko and one to President Podgorny. "According to experts, these interviews have led to the finding of a field of understanding for Soviet policies and Vatican diplomacy...." Do not forget that Paul VI, eager to alleviate the sad condition of the 60 million Catholics living in Communist dominated countries, has striven to restore the Vatican's relations with Communist governments right from the beginning of his Pontificate. To this end, he has not hesitated to make an ecumenical move and drop the inflexible standing of his predecessors.

What intrigues us is that a program of appeasement with the most violent and determined enemies the Church has ever had, could ever have been started. Even forgetting the clear and definitive old condemnations the Popes have launched against Communism, the monstrous crimes it has committed in all the countries it has dominated, and the impressive museum close to the Gregorian University of Rome showing the cruel and long-lasting martyrdom of the Church of Silence, I find it almost unbelievable that the Church, without betraying itself, and Communism, without changing its essentially anti-religious program, could have convened meetings, dialogue, and diplomatic activities that, according to the press dispatch, *in no way modified the basic situation.*

No doubt the Vatican and its messenger, Fr. Arrupe, try to conceal their aims behind the most ample veil of Conciliar ecumenism. The Father General told the Roman newsmen that the Society, his militia, "traditionally ... at the service of the Pope," had to help him promote contacts between Orthodox and Apostolic Roman Catholics. He was a messenger of Paul VI who "carried a

Christian greeting to our brethren in Christ." But the world press put it a different way. The news agencies told us this trip of the Father General of the Jesuits was the outcome of a long-lasting process of comings and goings of various top emissaries of Russia and the Church. The experts also affirm that "a field of understanding for Soviet policies and Vatican diplomacy" has been found. The agreement is so complete that this time the Pope will be represented by the "Black Pope." Perhaps this was a preparation for the Pontiff's spectacular trip to Communist countries.

Who has expedited this rapprochement, while the Communist plan of spreading slavery has not been abandoned, but on the contrary, has been intensified? Unless we are blind, we must see the action of mighty "hidden hands" which are patiently and skillfully moving the most important pawns in this devilish game. The immediate future of the Church and the world are at stake.

The following day the press announced Fr. Arrupe's arrival in Moscow. On arriving at his hotel, the Father General said his trip *was not political at all,* that he had been "invited by Nikodin" to visit Russia, but that he had no "official status or official mission to fulfill." Father General, it is not easy to change one's statements overnight and convince people the press has given wrong information to them. Nowadays this trick is well known, especially to us who really know the militia you lead. You use flexible moral probabilism in order to soothe the conscience of those who could react against the gelatinous casuistry of the "new wave" Jesuits.

The June 3, 1971 issue of *L'Osservatore Romano* can perhaps shed new light on our understanding of Pope Montini's complicated policies. On the feast of Pentecost, Paul VI refused to receive seven thousand Catholic pilgrims who came to Rome from all over the world to *beg the Pope to restore the Eucharistic Sacrifice* that Bugnini's liturgy had suppressed, but two days later, the "ecumenical Pope" welcomed a leading group of the Anti-Defamation League of the B'nai B'rith Jewish group. Below I reproduce the speech he addressed to them:

Dear friends,

It is our pleasure to welcome this distinguished group of the Anti-Defamation League of the B'nai B'rith.

On this occasion, we are pleased to repeat that it is the will of Vatican Council II "to foster and encourage mutual understanding and respect, which, above all, are the outcome of biblical and theological studies and fraternal dialogue" (*Nostrae Aetate,* 4).

As far as our own ministry of reconciliation and peace is concerned, we are particularly sensitive to every kind of discrimination that prevents fraternal charity among men, offends human dignity and God Himself. Recently we have spoken against all discrimination based on race, origin, color, culture, sex, or religion (Cf. Apostolic Letter, May 14, 1971).

We beg God, the Father of all, to bless your efforts to create a climate of love between Christians and Jews, for the well-being of all mankind.

Here we have the story of a drama of worldwide scope, in which the principal actors of yesterday and today, be it in Rome, Latin America, Australia, the Philippines, Russia, the Far East, or the United Nations, are Pope Montini, Fr. Arrupe, and the leaders of the Communist Party, the Anti-Defamation League, and international Jewry. The goal Paul VI revealed a few days after his election was "to soften Vatican relations with the Communist countries," a process that has been effected continuously, in spite of the difficulties Communist violence has posed in several parts of the world. The struggle has never ceased, just like the smiles, the diplomatic talks, the Pope's goodwill, and fretting flirtations with the enemies of Christ and His Church. Even the ceremony of the coronation of Paul VI was attended by an official delegation from Yugoslavia representing the Communist world.

John Baptist Montini has been subject to powerful and controlling influences which have shaped his thought, his attitudes, and his election to Peter's See. I am referring to the various compromising and indissoluble ties he has cultivated with the leading forces of Catholicism in the United States and the successive White House governments at the time of Pius XII, when Montini was the Under Secretary of State. Pope Montini's work is not new, but actually began to develop at the time of Pope Pacelli, and was based on the innovative doctrines of the Jewish convert, Jacques Maritain. Paul VI is a hundred percent Maritainian Pope. This explains why his position as Under Secretary of State, as Archbishop of Milan, as sovereign Pontiff, as Moderator of Vatican II, and world appeaser, has been so unstable, so tortuous and winding, because he moves on the unsteady soil of ecumenical pluralism.

At first his diplomatic activity as Under Secretary of State, Archbishop of Milan, and Pope seemed basically dedicated to cultivating relations with the United States. It appeared as though, in his mind, the military might, diplomacy, and baffling policies of Roosevelt, Truman, Eisenhower, Kennedy, and Johnson were the only forces capable of leading the world and saving the Church in these times of change, unsafety, and menacing dangers.

The vast wealth and unlimited generosity of the American Church, which entertains fraternal relations with the Jewish agencies and is practically pledged to the banks controlled by those agencies, unquestionably helped to soften resistance, and overcome obstacles, thus permitting the Church hierarchy and leaders of the United States to manipulate the management of the Church. Do not become frightened; in past times, emperors and kings with their armies used to press the Pope to render decisions not too consistent with his criteria and conscience. Now it is the dollars, the polite visits, and the personal representative of officially atheistic and anti-Catholic governments who work the miracle of invisibly controlling the mentality and policies of the Vatican.

To the experts in Vatican affairs, things have changed. Now the influence of the White House is not so obvious, and the leaders of Communism, Masonry, and international Judaism help shape Vatican policy. Without reservation or pretense, either these leaders openly go to the Vatican, and are cordially and officially received by Paul VI, or Vatican emissaries make spectacular trips and hold dialogue not only with the Orthodox Patriarchs, but with those who manage the Kremlin and promote world subversion. Who has performed this miracle? What hidden power is paving the way for the "fraternal dialogue" and "fraternal charity" mentioned by Paul VI in his speech to his personal friends and distinguished leaders of the Anti-Defamation League?

On August 29, 1971, FPA of Moscow gave us another important piece of news:

> *Podgorny Will Travel to Hanoi before China and the United States Make Up*—The President of the U.S.S.R., Nikolai Podgorny, will visit North Vietnam before President Nixon goes to Peking, according to well-informed diplomatic circles in Moscow.... This move of the Kremlin is aimed at preserving its positions in Indochina and Southeast Asia, before the prospect of a share of influence between the People's Republic of China and the United States, according to these circles.... Such being the main aim of President Podgorny, his trip to Hanoi will surely take place in September.... The Soviet Union wants to overcome a probable Chinese-American Yalta, and is determined to remain in an area where in many respects it can still play an important role. Seemingly its main card will consist of offering a third pole to those countries that wish to balance an alliance or fill the void of their neutrality.... In Hanoi itself, the Soviet head of state will rely on two other cards, namely, the amount of postwar economic aid the U.S.S.R. will be able to provide North Vietnam, and the pro-Sovietism of a segment of the North Vietnamese leaders .... However, it is doubtful whether the U.S.S.R. really wants to play the card of Hanoi's possible discontent before the prospect of Chinese-American understanding. The observers affirm that the North Vietnamese leaders are well-informed and sufficiently prudent not to let themselves be dragged along that field. Besides, the only ground for their eventual complaint against an agreement or improvement of relations between Washington and Peking would be that it would deprive them of their victory, even though it be acknowledged.... In that context, one of the missions of President Podgorny would consist of assuring the success of Soviet tactics, such as the transition from the sterile negotiations of Paris to Nixon's bargaining at Peking, where the Soviet Union will shine by its absence.... In order to achieve such a goal, the Kremlin will have to take into account the secret

preparatory conversations between representatives of China and the United States, that, according to well-informed sources, are currently being continued with the objective of preparing a specific format for President Nixon's visit. . . . These same sources had concluded that, after the Chinese-Soviet Friendship Treaty had been signed, Moscow's diplomacy for Southeastern Asia was reorganized on the basis of the visit of the head of the White House to the Chinese capital.

It appeared strange that, two days after Fr. Arrupe's arrival in Moscow on his trip of simple friendship and ecumenical rapprochement, the Kremlin lets the world know that its President Podgorny was about to travel to Indochina, the Gordian knot in the present policies of the great powers. Am I rash in questioning whether the White House, through its secret links with the Vatican, succeeded in having the Pope send Fr. Peter Arrupe, the Provost General of the Society of Jesus, as a confidential, efficient, and discreet emissary to Moscow to negotiate future steps to be made? Arrupe and his choice militia have already rendered very valuable services, in following papal directions for the realization of some world schemes. Is it perhaps the powerful Jewish agencies, mainly coordinated by the B'nai B'rith, that have been manipulating world politics through economic pressure, international Communism, international Masonry, and the invisible international political power of the United Nations?

I find certain parallel and similar connections between the visit of the Father General of the Jesuits to the Kremlin and the most famous visit of Pope Montini himself to the United Nations headquarters in New York. Why did Paul VI go to the U.N.? Apparently the masses got a simple and convincing answer: he was invited by the Secretary General of the U.N., the dynamic and faithful Mr. U Thant, to attend the celebration of the 20th birthday of that international institution. This was what Paul VI himself said, in opening his speech before that heterogeneous assembly:

> First, we want to express our deep gratitude to U Thant, your Secretary General. . . . *We introduce ourselves as friends.*

I believe that the Pope needed a certain degree of flexibility and adaptation to international forces to be acceptable to that world meeting and be invited to speak to them. Since the principles of the U.N. in its heterogeneity are so contrary to Catholic truth, were they perhaps going to observe him with curiosity and listen to him with implacable and dangerous criticism?

As far as compromise is concerned, the slope is always very steep. On any inclined plane, the first step may make one slip into unsuspected abysses. The rumor circulates, seemingly with good cause, that some most important concessions were demanded from the Pope as a condition for his being invited to the U.N., among which were the two famous statements of Vatican II on religious freedom and complete acquittal of the Jews from any liability for the Lord's Passion and death, as well as full Conciliar protection for these age-old enemies of the Church of Christ. Could Paul VI have appeared before the U.N. without being sure that these statements (which, at that time, were still being discussed in Vatican II) were going to be ultimately passed?

When they were approved, applause was heard in the Conciliar hall. Progressivists embraced each other, and the entire world press, controlled by the enemy, jubilantly published its victory over the Church's infallibility.

I still have another important point to mention to explain the success of the Vatican policies. Pope Montini's visit and speech at the U.N. were a kind of ratification of the *Pacem in Terris* of John XXIII, and a solemn proclamation of a doctrine completely alien to the Gospel, addressed to "all men of goodwill" by the Pontiff of Tolerance. Only within this context of laicism and surrendering ecumenism can Paul VI's visit and political speech at the U.N. be understood. Only within this same context can we understand the visit of the Father General of the Society of Jesus to Soviet Russia amid the current crisis. The official introduction of Fr. Arrupe to Moscow's official circles (let us remember that Russia's Orthodox Church is subject to the Kremlin's directions and mighty will) is already proof that the dialogue Vatican and Russian officers have been carrying up to now, has culminated in ecumenical concessions which only future history will one day reveal.

Chapter XXXVIII

THE TRAGEDY OF CHILE, TREASON WITHIN THE CHURCH, AND EXAMPLES TO BE IMITATED

The Republic of Chile was the second Latin American nation to fall under the yoke of international Communism. The Christian Democratic Party, *which has a Christian facade but is Communistic at heart,* acted as a bridge and opened the gates of power to the Marxists in our sister republic. To a larger extent, Salvador Allende owed his victory to a group of ecclesiastic radicals who drew their inspiration from the documents of Medellín, produced during the second general meeting of LAMEC, which was opened, blessed, and inspired by Paul VI, the solicitous Pontiff of *Populorum Progressio.* The 1968 Medellín document, whose chapters on social justice were drawn up by Fr. Roger Veckemans, S.J., is an almost complete victory of progressivists over conservatives. That was the victory of Pope Montini, his dialectics, and his compromise with the international agencies of the Jewish mafia.

The Latin American episcopate suddenly turned from its distinctive conservative and orthodox approach to a wild progressivism. They humbly accepted the classification of Pope Montini and Vatican II, according to which we are the Third World, the world of the *underdeveloped people,* where a determined, rapid, and audacious transformation of the old structures must be carried out. Without the cooperation of the clergy, the victories of neither Fidel Castro nor of Salvador Allende could have been possible.

In September of 1970, the Chilean episcopal conference released a communique at Punta de Tralca. They asked the priests "not to yield to the temptation of secularism," not to take part in party struggles, issue opinions on subjects they do not know well, or advance solutions to secular problems. The document said, "It is worth reflecting on the danger of neo-clericalism and ill-understood politics." The bishops insisted on intensifying the life of prayer and working for the unity of the Church. This communique carried no warning against Communism, but mentioned the political parties in general, and seemed to be aimed at smashing the defense of healthy and conscientious Catholic priests and believers against the irrepressible advance of Marxism.

In a collective pastoral letter, the episcopate gave the Church's full support to "agrarian reform," and condemned the ownership of land as "a capitalistic structure that impairs the dignity of man." In a letter of May 7, 1970, addressed to Msgr. José Manuel Santos, Bishop of Valparaíso and chairman of the episcopal conference, Sergio Onofre Jarpia, chairman of the National Party, energetically protested against the episcopate's opinion "on the capitalistic structure and the violence of the establishment. It is absolutely false," he wrote, "to maintain that Chile lives under a regime based on exploitation and injustice. If there be injustice, in no way does it constitute an institution."

Since the episcopal conference, motivated by charity or the directives of Rome and Medellín, paves the way for Marxism, one understands why the progressivist clergy boldly endorsed the most advanced radicals and revolutionaries. The leading agent of progressivist infiltration in Chile, under the guise of aid for development and social progress, was Fr. Roger Veckemans, S.J., of Flemish origin, a friend and political agent of President John F. Kennedy. He has been in Chile for almost 30 years, and is credited with being Edward Frei's[22] most outstanding aide. Veckemans founded DESAL, the Center for Latin American Social Development, actually a university of sociology with numerous branches in this continent. One of these branches is CIDOC of Cuernavaca, headed by the Jew Ivan Illich, whose portrait merited a place in the Museum of Militant Atheism in Moscow. Father Veckemans' influence on the Chilean episcopate has been enormous and nefarious.

On December 5, 1970, *Latest News (Ultimas Noticias)* of Santiago, affirmed that Fr. Veckemans and his Center were seriously threatened by Allende's regime, whose success they firmly backed and promoted, and that for reasons of security the Jesuit Father had to emigrate from Chile to Colombia. In fact, the motive for this restless Jesuit's movement was to transfer his subversion to another field of action. There is no ground to affirm that Fr. Veckemans' departure was due to the success of Marxism. On December 9, 1970, the *Journal of the Americas (Diario de las Americas)* tells us that Fr. Veckemans had spent millions of dollars on his Center for Development with the aid of the German group "Misereor" and the generous support of Washington.

In 1950 Fr. Veckemans had founded the Belarmine Center at Santiago, as well as *Message* magazine, edited by the economist of the Center, the Chilean Jesuit, Fr. Hernán Larrain Acuña. The Center was supposed to be "a place for a communal and solitary life" but in fact is a nest for subversive Jesuits. The January-February, 1950, release of *Message* carried the following statement:

> The hierarchy must respect and encourage the various political options that call for the general welfare and respect of man, but neither its words nor its silence may endorse a particular political tendency, to the exclusion of others that profess the liberation and dignity of man.

Chile, Treason in the Church, Examples to Imitate

On arriving in Colombia, Fr. Veckemans declared: "I am just a theologian and a sociologist [the way Fr. Pardinas was a humble anthropologist], and never have I paid any attention to economic problems." A surprising statement on the part of a Jesuit who spends millions of dollars and knows the influence exerted by the Belarmine Center upon the Christian Democracy-sponsored "revolution in liberty," including agrarian reform, "Chileanization" of copper and the growing intervention of the government in economic life, etc. "The policies, methods and practical moves of Christian Democracy," said the *Diario de las Americas,* "have handed Chile over to Marxism. One cannot understand how Fr. Veckemans, the spiritual father and fervent sponsor of such policies, can possibly deny the error of his ways."

Others, such as Fr. Arturo Gaeta, S.J., now come to make waves. Father Gaeta is ex-professor of philosophy at the Catholic University of Santiago, former vice-dean of the Catholic University of Valparaíso and a vice-editor of *Message* magazine. During a round-table discussion on "the evolution of moral codes in the Western World," Fr. Gaeta read some biblical texts along with quotations from Hegel, Marx, and Freud, "three of the four or five great men who have shaped modern mentality." To him, there is a principle of self-destruction and death in man, which Freud calls "Thanatos" and Saint Paul calls "sin." The task of creating a new man is not personal. "The reconciliation of man is realized first through the death of Christ and, as far as the rest of mankind is concerned, through love and struggle. Christians used to lay aside class struggle *a priori.* Understanding, however, is a result of struggle and conflict." *(Mercury [El Mercurio],* Jan. 25, 1971).

A group of *left-wing Christians* composed of religious, priests, and laity, founded the Medellín Centre at Santiago, with the aim of supporting and issuing directives for those Christians "who have opted for the revolutionary way." This initiative was approved by Msgr. Charles González and Bernardo Pinera of the diocese of Talca. Father Pablo Fontane, one of the members of the Medellíin Center at Santiago, declared that:

> ...[L]eft-wing Christianity, the one that really commits itself to revolutionary action, is undergoing an actual crisis of faith. This crisis presents itself as a struggle, from which purification or disappearance of the Faith can result.

Father Manuel Ossa, S.J., also a vice-editor of *Message* magazine, contended that "Christians have to understand their revolutionary role and work for it as Christians. Such is the goal of the Medellín Centre." In an article entitled, "Heavens Begin Down Here," Fr. Hernán Larrain, S.J., wrote on July 3, 1970: "I see no difficulty in working with Marxists. In fact, I insist that Marxists and Christians must join their forces to promote better justice and

The Montinian Church

equality."

Previously, Pope John XXIII had said:

> This is no ordinary dialogue, but a dialogue between men of goodwill. I believe that, in the current circumstances . . . if a concrete platform of struggle is established, from which a real effort is made to recover the land for man, form a greater fraternal relationship between men, and help people to attain equal possibilities and full realization, I see no reason why a Christian could not vote for a Marxist if he finds the latter to be more fit to follow such a political line and historical destiny.

On August 30, 1970, in *The Century (El Siglo)*, Fr. Darío Marcotti, from Valparaiso, wrote:

> The only way to be a Christian is to be one of the people, a worker who identifies with them. The only way of being faithful to the gospel of liberation and justice consists of turning it into action within the worker movement. Christ was always among His people and unmasked the oppressors.

Let it also be said that "comrade-priest Marcotti," as Allende called him on TV, was the founder of the "Church of the people."

On September 18, 1970, *The Century* published a document released by the Catholic University of Chile and signed by its dean. We quote a small part of it here:

> Faith in God, understood and lived in depth, is an impulse to liberate man and create a more just and fraternal society. Christian hope provides new grounds and fresh forces to break the economic, social, and cultural alienations, thus creating a society based on open relationships of truth, love, and justice.

Eroded by progressivism, the Catholic University is a focus of agitation. As a result of bloody clashes between police and students, Raúl Cardinal Silva Henríquez made an appeal on TV on July 1, 1970, to calm and convey a warning to his listeners:

> [We have] minority groups who are still fighting Communism, and who are trying to impose an environment of hostility, revolt, lack of confidence, and at times, terror upon the overwhelming majority of the Chilean people. Accepting [these revolts of minority groups] means destroying the basis of our civic consciousness.

On April 18, 1970, the centenary of Lenin's birth, a birthday celebration was held at Saint Catherine's Church in Salvador Cruz Gana (Muñoa). Fr. Hernán Larrain Acuña, S.J., had depicted Lenin in *Message* as "a real Communist, with ideas that fitted mankind." In *New Force* magazine in Madrid, Maximo Pacheco wrote: "I feel that Lenin is the most outstanding politician of our age who not only belongs to the Soviet Union, but to the whole world."

This Christian Democratic minister went on to say:

> I have set up a committee apart from the Chilean Ministry of Education, which will draw up a program of celebrations for this event. I am convinced it is the duty of the Chilean intellectuals to take part in the celebration of Lenin's hundredth birthday.

MY COMMENTS ON THE ALARMING TREASON AGAINST OUR CATHOLIC FAITH

Undoubtedly we are now in the middle of the darkest storm that we have ever seen on the Latin American continent. Ecclesiastics, Jesuits, monsignors, bishops, and cardinals are conducting a most treacherous treason against the Catholic Church. Not only have they made peace with the most satanic enemies that Christ's Church has ever had, but they have also deceitfully compromised the freedom and welfare of the Latin American people. Once again I denounce LAMEC and its Machiavellian documents from Medellín. I launch the anathema of the Church against those apostates, compromisers, and hirelings of the mafia.

Once again, I point to all those progressivist priests and religious as the real culprits of subversion, for they represent *"Chaos in the Church and treason to the government." Our Faith, our freedom and our national independence are at stake!* It is a lie that there is a different, more human and flexible sort of Communism. It is a devilish blasphemy that "Heavens begin down here" and that in the current circumstances "Marxists and Christians must join their forces to promote better justice and equality," because between Catholic truth, revealed truth and dialectic materialism there can be no compromise.

The Mexican Sun (Del Sol de Mexico) carried another bit of news:

> La Paz, Bolivia, August 31, 1971 (A.P.)—Three Jesuit priests abandoned this country after having been virtually expelled by the government: Pedro Negre, Federico Aguilo, and José Prats. All three priests had assumed a "progressivist" line. They belong to a Christian organization of laity and religious known as "Church and Society in Latin America."

I end this book invoking *the most Holy Virgin,* our Blessed Mother of *Tepeyac,* through whose ministry we receive the blessed gift of our Catholic

Faith. I beg her to protect this very Faith in our souls against the satanic dangers of religious progressivism, which as in Chile and Cuba, is trying to establish Communism among us, to prepare for the *world government of the mafia*. Let us open our eyes and wake up to reality. Let us not permit demagoguery to continue to conceal the sinister aims of our enemies.

AN EXAMPLE TO BE IMITATED, AND INTERCESSORS WHO WILL HELP US FROM HEAVEN

On October 25, 1970, forty martyrs from England and Wales were raised to the altar for having endured dreadful torments and having given up their lives amid unbelievable sufferings to uphold the orthodoxy of the Roman Catholic Church, to safeguard its supremacy, and to maintain the doctrine of the undefiled Virginity of most Holy Mary, Mother of God. They were determined not to pollute the crystalline purity of the Tridentine Mass of Saint Pius VI with the reformed rites of the Protestants.

Today the very Catholic, Apostolic, and Roman Faith is being threatened by destructive and subversive ideologies that are being spread with impunity in the very heart of the Church by those who should be keeping the deposit of the divine revelation intact. Unworthy ecclesiastics attack the devotion of the faithful to the most Holy Virgin with bold offenses, and the Virginity of our heavenly Mother is questioned. The supremacy of *Peter*, the rock on which Christ built His Church, is being questioned and doubted in a most vile and indecorous way by many apostates who remain in the Church, among whom are bishops and cardinals whose names are known to God's people. These enemies have also attacked the holy Sacrifice of the Mass according to the dogmatic doctrine of Trent, which was written in perpetuity by Saint Pius V. This Holy Mass which the reformist movement so seriously endangers, was the honor and glory of all Christianity, the spiritual source of its most heroic virtues. To defend it, forty saintly martyrs have been canonized in our days, after having unselfishly shed their blood for Christ. Let us remember what the great convert, Monsignor Ronald Knox, wrote about the persecution of Catholics begun by Henry VIII: *"They died to prevent the Mass from being adulterated."*

The crucial issue in the struggle between Catholic Tradition and the progressivist reformation is the Mass, which is also the *real defense* of Peter's Primacy, now being compromised by dialogue, *aggiornamento,* and ecumenism.

From the human aspect, it is necessary to warn all of Latin America of the danger threatening them. The directive has been given: It is necessary to *socialize*, that is to say, *Communize Latin America.* Several means can be used, such as guerilla warfare, constitutional or legal amendments, etc. The ultimate goal, however, is the same. Under the guise of social justice and a more equitable distribution of riches, attempts are being made to largely destroy *private property* and *"distinguishing property"* so as to establish the slavery of forced labor for everyone under the iron yoke of the Communist regime.

Chapter XXXIX

THE GREAT TREASON

The Gospel, Jesus Christ's "Good News" is, above all, the historic record of His Resurrection. On rising from the dead, the Incarnate God interrupted the natural process and gave human existence a new dimension. Instead of the death and decay that seemed to be the unavoidable end of all things, we now have everlasting life in front of us.

The apostles were the eyewitnesses of this unique phenomenon. They could say: "I saw Him; I spoke with Him; I learned from Him; I touched Him; I ate with Him after His resurrection from the dead." That was why those men were not afraid of death at the hands of the unbelievers, "in the certain hope of their own resurrection."

Today when the *Gospel* to most men is but a narrative, a legend about certain episodes in the life of Christ, and when an apostle is but a white-bearded itinerant master of the first century of the Church, it is almost impossible to imagine the impact of this "Good News," the abolition of death, that was "scandal to the Jews and foolishness to the Greeks." Although Christ's resurrection is the basis of our Catholic Faith, a large number of would-be Christians have replaced hope in their own resurrection for an insatiable interest in social progress, a preoccupation for the things of this world, which indicates they are convinced that "death is the end of everything," although they continue to say that they believe in the resurrection and eternal life.

Before His death and resurrection, Christ told His disciples the conditions necessary to attain everlasting life. At Capernaum's synagogue, a day after He announced and prefigured the Eucharist by feeding a crowd of more than five thousand souls with a few pieces of bread and a few fishes He had blessed, He said: "Unless you eat my flesh and drink my blood, you will have no life within you. He who eats my body and drinks my blood has eternal life and I will raise him up on the last day."

Since that time, many of His disciples have abandoned Him, saying: "How can this Man feed us with His body and give us His blood to drink?" This teaching, this truth, is too preposterous for human intelligence. Those who objected before the Lord's Passion and death, had the excuse that Jesus had not explained to them the supernatural fact of Transubstantiation, thanks to which we can really eat the body and drink the blood of God's Son. This explanation was kept for the twelve apostles, who, at Jerusalem, were with Him at the cenacle the night before He was executed as a criminal. When He, taking the bread, said *"This Is My Body,"* and taking a cup of wine, said: *"This Is My Blood,"* the apostles, among other ineffable emotions, were perhaps relieved, for the Master had finally fulfilled and explained the mysterious words He had uttered at Capernaum.

From this point of view, the Church is an organization set up to keep the truth that the Mass is the passport to eternal life. In a way, the other sacraments have been set up to protect it, as it is a kind of center of our whole religion. Through Baptism we symbolically and sacramentally participate in Christ's death and become eligible for the glorious resurrection. Once original sin is eliminated, we reach the state of grace we need to avoid "eating or drinking Christ's body and blood for our own condemnation." Through absolution, the Sacrament of Confession permits us to recover the state of grace that perhaps we had lost through grave personal sin. The Sacrament of Holy Orders is the guarantee that the miracle of Transubstantiation will be continually repeated by priests chosen for this office as successors to the apostles, and whose ministry therefore is valid.

Along with their perennial attacks against the Church, the forces of evil have always challenged the Mass in one way or another. Sometimes they have attacked the externals of the Eucharistic Sacrifice, such as the apostolic succession or the auricular confession, and at other times, the very Mass itself.

In the first centuries the heretics emphasized the denial of the Incarnation. The question of whether bread and wine had actually been changed into Christ's body and blood was a secondary one in respect to the fundamental question of whether God has or could have assumed a human body or, better yet, become a man without ceasing to be God. This is what we might call *the heresy* for, from the first century until our times, this has been the root of all heresies: the denial of the Incarnation because matter is always evil. The spirit, which is good, cannot dwell in the flesh, which is evil. *Gnosticism*, a philosophical and religious doctrine, a mixture of Christian doctrine with Jewish and Oriental beliefs, has taken various names and challenged the Church from the first years of its existence. During those first years, Saint Justin Martyr used the *resurrection of the flesh* as a cry to fight gnosticism which proclaimed only "the immortality of the soul," and to warn the believers that, "If you believe only in the immortality of the soul and fail to accept the resurrection of the body, you are not Christians."

The most dangerous and widespread recrudescence of gnosticism was that of the Cathars, in 13th century Europe. This was the religion of the "pure people," and Saint Dominic fought them with his Order of Preachers, while Simon of Montfort set up a crusade against them. Though the movement was smashed, it could not be completely destroyed. *Afterwards, it reappeared in*

The Great Treason

Puritanism, which insisted in affirming that "matter" was evil, and consequently, Transubstantiation could not be admitted or taught. They isolated some words taken from the New Testament: "God is a spirit, and those who worship Him must do so in spirit and truth." Puritans, then just as today, implicitly deny the essential doctrine of Christianity—the Incarnation of the Word, the Redemption on the Cross, and the Resurrection of Christ.

Neither they nor their successor Reformers could easily suppress the liturgical service of Communion, for this is clearly taught by Holy Scripture, so they and their successor heretics took away the orthodox meaning of the Sacrifice. The Cathars used the following *consecrating prayer* at the Last Supper: "O Lord, Jesus Christ, who blessed the five pieces of bread and the two fishes in the desert, and blessed the water that became wine: Bless, in the name of the Father, the Son, and the Holy Spirit this bread, fish, and wine, not as a sacrificial offering, but as a simple commemoration of the most Holy Supper of Jesus Christ and His apostles." This is the basis of the subsequent appearances of heretical doctrines regarding the Eucharist that reject the Oblation and the Sacrifice.

One of the responses of the Church against the threat of the Cathars was the institution in 1285, of the last reading of the Gospel by the priest, on coming back from the altar to the sacristy. His genuflection on pronouncing the words, "et Verbum Caro factum est" ("and the word became Flesh") was a guarantee that he was not a secret Cathar, and that he really had the intention of consecrating at the Mass he had just celebrated, thereby causing his words to accomplish the Transubstantiation.

When in 1965, after almost 700 years, the reading of the last Gospel was suppressed because of arguments "it did not belong to the primitive rite," those of us who knew our theology and the history of the Church understood that the attacks of the heresy against the Mass had begun again in our age.

Ecumenical Council XII, also known as Lateran IV, which met in 1215 and was attended by 400 bishops, 800 abbots and priors, and delegates of the Christian monarchies, issued a dogmatic definition against the Albigensians and the Cathars. We quote:

> One is the Universal Church of the believers, outside of which no one can be saved, and in which the priest himself is the Sacrifice, Jesus Christ, whose body and blood, under the species of bread and wine in the Sacrament of the Altar, really find themselves there, through the Transubstantiation of the bread into the body and the wine into the blood, by virtue of the divine power, in order that we receive from Him the same He took from us, thus perfecting the mystery of unity. And none can effect this Sacrament except the priest who has been duly ordained according to the power of the keys of the Church which Christ gave His apostles and their successors.

The Montinian Church

As an evident result of this Council and its definitions, devotion and worship of the divine Eucharist grew palpably during the 13th century. *The celebration of Corpus Christi was set up.* Saint Thomas Aquinas enhanced it with his magnificent hymns. Processions and the exposition of the Most Holy Sacrament became increasingly popular in that century and the following one, thus contributing greatly to the increase of Christian life among the believers.

However, the attacks of the heresy did not stop. In England, John Wycliffe, and in Bohemia his disciple John Hus, contended that Christ's words could not be literally construed. They had to be understood the following way: "This is my body" had to be translated: "This means my body." This was a preparation for the subsequent Protestant contentions. In 1577 a book was published in Germany, containing 200 different interpretations of the words, *Hoc est Corpus Meum.*

On denying Transubstantiation, both Wycliffe and Hus added other errors to back their heresy. Wycliffe challenged the apostolic succession and the exclusive right of the hierarchical priests of consecrating, teaching that only "good" men could *preside* at the Lord's Supper. Hus demanded Communion under both species in order to contradict the orthodox doctrine which affirms that under the appearance of only bread or wine we receive Christ as a whole, for Christ cannot be divided. Nowadays Communion under both species is demanded, the Sacrifice is denied, and the rite is becoming but a "memorial of the Last Supper."

In the 16th century, the anti-Catholic forces gathered themselves together around the three big heresiarchs: Luther, Zwingli, and Calvin. Though each of them taught a different doctrine and spoke of each other in a scarcely flattering way, they agreed in hating the Mass, "that cannot be sufficiently abominated" (Luther). They adopted all the heresies of the past and created some of their own, thus setting up and spreading what is now called the Reformation.

We know the means to which Archbishop Cranmer resorted to destroy the Mass in Protestant England. Along with two other Protestant leaders, Cranmer requested a public contest with Catholic theologians on Transubstantiation. This public discussion took place at Oxford and centered around three statements:

1. By virtue of the words of Christ which the priest utters, the body and blood of Christ are actually present in the Eucharist, under the appearance of bread and wine.

2. After the consecration, there is no remaining substance of bread or wine but only the body and blood.

3. The Mass is a real sacrifice that profits the living and the dead as a propitiation for their sins.

After a three-day dispute, the Protestants saw themselves obliged to repudiate the authority of Lateran Council IV "for not being in agreement with the Word of God." Although this repudiation was the logical outcome of Protestant doctrine, the Catholics, the arguing theologians, and the listeners, became quite surprised.

"What?" the presiding Catholic theologian exclaimed, "You do not accept the Lateran Council?"

"No; we do not," answered the Protestants.

There was nothing to be added. In repudiating a Catholic doctrine, the doctrine of Christendom, they repudiated the very idea of apostolic continuity and its development. Karl Adam said it in his work, *The Spirit of Catholicism:*

> Catholicism cannot and must not be identified with the faith of the primitive Church, the way a big bush cannot be identified with a tiny seed. There cannot be a mechanical identity, but only an organic identity. Christ's Gospel would not have been a living Gospel if it had remained the small seed sown in the earth in the year 33 of our age and had not developed deep roots to become a leafy tree. This is what 16th-century Protestants could not accept. To fight this principle they resorted to, or invented, the absurd historical theory that a modern historian named, "Search for the acorn." In other words: when you see a beautiful tree, look for the acorn similar to the one that germinated and developed to give birth to the tree, and say: "Do not pay any attention to the tree, for to be what it should, it would be necessary that it become an acorn."

To really understand this preposterous theory of "primitivism," who would now dare, for example, to ask that the House of Commons have its headquarters in Witanagemot and hold its meetings at Kingston-on-Thames or that Congress have its headquarters and sessions at Independence Hall in Philadelphia? Primitivism is not only absurd, but hypocritical. It should not mean that primitive customs are restored to the last detail but these examples indicate that primitivists have selected those primitive details prone to discredit today's customs. The reformers found, or thought they had found, in ancient documents what they believed justified their bold reforms. In the year 150 of our age, Saint Justin Martyr, wrote a letter to Emperor Marcus Aurelius to convince him that Christians were not involved in any criminal conspiracy as their enemies had claimed. The conditions and the places where, according to Saint Justin's description, the Mass was celebrated in those days, were imposed by persecutions and limited to utmost simplicity. In fact, Justin's description is not that of the normal worship of the primitive Church, the way a letter written inside a war airplane during a battle, would fail to depict England's regular 20th-century life.

This letter by Saint Justin served Protestants with an excuse plus the extra advantage that this document calls the celebrant a "president," so as not to convey to the emperor the wrong impression that he was identifying the

Catholic priest with the pagan priest.

Thus, whimsically choosing a letter written on a specific occasion for a specific purpose, Protestants invented the myth of "real Christianity" to back their absurd designs and the vernacular service of Communion. Replacing their altar with a table, stripping their churches of all images, and turning the Eucharist into a Memorial Supper, they made the celebrant the "president," who sits at the table facing the people.

Since people had been accustomed to consider the Mass as a sacrifice for centuries, the Protestants began to use the ambiguous expression, "sacrifice of praise and thanksgiving," which is still included in the prayer book of the Anglican Church. This gave the attendants the impression that the idea of "sacrifice" had not been eliminated, even in those strange rites.

To fight heresy, another ecumenical council was summoned, that of Trent. Besides ratifying the decrees of Lateran Council IV passed three centuries before, the Council of Trent passed new decrees and dogmatic definitions which are the expression of our Catholic Faith even today. As concerns the Sacrifice of the Mass, the most important subject, the Tridentine Council confirmed the old apostolic doctrine of the Church, namely:

> Should anyone contend the Mass is just a sacrifice of praise and thanksgiving or just a memorial of the sacrifice at the cross, instead of a propitiatory sacrifice; or that it only profits him who receives it and must not be offered for the living and the dead for expiation of sins, remission of penalties, impetration, and the other needs we have, let him be anathema.

After this Council, Pope Pius V published the Roman Missal, designed to safeguard in the whole Church the Faith so much fought by the heretics. The so-called Tridentine Mass was then prescribed by his apostolic Constitution, *Quo Primum* on July 17, 1570:

> Through this, our Constitution, that will stand perpetually, on penalty of our anger, we order that never be anything added, taken away or changed in our Missal.... In virtue of holy obedience we command ... that, laying aside all of the rites of other Missals, even though these be very old and have been used so far, from now on ... [priests and bishops] must read and sing the Mass according to the rite, the way and rules prescribed by us in this Missal ... we forbid that, in the celebration of the Mass, ceremonies or prayers other than the ones included in this Missal be added or recited.... And we permit and grant that this Missal be used in all sung or prayed Masses *without any scruple of conscience, without incurring any penalty, sentence or censorship from now on, with freedom and legitimacy, through our apostolic authority, by virtue of this document*, eiam perpetuo, *(perpetually)*.

The Great Treason

Thus the Tridentine Mass was an insurmountable wall against heresy until April 3, 1969, when the present Pope, through his Constitution, *Missale Romanum,* approved the new vernacular Mass, adapted to the practices and principles of the Protestants. It has to be celebrated on a table, and the priest has to face the people, as a "president" of the meeting.

In England and other parts of the world there was an immediate response to the new vernacular Mass. On May 10, 1969, the Pope's directions were translated. On the 17th of the same month, The Latin Mass Society sent the most Holy Father a petition asking that he preserve the Tridentine Mass according to Saint Pius V's Missal. In September, Cardinals Ottaviani and Bacci handed the Pope a critical analysis on the New Mass, prepared by outstanding theologians from Rome, demonstrating that the *Novus Ordo Missae* "as a whole and in every detail is impressively far from the Catholic theology of the Holy Mass." The Latin Mass Society immediately published a translation of this analysis, sending it to every single bishop, monsignor, priest, and religious in England. The hierarchy forbids the priests to comment on the document, and we may guess the 700 copies were thrown into the basket for waste paper.

In this important document, the theologians demonstrated that the New Mass had been essentially rebuked by the synod of bishops; never had it been put to the collegial wisdom of the episcopal conferences or requested by Christian people. It would please most modernist Protestants. Using ambiguous terms, it emphasizes the idea of "Supper" instead of "Sacrifice." It does not discriminate between divine Sacrifice and human sacrifice. It declares that the bread and wine are changed only spiritually, not substantially. It contains no reference to Christ's real presence, which seems to have been implicitly rebuked. The status of the priest and the people have been adulterated to such an extent that the celebrant is almost equated with a Protestant minister and the real nature of the Church is unbearably falsified. The abandonment of Latin signifies an attack on the unity of the Church, not only with respect to worship, but also with respect to beliefs.

The *Novus Ordo Missae* is no defense against heresy which, today like yesterday, continues to challenge the Eucharistic dogmas. The *Ordo* "impressively deviates from the dogmatic doctrine of the Council of Trent," which all Catholics must consciously profess on penalty of everlasting condemnation. In summary, the *Novus Ordo Missae* includes numerous ambiguities and not a few errors that stain the purity of the Catholic religion and smash all defenses of the deposit of faith.

The Vatican, the bishops of England and Wales and those of the rest of the world, see eye-to-eye in the way of pretending theological ignorance, and demand blind obedience to the new liturgy. To avoid suspicion, they executed changes in a most gradual way. In his pastoral letter of October 12, 1969, Cardinal John Heenan[23] put it this way:

The Montinian Church

Why does the Mass keep changing? The answer is that it would have been difficult to execute the changes simultaneously. Had all the changes been made at the same time, you would have all been shocked.

A month afterwards, Cardinal Heenan wrote a prologue to the English translation of the New Mass:

> Wise Pope Paul VI has made up his mind to put an end to experiments. He is happy, because the form of the Mass will need no further changes in the foreseeable future.... It is important to note that the revision has been carried on under the Holy Father's personal supervision. Thus, it cannot be accepted that the *Novus Ordo Missae* contains doctrinal errors.

The above words by the Cardinal imply that everything the Pope does or says is correct, *ipso facto*. This suggests that the Pope is a pagan oracle, whereas Catholic doctrine teaches that Peter's successor is infallible only when he defines *ex cathedra*, as Pastor and Teacher of the entire Church on penalty of everlasting condemnation, a doctrine contained in the deposit of divine revelation, regarding faith or morality. In all other cases, he is as fallible as any other human being.

The Pope's fallibility is, actually, the shield of his infallibility. He who affirms that the Pope, just because he is a Pope, cannot err, exposes our Faith to a bitter and fallacious criticism, such as that which our foes have launched against the Catholic dogma of the Pontiff's infallibility. For instance, Lytton Strachey wrote:

> In his bull, *Cum inter nonullos,* John XXIII affirmed that the doctrine of Christ's poverty was heretical, and his predecessor, Nicholas III, in his bull, *Exiit que seminat,* had written that the doctrine of Christ's poverty was a real doctrine, and only heretics could deny it. If John XXIII stated a Catholic truth, Nicholas III taught heresy. And if John XXIII was wrong, his teaching was definitively heretical. What about infallibility, then?

The opposition between those opinions does not impair papal infallibility. Those are the views of two men, and the solution will arise through the regular process of theological discussion. In like manner, the conflict between Paul VI and Saint Pius V regarding the *Ordo Missae* is a conflict between two men's opinions. Bearing in mind that Saint Pius V's *Ordo Missae* espoused the doctrine of Trent and was designed to defend our Faith against Protestant errors, our choice cannot be a hard one.

Professor Gordon Rupp, one of the most famous Lutheran theologians, in speaking about the Vatican's questioning the excommunication of Luther, said:

The Great Treason

It appears to be a logical step, since Vatican II agrees in so many fields with Luther's doctrine, for which he was condemned.

Paul VI himself is said to have been surprised at the extensive resistance to the New Order of the Mass. He devoted two allocutions, those of November 19 and 26, 1969, published by *L'Osservatore Romano* on November 27 and December 4, 1969, to defend the New Mass. He said, "The Mass with the new rite remains the same Mass as ever." He maintained that the new form was the Will of Christ, thus suggesting he had spoken infallibly when setting up the *Novus Ordo,* although he did not say so openly. He explained that the changes were made to shatter the apathy of the believers and to "help make the Mass a peaceful but efficient school of *Christian sociology.*" He affirmed that Latin is "the language of the angels" and provided simple people with a small consolation, since they would no longer be able to hear the divine services in a language used for nineteen centuries. He also promised to use that language for "the official acts of the Holy See." He ended by saying: *"Let us not talk anymore about the New Mass. Let us rather talk about the new age in the life of the Church."*

Every Catholic who really cares for his religion must have wondered: Why has all this taken place? We cannot believe what we are beholding; the Vatican is dismantling our Faith. This cannot succeed; it must be a nightmare from which, sooner or later we shall wake up and find every sacred thing untouched and in its original state. Anyway, why have the Pope and the bishops acted this way?

To give them an answer, we must give a brief explanation on *ecumenism.* When, on January 25, 1959, John XXIII announced "an ecumenical council," non-Catholic people, according to an article Cardinal Bea published in 1961, "thought the idea consisted of convening a council where the representatives of all Christian churches or communities would gather together to discuss the problems of unity." This interpretation was derived from the very term *ecumenism,* which is used in our times to mean rapprochement among so-called Christian religious groups. This meaning of the term, which describes the representatives of all the Christian denominations, was first used in the last century to establish unity among these groups. The wrong interpretation of it was cleared up afterwards.

Cardinal Bea was too optimistic. The meaning of the ambiguous term *ecumenism,* was never cleared up. Not even today do people know what it means. Many people keep believing that since Vatican II, like all general councils of the Church, called itself an ecumenical council, this meant, in a canonical sense, a gathering of all bishops in Communion with the Apostolic See. Protestants, of course, would construe these words in the same way, but Protestant ecumenism is the deadliest heresy of all. It is not only indifferentism, which says that all religions are good, but a denial of the very reality of the Church. It teaches that the real Church no longer exists, nor has it ever existed, but that it will exist in the immediate future through a blend of all viewpoints, beliefs, and religions that claim to be Christian. The World Council of Churches, which coordinates 239 sects, is the representative organ for the time being.

Despite Pope Paul VI's visit to the seat of the World Council of Churches in Geneva, the Catholic Church still refuses to accept this final apostasy of joining the World Council of Churches. Should it do so, it would be proclaiming that it is but one among the so-called Christian sects. Paul VI, however, has not hesitated to send delegates as observers to that organization, and he himself appeared before it to deliver an enigmatic speech. Moreover, he did not find any valid objection of faith or conscience in accepting some Protestant pastors to help prepare the *Novus Ordo Missae*.

Confusion between the classical Catholic meaning of the word, *ecumenical* and the Protestant version of the words, *ecumenical movement*, facilitated the activities of the World Council of Churches. To avoid confusion, Vatican II had to pass a decree on *ecumenism*. Though pretended charity could have moved the Conciliar Fathers to compromise, the decree is, undoubtedly, a statement of our Catholic Faith and an implicit condemnation of the Protestant ecumenical movement. It affirms that all Christian communities outside of the Catholic Church are defective; that "[o]nly through the Catholic Church of Christ can the necessary means for Salvation be fully achieved," that "[t]he unity Christ granted His Church when He founded it, still exists in the Catholic Church;" and that "[o]nly the Catholic Church possesses the total riches of revealed truth and all the means of grace."

The Vatican II document on ecumenism endorses Pius XII's great encyclical, *Mystici Corporis*, on the nature of the Church, and says:

> ... [I]n fact, among the members of the Church can be counted only those who have received the regenerating water of Baptism and who, professing the real Faith, have not themselves parted miserably from the body, nor have been removed from it by the *legitimate* authority because of their most grave guilt.

The decree on ecumenism is, in fact, a decree against the Protestants' ecumenical movement, for it confirms the doctrine of Pius XII. Unfortunately, Pius XII's encyclical continues to be disregarded by those bishops who invite heretics and schismatics to preach at Catholic pulpits, and foster other activities that impair the Catholic Church's exclusivity. In particular, they emphasize that Baptism, valid Baptism, unites all Christians in faith, but they omit an equally important truth expounded in *Mystici Corporis*, that the attachment of an adult to a non-Catholic sect breaks the relationship established by Baptism, since "schism, heresy, and apostasy, by their very nature, separate human beings from Christ's Body, the Church."

When the Vatican made a move of rapprochement toward the World Council of Churches, it deemed it necessary to change the Mass so as to please the ecumenical movement. To this effect, the very words of consecration pronounced by Christ Himself, which expressed Christ's Will on setting up the Eucharistic Sacrifice, were adulterated. Instead of saying His blood was shed for "many," it is now said it was shed "for all," this meaning not Redemption, but the application of the fruits of Redemption. This wicked and false doctrine of "the final salvation of all men," which is absolutely opposite to the Church's doctrine, is nowadays the fundamental rock of the entire structure of the modern heresy which bears the name of ecumenism.

Many centuries ago the heretics had attempted to change the phrase, *"for many"* to the phrase, *"for all,"* which is used nowadays. Saint Thomas Aquinas rebuked such attempts which contradict Christ's very words at the Last Supper: *"Ego pro eis rogo. Non pro mundo rogo, sed pro his, quos dedisti mihi.... Pater sancte, serva eos in nomino tuo, quos dedisti mihi, ut sint unum.... Quos dedisti mihi, custodivi, et nemo ex eis periit, nisi filius preditionis...."* ("I pray for them: I pray not for the world, but for them which thou hast given me... Holy Father, keep through thine own name those whom thou hast given me, that they may be one... those that thou gavest me I have kept, and none of them is lost, but the son of perdition...") (John 17:9-12). This sacerdotal prayer by Christ definitively states the Church's exclusivity. The world is saved through entering the Church. All men have the chance to save themselves through their entering the Church, but many exclude themselves freely, by their own will. The replacement then, of the words, "for many" by "for all," entails the idea of false ecumenism, according to which all men, whatever their creed or behavior, will be saved.

The history of this adulteration is an interesting one. In his already-mentioned allocution of Nov. 19, 1969, Pope Paul VI announced that "the changes had been introduced by eminent experts in sacred liturgy." He did not say however, that two Anglicans, a Lutheran, a Calvinist, and a representative of the World Council of Churches were among those experts, nor did he say, either, that the top "expert" was Joachim Jeremias, a non-Catholic, Jewish professor of the University of Göttingen, who had previously attacked Christ's divinity.

In his book, *The Eucharistic Words of Jesus*, published in 1966, Dr. Jeremias invented the ingenious theory according to which when Jesus said, "for many," he meant "for all," because the Aramaic language does not include the word, *all*. This argument also attacks Catholic theology, which since the Council of Trent, has repudiated the words, "for all men." Nevertheless, the argument of Dr. Jeremias has no value whatsoever. We find the word *all* in a passage from Daniel "all the inhabitants of the earth are reputed as nothing" (Dan. 4:32). Moreover, in a 1961 grammar of biblical Aramaic, an entire section is devoted to the Aramaic word, *all*.

The explanation of this particular point of the New Mass, like other points, can be explained through what a person who is not accustomed to the current episcopal ways of thinking, would call a lie. The gravity of the case is such that this change of Christ's words *definitely invalidates all the vernacular Masses*, since there is no solid ground to demonstrate the opposite. The *Latin* version of the *new* Canons keeps the words, *pro multis* (for many); nowhere in this version is the phrase, *pro omnibus* (for all) used. This clear argument should at least cause people who naively accepted the vernacular translation to be suspicious, and this Latin version of the new Canons is equally invalid. Before explaining why, it is convenient to say something about the Canon of the Mass itself, because the ecclesiastical authorities, in affirming that the Canon of Pius V's Mass is only 400 years old, attempt to make us believe that the changes accomplished in the Canon are unimportant and accidental.

In his prologue to the English version of the new "Westminster Mass," His Eminence Cardinal Heenan summarized the grounds for the radical changes accomplished in the liturgy of the Mass. We quote:

> The words and deeds that 400 years ago impressed people in the Elizabethan age would hardly suit the mentality and customs of 20th-century man.

This is not true, for the Canon of the Mass goes back to the early centuries of Christianity without any change whatsoever. This Canon was used before Saint Augustine began to evangelize Britain. The Canon he used in the first Mass he celebrated at Kent, was used in England with the very same words and language as were used in all Catholic Masses for the ensuing 1373 years, until Pope Montini abolished it in February of 1970.

Pius V's Tridentine reforms revised and unified the prayers and rites that had been introduced in certain places, but neither those reforms nor the prayers and rites modified the Canon, which was basically the same Canon of Christ. The Council of Trent itself makes us aware that the succession was unremitting:

> Whereas the holy things must be piously handled; and whereas of them all [the holiest one] is this most Holy Sacrifice, the Catholic Church many years ago instituted the Holy Canon so that the Sacrifice could be worthily offered and received. The aim was that the Canon be free of any error to such an extent (Canon 6) that it contains nothing that does not express great holiness and piety and lift up to God the minds of those who offer it .... [T]his is recorded *in the Lord's very words, the apostles' traditions and the Holy Pontiff's pious institutions*. (Denzinger, 942).

The Great Treason

Martin Luther, on the contrary, spoke of the Canon with utmost contempt. We quote Luther:

> That execrable Canon...is a summary of filthy traditions that have turned the Mass into a sacrifice. They have added offertories. The Mass is not a sacrifice nor the immolation of a priest. Along with this Canon we reject anything implying an oblation.

One of the chief architects of the New Mass, Msgr. Annibale Bugnini, seems to endorse this opinion of Luther, when he speaks about the famous *Formula Missae* (formula of the Mass) of 1523 published by the heresiarch as a *Missa Normativa*. The New Mass, which definitively destroyed the most ancient Canon, implies and incorporates all of Luther's principles.

As long as the Tridentine Canon was preserved, it was impossible to destroy the intention, the very essence of the Mass. That was why ecumenism demanded new and different Canons. One of them, the second one, is so innovating that any Protestant minister, or any renegade priest who does not accept Transubstantiation, can use it. Above all, according to Luther's recommendation, any reference to the Oblation has been eliminated.

On page 6 of Number 49 of the publication *Courier de Rome*, the outstanding theologian, Abbé R. Dulac, gives us the reason for it:

> According to Luther and his followers, since the risen Christ no longer dies, He cannot become a victim at the Mass. At most, He can be mystically represented in the state of a victim, under the species of bread and wine. The bread and wine are, consequently, parts of the Sacrifice.

Once they eliminated the offertory and laid aside the Oblation, the compilers of Canon II incurred Cranmer's concealed heresy. They wrote: "Sanctify these gifts with the effusion of the Spirit, in order that *they be to us the body and blood of our Lord Jesus Christ*. They did not say "they *be*, but *"be to us."* This form specifically denies Transubstantiation. It can be used by any member of the sects belonging to the World Council of Churches for their Communion service. And this *ecumenical* intention undoubtedly destroys the validity of the Mass. Certainly, the Tridentine Canon also includes the word *nobis*, but the great prayers of Oblation that precede it make indisputable the intention, the reality of the Sacrifice.

The validity of the other Canons has also been destroyed. Many people say that, since Father so-and-so undoubtedly believes in the Transubstantiation, his intention validates the Mass he celebrates. Here, however, we are dealing *with the intention of Christ and the Church*, not *with the celebrant's personal intention or belief.* For instance, although Talleyrand[24] was

The Montinian Church

a self-confessed atheist, the ordinations he performed and those performed by the people he ordained were not necessarily void. What is requested from the celebrant is that he have *Christ's* intention, the *Church's* intention, not *his* intention. This principle explains why, for example, a female Muhammadan might validly administer Baptism in case of need, provided she uses the right words, performs the right actions, and has the intention of doing what Christ's Church does, even though she does not believe in what she is doing and saying.

The Modernist Church incorporated Canon II, which denies Transubstantiation, in order to show its ecumenical intention. Hence, it appears, that *its* intention is no longer *Christ's* intention and, as a result, none of its Canons are valid. *No* priest can celebrate a valid Mass using these Canons, no matter how solid his theological knowledge and how great his devotion.

Many Catholics are groundlessly convinced that the Mass is valid if it is read in Latin. The Society for the Latin Mass has been organized all over the world, and, therefore, the faithful must be warned against the ambiguity these movements purport. On condition of saving the ecumenical structure of the New Mass, the hierarchy could consider sponsoring the movement and even graciously conceding the use of Latin.

We must repeat again and again that in the Church (we are not speaking of the Eastern churches) there is no valid Latin Mass other than the Tridentine Mass of Pius V, which was instituted to safeguard the Catholic Faith in perpetuity. In order to impose the New Mass on us and to prohibit the eternal Mass of Saint Pius V, the bishops remind us of the obedience we owe them, but they, in turn, must remember that obedience to one's conscience is above obedience to men who should not command what faith or reason condemn. Even in the army, no soldier can invoke obedience to his superiors as an excuse to commit a crime. By obedience the bishops mean a meaningless surrender, an absurd imposition contrary to conscience, the same obedience that apostate priests professed to apostate bishops during the Reformation of the 16th century. In *those* days, a bishop defended the Faith and died for it; in *our* days, we have yet to see a John Fisher[25] fight the current subversion.

Faced with grand treason on the part of the ecclesiastics, the defense of the Church demands that the laity exert all conceivable efforts to look for faithful priests, in catacombs if necessary, who wish to continue to say the eternal Tridentine Mass. This is being done in many places. We are back to the age of the catacombs, and we must not be afraid of canonical censorship. Pope Pius V said:

> We permit and grant [in perpetuity] that this Missal be used in all Masses ... without any scruple of conscience, without incurring any penalty, sentence, or censorship from this day forward, with all freedom and legitimacy, through our apostolic authority, by virtue of this doctrine, *etiam perpetuo*.

The Great Treason

It would be absurd to call schismatic those who, resorting to what Saint Pius V established perpetually in accordance with the standing doctrine of the Church for centuries, continue to celebrate the eternal Mass. It is not we faithful Catholics, but the ecumenists who are schismatics, heretics and apostates.

We do notice that the number of true Catholics is diminishing. Unfortunately, such has been the case whenever any schismatic or heretical movements have afflicted Christ's Church. Let us remember, however, that just because the Gospel has to be *preached* to the whole world, it does not mean that the whole world must *embrace* the Gospel. Christ, the apostles, and the Holy Fathers made the point that in this world the Church would be reduced to a small group. We have been warned of this great apostasy. We have been told by Hugh Ross Williamson:[26]

> ... [T]here will come a time, when people will not tolerate a sound doctrine, but will seek after masters who flatter their passions, and, closing their ears to the truth, will open them to fables, ... [so that] if it were possible, even the chosen ones would fall into error.

Chapter XL

DIVINISM, POPELATRY, AND THE DOCTRINE OF THE LESSER EVIL

Before thinking of the future, we must look back to find both the good that we can use and the bad that we must eliminate. Contemplating the wreckage of Christianity in Spain in just the last ten years permits us to discover three principal psychological causes responsible for that disaster. In chronological order of appearance, they were: divinism, popelatry and the doctrine of the lesser evil. These three were combined and interwoven due to minor causes such as laziness, lukewarmness, etc.

Divinism was a feature of the pre-Conciliar and Conciliar periods. It was responsible for the preparation, or rather *lack* of preparation, of our theologians. They received alarming news concerning what the Europeans thought. They knew the Europeans had succeeded in infiltrating their ideas into the Council's agenda and schemes, but our theologians did nothing. How could God permit the Council to approve such nonsense? That was the question they addressed to those of us who showed our concern at our most humble level of secular priests. "O, ye men of little faith," they kept repeating, while pushing us gently to the door. They also said: "Do not care for what is said during the discussions; what really matters is what is finally approved, for this will be sponsored by the Holy Spirit." This groundless confidence, this divinism, caused them to go to Rome without any more preparation than a cursory doctrinal review, and without any praxis. The Europeans certainly did not disregard this, for they brought huge loads of stationery, multicopiers, magnetic recorders, installations, clerks, and money.

Then came *popelatry*. When the seeds of catastrophe became obviously apparent in the acts of the Council, divinism could no longer be promoted, not even the clerical version of it, which consisted of blaming our Lord God for whatever evil takes place, with words such as: "He must have a good reason to permit it." Then divinism was either reinforced or in some cases replaced by popelatry. No one dares to say that certain concepts of the Council (or those at least authoritatively ascribed to the Council) that contradicted the previous Magisterium, were fruits of the Holy Spirit. To some people, the way out of certain death was to take refuge in devotion to the Pope. They confessed that they knew nothing of what had happened, of what they had seen or heard but,

The Montinian Church

since the Pope had said it, it was all right. Thus they even boasted of piety. This unconditional support of the non-infallible, Conciliar and post-Conciliar Pontifical Magisterium was not too consistent with Catholic orthodoxy itself, but to them it was not important, for they had convinced themselves through a romantic piety. Day after day, and disappointment after disappointment, reality undermined this psychological crutch until it became indefensible.

We cannot continue without mentioning that few people are as far off from this doctrine as Paul VI himself. A few days ago we read in the press that at an official meeting, some priests from Seville showed reticence toward sacerdotal celibacy, an issue about which the Pope has already uttered his opinion. Other priests from Toledo, in similar circumstances, discussed the same subject and submitted it to voting. I do not believe it is right to apply to those who used to practice popelatry (few people practice it now) the epithet of being "more Papist than the Pope," because those who deserve it the most are those who quantitatively prolong the Pope's wishes. Instead, now we are referring to a qualitative change and crediting a supreme authority with statements it has not issued. Devotion to the Pope, so widespread in Spain, is diminishing among us, because some people tried to take it out of context.

Having exhausted the expedience of excessive devotion to the Pope, some theologians fell back to a third defensive line, which, from the beginning, was far removed from the evangelical advice that "[t]he truth will make you free." This third line of defense is a false version of the "doctrine of the lesser evil."

The doctrine of the lesser evil, the capital sin in our religious and political history, has returned with this plan of action: "Certainly, we acknowledge that the Council and the Pontificate of Paul VI have yielded some bitter fruits, but proclaiming it and trying to cure them would be even worse; it is better that we dissimulate, yield, and quietly wait until our Lord God solves the problem..." (new divinism).

The moral doctrine of the lesser evil states that when there is no other remedy, when it is absolutely inevitable to choose between two evils, then, and only then, must the lesser evil be quietly accepted, but with the firm determination to get rid of it eventually.

We must clarify whether there is or isn't a solution different from the scandalous rebellion and resigned acceptance of "auto-demolition." In case there is no other way out, we should discern which of the two above-mentioned ways is *really* less evil.

I believe there is a third way out, that of the art of subterfuge: to obey, but not to accomplish anything, to do everything that is not expressly prohibited and which symbolizes the spirit of the real Church, to offer lawful and legal active and passive resistance to progressivist innovations, and to waste time and wait until personnel and their ideas change. If this solution were fully exploited, it would probably suffice to deliver us from the danger. If it were not sufficient

Divinism, Popelatry, and the Lesser Evil

and the option between scandalous rebellion and resigned acceptance were inevitable, I would still not believe acceptance to be the lesser evil. On one hand, rebellion would not be as scandalous as it might have been twenty years ago, for today greater scandal has caused lesser scandal to disappear. On the other hand, resigned acceptance has been the experimental way followed so far with such disastrous consequences, that we can hardly imagine any other tactics that would yield worse results.

(From the Spanish review ¿Qué Pasa? July 24, 1971).

FOOTNOTES

¹ Plutarco Elias Calles, Masonic President of Mexico from 1924 to 1928, was a nominal Catholic, who, like most Marrano Jews, openly practiced Catholicism but secretly practiced Talmudic Judaism. Marrano Jews also conspire to overthrow Christianity and Christian culture in order to establish a New World Order which, in reality, is the old Babylonian pagan world order imparted to the Pharisees during the Babylonian Captivity.

² Bishop Sergio Méndez Arceo, the "Red Bishop" of Cuernavaca, when visiting Cuba, declared himself to be a Marxist and a Communist.

³ *Matamoros* literally means "slayer of Moors." *Santiago* refers to St. James the Apostle; *Santiago Matamoros* was the war cry used by the Spanish soldiers who invoked the aid of St. James to achieve victory over the Moors.

⁴ Tito Casini, Italy's leading Catholic writer, in his book, *The Torn Tunic*, bitterly denounced Cardinal Lercaro for having devastated the Church. In April of 1976 he also exposed Monsignor Bugnini as being a Freemason, whereupon Bugnini's Congregation for Divine Worship was dissolved and the Monsignor was transferred to Iran to avoid the embarrassment of public disclosure.

⁵ This quote, taken from the proceedings of the Vatican Council, is also contained in the statutes of the CRSA.

⁶ The ephod was a special garment, similar to a chasuble, worn only by the Jewish High Priest, with two onyxes on which were engraved the names of the twelve tribes of Israel. Over it was the rational or breastplate of judgment, which was worn over the breast. On it were 12 stones in four rows of three, each stone being engraved with the name of one of the twelve tribes of Israel. It was called the rational of judgment because it admonished both the priest and the people of their duties to God, and partly because it gave divine answers and oracles, as if it were rational and endowed with reason. (References: Exodus 28:6-9 and 15-28; 39:2-4 and 12.) This is the ephod that Paul VI wore, not the ephod described in I. Kings 2:18, 22:18 and II. Kings 6:14; the latter is a linen garment worn by both priests and people for special occasions. (From the Catholic Home Encyclopedia, an appendix of *The Holy Bible*, Catholic Press, Inc., Chicago, 1952. Edited by the Rev. John P. O'Connell; *Imprimatur:* Samuel Cardinal Stritch.)

The Montinian Church

[7] MURO—a violent and belligerent group of university students headquartered in Guadalajara, Mexico.

[8] Max Lincoln Schuster, 1847-1971, a U.S. publisher and active Zionist, was co-founder of Simon & Schuster and of Pocket Books, Inc., the first large-scale publishers of paperback books in the U.S.

[9] Abraham Joshua Heschel, 1907-1973, was a well-known German rabbinical scholar who settled in the U.S. in 1940 and taught at the Hebrew Union College in Cincinnati. A radical liberal, he was active in the civil rights movement and was a personal friend of Martin Luther King.

[10] Father Noel Barbara, a Parisian, was a strong religious conservative and intimate friend of Fr. Saenz. He was the first to express the term, "Montinian Church," thereby providing Fr. Saenz with the title and impetus for this monumental work. He was also editor of *Fortes in Fides,* a worldwide booklet that became the official pamphlet of anti-Modernism.

[11] *Theandrical* is a theological term for the divine-human aspect of Christ, effected through the instrument of His humanity.

[12] Franziskus Cardinal König of Vienna frequently served in a liaison capacity for the Vatican with Communist countries. On April 7, 1965, Pope Paul VI appointed him head of the Secretariat for Non-Believers for the purpose of fostering dialogue with atheists.

[13] This refers to the Encyclopedists of the latter part of the 18th Century, a group of free thinkers, including writers such as Diderot, d'Alembert, Hume, and Halbach, who promulgated deism, atheism, hedonism, and materialism.

[14] IDOC is the acronym for the International Center of Information and Documentation of the Conciliar Church. It was organized to spread progressivist propaganda and to transform the Catholic Church into a desacralized, egalitarian new church at the service of Communism. It embraces important Catholic publishing houses and controls the religious sections of influential worldwide newspapers.

[15] Father Ivan Illich was a converted Jew who was assigned to work under Bishop Sergio Méndez Arceo of Cuernavaca where he organized *Emmaus,* a Marxist study center consisting primarily of the intelligentsia of North and South America. This group was chiefly responsible for introducing Marxism into the encyclicals, and psychoanalysis into the confessional.

Footnotes

[16] Father Chénu was an ultra-liberal French priest who, together with his associate, Fr. Ives Congar, formed a conciliary group to "modernize" (liberalize) the Church. In 1964, together with other Modernists such as Fathers Kueng and Schillebeeckx, they founded a Modernist theological journal entitled *The Concilium*.

[17] John Cardinal Newman (1801-1890) was an Anglican vicar who converted to Catholicism in 1845. He organized the Oxford Movement, which advanced the Anglo-Catholic revival in England and the United States.

[18] This refers to Februus, the Etruscan god of the underworld, the Roman god of purification, and corresponds to Dispater, the richest of all the gods.

[19] Father Ripalda was the author of the old standard Spanish catechism.

[20] *Charisma*—a divine supernatural gift that perfects the abilities of the individual for the spiritual good of the Church.

[21] Joseph Broz, the original authentic Tito, was killed in Moscow in 1941 and replaced by General Lebedev, a Russian Jew to whom he bore a marked resemblance. In 1978, Joseph's family finally received permission for a 20-minute audience with Tito after a lapse of 40 years. Afterwards, they privately stated that Marshal Tito was definitely not their brother. Moreover, Joseph had a finger missing from his left hand, whereas the "Tito" they met had all his fingers intact.

[22] Eduardo Frei, socialist ex-president of Chile, in a Kerensky-type fashion, prepared the way for Chilean Allende.

[23] John Cardinal Heenan (1909-1975) was an English cardinal of the Diocese of Westminster and an outspoken opponent of the *Novus Ordo*. He addressed a very serious warning to the Synod of Bishops in Rome who had met in October of 1967 to examine the proposed New Mass.

[24] Charles Maurice de Talleyrand de Périgord was a Bishop of Autun, French statesman, Freemason and Illuminist who played a major role in the French Revolution and the subsequent Napoleonic period.

[25] Saint John Fisher (1469-1535) was a Bishop of Rochester who was beheaded for denying the claim of Henry VIII to be supreme head of the English church.

[26] Hugh Ross Williamson, 20th century Anglican clergyman, converted to Catholicism following the creation of the Church of South India, formed by uniting Anglican and Free churches into one body. Along with many other Anglican clergymen, he

The Montinian Church

correctly interpreted this step as being incompatible with Anglican claims to apostolic orders. The liturgy of the Church of South India is the basis for the *Novus Ordo* celebration.

www.ingramcontent.com/pod-product-compliance
Lightning Source LLC
Chambersburg PA
CBHW032055230426
43662CB00035B/306